THE PRESIDENCY

The Presidency

RICHARD M. PIOUS
Barnard College and Columbia University

ALLYN AND BACON
Boston • London • Toronto • Sydney • Tokyo • Singapore

Vice President and Publisher, Social Sciences: Susan Badger
Senior Editor: Stephen P. Hull
Series Editorial Assistant: Susan Hutchinson
Marketing Manager: Karon Bowers
Editorial-Production Administrator: Deborah Brown
Editorial-Production Service: P. M. Gordon Associates, Inc.
Composition and Prepress Buyer: Linda Cox
Manufacturing Buyer: Aloka Rathnam
Cover Administrator: Suzanne Harbison
Photo Researcher: Sue C. Howard

A Simon & Schuster Company
Needham Heights, MA 02194

Library of Congress Cataloging-in-Publication Data

Pious, Richard M.
The presidency / Richard M. Pious.
p. cm.
Includes bibliographical references and index.
ISBN 0-02-395792-1
1. Presidents—United States. I. Title.
JK516.P553 1996
324.6′3′0973—dc20 95-12298
CIP

Printed in the United States of America

10 9 8 7 6 5 4 3 2 1 00 99 98 97 96 95

Photo Credits

Pages 2 and 386: Dirck Halstead/Gamma Liaison
Pages 13, 63, 129, 146, 202, 302, 426, and 461: UPI/Bettmann
Pages 22 and 191: The Bettmann Archive
Page 41: Art Resource, NY
Page 90: Library of Congress
Pages 121, 238, 265, 344, 424, 467, and 481: Reuters/Bettmann
Pages 170 and 372: AP/Wide World Photos

For my wife Sacha,
and for our children Samantha and Benjamin

The Presidency is not merely an administrative office. That is the least of it. It is pre-eminently a place of moral leadership.

—Franklin D. Roosevelt

Contents

Preface

The Presidency is a study of the Office of the President of the United States. The book deals with the creation of the presidency and its historical development; presidential nominations and elections; presidential leadership of party and public opinion; White House relationships with the Congress, the federal courts, and the bureaucracy; and presidential economic, diplomatic, and national security policy making.

My thesis is that the framers of the Constitution did not definitively settle either the role of the presidency or the limits of presidential power. The office possesses neither the constitutional nor the political resources necessary to resolve the problems for which the president takes political responsibility. To resolve the gap between the responsibilities of the modern presidency and its resources, presidents do three things: They use the expertise of the presidential advisory agencies to develop new programs (the programmatic presidency); they argue that their programs are in the national interest and attempt to gain public support for those programs (the public presidency); and, if necessary, they rely unilaterally on their constitutional powers (the prerogative presidency). Yet, at every turn, they find themselves caught in difficult or no-win situations. Their expertise is challenged and their authority diminished by intellectual critics inside government and in academia and the media; their public leadership is challenged both by established journalists and commentators and by the "new media" (primarily talk show radio); their assertions of constitutional prerogatives are challenged by Congress and not always upheld by the judiciary. Far from being a settled institution whose powers and authority have been fully legitimized, the American presidency is always being reinvented, always being simultaneously legitimized by its supporters and delegitimized by its critics.

I begin each chapter with a case study that illustrates some key issues. Then I describe the formal and informal powers of the presidency. I discuss the strategies and tactics presidents use to maximize their influence, and assess their failure or success. Many chapters conclude with a discussion of a leading theory about the presidency advanced by political scientists and historians. At the end of each chapter, I provide a list of books and data sources. Appendices at the end of the book present tables of presidents and vice presidents, relevant constitutional provisions about the presidency, and data on presidential election results.

What are the sources of presidential power? How do presidents try to maintain their authority and legitimacy with the American people? Under what circumstances do presidents succeed? Why do they so often fail? These are questions I have been thinking and writing about since I started teaching at Columbia University three decades ago. "No President has ever enjoyed himself as much as I have enjoyed myself," Theodore Roosevelt once wrote about his time in the White House, "and for the matter of that I do not know any man of my age who has had as good a time." I feel much the same way about my work as a presidency scholar, teacher, and writer. I hope those who read this book will share my enthusiasm for tackling the issues of presidential power that it poses.

R.M.P.
South Salem, New York, 1995

Acknowledgments

I thank my colleagues in the Departments of Political Science at Barnard College and Columbia University, most especially Demetrios Caraley, as well as Leslie Calman, Dennis Dalton, Flora Davidson, Michael Delli Carpini, Ester Fuchs, Charles Hamilton, Peter Juviler, Judith Russell, Robert Shapiro, and Phil Thompson, all of whom have given me ideas about presidential power. I also thank Mark Carnes, Herb Sloan, and Nancy Woloch of the Department of History at Barnard College, and my intellectual companions for more than two decades, the faculty members of the Barnard Round Table.

I have clarified my thinking about the presidency by participating in several conferences or ongoing seminars, including the following: a panel on "The Imperial Presidency," held at the American Political Science Association annual meeting in 1994 (with Arthur Schlesinger, Jr., I. M. Destler, Michael Nelson, and Michael Robinson); an American Politics Roundtable at Columbia University in 1994 (at which I presented a thesis about "Why Presidents Fail"); the Hofstra University Conference on Ronald Reagan in 1994 (at which I commented on presentations by Phillip Abbott and Michael Riccards); the Conference on Presidential and Parliamentary Democracies held by the Academy of Political Science in 1993 (for which I served as rapporteur); a panel at the Western Political Science Association annual meeting in 1993 (with Nelson Polsby, George Edwards, Bert Rockman, and Richard Brody); a 1987 American Political Science Association panel on presidential prerogative (with Jeffrey Tulis, James Franklin, and Ryan Barilleaux); a panel at the same convention on the modern Constitution (with Benjamin Page, David Mayhew, and David Greenstone); the Seminar on Comparative Social Welfare Policy in 1986, held at Columbia University and sponsored by the Ford Foundation; the Taipei Conference on American Foreign Policymaking in 1984; and the Montauk Conference on Presidential Selection in 1982, sponsored by the Sloan Foundation and organized by Alexander Heard.

I have had the good fortune to work with doctoral students from Columbia University and several other institutions whose dissertation topics dealt with presidential power, and I want to thank Sally Cohen, Dawn Farris, Charles Freilich, Jeffrey Helsing, Larry Jacobs, Nancy Kassop, Tom Langston, Brigitte Nacos, Kelly Patterson, and Paul Posner for sharing with me their ideas and enthusiasm.

The reference librarians at Barnard College and Columbia University were most helpful when I needed guidance and encouragement in conducting bibliographic searches. Nell Dillon-Ermers, the Political Science Departmental Administrator, saved me time and effort on numerous tasks. Barnard College awarded me a modest grant for a laptop computer; as always in such cases, it is primarily the thought that counts.

James Miller at Macmillan helped me conceive this book, and when the political science list was transferred to Allyn and Bacon, Stephen Hull saw the book through to completion. To both editors, my thanks for their encouragement and assistance. Thanks also to Suzanne Foreman, who first interested me in the project. I want to express my appreciation as well to Deborah Brown, the production administrator at Allyn and Bacon who supervised the copy editing and production, and to the principals and staff at P. M. Gordon Associates for their superb work on all phases of production.

Any merit this work may have I share gladly with colleagues, friends, and all of those presidency scholars whose research efforts are reflected in the pages that follow. In responsibility for defects, however, the buck stops here.

CHAPTER 1

Perspectives on the Presidency

The presidents made the highlights of American history, and when you tell about them, you've got it.

—Harry S Truman

INTRODUCTORY CASE: MR. CLINTON GOES TO WASHINGTON

> My fellow citizens, today we celebrate the mystery of American renewal. This ceremony is held in the depth of winter, but by the words we speak and the faces we show the world, we force the spring. A spring reborn in the world's oldest democracy that brings forth the vision and courage to reinvent America.

William Jefferson Clinton looked past the inaugural crowd gathered below him on the Mall behind the Capitol. In the distance he could see past the towers built to accommodate television cameras to the Washington Monument dominating the Mall, and beyond that he could make out the Lincoln Memorial. Washington and Lincoln had been presidents with the "courage to change." Now it was his turn. But the transition had been a disaster. Just hours after his election victory, his campaign team and transition advisors had fought over appointments to the White House jobs. The media had criticized his ethics guidelines for political appointees, even though they were the strongest any president-elect ever instituted. A prospective nominee for deputy chief of staff at the White House had to withdraw his nomination over newspaper allegations he had committed perjury in a court case in New York—allegations later shown to be false. Clinton planned to appoint excellent people, but critics complained that he was taking too much time and that he was establishing quotas for women and minorities. Zöe Baird, his nominee for attorney general, withdrew her name from Senate consideration (only the fifth nominee ever to do so) because of revelations that one of her domestic helpers was an illegal alien. When Donna Shalala, his nominee for Health and Human Services secretary, had testified before Congress about her plans and did not indicate that welfare reform would be one of her priorities, Senator Daniel Patrick Moynihan referred to the "clatter of campaign promises being cast off."

> Raised in unrivaled prosperity, we inherit an economy that is still the world's strongest but is weakened by business failures, stagnant wages, increasing inequality and deep divisions among our own people.

The economy, stupid! That's what he'd campaigned on; that's what he'd won on. Everyone knew his presidency would rise or fall on the economy. Already his stimulus proposals were being faulted by economists and assailed by Republicans. Should job creation or deficit reduction come first? How hard should he push trade liberalization, when his own party might be ripped apart by the issue? Already he had backed off his promise to cut the deficit by half, had dropped the idea of a middle-class tax cut, and had begun to float the idea of tax increases.

> The American people have summoned the change we celebrate today. You have raised your voice in an unmistakable chorus, you have cast your votes in historic numbers, and you have changed the face of Congress, the Presidency and the political process itself. Yes you, my fellow Americans, have forced the spring.

Americans wanted change, wanted to force the spring, but were divided on means and ends. Only 43 percent of the electorate had voted for him. He had received the lowest percentage of votes from the eligible electorate since John Quincy Adams had won the presidency in 1824.[1] He was not elected on a program of sacrifice, and he would have to take on part of his own party to push through his reforms. Were the people ready for sacrifice? To choose the public interest over their own?

> We know we have to face hard truths and take strong steps, but we have not done so. Instead, we have drifted, and that drifting has eroded our resources, fractured our economy and shaken our confidence.

The public was skeptical but hoped for the best: Polls showed that most people thought Clinton cared about "the needs and problems" of people like themselves; more than twice as many believed the economy would be better than thought it would be worse at the end of his term; close to two-thirds believed he could get health insurance for all Americans, improve education, and create jobs; and a slight majority believed he could improve government ethics and the environment.[2] It was time to conclude:

> Today we do more than celebrate America; we rededicate ourselves to the very idea of America: an idea born in revolution and renewed through two centuries of challenge; an idea tempered by the knowledge that but for fate we, the fortunate

William Jefferson Clinton regained the White House for the Democrats in 1993, ending twelve years of uninterrupted Republican control of the presidency. Two years later, however, Republicans won control of both houses of Congress for the first time since 1953.

> and the unfortunate, might have been each other; an idea ennobled by the faith that our nation can summon from its myriad diversity the deepest measure of unity; an idea infused with the conviction that America's long, heroic journey must go forever upward.

Clinton would need that reservoir of good will, for if presidential politics were anything like transition politics, he would need all the help he could get. Within two years his presidency was in peril. As a result of the midterm elections of 1994, his party had lost control of both the Senate and the House (the first time Democrats had lost the House since 1954), had retained control of only a minority of the governorships and state legislatures, and had lost their historic advantage in the South, which dated back more than a century. Some members of his party were even calling for him to withdraw from the presidential contest in 1996. Republicans, led by new House Speaker Newt Gingrich, had seized control of the domestic agenda with their "Contract with America." Clinton, by the spring of 1995, was reduced to claiming that he was "still relevant" in making national policy. If Clinton were not to become yet another failed president, he would have to engineer the political comeback of the century.

WHY STUDY THE PRESIDENCY?

If you are like most students enrolled in presidential politics courses, you already know a good deal about the office of the presidency and about American national politics, and you are probably studying the presidency to deal with the same issues that interest my students. In the falls of 1993 and 1994 I asked students at Columbia University to write their thoughts about the key issues of presidential power: what they admired or were impressed by about the presidency, what they feared about it, and what they did not understand.

"The public's tendency to rally around a president in crisis, regardless of where the fault for the crisis may lie, amazes me," a Columbia College student wrote. "What impresses me most about the office is, in a word, POWER," another said. "Although my view may be naive," he continued, "it seems that a person with as much clout as the President should be able to muscle through Congress any piece of legislation or idea he has." Another wrote, "I am amazed by the day to day demands and stress these men must endure as they are placed in a spotlight and under the microscope of public scrutiny."

Students wrote about their images of the president: "Waving atop the Air Force One stairway, flashbulbs popping and a marching band playing," or in the White House, like Abraham Lincoln during the Civil War, "a man, alone, deciding issues that will affect world history, and anything but confident in his ability to discern the correct solution." As one put it:

> When I think of the words Commander in Chief I see the black and white photographs of President Johnson in the Oval Office taken during meetings with his advisers. He is captured agonizing over the escalating situation in Vietnam, which will ultimately overshadow his War on Poverty. The photos show a man deeply

> concerned about the nation both domestically and internationally, who chooses the more difficult course of increased troop deployment in an unwinnable situation and who ultimately loses sight of the attainable goals at home.

A graduate student wrote, "What most impresses me about the presidency is presidential power." The student continued, "What most disturbs me about the presidency is presidential power." Another felt similar unease: "While we've had strong leaders who have tested the bounds of the office, their designs seem to be at odds with the general interests of the nation." A graduate student who had practiced law in Mexico added, "As a foreigner, what disturbs me the most is the influence that the president may have in some countries that he knows little about." Someone else worried that "Presidents often get to a point where they feel they are above the law and thus justify illegal covert actions." Yet one student noted how subjective issues of power can be: "When I don't agree [with a presidential policy] I don't think the president should have this power and when I do agree I'm all for it."

Most students come to the study of the presidency with questions about the role of the president in a democracy. "To what extent is a presidential election a mandate from the American people for a successful candidate's policies?" one wanted to know. "It often seems as though a President remains on the campaign trail throughout his term," another observed, "I fear that often the President takes a politically wise position over one that is beneficial to the entire community." Another wondered, "If you let public opinion polls dictate your actions why even be President?" adding, "Is it possible for a president to stay true to his beliefs and survive politically?" Still another wondered, "To whom are presidents truly accountable, special interests, or the public at large?"

Some students looked to the presidency for leadership and were bothered by a nation that seemed disinclined to support the person they had just elected. "He, in a sense, is America," wrote a student who had worked in the Clinton campaign, adding, "Today the President has become more of a scapegoat than a leader for everything that has gone wrong with America." Yet others were disturbed that the president would try to lead the nation unilaterally, and, as one put it, "I am disturbed by the arrogant posturing of some presidents who tend to presume that by being elected, they receive a mandate to do anything they choose and are above congressional and public oversight."

My students wanted to learn about the formal powers of the presidency, about the limits the Constitution places on them, and about the political constraints Congress can impose on presidential policies. "Although constitutional wording allows the presidency to grow, does it also allow it to shrink?" one asked. "The most confusing aspect of the President is the extent to which he can act on policy and security matters without consent of Congress," another wrote. "To what extent are these powers dependent on the personality and creativity of the individual man or woman, and to what extent are they inherent in the office?" another student pondered.

Some students want to study the presidency to "balance the impression given by the media that the Presidency is of limitless importance." Echoing that theme, a student from Jamaica wondered "why the President has so much difficulty getting his agenda across a Congress that seems to block every move?" Another was curious why it seemed "necessary to stumble through many deals and compromises in order to implement crucial pieces of legislation beneficial to all of America?" Many students are upset about the difficulties presidents have in getting things done in the bureaucracy that they presumably control. "I am particularly confused by the bureaucracy that a President faces," one student confessed, adding, "It appears that it is almost impossible for him to get anything done short of a national emergency."

"Why have we had no great presidents in my lifetime?" an undergraduate asked pointedly. Others wondered as well. "I find the office to be uniquely challenging and the men who have occupied it recently to be sorely lacking," wrote another student. "Why do the men who hold the office seem to be so fearful of taking a meaningful stance on many moral issues?" Why indeed?

THE DILEMMA OF PRESIDENTIAL GOVERNMENT

"We make our arches out of brick," the citizens of ancient Rome used to boast, "so that after the conquering hero passes through we have something to throw at him." Presidents succeed, sometimes beyond their wildest expectations, and then fall, fast and far, then proceed to make brilliant comebacks, and then fail again. "I used to say the White House theme song should be 'Riding high in April, shot down in May,' " said President Bush's media advisor Sig Rogich, "but it's more like 'Riding high at 8 o'clock, shot down at 9.' "[3] In the midst of the Whitewater scandal of 1994, a bemused Bill Clinton observed about his negative media coverage, "Sometimes I wonder what planet I'm on."

The Courage to Change

Far from being a stable institution that provides solidity or unity to our politics, the American presidency is the most unpredictable and unstable political institution in our nation. Every four years our presidential politics shakes things up and turns them around and upside down. Our presidential transitions become a time for innovations to percolate and bubble upward from the grassroots to the capital, and transfuse the top levels of national government with new appointees and new ideas—until the appointees (or even the nominees) are sent packing and their ideas go down in flames. Presidents rearrange the furniture in the Oval Office, redecorate the White House, and reorganize White House staff, executive office agencies, and the entire bureaucracy. They propose new economic and social programs, bring us to the brink of war, and sometimes take us beyond. They dominate the front pages of newspapers and the evening network newscasts because they are news, and they are news because everyday what they and their colleagues in the White House are doing is new.

In Clinton's inaugural address we heard the uplifting themes of presidential rhetoric: the "courage to change" that the president calls for from the people, the courage to "force the spring." In Clinton's troubled transition and term of office we see the gritty reality of presidential politics. Nothing comes easy to those who sit in the Oval Office. The easy issues are settled elsewhere in government; what comes to the president are issues that are intractable or unmanageable. "If people thought I'd be president, and 90 days later every campaign commitment I made would be written into the law, and everybody's life would be changed, I think that's just not realistic," Clinton told a meeting of newspaper executives just before the end of his first 100 days.[4] The President must, day in and day out, figure out how to solve the unsolvable and manage the unmanageable. "When I read the other day in the *Los Angeles Times* that I had the best record of any President in 40 years," Clinton concluded near the end of his first year, "I said, 'Pity the others.' "[5]

Is There an "Expectations Gap"?

Because the president is chief of state, he becomes a father figure to us. We are socialized in the lower grades to think of the president, like the police officer or the teacher, as a figure who is all-knowing, all-powerful, and benevolent—a combination of George Washington and Abraham Lincoln. As we grow up in front of the television set, we find the news concentrating on the White House rather than on the complexities of Capitol Hill, on executive actions and speeches rather than on congressional proposals and debate. We grow up with an underlying set of assumptions about the way American government works:

- Presidents run the government because they head "the Executive Branch";
- Other officials work under them and follow their orders;
- By virtue of their election they embody the will of the people;
- Presidents use their party to control Congress and get their campaign platform and other programs enacted.

Each of these assumptions is incorrect. A president can run some of the government some of the time, and a small part of the government all of the time, but no president can run all of the government all of the time. Officials work under Congress as well as under the president (and are subject to the courts as well). No president receives a "mandate" on more than a few issues from the voters. Party support for the president can be obtained, but no president can take it for granted, and most need support from the opposition party as well. The best of presidents do not dominate their party or Congress on most issues most of the time. Some do not even try to lead Congress, but prefer to bypass it, especially when it is controlled by the opposition party—as it is so much of the time.

"The nation expects more of the president than he can possibly do," wrote Louis Brownlow, a political scientist who helped Franklin Roosevelt create the Executive Office of the President. "Thus, expecting from him the impossible, inevitably we shall be disappointed in his performance."[6] Some people believe that the "expectations gap" between what the public expects and what presidents can accomplish explains much of why presidents fail.[7] Do presidents raise expectations they cannot meet because they lack sufficient constitutional power and political support to accomplish all they promise and all we ask of them? Although the "expectations gap" approach has some merit, it is somewhat misleading on the following four counts:

- The public does not have confidence in any governmental institution, especially the presidency. Between 1973 and 1993 the proportion of the public saying they had a "great deal of confidence" in the executive fell from 29 to 12 percent; the proportion with "hardly any" confidence rose from 18 to 32 percent.[8]
- Since the 1970s the public has not expected presidents to solve every problem. Approximately 70 percent of the voters say "yes" in national polls when asked if they are optimistic about the next four years with a new president. In 1993, however, a majority of voters agreed with the statement "The problems this country faces today are so large that no President could do much to solve them" (only 38 percent thought so in 1991). Less than half the public thought Clinton could deal effectively with drugs and crime, or budget reduction, though, on the economy, a majority assumed he would make a difference. Two years into his term those who thought he could be effective were in a shrinking minority. Most voters think that presidents will renege on their campaign promises.[9]
- In presidential elections many people vote for "the lesser of two evils." On average this "negative voting" accounted for 14.8 percent of the vote between 1952 and 1960, 25.2 percent of the vote between 1968 and 1976, and a huge 40.7 percent of the vote between 1980 and 1988.[10] Enthusiasm for presidential candidates has been steadily declining over the past three decades: the percentage of voters expressing reservations about their choice increased in each election. Between 1952 and 1980 there was a 31 percent drop in voters giving a "highly favorable" rating to the nominees of the two parties. In most elections approximately 65 to 75 percent of those eligible to vote did not cast ballots for a new president. Both voters and nonvoters have low rather than high expectations for the candidate who wins the White House.[11]
- The relationship between public expectation and presidential accomplishment is sometimes inverse. No one expected much from Abraham Lincoln, or for that matter from Franklin Roosevelt, two of the strongest presidents in American history. On the other hand, Herbert Hoover was expected to be an effective and energetic president because of his prior career in the cabinet and his efforts as relief administrator in Europe after World War I, but to many Americans he seemed ineffective during the Depression. No one thought Lyndon Johnson would go from triumph in domestic affairs to disaster in the Vietnam War in his elected term.

Expectation gap theorists have the problem the wrong way round: by the 1990s Presidents Bush and Clinton entered office without popular mandates or great expectations that they could accomplish much at all, yet they had awesome constitutional and political responsibilities. As it turned out, popular expectations had little impact on their actual performance. President Bush, even with a modest domestic agenda, enjoyed several years of high popularity, during which time no gap between his modest accomplishments and presidential demands for action could be detected.[12] Conversely, President Clinton suffered from low public approval ratings in his first two years, yet during that time his legislative accomplishments and the strong performance of the economy ranked him among the most effective presidents since World War II. Nevertheless, he presided over a midterm disaster in spite of his legislative record—or perhaps because of it. How to explain these inverse relationships remains one of the unanswered questions of American politics.

Mistrust of Executive Power

If we have a president who is strong enough to govern, is that, as Alexander Hamilton asked after the Constitutional Convention, "inconsistent with the genius of republican government"?[13] Hamilton answered no, but many Americans remain ambivalent about presidential power and are suspicious of its exercise. "We give the President more work than a man can do, more responsibility than a man should take, more pressure than a man can bear. We abuse him often and rarely praise him. We wear him out, use him up, eat him up," John Steinbeck observed in 1966.[14] Our presidents are our national heroes, and at the same time they are national scapegoats and fall guys for late-night comics. Our attitude problem with presidents goes all the way back to colonial times. The Puritans who started the early settlements left England to get away from the King. Royal governors abused their powers routinely in the colonies. The Declaration of Independence is a list of complaints against a tyrannical monarch. Yet the weak state governors installed after the Revolution proved incapable of providing effective government. We have never figured out what we wanted from the presidency or, for that matter, from our presidents.

Ambivalence about Presidents

Is Clinton Our Boy Bill or Slick Willie? We can change our minds in a minute. Was Jimmy Carter a passionless technician or a feeling moralist crusader? At different times we perceived him each way. When George Bush was on top of the world after the Persian Gulf War, we thought of him as the patrician progressive; a year later when the economy tumbled he seemed aloof and out of touch. Gerald Ford took office as a homespun regular kind of guy who made his own breakfast in the White House; after issuing a pardon to Nixon, though, he was viewed as a bumbler who could not walk and chew gum at the same time. When Lyndon Johnson assumed the presidency he was hailed as the consummate politician; when his support ebbed because of the Vietnam War he was portrayed as an arrogant loudmouth and corrupt wheeler-dealer, presiding over a White House of sycophantic courtiers.[15] Each quality has a positive or negative attribution, and these can spin around in minutes.

No matter what presidents do, in some ways they are locked into no-win situations. We want contradictory qualities in our chief executive. We want a decent and honest leader who can manipulate the system. We want someone with strong inner convictions who is also flexible and adaptable. We want someone who innovates and leads yet also responds to majority sentiment and does not get out of touch. We want a politician who knows how to wheel and deal, but we also want a statesperson who is above the grimy game. We want someone with the common touch yet with an aura of greatness about him or her. When we think of past presidents, we conjure up an "idealized" composite that no modern president can match: the exuberance of Teddy Roosevelt, the erudition of Woodrow Wilson, the aristocratic bearing of Franklin Roosevelt, the common touch of Harry Truman, the father image of Dwight Eisenhower, the wit of John Kennedy, the political instincts of Lyndon Johnson, the diplomatic expertise of Richard Nixon, the modesty of Gerald Ford, the religious values of Jimmy Carter, the dramatic flair of Ronald Reagan, the experience of George Bush.[16] And every president's weakness can always be contrasted with the corresponding strength of one or more of his predecessors: Why did Bill Clinton lack the political skills of Franklin Roosevelt or the plain dealing of Harry Truman? Why couldn't George Bush articulate a vision the way Ronald Reagan could? Why wasn't Richard Nixon blessed with the integrity of Dwight Eisenhower?

The Fall Guy

"America has a manic-depressive cycle with its leaders," observes historian Michael Beschloss, "and it's a bad thing, because it inevitably sets these presidents up for a terrible fall."[17] Voters are quicker than ever to decide that "the honeymoon is over." Ford's popularity dropped 30 points after his pardon of Nixon; Reagan's plummeted 40 percent in two years because of a steep recession; Clinton's dropped from 60 to 43 percent approval in his first hundred days because of a widespread perception that his administration was disorganized and unfocused and that he was backing away from his commitments. By the end of his first year his popularity was lower than that of any president since 1945. By March of his second year, he was defending his wife against gutter journalism charges that she might have had something to do with the death of White House aide Vincent Foster; by the fall of 1994 he was setting up a legal fund to pay lawyers defending him against a lawsuit charging him with sexual harassment.

Media Coverage

Part of our ambivalence, indeed our schizophrenia, about presidential power, is derived from the confusing media coverage of Oval Office occupants. Critical coverage in the presidential primaries (*Time* magazine had a Clinton cover in the spring of 1992 with the tag line "Why Voters Don't Trust Clinton") is followed by a celebration of the party nominee, then by more critical coverage of the general election efforts. The new president is greeted favorably (the January 7 *Time* celebrated Clinton as "Man of the Year"), then a few months later is cast over (the June 7 *Time* cover story analyzed "The Incredible Shrinking Presidency"), then by late fall is celebrated once again (as "Standing Tall" in a *Newsweek* story). After two months of savaging of Clinton in the Whitewater scandal, a spate of articles appeared in the same newspapers criticizing journalists for making a mountain out of a molehill and relying on rumor and innuendo instead of hard evidence.

In classic movie comedies the Keystone cops chased criminals by running across the screen from left to right, then moments later reappearing and running from right to left, but no matter how ridiculous they appeared, they do not begin to compare with the American press corps as its pundits change their mind about presidential performance from week to week. We cannot possibly hope to gain any good understanding of presidential politics from media coverage of current events.

LEARNING ABOUT THE PRESIDENCY

How can we learn about the presidency? How can we sort out our own attitudes about presidents and their exercise of power? We can start by learning about how the office works, how presidents interpret and use their constitutional powers, and how they try to gain influence with Congress, the bureaucracy, and the public. Once we do so we are less likely to rush to judgment about presidents and more likely to understand the limits of presidential leadership in our democracy.

What Do We Know about the Presidency?

Public opinion polls tell us that Americans know a great deal about the people in the White House and about their personality traits. Almost everyone (usually 99 percent) knows who the U.S. president is, and approximately 80 percent of the American people can name a secretary of state and other key cabinet members. Most of the public knows the president's position on key issues, as well as the important facts about the presidency: who the first president was, what Lincoln did to save the Union, the length of the presidential term, what a presidential veto is. Unfortunately, only a minority know that the president does not declare war, what the electoral college does, how convention delegates are selected to nominate a president, or the percentage of votes needed in Congress to override a presidential veto.[18]

What We Know That Is Not So

The good news is that we know a great deal about the presidency; the bad news is that much of what we think we know proves to be incorrect, in large measure because pundits (magazine and newspaper columnists and talk-show commentators) seem incapable of adequate description or prediction. In 1992 we were told that Bush was a lock-in for reelection with his 91 percent popularity rating; Clinton defied the odds and made Bush history. Pundits reported in 1981 that a "Reagan Revolution" would make the Republicans the dominant party in the nation, but by 1989 when President Reagan left office, Republicans held fewer elected posts than in 1981. In the 1970s pundits observed that Jimmy Carter was a bumpkin small-state governor who did not know anything about foreign affairs; we found out that he could handle himself in the world arena when he brokered a peace agreement between Israel and Egypt at the Camp David Summit. In the 1960s we were told that Richard Nixon was a consummate anticommunist who would heat up the Cold War, but Nixon ushered in an age of détente with the Soviet Union, ended American involvement in the Vietnam War, and inaugurated low-level diplomatic relations with communist China after making a historic trip there. In the 1950s most observers told us that Eisenhower was a military man with no talent for civilian politics: he won two elections (and could easily have won a third), kept infla-

The Presidential Job Description

We sometimes think the president "runs" the government, but in fact the Constitution created a system of separated institutions (the presidency, Congress, and the federal courts) that share in, and sometimes compete for, the power to govern. Consider the following presidential roles and their limits.

Chief of State

Role. Presidents are heads of state, presiding at ceremonial occasions and symbolizing our values and traditions. Presidents issue proclamations (Thanksgiving Day, for example), receive honored guests in the name of the American people, and unify the people at times of national mourning or in national emergencies.

Limits. The Constitution does not make presidents the head of state, and presidents do not embody the sovereignty of the nation, which is exercised concurrently by Congress, the Supreme Court, and the president. Although the incumbent sometimes serves as a figure of national unity, he or she will divide the American people during elections.

Commander in Chief

Role. Presidents command the armed forces in peace and in war. They and their appointees determine overall defense policy and the deployment of the armed forces. Presidents order the armed forces into combat and engage in war making on their own authority.

Limits. The Constitution does not specify anything other than that the president is commander in chief. It does not empower the president to command troops, direct military operations, or make war policies. There are no clear boundaries between presidential responsibilities and the specific constitutional duties of Congress.

Chief Diplomat

Role. Presidents and their appointees communicate with other governments, take the lead in forging and maintaining our alliances, and negotiate bilateral and multilateral international agreements and treaties. Presidents receive foreign ambassadors, appoint (by and with the advice and consent of the Senate) our ambassadors to other nations, and recognize foreign governments.

Limits. The Constitution does not make the president the sole organ of American foreign affairs. The Senate plays a major role in presidential appointments

Continued

The Presidential Job Description *(continued)*

and consents to treaties. The House and Senate fund foreign affairs activities. Laws passed by Congress on trade, immigration, foreign aid, patents and copyrights, and other matters have a major impact on foreign affairs.

Chief Executive

Role. Presidents supervise the work of the departments and agencies of government. They appoint (by and with the advice and consent of the Senate) the executives to run these agencies, propose policies, and are responsible for their implementation once passed into law.

Limits. Congress conducts legislative oversight and strongly influences the work of executive officials. It determines the organization of departments, and the powers of its agencies, sets the pay scales and personnel policies, and funds the activities of each agency.

Chief Legislator

Role. Each year the president prepares a domestic legislative program and a budget and sends them to Congress for its consideration. Presidents lobby with Congress for their programs, threaten to use the veto on legislation they deem unsatisfactory, and implement laws passed by Congress according to their own interpretation.

Limits. The legislative parties develop much of the congressional program independently. Presidents do not control legislative party or committee leaders. They have only marginal influence on congressional consideration of legislation. Their interpretations of laws are subject to judicial checks.

Chief of Party

Role. Presidents are titular leaders of their parties. They choose the national chairperson and influence the work of their party's national committee.

Limits. Legislative party leaders control the party's Senate and House campaign committees. The White House does not control state, county, and local parties. Presidents may help recruit candidates for office, but they cannot purge them.

tion low, reduced military expenditures, and steered clear of foreign wars—not a bad record for an amateur in the White House, or for any president. No matter how much we think we know about a president, his or her administration is bound to surprise us. No president will be predictable in office—that is the only prediction that we can make.

President Nixon conferring with Chinese Communist Party Leader Mao Zedong on February 21, 1972, during Nixon's historic diplomatic mission to China. Nixon ended more than two decades of American nonrecognition of the communist regime, after having been one of that policy's chief architects.

Similarly, what we think we know about the *office of the presidency* may not always be so. Many of us think that the Constitution defines the president's powers and makes him or her the undisputed head of the executive branch of government. But the Constitution is usually silent, underdefined, or ambiguous about important presidential powers, and, when a serious issue arises, the Constitution usually does not provide an answer. We think that a president is the head of the cabinet and the executive branch, and that he or she has vast powers and can order the government to do what he or she wants done. The Constitution does not mention an executive branch of government or the cabinet. Often presidents who issue commands do so out of weakness and not strength, and sometimes their commands are not obeyed, even by their subordinates. We think that a president is the leader of his or her party and can count on its support. Sometimes the most dangerous of the enemies that do a president in come from his or her own party.

Judging Presidents: The Verdict of History

Who are the successful presidents? What accounts for their success? In 1948, distinguished historian Arthur Schlesinger, Sr., asked 75 of his colleagues to rank the presidents. Not surprisingly they ranked (in order): Abraham Lincoln, George Washington, Franklin Roosevelt, Woodrow Wilson, and Andrew Jackson.[19] In 1962, Schlesinger found similar results (Jackson had been dropped to "near great" from "great"). These presidents had several things in common. They were powerful ambitious leaders who left the office stronger than it had been when they entered it. Each used his constitutional powers to the maximum. Washington excepted, each was willing to appeal to the people over the heads of Congress for political support to advance his agenda. They were all victorious in wartime (or in Jackson's case, in threats to use force against secessionists).

It is impossible to make a serious judgment about a president's performance while he or she is in office. It takes the passage of time (and the opening up of presidential libraries) to make an informed judgment. Even public approval scores for most presidents rise and fall from generation to generation.[20] Harry Truman in 1952 had so little support he withdrew from consideration for reelection. His average approval rating was 41 percent when he was in office. Yet it rose to 68 percent in 1990, after his Cold War policies had been vindicated by the collapse of the former Soviet Union. In contrast, Lyndon Johnson's average rating was 56 percent during his term, but by 1990 the legacy of his disastrous Vietnam War policies had lowered his approval rating to 40 percent. Richard Nixon's average rating was 48 percent when in office, but was stuck at 32 percent in 1990, despite his Herculean efforts to rehabilitate himself after abusing his presidential powers in the Watergate scandal. Why do presidents rise and fall, or vice versa, in public esteem? Why do they go from being heroes to being (in the words of President Carter's chief of staff Jack Watson) the "javelin catchers" of American politics? And vice versa? Often their policies are later vindicated by events. Values change, and presidents who exemplify the ones we appreciate more may find their popularity increasing as the decades pass—as are the cases with Truman's plain speaking and Carter's emphasis on ethics in government and human rights in world politics. Historians, political scientists, and investigative reporters are constantly discovering things about presidents; hence later generations have more information on which to base their judgments.

THE RESEARCH AGENDA

Political scientists and historians divide presidency research into several subfields. These parallel the questions that students of the presidency are interested in; we do our best to provide answers, or if not answers, at least ways of thinking about how answers might be found.

One field concentrates on the character of those who have held the office. How have conscious (and perhaps subconscious) factors affected their styles of leadership? Another focuses more directly on presidential leadership: Does the president deal step-by-step with issues or go for broke and gamble everything? Is the president a skilled political infighter, or does he or she act the part of a statesperson above the political fray? Can the president persuade Congress and the nation, or does he or she rely primarily on unilateral actions and constitutional powers? Is the president flexible and cool under fire, or does he or she "rigidify" and "freeze up" in a crisis?

Political scientists sometimes concentrate on the presidency as an institution—the personnel and staff agencies surrounding the president, including the White House Office (the president's staff) and the Executive Office of the President (agencies that handle presidential business). We want to know how effective these offices are in helping presidents with their priorities: How useful is their advice?

What happens when advisors disagree? In what ways might the presidential advisory system be improved?

Another way to study the presidency is to consider how presidents deal with constituencies: political party organization, electoral coalitions, and interest groups. We want to know how they maintain and broaden their coalitions of voters and interest groups, and how they prevent their opponents from splitting their followers. How well do presidents use the media, and what are the relationships between public approval of their performance and their success with Congress?

We often study the formal powers of the presidency, especially those left indeterminate by the Constitution. How do presidents interpret their constitutional powers, restrictively or expansively? What are the costs and benefits involved in the "constitutional opportunism" of those presidents who seek to expand their powers? How have presidents expanded the responsibilities and powers of their office? What are the prospects that their powers will expand or be limited in the future? Do we have an imperial presidency, riding roughshod over the Constitution and the laws? Or do we have, as President Gerald Ford suggested, an "imperiled" presidency, one that is too weak to the govern because of Congressional usurpations of power? Or do we simply have the normal workings of checks and balances, in which presidents and legislators will continue to frustrate each other by exercising their constitutional powers?

The Plan of the Book

Whatever our particular subfields, we study the presidency because we want to know its impact on our lives. We need to understand how presidents manage the economy, guide American diplomacy, and make decisions about peace and war. Why do our presidents fail so often? Under what circumstances are they likely to succeed? What kind of presidential office is best for American democracy? How is the presidency evolving? These are the issues we will be exploring in the remainder of this book.

In Chapter 2 we examine the origins of the presidency. We want to know why it was created and what problems it was meant to solve. The Constitutional Convention provided the presidency with some explicit powers, but in addition, the wording of the Constitution was vague and ambiguous and incomplete. Why weren't the framers more precise about enumerating presidential powers? Understanding their reasons will give us a start in understanding how the presidency works.

In Chapter 3 we look briefly at the evolution of the presidential office. In the nineteenth century presidential candidates did not attend nominating conventions and did not go on the campaign trail. Once in the White House, the president was not expected to present a legislative program or appeal to the American people for support. He had hardly any staff assistance. His powers were limited, and he did not have any budgetary or administrative powers. How this weak office was transformed into a powerful instrument of democratic leadership is the subject of this chapter.

In Chapter 4 we consider the formal constitutional powers of the president from another angle: although the Constitution did not provide the president with extensive powers, the occupants of the Oval Office have been able to develop a "prerogative style" of government that allows them to exercise vast governmental powers unilaterally, without the participation of Congress, and sometimes in secret so the American public is not informed of what they are doing. Is prerogative government compatible with checks and balances and separation of powers? Does it pose a danger to American democracy, or is some exercise of prerogative essential to its preservation? No questions about the American presidency are more important to consider.

In Chapters 5 and 6 we consider how presidents are nominated and elected. Nominations were once controlled by members of Congress, then they were transferred to state and local party leaders at national conventions. Since the 1970s the voters in each party, through state primary contests, have made the final determinations. Do we get better candidates through the modern system, or did state party bosses provide us with better candidates? We examine this and other questions in Chapter 5. In chapter 6 we consider whether presidents gain a mandate on issues in presidential elections. To what extent can their election be considered a mandate from the majority of the American people?

In Chapters 7 and 8 we consider the political resources the victorious presidential candidate brings to the White House. Can he or she be an effective party leader? To what extent does a president have "coattails" that translate into support for congressional and state and local candidates? Once in office, can the president use the "bully good pulpit" (in Theodore Roosevelt's words) to convince the public to support his or her program?

In Chapters 9 through 12 we examine the way the president interacts with legislators, department and agency officials, and the judges and justices of the federal courts. To some extent the Constitution permits the president to substitute his or her own powers for theirs: presidents may "legislate" by issuing executive orders and proclamations, for example. Yet in other ways the president is more limited than we might suppose: A combination of congressional committees and government bureaucrats and federal judges can block presidential orders, prevent the White House from controlling the bureaucracy, and limit the president's administrative and budgetary powers. How modern-day political practices prevent the creation of an "Executive Branch" dominated by the president is the theme of these chapters.

Chapters 13 through 15 deal with presidential economics, diplomacy, and war-making. Do Presidents have adequate information and valid theories about the economy and international affairs to make rational decisions? How much help do they get from their advisors? Do they have enough constitutional and statutory power to manage these affairs, or should they be provided with more?

How can we improve the way decisions are made? Chapter 16 takes up various proposals to reform the American system: giving the president more power, installing a form of cabinet government to replace our presidential system, or establishing a better system of shared decision making by president and Congress. We consider the pros and cons of each idea, so that readers will have some ideas about what will not work—and what might.

FURTHER READING

Books

Philip Abbott, *The Exemplary Presidency,* Amherst, MA: University of Massachusetts Press, 1963.

Barbara Hinckley, *The Symbolic Presidency,* New York: Routledge, 1990.

Thomas Langston, *With Reverence and Contempt: How Americans Think about their Presidents,* Baltimore, MD: The Johns Hopkins University Press, 1995.

Lewis Lapham, *The Wish for Kings,* New York: Grove/Atlantic Press, 1993.

William Leuchtenberg, *In the Shadow of FDR,* rev. ed., Ithaca, NY: Cornell University Press, 1984.

Theodore Lowi, *The Personal President: Power Invested, Promise Unfulfilled,* Ithaca, NY: Cornell University Press, 1985.

George Reedy, *The Twilight of the Presidency,* New York: Mentor, 1970.

Steven Wayne and George Edwards, eds., *Studying the Presidency,* Knoxville, TN: University of Tennessee Press, 1987.

Aaron Wildavsky, *The Beleaguered Presidency,* New Brunswick, NJ: Transaction Books, 1991.

Presidents on the Presidency

Jimmy Carter, *Keeping Faith: Memoirs of a President,* New York: Bantam, 1982.

Dwight D. Eisenhower, *The White House Years,* Garden City, NY: Doubleday, 1965.

Gerald R. Ford, *A Time to Heal,* New York: Harper and Row, 1979.

Herbert Hoover, *Memoirs,* 2 vols, New York: Macmillan, 1951.

Lyndon Johnson, *The Vantage Point,* New York: Holt, Rinehart and Winston, 1971.

Richard Nixon, *R. N.: The Memoirs of Richard Nixon,* New York: Grosset & Dunlop, 1978.

Ronald Reagan, *An American Life,* New York: Simon and Schuster, 1990.

Theodore Roosevelt, *An Autobiography,* New York: Macmillan, 1919.

Harry S. Truman, *Memoirs,* 2 vols, Garden City, NY: Doubleday, 1955.

Reference Works

Leonard W. Levy and Louis Fisher, eds., *The Encyclopedia of the American Presidency,* New York: Simon and Schuster, 1994.

Michael Nelson, ed., *Guide to the Presidency,* Washington DC: Congressional Quarterly Press, 1990.

Richard M. Pious, *The Young Oxford Companion to the Presidency of the United States,* New York: Oxford University Press, 1993.

NOTES

1. Calculated by multiplying Clinton's percentage of the three-candidate vote (43%) times the turnout of eligible voters (55%). Presidents Lincoln (1860), Wilson (1912), and Nixon (1968) received a lower percentage of the vote, but turnouts were much higher, giving them higher overall support among the adult Americans eligible to vote.

2. Dan Clymer, "Americans Have High Hopes for Clinton, Poll Finds," *New York Times,* January 19, 1993, p. A-13.

3. Quoted in Maureen Dowd, "Clinton as National Idol: Is It Only Puppy Love?" *New York Times,* January 3, 1993, p. A-18.

4. Gwenn Ifill, "President Asks for Time and a Little Tenderness," *New York Times,* April 26, 1993, p. B-9.

5. Address by President Clinton at Georgetown University, Washington, DC, December 1, 1993.

6. Louis Brownlow, "What We Expect the President to Do," in Aaron Wildavsky, ed., *The Presidency,* Boston: Little, Brown, 1969, p. 35.

7. This question is considered in Richard W. Waterman, ed., *The Presidency Reconsidered,* Itasca, Ill.: F. E. Peacock, 1993.

8. National Opinion Research Center polls, *The American Enterprise,* November/December, 1993, p. 94.

9. The Wall Street Journal/NBC Poll, January 20, 1993, *Time Magazine/CNN Poll,* August 15, 1994.

10. Michael M. Gant and Lillian E. Richardson, Jr., "Presidential Performance, the Expectations Gap, and Negative Voter Support," in Richard Waterman, ed., *The Presidency Reconsidered,* Itasca, IL: F. E. Peacock, 1993, pp. 47–74, data from Table 3.2, Negative Voter Support, 1952–58, p. 59.

11. Martin Wattenberg, *The Rise of Candidate-Centered Politics,* Cambridge, MA: Harvard University Press, 1991; Anthony King, "How Not to Select Presidential Candidates," in Austin Ranney, ed., *The American Elections of 1980,* Washington, DC: American Enterprise Institute, 1981; Table 9-1, p. 306; also *Washington Post/ABC Poll,* January 14–17, 1993.

12. Charles Jones, "Meeting Low Expectations: Strategy and Prospects of the Bush Presidency," in Colin Campbell, S.J., and Bert Rockman, eds., *The Bush Presidency: First Appraisals,* Chatham, NJ: Chatham House, 1991, pp. 37–38; George Edwards, "George Bush and the Politics of Inclusion," in Campbell and Rockman, op. cit., p. 145.

13. Alexander Hamilton, *The Federalist Papers,* no. 70.

14. John Steinbeck, *America and Americans,* New York: Bonanza Books, 1966, p. 46.

15. George Reedy, *The Twilight of the Presidency,* New York: New American Library, 1970.

16. Michael Nelson, "Evaluating the Presidency," in Michael Nelson, ed., *The Presidency and the Political System,* Washington, DC: Congressional Quarterly Press, 1984, pp. 5–28.

17. Quoted in Maureen Dowd, "Clinton as National Idol," p. A-1.

18. Data from polls conducted by Michael Delli Carpini and Scott Teeter, *What Americans Know about Politics, and Why It Matters,* New Haven, CT: Yale University Press, forthcoming.

19. Arthur M. Schlesinger, Sr., "Historians Rate U.S. Presidents," *Life,* November, 1948; also Arthur Schlesinger, Sr., "Our Presidents: A Rating by 75 Historians," *New York Times Magazine,* July 29, 1962, p. 12 ff.

20. *New York Times,* January 24, 1993, reporting on Gallup polls, p. 3.

CHAPTER 2

The Creation of the Presidency

In framing a government which is to be administered by men over men, the great difficulty lies in this: you must first enable the government to control the governed; and in the next place oblige it to control itself. A dependence on the people is, no doubt, the primary control on the government, but experience has taught mankind the necessity of auxiliary precautions.

—*James Madison*

INTRODUCTORY CASE: SHAYS'S REBELLION

They were farmers in Massachusetts, most of them veterans of the Revolutionary War, and in the summer of 1786 their taxes were high and prices for their crops low. Creditors were foreclosing on their lands and taking their crops and livestock. In the hills of western Massachusetts they drafted petitions to the state legislature in Boston, but it adjourned without passing a law to stay foreclosures. On August 31 farmers prevented a court from sitting in Northampton, and on September 5 court proceedings in Worcester were disrupted. Crowds freed farmers from debtors' prisons. When the state supreme court convened in Springfield, 600 farmers led by Daniel Shays, a former captain in the Revolutionary War, squared off against an equal number of militiamen sent by Governor James Bowdoin, and to prevent bloodshed the judges went back to Boston.[1]

Governor Bowdoin suspended habeas corpus (so he could arrest people and hold them without trial), and sent an enlarged militia back to crush the farmers. On January 25, 1787, Shays and 1200 of his followers confronted General William Shepherd and his militia at the federal arsenal at Springfield. If Shays had been able to take control of the arsenal, his army of farmers might have dominated the western part of the state. Instead the militia routed Shays, and he and 150 of his followers were soon captured. On March 14 Shays and a dozen other leaders were tried, convicted, and sentenced to death. Governor Bowdoin, however, soon to leave office, granted a reprieve, and his successor, John Hancock, pardoned all of them. The legislature, realizing that the farmers had legitimate grievances, passed a bill exempting clothing, household goods, and farm implements from court judgments.

Shays's Rebellion shocked American leaders. "For God's sake tell me what is the cause of all these commotions," George Washington wrote his friends. "Do they proceed from licentiousness, British influence disseminated by the Tories, or real grievances which admit of redress?" To conservatives like Abigail Adams, wife of John Adams, American minister to London, the rebels were simply "ignorant, restless desperadoes, without conscience or principles," acting on "grievances which have no existence but in their imaginations." To Thomas Jefferson, however, minister to Paris, the rebels might prod the nation to make reforms. "I like a little rebellion now and then," he wrote to Abigail Adams. "It is like a storm in the atmosphere."

The troubles in the Berkshire mountains of Massachusetts had far more impact than the farmers could have known. Even as they were being dispersed and tried for treason, George Washington and a circle of influential politicians that looked to him for national leadership were making plans for a constitutional convention in Philadelphia, one that might be the last chance to preserve and strengthen democratic government in the states and the nation. The thirty-nine signers of the Constitution and the hundreds of state convention delegates who ratified it did so because they were convinced that without it they could not preserve their states and territories against European powers, maintain domestic order against insurrection, or provide for national prosperity.

The Constitution was an experiment crafted by politicians who made pragmatic accommodations to achieve common purposes. Within this experiment was contained another: the presidency, an office that did not rely on the forms of monarchy for its legitimacy. The creation of the presidency is often viewed as a reaction to monarchy, and to some extent it was, for the framers did not want executive power to be associated with the abuses they had suffered under King George III.[2] But it was also a response to the failure of governance under the Articles of Confederation, which provided no executive power at all. It was an experiment, to be sure, but one that represented a distillation of all that Americans had learned in one hundred fifty years of experimenting with the use of executive power.

THE FAILURE OF THE ARTICLES OF CONFEDERATION

"Our situation is becoming every day more and more critical," James Madison wrote to Virginia Governor Randolph from the Continental Congress. "No money comes into the federal treasury; no respect is paid to the federal authority; and people of reflection unanimously agree that the existing confederacy is tottering to its foundation."[3] In the Northwest Territory the British had not evacuated their garrisons according to the treaty ending the Revolutionary War. The Spanish in Florida and their Indian allies threatened settlers in Georgia. Foreign nations did not recognize the Confederation as a sovereign power, often dealing instead with the separate states.[4] Pirates in the Mediterranean menaced American shipping with impunity, for there was no American navy to punish them and no funds in the treasury to pay their tribute. The talk among politicians in 1786 was of creating three new regional confederacies, linked to each other by treaties. At the Harvard College Commencement of 1787, John Quincy Adams, the valedictorian of the senior class, talked of the American people "groaning under the intolerable burden of accumulated evils."

The Newburgh Mutiny

The army was a volatile factor in American politics. In 1782 army units quartered at Newburgh, New York, threatened to mutiny over back pay and put George Washington in as a monarch. Washington got wind of the "Newburgh conspiracy," raced to their encampment, declined to participate in the plot, and promised he would intercede with Congress for their pay.[5] The following year troops ransacked arsenals in Philadelphia and forced the Confederation Congress to flee to Princeton, while the Pennsylvania militia rounded up the mutineers. Congress could not devise a funding plan to pay army claims that would be acceptable to the states, so the Confederation remained unstable.

Without a reliable army, Congress was virtually powerless to intervene in Shays's Rebellion or other debtors' insurrections that might follow. Washington, responding to a plea from Congress that he use his influence with Captain Shays to end the rebellion, replied, "I know not where that influence is to be found, or if attainable, that it would be the proper remedy for the disorders. Influence is no government. Let us have one by which our lives, liberties and properties will be secured, or let us know the worst at once."[6] Political leaders corresponded with one another to consider changes in the governmental system. As Washington wrote to Jefferson just before the Constitutional Convention, "The situation of the General Government (if it can be called a government) is shaken to its foundation and liable to be overset by every blast—In a word, it is at an end, and unless a remedy is soon applied, anarchy and confusion will inevitably ensue."[7]

George Washington: The National Idea

Throughout the 1770s and 1780s Washington had proposed a stronger central government. During the Revolutionary War he had proposed a single national army and had only reluctantly accepted the congressional plan for a mixed national army and set of state militias. Washington chafed under a system in which Congress could not tax but had to ask states for requisitions and assessments. He called for centralized economic regulation as well.[8] He wanted a revamping of the agencies in charge of diplomacy, military matters, and the treasury, so his forces could be supplied, and pressured Congress to change from boards and commissions under its direct supervision to department secretaries able to act efficiently. He came out of the war believing that a strong national government was essential to safeguard American territory and national security.[9]

Many of the former war officers and state politicians, the "young men of the Revolution" who looked to Washington for leadership and corresponded with him, had already become strong nationalists by 1785, ready to back a new system that would provide for much greater executive power.[10] Washington corresponded with many of these leaders in 1786–1787, asking them to propose ideas for a new national government. He feared "the worst consequences from a half-starved, limping government, always moving on crutches and tottering at every step." He was particularly impressed with ideas submitted by Secretary of War Henry Knox and by John Jay, both of whom called for the creation of an executive branch of government led by a "Governor General."[11]

George Washington bids farewell to his officers after resigning from the army. Washington established the principle that no officer on active duty runs for the presidency.

Executive Power in the Confederation

Washington was particularly upset that the Articles of Confederation and Perpetual Union, adopted in 1781, made no mention of an executive branch. In 1777 the Continental Congress had rejected a proposal for an executive in the "Dickinson Draft" prepared by New Jersey delegate John Dickinson. He wanted a "Council of State" to "manage the general affairs of the United States," exercising broad military, diplomatic, and financial powers, even while Congress was in session. Instead the version that the Continental Congress adopted provided for a "Committee of States" that would sit only when Congress was in recess and would exercise only such powers as nine states or more of the Congress would vest in it. The Committee would not be able to exercise military, diplomatic, or fiscal powers.[12]

To administer these functions Congress created ad hoc or standing committees, supplemented by boards of commissioners operating under their direction. The Marine Committee dealt with the Navy, the Board of War and Ordnance with the Army, and the Committee of Secret Correspondence handled diplomacy. Those who wanted efficient administration, like Washington's aide-de-camp Alexander Hamilton, proposed that Congress create departments headed by secretaries, but Congress resisted, going so far as to replace the superintendent of finance, Robert Morris, with a treasury board it could control. Hamilton wrote bitterly to a colleague in 1780 that "Congress is properly a deliberative corps, and it forgets itself when it attempts to play the executive."[13] By 1781, after prodding by Washington, several departments were created, among them Foreign Affairs, War, Marine, and Treasury, but no council of state, prime minister, or president gave direction to the departments and other boards. Governance remained chaotic, especially when Congress insisted that secretaries report to its committees and take directions from them. The departments remained appendages to the legislature and did not form a coherent executive branch.

The Confederation Congresses were chaired by presidents, but these were simply presiding officers, not chief executives. They were elected by Congress for one-year terms, and many were men whose reputations and talents matched their limited powers. They handled correspondence with foreign dignitaries but conducted no diplomatic discussions unless the entire Congress were present. They signed the drafts of diplomatic correspondence prepared by the foreign affairs committee, but did not author them. They were not expected to introduce a legislative program, organize followers, or use personal influence on policy. They had no control over the legislative agenda, did not monitor the work of the committees, and in transmitting committee instructions to executive officials, did not include their own views. They were so insignificant that several did not even show up for some or all of the sessions of the Congresses for which they had been elected to preside.[14]

Viewed from the perspective of the delegates to the Continental Congresses that had worked in the 1770s on a plan of government, the Articles of Confederation was a success. It had not really formed a government but rather a "defensive alliance" that had successfully fought the British and had obtained aid from the French and Dutch. It had served as a forum that kept the newly independent states from making war on each other. It had secured the sovereignty of the individual states, and at the time that had seemed far more important than erecting a national government over all of them.[15]

Executive Power in the Colonies and States

Although government under the Articles was, according to Noah Webster, "but a name, and our confederation a cobweb," the American experience with colonial and state government provided an alternative model that separated executive and legislature power.[16] Separation of powers was instituted in colonial governments in the seventeenth century because royal governors could not simultaneously represent the interest of the Crown, the wealthy proprietors who provided funding for the colonies, and the settlers. Governors and judiciaries took the part of the Crown, their advisory councils represented the interests of the wealthiest landowners, and legislative assemblies represented the colonists. Between 1660 and 1730 assemblies began to sit without governors present and pass legislation on their own initiative. Between 1730 and 1750 the governors' councils began to sit without the governor and started functioning as "upper houses" of the legislature, to represent the interests of landowners and merchants.

Colonists developed a system of checks and balances to prevent any single institution from dominating.[17] Legislation was subject to absolute veto by the governor. Clashes between governors and assemblies over appointments and direction of the militia were regular features of colonial politics, and governors often exercised their formal powers in ways desired by the assembly in return for the funds they needed for their administration. A governor who ignored the assembly in filling offices might find that it would refuse to vote funds to pay salaries—including his own. Although the governor was captain-general and vice admiral of the colony's forces, the assemblies often placed officers of their choice in command and determined military strategy in wars against the Indians and French. But as Benjamin Franklin recounted at the Constitutional Convention, colonial governors also had powers:

> No good law could be passed without a private bargain with him. An increase in his salary, or some donation, was always made a condition; till at last it became the regular practice to have orders in his favor on the Treasury presented along with the bills to be signed, so that he might actually receive the former before he signed the latter.[18]

The period between 1763 and 1774 was a departure from the system of legislative supremacy. Governors carried out repressive British tax and regulatory policies based on "Orders in Council" issued by the Crown. During the Revolution the traditional pattern of legislative dominance reasserted itself when state governments we reformed.[19] The Virginia Constitution of 1776, for example, restricted the powers of the governor with the following provision:

> He shall, with the advice of a Council of State, exercise the executive powers of government, according to the laws of this Commonwealth, and shall not, under any pretence, exercise any power or prerogative, by virtue of any law, statute, or custom of England.

In Massachusetts the governor was controlled by a nine-member privy council, whose assent was required for appointments, vetoes, and public spending. In most states the governor had no veto or appointment power without the concurrence of a council of state. In New England states and in New York, governors were elected by the voters, but in other states they were elected by the legislature. All states provided for removal of their governors by impeachment.

A few states provided their governors with real power. The New York Constitution of 1777 provided that the governor would be popularly elected and would serve a three-year term and be eligible for reelection. He could exercise, in conjunction with a Council of Revision, a veto over legislation he thought "inconsistent with the spirit of the Constitution or with the public good." Governor George Clinton used this power to veto fifty-eight bills, at one point using his constitutional power to dismiss the legislature to a later time. He could also recommend measures to the legislature. He was to "take care that the laws be faithfully executed," which gave him power over the departments, and he had the power to grant pardons and reprieves. He commanded the state militia effectively and helped Massachusetts put down Shays's rebellion. Massachusetts and New Hampshire also gave their governors more powers than most other states.

Not coincidentally, the drafters of the New York Constitution—Gouverneur Morris, John Livingston, and John Jay—were among those politicians most in favor of a strong executive branch for the national government. Men of property in Pennsylvania, the "Republican" faction in state politics, led by James Wilson and Robert Morris, attempted to revise their state's constitution to provide for a "principal executive magistrate" to replace the existing Executive Council (a collective governorship). They failed to win their point, but they were to exert considerable pressure at the Constitutional Convention of 1787 in favor of a strong presidency.

Washington Rejects a Monarchy

"Shall we have a king?" John Jay asked George Washington at the height of Shays's Rebellion. Monarchy was the obvious model for a national executive. But George Washington, the obvious choice, rejected the idea, referring to it as a "triumph for the advocates of despotism." During the Newburgh mutiny he had warned his aides, especially Alexander Hamilton, against monarchist intrigues.[20] If Washington would not accept a crown, no other American pretender or prince could hope to do so, because no king could govern in the colonies without the support of the army, the ex-military officers banded together in the Society of the Cincinnati, and the leading state politicians, all of whom wanted Washington to be the nation's leader. Moreover, a monarchy would require an established church (because kings ruled by "divine right" and had to be invested by religious authority) and a titled nobility, neither of which existed in America. To create an established church would go against the tendency in the new state governments to disentangle the clergy from government and would create religious conflict among Puritans of New England and Anglicans of the South. The small farmers and merchants would be unlikely to suffer patiently the ceremonial extravagance of transplanted royalty and nobility. For that matter, neither Yankee merchant nor Tidewater planter would relish paying taxes to support a royal court; they wanted public funds for payment of war debts and the settlement of the back pay issue with the army. The men of property in America intended to make their fortunes through commerce, finance, land speculation, and farming. To retain power a monarch would give the nobility land patents, manufacturing and trading franchises, and other privileges that would interfere with the ambitions of the "gentry." Americans preferred capitalist enterprise and representative government to mercantilism and monarchy.

CHOICES FOR THE CONSTITUTIONAL CONVENTION

"It is the most difficult of all rightly to balance the Executive," Gouverneur Morris observed of the problem that faced the fifty-five delegates to the Constitutional Convention (thirty-two of them former members of the Continental or Confederation Congresses) that met in Philadelphia in the spring of 1787. "Make him too weak: the Legislature will usurp his powers: make him too strong, he will usurp the Legislature."[21] The delegates had three questions to answer about the organization of the executive: first, should it consist of a single person or a council; second, should the executive be chosen by Congress, or by some other means; and third, what should be the extent of its powers?

Initial Assumptions

Most delegates began work assuming that they would create a "Council of States" as a plural executive to administer the departments, exercising only such powers as granted it by Congress. As Roger Sherman described the idea, it would be "no more than an institution for carrying the will of the legislature into effect," and its members would be appointed by the legislature itself, because that institution reflected "the supreme will of Society."[22] This approach was favored by delegates with suspicions about executive power, such as Pierce Butler, who warned delegates that "in all countries the Executive Power is in a constant course of increase," and prophesied a "Cataline or Cromwell" might arise in the Americas, and like their Roman and British counterparts, demagogue with the masses and exercise dictatorial power.[23] A second approach, advanced by James Madison, was to provide the executive with checks and balances against the will of the legislature; he warned of "a tendency in our governments to throw all power into the legislative vortex" and wanted the executive to check Congress to avoid the possibility of "legislative tyranny."[24] Madison, James Wilson, and Gouverneur Morris all emphasized that a strong and independent president was necessary precisely because the powers of Congress were being greatly increased.[25] Still a third approach, favored by Alexander Hamilton and Gouverneur Morris, was to grant the executive very broad constitutional powers of its own. "If a good organization of the Executive should not be provided," Gouverneur Morris warned the delegates, the nation might wind up with "something worse than limited monarchy" they were guarding against.[26]

As the Convention opened most delegates were "congressionalists": deeply skeptical of executive power because of their experience with the British monarchy, they nevertheless were prepared to accept a separate executive branch because they recognized the need for more efficient governance. But they were skeptical of arguments by Wilson and Hamilton. Few understood the Madisonian doctrine of checks and balances, and only a small group of "presidentialists" centered around George Washington understood the need for a strong and independent executive branch.[27]

Convention deliberations began with Robert Morris's motion, carried unanimously, to elect Washington the presiding officer. At Hamilton's suggestion the convention resolved to deliberate in secrecy, so delegates could consider major changes in the form of government without being influenced by public opinion. It was obvious from the start that the delegates expected Washington to lead the new government. All deliberations about the creation of the presidency were debates about the powers to be accorded Washington. Pierce Butler later observed that the powers of the office would not have been so great "had not many of the members cast their eyes toward General Washington as President; and shaped their ideas of the Powers to be given a President, by their opinions of his Virtue." Washington helped prepare the initial Randolph Resolutions with which the convention began its work, was influential within the Virginia delegation, and lobbied delegates from other states for a strong executive. His votes as a member of the Virginia delegation always supported maximum presidential power.[28]

A Plural or Single Executive?

The Convention began work with the "Virginia Plan," which increased the powers of the legislature, provided for a congressional veto over state laws (favored by Madison), and created a "National Executive" consisting of several officials (the exact number was left blank in the draft) elected by Congress for a seven-year term with no possibility of reelection. The powers of this plural executive body would derive solely from "the Executive rights vested in Congress," so it would be merely an agent of the legislature with no independent powers. A Council of Revision, including the National Executive and the members of the Supreme Court, would be able to veto laws passed by Congress and could stay the congressional veto of laws passed by the state legislatures. Congress could then repass the law (or the negative over a state law), and it would go into effect over the disapproval of the Council of Revision. Elbridge Gerry talked of "annexing a Council to the Executive in order to give weight and inspire confidence."[29] But James Wilson pointed out that a council was more likely to cover up than to reveal malpractice and abuses of power.

James Wilson and other "presidentialists" tried to replace the plural executive with a single official, arguing that it would promote better accountability. This proposal alarmed Edmund Randolph, who remarked that "he regarded it as the foetus of monarchy." After the proposal passed Colonel Mason warned, "We are not indeed constituting a British Government, but a more dangerous monarchy, an elective one."[30] After two weeks of debate the Convention approved a constitutional article calling for a single executive, chosen for a seven-year term by Congress and ineligible for reelection, with powers derived solely from the legislature and a veto that could be overridden only by a two-thirds vote of each house. They had opted for a weak presidency that would be dominated by Congress. Shortly after that, an even weaker presidency was proposed by small state delegates presenting the New Jersey Plan.

The "weak presidency" model of government had been supported by a coalition consisting of northern and deep southern states, with most of the mid-Atlantic voting in favor of a stronger office. As the work of the Convention proceeded, the Committee on Detail, Committee on Postponed Matters, and Committee on Style all reported drafts of a Constitution with increasingly greater powers for the presidency, and the mid-Atlantic coalition continued its struggle for a stronger presidency.[31]

Congressional Selection or Popular Election?

In the last weeks of July the Convention wrestled with issues of election, tenure in office, and eligibility. The Virginia Plan had called for a legislative election. James Wilson and Gouverneur Morris argued that legislative election opened the possibility of foreign or domestic conspiracy and corruption and violated the doctrine of separation of powers by making the presidency an instrument of the legislature: any president seeking reelection would tend to curry favor with Congress. They proposed that the president serve a shorter term, be eligible for reelection, and be accountable to the people rather than to Congress—all measures that would strengthen the presidency. Morris argued that "If the people should elect, they will never fail to prefer some man of distinguished character, or services; some man, if he might so speak, of continental reputation."[32] But even this veiled reference to Washington did not move the Convention. Colonel Mason expressed the prevailing sentiment when he cracked that "it would be as unnatural to refer the choice

Three Who Created the Presidency

James Madison

Often called the Founder of the Constitution, Madison helped organize the revolutionary activities in Virginia in 1774 and helped write the state's convention in 1776. He served in the Virginia legislature and in the Continental Congress. "I have scarcely ventured as yet to form my own opinion either of the manner in which [the executive] ought to be constituted or of the authorities with which it ought to be clothed," he wrote to George Washington shortly before the Constitutional Convention. Madison wanted an executive that would be able to check and balance the legislative branch, for otherwise he believed the legislature would become as tyrannical as the British Crown. He wanted the presidency to be given a seven-year term (with no reeligibility), provisions that would make it independent of the legislature. He supported the idea of an electoral college rather than congressional election of the president. He was a strong proponent of separation of powers, arguing for "guarding against a dangerous union of the legislative and executive departments." Once the small states had won equal representation in the Senate, Madison shifted from his early position calling for the Senate to make appointments to the judiciary and instead favored presidential appointments. Similarly Madison opposed giving the treaty-making power to the Senate, instead urging it for the executive. Not everything Madison proposed was adopted. He favored a joint executive–judicial Council of Revision that could veto legislation. He argued that the judges on the council would help the president retain the confidence of the people when it opposed Congress. He favored a unitary executive, but only if it were assisted by an advisory Council of State. Neither of these councils were approved by the Convention. Nevertheless, Madison was instrumental in convincing skeptical delegates, especially in the South, that a strong Congress must be checked and balanced by a strong executive.

Further Reading. Jack Rakove and Susan Zlomke, "James Madison and the Independent Executive," *Presidential Studies Quarterly,* Vol. 17, no. 2, Spring 1987, pp. 293–300.

James Wilson

Perhaps no delegate made more cogent arguments for presidential power at the Convention. Wilson was the foremost legal scholar of his day. He had signed the Declaration of Independence, then wrote influential essays on the need to separate from England. At the Constitutional Convention he wrote the draft reported from the Committee on Detail, and he also had a hand in the final draft reported by Committee on Style (though he was not a member). Wilson called for a single rather than a plural executive, for only a single president would have the "energy, dispatch and responsibility" required. He spoke against Madison's call for a council to be attached to the presidency, because with such a council the president could evade accountability for his actions. Wilson was a vocal proponent of direct popular election of the president, but he supported the electoral college mechanism as the best alternative to congressional selection. He favored a short term of three years coupled with indefinite reeligibility, because it would give the president an incentive to act in the public interest, and because he believed that the people had a right to choose whomever they wanted. Wilson opposed giving the Senate a role in the contingency election of the president, and on his motion the Convention gave that function to the House of Representatives. As a member of the Committee of Detail, Wilson wrote a draft that granted the president a large number of specific enumerated powers. But some of his ideas were rejected. He favored an absolute veto for the president that could not be overridden by Congress, and a judicial–presidential Council of Revision. Once these proposals failed, he proposed that Congress be required to obtain three-fourths rather than two-thirds votes to override presidential vetoes, a motion also rejected. Wilson opposed the small-state demand for equal representation in the Senate, and once it was granted, he became an implacable foe of the institution. He wanted presidentially drafted treaties to be consented to by a majority rather than two-thirds vote of the Senate to limit its influence. He wanted the president to appoint justices of the Supreme Court and executive officials without Senate confirmation. Although many of Wilson's specific proposals were rejected, his vision of the president as a "man of the people" who would "hold the helm" of the American ship of state and set its course has been vindicated by the subsequent evolution of the office into a sometime instrument of American democracy.

Further Reading. Robert DiClerico, "James Wilson's Presidency," *Presidential Studies Quarterly,* Vol. 17, no. 2, Spring, 1987, pp. 301–317.

Gouverneur Morris

One of the wealthiest and most influential friends of George Washington, Morris drafted the final version of the Constitution as chair of the Committee on Style. Morris graduated from King's (now Columbia) College at age 16 and received a masters degree at 18. He drafted the New York State Constitution during the Revolution, a document that provided for a strong executive. Morris served in the Continental Congress as a delegate from New York, but after various run-ins with Governor Clinton, he moved to Pennsylvania and became active in its state politics and finance. At the Constitutional Convention he spoke more than any other delegate. His views were often considered to reflect the ideas of George Washington, because the two were close friends: Washington lived at Morris's home during the Convention, and the two men went on vacation break in July to Valley Forge, Pennsylvania, to revisit Washington's campsites. Morris opposed legislative election of presidents. Like Wilson, he favored

Continued

Three Who Created the Presidency *(continued)*

direct popular election but compromised on an electoral college. Morris was the single most influential delegate in getting the electoral college mechanism adopted, putting the proposal into his final drafts of the Constitution, even though a majority of the Convention had continually voted for legislative election. But the Convention did not adopt all his proposals. Like Wilson, Morris believed that the president should have exclusive power over judicial and executive appointments, but his ideas were rejected. He did insert language stating that the president "shall" rather than "may" recommend to Congress measures about the state of the Union. He got the Convention to strike out a provision for Congressional appointment of the treasurer—providing instead that the treasurer would be appointed by the president by and with the advice and consent of the Senate. Morris began his final draft of the Constitution by granting the president "The Executive Power"—a vague term that could be expanded to include powers not enumerated at the time. This language reflected his vision of the presidency as a unitary, independent office that would be an instrument of the people and would act for the common national interest against the narrow-minded and conservative property interests of the upper classes dominating the legislature.

Further Reading. Donald Robinson, "Gouverneur Morris and the Design of the American Presidency," *Presidential Studies Quarterly,* Vol. 17, no. 2, Spring, 1987, pp. 319–328.

of a proper character for chief magistrate to the people, as it would to refer a trial of colors to a blind man."[33]

Madison had spoken for many at the Convention when he argued for a system of "successive filtration" that would "refine" popular sentiment and allow a president to be shielded from its excesses.[34] Few delegates would consider direct popular election. Wilson then proposed that an electoral college choose the president: it would consist of *electors* chosen by each state. The election would be removed from Congress, ensuring executive independence, and from the people (giving the proposal a chance to pass the Convention).

The issue was thrashed out between July 17 and July 26, just after the Convention agreed in the Connecticut Compromise to provide for equal state representation in the Senate.[35] With that small state versus large state issue resolved, the Convention considered (in 39 separate votes) the questions involved in electing the president. In every vote but one, a peripheral coalition of deep south and far-northern states voted for election by Congress.[36] On July 19, Oliver Ellsworth proposed that the president be elected by an electoral college—for the first and only time the Convention approved, by six to three with one abstention, a victory for a coalition of mid-Atlantic states. Even on that vote, the Convention was inconsistent, providing for a lengthy six-year term with no re-eligibility, part of the "weak presidency" package. The mid-Atlantic coalition of states could not maintain its cohesion on this issue, however, because the large states soon disagreed with Delaware and New Jersey on how delegates in the electoral college would be proportioned. Because electors would be apportioned to the states based on their populations, the small states (New Jersey and Delaware) soon defected to the peripheral coalition favoring congressional election, which was once again passed by the Convention on July 23.[37]

Meanwhile, large states insisted that if a system of congressional election were adopted, each legislator should cast an individual vote, and the small states insisted that each state's delegation be given a single vote, thus canceling out the numerical advantage of the larger states. With small and large states in opposition on both the congressional or the electoral college method, and neither the peripheral nor the mid-Atlantic coalition able to muster enough support to resolve the issue, the question of how to elect the president was referred to a Committee on Postponed Matters. That committee was dominated by delegates favoring a strong executive. It reported its compromise to the Convention: a college of electors, meeting separately in each state, would cast ballots for president. Electors would be assigned to states based on population (plus additional delegates based on senate representation), which was a system favored by large states. In the event no candidate received a majority, the final choice would be made by the Senate, where each state would cast an equal number of votes (a feature designed to win small-state support).[38] The delegates assumed that after the certain election of Washington, no candidate would subsequently obtain a majority of the electoral college vote, and they calculated that elections would be decided by the Senate. In their view, the electoral college would serve as a screening device, to nominate five candidates (most likely one from each of the larger states), and the Senate would then make the final selection. The proposal was a compromise between the mid-Atlantic and peripheral states (because it would involve an electoral college nomination followed by a congressional selection) as well as a compromise between large and small states, because the nominees would come from large states, but all states would have an equal voice in their selection.

The Convention approved the plan but replaced the Senate with the House, where each state delegation would cast a *single* vote in the contingency election for the president (reassuring the smaller states that they would be treated equally). The House was substituted because many delegates thought there might be a tendency for the president to combine with the Senate in a conspiracy to subvert the Constitution, or that the president might, in the words of James Wilson, become simply the "Minion of the Senate."[39] The Convention delegates never voted separately on the provision for an electoral college. But by accepting the Constitution in its entirety, with the provision for an electoral college included, the delegates finally cut loose from the notion that the president should be politically accountable to the legislature.[40]

The Convention provided that to serve as president one must be a natural-born citizen, thirty-five years of age on assuming the office, and fourteen years a resident of the United States. It barred any religious test for the office. (Later, the Twelfth Amendment would provide that the vice president meet the same qualifications.) The president would serve a four-year fixed term and be eligible for reelection to an unlimited number of terms. (After FDR, the Twenty-Second Amendment would limit the president to two elected terms.) The president was to be chosen by an electoral college, whose method of selection would be determined by the legislatures in each state. If the electoral college could not provide a majority for a candidate, the presidential election would be settled in the House (each state having one vote) and the vice presidential election in the Senate. The president would be inaugurated in March after his election, and Congress would hold its first session the subsequent December, fourteen months after its election. (The Twentieth amendment later set the presidential inaugural date for the 20th of January and provided that Congress would convene beforehand, on January 3.)

Enumerating Presidential Powers

Many delegates wanted to provide the presidency with specific powers granted directly from the Constitution. In addition to the veto power of the Virginia Plan, the subsequent New Jersey Plan added that the executive "would appoint all federal officers not otherwise provided for" and would "direct all military operations." Later the Committee on Detail, chaired by James Wilson, reported a draft of the Constitution that provided a number of enumerated powers: The president was to appoint officers otherwise not provided for, give Congress information on the state of the Union and recommend measures for its consideration, receive ambassadors, grant reprieves and pardons, convene Congress on extraordinary occasions, ensure that the laws be faithfully executed, command the armed forces, and command the militia when called into federal service. These provisions were authored by Wilson and based in part on a draft written by Charles Pinckney, which in turn had been inspired by the powers granted to the governor in the New York State constitution.[41] The Committee on Postponed Matters added the presidential power to appoint, by and with the advice and consent of the Senate, ambassadors and justices of the Supreme Court, and provided that the president "may require the opinion in writing of the principal officers in each of the executive departments, upon any subject relating to the duties of their respective offices."[42] No longer would department heads report only to Congress; the foundation for an executive branch of government, far more efficient than anything that had been known before, had been laid.[43]

The Executive Power

James Madison had told the Convention that the presidency must be granted sufficient power to check and balance Congress, but he called on the Convention "to fix the extent of the Executive authority," which "should be confined and defined."[44] But not all delegates agreed, especially not those who wanted a strong executive. They wanted more general terms and ambiguous language that could be interpreted broadly. The Committee on Detail provided that "The Executive Power of the United States shall be vested in a single person," without specifying the limits of such a power. Gouverneur Morris, chairman of the Committee on Style, later revised this provision into the opening words of Article 2, "The Executive Power shall be vested in a President of the United States of America." This was a general term, sufficiently ambiguous so that no one could say precisely what it meant. It was possible that the words referred to more than the specific powers that followed and might confer a set of otherwise unspecified executive powers: the power to give orders to department secretaries; and the power to remove officials who did not follow presidential policies. When Morris and his allies used the term "The Executive Power," they were seeking deliberately to build into the Constitution an open-ended clause that might later expand the powers of the presidency. As a result of their efforts, the limits to presidential power were not fixed in the Constitution.

Sovereign Powers in Internal Affairs

The new Constitution was designed to limit the power of the states: no state could coin money or pass a law impairing the obligation of contracts, two provisions that would benefit men of property. If debtors like Shays gained control of state governments, then the army or the state militia called into national service could be used by the president to enforce the orders of federal courts enjoining any state actions in violation of the Constitution. The president could uphold Article 6, the Supremacy Clause, providing that the Constitution, laws, and treaties of the United States are the "supreme law of the land." Congress under Article 1 was given the power to specify by law the procedures and circumstances under which the president could call forth the militia to enforce national law and suppress domestic violence. The framers had remedied a major defect of the Confederation—the lack of institutions that would enforce the laws and preserve domestic tranquillity.

The president was given the power "to grant reprieves and pardons for offences against the United States, except in cases of impeachment." This power, proposed by Alexander Hamilton, was included by the Committee on Detail. The Convention defeated a motion requiring the Senate to consent to the exercise of the pardon power. It also defeated a motion to limit pardons to persons already convicted of a criminal offense. James Wilson argued that it should extend to persons not yet convicted for the purpose of obtaining confessions that could be used in prosecuting others involved in the same crime. He also blocked a proposal that would have prevented the president from offering pardons to traitors. Hamilton proposed the pardon power, and Wilson fought against limitations on it, because they saw the pardon power as an instrument to put down domestic insurrections such as Shays's Rebellion. As Hamilton explained after the convention in *The Federalist Papers:*

> The principal argument for reposing the power of pardoning in this case in the Chief Magistrate is this: in seasons of insurrection or rebellion, there are often critical moments when a well-timed offer of pardon to the insurgents or rebels may restore the tranquillity of the commonwealth; and which, if suffered to pass unimproved, it may never be possible afterwards to recall.[45]

War and Peace Powers

The King of England had the power to make war, and some presidentialist delegates wished to confide the same decision in the president. But outright adoption of British practice was unacceptable to most Americans, who viewed this particular royal prerogative with extreme distaste. They assumed that George III had initiated the war against the Colonies, and they sympathized with the British Whigs who stressed the war powers of Parliament and had finally forced the king to end hostilities. When the Committee on Detail submitted its draft, it stated that Congress would "make war." That left two key issues unresolved: Did it mean that Congress would make the decision for peace or war? Would Congress control the conduct of war once begun? When the delegates debated the issue, Pinckney proposed that the power to make war be lodged in the Senate, but Pierce Butler "was for vesting the power in the President, who will have all the requisite qualities, and will not make war but when the Nation will support it."[46] Speakers in the debate appear to have used the word "make" in the broad sense of conducting as well as declaring hostilities. To clarify matters, Madison and Elbridge Gerry moved to insert "declare" and strike out "make" war, "leaving to the Executive the power to repel sudden attacks."[47] The motion left the president with the power to repel invasions on his or her own initiative.

The delegates intended to leave the decision for peace or war with Congress, except in the case of invasion, because in that event, if the president had to wait for Congress to declare war, an enemy that invaded and prevented Congress from convening would win the war by default. It was not clear whether the new wording would limit congressional power to *conduct* a war. Had the change from "make" to "declare" reduced the congressional role? Perhaps the president had the power to determine war policies based on the commander-in-chief clause. Or perhaps war powers remained with Congress, expressed through its legislation. Had the delegates cared to settle the issue, they could have followed the Massachusetts constitution and provided specific powers for the president after the title of commander in chief; because they did not, both branches of national government were left to compete for war powers.

During the debate, Pierce Butler proposed to give the legislature the power to make peace, but the proposal was defeated. Madison then proposed that the Senate, by a majority vote, be able to approve a peace treaty submitted by the president, or by a two-thirds vote be empowered to make a peace treaty without the concurrence or participation of the president. "The President," he forecast, "would necessarily derive so much power and importance from a state of war that he might be tempted, if authorized, to impede a treaty of peace."[48] Gouverneur Morris led the opposition that defeated the motion. The Convention twice refused to lodge any peace powers with the Senate or Congress and indeed said nothing about peace powers at all.

Diplomatic Powers

Which branch of government should conduct the diplomacy of the United States? The Convention left the issue unresolved. The president was granted the power to receive ambassadors and ministers. Most delegates thought of this as a ceremonial function without significance. They intended to assign the power to recognize foreign nations in the president and Senate, who were to jointly agree on the nomination of ambassadors to foreign nations. The collaborative pattern was extended to treaty making, which was confided to the president by and with the advice and consent of the Senate. The language anticipates that the president would permit the Senate to participate in treaty negotiations; the Convention did not assume that the president would simply lay the completed draft of a treaty before the Senate for its consent. The Constitution also assigned Congress jurisdiction over tariffs and commerce with foreign nations. From these limited grants of power the two branches would find it necessary to construct a set of diplomatic powers, and the president would ultimately find his greatest powers in the silences of the Constitution.[49]

Alexander Hamilton's "Supreme Governor"

On June 18 Alexander Hamilton stood at his desk in Independence Hall, looked around at the delegates, and began a speech that one member of his audience was later to say "was admired by all and influenced none." Hamilton had been frustrated by the way the Convention debates had been going, and in this speech he intended to have his say, to shock the delegates out of their complacency, and to make them understand the need for a strong executive. He told the delegates that he "was unfriendly" both to the Virginia and New Jersey Plans. He told them that "the English Model" of an executive was "the only good one on his subject," and that the Constitution should "go as far in order to attain stability and permanency, as republican principles will admit." Then he presented his plan, which went beyond even constitutional monarchy to come close to dictatorship. His proposals bore a striking resemblance to the *Instrument of Government* instituted in England by the dictator Oliver Cromwell in 1653. Cromwell had named himself "Protector for Life": Hamilton's proposed "Governour" would be chosen by electors to serve on "good behavior," that is, for life. The Protector had the "exercise of the chief magistracy and the administration of government": Hamilton's plan gave the "supreme Executive Power" to the "Governour." Cromwell provided himself with a veto effective for twenty days against laws passed by Parliament: the governour was to have an absolute "negative on all laws about to be passed, and the execution of all laws passed" by Congress.[50]

Where had Hamilton gotten these ideas? As a sophomore at King's College (now Columbia College) in New York City, he had studied Cromwell's Instruments of Government, as well as William Blackstone's *Commentaries on the Laws of England.* He relied on them for structure and phrasing when writing his Revolutionary War pamphlets in 1774, studied Blackstone again when preparing to become a lawyer in 1781, and used Blackstone's language from the chapters "On Parliament" and "On Prerogative" in his speech to the Convention. Hamilton was attracted particularly to Blackstone's description of "Crown Prerogatives." With the exception of taxing power, granted to Parliament, Blackstone assigned almost all important governing powers to the British Monarch: war powers and command of the armed forces, the power to raise fleets and armies, to enforce embargoes, to make treaties, to make peace, to recognize foreign nations, and to exercise diplomatic powers. In domestic affairs the sovereign could coin money, erect corporations, arbitrate commerce, pardon offenses, and create offices. The Crown exercised an absolute veto on legislation, supervised the courts, and appointed judges. Although in no sense an accurate description of British constitutional practice in the eighteenth century,

Blackstone's *Commentaries* could serve as a model of executive power operating under a constitution in its most extreme form.

Hamilton could not expect Convention delegates to accept most of his argument or vote openly for monarchical prerogatives. The country had just fought a revolution against the royal prerogative, which was equated with tyranny. His speech to the Convention was tactical; it was designed to shock, and it did. In turn, other "presidentialists" like James Wilson and Gouverneur Morris appeared moderate. Hamilton's speech had the intended effect of giving his allies some room to maneuver in expanding the powers of the presidency. Nevertheless, Hamilton was disappointed at the tepid response of the other delegates, and he left for New York City to spend most of the summer away from the Convention. He was absent while most of the enumerated powers were drafted. But he and Gouverneur Morris, together with Hamilton's protégé Rufus King, were members of the Committee on Style, and they shaped the final ambiguous language of Article 2, which was later to be used to legitimize vast claims of executive power.

AUXILIARY PRECAUTIONS

Once the convention had granted constitutional powers directly to the president, it had to consider ways to prevent abuses of power. Although they relied on the "republican virtue" of men like Washington to steer clear of corruption or treasonous relations with European powers, delegates understood that institutional arrangements provided greater safeguards than trust in good character. The irony of the Constitution, however, lies in the fact that many of the arrangements made to limit the powers of the presidency actually opened the door to their vast expansion.

Partial Separation of Powers

James Madison called for *partial* rather than *complete* separation of powers; the three separate institutions would have overlapping grants of authority and would sometimes have to collaborate in performing a function.[51] Madison believed, along with most other delegates, that the experience of state government since independence had demonstrated conclusively that the legislative power was the strongest, and that unless some of its powers were shared, the Congress might dominate the government and institute a legislative tyranny. One way to control the legislative power was to divide it: a bicameral system consisting of a House and Senate was instituted. Another way was to give the president a share in the legislative business by calling Congress into special session, by deciding on a date that Congress would reconvene in the event the two houses disagreed, and by recommending measures to the legislators that the president considered expedient. Conversely, Congress would have a share in the executive's business: it would have the power to pass laws "necessary and proper" for the exercise of the powers of the presidency as well as for its own powers.

Checks and Balances

The idea that each institution should check and balance the others was also contributed by Madison. The president could veto laws passed by Congress, and such vetoes could be overridden only by two-thirds of each legislative chamber. (The delegates defeated a proposal, favored by George Washington, that a three-fourths vote be necessary to override a presidential veto). Madison wanted to go even further and provide a set of "interior contrivances" to balance power within the executive branch. He proposed a Council of Revision (that would have included justices of the Supreme Court) to share in the veto power. He proposed an executive council to share in "The Executive Power" of the United States, and he gathered a distinguished group of allies, including James Wilson, Oliver Ellsworth, George Mason, John Randolph, and Benjamin Franklin. To forestall Madison, Gouverneur Morris and Charles Pinckney proposed a "Council of State" to consist of the president and his department secretaries. This council would have had only advisory powers, without any checks on the president. Their language also contained a detailed description of the powers of the governmental departments.[52] Many delegates correctly recognized the proposal as a ploy to place in the Constitution itself a detailed blueprint for an executive branch with vast powers rather than allow Congress to pass laws organizing the executive branch after the new government was set up. In any event, neither the Committee on Detail nor the Committee on Postponed Matters recommended an executive council. A last-ditch attempt by Madison, Randolph, and Mason to create a six-member council consisting of two members each from northern, central, and southern states was defeated at the end of the convention, ending Madison's attempt to provide internal checks and balances within the executive.

Impeachment

The Convention provided for impeachment: a means of removing a president who abused his powers. Impeachment owed something to British precedents, but adapted to American needs, it was in some respects a major improvement on British practices. In Britain, impeachment had been used against ministers who pursued policies favored by the Crown that were opposed by a majority of the House of Commons. But the actual proceedings were conducted not as a vote on a parliamentary motion, but rather as a trial in the House of Lords, and conviction could lead to stiff fines or even imprisonment. Making criminal cases out of what were actually political disputes made no sense: between 1660 and 1717 many impeachments were voted, but not one resulted in a guilty verdict. After 1782 the British substituted a parliamentary motion of "no confidence" in a government, which if passed would lead to the fall of the ministry and its replacement with another.

The Convention revised the British practice. It refused to permit impeachment on political grounds. It voted down a proposal to make the executive removable by a majority of the state legislatures, or removable on the application of a majority of state governors. By refusing to pass these proposals, the Convention established the principle that a president may retain office even without the confidence of a majority of Congress or the institutions of state government. But the Convention wanted to give Congress the power to remove a president who abused his powers. George Mason, an opponent of the strong presidency, gained support for an impeachment mechanism when he asked, "Shall any man be above justice? Above all shall that man be above it, who can commit the most extensive injustice?" Few delegates supported Rufus King, who warned that impeachment would destroy the separation of powers, or Gouverneur Morris, who argued, "If he is to be a check on the legislature, let him not be impeachable."[53] Morris and Pinckney proposed to strike out proposals for impeachment, while Madison and others defended them. As the debate wore on, Morris realized that the only way to win delegates over to his conception of a strong presidency was to reassure them that abuse of presidential power would be punished. Shifting his ground, he agreed with Madison's comment that a president "might lose his capacity after appointment. He might pervert his administration into a scheme of peculation or oppression. He might betray his trust to a foreign power."[54] Morris then suggested that "the Executive ought therefore to be impeachable for treachery; corrupting his electors and incapacity were other causes of impeachment."[55]

The Committee on Detail placed the impeachment power in the House of Representatives and the power to try impeachment in the Supreme Court. Grounds were limited to "treason, bribery and corruption." The Committee on Postponed Matters, as part of a compromise with small states designed to increase the powers of the Senate (where they had equal representation with the large states), placed the power to try impeachments in the Senate, with the Chief Justice of the United States presiding. The committee removed "corruption" as a grounds for impeachment, when the delegates realized that the word might forbid a president from using patronage and incentives to lead Congress. Debate further defined the purposes of impeachment. Mason proposed adding "maladministration" to the list of offenses. Madison responded that "so vague a term will be equivalent to tenure during the pleasure of the Senate."[56] Mason compromised and moved that the phrase "other High Crimes and Misdemeanors" be substituted.

Mason took that phrase from British impeachments. The offenses it referred to were not limited to the criminal laws of England but included misapplication of public funds, abuse of authority, criminal conduct, corruption, and encroachment on the prerogatives of the legislature.[57] The Convention adopted this phrase so that abuse of power, rather than ordinary criminal conduct, would be grounds for impeachment. The language was a compromise: Those favoring a strong presidency wanted to restrict the grounds for impeachment to charges of criminal conduct; those favoring a weak presidency wanted a provision similar to a "vote of confidence" to remove an executive on political grounds or "maladministration."

The impeachment provision reversed a second British practice: conviction did not result in criminal penalties but extended only to removal from office and possible disqualification from holding office in the future. If the offense involved a crime, judicial proceedings could be instituted after removal from office. The framers did not intend impeachment to mete out criminal justice but rather to serve as the ultimate political check and balance.

What the framers did not anticipate was the use to which presidents themselves might put the impeachment process. When they expanded the scope of their powers, they reassured the nation that they were not exceeding their powers, and challenged their critics, in effect, to "put up or shut up" by instituting an impeachment proceeding. The presence of the impeachment mechanism also gave presidents ammunition when they argued that they should have total control over the departments and agencies of government: they argued that because they could be impeached for abuse of power, it was necessary that they have the administrative powers needed to prevent abuses of power by their subordinates, such as the removal power. What had originally been intended as a check on presidents became their ultimate justification for expanded powers.

PRESIDENTIAL VERSUS PARLIAMENTARY GOVERNMENT

Most Convention delegates believed they were adapting British precedents to American conditions. True, they had rejected a monarchy, but they created the next best thing, an "elective kingship," albeit of short duration, to run an executive branch. As they read British commentators such as John Locke, author of the philosophical treatise *On Government,* or William Blackstone, author of the constitutional law text, *Commentaries on the Laws of England,* a constitutional system required separated institutions exercising executive, legislative, and judicial powers. But the Convention was laboring under the delusion that it was adapting a British system. In theory the Crown and Privy Council exercised royal prerogatives and executive power, and in theory legislative power was exercised by a House of Commons and House of Lords independent of royal control. These late–seventeenth-century approaches to constitutional government, however, were being discarded even as the Convention was doing its business. Americans adopted the principles of separation of powers and checks and balances just as the British abandoned them. Throughout the eighteenth century the Hanoverian monarchs used "pensions and places" (bribery and patronage) to corrupt and control Parliament and "unbalance" the seventeenth-century constitution. After the loss of the American colonies a struggle broke out between Crown and Parliament over control of the ministries of government. The House of Commons in 1782 condemned "farther prosecution" of the Revolutionary War, and when the King's ministers ignored this warning, a resolution was passed stating that the House "will consider as enemies" those ministers favoring a continuation of the fighting. Faced with a threat of impeachment, the King's prime minister, Lord North, informed King George that he could not govern because he lacked the confidence of the House of Commons. North's communication to the King was the first step toward parliamentary government: a system in which the prime minister and cabinet govern only with the support of a parliamentary majority and remain accountable to it. A parliamentary system does not separate powers and check and balance them: instead, it unites the legislative power of parliament with the executive power of a prime minister and cabinet, as well as with the remaining royal powers of the monarch.

Although Convention delegates looked to the British system to support their proposals, they misunderstood what was happening on the other side of the Atlantic. Madison, for example, analyzed the fall of Lord North's government in 1782 and the subsequent accession of Whig leaders opposed to the King's war policies as a sign that separation of powers was alive and well in Britain, and that checks and balances was one of the reasons why the war had come to an end. For Alexander Hamilton the significant event was the smashing victory that William Pitt, a member of the pro-monarchy Tory Party, won over the Whigs in the succeeding elections. To Hamilton, Pitt's victory seemed to show that the Crown could continue to dominate Parliament and that executive power would remain the dominant factor in the British constitution. In fact, separation of powers, checks and balances, and royal powers had little influence on British politics in the next century. Had the American constitutional convention been delayed by twenty years, delegates would have seen clearly that the Crown no longer ran the ministries of government, and that conflict between King and Parliament had given way to cabinet government and the fusion of legislative and executive powers. They might then have adapted British practices and created a system of cabinet government in which the president was elected by and remained completely accountable to Congress.

RATIFICATION DEBATES

The unsettled issue of presidential power was to trouble many of the delegates to state conventions called to ratify the Constitution. Although ratification by state conventions did not turn on the question of presidential power, debates over the office were significant.[58] "Your president may easily become a king," thundered Patrick Henry in Virginia, and he predicted, "There will be no checks, no real balances in this government. What can avail your specious, imaginary balances, your rope-dancing, chain-rattling, ridiculous ideal checks and contrivances?" Henry warned that "the President, in the field, at the head of his army, can prescribe the terms on which he shall reign master." James Monroe gloomily foresaw a President who might be reelected for life. George Mason, who had refused to sign the Constitution, warned of a dangerous combination between the president and Senate that "could destroy all balances" unless a council of state were provided for by amendment. Mason warned that the president might use his pardon power "to screen from punishment those whom he has secretly instigated to commit the crime, and thereby prevent a discovery of his own guilt." In Paris Thomas Jefferson noted tartly after receiving a copy of the Constitution from Madison that the president "seems a bad edition of a Polish King" because he could be reelected indefinitely and commanded the armed forces.[59] New York Governor George Clinton warned that "if the President is possessed of ambition, he has the power and time sufficient to ruin the country." He attacked the presidency because it resembled his own office, arguing that it was one thing to have a strong state governor, but quite another to have a strong president. "This government is no more like a true picture of your own," he warned New Yorkers, "than an Angel of Darkness resembles an Angel of Light."[60] The Virginia and North Carolina conventions submitted pro-

Patrick Henry cautions Virginians against the excesses of the strong presidency after the Constitution's provisions were made public at the end of the Philadelphia Convention.

posed constitutional amendments to limit tenure in office to eight years in any sixteen-year period, and New York also recommended a term limit. A minority faction in the Pennsylvania convention proposed that "a constitutional council be appointed to advise and assist the President." In the Albany Manifesto, New York anti-Federalists proposed a Council on Appointments, stripping the president of his power over the armed forces, congressional consent to presidential pardons, and a two-term limit.

For tactical reasons the supporters of a strong presidency tried to minimize the extent of its powers when describing the Constitution. They pointed out that the president could not become a king because the nation lacked an established church or nobility. The president would not appoint the Senate and was unlikely to combine with senators in the conspiracy suggested by anti-Federalists. The president would have no hereditary income or honors to bestow on followers, and would have little patronage or influence with the legislature. The president would have no royal prerogatives, and the office's limited diplomatic authority would be subject to check by the Senate. The president would be nominated and elected by the electoral college or by the House of Representatives. As James Wilson pointed out to the Pennsylvania delegates: "The President, sir, will not be a stranger to our country, to our laws, or to our wishes. He will, under this Constitution, be placed in office as the President of the whole Union, and will be chosen in such a manner that he may be justly styled the man of the people."[61]

Presidentialists claimed that the president would possess no monarchical powers. Madison noted that the proposed national army would be ten times smaller than the state militias, and these militias would serve as a check on the presidential power as commander in chief.[62] Wilson and Hamilton pointed out that the executive power would extend only to the faithful execution of the laws and was not intended to give the president additional powers. But as Hamilton reminded the New York convention:

> When you have divided and nicely balanced the departments of government, when you have strongly connected the virtue of the rulers with their interest, when, in short, you have rendered your system as perfect as human forms can be, you must place confidence, you must give power.[63]

Hamilton, Madison, and John Jay wrote a series of essays defending the Constitution and designed to influence public opinion and thus the delegates to the ratifying conventions in New York and other states. First published in the *Independent Journal* (a New York City newspaper), then reprinted in newspapers around the nation, they were finally reprinted in book form in 1788 and today are known collectively as *The Federalist Papers.* Madison reassured his readers that the checks-and-balances system resembled state practices, and that each of the branches had "the necessary constitutional means and personal motives to resist the encroachments of the others." Hamilton took great pains to point out the dissimilarities between the president and the British monarch, going so far as to list the prerogative powers of the Crown (as Blackstone had listed them) to deny that the president possessed them.[64] Hamilton was guilty of deliberate deception on two counts: he overstated the powers of the British monarch and understated the powers of the president by sliding over the ambiguous language of Article 2. He deliberately misstated his own position on "The Executive Power" by denying that it granted any power to the president at all. Because the Convention proceedings had been kept secret, the public was not aware that Hamilton had given a speech at the Convention calling for an elective king, or that he had pressed a version of his plan on Madison at the very end of the Convention. As a pragmatic politician Hamilton was supporting the Constitution as the best form of government that could be achieved at the time, and in *The Federalist Papers* he supported precisely those limitations on presidential power that he and other Convention delegates had previously fought and voted against.[65] Nevertheless, he and James Madison did point out that the executive would infuse the new government with the energy necessary to defend the nation against foreign attacks, conduct effective diplomacy, and prevent internal disorders that would otherwise endanger property rights.[66] Hamilton was able to turn a 2–1 anti-federal majority in New York's Convention into a narrow 30–27 vote in favor of the Constitution.

After ratification, the Congress under the Articles of Confederation passed a law providing for a transition from the old to the new form of government. Under its provisions, electors were chosen by states for the electoral college by winter 1788. On February 4, 1789 they picked George Washington unanimously to be the first president. According to procedures adopted by the outgoing Congress, the new government assembled in New York City, which was to be the temporary capital until a new federal district could be established. Late in March, George Washington entered the city at the head of a parade of exuberant citizens. In early April the new Congress convened, and on April 30th Washington took the oath of office on the balcony at Federal Hall. "Our Constitution is in actual operation," Benjamin Franklin reported to his friends abroad. "Everything appears to promise that it will last," he added, "but in this world nothing is certain but death and taxes."

A CONSTITUTION OF ORIGINAL INTENT?

Is it possible to understand fully the intent of the framers of the Constitution? Although we must rely on the recollections and notes of several of the delegates to the Convention, we should not assume that the records they left us provide the entire story. For one thing, the official journal of the Convention (including the votes) was kept in somewhat haphazard fashion, and the editing of it done years later involved reorganizing and rearranging material; some had even been thrown away at the Convention's end. Madison took careful notes from his front seat, but he participated so energetically in the deliberations that he could not record all that occurred: his notes are selective summaries of the main points of each speaker, not necessarily a verbatim transcript of what they said. Moreover, in editing his work for publication many years later, Madison made extensive changes: some to conform to the Journal of the Convention and correct errors he had made in tabulating votes; other changes for reasons about which we can only speculate. Notes of other participants were generally fragmentary. Although these sources provide the best information about the Convention proceedings, anyone who has read them knows that they only offer us a glimpse of each day's proceedings and brief summaries of the main points of key speakers.

Neither can we rely on *The Federalist Papers* or debates in the state conventions to give us authoritative meanings of particular constitutional clauses. The Federalists used arguments in winning ratification that they were later to discard when the new government was in power. Hamilton, for example, stated that a president would not be able to end a treaty obligation without the concurrence of the Senate. Once in Washington's administration as secretary of treasury, he counseled the president to abrogate a treaty with France in 1792 without any mention of the need for Senate approval. These documents are brilliant expositions of the overall political theory underlying the new form of government, but they should not be taken as authoritative treatises on specific issues of presidential power.

We reconstruct the work of the Convention as best we can to understand the motivations of those who created the presidency, and we try to experience for ourselves the dangers they faced and their brilliant talent for improvising bold solutions. But we do well to keep in mind the caution of Supreme Court Justice Robert Jackson: "Just what our forefathers did envision, or would have envisioned had they foreseen modern conditions, must be divined from materials almost as enigmatic as the dreams Joseph was called upon to interpret for the Pharaoh."[67] We cannot know for certain what they intended, and it makes no sense at all to run back to these texts as if they were sacred documents that could answer all our questions about how to define and confine presidential power to safeguard constitutional government.[68]

THE CONSTITUTIONAL EXPERIMENT

Readers of the Convention debates are struck by the experimental nature of the enterprise. Many of the politicians who made the historic compromises were actually quite disappointed in their work. Madison, who had not won his council of state, proportional representation in the Senate, a congressional "negative" over state laws, and most of his other specific proposals, signed the final document, but wrote in disgust to Jefferson that "the plan should it be adopted will neither effectually answer its national object nor prevent the local mischiefs which everywhere excite disgusts against the state governments." Hamilton, although in public the strongest proponent of the presidential article of the Constitution, was in private quite disappointed. He began thinking about ways to establish an American branch of the Hanoverian monarchy if the states rejected the proposed Constitution. "The most plausible shape of such a business," he wrote in his diary shortly after the convention ended, "would be the establishment of a son of the present monarch in the supreme government of this country with a family compact."[69] Just two years before his death in 1804, Hamilton wrote a friend about the Constitution that he was "still laboring to prop the frail and worthless fabric."[70]

As George Washington assumed office in 1789, no one could foresee whether the Union would survive or the new Constitution would work. Washington expressed the mood of the people when he referred to the new government as "an experiment entrusted to the hands of the American people."[71] The presidential experiment would be carried out by the politicians who had created it—as well as by the people who elected them and to whom they would be accountable. The American experiment with presidential governance had begun.

FURTHER READING

Books

Joseph Bessette and Jeffrey Tulis, *The Presidency in the Constitutional Order,* Baton Rouge, LA: Louisiana State University Press, 1981.

Jacob Cooke, ed., *The Federalist,* by Alexander Hamilton, James Madison and John Jay, Cleveland, OH: Meridian Books, 1961.

Thomas Cronin, ed., *Inventing the American Presidency,* Lawrence, KS: University Press of Kansas, 1989.

Calvin Jillson, *Constitution Making: Conflict and Consensus in the Federal Convention of 1787,* New York: Agathon Press, 1988.

Cecilia Kenyon, *The Anti-Federalists,* Boston: Northeastern University Press, 1966.

Glenn A. Phelps, *George Washington and American Constitutionalism,* Lawrence, KS: University Press of Kansas, 1993.

Michael P. Riccards, *A Republic, If You Can Keep It: The Foundation of the American Presidency,* Westport, CT: Greenwood Press, 1987.

Donald Robinson, *To the Best of My Ability: The Presidency and the Constitution,* New York: W. W. Norton, 1987.

Robert Rutland, *The Ordeal of the Constitution: The Antifederalists and the Ratification Struggle of 1787–1788,* Norman, OK: Oklahoma University Press, 1966.

Herbert Storing, *What the Anti-Federalists Were For,* Chicago: University of Chicago Press, 1981.

Charles Thach, *The Creation of the Presidency, 1775–1789: A Study in Constitutional History,* Baltimore, MD: Johns Hopkins University Press, 1923.

Gordon Wood, *The Creation of the American Republic, 1776–1787,* Chapel Hill, NC: University of North Carolina Press, 1969.

Documentary Sources

Jonathan Elliot, ed., *The Debates in the Several State Conventions on the Adoption of the Federal Constitution,* 1861, 5 vols., New York: Franklin Burt Publishers, 1974.

Max Farrand, *The Records of the Federal Convention of 1787,* 4 vols., rev. ed., New Haven, CT: Yale University Press, 1966.

Philip Kurland and Ralph Lerner, eds., *The Founders' Constitution,* 5 vols., Chicago: University of Chicago Press, 1987.

Leonard W. Levy and Dennis J. Mahoney, eds., *The Framing and Ratification of the Constitution,* New York: Macmillan, 1987.

Herbert Storing, *The Complete Anti-Federalist,* 7 vols., Chicago: University of Chicago Press, 1981.

NOTES

1. Jonathan Smith, "The Depression of 1785 and Daniel Shays' Rebellion," *William and Mary Quarterly,* 3rd series, Vol. 5, January 1948, pp. 77–94; Robert A. Feer, "Shays's Rebellion and the Constitution: A Study of Causation," *New England Quarterly,* Vol. 52, no. 3, September, 1969, pp. 388–410.

2. William D. Liddle, " 'A Patriot King or None': Lord Bolingbroke and the American Renunciation of George III," *Journal of American History,* Vol. 65, no. 4, March, 1979, pp. 951–970; Winthrop D. Jordan, "Familial Politics: Thomas Paine and the Killing of the King, 1776," *Journal of American History,* Vol. 60, no. 2, September, 1973, pp. 294–308.

3. Jonathan Elliot, ed., *The Debates of the Several State Conventions,* 2nd ed., New York: Franklin Burt Publishers, 1888–96, Vol. 5, p. 107.

4. Claude H. Van Tyne, "Sovereignty in the American Revolution: An Historical Study," *American Historical Review,* Vol. 12, 1907, pp. 529–545; Merrill Jensen, "The Idea of a National Government during the American Revolution," *Political Science Quarterly,* Vol. 58, no. 3, Autumn, 1943, pp. 356–379; "Note: The United States and the Articles of Confederation: Drifting toward Anarchy or Inching toward Commonwealth," *Yale Law Journal,* Vol. 88, no. 1, November, 1978, pp. 142–166.

5. Richard H. Kohn, "Inside History of the Newburgh Conspiracy," *The William and Mary Quarterly,* Vol. 28, no. 2, April, 1970, pp. 187–220.

6. Jared Sparks, ed., *The Writings of George Washington,* Vol. 9, New York, Aubern: Derby and Miller, 1852, p. 204.

7. Julian Boyd, ed., *The Papers of Thomas Jefferson,* Vol. 9, Princeton, NJ: Princeton University Press, 1955, p. 389.

8. Glenn A. Phelps, *George Washington and American Constitutionalism,* Lawrence, KS: University Press of Kansas, 1993, pp. 23–90.

9. Ibid., p. 58.

10. Stanley Elkins and Eric McKitrick, "The Founding Fathers: Young Men of the Revolution," *Political Science Quarterly,* Vol. 76, no. 2, Summer, 1961, pp. 181–216.

11. Library of Congress, Washington Papers, Series 4, George Washington, "Sentiments of Mr. Jay, General Knox, and Mr. Madison on a Form of Government, Previous to the General Convention Held at Philadelphia in May, 1787."

12. Merrill Jensen, "The Articles of Confederation: A Re-Interpretation," *Pacific Historical Review,* Vol. 6, 1937, pp. 120–142; Jack Greene, "The Background of the Articles of

Confederation," *Publius,* Vol. 12, no. 4, Fall, 1982, pp. 15–44; Jack Rakove, "The Legacy of the Articles of Confederation," *Publius,* vol. 12, no. 4, Fall, 1982, pp. 45–66.

13. Harold Syrett, *The Papers of Alexander Hamilton,* New York: Columbia University Press, 1962, Vol. 3, p. 404.

14. Calvin Jillson and Rick Wilson, "Leadership and Coordination in Legislatures: The 'President' of the First American Congress: 1774–1789," *Congress and the Presidency,* Vol. 17, no. 2, Autumn, 1990, pp. 85–105.

15. Peter S. Onuf, "The First Federal Constitution: The Articles of Confederation," in Leonard W. Levy and Dennis J. Mahoney, eds., *The Framing and Ratification of the Constitution,* New York: Macmillan, 1987, p. 88.

16. Quoted in Clinton Rossiter, *1787, The Grand Convention,* New York: Macmillan, 1966, p. 50.

17. Evarts Greene, *The Provincial Governor in the English Colonies of North America,* New York: Longmans Green, 1898.

18. Max Farrand, ed., *The Records of the Federal Convention of 1787,* rev. ed., New Haven, CT: Yale University Press, 1966, Vol. 1, p. 99 (hereafter Farrand, *Federal Convention*).

19. William Webster, "A Comparative Study of the State Constitutions of the American Revolution," *The Annals of the American Academy of Political Science,* Vol. 9, Philadelphia: 1897, pp. 380–419.

20. Harold Syrett, op. cit., Vol. 3, pp. 309–310.

21. James Madison, *Notes of the Debates in the Federal Convention of 1787,* Athens, OH: Ohio University Press, 1966, p. 361 (hereafter Madison, *Notes*).

22. Farrand, *Federal Convention,* Vol. 1, p. 65.

23. Farrand, *Federal Convention,* Vol. 1, p. 100.

24. Farrand, *Federal Convention,* Vol. 2, p. 35.

25. Gordon Wood, *The Creation of the American Republic,* 1776–1787, New York: W. W. Norton, 1969, pp. 430–438.

26. Madison, *Notes,* p. 360.

27. Arthur N. Holcombe, "The Work of Washington in the Framing of the Constitution," *The Huntington Library Quarterly,* Vol. 19, no. 4, August, 1956, pp. 317–334.

28. Glenn A. Phelps, op. cit., pp. 91–120.

29. Madison, *Notes,* p. 46.

30. Farrand, *Federal Convention,* Vol. 2, p. 101.

31. Calvin C. Jillson, *Constitution Making: Conflict and Consensus in the Federal Convention of 1787,* New York: Agathon Press, 1988, pp. 101–102.

32. Ibid., p. 29.

33. Ibid, p. 31.

34. Madison, *Notes,* p. 40.

35. Shlomo Slonim, "The Electoral College at Philadelphia: The Evolution of an Ad Hoc Congress for Selection of a President," *Journal of American History,* Vol. 73, no. 1, June, 1986, pp. 35–58.

36. Jillson, op. cit., p. 111.

37. Jillson, op. cit., pp. 116–20; Farrand, *Records,* op. cit., Vol. 2, p. 95.

38. Farrand, *Federal Convention,* pp. 493–494.

39. Madison, *Notes,* p. 587.

40. Judith Best, "Legislative Tyranny and the Liberation of the Executive: A View from the Founding," *Presidential Studies Quarterly,* Vol. 17, no. 3, Fall, 1987, pp. 697–709.

41. Charles Thach, *The Creation of the Presidency, 1775–1789,* Baltimore, MD: Johns Hopkins University Press, 1922, pp. 110–112.

42. Farrand, *Federal Convention,* Vol. 2, p. 499.

43. Louis Fisher, "The Efficiency Side of Separation of Powers," *Journal of American Studies,* Vol. 5, no. 2, August, 1971, p. 113–131.

44. Farrand, *Federal Convention,* Vol. 1, pp. 66–67, 70.

45. Alexander Hamilton, *The Federalist Papers,* no. 74.

46. Farrand, *Federal Convention,* Vol. 2, p. 318.

47. Ibid., p. 318.

48. Madison, *Notes,* p. 599.

49. Frederick W. Marks III, "Power, Pride and Purse: Diplomatic Origins of the Constitution," *Diplomatic History,* Vol. XI, 1987, pp. 303–319.

50. Farrand, *Federal Convention,* Vol. 1, pp. 282–293.

51. James Madison, *The Federalist Papers,* no. 51.

52. Farrand, *Federal Convention,* Vol. 1, p. 342–344.

53. Ibid., pp. 65, 52.

54. Ibid., p. 65.

55. Ibid., p. 68.

56. Ibid., pp. 550–551.

57. Raoul Berger, *Impeachment,* Cambridge, MA: Harvard University Press, 1973, pp. 53–102.

58. Michael Riccards, "The Presidency and the Ratification Controversy," *Presidential Studies Quarterly,* Vol. 7, no. 1, Winter, 1977, pp. 37–46.

59. Jonathan Elliot, *The Debates of the Several State Conventions,* Philadelphia: J. B. Lippincott, Vol. 2, pp. 54, 58, 220–221 (hereafter Elliot, *Debates*). On the position of the anti-Federalists, see Cecilia Kenyon, "Men of Little Faith, The Anti-Federalists on the Nature of Representative Government," *William and Mary Quarterly,* 3rd Series, Vol. 12, 1955, pp. 3–43; Raymond B. Wrabley, Jr., "Anti-Federalism and the Presidency," *Presidential Studies Quarterly,* Vol. 21, no. 3, Summer, 1991, pp. 549–570.

60. Cato, "Various Fears Concerning the Executive Department," *New York Journal,* November 8, 1787.

61. Elliot, *Debates,* Vol. 2, p. 448.

62. James Madison, *The Federalist Papers,* no. 46.

63. Elliot, *Debates,* p. 348.

64. James Madison, *The Federalist Papers,* nos. 51 and 69.

65. Frederick W. Marks III, "Foreign Affairs: A Winning Issue in the Campaign for Ratification," *Political Science Quarterly,* Vol. 86, no. 3, September, 1971, pp. 444–469.

66. *The Federalist Papers,* nos. 70 (Hamilton) and 37 (Madison).

67. Concurring opinion in *Youngstown Sheet and Tube v. Sawyer,* 343 U.S. 579 (1952), p. 634.

68. Richard Loss, "Presidential Power: The Founder's Intentions as a Problem of Knowledge," *Presidential Studies Quarterly,* Vol. 9, no. 3, Fall, 1979, pp. 379–386; James H. Hutson, "Robert Yates Notes on the Constitutional Convention of 1787," *Quarterly Journal of the Library of Congress,"* Vol. 35, 1978, pp. 173–182; Charles Ray Keller and George Wilson Pierson, "A New Madison Manuscript Relating to the Federal Convention of 1787," *American Historical Review,* Vol. 36, no. 1, 1930, pp. 17–30.

69. Julian Boyd, ed., op. cit., Vol. 12, p. 103; Harold Syrett, ed., op. cit., Vol. 4, p. 275.

70. Adrienne Koch, *Power, Morals and the Founding Fathers,* Ithaca, NY: Cornell University Press, 1961, p. 176.

71. *Inaugural Addresses of the Presidents of the United States,* Washington, D.C.: Government Printing Office, 1965, p. 3.

CHAPTER 3

The Evolution of the Presidency

The people of the United States have not failed. In their need they have registered a mandate that they want direct, vigorous action. They have asked for discipline and direction under leadership. They have made me the present instrument of their wishes. In the spirit of the gift I take it.

—Franklin D. Roosevelt

INTRODUCTORY CASE: TEDDY ROOSEVELT TRANSFORMS THE PRESIDENCY

Vice President Theodore Roosevelt was on vacation when a messenger brought him the tragic news: President William McKinley had been shot by an anarchist named Leon Czolgosz during the celebration of the Pan-American Exposition in Buffalo, New York. On taking the oath of office in 1901, Roosevelt became the youngest president of the United States. He was viewed as a maverick and completely unpredictable: "Anything can happen now that that damn cowboy is in the White House," grumbled Mark Hanna, the chairman of the Republican National Committee.

Hanna was right: once in the White House Roosevelt used the powers of the presidency to the hilt, to push an economic reform agenda opposed by conservative leaders of his own party. He thought that the president should act as a chief executive and that he should take all measures necessary for the welfare of the American people, even if not specifically mentioned in the Constitution. His Justice Department brought more than thirty lawsuits against corporations, charging them with violating antitrust laws. He insisted that coal mine owners negotiate with striking mineworkers; for the first time an American president acted as a neutral umpire in management–labor disputes rather than take the side of management. Without congressional authorization he acted to increase the acreage of national parks and forests fivefold.

Roosevelt won passage of three important laws: the Pure Food and Drug Act and the Meat Inspection Act, both of which established new safety standards for consumers, and the Hepburn Act, which strengthened the enforcement power of the Interstate Commerce Commission over railroads. His victories were achieved in spite of congressional reluctance to act because Roosevelt was the first president ever to mobilize public opinion behind him by using the presidency as a "bully good pulpit." He went across the nation by railroad, speaking out on behalf of a bill to regulate the freight charges of the very railroads he was traveling on to reach the public. "I achieved results only by appealing over the heads of the Senate and House leaders to the people, who were the masters of both of us," he observed about his tactics to break the opposition to his bills by his own party leaders in the Senate.[1]

In foreign affairs Roosevelt sent the "Great White Fleet" on a tour around the world between 1907 and 1909 to demonstrate America's power to other nations. Congress had not appropriated funds for the tour, but Roosevelt was not worried: he knew if he sent the fleet halfway around the world, Congress would eventually provide the funds to get all the way round. Roosevelt could find a way past any obstruction: when the government of Colombia refused to ratify an agreement to permit the United States to begin construction of an isthmian canal, Roosevelt encouraged Panamanians to secede from Colombia, then ordered the U.S. Navy to prevent Colombian warships from quelling the revolt. Afterwards he concluded an agreement with the new nation of Panama granting the United States a zone in which to construct a canal.

"While President, I have *been* President, emphatically," Roosevelt summed up shortly before leaving office, adding, "I believe in a strong executive; I believe in power . . ."[2] A president dominating a political party, appealing over the heads of the members of Congress to the voters, acting as a world leader, and immersing the United States in the affairs of other nations without the advice of the Senate—these actions would have astonished the framers of the Constitution of 1787, though they are commonplace presidential activities today. Roosevelt was not only the first twentieth-century president, he was also the first *modern* president.

THE PREMODERN PRESIDENCY

The "young men of the Revolution," who had created the presidency in 1787, built up the powers of the office through the 1820s. As they gave way to the leaders of the political parties created in the 1830s, the presidency itself underwent a fundamental transformation that converted it into an instrument of Congress throughout much of the nineteenth century.

Washington and Hamilton: The President and the "Prime Minister"

As with most new nations, the preeminent military leader in the struggle for independence became the head of the government: George Washington was unanimously chosen president by the electoral college and inaugurated in 1789. Washington adapted some monarchical customs and briefly insisted on British court etiquette, but after criticism by many of his own followers, a simpler, more "republican" approach was adopted, including the title "Mr. President." Washington played only a limited role in running the government. For the most part he did not concern himself with the details of laws passed by Congress, especially in the first year, when the structure of government was set up. Even in diplomatic matters, he left the conduct of crucial negotiations with the British to his envoy John Jay.

The most important decision Washington made was to appoint Alexander Hamilton as his secretary of the treasury. Hamilton believed in energetic government and produced a series of "Reports" to Congress calling for an industrial policy for the new nation, complete with high tariffs on imports, subsidies for manufacturing, development of roads, canals, bridges, and harbors, creation of a national bank, and imposition of high taxes (on commodities such as whiskey). Hamilton was soon functioning as if he were a "prime minister" in Washington's administration, organizing the Federalist party in Congress to pass his programs.[3]

"He was an aegis essential to my plans," Hamilton said of Washington, for without presidential support his program would go nowhere. He relied on Washington's prestige as a statesman and his authority with the American people, combined with his own energy and talents for intrigue. Had Washington been content with a purely ceremonial role, the presidency might have quickly evolved into a figurehead. As it turned out, Washington lent his support to Hamilton when Hamilton's programs coincided with his own priorities: when they did not, he withheld support, and Hamilton failed to get his plans passed into law. Hamilton was defeated on plans to develop western lands and subsidize industry. The "prime ministerial" system never became institutionalized because Hamilton was unpopular with many politicians and trusted by very few. He was unable to control Washington's cabinet because of policy disagreements with Secretary of State Jefferson: Hamilton favored a pro-British policy, and Jefferson favored the French. Washington used Hamilton as much as Hamilton used Washington: when his controversial treasury secretary had run out of influence with cabinet and Congress, Washington discarded him, and by 1794 both Hamilton and Jefferson found themselves out of Washington's cabinet. Hamilton's attempt to institute prime ministerial government and convert the presidency into a ceremonial unifying office had ended, as followers of Hamilton and Jefferson created opposing factions—soon to be known as Federalists and Republicans—to compete for power.

In 1796 John Adams was narrowly elected to the presidency over Thomas Jefferson (who became his vice president). Adams retained Washington's cabinet—a bad mistake, because its members looked to Hamilton rather than to Adams for political direction. Adams was unable to control his Federalist supporters, and by 1798 Congress had pushed him into an unfortunate "undeclared naval war" with France, even going so far as to name George Washington the "commander-in-chief" of the military and Hamilton as his principal aide. Though Adams managed to get out of the war with quiet diplomacy and then overhauled his cabinet, his presidency never recovered from these internal intrigues and plots hatched by Hamilton.

The first dozen years under the Constitution had dashed the framers' hopes that the president would be above party and insulated from public opinion. Though Washington had warned on leaving office against the "baneful influence of faction" in his farewell address to the nation, factions existed and could not be suppressed. The Federalists spent too much of their time in political intrigue in the capital, while Jefferson and Madison went around the country building up state parties. The result was a Republican victory in the elections of 1800.

Jefferson: Presidential Party Government

In 1801 Thomas Jefferson became President, and his Republican supporters took control of Congress.[4] "We are all Federalists, we are all Republicans," Jefferson told the nation reassuringly at his inauguration, but in fact the new president intended to use his party (formally known as the Democratic–Republicans) to bridge the constitutional separation of powers: he would fuse the executive power of the presidency with the legislative powers of Congress to create *party government.* He presided over meetings of his party's legislators (known as a congressional caucus), organized the congressional committees and handed out committee assignments to supporters, and got Congress to name his close allies to leadership positions. Because Washington City (at that time the name of the nation's capital) was just rising from the swamps, most legislators lived in boarding houses, and Jefferson would ride out to the inns, join them for dinner, and cement personal ties with his followers and lobby them for support.[5] Jefferson got Congress to pass bills to dismantle much of the Federalist economic program and return power to the states.

But Jefferson soon discovered that the Madisonian checks and balances instituted in the Constitution were stronger than the party government he was trying to create. "Ambition must be made to counteract ambition," Madison had argued in *The Federalist Papers,* "The ambition of the man must be connected to the constitutional rights of the place."[6] The institutions that had been separated constitutionally could not be unified politically by Jefferson for long. He was able to get the unpopular Federalist Supreme Court Justice Samuel Chase impeached in the House (he was charged with unbecoming conduct and disregard of the law), but the Senate refused to convict him, with some members of Jefferson's own party preferring to vote to keep the judiciary independent.

Judicial independence was demonstrated in the case of Aaron Burr, Jefferson's vice president during his first term. Burr fled west after killing Alexander Hamilton in a duel and organized a group of armed men in Kentucky. No one knew for sure what they were up to (perhaps they intended to detach western territories from the Union, or perhaps invade Mexico, or even overthrow the U.S. government), but Jefferson took no chances. He had Burr arrested and brought back east for trial. Burr was acquitted of treason in the federal courts, and when Jefferson subsequently brought Congress a bill defining treason that would cover cases like Burr's, Congress refused to pass it.

Jefferson was unable to dominate Congress for long. His hand-picked choice to lead the House of Representatives, his cousin John Randolph, disappointed him, and soon he had to lead a "coup" to change congressional leaders. By the middle of his second term his congressional allies abandoned him on key issues: he was unable to control committees or the leaders of the House and Senate, though he had been responsible for placing these men in their posts. His foreign policy of "nonintercourse" with Britain and France in the Napoleonic Wars was unpopular with his party and was scrapped as he left office. Party government worked intermittently for Jefferson, but his successors would have to share power with other party leaders in Congress and the cabinet.

Jefferson, Madison, Monroe, and Adams: Cabinet Government

At the Constitutional Convention of 1787 James Madison had fought unsuccessfully for a council of state to serve as an "interior check" on the president's exercise of executive power. The evolution of the cabinet in the early nineteenth century made it the functional equivalent of the council the Convention had rejected. Jefferson and his successors, Madison, James Monroe, and John Quincy Adams, all instituted forms of "cabinet government." When an important decision was to be made, the president would read a state paper outlining his proposed policy to the cabinet: if a majority could not support his policy, it would be modified, deferred, or scrapped. In 1819, for example, James Monroe read a seventy-page position paper on his opposition to signing laws passed by Congress providing for roads and other internal improvements: the cabinet was divided and prevailed on Monroe *not* to send the document to Congress as part of his annual message.[7] A president did not make or implement policy without full discussion with the cabinet, and usually would not act without either the consensus of his cabinet or a majority vote of its members. So "the executive power" of the president was exercised "in commission." As Jefferson described the practice in his administration:

> All matters of importance or difficulty are submitted to all the heads of departments composing the Cabinet: sometimes by the President consulting them separately and successively, as they happen to call on him; but in the gravest cases, by calling them together, discussing the subject maturely, and finally taking the vote, in which the President counts himself but one.[8]

Cabinet government evolved because cabinet secretaries were politically powerful figures whom the president appointed to consolidate his party position. In turn, cabinet politics until the 1830s was bound up in the procedures for presidential nominations: the Democratic–Republican Party selected its presidential nominees through the "Congressional Caucus." At the end of the congressional session in a presidential election year the party members in Congress would caucus (i.e., meet behind closed doors) and decide on a candidate for the presidency. Having made their choice, they would communicate it through a Committee of Correspondence, which would publicize their endorsement to newspapers around the country. The party's candidates for the electoral college in each state were expected to support congressional caucus choice. Most of the contenders for the endorsement of the caucus were already members of the cabinet or congressional leaders, and they held "salons" in the capital (gatherings with plenty of food, drink, and politics) to lobby for the support of the legislators. Members of Congress endorsed politicians whom they knew—those who were on the scene in Washington—and they passed over state governors.

A newly elected president, to reunify his congressional party after the divisive struggles for the caucus endorsement, would choose for his cabinet other leading politicians who had strong support from factions of the Democratic–Republican Party. As cabinet secretaries they functioned almost as equals to the presidents who appointed them, and many maneuvered for subsequent presidential nominations.[9] Presidents could not just boss these secretaries around as if they were menial subordinates but had to treat them as political equals; a conflict with a secretary might mean a loss of support from his followers in Congress. Moreover, by education, experience, and reputation, the secretaries of state were considered the equals of the Presidents and their potential successors.

By the late 1820s a weak and ineffective national government was faced with sectional division and paralysis. The Federalists had disappeared, and the Democratic–Republicans were the only party, presiding over an entrenched clique of civil servants running the departments who had served since the early 1800s. It was not clear that the presidency could remain more than an instrument of cabinet politicians and congressional party leaders.

Jackson: The Plebiscitary Presidency

Andrew Jackson completely upended American politics and the Republican conception of the presidency. To begin with, he delegitimized the congressional caucus. He had been defeated for the caucus nomination in 1824 but had run for president anyway in a four-candidate contest (all were members of the Democratic–Republican party) and received a plurality of the popular vote. Because no one had received a majority of electoral college votes, the election went to the House of Representatives, which chose John Quincy Adams. When Adams promptly named House Speaker Henry Clay (himself one of the four candidates) to his cabinet as secretary of state, after Clay had worked for Adams's election in the House, Jackson and his followers denounced the "corrupt bargain."[10] Jackson then proclaimed as a matter of political principle that the candidate who had received the most popular votes should become President: this idea, reinforcing the democratic elements of American politics, delegitimized the Madisonian notion that selection of a president should be "filtered" by national leaders more experienced than the people and more likely to make a wise choice. Nevertheless, the country was ready for the idea (which had been put forth at the Constitutional Convention by James Wilson and Gouverneur Morris) that the will of the popular majority should prevail in the selection of a president. By 1828 all states except South Carolina provided that the presidential electors would be chosen by popular vote rather than by state legislatures.

In 1828 Jackson bypassed the discredited "King Caucus" and "nominated" himself. He abandoned the Democratic–Republicans, ran as an independent candidate, and created a movement in each state to support him.[11] The Democratic–Republicans split, with some supporting Jackson and others, calling themselves "National Republicans," supporting the incumbent Adams. When Jackson won the presidency in 1828, neither his nomination nor his election had been "filtered" by an elite. He could plausibly claim to be the choice of the people, a claim made even more credible by the fact that under the new system of direct selection of presidential electors the voters had turned out in huge numbers: the number of voters casting ballots quadrupled between 1824 and 1828.[12] The president was now chosen by a mass electorate, and its legitimacy was now based on the will of the people.

With a popular base Jackson expanded the powers of the office he had won: he scrapped cabinet government and exercised "The Executive Power" by himself. For much of his first term he ignored the cabinet because he was infuriated by most of the secretaries and their wives: they were ostracizing Peggy Eaton (the new wife of his secretary of war) because of rumors that in her first marriage she had been an adulteress. Jackson took Mrs. Eaton's side, refused even to convene his cabinet for a long time, and instead took advice from a "Kitchen Cabinet" of personal advisors.[13]

When he met with his cabinet secretaries, he treated them as subordinates rather than as equals. Instead of following Republican precedent and soliciting their advice and giving them a veto on his policies, he issued instructions and told them what to do. He extended his political direction over the secretary of the treasury, long considered primarily accountable to Congress, because Congress had been granted the constitutional power of the purse. He fired Treasury Secretary William Duane when he refused a presidential order to shift government funds from the Bank of the United States (controlled by Jackson's political opponents) to state banks controlled by friendly Democrats, even though the Constitution is silent on a presidential removal power.[14] Duane cited his obligations and accountability to Congress, but Jackson informed him that his duty was to obey the President—and then fired him for insubordination.

The power of cabinet secretaries had been diminished because Jackson had eliminated the congressional caucus. No longer would a contender for a party's presidential nomination have to curry favor with cabinet secretaries or members of Congress. In 1832 Jackson's followers, now organized as the Democratic Party, held a national convention of state party leaders to choose a vice presidential candidate for his second term. By 1836 both the Democrats and their Whig opponents were nominating presidential candidates at national party conventions controlled by state party leaders.[15] Cabinet secretaries no longer influenced nominations, nor were they the leading contenders, because state politicians naturally looked to their peers in the statehouses (or to Senators whom their state legislatures had chosen). Presidents now came *to* Washington rather than *from* Washington.

Jackson changed the way presidents dealt with Congress. Unlike Jefferson, he did not control Congress after reshaping the party system, and it challenged him on key elements of his economic program. He was the first president to veto laws on policy grounds rather than on grounds of unconstitutionality. Jackson's threat to veto bills inserted him directly into the legislative process. He appealed to the people directly over the heads of Congress: he organized party newspapers, run by the leading Democratic state politicians, to spread his ideas and defend his actions against attack. Their reporters sent him daily dispatches about state politics, serving him as an informal White House intelligence network.

Jackson and his Vice President Martin Van Buren invented the American two-party system. They did not believe that a party and a president should try to be all things to all voters, because to do so unsatisfactory compromises of principles would have to be made. Jackson had strong beliefs and was not much interested in compromising them: by trying to satisfy a small majority of voters rather than everyone, he believed that he could retain his principles and still govern effectively. Nor did he believe that members of the opposition were "disloyal" and their presence illegitimate—as Federalists and Democratic–Republicans had treated each other. Instead, Jackson and Van Buren believed that a vigorous two-party system—similar to the one that functioned in New York State—would provide the people with a choice and would validate the principle that a president has the right to exercise power because he represents the majority.[16]

What cemented Jackson's followers to his party was the prospect of presidential patronage. "To the victors belong the spoils" was the motto of the Jacksonians, who ended a decades-long practice of allowing almost all national officials to remain in power from one administration to the next. John Quincy Adams, for example, hardly ever had removed department officials, and had lost his chance to dominate departmental business or influence Congress. Under Jackson, more than one-tenth of the civil officers were removed so that Jackson's loyal party followers could get their jobs. "Rotation in office" rather than "expertise" became the order of the day.[17] It was the era of the Common Man: any American could fill any position, Jacksonians claimed rhetorically (though in practice they kept the experts on in key posts). Presidential patronage built political parties, and in turn these parties mobilized voters in presidential elections to provide the winning candidate with majoritarian legitimacy.

But Jackson's conception of the presidency based on plebiscitary leadership did not survive, for much the same reasons that Jefferson's party government eventually failed. Absent the dominant personality of the party's founder, the practices of American politics at the time were uncongenial to strong national government or strong presidential leadership. Both Jefferson and Jackson had won the presidency in large measure by expressing great distrust for the exercise of national governmental power. The Democrats and Whigs in the post-Jackson era nominated candidates for the presidency who were not prepared to exercise such power vigorously.

Harrison and Taylor: The Whig Presidency

Jackson's opponents organized the Whig Party and used the techniques of popular government pioneered by Jackson to win the presidency in 1840, defeating Jackson's successor Martin Van Buren in his bid for a second term. Whigs were united in opposition to the principles of the Jacksonian presidency. They believed that presidents should serve only one term, that they should not try to influence Congress on legislation or lead a congressional party, that they should take direction from party leaders in Congress (who would write their Inaugural Addresses and State of the Union messages), that they should not remove department officials except at the request of congressional leaders, and that they should simply preside over the government and see that the laws were faithfully executed.[18]

The Whigs elected two military heroes with no prior civilian political experience: General William Henry Harrison in 1840 and General Zachary Taylor in 1848. In their view, the less the president knew about government and politics the better. Their candidate's job was to win the White House and act as a figurehead, allowing Congress to control the government. Harrison died after his first month in office, and Taylor never finished his term—it is not too much of an exaggeration to say that by dying in office these presidents simply carried the Whig approach to the presidency to its logical conclusion.

The Weak Presidency and Congressional Government

The Democrat and Whig presidents who served after Jackson up to the start of the Civil War were unable or unwilling to capitalize on the newly democratized system to extend presidential power. All held office for a single term, most because they were unable to win renomination or reelection, or because (like Polk) they pledged to serve only a single term. Congress, not the president, took the initiative on domestic issues such as currency and commerce, slavery and sectionalism, and tariffs and taxation. The sectional compromises on slavery of 1850 and 1854 that temporarily preserved the Union were the work of legislators such as Henry Clay, John Calhoun, Stephen Douglas, and Daniel Webster, with presidents ineffectually standing on the sidelines or intervening in ways that sometimes reduced chances for passage. President James Buchanan, believing himself powerless to intervene to preserve the Union when Southern states began to secede in the winter of 1861, symbolized the failure of party government and presidential politics before the Civil War.

Although Abraham Lincoln got his start in national politics as a congressional Whig opposed to President Polk's leadership in the Mexican-American War, in the 1850s, as the Whigs disintegrated, he helped form a new party, the Republicans (no relation to Jefferson's party of the early 1800s). Once in the White House in 1861, he demonstrated the bankruptcy of the Whig–Democrat conception of presidential power in times of emergency. Lincoln exercised enormous powers, bypassing Congress when he thought he had to, and created what some historians later referred to as a "constitutional dictatorship" to save the Union. His powers were so extraordinary that they did not serve as a precedent through the remainder of the nineteenth century. Constitutional law scholars after the Civil War distinguished between the powers of the "State" (which Lincoln exercised in an emergency situation) and the routine powers of "the government" as specified by the Constitution. By making that distinction, a weak presidency functioning within a weak national government reemerged after the Civil War.[19]

After Lincoln's assassination by John Wilkes Booth, the power of the presidency once again plummeted. Lincoln's successor, Andrew Johnson, was a Tennessee Democrat who had remained loyal to the Union and who had been put on Lincoln's "Unionist" ticket in 1864 to win support from the border states. Johnson had no political support among Republicans in Congress (some of whom even thought he had been part of the assassination plot), and when he attempted his own lenient policy of postwar Reconstruction for the South, he was impeached by the House and nearly convicted by the Senate. Johnson was acquitted by one vote, but his acquittal did not restore the power of the presidency, because to remain in office he had to promise Congress that he would give up his attempt to control Reconstruction.

With the election of General Ulysses S. Grant, a period of congressional supremacy was begun that would last for the remainder of the nineteenth century. When the writer Henry Brooks Adams saw the corrupt party hack politicians Grant had appointed to his cabinet, he observed that "the progress of evolution from President Washington to President Grant, was alone evidence enough to upset Darwin."[20] Grant's cabinet secretaries were involved in a number of scandals, all of which reduced the influence of the presidency, and at the end of his second term Grant apologized to the nation for his corrupt administration, blaming his own political inexperience and naivete.

Grant was followed by a succession of politicians (many of whom had served as generals in the Civil War after being given political appointments to state militia) who were willing to do the bidding of their party. "Congressional government" was the term used by a young graduate student named Woodrow Wilson to describe

American politics after the Civil War.[21] Weak and ineffectual presidents presided over cabinets composed of party hack politicians, who themselves had received office because of deals made at the national nominating conventions. The cabinet secretaries and congressional committee leaders bypassed the White House and worked together to formulate and implement laws, which produced a cornucopia for their followers of subsidies, contracts, commissions, franchises, protective tariffs, land grants, veterans' pensions, and public works. Interest groups financed the parties and bought influence directly from legislators and cabinet secretaries.

Presidents had no advance notice of the raids on the Treasury conducted by congressional committees on behalf of their constituents. Presidents did not introduce a comprehensive legislative program (though they occasionally recommended measures), nor did they prepare a budget. They might be intimately involved with patronage requests from state parties, but often matters involving state politicians would be handled by department secretaries without presidential supervision. The nexus of interest group lobbyists, congressional committees, and department secretary ran each department. Cabinet meetings resembled local party "clubhouses," where patronage requests and other matters were the order of business.

To the extent that presidents demonstrated any independence from Congress, they were "nay-sayers" like Hayes and Cleveland, who used the veto power against congressional barons when their raids on the Treasury went too far, or McKinley, who stood firm against calls for "easy money." Late–nineteenth-century presidents set themselves against the excesses of the party spoils system, and acquiesced in the creation of a nonpartisan merit form of civil service appointment for a small minority of federal officeholders, but their powers were limited and their conception of the office narrow.

THE MODERN PRESIDENCY

The presidency was transformed at the beginning of the twentieth century, in large measure because of the changing place of the United States in world politics, the development of the United States as a modern industrial economy with an expanded social welfare state, and the continuing democratization of the electoral system.[22]

Roosevelt versus Taft: Steward of the People or Chief Magistrate?

Theodore Roosevelt's debate about presidential leadership with his successor William Howard Taft illuminates the changing conceptions of the presidency during the early twentieth century. Roosevelt wanted the president to exert energetic leadership on all occasions. "My view," he later was to write, "was that every officer, and above all every executive officer in high places, was a steward of the people."[23] He argued that the president could take any action not expressly prohibited by the Constitution, a position similar to Alexander Hamilton's (about whom he had written a biography). Taft, whose life's ambition was to be a justice on the United States Supreme Court, believed that the president should act as a judge to resolve disputes within his administration: he referred to the president as "Our Chief Magistrate."[24] He believed that a president could exercise only those powers that were expressly granted, or could be fairly construed to be granted, to the president by the Constitution and laws. Roosevelt had formulated a program (the Square Deal) and had led the nation; Taft presided over a cabinet and tried (unsuccessfully) to keep it on an even keel, and his idea of a major initiative was to propose reforms in the budget process. Taft simply was not willing to use the "bully pulpit" that Roosevelt had understood was the essential source of power for the modern presidency.

Wilson versus Coolidge: The Rhetorical versus the Taciturn Presidency

Woodrow Wilson had been a political science professor and president of Princeton University before becoming governor of New Jersey and then president of the United States. He came into the White House having already thought and written about the powers of the presidency. "Whatever else we may think or say of Theodore Roosevelt," he had written, "he led Congress—he was not driven by Congress. We may not approve of his methods but we must concede that he made Congress follow him."[25] Wilson intended to use political rhetoric for even bolder ends: he would lead Congress by leading its majority party—and he would also lead it by influencing public opinion.

Wilson was determined to use party leadership as Jefferson had done before him to bridge the separation of powers. Democrats controlled Congress, and Wilson set about to reorganize the legislative party to make it an instrument of his leadership. Like Jefferson, he dominated his party's Senate and House caucuses, and like Jefferson, he installed his supporters on key congressional committees. Wilson's party went against its own "seniority" customs, which would have granted senior Democrats certain committee assignments, to line up Wilson loyalists on key committees. Democrats even agreed that caucus decisions to support legislation should be binding rather than advisory; a rule that would promote party discipline. With these procedures Wilson thought that presidential party government would replace congressional government.[26]

Yet Jefferson had thought he could create party government, and he had been disappointed. How could Wilson avoid Jefferson's failure? His solution was to combine inside maneuvering within the congressional power structure with influence over public opinion: he would speak directly to the people, something Jefferson had never done. He reinstituted the practice (dropped by Jefferson in 1801 as demagogic and monarchic) of delivering a message on the state of the union personally to Congress at the beginning of its sessions, rather than sending it a message and accompanying reports of the departments. He also made it a point to present some of his most important measures to Congress in person.

Wilson believed that his speeches and messages to Congress, widely reported by newspapers, would help him shape public opinion, because his language was directed as much to the voters as to the legislators. He believed that his rhetoric could convert political conflicts into issues of principle and would get the public interested in what was happening in Washington. The president would simplify issues to attract public interest. Like Roosevelt, Wilson would use stirring rhetorical devices to appeal to his audience rather than ponderous and solemn language. He would offer the people his policies and give them the information they needed to press their priorities on the government.[27]

How would Wilson avoid demagoguery? First, he would adhere to the norms of parliamentary debate, and would avoid logical fallacies, ad hominem arguments (that attacked individuals), and other ways of stirring up emotions and hatreds that would threaten the stability of the system. Second, he would use rhetoric that would enhance the public's confidence in his leadership and character. Wilson was confident that a demagogue could not survive public scrutiny. Finally, Wilson believed it was so difficult to move public opinion that no demagogic president would be able to gain mastery; he placed his confidence in the ability of the people to sift through presidential rhetoric and support what was in their own interest. In his belief that the public would support him if he presented complex issues in a complex way, Wilson was mistaken, with disastrous consequences for his presidency.

The failure of Wilson's rhetorical presidency involved the controversy over American participation in the League of Nations. In the aftermath of the Allied victory in World War I, Wilson went to Europe with his Fourteen Point program for "peace without victory." Wilson won Allied acceptance of a League of Nations, but he faced a harder task in gaining American acceptance. Wilson believed that he could rally American public opinion behind the League of Nations and that it would not be difficult to get the Senate to approve the Treaty of Versailles ending the war, even though he had broken with previous precedents by not taking a bipartisan delegation of senators with him when he negotiated the peace treaty (he included only one Republican on his delegation and did not take any influential Senate leaders). Many Republicans in Congress, urged on by former President Roosevelt, sensed that America wanted no foreign entanglements, and they opposed the treaty and the League. Even before sailing for the peace conference, Wilson had appealed to the nation to elect a Democratic Congress in the midterm elections, but instead the voters gave the Republicans majorities in both houses, making his task even harder.

Wilson soon learned that the same techniques used by a president to mobilize public opinion could also be used against the White House. On the Republican side of the aisle, some senators had turned isolationist and this "irreconcilable" bloc was prepared to vote against any treaty at all. Other Republicans, led by Senator Henry Cabot Lodge of Massachusetts, would accept a treaty only if it placed strict congressional limitations on the power of the president to commit the United States to peacekeeping duties.

Wilson embarked on a nationwide speaking tour to win public support. If the treaty were to be defeated, he warned the crowds, "I can predict with absolute certainty that within another generation there will be another world war." On September 25, 1919, while making a speech in support of the League in Pueblo, Colorado, he collapsed and was brought back to Washington, where he suffered a stroke on October 2. Paralyzed on his left side, confined to bed or a wheelchair, and totally dependent on his wife as his link to the outside world, Wilson was in no position to control the outcome of the struggle for the treaty. The Senate considered a series of "Reservations" sponsored by Senator Lodge, some of which seemed to limit the power of the president as commander in chief to use military force in support of the League. Wilson called on his supporters to vote against the treaty if it were amended. On November 19 and 20, 1919, a coalition of Republican "irreconcilables" and Democrats following Wilson's orders defeated Lodge's version of the treaty. (Later, by a simple resolution in 1921, the Senate ended the state of war with Germany.)

Wilson remained ill and under the close supervision of his wife. He was awarded the Nobel Peace Prize in December 1920, but that prize was small consolation for his party's defeat in the presidential elections at the hands of Warren Harding and his corrupt "Ohio Gang," a group that represented everything Wilson despised in American party politics. The rhetorical presidency was dead as well: the model of an effective president in the 1920s became "Silent Cal" Coolidge (who succeeded Harding after his death in 1923): supposedly Coolidge said, "You lose," when his dinner companion told him she had made a bet that she could get him to say more than two words that evening. By the time Herbert Hoover tried to exhort the nation during the Depression with his slogan that "Prosperity Is Just around the Corner," the rhetorical presidency seemed to be a doomed proposition. If anything, the passage of the Seventeenth Amendment, providing for direct election of senators, seemed to increase the democratic legitimacy of Congress as the preeminent institution of government.

Roosevelt versus Eisenhower: The Open versus the Hidden Hand

Walter Lippmann, a leading newspaper columnist of the 1930s, once wrote that Franklin D. Roosevelt was "a pleasant man who, without any important qualifications for the office, would very much like to be President." Lippmann not only was wrong about Roosevelt's qualifications, he also missed a shift in party politics that had occurred since the early 1900s. No longer were political bosses at the nominating conventions choosing men like themselves to be president: now that the United States was a world power, they had recognized the importance of backing experienced and intelligent leaders for the nomination: Taft, Wilson, Hoover, and Roosevelt (Warren Harding excepted) were all highly qualified nominees (as were most of their opponents) whose education, governmental experience and ethical standards contrasted favorably with most of their nineteenth-century predecessors. If we had not completely returned to the elitist era of the Federalist and Republican candidates, we had nevertheless come a long way from the level of the presidential nominees in the nineteenth century.

Between 1933 and 1945 Franklin D. Roosevelt drew on the precedents set by his cousin Theodore and Woodrow Wilson, and reinstituted a programmatic and rhetorical presidency. His administration relied on experts in task forces and commissions. A "Brains Trust" of Columbia University professors, who had ably assisted him when he was governor of New York, also helped to develop the New Deal program. Roosevelt was impatient with theorizing when action was needed. He was a problem solver, willing to try anything once. "It is common sense," he said, "to take a method and try it. If it fails, admit it frankly and try another. But above all, try something." Like Wilson, Roosevelt was a rhetorician, whose speeches first calmed the people in the midst of the Depression and then mobilized them to support his initiatives.

Roosevelt tried to revive the Jeffersonian and Wilsonian strategy of party government, but with mixed success. After his initial great successes in the First Hundred Days, Congress blocked some of his initiatives, made extensive modifications in others, and passed many programs of its own. In a replay of Jefferson's tampering with a conservative judiciary, Roosevelt lost the support of many members of his own party when he asked them to pass a bill increasing the membership of the Supreme Court; his "court-packing" plan was defeated in 1937, but more importantly, Southern Democrats joined conservative Republicans to block most New Deal measures thereafter.[28] When Roosevelt tried to intervene in party primaries to defeat prominent opponents of the New Deal, his attempts at a "purge" were rebuffed by voters, who resented White House interference in what they considered to be local contests.[29] Nevertheless, he restored confidence in the national government, and he ameliorated the suffering of millions, even if his measures did not end the Depression. With American entry into World War II, Roosevelt doffed his "Dr. New Deal" hat and instead donned his "Dr. Win the War" hat. He asked Congress for vast delegations of powers to mobilize the economy and conduct the war, powers Congress granted. His successor, Harry Truman, tried to continue the Roosevelt domestic agenda after World War II, but the election of a Republican Congress in 1946 put the brakes on his program. Nevertheless, by the late 1940s, progressive presidents of both parties had institutionalized a "presidency of powers" that involved strong legislative leadership, presidential control over the departments of government, activism in domestic affairs, and vast delegations of power for diplomacy, national security affairs, and war making.

The most successful president since Franklin Roosevelt was in many ways his antithesis: the political success of Dwight Eisenhower provides us with at least a second formula for operating in the White House: a president who uses a "hidden hand" to disguise his formidable political resources. For much of his presidency Eisenhower seemed to be a political novice. He seemed to rely on his chief of staff Sherman Adams to an excessive extent for domestic policy and on his secretary of state John Foster Dulles for foreign policy. He seemed a captive of his staffing system, which was rigid, unimaginative, and cautious to an excess. Years later, when scholars were able to examine Eisenhower's papers, they drew different conclusions.[30]

Eisenhower was actually a skillful politician who chose not to let others realize that fact. He camouflaged his participation in partisan Republican politics by relying on others to conduct his political business and concealing his own role. He did not put political appointments on the official White House calendar of daily presidential events, for example. Rather than act as leader of his party, he acted as if he were above party. Although Eisenhower was no Woodrow Wilson or Franklin Roosevelt when it came to making public addresses, he converted his weakness into a strength. He often used language that was ambiguous and spoke in an evasive, noncommittal, or seemingly confused fashion. His speech made his adversaries underestimate him. His use of jumbled syntax at press conferences was a deliberate ploy to enable him to avoid taking stands on controversial issues, such as pending civil rights legislation that might divide his party. He did not try to polarize opinion or ascribe evil motives to his opponents. He was adept at hiding his personal feelings about those whom he despised. He tried never to attack anyone's motives or make personal comments about them in public. His rhetoric was never overheated; consequently, he did not convert opponents into enemies.

Eisenhower was a shrewd judge of character. He could step into other people's shoes and understand situations from his adversaries' point of view. He could anticipate how others might respond and could shape his strategy and tactics accordingly. He could assess his opponents' intentions as well as their capabilities. He never felt comfortable dealing with a situation until he had some idea of how his opponents might be thinking about it.

Eisenhower knew how to delegate responsibility. He delegated much presidential business, but never to the extent that he lost control of policy. Though some people thought Secretary of State John Foster Dulles was running American foreign policy, Eisenhower personally knew the leaders of the other great powers (Dulles did not), and Eisenhower dominated foreign policy. He also kept close control over the Defense Department and its "more bang for the buck" strategy of substituting nuclear for conventional forces. Eisenhower would share credit for the successes of his subordinates, and more importantly, he would see that subordinates deflected criticism and blame away from him.

Eisenhower had been a career military officer (except for a few years as president of Columbia University), and his style of leadership was based on military strategy and tactics. Generals must know how to deceive the enemy, to make opponents think they are weak and disorganized, and to gull them into making a premature attack. Military leaders try to find out all they can about the opposing generals or admirals, and what they might be expected to do in a given situation. Officers stay out of civilian politics, but within their own ranks they must be consummate politicians to get promoted. They must be adept at finding sponsors, obtaining the right assignments (they refer to it as "getting your ticket punched"), and keeping out of trouble. Eisenhower began his career under a cloud (he was accused of misappropriating military funds) and earned the ill will of several senior officers, and it took him a decade to emerge from obscurity and get his career back on track. His abilities as a commander in war games, as well as the patronage of President Franklin Roosevelt (and his wife Eleanor Roosevelt), enabled Eisenhower to jump over many senior commanders at the start of World War II. During the war he was responsible for pulling together Allied forces into a single European command, an assignment that required diplomatic skills of the highest order. Eisenhower was a consummate politician, even though he had never held elected office.

Once in the White House, Eisenhower used a "hidden hand" that left his opponents bewildered. He hid his role in efforts to neutralize Senator Joseph McCarthy (a Republican senator from Wisconsin, who meddled in diplomatic and military matters while on a supposed hunt for communist spies in the government), allowing Vice President Nixon and Senate Majority Leader Lyndon Johnson to take the lead, but orchestrating much of the effort himself. Eisenhower forged a bipartisan consensus in foreign policy that got us out of the Korean War and kept us at peace, while using the intelligence agencies to subvert foreign governments or overthrow them—activities involving Iran and Guatemala kept secret from the American people. He presided over the consolidation of New Deal social programs and even expanded them, giving these agencies cabinet status for the first time by creating the Department of Health, Education, and Welfare. Eisenhower gained influence in Congress by relying on the Democratic congressional leaders (Lyndon Johnson and Sam Rayburn), men who were his poker and drinking partners, and they often had more influence in the administration than the Republican leaders (William Knowland and Joe Martin), both of whom he despised.

Sometimes Eisenhower's hand was too hidden. He exerted no moral leadership on one of the key domestic issues of the time, racial desegregation of the public schools, and did what he could to pressure Chief Justice Earl Warren to slow the pace of desegregation. While he preserved his own reputation and popularity, he never transferred them to his party: by 1954 the Democrats had regained the Senate; after his own victorious reelection victory the Republican Party suffered disastrous defeats in state and congressional elections in 1958 and lost the chance to convert itself from minority to majority-party status. Eisenhower's hidden-hand efforts to deny Nixon the vice presidential renomination in 1956, as well as his efforts to designate Treasury Secretary Robert Anderson as his political heir apparent in 1960, weakened Richard Nixon's chances to win the White House. He did not campaign for Nixon until the very end of the campaign, and the Democrats won the White House, reinstituting FDR-style presidential leadership.

President Eisenhower jokes with Senate Majority Leader Lyndon Johnson just before addressing the Bi-Partisan Foreign Aid Conference on the need for both parties in Congress to support the administration's $4 billion foreign aid program.

THE INSTITUTIONALIZED PRESIDENCY

Since the late 1930s, the presidency has become institutionalized: the president now employs hundreds of aides and many agencies to conduct his or her business. Franklin Roosevelt created the White House Office (WHO) and the Executive Office of the Presidency (EOP). These agencies give the occupant of the Oval Office the staff resources to gain more influence over the government.[31] The vice president and the presidential spouse, both figures with almost no influence until the 1930s, also began to participate in presidential decision making.

The White House Office (WHO)

Franklin Roosevelt's predecessors had run the Oval Office with a few clerks and confidential assistants and aides, some of whom had to be put on departmental payrolls because the White House had no funds for their salaries. At Roosevelt's suggestion, Congress passed a reorganization law that established a White House Office (WHO) of six senior officials to carry out the president's political business. These "assistants to the president" were supposed to have a "passion for anonymity," according to Louis Brownlow, a political scientist who headed a committee of public administration experts that recommended creation of the WHO.[32] The reorganization plan also created the Executive Office of the President, which grouped a number of agencies under the president to supervise personnel and civil service matters, the preparation of the budget, and efforts to alleviate the Depression.

The WHO was created by Reorganization Act Number One in 1939. Until that year the president had no senior aides on his payroll, though Congress had provided salaries for several clerks and for the housekeeping staff that ran the mansion. (Franklin Roosevelt had once wisecracked that Herbert Hoover's main accomplishment had been in getting Congress to fund a third clerk.) Presidents had used assistant secretaries in the departments who had been detailed to the White House to handle presidential business such as liaison with Congress. By 1940 Roosevelt's office consisted of three "secretaries to the President," four "administrative assistants," a "personal secretary," and an "executive clerk." By the end of World War II the number of aides had increased to forty-five, by the end of the Eisenhower administration it was up to four hundred, and there were more than six hundred staffers during the Nixon administration, stabilizing at around five hundred thereafter.

The WHO concentrates on communications. The Appointments and Scheduling Office handles the flow of visitors in and out of the White House. The Advance Office handles the president's calendar and the logistics for his or her public appearances around the nation. The Director of Media Affairs (and the press secretary) handle news conferences and the dissemination of information to the media by the president and other White House aides. The Speechwriting Office prepares drafts of presidential speeches and messages to Congress, and other written documents. The White House Research Unit checks the facts contained in any presidential statement, especially quotations, dates, figures, and historical references. The Office of

Congressional Liaison helps the president persuade Congress to pass his or her legislative program. The Office of Intergovernmental Affairs keeps in contact with governors and mayors. The Political Affairs Office keeps the president in close touch with his or her party's leaders in state and local government. The Public Liaison Office helps the president gain support from interest groups and their lobbyists.

Some units have substantive responsibilities. The Office of Personnel helps recruit the political executives into the White House, Executive Office of the President, and the cabinet and subcabinet positions that constitute the "administration." The Cabinet Secretariat makes sure that department secretaries and other administration officials implement presidential decisions, and it coordinates the travel and speechmaking of cabinet secretaries so that they can advance the president's agenda around the nation. The Domestic Policy Assistant, the Assistant to the President for Economic Policy, the Assistant to the President for Science and Technology, and the National Security Adviser all promote new policy initiatives.

The White House Counsel's Office provides legal advice to the president and his or her aides. It consists of approximately twenty lawyers and is headed by the White House Counsel, who is appointed by the president. They review requests for presidential pardons and commutation of sentences; advise the president on which gifts he or she may accept for the nation, ensure compliance with campaign finance laws during reelection campaigns; deal with subpoenas from Congress or courts, and advise whether to invoke executive privilege. White House Counsel also participate in decisions about vetoing laws. The Office reviews data on appointments with the Personnel office and the Office of Government Ethics, and may show copies of FBI reports and tax-compliance summaries prepared by the Internal Revenue Service to Senate committees handling nominations. It plays an important role in advising the president on suitable nominees for the federal district and appeals courts and for justices of the Supreme Court. The White House Counsel increasingly takes a public role in reassuring the media that the president is ethical and law abiding.

Other units in the White House perform essential "housekeeping" functions: these include, among many others, the Office of Correspondence and Messages, which handles the mail; the White House Military Office, which handles the "football," which contains codes that allow the president to launch a nuclear attack; and the White House Communications Agency, which keeps the president in touch with military, diplomatic, intelligence, and other national security communications networks. There are also units of the Secret Service assigned to guard the First Family. The White House Physician is responsible for keeping close tabs on the president's physical condition.

Whatever their title or formal job description, the top staffers, with titles such as "senior political adviser to the president," are best thought of as protectors of the president's political stakes in any situation. They are adept at communication, liaison, negotiation, and transacting political business. Many come from the campaign (and others from the mass media) and have experience in image projection. They take on whatever assignments the president parcels out to them. They enforce presidential priorities on department secretaries and other members of the administration. They organize and supervise presidential commissions and task forces to develop new government programs. They are the "firefighters" on whom the president calls to deal with political crises, such as scandals, a plunge in the polls, adverse media coverage, and the like. They may run a "situation room" or "war room" organized to manage a particular presidential initiative, in which public liaison, communications, congressional liaison, and other communications functions are integrated into a single strategy to get a bill passed.[33] They are the "spin artists" sent to manipulate the media and give the administration version of events. They are the "fixers" for presidential business in the bureaucracy, which may involve specific favors and transactions to secure votes in Congress. They are sounding boards for the president, who develops political strategy with his or her top aides. They are buffers who protect the president's time and try to handle departmental business without bothering the president on issues of lesser concern.

Unless the White House staff operation is organized carefully, these assistants will have overlapping responsibilities, and friction is bound to occur as they jockey for access, position, and power in a modern version of "palace guard" politics. They have become media figures in their own right, and what they do may give the president political pluses and minuses. The pluses come when aides are portrayed by the media as energetic, intelligent, and engrossed in working for the public interest. If they are seen as arrogant, or as inexperienced youngsters, or as "professorial" types divorced from the real world, or as Machiavellian maneuverers who treat politics as an extension of the warfare of the campaign, unable either to manage or negotiate on behalf of the president, that advantage is dissipated. White House staffers may get involved in sex scandals, abuse of power, or improper use of the "perks" of office—such as the White House limousines or helicopters. Presidential aides, no matter how powerful, are "suspended from above" rather than "supported from below," because they have only a single constituency—the occupant of the Oval Office. The president can build them up or drop them at will once they become a liability. As Lyndon Johnson once told his staff, "Now you very important guys ought to keep one thing in mind. The folks tonight who tell you how smart you are and how charming you are don't give a pig's a– – about you personally. They think you can get to me."[34]

Critics argue that the president had too many staffers tripping over each other, and during campaigns it became good presidential politics to pledge to reduce the size of the White House Office. Although several presidents claimed to have done so, often it merely involved shifting staffers from the White House payroll to some other agency. President Clinton's pledge to reduce the staff by 25 percent was accomplished in large measure by a reduction in the number of clerical and housekeeping aides, as well as by the transfer of some officials to executive agencies. But some reductions were real—about 40 in WHO and over 300 in the EOP—leading to complaints that the staff was overworked, that turnaround time in dealing with problems had lengthened, that there was less reaching out and follow-up, and less communication going on (in a staff whose main job is to communicate).[35]

The Chief of Staff

Starting in the 1950s under Dwight Eisenhower, a "chief of staff" presided over the WHO and the EOP, assisted by a deputy chief of staff. Presidents usually appoint trusted friends, sometimes from their home state and almost always from their campaign. The chief of staff serves as a principal counselor and political advisor, as well as being the "gatekeeper" who determines who can see the president, at what time, and on what business. An effective chief of staff keeps the paperwork running smoothly, heads off conflict among aides, and gives the media the impression that the work of the presidency is being performed smoothly and competently. The best chiefs seem to be those who come to the position with broad expertise in a variety of political settings, gain the confidence of key members of Congress, and can take charge of the staff without being overbearing or arrogant.[36]

Unfortunately, many chiefs of staff cause more problems for presidents than they solve. Dwight Eisenhower had to dismiss Sherman Adams because he had accepted gifts from a Boston financier that constituted a conflict of interest. Richard Nixon's chief of staff, H. R. "Bob" Haldeman, resigned after it became known that he participated in the cover-up of the Watergate crimes. President Reagan's chief of staff, Don Regan, was forced out by Nancy Reagan and other top White House aides in the aftermath of the Iran–contra scandal, in large measure because he seemed overbearing and lacking the confidence of Congress (he was replaced by former Senator Howard Baker). President Bush's chief of staff, John Sununu, was considered a liability in dealing with Congress because of his arrogant manner and refusal to compromise—even with Republicans in Bush's own party. President Clinton's first chief of staff, Thomas "Mack" McClarty, an Arkansas business executive and one of Clinton's boyhood friends, left the impression that he was politically naive and completely out of his league in protecting the political interests of the president. His second, Leon Panetta, was a Washington insider (a former member of the House and budget director), and he quickly took charge of communications, political strategy, and passing the president's program in Congress, focusing on these political responsibilities rather than working on administrative issues. Presidents who try to function without an experienced chief of staff—such as Jimmy Carter and Bill Clinton in their first two years—find that the free-wheeling chaos in the White House is worse, and soon revert to the chief of staff system.

The Executive Office of the President (EOP)

The Brownlow Committee recommended the creation of an Executive Office of the President (EOP) to assist the president in supervising the departments. The EOP was created by Congress, on President Roosevelt's recommendation, in Reorganization Act One in 1939 (see Figures 3.1 and 3.2 and the box on pp. 70–71). Most of its units provide the president with essential support in coordinating the work of the departments, though some of the more than eighty units that existed at one time or another in the EOP have dealt with particular policies of public concern (drugs, crime, poverty, energy, or the environment). As of 1994 the EOP agencies had approximately 1,800 employees and budgets totalling more than $210 million.

In theory each of the EOP agencies provides the president with indispensable technical assistance in formulating or implementing his or her program. In practice, these agencies have been politicized since the early 1970s, and the top officials function as White House aides, using the agencies as their own resources in promoting their own agendas within the White House. They serve up intelligence and

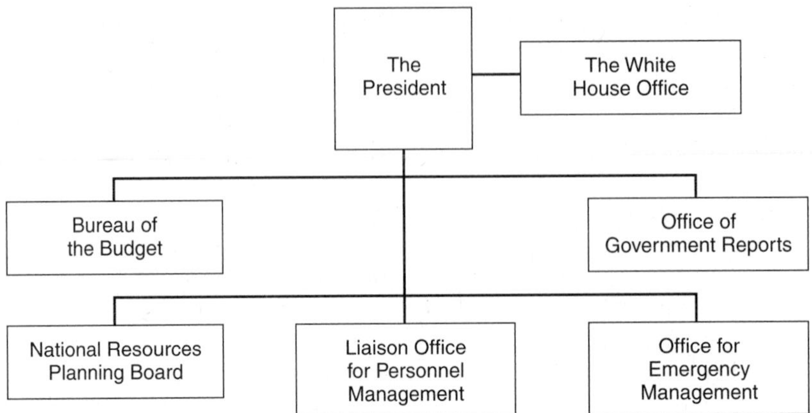

Figure 3.1 The Executive Office of the President in 1940.
Source: United States Government Organizational Manual, 1941, p. 592.

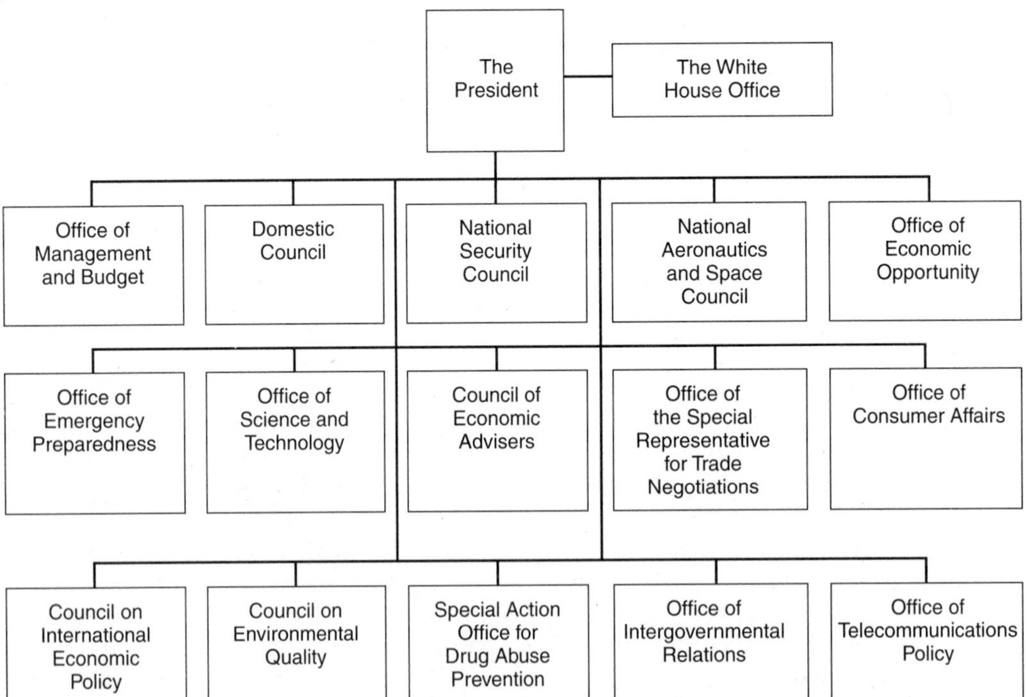

Figure 3.2 The Executive Office of the President in 1971.
Source: United States Government Organizational Manual, 1972, p. 68.

policy options, and provide advice to the president, and once decisions have been made, they help with their implementation.

Critics have faulted these agencies on three grounds: First, they are not nearly as institutionalized as they might be; they are highly politicized, most of their higher-level personnel enter when a new president assumes office and remain only for his term, and they have little "institutional memory" to provide continuity or expertise when a new administration takes office. Each of these agencies is constantly "reinventing the wheel." Second, they rarely engage in serious long-range planning, and their program perspectives seem to be coterminous with the presidential term. Finally, they are less adept at effective implementation, monitoring, and evaluation of programs than they are at proposing new initiatives. For the programmatic presidency, the actual performance of government seems to be a low priority, yet poorly administered government feeds on public disillusionment and cynicism, and accounts for much of the weakness of the modern programmatic presidency.

The Vice President

The vice presidency was an afterthought for the Constitutional Convention, put into the document by the Committee on Postponed Matters to provide for orderly succession in case of presidential death, disability, resignation, or impeachment. The vice president has no constitutional responsibilities other than serving as president of the Senate and presiding over that body (except in impeachment trials, when the Chief Justice of the United States presides) and voting to break ties. Vice presidents usually do not preside over the Senate unless a tie vote on an important issue is likely to occur.

The vice president is *not* constitutionally a member of either the executive or legislative branches. The vice president is not a subordinate of the president, who has no power to issue orders to the vice president and cannot remove him from office. But vice presidents have found that the way they gain influence in Washington is by subordinating themselves to the president. They have become, since the Eisenhower administration, part of the inner circle of senior White House advisors.[37] Vice presidents are usually assigned by the president to chair commissions dealing with the space program, nondiscrimination in government contracting, improving the administration of intergovernmental grant programs, and deregulation of the economy. Vice President Gore chaired a commission on "reinventing government" for President Clinton. They usually serve as White House liaison with the National Governors Association and the U.S. Conference of Mayors. The vice president participates in cabinet meetings, a custom established by Warren Harding. Since the Eisenhower administration vice presidents have presided over cabinet meetings and the National Security Council in the absence of the president; Richard Nixon chaired twenty such meetings during Eisenhower's illnesses and trips.[38] Nixon, Walter Mondale, and Al Gore all assisted their presidents in rounding up votes in Congress for White House measures, while George Bush was primarily active in national security affairs, serving as a presidential emissary to foreign rulers.

The Executive Office of the President, 1995

The Office of Management and Budget was created by the Budget and Accounting Act of 1921. It prepares the Budget of the United States, oversees departmental requests for legislation from Congress, develops new management initiatives, formulates reorganization plans, assists the president with veto messages, and ensures that new government regulations are in accordance with presidential priorities. Its director is one of the president's principal advisors on economic issues. Included within it is the Office of Federal Procurement Policy.

The National Economic Council, established by Executive Order in 1993, coordinates the national and international economic policy making of the departments of the national government.

The Council of Economic Advisers was created by Employment Act of 1946. Its three members prepare the Economic Report of the President, conduct research on economic issues, and give the White House advice on economic policy. Its chair serves as the president's principal spokesperson on fiscal policy making.

The National Security Council was created by the National Security Act of 1947. Members consist of the president, vice president, and secretaries of state and defense. Principal advisors consist of the chair of the Joint Chiefs of Staff and the director of the Central Intelligence Agency. The NSC provides advice to the president on foreign policy and military matters, and its staff conducts research on strategic defense and diplomatic issues.

The Office of United States Trade Representative, established by the Trade Act of 1974, conducts studies of the impact of bilateral trade patterns on the U.S. economy and negotiates trade policies with other nations. It is headed by the United States Trade Representative, a cabinet-level officer with the rank of ambassador who reports directly to the president. The Trade Representative is the chief representative of the United States for all activities concerning multilateral trade agreements such as GATT and NAFTA.

The Office of Science and Technology Policy, established by the National Science and Technology Policy, Organization, and Priorities Act of 1976, recommends new government programs in science, and prepares reports on science and technology that are mandated by Congress. The director chairs the cabinet-level Federal Coordinating Council for Science, Engineering and Technology, which uses task forces of government officials to recommend policies that affect more than a single federal agency or department.

The Office of Policy Development was established by Executive Order in 1970 as the Domestic Council, abolished by Carter in 1977 (who replaced it with a Domestic Policy Staff run by the vice president), and reestablished in 1981 as the OPD. It provides long-range planning studies for cabinet councils in charge of proposing new domestic legislation. (In the Clinton administration it is an umbrella agency for the national Economic Council, Domestic Policy Council, and Office of Environmental Policy.)

The Office of National Drug Control Policy, established by the National Narcotics Leadership Act of 1988, coordinates federal, state, and local efforts to control illegal drug abuse.

The National Critical Materials Council, established by the National Critical Materials Act of 1984, ensures that strategic minerals and materials are maintained for U.S. national security and economic development.

The Office of Administration, established by Reorganization Plan One of 1977, provides management support for the other agencies, including payroll and accounting, central purchasing, and the law and reference libraries. Its Reference Center, with access to government and commercial computer databases, provides the president and White House staff with background research under deadline pressures.

The President's Spouse

The president's spouse also serves as an adviser and policy innovator. From a suite of offices in the East Wing, the "First Lady's" staff handles her correspondence, plans speaking engagements, and coordinates other communications. Eleanor Roosevelt was the first presidential wife to have had a significant career: as a teacher, journalist, and Democratic Party activist. She served as her husband's "eyes and ears" and as one of his most important advisers on New Deal legislation. Rosalynn Carter was the first to play an active role within the White House Office: she testified before Congress on legislation, supported the Equal Rights Amendment, was active in promoting mental health initiatives in government, met foreign heads of state as her husband's representative, and was the first spouse to attend cabinet meetings. Hillary Rodham Clinton played an unprecedented role as a policy formulator by chairing a presidential task force on health care reform. She later became one of the most influential administration spokespersons in defending the plan (unsuccessfully) against its critics. Known as one of the president's most influential advisors, she played a major role in recruiting potential officeholders and in approving presidential appointments to the administration.

THE PARTISAN PRESIDENCY

Between the 1930s and early 1990s, there was a divergence between the Democratic and Republican conceptions of an effective presidency. Democrats usually controlled Congress and were more likely to develop collaborative approaches with Congress; Republican incumbents had to develop a governing strategy to take into account split government: control by the opposition party of one or both chambers of Congress, as well as a majority of governorships and state legislative chambers.

Democrats: The Persuasive Presidency

Democratic presidents after Franklin Roosevelt—Harry Truman, John Kennedy, Lyndon Johnson, Jimmy Carter, and Bill Clinton (through 1994)—presided over a party that controlled Congress (except for part of Truman's and Clinton's terms) and a majority of state and local governments. They succeeded with their ambitious domestic agendas when they unified their party and divided their opponents, and they failed when their own party split between liberal and conservative positions and their Republican opponents united. The White House engaged in constant attempts to win over public opinion and congressional majorities. A president's reputation as an astute negotiator and bargainer could serve him well in dealing with the small group of legislators and top officials in the administration whose support he needed. A president who understood his power stakes in any situation (how a decision made at that time might affect future bargaining situations) could maneuver effectively to maximize his limited power. Democratic presidents (Carter excepted) prided themselves on their skills as professional politicians, able to understand what other politicians needed from them, and able to transact political business with them.[39]

Republicans: The Administrative Presidency

Beginning with Richard Nixon in 1969, Republicans occupied the White House for twenty of the next twenty-four years. For that entire period Democrats controlled the House of Representatives. For eighteen of those years they controlled the Senate (Republicans won the Senate in the 1980 elections and lost it in the 1986 contest.) Throughout that time Democrats controlled a large majority of governorships, state legislatures, and county and city governments. Neither party government nor public opinion leadership could provide Republicans Nixon, Ford, Reagan, or Bush with the political resources they needed to advance their agendas.

Republican presidents developed a twofold strategy to govern: first, they relied on control of the departments to implement the substance of Republican economic and domestic policies, which often involved attempts to dismantle or cripple Democratic programs—even without legislation, or sometimes in the face of the laws.[40] Second, they used communication tactics honed in the presidential campaign to boost the president's popularity, defend the administration from Democratic attacks that the president had bypassed Congress or violated the laws, divert public attention from their dismantling of programs, and keep the Democrats in Congress off balance. In effect, they created a "semisovereign" presidency, by which they could govern without Congress by undermining its legislative powers.[41]

To govern without Congress or against its strong opposition to their policy agenda, Republican presidents:

- Submitted fewer requests for legislation and won passage of fewer bills than Democrat presidents, even when they enjoyed high public approval ratings;[42]
- Issued "signing statements" when signing laws passed by Congress that would offer an interpretation of the law at odds with the intent of Congress. Agencies were directed to follow the White House interpretation;[43]
- Vetoed bills passed by Democratic Congresses more often than Democratic presidents, and when bills passed over their vetoes sometimes delayed or refused to implement the laws;[44]
- Relied on executive orders to make and implement policy instead of asking Congress for legal authority. Congress responded by passing laws "micro-managing" the work of the departments and increasing oversight and investigations of their work;[45]

- Established regulatory review mechanisms staffed by White House aides who did not have the legal authority from Congress to review, delay, or modify agency regulations;[46]
- Shut down or withheld funds for programs they opposed, even when Congress had already appropriated funds for them, until federal courts ordered these programs continued.[47]

Although many journalists applied the term *gridlock* to the era of split-party government, the reality was more complex. Gridlock implies that nothing was getting done in Washington, but that was not the case. Republican presidents still introduced legislative proposals, and when they could rally public opinion they might get much of them through Congress. Democratic Congresses passed many of their own measures that Republican presidents were unwilling to veto. Presidents instituted many policies by executive order, and Congress responded by countervailing legislation. Far from being an era of gridlock, it was an era of activist government—the problem was that each institution worked at cross-purposes to the other, so the activism was not coherent or coordinated, but rather competitive and contradictory.[48]

Clinton: The Technocratic Presidency

The election of Bill Clinton in 1992 was the second time (the first being Carter's election in 1976) since 1968 that the Democrats were able to restore party government, at least until the midterm losses in 1994. With 43 percent of the vote, Clinton's political resources did not come close to matching his inflated campaign and governing rhetoric. Nevertheless, he offered an ambitious and somewhat scattershot legislative agenda, which did have a certain internal coherence: In program after program, from trade promotion to environmental protection to welfare and health care reform, the Clinton strategy involved having government do more, but do it more efficiently, based on scientific, technical, and professional problem analysis and problem solving. Hillary Clinton observed that inoculating poor children cost less than later treating them for serious diseases; her husband said that it was cheaper to provide medical insurance and doctor's visits for low-income families than to pay for their treatment in hospital emergency rooms. The Clinton presidency was technocratic: Its authority rested on the expertise of the "policy wonks" who claimed to be able to craft "tough and smart" programs.

Clinton ran risks similar to those of his predecessors, particularly Lyndon Johnson and Jimmy Carter. The first was that the compromises he found necessary to make within the Beltway to pass measures would allow him to be characterized by talk-show hosts and editorial writers as a president lacking principles, character, and backbone. The second risk, related to the first, was that each part of his coalition could find as much to oppose as to support in his program. "We know we have to face hard truths and take strong steps," Clinton had warned the American people in his inaugural, but it was not clear that his party or the voters were ready for the truths or the steps. ("It is a terrible problem," Franklin Roosevelt once said, "to look over your shoulder when you are trying to lead and find no one there.") Clinton had appealed to a common public interest and had called on Americans to "contribute" (i.e., sacrifice) rather than continue to promote their private interests. He might push himself over the precipice if the American people were not ready to make their "contribution," especially if voters believed that Clinton had called on them to sacrifice but was still distributing largesse to others. The final risk that Clinton ran was that his programs would not work as advertised—that the technocratic presidency might fail.

As of 1995, facing Republican majorities in Congress, it appeared that an unusual pattern of divided government had emerged: a Democratic president committed to activist government confronting a Republican Congress seeking to reduce the role of the national government and cut his presidency down to size. The resulting pattern might involve gridlock and paralysis, or capitulation by the president and a return to "congressional government," or possibly a "Grand Compromise" between the parties to tackle pressing national problems. Clearly the brief era of programmatic politics and strong presidential leadership Clinton hoped would characterize his presidency were at an end.

THE POSTMODERN PRESIDENCY

Some political scientists believe that beginning with Jimmy Carter in 1977 the modern presidency has been superseded by a postmodern presidency. They argue that the resources of the White House have not proved sufficient to meet its international responsibilities.[49] The United States has collective security obligations to other nations around the world; the continued vitality of its economy requires collaboration with other industrialized and developing nations; and without party, public, and congressional support the president cannot meet these international obligations. The modern president could use the United States's stature in world affairs to dominate its allies, but in the era of the postmodern presidency the United States no longer can impose its will on allies or adversaries. Since the Vietnam War the American people have been more leery of military interventions; because its economy has weakened relative to those of other leading industrial nations (while its budget and trade deficits have soared), the United States cannot afford the kind of economic leadership it exercised for two decades after World War II. We cannot spend large sums of money on international initiatives (foreign aid to other nations has dropped by more than half); we cannot afford to finance wars to repel aggression (the Persian Gulf War was paid for by our allies); we cannot pressure other nations on human rights (the United States backed off a confrontation with China in 1994); and we cannot project U.S. military power effectively (the United States backed away from confrontations in Haiti, Bosnia, and Somalia in 1993). Other nations now influence the United States as much as the United States influences them.

The Postmodern President at Work

According to this theory, the success or failure of the "postmodern" president happens as much in international arenas as in Congress. The president must work with

NATO and the United Nations in peacekeeping and humanitarian missions. He or she must gain the support of Russia and other members of the Commonwealth of Independent States (what was once called the Soviet Union) for diplomatic initiatives in the Balkans and the Middle East. Presidential arms control initiatives require support of the European Conference on Peace and Security. The White House wins or loses in such forums as the General Agreement on Tariffs and Trade, the World Bank and International Monetary Fund, and the United Nations conferences on the environment and population.

The modern president led by gaining public support for his policies: the postmodern president faces an international as well as a domestic audience, and each may want different things. A president may gain domestic support by calling for an "America first" policy on trade and jobs and immigration; at the same time he or she will lose support of our allies. Or the president may win support of allies by promising to supply U.S. forces as peacekeepers, while losing domestic support in the process. The president not only must appeal to Congress by "going Washington" and to the American people by "going public," he or she must also appeal to a foreign constituency by "going international."[50] A postmodern president who has a great deal of influence in world politics, and is reinforced by other nations, will be a world leader; he or she will become vulnerable if other nations oppose his or her initiatives; he or she will be isolated if the American people do not support his or her foreign policies, and he or she will be a "global failure" if neither the American people nor foreign governments offer support.[51]

Critique of the Postmodern Presidency Theory

Not everyone agrees that the modern presidency has been superseded by a postmodern presidency. For one thing, while the modern presidency was being created in the first half of the twentieth century, the United States was not a superpower; it was merely one of the "Great Powers" and did not dominate its allies, but worked alongside of them. To the extent that the United States dominated the "Free World," it was for a brief period in the postwar period under Truman and Eisenhower. John Kennedy was unable to dominate the French government led by Charles de Gaulle, and Lyndon Johnson and Richard Nixon had little support for many of their foreign policies from our allies, including the escalation of the Vietnam War and the invasion of the Dominican Republic in 1965, the invasion of Cambodia in 1970, and the resupply of Israel in the 1973 war. If in the 1980s and 1990s, presidential success may be judged on the basis of collaboration with allies, that was also the case during World War I, World War II, and much of the postwar period, when presidents worked with allies to implement the Point Four foreign aid program, military assistance to Greece and Turkey, the Marshall Plan to reconstruct Western Europe, the North Atlantic Treaty Organization (NATO) to defend Western Europe, the Rio Pact for Western hemisphere collective security, and the Bretton Woods agreement for monetary coordination by the industrial nations.

With the collapse of the Soviet Union in 1991, the United States for the first time in its history had the opportunity to become the sole superpower. Presidents in the early 1990s had opportunities to shape a "new world order" denied to their predecessors. If there is a postmodern presidency, it may not fit the description of a weakened president presiding over a weakened United States. George Bush projected American power in Panama and the Persian Gulf with enormous success—and did so without the support of a majority of the American people at the time (a majority opposed military action against Iraq when President Bush ordered U.S. forces into action). The U.S. economy was weaker in the 1990s than it had been in the 1960s, but only relative to other nations. In the 1990s it remained by far the largest producer of goods and services and new technologies in the world and was still the major influence on world prosperity. In international crises, the real "postmodern" presidency may yet prove to be an enlarged rather than diminished version of the modern presidency.

THE TRANSFORMATION OF THE PRESIDENCY

The presidency has not evolved smoothly, nor has it inevitably obtained more power and influence in the American political system. There has been an ebb and flow to presidential power. Activist presidents like Jefferson, Jackson, Lincoln, and the two Roosevelts used the resources they found at hand, and they did not hesitate to invent new mechanisms, claim new powers, experiment with new procedures, or find new resources—such as the use of the mass media—to transform their office. The history of the presidency is one of constant innovation and adaptation. The great presidents do not play by existing rules: they make up new ones as they go along.

Yet the intent of the constitutional framers continually trips up even the strongest presidents: they have not managed to bridge the separation of powers, limit the impact of checks and balances, dominate Congress, or completely control the departments of government. Sometimes an evolution in the office of the presidency is aborted when the American public finds the innovation insupportable or illegitimate. We have not developed a system of presidential governance to replace original constitutional understandings calling for separated institutions competing for power.

From the premodern to the modern presidency, the development of the office in large measure corresponds to the democratization of American politics. Whenever a new mechanism of democracy or communication appeared, presidents (or presidential candidates) took advantage of it: Jefferson as he organized the first party organization; Jackson as he organized the first mass party and transformed nominating and election procedures; Theodore Roosevelt as he used the "penny press" and the muckraking magazines to make the presidency a "bully good pulpit"; Woodrow Wilson as he took advantage of the Progressive Era political reforms such as the direct primary; Franklin Roosevelt and his successors as they relied on mass media and public opinion polls to mobilize voter support for his New Deal programs; Ronald Reagan as he relied on public opinion to pressure Congress to dismantle those New Deal programs.

One president's resource is another's constraint: Jefferson's party and its congressional caucus system helped cabinet secretaries become influential and led to cabinet government; Jackson's popular government resulted in a backlash against presidential power, and his creation of the Democratic party led to the organization of a Whig opposition that weakened the presidency. After the Civil War the political parties put mediocre men into the White House and instituted the congressional government that left presidents presiding over rather than making policy. Woodrow Wilson's rhetoric was countered by members of Congress who were just as effective in leading public opinion. Presidents often are opposed by interest groups that have tens of millions of dollars for advertising campaigns. As a public leader a president is often outspent and outmaneuvered by the private sector. A president may claim authority because he or she has "the experts" giving advice; yet the resources of the institutionalized presidency—the White House staffers, the experts in presidential agencies, and task forces—have been countered by congressional staff agencies and their own experts.

To its original constitutional base the presidency has added formidable political and institutional resources. These, though, can also become constraints on presidential power when incumbents lose their authority because of unpopular policies or their legitimacy because of their abuses of power. There has been no linear "evolution" of the presidency into a form of "presidential government." Instead, the game of presidential politics has evolved into a particularly American form of Russian roulette.

FURTHER READING

The Premodern Presidency

Wilfred Brinkley, *Presidents and Congress,* New York: Random House, 1947.
James Bryce, *The American Commonwealth,* rev. ed., Vol. I, New York: Macmillan, 1926.
Henry Jones Ford, *The Rise and Growth of American Politics,* London: Macmillan, 1898.
Henry Lockwood, *The Abolition of the Presidency,* New York: R. Worthington, 1884.
Sidney Miklis, and Michael Nelson, *The American Presidency: Origins and Development,* Washington, DC: Congressional Quarterly Press, 1990.
Michael Riccards, *The Ferocious Engine of Democracy: From the Origins Through McKinley,* Lanham, MD: Rowman and Littlefield, 1995.
Augustus Woodward, *The Presidency of the United States,* New York: D. Van Veighton, 1825.

The Modern and Postmodern Presidency

James MacGregor Burns, *Presidential Government,* New York: Avon Books, 1965.
Fred Greenstein, ed., *Leadership in the Modern Presidency,* Cambridge, MA: Harvard University Press, 1988.
John Hart, *The Presidential Branch,* New York: Pergamon Press, 1987.
Richard Neustadt, *Presidential Power and the Modern Presidents,* New York: Free Press, 1991.
Richard Rose, *The Postmodern President,* 2nd ed., Chatham, NJ: Chatham House, 1991.
Clinton Rossiter, *The American Presidency,* New York: Harcourt Brace, 1956.
Malcolm Shaw, *The Modern Presidency: From Roosevelt to Reagan,* New York: Harper and Row, 1987.

Presidents on the Development of the Presidency

Theodore Roosevelt, *An Autobiography,* New York: Scribner's, 1931.

William Howard Taft, *Our Chief Magistrate and His Powers,* New York: Columbia University Press, 1916.

Woodrow Wilson, *Congressional Government,* New York: Houghton Mifflin, 1885.

Woodrow Wilson, *Constitutional Government in the United States,* New York: Columbia University Press, 1908.

Documentary and Reference Sources

Henry Graff, ed., *The Presidents: A Reference History.* 2nd. ed., New York: Scribner's, 1996.

James Richardson, *Messages and Papers of the Presidents of the United States,* 10 vols., Washington, DC: Bureau of National Literature and Art, 1900.

The Public Papers of the Presidents, Washington, DC: Government Printing Office, annually.

Edward Stanwood, *A History of the Presidency,* 2 vols., Boston: Houghton Mifflin, 1898.

NOTES

1. Theodore Roosevelt, *An Autobiography,* New York: Scribner's, 1926, p. 352.

2. John Morton Blum, *The Progressive Presidents,* New York: W. W. Norton, 1982, p. 58.

3. James MacGregor Burns, *Presidential Government,* Boston: Houghton Mifflin, 1965, pp. 3–31.

4. Paul Goodman, "The First American Party System," in William N. Chambers and Walter Dean Burnham, eds., *The American Party System,* New York: Oxford University Press, 1967, pp. 56–89.

5. James Sterling Young, *The Washington Community, 1800–1828,* New York: Columbia University Press, 1966.

6. James Madison, *The Federalist Papers,* no. 51.

7. Stephen Skowronek, *The Politics Presidents Make,* Cambridge, MA: Belknap Press, 1993, p. 103.

8. Jefferson, *Works* (Ford ed.), vol. IX, p. 69; also see Edward Corwin, *The President: Office and Powers,* New York: New York University Press, 1957, p. 19.

9. Edward Stanwood, *A History of the Presidency,* Boston: Houghton Mifflin, 1898, pp. 125–141.

10. C. S. Thompson, *The Rise and Fall of the Congressional Caucus,* New Haven, CN: Yale University Academical Department, 1902.

11. Edward Stanwood, *A History of the Presidency,* Boston: Houghton Mifflin, 1898, pp. 125–150.

12. Robert V. Remini, "The Election of 1828," in Arthur M. Schlesinger, Jr., ed., *The Coming to Power,* New York: Chelsea, 1981, pp. 67–90.

13. Glyndon G. Van Deusen, *The Jacksonian Era, 1828–1848,* New York: Harper and Row, 1959, pp. 32–34.

14. Robert V. Remini, *Andrew Jackson and the Bank War,* New York: W. W. Norton 1967, pp. 116–124.

15. James S. Chase, *Emergence of the Presidential Nominating Convention, 1789–1832,* Urbana, IL: University of Illinois Press, 1973.

16. Richard Hofstadter, *The Idea of a Party System,* (Berkeley, CA: University of California Press, 1969, pp. 212–271.

17. Arthur M. Schlesinger, Jr., *The Age of Jackson,* Boston: Little, Brown, 1945, pp. 45–47.

18. Leonard White, *The Jacksonians,* New York: Free Press, 1965, pp. 20–24.

19. John Burgess, *Political Science and Comparative Constitutional Law;* Christopher Tiedemann, *The Unwritten Constitution of the United States;* W. W. Willoughby, *The American Constitutional System,* all edited by Richard M. Pious, New York: Dabor Social Sciences Publications, 1982.

20. Henry Brooks Adams, *The Education of Henry Adams,* Boston: Houghton Mifflin, 1927, p. 266.

21. Woodrow Wilson, *Congressional Government,* Boston: Houghton Mifflin, 1885.

22. Clinton Rossiter, "The American President," *Yale Review,* Vol. 37, Summer, 1948, pp. 619–637; Richard E. Neustadt, "The Presidency at Mid-Century," *Law and Contemporary Problems,* Vol. 21, no. 3, Autumn, 1956, pp. 609–645.

23. Theodore Roosevelt, *op. cit.,* p. 388.

24. William Howard Taft, *Our Chief Magistrate and His Powers,* New York: Columbia University Press, 1916.

25. Woodrow Wilson, *Constitutional Government in the United States,* New York: Columbia University Press, 1908.

26. John Whiteclay Chambers, *The Tyranny of Change,* New York: St. Martin's Press, 1992, pp. 190–200.

27. Jeffrey Tulis, "The Two Constitutional Presidencies," in Michael Nelson, ed., *The Presidency in the Political System,* 3rd ed., Washington, DC: Congressional Quarterly Press, 1991, pp. 85–116.

28. James T. Patterson, *Congressional Conservatism and the New Deal,* Lexington, KY: University of Kentucky Press, 1967, pp. 109–127, 288–325.

29. Patterson, ibid., pp. 250–288.

30. Fred Greenstein, *The Hidden Hand Presidency,* New York: Basic Books, 1979.

31. John P. Burke, *The Institutional Presidency,* Baltimore, MD: Johns Hopkins University Press, 1992, pp. 1–24.

32. President's Commission on Administrative Management, *Report with Special Studies,* Washington, DC: Government Printing Office, 1937, p. 5.

33. "A Modish Management Style Means Slip-Sliding around the West Wing," *National Journal,* October 30, 1993, pp. 2606–2607.

34. Jack Valenti, "Life's Never the Same after the White House Power Trip," *Washington Post National Weekly Edition,* March 19, 1984, p. 21.

35. "Scrimping on White House Staff Could Damage Clinton's Fortunes," *National Journal,* August 14, 1993, pp. 2046–2047.

36. Michael Medved, *The Shadow Presidents,* New York: Times Books, 1979, p. 352.

37. Joel K. Goldstein, *The Modern American Vice Presidency,* Princeton, NJ: Princeton University Press, 1982; Paul C. Light, *Vice-Presidential Power: Advice and Influence in the White House,* Baltimore, MD: Johns Hopkins University Press, 1984; Ronald Moe, "The Institutional Vice Presidency," in James Pfiffner and Gordon Hoxie, eds., *The Presidency in Transition,* New York: Center for the Study of the Presidency, *Proceedings,* Vol. 6, no. 1, 1989, pp. 391–424.

38. Bradley H. Patterson, Jr., "Teams and Staff: Dwight Eisenhower's Innovations in the Structure and Operations of the Modern White House," *Presidential Studies Quarterly,* Vol. 24, no. 2, Spring, 1994, p. 278.

39. Richard E. Neustadt, *Presidential Power,* New York: John Wiley, 1960.

40. Richard Nathan, *The Administrative Presidency,* New York: John Wiley, 1983.

41. Charles Tiefer, *The Semi-Sovereign Presidency,* Boulder, CO: Westview Press, 1994.

42. Tiefer, ibid., p. 13.

43. M. N. Garber and K. A. Wummer, "Presidential Signing Statements as Interpretations of Legislative Intent: An Executive Aggrandizement of Powers," *Harvard Journal of Legislation,* Vol. 24, no. 1, Summer, 1987, pp. 154–164.

44. A. L. Weil, "Has the President of the United States the Power to Suspend the Operation of an Act of Congress?" *California Law Review,* Vol. 1, March, 1913, pp. 230–250; Arthur S. Miller and Jeffrey H. Bowman, "Presidential Attacks on the Constitutionality of Federal Statutes: A New Separation of Powers Problem," *Ohio State Law Journal,* Vol. 40, no. 1, Spring, 1979, pp. 51–80; Arthur Miller, "The President and the Faithful Execution of the Laws," *Vanderbilt Law Review,* Vol. 40, no. 2, March, 1987, pp. 389–406.

45. Joel D. Aberbach, *Keeping a Watchful Eye: The Politics of Congressional Oversight,* Washington, DC: The Brookings Institution, 1990, pp. 48–78.

46. Charles Tiefer, op. cit.

47. *Impoundment of Appropriated Funds by the President,* Joint Hearings Before the Committee on Government Operations and the Committee on the Judiciary, U.S. Senate, 93rd Cong., 1st Sess. (1973); Louis Fisher, "Impoundment of Funds: Uses and Abuses," *Buffalo Law Review,* vol. 23, no. 1, Fall, 1973, pp. 141–200; James Pfiffner, "Impoundment as a Presidential Policy Tool," in James Pfiffner, *The President, the Budget and Congress: Impoundment and the 1974 Budget Act,* Boulder, CO: Westview Press, 1979, pp. 27–48.

48. David Mayhew, *Divided We Govern,* New Haven, CN: Yale University Press, 1991.

49. Richard Rose, *The Postmodern President,* Chatham, NJ: Chatham House, 1988, p. 25.

50. Richard Rose, op. cit., p. 39.

51. Richard Rose, op. cit., Figure 3.3, p. 56.

CHAPTER 4

The Presidential Prerogative

The President must place himself in the very thick of the fight . . . and be prepared to exercise the fullest powers of his office—all that are specified and some that are not.

—*John Kennedy*

INTRODUCTORY CASE: LINCOLN'S CONSTITUTIONAL DICTATORSHIP

Abraham Lincoln arrived in Washington for his inauguration in March 1861, even as the Union was disintegrating. South Carolina, Georgia, Florida, Alabama, Mississippi, Louisiana, and Texas had seceded and formed the Confederate States of America in February. In his inaugural address Lincoln appealed to Southerners not to take irrevocable steps, and spoke favorably of a constitutional amendment proposed by the House Committee of Thirteen that would guarantee slavery in the states where it already existed. But he insisted that the laws must be faithfully executed: "You have no oath registered in Heaven to destroy the government," he told them, "while I shall have the most solemn one 'to preserve, protect and defend' it. You can forbear the assault; I can *not* shrink from the *defense* of it."[1]

Lincoln did not wait for events to unfold. During the transition period after the election, he had opposed the Crittenden Compromise, a plan to extend slavery to the west coast below the 36°30' latitude, and had also rebuffed overtures from a Peace Convention in Richmond, Virginia, attended by delegates from twenty states and presided over by former President John Tyler. Two weeks after his inauguration Lincoln forbade Secretary of State William Seward from receiving officials of the states in secession or negotiating with them. Despite the misgivings of a majority of his cabinet, he overrode Seward's promise to Confederate President Jefferson Davis that the federal garrison at Fort Sumter would not be resupplied. If he calculated that the South, faced with this show of force, would capitulate or compromise, he was wrong.

The Confederate bombardment of Fort Sumter began at 4:30 AM on April 12; three days later the 127 Union soldiers under the command of Major Robert Anderson surrendered. Lincoln responded to the fall of Fort Sumter with emergency powers, most of them *not* assigned to the president by the Constitution. On April 15, 1861, he issued a proclamation calling forth the state militias and asked for 75,000 volunteers to aid in executing the national laws—a call that led to the secession of the states of the upper South, including Virginia. According to the Constitution, Lincoln should have received congressional authorization to call for the volunteers, but Congress was not due to convene until the following December. Without congressional approval he also accepted 188,000 volunteers in the militias for three years of service, and raised 42,000 men for the regular army and 18,000 naval volunteers, all of which violated ceilings in existing laws and disregarded the constitutional powers of Congress in Article 1 "to raise and maintain an army" and provide for a navy. He organized ten army regiments and authorized the construction of nineteen warships, all on his own authority. He proclaimed a boycott of southern ports, in effect making war without a congressional declaration. He sent weapons and $2 million in gold from the federal Treasury to Union loyalists in the northern part of Virginia, enabling them to set up the State of West Virginia, all without any congressional appropriation of funds. He issued six proclamations suspending the privilege of the writ of habeas corpus so that thousands of Confederate sympathizers and secessionists in the border states and Florida might be arrested by the army and tried by military courts.[2]

Lincoln called Congress into special session on July 4, 1861. "These measures," he told the legislators, "whether strictly legal or not, were ventured upon, under what appeared to be popular demand and public necessity, trusting . . . that Congress would readily ratify them. It is believed that nothing has been done beyond the constitutional competency of Congress."[3] In his message Lincoln avoided the question of whether he had exceeded his own constitutional powers as president.

Congress ratified Lincoln's emergency actions and usurpation of congressional powers by passing a spending bill specifying that all his acts, proclamations, and orders involving the military "are hereby approved and in all respects legalized and made valid, to the same effect as if they had been issued and done under the previous express authority and direction of the Congress of the United States."[4] Congress later ratified other presidential emergency measures: in 1862 it passed a law giving the president authority to censor telegraph lines (he had already done so) and it passed the Militia Act enabling him to draft an additional 300,000 troops (which he was already doing); in 1863 it passed a draft law sanctioning his previous enlistment of troops and a law allowing the president to suspend habeas corpus (he had been doing that since 1861). In 1863, by a bare five to four majority, the Supreme Court ruled in The Prize Cases that the war had constitutionally begun two years earlier with Lincoln's proclamations.[5]

Even Lincoln's emancipation of slaves during the war was constitutionally suspect. The Emancipation Proclamations of 1862 and 1863 were war measures designed to strike at enemy property, relying on Lincoln's powers as commander in chief—only slaves in areas controlled by secessionists were freed, and not those slaves in states that had remained within the Union. The practical effect was that military commanders could use ex-slaves in their armies when they advanced into Confederate territory. But slavery had been explicitly protected by the Constitution and its regulation entrusted to Congress. The Supreme Court in 1857 in *Dred Scott v. Sandford* had ruled that slaves were property.[6] According to the Fifth Amendment Lincoln should not have seized property (for that is what the slaves were considered) without due process of law, but there was no national law by which he acted. Congress in the Confiscation Act of 1861 had limited the authority of military commanders: they could only free slaves put to hostile use against them, or those crossing over to Union lines, or those owned by secessionists who had joined the Union armies.[7] Many in Congress, even some members of Lincoln's own party, argued that he had gone beyond his presidential authority and should have waited for Congress to pass an Emancipation Act. "I felt that measures, otherwise unconstitutional, might become lawful, by being indispensable to the preservation of the Constitution through the preservation of the nation," Lincoln wrote in 1864 to a friend who had questioned him about his use of emergency powers.[8]

Lincoln's expansive interpretation of his constitutional powers became an issue in the 1864 presidential elections. The Republican platform commended Lincoln for his "fidelity to the Constitution" in the way he discharged his office, and endorsed all his measures, including emancipation. The Democrats in the northern states, in response to those claims, stated that they "consider that the administrative usurpation of extraordinary and dangerous powers not granted by the Constitution . . . is calculated to prevent a restoration of the Union and the perpetuation of a Government deriving its just powers from the consent of the governed."[9]

Lincoln had fused the powers of Congress with his own in the early stages of the emergency, but he had not ruled without the consent of the governed. He had called Congress into session (dictators usually dismiss the legislature). He had presided over midterm elections and presidential elections in 1862 and 1864 (dictators usually dispense with elections, especially during a civil war). The elections had been fairly and honestly run (Democrats increased their strength in Congress in 1862 and made a strong run at the White House in 1864). At any time Congress could have impeached and removed Lincoln from office if he had abused his emergency powers. Instead, it validated his actions and the people reelected him. Perhaps the best verdict on Lincoln came from his secretary of state, William Seward, who observed, "We elect a king for four years, and give him vast powers, which after all he can interpret for himself."

PREROGATIVE POWER AND THE CONSTITUTION

The framers of the Constitution did not explicitly provide the president with prerogative powers, because the term *prerogative* was associated with the British monarch's "Crown prerogatives." The Declaration of Independence and other American resolutions passed before the Revolutionary War roundly condemned King George III for exercising royal prerogatives, and Americans viewed them as synonymous with tyranny. At the Constitutional Convention, Alexander Hamilton and other delegates had substituted the word *administration* for *prerogative,* or used the phrases *energetic government* or *vigorous administration* to describe the kind of government they sought to institute.[10] The Committee on Style that wrote the final version of the Constitution left Article 2 with ambiguities, omissions, and general terms, all of which might provide an opportunity for a president to claim vastly expanded prerogative powers.

Claiming Prerogatives

Presidents claim constitutional prerogatives in several different ways. First, they go beyond the literal text of the Constitution to lay claim to the *sovereign powers* of the United States: the powers that the government may exercise by virtue of the independence and sovereignty of the American people. Thomas Jefferson decided to acquire the Louisiana Territory by treaty from France, although the Constitution makes no mention of a power for the government to acquire territory, only establishing the method by which states may join the Union. "The less said about any constitutional difficulties, the better," Jefferson cautioned his attorney general.[11] Any sovereign nation may acquire territory, and Jefferson (and the Congress) were exercising powers that any nation may exercise.

Presidents also exercise the *sovereign powers* of the United States to meet the nation's international commitments. They claim that the general terms of the Constitution (commander in chief, executive power, the "take care" clause) provide them with authority to act unilaterally. Presidents send U.S. armed forces on humanitarian missions and peacekeeping assignments, mediate between other nations in international disputes, take steps to combat international terrorism, and claim the power to uphold collective security treaty commitments without further congressional action.

Presidents exercise *emergency powers* when necessary to preserve the nation. John Locke, the English philosopher, referred to the power of the Executive "to act according to discretion, for the publick good, without the prescription of the Law, and sometimes even against it."[12] To defend his suspension of habeas corpus, Lincoln put the question to Congress in his message of July 4, 1861: "are all the laws, *but one,* to go unexecuted, and the government itself go to pieces, lest that one be violated? Even in such a case, would not the official oath be broken, if the government should be overthrown, when it was believed that disregarding the single law, would tend to preserve it?"[13] Presidents will not bind themselves to the strict terms of the Constitution when a strict reading might bring the nation to ruin. They claim the right to preserve the "peace of the United States," by intervening with the military in civil disorders or strikes, and by using wiretaps and surveillance against suspected foreign and domestic enemies.[14]

Presidents have vast *discretionary power* in executing the laws. They may combine their constitutional powers with statutes passed by Congress to vastly expand their administrative, diplomatic, and military powers. They issue executive orders, in effect asserting their own *legislative power,* and these orders may go way beyond the scope of the laws Congress passed to deal with a subject, sometimes covering matters Congress has not legislated on at all. Such orders were used in the nineteenth century to establish and expand Indian reservations, establish nature preserves, and withdraw public land from excessive exploitation.[15] Presidents have an ordinance-making power, by issuing these executive orders, that at times can displace the Congressional lawmaking function.

Presidents claim a *dispensing power:* a prerogative to refuse to execute the provisions of a law, if obeying those provisions might be harmful to the nation. Although they do have an obligation to "take care that the laws be faithfully executed," that obligation does not appear in the oath of office. Presidents use the dispensing power even when preservation of constitutional government is not at stake. They claim that when laws conflict, they have the prerogative to decide which laws are to be enforced and which are subject to the "dispensing power."

Presidents claim *inherent powers* of a "chief executive" based on an expansive reading of specific constitutional clauses, claiming that separation of powers makes them the head of an "executive branch." Similarly, they claim *implied powers.* They argue that, like Congress, they may take actions "necessary and proper" to put their executive powers into effect, having all the means at their disposal that are not forbidden by the Constitution. The congressional "necessary and proper" clause appears explicitly in Article 1, sec. 8, paragraph 18; nowhere does a similar clause appear in Article 2, yet presidents claim that such a clause is implicit.

The Use of Precedent

Presidents claim each of the prerogative powers described above by pointing to past instances of their use. To some extent the "living presidency" is defined by past custom. These may be considered precedents if presidents have invariably responded to an issue by using their prerogatives powers in a certain way; if they have asserted their prerogatives on many occasions; and if they have exercised their prerogative in modern times.[16] Merely dredging up an isolated example of a successful claim of power from the premodern presidency is not enough to be considered a strong precedent.

The response of Congress to a presidential use of prerogative power is also important in determining its precedential value. Congressional acquiescence sometimes may be taken by the courts as consent. But consent may only be granted if Congress knows about the use of power—in secret operations Congress may not be in a position either to acquiesce or to oppose the action. In weighing the constitutionality of a claim of presidential prerogative, federal courts give great weight to three factors: Has Congress passed laws that are consistent with the subsequent exercise of presidential prerogative?[17] Has Congress consented to the use of prerogative by its silence?[18] Has Congress directly sanctioned it by passing legislation in support of the president's policy?[19]

THE PREROGATIVE STYLE OF GOVERNANCE

Presidential use of prerogative power has been controversial: some presidential actions have become a part of the "unwritten Constitution." Others have been checked by the courts or Congress. Prerogative governance is a high-risk strategy. Why do presidents opt for it?

Motives for Using Prerogative Power

When presidents rely extensively on their constitutional prerogatives we say they have adopted a prerogative "style." They often do so out of political weakness, using prerogative powers as a last resort to resolve issues when it appears they lack political support in Congress and the nation. Prerogative governance is most likely under the following circumstances:

- When presidents believe that an issue must be resolved successfully or the consequences will be serious for the welfare of the nation;
- In situations where inaction might weaken the credibility of the president and the rest of the government;
- When they cannot obtain support in Congress for their proposed courses of action;
- When they cannot count on public support for their decisions;
- When a crisis requires timely action and they face congressional delay.

When presidents rely on their constitutional powers to manage an issue, they leave themselves open to two lines of attack: first, their authority may be challenged by critics who claim they don't know what they are doing; and second, opponents may claim that they lack the constitutional powers to act, and that they have usurped congressional powers or gone beyond the constitutional powers of the government as a whole. When a president can rely on bipartisan support in Congress, he or she need not rely on his or her prerogatives, but instead can ask Congress for legislation to delegate necessary powers to resolve the issue. Prerogative politics is a high-risk gamble, because it cuts against the grain of American democracy and limited constitutional government.

Instituting Prerogative Government

When presidents institute prerogative government, they often impose tight secrecy at the top levels of government until they are ready to go public. Presidents usually confine their deliberations to a very small group, usually two or three top aides, and may cut out the cabinet and other top-level policy councils completely. When presidents are ready to take action, they issue proclamations, executive orders, and national security directives; institute a chain of command flowing from the White House directly to the officials who will carry out the orders; give instructions to subordinates so that they will execute the orders and follow the policy; and have White House aides monitor the actions of officials carrying out the policies from a "situation room."

The Politics of Prerogative Governance

The Madisonian constitution—partial separation of powers, collaborative government, interior contrivances, and checks and balances—assumes that before a president makes a decision he or she will review it with his or her top aides, take it before the cabinet or another policy council, and then present the decision to Congress for prior legitimation in the form of a law, an appropriation of funds, or a resolution of support. Prerogative government is the antithesis of Madisonian principles: it involves governance by fait accomplis. The president decides, his or her subordinates implement the policy, and the president then informs Congress. (Sometimes presidents do so years or decades later, as in the case of covert operations.) The president may make a nationwide television address to Congress, speak directly to the American people from the Oval Office, or announce his or her actions at a news conference. At that point the politics of prerogative government begins: the president must defend his or her actions against the attacks of the opposition.

Defending Prerogative Government

Presidents vigorously defend themselves against charges they have usurped congressional or judicial power. No president has ever admitted that he violated the Constitution or usurped the power of another institution. All have obtained opinions from their Attorneys General, White House Counsel, and counsel for the relevant departments (especially State, Defense, and the Central Intelligence Agency) arguing for the constitutionality and legality of their actions. The Solicitor General of the Justice Department defends the constitutional prerogatives of the president before the Supreme Court if necessary. In fashioning their arguments, these constitutional lawyers may rely on past precedents and legal doctrines. Yet for every argument a president makes, a counter argument exists. "A century and a half of partisan debate and scholarly speculation," Justice Robert Jackson concluded in a case involving presidential prerogatives, "yields no net result but only supplies more or less apt quotations from respected sources on each side of any question. They largely cancel each other."[20]

Presidents know that if they can defend the wisdom of the policy, most of the constitutional criticism will not harm them. Winning in the court of public opinion may be more important than winning in a court of law. The courts usually abstain from deciding cases involving presidential prerogatives, or else declare them constitutional exercises of power; yet many presidents who won in court later found themselves politically damaged or destroyed after their exercise of such powers. Lyndon Johnson, for example, successfully defended presidential war making in the federal courts, yet his escalation of the war in Vietnam eventually cost him public support and a chance to win a second elective term as president.

Maintaining Authority

When they use prerogative power, presidents have two problems in trying to maintain their authority with the American people—that is, the public's sense that they know what they are doing. First, the people have always been averse to the unchecked exercise of executive power, equating it with monarchs and dictators, so critics will claim the president was autocratic rather than democratic; second, the exercise of prerogative power, if it involved secrecy and a fait accompli, will be characterized by critics as deceptive or evasive. How do presidents respond? By discrediting their critics as best they can. They argue that their actions were required in the national interest: opponents of their policy either lack the facts to understand the national interest or do not have the national interest at heart. Why might their critics be misinformed or uninformed? Because in national security matters presidents have intelligence sources that they cannot reveal (or else they might be compromised). They have information that must remain top secret. They know things about the situation that their critics cannot know—and that the American people cannot know. Presidents argue that the critics should reserve judgment, and that the American people should trust them and other top officials to act in the national interest.

To members of his or her own party, the president will argue that those tempted to desert the White House are also sealing their own fate, because a party split will only help the opposition. To members of the opposition party the president will argue that his or her diplomatic prerogatives should be supported in a spirit of bipartisanship; that war-making prerogatives should be supported because to do otherwise would give "aid and comfort to the enemy" (i.e., treason); and that in intelligence matters the president's prerogatives should not be challenged because it might lead to embarrassing revelations that would damage the standing of the United States and its intelligence capabilities.

A president who can convince people of the soundness of his or her policy will be able to get away with constitutional shortcuts and violations, as Jefferson and Lincoln did. A president who loses authority will also face a greater challenge to the legitimacy of his or her prerogative power, as Lyndon Johnson and Richard Nixon endured with the war in Vietnam. It is rare for politicians who support the president's policy to attack its constitutionality—either they will remain silent on the constitutional issues or they will change their position on them. A generation of scholars and politicians who supported presidential war powers when exercised by Wilson, Roosevelt, and Truman executed an about-face on the constitutional issues during the Vietnam War, for example, and for many policy considerations drove that shift. Rarely do politicians decide to oppose a policy because they believe it is being implemented unconstitutionally. Confidence in the president—or a lack of it—is what induces politicians to change their approach to the limits of presidential power.

Partisan Responses to Presidential Prerogatives in Congress

For most members of Congress, partisan factors are more important than any consistent or principled constitutional position about presidential powers: legislators usually support presidents of their own party, even if they have to give them the benefit of the doubt, while their partisan opponents will attack their exercise of prerogative. President Franklin Roosevelt won support of most Northern Democrats but only a small percent of Republicans on votes involving presidential powers, a pattern similar for Truman and Kennedy. Only Lyndon Johnson won majorities from both parties on issues involving his prerogatives. Similarly Republican presidents Nixon, Ford, and Reagan gained far more support from Republicans than Democrats in Congress on issues of presidential power: only Eisenhower won bipartisan majorities.[21] Dramatic changes, sometimes referred to as "situational constitutionalism," occurred as Democrats, who had once supported expansive diplomatic and military powers from Roosevelt through Kennedy, later shifted to criticize these powers when exercised in ways they disapproved of by Nixon, Ford, Bush, and Reagan. A similar reversal occurred after 1995, when Democrats defended President Clinton's constitutional prerogatives in foreign affairs, while Republicans insisted that Congress play a greater role based on its constitutional powers.

THE OUTCOMES OF PREROGATIVE GOVERNANCE

Presidents who use their prerogatives are like tightrope walkers who do their stunts without a net, or acrobats who fly through the air from the trapeze, uncertain of whether they will meet the hands of their partner or find only empty air. Presidents may succeed with their policies and find the powers they assert are incorporated into the Constitution without much controversy; alternatively, even if they manage the crisis successfully, they may discover that the parties in Congress and the American people were opposed to their constitutional claims, and the powers they asserted may be denied (by courts or Congress) to their successors. In a few situations prerogative governance has resulted in a total fiasco for the White House.

Frontlash

When a president uses expansive powers and his policy works, he may benefit from a frontlash effect: the successful assertion of power will not only yield political dividends, it will also strengthen the office of the presidency itself. George Washington's diplomacy provides a good example. He issued a Neutrality Proclamation in 1792 on his own prerogative when the British and French were at war, even though the United States and France were obliged to come to each other's aid by the terms of a treaty. Washington argued that the treaty had been made with the French king (later killed in the French Revolution) and that the United States had no obligations to the revolutionary government. He further claimed that the president could declare neutrality on his own, without any congressional authorization, and could enforce it with sanctions. His proclamation was defended by Secretary of Treasury Hamilton, who (writing under the pen name Pacificus) argued that the president had all constitutional powers over foreign affairs, except those specifically granted to Congress.[22] The pro-French secretary of state Thomas Jefferson wrote to Madison after he had read Hamilton's essays, and implored him "to take up your pen, select the most striking heresies, and cut him to pieces in the face of the public."[23] Writing as Helvidius, Madison argued that foreign affairs were legislative in nature, and that the president could exercise only those powers specifically granted to him by the Constitution.[24] Congress, Madison argued, was to exercise all other powers of the sovereign nation. Although Washington's actions were unpopular at the time (pro-French mobs even burned him in effigy), American neutrality promoted friendship with Great Britain, and that in turn kept the nation out of war with England and ensured its funds for investment in the American economy. Congress approved of Washington's action, and the following year it passed a neutrality act that vindicated Washington's position.

A century and a half later, roles were reversed: President Franklin Roosevelt tried to institute "pro-British" neutrality at the outbreak of World War II while Congress wanted to remain strictly neutral. Congress had already passed a Neutrality Act in 1933 instructing the president to declare an arms embargo against all belligerents. A law passed in 1936 required him to impose an embargo against all third parties entering hostilities and forbade loans to belligerents. In 1939 Congress passed a third neutrality measure providing that these laws could be invoked by concurrent resolution (i.e., by both houses) of Congress.

When war began in Europe President Roosevelt proclaimed neutrality and imposed an arms embargo. But in November 1939 Congress passed his proposal for "cash and carry" arms sales to the British and French. In March 1940 he proposed "lend-lease" military assistance to the allies (who could no longer pay for arms), but his proposals languished in Congress. Roosevelt then used prerogative power to bypass the isolationists in Congress. By executive agreement (not requiring Senate consent) the United States participated in the Pan American Union policy of keeping French possessions in the Western hemisphere out of the hands of pro-German officials of the Vichy regime. Also by executive agreement a Permanent Joint Board of Defense involving Canadian and American military staffs was established.

The most controversial use of presidential prerogative power involved a deal Roosevelt made with British Prime Minister Winston Churchill to swap fifty overage American destroyers for leases to several Caribbean island bases controlled by the British. The administration not only circumvented the senatorial treaty power with the presidential prerogative to conclude executive agreements, it also ignored the letter and spirit of the Neutrality Act of 1940, which prohibited the transfer of usable military equipment to other nations. Even though the Chief of Naval Operations certified the destroyers were useless, that was an absurd finding. (They were not useless to the British, who needed them desperately!) Moreover, although a 1917 law prohibited the use of American warships by a belligerent power, Roosevelt claimed that the law only prohibited construction of ships built for a belligerent, and did not prohibit transfer of ships originally built for the U.S. Navy. This was an interpretation of the law at variance with the congressional intent. To get around the law, Attorney General Robert Jackson issued a legal opinion in which he construed the president's power as commander in chief not only to include the power to dispose American forces, but also the power to dispose *of* them.[25] Jackson further argued that the agreement involved a single transaction, with no further obligations on either party, and therefore was not suitable for a treaty, but rather should be consummated as an

On the campaign trail, September 3, 1940, President Roosevelt announces an exchange of surplus U.S. destroyers, badly needed by Great Britain, for eight Caribbean naval bases. He had the secret approval of his Republican opponent, Wendell Willkie, but did not ask for congressional authorization.

executive agreement. This distinction was spurious, because Roosevelt and Churchill meant the agreement to cement their anti-Nazi alliance, but it permitted Roosevelt to bypass the Senate and implement the agreement on his own prerogative. By construing presidential constitutional powers expansively and statutes so that they defied common sense and congressional intent, Roosevelt was able to consummate his deal and forge an alliance with Great Britain.

Roosevelt, like Lincoln, was no autocrat in these matters. He kept congressional leaders fully informed and consulted with them in advance of the deal. He gained the approval of the Republican presidential candidate Wendell Wilkie, which kept the issue out of the 1940 elections. A majority of senators were relieved that his executive agreement let them off the hook, because they would not have to vote to approve a treaty opposed by their constituents.

The "frontlash" effect was soon apparent. Roosevelt continued with his policy of confrontation against the Axis dictatorships. Presidential emissary Harry Hopkins took two trips to Moscow in January and July 1941 to arrange for $3 billion in lend-lease supplies for the former Soviet Union, establishing an even more controversial alliance without congressional involvement. The U.S. military occupied Greenland in 1941 and took over the defense of Iceland. Roosevelt ordered the navy to protect convoys on the open seas and to sink Axis submarines—the start of the undeclared naval war in the North Atlantic. Roosevelt and Churchill met at sea and produced the Atlantic Charter with its "Four Freedoms" defining the war aims of the democracies. In the fall of 1941 the President instituted a "shoot on sight" policy against Axis ships near allied convoys in the Atlantic. In October Roosevelt armed merchant vessels and gave the navy orders to sink Axis ships anywhere in the Atlantic. Roosevelt even ordered the navy to provide "neutrality patrols" near Allied convoys, in spite of a law passed by Congress prohibiting the navy from convoying duty for allied vessels.

Roosevelt's policy of preparedness was vindicated by the Japanese attack on Pearl Harbor, which brought the United States into the war on December 7, 1941. Waiting for Congress to act would have been a disaster: lawmakers took a year to pass the lend-lease program, and they almost repealed a draft law in August 1941, an action that would have left the nation defenseless. Even so, Congress cut construction funds for naval bases in the Pacific and procurement of advanced arms. The legislators lacked foresight, courage, or common sense: Roosevelt's use of constitutional prerogatives was the only way to prepare the nation for the inevitable conflict between the democracies and the Axis powers.

In both Washington's strict neutrality policy and Roosevelt's pro-British neutrality and preparedness policies, presidents were vindicated by events. In both cases, the president's followers united while the opposition split. Both presidents won their next elections, and their parties maintained congressional majorities. Congress did not check the presidents but passed legislation consistent with their actions, and the courts did not interfere. The powers asserted by these presidents become part of the "living Constitution" because they were legitimated by the party system and the people. Senator William Fulbright, who headed the Senate Committee on Foreign Affairs in the 1950s, drew the lesson from events during and after World War II that Congress should defer to presidential leadership and provide the president with bipartisan support: the frontlash effect gave the presidency the initiative in foreign policies from 1941 until the Vietnam War in the mid-1960s.[26]

Backlash

Many presidents suffer serious setbacks when they use their prerogatives, and a "backlash" effect may result: in one variation, the presidency will lose politically even as the president expands the constitutional powers of the office; in another variation, the president will be checked by Congress or the judiciary and his prerogative power will be eliminated or sharply reduced by their actions.

The first variation is illustrated by two nineteenth-century presidents: John Tyler and Grover Cleveland. Tyler was a Democrat who bolted his party in 1840 to accept the Whig nomination for vice president. After President William Henry Harrison's death he succeeded to the presidency and faced a dilemma: If he put forth a Democratic program, the Whigs in Congress and in his cabinet would desert him. If he opposed Whig programs he would have to rely on the prerogative powers exercised by Andrew Jackson—powers that had originally caused Tyler to defect from the Democratic Party. Tyler chose Democratic public policies over his former constitutional principles. He began his presidency with an exercise of prerogative. It was not clear from the wording of the Constitution whether a vice president succeeded to the "office of president" in the event of a vacancy, or only exercised the "powers and duties" of the office, serving as "acting president." Tyler settled the issue by taking the presidential oath and issuing a statement couched in the form of an inaugural address. The House promptly passed a resolution referring to him as president, and the Senate defeated a resolution referring to him as vice president, settling the issue in his favor. But much of the nation still referred to him as "His Accidency."

The Whig cabinet moved to take control of policy. At the first meeting Secretary of State Daniel Webster told Tyler that his predecessor had settled questions by majority vote (reviving the "cabinet government" of Madison). "I, as President, shall be responsible for my administration," Tyler responded, echoing Andrew Jackson's theory of presidential supremacy, adding, "I hope to have your hearty cooperation in carrying out its measures. So long as you see fit to do this, I shall be glad to have you with me. When you think otherwise, your resignation will be accepted."[27]

Whigs brushed aside Tyler's proposals for a national bank and instead passed their own version, which the cabinet urged him to sign. Tyler vetoed the bill, which was sustained by the Democrats in the Senate. After Tyler vetoed a second bank bill and it was sustained, the entire Whig cabinet resigned (with the exception of Webster, who was finishing up treaty negotiations with Great Britain). The Whig Party issued a manifesto disassociating themselves from Tyler, who was left to occupy the White House without an electoral mandate, party affiliation, or cabinet. The Whigs demanded that he resign, to be succeeded by the Whig president pro tem of the Senate as "acting president" under existing succession laws. Tyler refused. He formed a cabinet of Democrats through recess appointments that did not require approval by Whig Senate majorities. Democrats provided support for Tyler that made conviction on impeachment charges impossible. The result was a stalemate: the Whigs could not obtain their national bank, nor a high tariff, nor a program of public works. They were unable to pass an impeachment resolution in the House, though the Senate managed to pass a resolution of censure.

Tyler was successful at using prerogative politics to keep his opponents on the defensive, but was a political failure because of a public backlash against his assertions of powers, especially the use of the veto on policy grounds against the banking proposals of the Whigs. He did not win the Democratic presidential nomination in 1844. Historians generally rate him as ineffective because of the deadlock in domestic policies. But he showed that a president without a shred of popular or congressional support could still exercise the power to stalemate opposing congressional majorities.

Grover Cleveland was a New York Democrat who had the distinction of being the only president to serve two nonconsecutive terms in office (being defeated at his first try for a second term in 1888 by Republican Benjamin Harrison). He too wielded the veto power against Congress, though it was against his own party's Democratic congressional majorities. Cleveland was a conservative in spending matters: he vetoed two hundred of the seventeen hundred private pension bills Congress passed for veterans of the Civil War, arguing that many of these claims were fraudulent. He also vetoed measures to relieve farmers in the West from drought. He was a strong "law and order" president: he used federal troops to protect Chinese workers in the western states after white coal miners had killed and injured five hundred of them in the Rock Springs massacre of 1885. In his second term Cleveland was just as much of a "naysayer." The Panic of 1893 led populists and progressives to call for national action on currency reform, but Cleveland turned a deaf ear. He refused to inflate the currency and forced repeal of the Silver Purchase Act, leading to a contraction in the supply of money that added to hard times in the West. He bought gold for the Treasury from financiers J. P. Morgan and Augustus Belmont that returned them large profits. He refused to compromise with high tariff interests in the Northeast, threatened to veto any high tariff bill, and lost support in his own state.

Labor unrest added to his troubles. When Jacob S. Coxey led "Coxey's Army" of unemployed people to the capital to demand public service jobs, Cleveland had the army disperse them. When Pullman railway car workers went on strike in 1894, "Sheriff Cleveland" (as strikers called him) won a court injunction and then sent two thousand federal troops into Illinois to break the strike, arguing that the workers had breached "the peace of the United States." This action was sharply criticized by many members of his own party, including the Democratic governor of Illinois, John P. Altgeld, who had told Cleveland before he intervened that state authorities were capable of maintaining order. At the behest of Attorney General Richard Olney, a former railroad lawyer himself, the government jailed socialist leader Eugene V. Debs, at that time the head of the American Railway Union, for organizing a boycott of Pullman railway cars in support of the strikers. The Supreme Court case *In re Debs* upheld the conviction and Cleveland's contention that he could use presidential power to enforce the "peace of the United States" even in the absence of a specific statutory violation by strikers.[28]

The political backlash against Cleveland in each of his terms led to his defeat by Republican opponents. The Democratic Party abandoned his positions on currency, pensions and relief for the poor, and labor in 1896 when it nominated William

Jennings Bryan. Years later Cleveland wrote a book entitled *Presidential Problems,* much of which was devoted to a defense of his prerogative powers, and none of which had any influence on his party.[29]

The second backlash variation—loss of constitutional authority through checks and balances—is exceedingly rare but is illustrated by the outcome of President Harry Truman's seizure of steel mills. Truman used his prerogative powers to seize steel mills during a 1950 strike to maintain steel production for the Korean War and the reconstruction of Europe. He relied on his power as commander in chief to seize the mills as a war measure: he issued Executive Order 10340, directing his secretary of commerce "to take possession of and operate the plants and facilities of certain steel companies." In issuing his order, Truman ignored three laws passed by Congress that regulated labor–management relations:

- *The Selective Service Act of 1948* allowed the president to seize factories if direct orders to the government were not fulfilled, but the government had not placed those orders yet, and to do so and then wait for nonfulfillment would be too time consuming.
- *The Defense Production Act of 1950* provided that the two sides could create an arbitration board and enter into compulsory arbitration if both agreed, but did not require it. The unions were adamantly opposed to it.
- *The Taft-Hartley Labor Relations Act of 1946* provided that in a national emergency the president could appoint a board of inquiry to determine the facts, and then order the attorney general to seek a federal court injunction for a sixty-day "cooling off" period. Then the National Labor Relations Board would order a union vote on the last offer of the employers. If all else failed, the president could ask Congress for legislation to settle the strike.

Truman had vetoed the Taft-Hartley Act, which Congress had then repassed, and would not want to use its provisions, widely regarded by labor as tilted to management. He was not sure that the courts would grant an injunction or that Congress would require a settlement.

Truman knew that the companies would challenge the seizure in the courts, but calculated that his actions would be upheld. Not since 1866 had the courts decided against a president in a case involving prerogative power, and the president against whom that decision had been directed, Abraham Lincoln, was already dead.[30] Wilson had seized property during World War I, Roosevelt had done so during World War II, and surely, Truman thought, the court would uphold his doing so during the Korean War. Justice Jackson had written the *Opinion of the Attorney General* for Roosevelt to legitimize the destroyer deal, and was a strong supporter of presidential power. Justices Black and Douglas were sympathetic to labor. Justices Clark, Minton, and Burton were Truman appointees.

But Truman's speech to the American people justifying the seizure backfired. The subsequent radio address by a steel company executive warned of a usurpation of power and a payoff to the unions. Industry won the battle for public support, with 43 percent opposing and 35 percent supporting the president.[31] Truman compounded his political problems when he remarked, just before the Supreme Court was to decide the case, "The President has the power and they can't take it away from him." When reporters at the news conference asked the president if he meant the courts, he added, "Nobody can take it away from the President because he is the Chief Executive of the Nation, and he has to be in a position to see that the welfare of the people is met."[32]

The Supreme Court did take the power away from Truman: By a 6–3 vote in *Youngstown Sheet and Tube Co. v. Sawyer,* the Court ruled that Truman did not have the power to seize property in this instance.[33] The justices pointed out that Congress had legislated on the subject of strikes and seizures, preempting the field, and presidential prerogative power could not be exercised after Congress had spoken. Justice Jackson, in a concurring opinion, offered a test for weighing prerogative powers. When the president takes action compatible with the express will of Congress, his use of constitutional powers should be presumed constitutional. When Congress has not legislated on a matter and the president acts, the courts should scrutinize the action more carefully. And, most important, Jackson held:

> When the President takes measures incompatible with the expressed or implied will of Congress, his power is at its lowest ebb, for then he can rely only upon his own constitutional powers minus any constitutional powers of Congress over the matter. Courts can sustain exclusive presidential control in such a case only by disabling the Congress from acting upon the subject. Presidential claim to a power at once so conclusive and preclusive must be scrutinized with caution, for what is at stake is the equilibrium established by our constitutional system.[34]

Not only had the Supreme Court checked Truman (who returned the mills promptly to their owners), but the backlash against his actions precluded his successors from exercising similar powers. In the coal strike of 1978, for example, Jimmy Carter could not make a credible seizure threat, at least not without asking Congress for emergency legislation.

Political constraints on presidential power are often more significant than formal checks: In a backlash situation the president's party divides on the issue, while the opposition, sensing opportunity, unites. The president loses the battle for public opinion, and in the subsequent elections either does not run (as Truman decided in 1952) or does not win. The checks and balances involved in a backlash against the prerogative power sometimes weaken the presidency: The courts may come down with a decision that limits presidential powers, or Congress may pass a law that establishes procedures for the exercise of his powers, with the practical effect of limiting their exercise.

Overshoot and Collapse

The assertion of prerogative power can lead to the complete collapse of a presidency, for part or all of a president's term. The constitutional claim a president makes may be so sweeping, or his abuse of power so transparent, that Congress and the courts feel compelled to act. A president may be impeached (though none has yet been removed from office) or his administration tied up in congressional investigations and legal proceedings conducted by a special prosecutor or independent counsel (an official appointed by a special panel of judges to investigate wrongdoing in the executive branch and seek indictments and convictions of his principal aides in the federal courts if warranted).[35] His popularity takes a nosedive and his credibility as a leader is eroded, many of his party members desert him openly while others distance themselves from him, and his program is stalled in Congress. A president suffers his own personal collapse, either mental or physical, in these trying conditions, growing ever more distracted and distressed as events unfold. The institutional effects of a collapsed presidency may be enormous: after the impeachment trial of Andrew Johnson, a succession of weak presidents were hemmed in by congressional statutes through the turn of the century; after the impeachment proceedings against Richard Nixon, a resurgent Congress passed hundreds of statutes regulating presidential powers, and approval of the legislature's performance rose sharply in public opinion polls.[36]

THE WATERGATE SCANDAL

A prime example of overshoot was the Watergate scandal that triggered the impeachment proceedings against Richard Nixon. The problem for Nixon started at 1:00 AM on June 17, 1972, when five burglars entered the Watergate apartment complex offices of Lawrence O'Brien, chairman of the Democratic National Committee. Security guard Frank Wills noticed a garage door had been forced and called the police, who arrested them. The police also caught James McCord, head of security for the Committee to Re-Elect the President (CREEP), Nixon's campaign organization. All these men were on the payroll of CREEP.

Nixon's Surveillance Operations

When questioned by reporters, Nixon's press secretary Ron Ziegler referred to it as a "third rate burglary" and denied any involvement by the White House. But the White House had been involved: McCord's supervisor was G. Gordon Liddy, Counsel to CREEP. Liddy in turn had worked with E. Howard Hunt, a presidential staffer who had set up Operation Gemstone, a White House intelligence operation that had engaged in several illegal burglaries. Liddy had received $200,000 in illegal campaign contributions for these operations, most likely authorized by former Attorney General John Mitchell.[37] The burglars (known as the "plumbers" in the White House) were part of an ongoing intelligence operation that obtained information by illegal surveillance, burglaries, and wiretaps.[38]

Why had CREEP burglarized the opposition's party headquarters? One reason was that Nixon was running scared: the May Harris Polls had Nixon behind the leading challenger for the Democratic nominations, Edmund Muskie, by a 47 to 39 margin. Already he had dispatched White House "dirty trick artists" led by Donald Segretti (under the supervision of White House appointment secretary Dwight Chapin) to disrupt the Muskie campaign and obtain political intelligence on all Democratic contenders for the nomination. Other White House aides directed the Internal Revenue Service to conduct investigations of individuals on Nixon's "enemies list," and wiretaps had even been placed on members of the National Security Council staff suspected of leaking sensitive information to the opposition.[39] Another possible reason: Nixon may have wanted to find out what Larry O'Brien, head of the Democratic National Committee, knew about his own links to financier Howard Hughes, particularly if O'Brien had evidence of an illegal $100,000 cash payment (ostensibly a campaign contribution in 1968) to Nixon from Hughes that might be leaked during the elections.[40]

Nixon's Cover-Up

There is no direct evidence that Nixon ordered the burglary of the Democratic National Committee or knew about it in advance, though his chief of staff H. R. Haldeman had been briefed about prior operations. As soon as Nixon was briefed about the arrests by his top aides, however, he began to cover up any trail that might lead to the White House. "The White House has had no involvement whatever in this particular incident," Nixon told reporters at a June 22 press conference.[41] Then he set to work to make sure his story would stick. On June 23 he met with Haldeman and senior White House aide John Erlichman: they agreed on a plan to derail the FBI investigation, by claiming that the burglary had involved a national security operation. Nixon also began to consider pardoning the burglars or paying "hush money" to ensure their silence.

The White House "plumbers" were tried in a federal district court and convicted of breaking and entering. Judge John Sirica, a tough "law-and-order judge," sentenced them provisionally to excessive jail terms, in the hope that it might induce them to reveal who had ordered the burglaries. The Senate, controlled by the Democrats, launched an investigation into the matter as the Senate Select Committee on Presidential Activities of 1972 opened televised hearings in the spring of 1973. White House Counsel John Dean testified that he had warned Nixon about "a cancer on the presidency" but that Nixon and other top aides were involved in a cover-up. On April 30, 1973, with the cover-up by top staffers unraveling, Nixon accepted the resignations of his two top aides, Haldeman and Erlichman, who had approved the payments for the plumber and dirty tricks operations.

The White House Tapes

John Dean's testimony before the Senate implicated Nixon directly in the cover-up, but there was no corroboration by other witnesses or any other evidence to back Dean's contention. Then Alexander Butterfield, an aide to Haldeman, testified at the hearings that the White House had taped most of the conversations held in the Oval Office. If these tapes could be obtained by the Senate Committee, they might provide evidence to link Nixon to the cover-up, or even to the burglary itself. The Senate Committee demanded access to the tapes, and so did Archibald Cox, the special prosecutor in the Justice Department in charge of criminal investigations of the Watergate case. When Nixon refused, Judge Sirica issued an order that he turn the tapes over. Nixon refused and prepared to defend himself in court. The Court of Appeals for the District of Columbia ordered the president to turn over the tapes: he complied with part of the order but told Cox not to request the remainder. Cox won a new court order requiring that nine contested tapes be turned over. Nixon said he would provide summaries of the tapes: Cox refused and demanded all the evidence.

On October 20, 1973, Nixon ordered Attorney General Elliott Richardson to fire Cox. Richardson resigned in protest, because he had given the Senate his word when he had been confirmed that he would protect the independence of the special prosecutor. Alexander Haig, Nixon's chief of staff, then ordered Deputy Attorney General William Ruckelshaus to do the firing. When Ruckelshaus refused, Nixon fired *him.* Robert H. Bork, the Solicitor General (the official in the Justice Department in charge of presenting the government's case before the Supreme Court), became the highest-ranking official in the Justice Department, and he agreed to fire Cox. This "Saturday Night Massacre" unleashed a fire storm of protest across the nation. Within four days Nixon told Judge Sirica that the nine contested tapes would be turned over to the grand jury. They were, but a tape of the first meeting Nixon had held with Erlichman and Haldeman on June 20—during which they may have discussed the cover-up—had an eighteen and one-half minute segment erased. Nixon denied knowing anything about the missing segment or who might have erased it.

The Claim of Executive Privilege

Faced with the prospect that Congress would create its own independent counsel office to continue the investigation, Nixon reestablished the office of special prosecutor, appointing Leon Jaworski, a respected Texas lawyer and past president of the American Bar Association, to take Cox's place. Jaworski continued with the court case, demanding that Nixon turn over the tapes to the grand jury. On March 1, 1974, the federal grand jury indicted several top White House aides. It also named Nixon an "unindicted co-conspirator" in the cover-up.

President Nixon claimed that he did not have to turn over his tapes or other White House materials, either to the congressional committee investigating Watergate or to the grand jury and the special prosecutor. He claimed executive privilege, the constitutional right to withhold information from Congress and the courts about any conversations held or decisions made in the White House. Executive privilege is not mentioned in the Constitution: It is a prerogative power that the president asserts by interpreting clauses of the Constitution broadly.[42] Nixon argued that the privilege was "necessary and proper" for the functioning of his office. Confidentiality is essential in the Oval Office if the president is to obtain good information. He cannot obtain that information if Congress and the courts can later get at it. "No President could function if the private papers of his office, prepared by his personal staff, were open to public scrutiny," Nixon told the Senate committee. His lawyer, Charles Alan Wright, told Judge Sirica that withholding the tapes served "the public interest in having the president able to talk in confidence with his closest advisors."[43] Nixon argued that he alone must make the decision about the evidence. A holding that the president is personally subject to orders of a court would effectively "destroy the status of the executive branch as an equal and coordinate element of government," Nixon's lawyers argued.[44]

Nixon claimed that because he had "The Executive Power of the United States" and the responsibility to see that the laws were faithfully executed, he supervised the Department of Justice and could be considered the "prosecutor-in-chief" of the United States. Nixon argued that prosecutors have discretion about whether to bring cases to trial, and what evidence to pursue when doing so. It was up to him, and not the courts, grand jury, or special prosecutor, to determine what evidence to use in the Watergate prosecutions. "It is exclusively for the Executive Branch, and not for the Courts, to decide whether other governmental interests outweigh the interests in a particular criminal prosecution." The president must decide whether or not to "sacrifice the confidentiality he deems essential to the proper functioning of the office." Nixon need not obey a court order to produce the tapes as evidence: "The court may tell the Executive that it is to produce [the tapes] but if the Executive chooses not to do so, it is free to make that choice. . . ."[45]

Ordinarily when the government does not produce evidence required by a court the trial judge may dismiss the case. Most of the time the top officials in the administration want a case to go forward and must weigh national security interests that might be involved in disclosing secret matters in open court against their desire to continue prosecuting the case. But Nixon did not want the special counsel to prosecute people in his administration. By withholding evidence, he would be not only protecting himself, but also ending the possibility that top officials could be convicted for crimes, and that, in turn, would keep him from being linked to the conspiracy.

Nixon's arguments were rejected by the Supreme Court in *U.S. v. Nixon.*[46] Although the court found the president had a claim of executive privilege, it did not find the claim absolute. It would have to be weighed against the public interest involved in the grand jury investigation of Watergate crimes. A federal grand jury is entitled to every person's evidence—including the president's.[47] In the Watergate matter the grand jury was gathering evidence about a conspiracy in which Nixon had been held by it to be an unindicted coconspirator, and that did not involve a national security matter. Absent a valid claim of national security, "the generalized assertion of privilege must yield to the demonstrated, specific need for evidence in a pending criminal trial."[48] Even if the president does have supervisory powers over the Department of Justice, that gives him no "prosecutorial discretion" to withhold evidence or even drop an investigation. The grand jury, not the prosecutor, determines whether to drop a case or go forward.

Who weighs the competing interests? Nixon argued that he must make the decision himself, but the court rejected that claim. "The President cannot be a proper judge of whether the greater public interest lies in disclosing evidence, when that evidence may have a material bearing on the guilt or innocence of close aides and trusted advisors," the special prosecutor had argued before the high court, especially when there is a prima facie case that the president and these advisors were "members of a conspiracy to defraud the United States and to obstruct Justice."[49] The Supreme Court agreed.

The Move to Impeach

In the spring of 1974, some months before the Supreme Court issued its ruling, the House Judiciary Committee began an inquiry on the possible impeachment of Richard Nixon. The issue turned around a question of constitutional interpretation: what exactly is the impeachable offense of a "High Crime and Misdemeanor"? Most Republicans on the Judiciary Committee agreed with Nixon, who stated at a press conference that "a criminal offense on the part of the President is the requirement for impeachment."[50] Democrats on the committee argued that "the framers intended impeachment to be a constitutional safeguard of the public trust." In their view, a serious abuse of the presidential office, even if not a criminal offense, could be considered a "high crime and misdemeanor." If the president took action that exceeded the powers of his office, or if he "behaved in a manner grossly incompatible with the proper function and purpose of the office," he could be impeached, the Democrats concluded. As Democrat George Danielson put it, they were dealing with "crimes or offenses against the very structure of the state, against the system of government."[51]

The positions of the Democrats and Republicans were the opposite of those their parties had taken in 1867 in the impeachment proceedings against Andrew Johnson. Then the Democrats, supporting the president, had insisted that an impeachable offense had to involve commission of a federal crime. "The House of Representatives," they argued, "may impeach a civil officer, but it must be done according to law. It must be for some offense known to the law, and not created by the fancy of the members of the House." According to the Democrats, no impeachment could be voted for an offense that would not result in a criminal indictment if brought to a federal court. Republicans trying to remove Johnson had argued for a broader definition, one that did not require an offense against the laws already passed by Congress. They argued that Johnson's attempt to make a Reconstruction policy, going against the priorities of Congress, "was a high crime" against the nation and a usurpation of legislative power for which impeachment was a valid remedy.[52]

The grounds for impeachment voted against Nixon took a middle ground between the broad view expressed by Republicans and the narrow view expressed by Democrats in 1867. The House Committee deliberated until July 24, 1974, at which time six of the seventeen Republicans voted with all twenty-one Democrats for the first article of impeachment. Of the three articles passed by the committee, one involved obstruction of justice (the cover-up of the Watergate burglary), itself an indictable legal offense; another involved abuse of power (the White House use of government agencies such as the IRS, the CIA, and the FBI to harass opponents of the administration); and the last cited Nixon's refusal to answer committee subpoenas for evidence.[53]

When Nixon eventually released the contested tapes after the Supreme Court ordered him to do so, the June 23 tape indicated that he had conspired to cover up White House involvement in Watergate by using the CIA. Nixon had committed a federal crime after all. Republicans who had defended the president were devastated. Republican Senate Minority Leader Hugh Scott, after reading the transcript, called it "a shabby, disgusting, immoral performance by all those involved."[54] The Republicans on the Judiciary Committee, in their final report, conceded that "The charges of conspiracy to obstruct justice, and obstruction of justice . . . may be taken as substantially confessed by Mr. Nixon," and they concluded, "Richard Nixon, as President, committed certain acts for which he should have been impeached and removed from office."[55]

On August 7, 1974, a delegation of senior Republicans in Congress met with President Nixon. They did not pressure him to resign, but they did let him know he had no support in the Senate, with only ten senators supporting him, and of those, six were really undecided about his guilt. Barry Goldwater, the dean of Republican conservatives, had already told Vice President Gerald Ford that "the best thing Nixon can do for the country is to get the hell out of the White House."[56] On August 8, at 9:00 PM Nixon went on national television. "In the past few days it has become evident that I no longer have a strong enough political base in the Congress," he told the audience. "As President I must put the interests of America first." Then came the hardest part of any speech he had ever made: "Therefore I shall resign the Presidency effective at noon tomorrow." Richard Nixon's last official act was to sign a short letter of resignation addressed to his Secretary of State Henry Kissinger: "Dear Mr. Secretary: I hereby resign the Office of the President of the United States. Sincerely, Richard Nixon."

As a result of Nixon's actions, the presidency was diminished morally, politically, and constitutionally. The White House staff had been decimated, and several staffers would soon serve prison terms. In the last months of Nixon's term the cabinet was held together by Secretary of State Kissinger and Secretary of Defense James Schlesinger, both of whom had been running the government in international crises while Nixon remained preoccupied with Watergate. The president had spent little time in Washington or at the White House in his last months in office (most of his time was spent at Camp David or elsewhere), and when he was there he seems to have been distracted with Watergate, spending little time on presidential business. It is not too much of an exaggeration to say that the misuse of presidential prerogative led not only to the collapse of the presidency, but also to the collapse of Richard Nixon.

THE IMPERIAL PRESIDENCY

"When the President does it, that means it's not illegal." That was how Richard Nixon described the unlimited scope of presidential power to television interviewer David Frost as he tried to justify his actions and rehabilitate his reputation.[57] The claim that the president is above the law and not restrained by it, and that what he orders *is* the law—provisions of the Constitution or statutes passed by Congress notwithstanding—is the very definition of the imperial presidency.[58]

Characteristics of the Imperial Presidency

The imperial presidency shows a disregard for certain provisions of the Constitution, particularly regarding the power of the Congress to declare war, appropriate funds, and oversee covert intelligence operations. Truman and Johnson entered into wars without gaining congressional authorization; Nixon expanded the Vietnam War into Cambodia and conducted a secret bombing campaign there, and he withheld funds Congress had appropriated; Reagan's subordinates did not follow the procedures of laws regulating arms sales and intelligence operations when they sold weapons to Iran and transferred the funds to the contras (a group trying to overthrow the leftist government in Nicaragua). The imperial presidency substitutes presidential prerogatives for congressional authority on such a massive scale that the balance between president and Congress tilts overwhelmingly to the executive. Presidential war making substitutes for joint decision making by president and Congress, and legislators no longer participate meaningfully in crucial decisions about national security.

The imperial presidency involves excessive reliance on White House aides and executive office agencies at the expense of the cabinet secretaries, who are required to obey statutes and agency regulations, and the establishment of a "palace guard" of presidential staffers, seemingly protected by executive privilege, who stand above officials consented to by the Senate to run the government. These officials convert politics from a contest between adversaries into a form of warfare against enemies. All means are used to defeat opponents, including surveillance, investigation, burglary, and use of "dirty tricks."

Congress, the media, and the American people are deliberately deceived about the use of prerogative power through excessive White House use of secrecy systems and executive privilege, all of which results in a "credibility" gap. Eisenhower claimed that the United States had not spied on the Soviet Union but then recanted his claim when the Soviets produced a downed U.S. pilot; Johnson denied that the United States had plans to escalate the Vietnam War in 1964, then announced a massive escalation after the elections; Nixon denied the White House had been involved in Watergate, then changed his story when the burglars began to confess; Reagan proclaimed that the United States would not negotiate with terrorist nations just at the time his national security staffers were negotiating to sell arms to Iran in exchange for release of U.S. hostages; later he laid out the details of the operation at a televised news conference.

The imperial presidency has been subject to congressional and judicial checks and balances. Congress cut off funds for Nixon's war in Cambodia in 1971 and ended the bombing in Indochina in 1973. It prevented him from abolishing domestic programs or cutting back on spending for them.[59] Secrecy and the claim of executive privilege have been relied on by several presidents, including Eisenhower and Kennedy, but in the era of the "imperial presidency" the Supreme Court put limits on its use during the Watergate crisis. The Iran–contra scandal resulted in the resignation of top Reagan aides, a complete reorganization of the National Security Council operations, and lengthy court cases against the key figures involved.

Reassessing the Imperial Presidency

Some observers argue that the imperial presidency of the 1970s has been converted into an "arrogant presidency" of the 1980s—because presidents and their aides have challenged not only the legitimacy of congressional checks and balances, but also the role of the legislature in making policy, and have done all they could to subvert the role of Congress in making national policy, even in routine domestic matters.[60] Other observers claim that in the post-Nixon era, the presidency has been more "imperiled" than "imperial" because of congressional oversight, investigation, micromanagement through legislation, and judicial checks and balances.[61] When Carter negotiated the Panama Canal treaty, the Senate insisted on renegotiations and new amendments. When Bush decided to use force against Iraq to obtain its withdrawal from Kuwait, he found it expedient to ask Congress for a resolution authorizing hostilities. When Clinton converted a U.S. humanitarian mission in Somalia to a police action, Congress required him by law to meet stiff criteria for continuing the American presence. In the post–Cold War era, a diminished national security threat against the United States may be leading to the evolution of a "postmodern" presidency rather than a reassertion of an imperial presidency.

PROSPECTS FOR PREROGATIVE GOVERNANCE

Presidents rely on prerogative power more out of political weakness than constitutional strength. The transformation of the presidency during the New Deal and Cold War periods has expanded the political responsibility of the incumbent well beyond his resources as a partisan and public leader.[62] In crisis times the system of partial separation of powers and checks and balances often seems too slow and unworkable; for important noncrisis issues, the president and his advisers may be so anxious to resolve the issue and avoid political danger that they are prepared to take constitutional shortcuts to do so. The powers of the presidency become a two-edged sword: they enable the president to take decisive action and manage the crisis as he wishes, provided he maintains his authority as a national leader. These same powers can cut his presidency to shreds if his opponents seize on his use of them to charge him with usurpation of power and bad decision making.

The history of the presidency involves a slow but generally steady accretion in the political power and responsibilities, combined with sudden and dramatic increases or decreases in the constitutional and legal powers in times of crises. If the postmodern presidency theory is valid, weak presidents will remain tempted to use prerogative power to resolve international crises, but the very lack of domestic and international support that compels them to consider using prerogative power may undercut them in the event that they do so. An international backlash, as well as a domestic backlash, may then result: checks and balances can be wielded by international organizations as well as by Congress and the courts.

As citizens of a constitutional democracy we can question the use of presidential prerogatives. Did the president act to secure personal or partisan advantage, or were his actions in the national interest? Were his actions intended to interfere with elections? Were they exercised when no statute provided a viable alternative, or were they designed to secure an advantage by circumventing Congress? Did the president use secrecy and deception to meet legitimate national interests, or did he do so to circumvent the checks and balances of the courts and Congress?[63] Although no criteria can provide absolute protection against abuses of power, these questions provide criteria by which voters can hold presidents accountable.

FURTHER READING

Books

Michael Benedict, *The Impeachment and Trial and Andrew Johnson,* New York: W. W. Norton, 1973.

Edward S. Corwin, *The President: Office and Powers, 1787–1957,* 4th rev. ed., New York: New York University Press, 1957.

Martin Fausold and Alan Shank, *The Constitution and the American Presidency,* Albany, NY: State University of New York Press, 1991.

Louis Fisher, *Constitutional Conflicts between Congress and the President,* Princeton, NJ: Princeton University Press, 1985.

Harold Koh, *The National Security Constitution,* New Haven, CN: Yale University Press, 1990.

Stanley Kutler, *The Wars of Watergate,* New York: Alfred A. Knopf, 1990.

Harvey Mansfield, Jr., *Taming the Prince: The Ambivalence of Modern Executive Power,* New York: Free Press, 1989.

Maeva Marcus, *Truman and the Steel Seizure Case,* New York: Columbia University Press, 1977.

Richard Pious, *The American Presidency,* New York: Basic Books, 1979.

Christopher Pyle and Richard Pious, *The President, Congress and the Constitution,* New York: Free Press, 1984.

Clinton Rossiter, *Constitutional Dictatorship,* New York: Harcourt Brace and World, 1948.

Arthur Schlesinger, *The Imperial Presidency,* Boston: Houghton Mifflin, 1973.

Theodore Sorensen, *Watchmen in the Night,* Cambridge, MA: MIT Press, 1975.

Documentary Source

William M. Goldsmith, ed., *The Growth of Presidential Powers,* 3 vols, New York: Chelsea House, 1974.

NOTES

1. *The Inaugural Addresses of Presidents of the United States,* Washington, DC: Government Printing Office, 1965, p. 126.

2. James G. Randall, *Constitutional Problems under Lincoln,* Urbana, IL: University of Illinois Press, 1964; Clinton Rossiter, *Constitutional Dictatorship,* Princeton, NJ: Princeton University Press, 1948, pp. 224–230; Herman Belz, "Lincoln and the Constitution: The 'Dictatorship Question' Reconsidered," *Congress and the Presidency,* Vol. 15, no. 2, Autumn, 1988, pp. 147–164.

3. James D. Richardson, *A Compilation of the Messages and Papers of the Presidents,* Washington, DC: Bureau of National Literature and Art, 1900, Vol. 7, pp. 3215–3219 (hereafter Richardson, *Messages and Papers*).

4. *Appropriations Act of August 6, 1861,* 12 U.S. Stat. 326.

5. *The Prize Cases,* 2 Black 635, 1863.

6. *Dred Scott v. Sandford,* 19 Howard 393, 1857.

7. *An Act to Confiscate Property Used for Insurrectionary Purposes,* 12 U.S. Stat. 319, sec. 4.

8. Roy B. Basler, ed., *The Collected Works of Abraham Lincoln,* New Brunswick, NJ: Rutgers University Press, 1953–1955, Vol. 7, pp. 281–282.

9. Kirk H. Porter and Donald Bruce Johnson, *National Party Platforms, 1840–1960,* Urbana, IL: University of Illinois Press, 1961, pp. 34–36.

10. Harvey Flaumenhaft, "Hamilton's Administrative Republic and the American Presidency," in Joseph M. Bessette and Jeffrey Tulis, eds., *The Presidency in the Constitutional Order,* Baton Rouge, LA: Louisiana State University Press, 1981, pp. 65–112; Broadus Mitchell, "Alexander Hamilton, Executive Power, and the New Nation," *Presidential Studies Quarterly,* Vol. 17, no. 2, Spring, 1987, pp. 328–343.

11. Paul Leicester Ford, ed., *The Writings of Thomas Jefferson,* New York: Putnam, 1892–1899, Vol. 8, p. 246.

12. Arnhart, Larry, " 'The God-Like Prince': John Locke, Executive Prerogative, and the American Presidency," *Presidential Studies Quarterly,* Vol. 9, no. 1, Spring, 1979, pp. 121–130; for a more restrictive view, see Thomas Langston and Michael Lind, "John Locke and the Limits of Presidential Prerogative," *Polity,* Vol. 24, no. 1, Fall, 1991, pp. 49–68.

13. Roy P. Basler, op. cit., Vol. IV, 1953–1955, pp. 429–430.

14. *In re Neagle,* 135 U.S. 1, 1880; *In re Debs,* 158 U.S. 564, 1895.

15. Louis Fisher, "Laws Congress Never Made," *Constitution Magazine,* Fall, 1993, pp. 59–66; James Hart, "Ordinance Making Power of the President," *North American Review,* Vol. 218, July, 1923, pp. 59–66; William Hebe, "Executive Orders and the Development of Presidential Power," *Villanova Law Review,* Vol. 17, no. 3, March, 1972, pp. 688–712.; Joel L. Fleishman and Arthur H. Aufses, "Law and Orders: The Problem of Presidential Legislation," *Law and Contemporary Problems,* Vol. 40, no. 1, Summer, 1976, pp. 1–45.

16. Michael Glennon, *Constitutional Diplomacy,* Princeton, NJ: Princeton University Press, 1990, pp. 54–59.

17. *Dames and Moore v. Regan,* 452 U.S. 654, 1981.

18. *U.S. v. Midwest Oil Co.,* 236 U.S. 459, 1915.

19. *Korematsu v. U.S.,* 323 U.S. 214, 1944; also *Mitchell v. Laird,* 488 F. 2nd 611 (DC Cir. 1973).

20. Concurring opinion in *Youngstown Sheet and Tube v. Sawyer,* 343 U.S. 579, 1952, pp. 634–635.

21. J. Richard Piper, " 'Situational Constitutionalism' and Presidential Power," *Presidential Studies Quarterly,* Vol. 24, no. 3, Summer, 1994, using data from "Table 1: Northern Democratic and Republican Support for Presidential Powers on Key Congressional Roll Calls, 1933–1989," p. 584.

22. Pacificus, Letter Number 1, June 29, 1793, reprinted in Christopher Pyle and Richard Pious, *The President, Congress and the Constitution,* New York: Free Press, 1994, pp. 55–57.

23. Jefferson, *Writings,* VI (Ford ed., 1892–1899), p. 338.

24. Helvidius, Letter Number 1, August–September, 1793, reprinted in Pyle and Pious, op. cit., pp. 58–60.

25. Quincy Wright, "United States and International Agreements: Treaties and Executive Agreements," *American Journal of International Law,* Vol. 38, no. 3, July, 1944, pp. 341–355; Edwin M. Borchard, "Shall the Executive Agreement Replace the Treaty?" *American Journal of International Law,* Vol. 38, no. 3, October, 1944, pp. 637–643.

26. J. William Fulbright, "American Foreign Policy in the 20th Century Under an 18th Century Constitution," *Cornell Law Quarterly,* Vol. 47, no. 1, Fall, 1961, pp. 1–13; Barry M. Goldwater, "The President's Constitutional Primacy in Foreign Relations and National Defense" *Virginia Journal of International Law,* Vol. 13, no. 4, Summer, 1973, pp. 463–484.

27. Oliver Chitwood, *John Tyler,* New York: Russell and Russell, 1939, p. 270.

28. *In re Debs,* 158 U.S. 564, 1895.

29. Grover Cleveland, *Presidential Problems,* New York: The Century Co., 1904; Richard E. Welch, *The Presidencies of Grover Cleveland,* Lawrence, KS: University Press of Kansas, 1988.

30. *Ex Parte Milligan,* 71 U.S. 2, 1866.

31. Maeva Marcus, *Truman and the Steel Seizure,* New York: Columbia University Press, 1977, p. 92.

32. Ibid., pp. 166–167.

33. *Youngstown Sheet and Tube Co. v. Sawyer,* 343 U.S. 579, 1952.

34. Ibid., p. 637.

35. Katy J. Harriger, *Independent Justice: The Federal Special Prosecutor in American Politics,* Lawrence, KS: University Press of Kansas, 1991.

36. "What the Public Thinks of Congress," citing Gallup Polls, in *Washington Post National Weekly Edition,* July 11–17, 1994, p. 7.

37. Stanley Kutler, *The Wars of Watergate,* New York: Alfred A. Knopf, 1990, p. 109; Fred Emery, *Watergate: The Corruption of American Politics and the Fall of Richard Nixon,* New York: Times Books, 1994.

38. Stanley Kutler, op. cit., pp. 111–119, 191.

39. Ibid., pp. 204–205.

40. Daniel Schorr, "The Roots of the Nixon Resignation," *Washington Post National Weekly Edition,* August 15–21, 1994, p. 24.

41. Stanley Kutler, op. cit., p. 191.

42. The term was first used by the Justice Department in 1958 to defend Eisenhower's refusal to turn over personnel files to a Senate committee; it was later used by Kennedy and Johnson on several occasions involving defense policies, also against congressional committees. See Senate Committee on Government Operations, Committee on the Judiciary, *Executive Privilege, Secrecy in Government, and Freedom of Information,* Vols. 1–3, Hearings, 93rd Congress, 1st Sess., Washington, DC: Government Printing Office, 1973.

43. Nixon letter to Ervin, July 6, 1973; Oral argument before Judge John Sirica, August 22, 1973.

44. Brief of August 7, 1973.

45. Brief of August 7, 1973.

46. *U.S. v. Nixon,* 418 U.S. 663, 1974.

47. In trials one may assert a Fifth-Amendment right against self-incrimination, but in federal grand jury proceedings the prosecutors may ask the federal judge for a ruling requiring that testimony be given. The witness before the grand jury then receives either transactional immunity (his or her testimony may not be used in a trial) or use immunity (no criminal charges can be brought after the witness testifies about his or her involvement in the crime). The granting of such immunity is regulated by an act of Congress passed in 1954 to counter the growing influence of organized crime, and may also be granted by congressional committees.

48. *U.S. v. Nixon,* 418 U.S. 663, 1974, p. 713.

49. Brief of July 1, 1974.

50. White House Press Conference, February 25, 1974.

51. House Committee on the Judiciary, *Constitutional Grounds for Presidential Impeachment,* February 20, 1974; House Committee on the Judiciary, *Debate on Articles of Impeachment,* 93rd Congress, 2nd Sess., Washington, DC: Government Printing Office, 1974, p. 337.

52. House of Representatives, Committee on the Judiciary, Series No. 134, Report 7, 40th Congress, 1st sess., 1867; Michael L. Benedict, *The Impeachment and Trial of Andrew Johnson,* New York: W. W. Norton, 1973.

53. House Committee on the Judiciary, *Debate on Articles of Impeachment,* 93rd Congress, 2nd Sess., Washington, DC: Government Printing Office, 1974.

54. Robert Woodward and Carl Bernstein, *The Final Days,* New York: Simon and Schuster, 1976, p. 155.

55. House Committee on the Judiciary, *Report: The Impeachment of Richard M. Nixon,* Washington, DC: Government Printing Office, 1974, pp. 359–360.

56. Kutler, op. cit., p. 539.

57. *New York Times,* May 20, 1977, p. B-10.

58. Arthur M. Schlesinger, Jr., *The Imperial Presidency,* Boston: Houghton Mifflin, 1973; Arthur Schlesinger, Jr., *Cycles of American History,* Boston: Houghton Mifflin, 1986, pp. 277–336; for similar argument about Reagan, see Theodore Lowi, "Presidential Power: Restoring the Balance," *Political Science Quarterly,* Vol. 100, no. 2, Summer, 1985, pp. 185–213; Daniel P. Moynihan, "Imperial Government," *Commentary,* Vol. 65, no. 6, June, 1978, pp. 25–32.

59. Louis Koenig, "Reassessing the 'Imperial Presidency,' " in Richard M. Pious, ed., *The Power to Govern,* New York: Academy of Political Science, 1982, pp. 31–44.

60. Nancy Kassop, "The Arrogant Presidency II: The Bush Administration Confronts Separation of Powers," Paper delivered at the Western Political Science Association Annual Meeting, Albuquerque, NM, March 10–12, 1994.

61. Thomas E. Cronin, "A Resurgent Congress and the Imperial Presidency," *Political Science Quarterly,* Vol. 95, no. 2, Summer, 1980, pp. 209–237.

62. Clinton Rossiter, "Constitutional Dictatorship in the Atomic Age," *Review of Politics,* Vol. 2, no. 4, October, 1949, pp. 395–418.

63. Arthur Schlesinger, Jr., *The Imperial Presidency,* op. cit., pp. 450–451.

CHAPTER 5

Presidential Nominations

I've been going to conventions since 1928, and this one is the best of all.

—Lyndon Johnson (at the 1964 Democratic Convention)

INTRODUCTORY CASE: AN AMBUSH IN NEW HAMPSHIRE

They called themselves "clean for Gene," and in the winter of 1968 these college students shaved off their beards, cut their long hair, and tramped through the snows of New Hampshire, campaigning for Senator Eugene McCarthy, a fierce opponent of the Vietnam War, in the New Hampshire Democratic presidential primary. Their goal was to topple Democratic President Lyndon Johnson. Could they pull it off? Commentators gave them no chance: sitting presidents seeking reelection did not have to worry about primary fights. Not since Chester Arthur in 1884 had an incumbent president been denied renomination by his party. Democratic Governor John King and Senator Thomas McIntyre were supporting Johnson, and they had the party organization with them. The students did not heed the history lessons; they just shrugged and rang doorbells. There was no way New Hampshire voters would repudiate the president, the media pundits claimed. The students kept ringing doorbells and canvassing for support. McCarthy later recalled that many voters "had not talked to their own children in years as they talked with the young workers in my campaign."[1] More than five thousand students gave up their weekends to the effort (including McCarthy's daughter Mary): newspaper reporters dubbed it the Children's Campaign, and reported that crowds were sparse and the candidate was putting them to sleep. Pollsters gave McCarthy no chance. McCarthy appealed for funds, running a newspaper ad with the following copy: "Senator McCarthy is backed by the most improbable political machine in American history. It works for nothing, runs on peanut butter sandwiches and soft drinks, and spends the night in sleeping bags or empty warehouses. . . ."[2]

On primary day, March 12, 1968, President Johnson got the shock of his life. Eugene McCarthy did not win, but it appeared that he had received 42 percent of the vote. (After write-in votes were counted, McCarthy received 49 percent and lost by just 230 votes.) In other states jubilant "clean for Gene" volunteers began gearing up for a real nomination fight, and on March 14 Senator Robert Kennedy entered the race. President Johnson made a speech to the nation on March 31 in which he announced that he was ordering a pause in the U.S. bombing of North Vietnam. Then, looking straight into the cameras, Johnson continued, "I shall not seek and I will not accept the nomination of my party for another term." Two days later McCarthy won the Wisconsin primary. The Children's Brigade had demonstrated the power to topple a president and open up a nominating contest, and American presidential politics would never be the same.

Since 1968, the presidential nomination contest has undergone a vast transformation: once controlled by state party leaders, nominations are now granted or withheld by millions of voters in primary contests. Although, through 1992, no sitting president since Johnson has been run out of the race, Gerald Ford in 1976 and Jimmy Carter in 1980 came close to losing to party rivals, and George Bush had to stave off a challenge in 1992. Bill Clinton's rivals were considering attempts to unseat him after the midterm reverses of 1994. Nomination politics affects what a first-term president does when he gets into office, because as soon as he takes the oath, he has to start thinking about the prospects for his own renomination.

MAKING THE RACE

From the organization of political parties in the nineteenth century through the 1992 elections, only major-party candidates won the White House. To win a major-party nomination a contender almost always must have prior experience in public office, access to large amounts of money, and considerable experience in running a media campaign.

Incumbents and Heirs

A president who does not seek another term or has already served two terms may try to arrange for the succession by passing the nomination on to an heir apparent, but rarely does this work. Calvin Coolidge did not want his secretary of commerce, Herbert Hoover, to succeed him, but had no influence at the Republican convention of 1928. Dwight Eisenhower wanted Treasury Secretary Robert Anderson, but his behind-the-scenes maneuvers to "dump" Vice President Richard Nixon in 1956 from the ticket were unsuccessful, and in 1960 Anderson declined to run, allowing Nixon to assume the mantle of heir apparent, even though Eisenhower did not believe he had grown sufficiently to make a good president. Heirs that have made it to the White House have disappointed their predecessors: Teddy Roosevelt was so upset with William Howard Taft's actions that he ran against him in 1912 for the Republican nomination. Taft was renominated, but the party split allowed Democrat Woodrow Wilson to win the election.

Cabinet Secretaries

One might think that secretaries of state, defense, and treasury, heads of the most important cabinet departments, with executive experience in national government, would be odds-on favorites to win nominations. Department secretaries, however, were favored only in the congressional caucus system. Since the rise of state party leaders to influence in nominating politics in the 1830s, most cabinet secretaries have been ignored: although many are "mentioned" as potential contenders (for

1996 these included former Secretary of State James Baker and former Secretary of Defense Richard Cheney), few ever make the race (neither Baker nor Cheney did so, though former Education Secretary Lamar Alexander threw his hat in the ring), and through 1992 only Taft (1908) and Hoover (1928) won a major-party nomination while serving in the cabinet.

U.S. Representatives

Through 1992, only one sitting member of the House of Representatives, James A. Garfield, has ever been elected president, and that was in 1880. Only one other major-party presidential nominee came directly from the House, also in the nineteenth century. Few serious contenders have competed for nominations while serving in the House. (Speaker Champ Clark won 40 percent of the Democratic delegates in 1912, losing to Woodrow Wilson.) Many presidential nominees at one time or another in the course of their careers did serve in the House. In the nineteenth century these included Jefferson, John Quincy Adams, Monroe, Jackson, William Henry Harrison, Polk, Fillmore, Buchanan, Lincoln, Johnson, Hayes, Garfield, and McKinley. In the twentieth century far fewer presidents have had House experience: these include Kennedy, Johnson, Nixon, Ford, and Bush.

U.S. Senators

One or more senators are almost always in the field of contenders, including Robert Dole, Phil Gramm, Richard Lugar, and Arlen Specter in 1996. Some political scientists and pollsters once argued that senators were likely to win presidential nominations because they serve in Washington, get national media attention and have high name recognition, and deal with important national issues. Yet senators rarely win major-party presidential nominations: the anti-Washington mood of the voters makes them less attractive to voters than governors. Only two senators in the nineteenth century (Jackson and Benjamin Harrison) and two in the twentieth (Harding and Kennedy) have gone directly to the White House from the Senate, as of 1995.

Vice Presidents

Between 1789 and 1900 seven vice presidents became president, three by winning party nominations and getting elected (John Adams, Jefferson, and Van Buren) and four by succession (Tyler, Fillmore, Johnson, and Arthur). None of them subsequently won their party's nomination for another term. Between 1900 and 1992 seven vice presidents also became president: George Bush immediately won his party nomination and the subsequent election; Richard Nixon was nominated for president, lost the election, then eight years later was nominated and elected president; Theodore Roosevelt, Coolidge, Truman, and Johnson succeeded to the office and won subsequent renomination and election; and Gerald Ford entered the vice presidency through procedures of the twenty-fifth Amendment, then succeeded to the presidency when Nixon resigned. In addition to Nixon, two other vice presidents won their party's presidential nominations but lost the general election: Hubert Humphrey in 1968, and Walter Mondale in 1984 (after a four-year hiatus).

Governors

Governors do better than members of Congress in winning major-party nominations and presidential elections. In the nineteenth century four won the presidency, including Polk, Hayes, Cleveland, and McKinley; the list of those elected in the twentieth century, through 1992, includes Wilson, Franklin Roosevelt, Carter, Reagan, and Clinton. Ten other governors have lost presidential elections after winning nominations: two in the nineteenth century and eight in the twentieth. Governors win nominations because of an anti-Washington mood in the electorate: They portray themselves as Washington outsiders, ready to shake up the capital, and as vigorous executives who know how to solve problems. Governors also seem to be better able to organize efficient campaigns and fund them adequately, often relying on a core of in-state private and corporate contributors who have dealt with their state governments.

Army Generals

Few military officers have ever run for the presidency, and the only ones who have ever won have been successful commanders in major wars: Washington, Jackson, William Henry Harrison, Taylor, Grant, and Eisenhower. A number have won nominations and been defeated, including William Henry Harrison in 1836, Winfield Scott in 1852, John Frémont in 1856, George McClellan in 1864, and Winfield Hancock in 1880. Nevertheless, the temptation is great for a party to think about nominating an authentic war hero: in 1995 former Chairman of the Joint Chiefs of Staff Colin Powell was mentioned as a Republican possibility for 1996 because of his prominent role in the Persian Gulf War.

Demographics

Until recently the field of contenders was composed almost entirely of married white Protestant men of English, Scottish-Irish, Dutch, or German descent. But times have changed, and in a pluralistic nation contenders now come from a broader spectrum of the population. Catholics Al Smith and John Kennedy won Democratic nominations, and other Catholics have competed strongly, including Robert and Ted Kennedy, Edmund Muskie, and Jerry Brown. The Democratic candidate in 1988, Michael Dukakis, was the first Greek Orthodox candidate. Adlai Stevenson in 1952 was the first nominee to have been divorced, and Ronald Reagan was the first candidate who had been divorced to win the White House (unlike Stevenson, he had remarried). The post–Civil War taboo against nominating southerners was broken by the transplant Woodrow Wilson in 1912, then by Lyndon Johnson in 1964 (he argued that Texas was a "Western" state) and since then southerners Jimmy Carter and Bill Clinton have won nominations and elections.

Nonwhites, non-Christians, and women still have not won a major-party presidential nomination, though in 1988 African-American Jesse Jackson made a strong run, and African-American Colin Powell was a potential contender for 1996. Through 1992 no woman had been considered as a serious presidential contender by either major party, though several women have received a smattering of votes at

Prior Public Offices Held by Presidents Elected between 1789 and 1992

	Nineteenth Century	Twentieth Century
National Office		
Vice President	7	7
Cabinet Secretary	7	2
Subcabinet Official	1	6
U.S. Representative	13	5
U.S. Senator	8	5
U.S. Supreme Court Justice	—	—
Federal Judge	—	1
Diplomat	7	2
Army General	5	1
State and Local Office		
Governor	11	7
State Legislator	17	5
State Executive	10	3
State Judge	1	3
Mayor	2	1
City Official	1	3

national conventions since Representative Shirley Chisholm won 172 votes at the 1972 convention. There is no question that women will soon be serious contenders, given the increased representation of women in Congress since 1992.

Running the Media Gauntlet

David Broder, a columnist for the *Washington Post,* once argued that an "inner-club" of newspaper editorialists and columnists acted as a kind of screening committee to winnow the field. Columnists for major newspapers acted as "talent scouts" who sought out and identified presidential possibilities who might otherwise have been overlooked by party professionals. Contenders courted them and appeared on Sunday morning talk shows, hoping that what columnist Russell Baker calls "The Great Mentioner" would mention them. Yet often the "club" has had little or no influence on nominations, for if it did, Nixon, Carter, Reagan, and Clinton—none of them media favorites—would never have made it to the White House, and such contenders as Perot, Jackson, Robertson, and Buchanan would never have been included in the field. Conversely, if the "club" had real power, Governor Mario Cuomo, Senator Howard Baker, and Senator Robert Dole might have been nominated by their parties in the 1980s.

Changes in the media and public attitudes have made media endorsement as much of a liability as an asset. Columnists are considered by many voters to be part of the "elitist" Washington establishment. Many contenders bypass the dull weekend public service news programs with their miniscule viewership and egotistical "talking heads." Instead, contenders favor late-night television and all-day radio "talk shows" hosted by personalities who act primarily as conduits for the voters to ask their own questions; these shows give contenders the chance to "kick back" and reveal something of themselves to the voters. Candidates can bypass tough scrutiny on national issues by informed journalists in favor of "soft" interviews in which empathy rather than knowledge bonds them to their viewers and listeners. Bill Clinton went on the late-night Arsenio Hall program and played jazz riffs on the saxophone in front of a national audience of millions. That scene alone was worth a thousand words from newspaper columnists.

To the extent that contenders are "winnowed out" by the media, it is not by the commentators, but rather by investigative journalists or the "junkyard dogs" of the tabloid press.[3] Gary Hart was discovered in an extramarital affair in 1988, and the revelation soon forced him from the campaign. Allegations that Bill Clinton had been involved in an extramarital affair in 1992, however, did not drive him out, so the "winnowing effect" even of the tabloid press may be overrated.

Poll Standings

Only five or six politicians achieve contender status in the prenomination polls in any election year.[4] Yet a contender can come out of nowhere and win a nomination, and high standing in the polls does not guarantee anyone the nomination. Jimmy Carter, an obscure former governor from Georgia, won the Democratic nomination and the presidency in 1976, though he had not even been included in the polls the previous year. In 1986 Michael Dukakis was not even included on a list of eighteen likely Democratic candidates in the Gallup polls, yet in 1988 he won the Democratic nomination. Preprimary polls are sometimes inaccurate: In 1984 the *New York Times* published poll results before the first set of primaries indicating that Walter Mondale had a commanding lead. Shortly thereafter Mondale was in the fight of his life against rival Gary Hart—a fight he barely won.

Presidential Entrepreneurs versus Parliamentary Apprentices

Perhaps the most serious problem with our nominating system is that those who emerge with the nomination often are those least experienced, a situation that rarely occurs in other nations. In European parliamentary systems most party and government leaders have served long apprenticeships before heading the government. British prime ministers, like Margaret Thatcher and John Major, start on the "back benches" and demonstrate their talents with minor assignments. They then become junior ministers, assisting senior colleagues in running a department and defending its policies in debates, or hone their skills as "shadow ministers" assigned to debate with the government on particular issues. Later they become ministers, then parliamentary leaders. They spend many years rising to the top of their party by

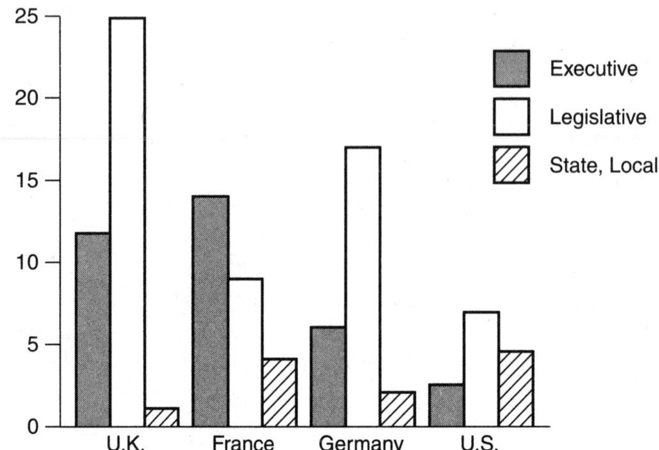

Figure 5.1 Average years of political experience of major party leaders since 1945.

gaining the respect and friendship of their colleagues. Figure 5.1 indicates that other democratic nations also select leaders with experience in national government.

In the United States there is no orderly line of succession, no "shadow cabinet" in the opposition waiting to form a government if elected. There is no opposition party leader, unifying the party and preparing for the time the electorate returns his party to power. Given the anti-Washington mood of voters, outsiders such as Carter, Reagan, and Clinton stand a good chance of winning their party's nomination and the White House. When they come into office, their prior careers have not prepared them for the challenges of working with other Washington officeholders.

ORGANIZING A CAMPAIGN

In the days of party-dominated national conventions a contender's campaign organization consisted of a few agents who would negotiate in his name with the state party bosses. Starting in the 1950s, candidates created their own campaign organizations to raise money, conduct research and public opinion polling, organize volunteers in key states, develop campaign commercials, obtain good media coverage, and do "advance work" when they made appearances around the country.

The Preliminary Organization

In the nineteenth century, candidates could wait until a few months before the Convention to announce their candidacies, because the politicking would occur just before and at the Convention. By the 1930s, candidates announced at the beginning of the new year, giving themselves five months to campaign. By the 1980s, candidates were announcing more than a year in advance, and as of summer 1994,

Robert Dole indicated he was seriously considering a run for the 1996 Republican nomination.[5] Contenders begin by setting up a preliminary organization, which consists of one or more of the following:

- *Research foundation.* A nonpartisan research and educational organization (to which contributions are tax deductible) that conducts research on issues that the candidate may later use in the campaign. The foundation may not spend money in a political campaign.
- *Candidate PAC.* An organization that raises and spends funds in federal elections. A politician may create his or her own PAC (political action committee) to contribute to House and Senate campaigns and win support from other politicians.
- *Exploratory committee.* An organization permitted to pay for certain prenomination campaign expenses in the months preceding a formal announcement of candidacy.
- *Presidential campaign committee.* The exploratory committee transforms itself into the formal campaign organization when the contender makes an announcement that he or she is in the race for the nomination. The committee pays for the expenses of running the contender's campaign through the nomination.

Field campaigns are organized as much as two years in advance of the nominating season in key states such as Iowa and New Hampshire, which hold contests early and are used by the national media to assess the race. Their first job is to get the candidate on the ballot by complying with complex ballot-access laws in each state. Campaigns then hire organizers who have worked these states before and know the local party leaders. During the primary season contenders often run "tarmac campaigns," speeding across the country from airport to airport. Armed with minicams and microwave transmitters, news crews can conduct live interviews with a candidate. Contenders can cut down on their travel by taping speeches and "interviews" and using "uplink" transmitters to send them to satellites, which in turn can send the signals to any of the thousand or so television stations equipped with corresponding "downlinks," allowing a contender access to hundreds of major media markets simultaneously.

Fund-Raising

"You need three things to run for public office," House Speaker Tip O'Neill used to say, "money, money, and money." Nowhere is this more true than in nominating politics. A contender must raise a great deal of money to create an organization to communicate with the voters. And he or she must continue raising money ("dialing for dollars") at a fast clip: failure to do so almost inevitably brings about a quick exit from the race. This situation discourages some potential contenders, such as Dan Quayle and Jack Kemp, who were reluctant to make the strenuous efforts to raise the $20 million or so necessary to run a credible race for the nomination in 1996.

The Federal Election Campaign Amendments of 1974 placed a spending limit on each contender's prenomination campaign of $10 million, with an additional $2 million for expenses (to be adjusted upward each election for inflation). To reduce the impact of the wealthy in the nominating process, the law specified that no candidate could spend more than $50,000 in personal funds (a provision later ruled unconstitutional by the Supreme Court if a candidate decided to forego public funding). No individual could contribute more than $1,000, and no political action committee or political party committee could contribute more than $5,000 to a contender in the preconvention period.

Each contender was eligible for matching funds from the Treasury, if he or she could raise $5,000 in each of twenty states in amounts of $250 or less. The Treasury then would match, dollar for dollar, all contributions of $250 or less an eligible contender received. A candidate could raise $5 million in small contributions and receive another $5 million from the Treasury. As a result of the Supreme Court's *Buckley v. Valeo* decision, a candidate who chose not to accept matching funds was not limited to the $10 million (plus inflation) ceiling.[6] (The only serious major-party contenders for a presidential nomination who had not accepted federal funds through 1992 were Pat Robertson in 1988 and John Connally in 1980.) Candidates who received less than 10 percent in two consecutive primary contests would lose their eligibility for funding. In effect, the public funding provisions help winnow out the weaker candidates by drying up their funding almost immediately, narrowing the field down to three or four candidates at the most within a few weeks after primary contests begin.

Since 1980 every contender who eventually won a major-party nomination led the field in funds raised on December 31 of the year before the convention. In 1992, for example, the well-funded Clinton campaign was able to outlast opponents who ran out of money after the early primaries, and his funding advantages made a big difference in the race. By 1996, a good $20 million in the bank before the primary season starts seems to be necessary to play the game. Candidates do not necessarily have to outspend their opponents state by state to win the nomination. In 1988, for example, Robert Dole outspent George Bush in eleven and Pat Robertson outspent Bush in four contests that Bush won. On the Democratic side, Michael Dukakis was the "big spender" in only thirteen of twenty-seven contests, and managed to lose four of them; nevertheless, he won in three states in which he was outspent, and won the nomination.[7]

The contribution and spending limits have meant that candidates can no longer rely on huge warchests raised from the super-rich in the primary season. Nor has it made much sense to receive funds from PACs, because the money would not be eligible for matching funding. Since the 1970s direct-mail fund-raisers have developed lists of contributors for the early stages of a campaign. PACs, rather than make direct and visible contributions, steer their members into making $250 donations to contenders they favor.

The spending limits have placed a premium on being able to raise funds from the grassroots and gain interest group support, make an intelligent allocation of funds, and plan in advance for each state contest. Campaign fund-raising itself is a good test of qualities needed by a president.

WINNING DELEGATES

A patchwork quilt of caucuses and primaries held in fifty states and the District of Columbia (as well as in Puerto Rico and several other U.S. commonwealth territories such as the U.S. Virgin Islands) to choose delegates to the national convention requires contenders to travel all over the country in the space of fifteen weeks. Racing from airport to airport gives them little time to think, to read, to reflect on issues, or to work with people they might want in their administration. Staffers and media advisors with little experience in government peddle their own policies to campaigns starved for ideas and position papers. The campaign functions in its own enclosed universe, with candidates surrounded by advisers and the attending journalists. Real face-to-face contact and communication with voters (as opposed to staged media events) is limited, though it stands as a refreshing contrast to manipulative campaigning when it occurs.

Caucus-Convention Contests

One-third of the states use the caucus-convention system. In each, hundreds of precinct caucuses (known as the "first round") are held in meeting halls (such as a high school gymnasium or auditorium) on a designated day. Those attending nominate their choices for delegates to attend subsequent district conventions covering a larger area of the state ("second round"), which in turn sends delegates to a state convention ("final round"). There the composition of the state's delegation to the national convention will be determined.

Each precinct caucus is run as a meeting, in which supporters of each contender make speeches that are designed to sway the opinion of those attending. After the discussion period, some caucuses provide for an open vote, often taken by having those attending move to different corners of the room to demonstrate support for competing slates of delegates, known as "grouping." If a contender fails to attract a minimum "threshold" in a group, the attendees are invited to move to other groups so as not to waste their vote. In other states party rules may allow a secret ballot. Delegates are allotted in the Democratic Party according to the rule of proportional representation. In the Republican Party a winner-take-all system is often used.[8]

Some states attract as much as 10 to 15 percent of the registered party voters. The 1992 Iowa, Minnesota, and Washington State Democratic caucuses had between 30,000 and 60,000 voters attending. (In Wyoming and Alaska, the turnout at meetings was a mere 1,500 and 1,100.) The overall rate of participation in caucuses averages around 3 percent of registered party voters, though it may vary significantly from one contest to the next. With their low turnout, caucuses cannot represent mass public opinion in the states that use them. They are not an exercise in mass voter mobilization but are a forum for organized interests.[9]

Until the 1970s party leaders controlled who attended caucus meetings, and their rules usually provided that only party workers were eligible to participate. By excluding all but their own followers, they were able to choose "uncommitted" delegations to the national conventions that would follow their bidding. In 1972 Democrats changed their rules to provide that caucus meetings must be open to all registered party voters, and Republicans soon followed suit. Since then, candidates have competed for convention delegates at every stage of the process, and state party leaders rarely have enough strength to keep delegations uncommitted. Contenders flood caucus meetings with their followers. The only way they can do this, however, is by relying on the support of unions, ethnic groups, professional associations, or church groups, and others who can bring their members out to the meetings. Caucus states favor candidates who can rouse ideologically committed supporters, who have endorsements from interest groups (like the National Educational Association) or from minority groups. Pat Robertson and Jesse Jackson did well in the Michigan contests in 1988, for example: Jackson's followers were organized by the African-American churches, and Robertson benefited from the support of fundamentalist Christians.

Because the Iowa caucuses involve the first contest held by any state for convention delegates, at times they have assumed great importance in the presidential race. The winner and second-place finishers in Iowa receive much more media coverage than other contenders and a boost in campaign contributions. Those who fare poorly in Iowa may be forced to drop out of the race. In 1984, for example, Gary Hart took second place and George McGovern finished third, with fewer than fifteen hundred votes separating them. Yet Hart received a boost in his campaign from the press, and McGovern was ignored and soon dropped out. At other times Iowa may mean little: in 1988 the Democratic and Republican winners (Richard Gephardt and Robert Dole, respectively) were both out of the race within a month. In 1992, with Iowan Tom Harkin running in the Democratic contest, its importance further diminished.

Winning early caucus contests or a large number of caucus contests does not mean much in the presidential sweepstakes, because there are so few delegates at stake. In 1992 Bill Clinton won only four state caucuses out of seventeen (Figure 5.2), yet still won the nomination by virtue of his successes in the other method of delegate selection—the primaries.

Primary Contests

A presidential nominating primary is an intraparty election in which voters choose delegates to the national convention. Between two-thirds and three-fourths of the national convention delegates are chosen in such primaries. Primaries take influence away from the party organization (which had controlled delegations in the era of closed party caucuses) and interest groups (which may flood caucuses with their followers) and give it to the party-in-the-electorate.[10]

Primaries began as part of the Progressive movement, whose reforms were designed to weaken boss-dominated parties. The first presidential primary was held in Florida: in 1904 it established a "preference primary" that allowed voters to signal their preference for the nomination. The state's convention delegates were chosen by a caucus-convention and were not bound by the results of the primary. In 1905 Progressive Governor Robert M. La Follette won passage in Wisconsin of a law creating a delegate-selection primary for the 1908 conventions. Oregon in 1908 used a "first ballot primary," which bound the state delegation to vote for the winner of the primary on the first national convention ballot but thereafter permitted it discretion; its lead was followed by North Dakota, Nebraska, Wisconsin, and New Jersey. By 1912 a dozen states had established primaries, but many were like Florida's preference primary, whereas others had separate "preference" votes for candidates and votes for convention delegates. At times this could lead to mixed results: In 1912 in Massachusetts voters selected Theodore Roosevelt's supporters to go to the

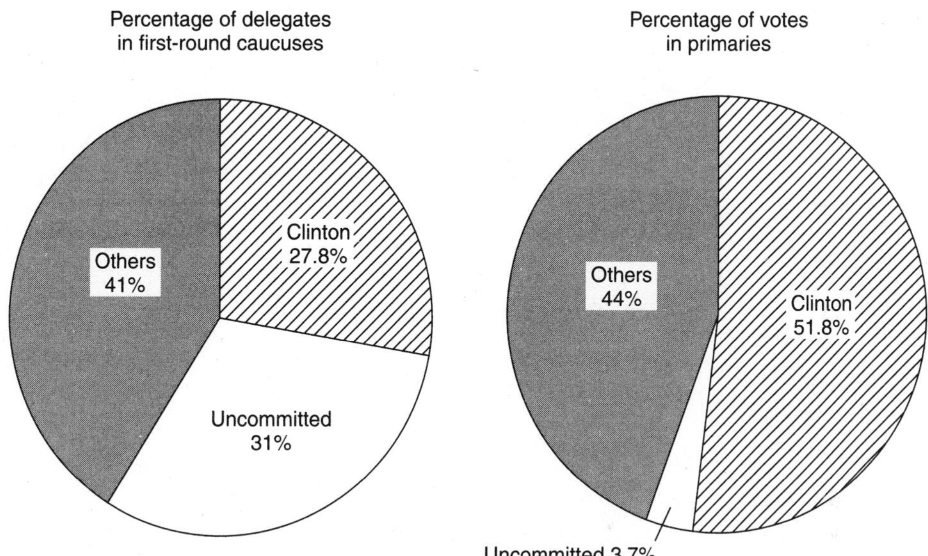

Figure 5.2 How Bill Clinton fared in primaries and caucuses, 1992.
Source: Data from *Congressional Quarterly Weekly Reports,* July 4, 1992, pp. 69–70.

convention, but also expressed their "preference" for William Howard Taft. Twenty states held primaries in 1916. In the 1920s, because of high cost and low voter participation, eight states dropped primaries and returned to the caucus system. By 1960 only fifteen states held primaries (a low after 1916), and in many of these states delegates were still selected by party leaders.

Because so few states actually permitted the voters to select convention delegates, contenders could lose a majority of primaries or not enter them at all and still win their party's presidential nomination. The list of such nominees includes Woodrow Wilson and William Howard Taft in 1912; Warren Harding in 1920; Herbert Hoover in 1932; Thomas Dewey in 1948; Adlai Stevenson and Dwight Eisenhower in 1952; and Hubert Humphrey in 1968. Overall, only two-fifths of the top vote-getters in the primary season were nominated between 1912 and 1968.[11]

In those days candidates entered primaries to dispel doubts about their electability so they could gain the support of political bosses who controlled most of the convention delegates. In 1960 John F. Kennedy won primaries in Wisconsin and West Virginia, demonstrating that a Catholic could do well with Protestant voters, and only then gained the crucial support of skeptical big-city bosses (many of them Catholic). In 1968 Richard Nixon won enough primaries to dispel the "loser" reputation he had acquired after losing the presidency in 1960 and the California governor race in 1962.

In 1968 Hubert Humphrey won the Democratic nomination without having entered a single Democratic primary, because he was supported by party bosses who controlled more than 60 percent of the delegates. To many rank-and-file Democrats, especially those supporting Humphrey's rival Eugene McCarthy, the system seemed undemocratic. Media commentary, focusing on "smoke-filled rooms" and boss-dominated conventions, also delegitimized the system, in much the way that "King Caucus" had been delegitimized by the Jacksonians in the 1820s. Stung by their defeat in the subsequent presidential election, Democrats established a Commission on Party Structure and Delegate Selection (the McGovern-Fraser Commission). As a result of its recommendations, the Democrats adopted party rules requiring either primaries or open caucuses (at which any registered Democrat could participate) to select delegates. In both parties rules require that the preferences of the voters be translated directly into election of delegates. Gone were the "preference primaries" that had no effect on the composition of the state delegation. Most state parties and legislatures opted for primaries: there were thirty-eight such state contests by 1992, choosing three-quarters of the convention delegates. As a result of these reforms, contenders since 1972 have had to enter every primary and win in many. Gone are the days when a front-running contender could win the nomination without entering most primaries, or a Hubert Humphrey could be put over by party bosses.

Proponents of state primaries point out that since 1972 they have become mass-participation exercises in intraparty democracy, with almost 20 million voters participating in the 1992 Democratic contests (and somewhat less on the Republican side). One-quarter to one-third of the eligible voters turn out in competitive state contests. Overall turnout is lower (in 1992 it was 19 percent) because some states hold primaries after the nomination has been wrapped up.[12]

Critics of these reforms argue that primaries are undemocratic. First, because candidates tend to drop out early if they do not do well in the early going, many voters do not get a chance to express preferences among the full field. If a candidate wraps things up quickly, voters in states holding late primaries have no choice at all. To meet this criticism, California moved its primary up from June to early March for 1996 and New York quickly followed suit. About 80 percent of the delegates in 1996 were scheduled to be chosen by mid-March, giving most voters the opportunity to cast a meaningful ballot, a situation that should increase turnouts. Second, critics argue that primaries draw a disproportionate number of voters from higher socioeconomic groups and that the primary electorate is not representative of the diversity of the population.

Defenders respond that surveys taken since primary participation tripled in the 1970s have shown that there is little difference between the characteristics of primary and general election voters, though primary voters are slightly better educated and somewhat older and more affluent. The biggest differences are ideological: Democratic primary voters are more likely to be liberal and less likely to represent the conservative wing of the party; Republican primary voters are heavily skewed toward the conservative end of the spectrum and underrepresent moderates.

Critics argue that the unrepresentativeness of the primary electorates leads to nominations that do not reflect the preferences of the majority of party voters. Yet in all cases since 1972 the winner of the primary season (and the eventual nominee) *becomes* the first choice of party voters as expressed in public opinion polls. The winner of each party's nomination since 1972 (with the exception of the 1976 Republican convention that nominated incumbent President Gerald Ford) has been the candidate with the largest share of primary votes. In 1992, for example, Clinton won 52.1 percent of the Democratic primary vote, and Bush won 73.4 percent of the Republican. The primary winner is transformed into party leader by virtue of subjecting himself or herself to the endurance contest and coming out victorious.[13]

By tradition (as well as party rules), the first primary is held in New Hampshire, a contest that has been won by all presidents since 1960—until Clinton's second-place finish in 1992. The Democratic primary brings a large turnout of about two-thirds of the state's registered Democrats, including Catholic blue-collar working class and middle class voters, as well as some of the new professionals in high-tech industry. Republican voters are predominantly Protestant "Yankees" from the smaller towns, suburbs, and countryside. Because of the enormous media exposure it generates for the winner, it is one of the most important contests.[14] Consider Jimmy Carter's experience after his first-place finish in 1976: he appeared on the cover of major news magazines, and went from less than 1 percent support in the polls to more than 30 percent on the basis of his victory. Gary Hart's surprise victory in 1984 over Walter Mondale gave him the same media boost, resulting in a huge jump in the polls, from 4 to 40 percent in two weeks. Yet as Hart's ultimate defeat demonstrated, victory in New Hampshire must be followed by many other

Republican presidential hopefuls testing the waters in Manchester, New Hampshire, on February 19, 1995, a year before the New Hampshire primary. From left to right, Pat Buchanan, Phil Gramm, Arlen Specter, Bob Dole, Lamar Alexander, Bob Dornan, Alan Keyes, and Richard Lugar.

primary victories—it is no guarantee of success. Conversely, losing in New Hampshire need not be fatal, as Walter Mondale demonstrated in 1984. In 1992 Bill Clinton did not win a majority of votes in New Hampshire, but by coming in second to a regional candidate (Paul Tsongas of Massachusetts), he "won" the contest, and kept his candidacy viable until he could return to the South.

Until 1988 the primary season after New Hampshire involved widely separated contests over the next eight weeks, with candidates criss-crossing the nation. But in 1988 fourteen southern and border states decided to hold their primaries on March 8, and six other states joined in as well. The result: more than one-third of the convention delegates were chosen on that date, making "Super Tuesday" not only a large regional primary, but a make-or-break proposition as well. In 1988 victories on that day gave a major boost to the candidacy of Jesse Jackson. In 1992 it gave Bill Clinton front-runner status after his lackluster showings in Iowa and New Hampshire.[15]

The Shakeout

Contenders must do well in early contests or face quick elimination, given the high cost of campaigning. Those who get less than 10 percent of the vote in primaries lose their matching funding from the Treasury, which quickly sinks their campaign in a mountain of debt and often forces them from the race. Since 1992, Democratic candidates who fail to win 15 percent of the votes in each state in which they compete are not eligible to win delegates, which has the effect of dropping the weakest candidates out. Because Democrats forbid a statewide "winner-take-all" contest, requiring either proportional allocation of delegates or district contests, the momentum of the front-runner is slowed, and the contest may continue for a long time. On the Republican side, front-runners *are* boosted by the statewide "winner-take-all" system permitted by their party. In most states all convention delegates go to the contender with a plurality of votes, which reduces the GOP field quickly.

Front-runners tend to employ a twofold strategy: first, eliminate rivals who share the same ideology or come from the same region in the early primaries; then in the "shakeout" period when states in a specific region hold contests on the same day ("Junior Tuesday" and "Super Tuesday"), defeat other opponents. Long-shot candidates, after intensive campaigning in Iowa or New Hampshire, hope for an immediate breakthrough from the pack and front-runner status.[16] A candidate who does well in the early going will move up in the polls, get more PAC and direct-mail contributions (which in turn triggers more Treasury matching funds); by doing so he hopes to parlay the momentum ("Big Mo" as George Bush put it) into victory.[17] The network news provides more than twice as many "horse race" stories in the primary season as it does stories about substantive issues dividing the contenders; in consequence, a front-runner will get favorable publicity, and other contenders will find it harder to get their message out.[18]

A contender need not win a majority of the primaries or their delegates; it is enough to come out of the primary season with front-runner status. A contender leading the field with 41 percent or more of the delegates going into the national convention has always won the nomination, as Jimmy Carter did in 1976. The front-runner wins by convincing the remaining uncommitted delegates to support him.[19]

CONVENTION POLITICS

Delegates selected in the caucus and primary contests meet over four days to nominate a presidential candidate. They also agree on a platform and approve that candidate's choice of a running mate. The most important thing delegates must do is win over a national television audience. The nominee, in turn, must convert intraparty enemies into willing allies for the contest against the opposing party. Intense friction or an intraparty convention bloodbath makes it far more difficult for a candidate to win the White House.

Boss-Dominated Nominating Conventions: 1836–1968

The Russian political scientist Moisei Ostrogorski, visiting a late-nineteenth-century convention, described his impressions of a convention dominated by state and local party bosses:

> You realize what a colossal travesty of popular institutions you have just been witnessing. A greedy crowd of officeholders, or of office seekers, disguised as delegates of the people, on the pretense of holding the grand council of the party, indulged in, or were the victims of, intrigues and maneuvers, the object of which was the chief magistracy of the Greatest Republic of the two hemispheres—the succession to the Washingtons and the Jeffersons.[20]

Yet even Ostrogorski was compelled to admit that in assessing the line of American presidents nominated by these conventions, "you find that if they have not all been great men—far from it—they were all honorable men, and you cannot help repeating the American saying, 'God takes care of drunkards, little children, and the United States of America.' "[21]

"Less than one hundred men in any convention . . . really dictate what occurs," explained Bronx County's Democratic Party boss Ed Flynn in 1948.[22] The bosses of the delegations would pack them with loyal followers. The leaders would hold the proxies of the rank-and-file. In many states a "unit rule" would require the delegation to "caucus" (hold a meeting off the convention floor), and a majority of delegates under the guidance of the leaders would determine the entire state's votes, which would then be cast as a single unit, preventing defections by individual delegates to other candidates from affecting the state's vote. In 1932, for example, only 15 percent of the state delegations cast divided ballots.[23] The delegation might go to the convention uncommitted, nominally supporting a "favorite son" governor or senator, whom the delegation would support until the bosses were ready to make their move and support a real contender.

"What the party wants," British observer James Bryce observed late in the nineteenth century, "is not a good President but a good candidate," meaning someone who would win by uniting the party and assembling a majority coalition of voters, and then on becoming president, would distribute the spoils of victory to the bosses that had given him the nomination.[24] So contenders (or more precisely, their campaign managers, because contenders did not even attend conventions until Franklin Roosevelt accepted his nomination in 1932) dealt with the state party leaders. "In reality it is all a matter of bargaining," Ostrogorski observed. "They calculate, they appraise, they buy, they sell, but the bargain is rarely stated in definite terms: there is a tacit understanding that the delegate who gives his vote will have a claim on the lucky winner."[25]

"I authorize no bargains and will be bound by none," Lincoln telegraphed his managers in 1860 at Chicago's Wigwam Hall, site of the Republican convention. "Damn Lincoln," his zealous managers responded, and won over Indiana by offering Caleb Smith the job of Secretary of the Interior, Pennsylvania by giving Simon Cameron the War Department, and New York on the third ballot by offering Salmon Chase the Treasury Department. In 1912 Woodrow Wilson's campaign managers dealt away one cabinet position after another, as well as a promise of a vice presidential nomination. They also made a deal with Oscar Underwood: his supporters would give Wilson a chance to put together a coalition: if Wilson failed, he would then support Underwood against House Speaker Champ Clark. Wilson finally managed to win on the 46th ballot. In 1932 Franklin Roosevelt's campaign manager James Farley made a deal with Virginia to put Senator Claude Swanson in the cabinet, won Missouri by getting the Pendergast machine's support in return for promises of patronage, won Louisiana by seating a delegation headed by Huey Long in a fight over credentials of rival party factions (and Long then helped keep Alabama and Mississippi from bolting away from FDR on the third ballot), and won Texas by offering FDR's rival John Garner the vice presidency. But there were limits to deal making. The corrupt Tammany Hall organization offered to support Roosevelt instead of his rival Al Smith if Roosevelt would guarantee New York City Mayor Jimmy Walker immunity from federal prosecution; Roosevelt turned down the deal. Instead he ran against the corruption of Tammany Hall.

In a few conventions bosses might unite on a single candidate or a president's designated heir. Until the 1960s, however, most conventions either required a compromise or a factional victory. Politicians played games of bluff and counterbluff, with many ballots, as a front-runner tried to build a critical coalition (until 1936 it took a two-thirds vote in the Democratic convention) by convincing uncommitted delegations to join their bandwagon. Other candidates might gang up, encourage defections, and block the front-runner. In 1852 Democrats took forty-nine ballots before Pierce won; in 1912, forty-six for Wilson; and in 1924 it took 103 ballots to nominate John W. Davis. On the Republican side, things tended to move faster; yet it still took thirty-six ballots for Garfield in 1880, ten for Coolidge in 1920, and six for Willkie in 1940.

To stop a front-runner, a rival coalition would challenge credentials of some of his delegates on the first day, provoke a platform fight to try to divide the front-runner's coalition on the second, or raise a procedural issue that might cause defections on the day of the nomination. The votes on these procedural challenges became tests to see if a front-runner could control the convention. If so, delegates would not be diverted or divided by extraneous issues, nor would they desert the coalition and spark a bandwagon to a rival camp. Eisenhower defeated "Mr. Conservative," Senator Robert Taft, after winning procedural votes in a closely divided contest in 1952. Even as late as 1980 Edward Kennedy used these tactics against Jimmy Carter at the Democratic convention: he made the convention vote on whether to maintain or overturn a rule requiring that delegates be "pledged" to candidates who had won them in primaries; he hoped to abolish the rule under the rubric of allowing a "conscience" vote, that would then allow him to obtain support from delegates

Carter had won in the primaries. His failure to win on the procedural votes sealed his fate at the convention.

Boss-dominated conventions might reject all the leading contenders and choose a "dark horse" initially given little chance of success. The dark horse might have been the second or third choice of many delegates but the first choice of few. The strategy of the dark horse was to block the favorite and create a deadlock among front-runners. James K. Polk was the first dark horse, winning the Democratic nomination in 1844 on the ninth ballot. Franklin Pierce won the Democratic nomination on the 49th ballot in 1852. In 1876 Rutherford B. Hayes won the Republican nomination on the seventh ballot. Recent Republican dark horses have included Warren Harding in 1920, and Wendell Willkie in 1940. Dark horse nominees have done well in the elections: all but Willkie turned out to be winners, which may say something for the political acumen of the bosses who arranged for their nomination. The changes in party rules that made the conventions registering devices for the preferences of voters in primaries ended dark horse candidacies.

Candidate-Dominated Nominating Conventions: 1972 to the Present

Since 1972, convention delegates have voted for the presidential candidate who won them in the caucuses and primaries. In 1980 the Democrats passed rule 11-H to make it absolutely clear that: "All delegates to the national convention shall be bound to vote for the presidential candidate whom they were elected to support for at least the first convention ballot, unless released in writing by the presidential candidate." Delegates who try to violate the rule may be replaced by the candidate with an alternate. This "pledge" rule was abolished at the next convention (the Republicans had a similar rule in 1976 and abolished theirs in 1980), but the idea that the delegate was bound to vote the way the primary and caucus contests had turned out remains the fundamental legitimating principle of the modern convention.[26] This principle also required the parties to do away with the unit rule: a majority no longer casts the ballots of the entire state's delegation, and divided balloting is now the norm, with less than 14 percent of the states casting unified ballots since 1972.[27]

Delegates are not demographically representative of the party rank-and-file. They are better educated and more affluent than most voters. More than two-thirds have finished college, and more than half the Democrats and one-third of the Republicans hold advanced degrees; more than one-fifth have law degrees; another fifth have masters and doctorates. More than half have incomes over $50,000, with one-third having incomes over $100,000, well above the average family income. Democratic party rules require that half the delegates be women; Republicans do not have a formal rule, but more than two-fifths of their delegates are women. Democrats in 1992 had more Catholic (30 percent), Jewish (10 percent), and African-American (16 percent) representation at their conventions than did Republicans (with 27 percent, 2 percent, and 4 percent, respectively), reflecting differences in their electoral coalitions.[28]

Until the 1970s many governors and members of Congress attended conventions as part of their state delegations. Initially the reforms induced members of the party-in-government to drop their attendance, because they felt uncomfortable and unwelcome. But since then the pendulum has once again swung the other way. Convention delegates are experienced in elective politics: more than two-thirds at most conventions have had prior experience holding public or party office, and more than half have attended previous conventions.

Because convention delegates today merely register the results of primary and caucus contests, the element of peer review has been eliminated. In the past, professional politicians got to know contenders personally and could observe their political skills and judge their character on the basis of firsthand observation. But there is no way for voters to take the measure of contenders in person and separate those with character and ability from the media hypesters. To remedy the situation, since 1984, Democratic rules have provided for a category of superdelegates: Most Democratic members of the House and Senate are added automatically to their state delegations, as well as the members of the Democratic National Committee. These delegates, pledged to no particular candidate, accounted for 14 percent of convention delegates in 1984 and were increased to 18 percent by 1992.[29] Their presence was supposed to restore some element of professional peer review, and in theory they might hold the balance of power if two candidates came into the convention and neither had a majority of the delegates. In fact, these delegates, although nominally uncommitted, have voted heavily for the front-runner at the end of the primary season. In 1992, bowing to the reality, Democrats adopted a rule providing that the state party officials added to the delegations would be required to reflect the state's primary or caucus vote, though the congressional superdelegates would remain nominally uncommitted.

In most conventions a majority of Republican delegates call themselves conservatives (60 percent in 1988 and 70 percent in 1992), with the remainder self-described moderates. Democratic delegates are fairly evenly divided between liberals and moderates (the split was 47 percent liberal and 44 percent moderate in 1992), as the party since 1972 has moved from a liberal to a centrist position. Republicans find it increasingly difficult to moderate extreme right-wing groups at the convention, which may get more media attention than their numbers deserve. Democrats have to deal with issues of "cultural politics": the impact of women, young delegates, and gays in delegations, as well as many minorities (20 percent of the 1988 convention was African American) may lead many potential voters to assume that the Democrats do not represent white "middle Americans" or their values. In an era in which stereotyping of groups has great political potency, Republicans must manage at their convention to avoid charges that they are a lily-white party excluding others in the American mosaic. In turn, Democrats at their convention must convince voters that they are not simply a disparate collection of minorities.

What the Convention Does

"The rise of the primaries has made it inevitable that the nomination is settled before the convention begins," observed New York Democratic Senator Daniel Patrick Moynihan, adding "the convention does not decide and it does not debate."[30] If the country knows who will be nominated on the first ballot, what then is the value of holding a convention? "Our activists and leaders still need to meet with each other," Georgia Republican Representative Newt Gingrich pointed out, to converse about "their beliefs and about the future." What the delegates do at the convention, as they listen to speeches, accept or reject platform amendments, decide on party rules, and speak to the television reporters roaming the hall, may divide or unify the party, bring it new supporters from the television audience, or alternatively, alienate voters and show a party in disarray on the evening network news.

The national party committee organizes the convention business into staged segments, or "podium events," including addresses by party notables, showcasing of elected officials running for other office, presentation of documentary films about past presidents, and floor demonstrations for candidates. In 1984 Republicans began producing a "convention film" highlighting the accomplishments of the incumbent president—their eighteen-minute effort, "America's Back," cost $435,000. In response to this canned propaganda, television networks have increasingly cut away from podium events: they go to commercial breaks, discussion by their own anchors and commentators, interviews with delegates on the floor, or they bring in guests to comment on the proceedings.

The nominee addresses the convention and a nationwide audience and may obtain a convention "bounce" in the form of higher poll ratings. Between 1964 and 1992, the bounce has averaged 6 percent, and although temporary, it can provide the presidential campaign with some initial momentum. But it may do a candidate no ultimate good: according to NYT/CBS polls, in 1980 Carter increased his ratings 17 points; in 1984 Mondale went up 16 points; in 1988 Dukakis went up 9 points; but all three lost. However, in 1992 Clinton bounced an incredible 24 points, taking a 56–31 lead against George Bush, who had been in the lead until the Democratic conclave. Clinton's advantage then proved insurmountable.

A candidate can self-destruct at the convention. Barry Goldwater destroyed his chances in 1964 when he told his cheering supporters that "extremism in the defense of liberty is no vice," allowing Lyndon Johnson to paint him as an extremist who would start World War III. (After the convention, when Goldwater commercials appealed to voters with the slogan, "In your heart, you know he's right," comedians unfairly retorted with the line, "In your heart, you know he's crazy.") Walter Mondale's candor in 1984—"Taxes will go up, and anyone who says they won't is not telling the truth"—provided the opening wedge for Ronald Reagan to portray him as a traditional Democratic "tax and spend" liberal, thus securing Reagan's landslide reelection victory.

Above all, the nominee uses the convention to try to avoid a "carryover" effect from the bitter primary fight. The candidate wants to unify the party, mollify rank-and-file voters who supported other contenders, and give them a reason to vote for him in the general election.[31] If a candidate successfully positions him- or herself and bridges the gap between different demographic, ideological, and regional wings, his or her nomination should not result in too many defections from the party.[32]

Forming the Ticket

Before the election of 1804, tickets were informal, because all candidates ran for presidential electoral votes. The twelfth Amendment, which took effect that year, separated electoral votes for president and vice president, and party leaders in the congressional caucus responded by making separate informal "nominations" for vice president. With the 1832 Democratic convention Andrew Jackson established two principles: party conventions would nominate the vice presidential candidate, and in doing so they would follow the wishes of the president. Yet the custom was not always followed: in 1840 Martin Van Buren ran for president with different vice presidential candidates on his ticket in each state, because the Democratic national convention had resolved not to endorse any candidate for the office, and left it instead to state parties to "nominate" their own vice presidential candidates to appear on the ballot with Van Buren. The failure of that experiment (Van Buren lost the election) led to a return to Jackson's approach.

Occasionally a party has nominated a vice presidential candidate from the opposition party to create a "unity" ticket and divide the opposition. John Tyler ran for vice president on the Whig ticket in 1840 but was himself a Democrat. In 1864 Republican Abraham Lincoln ran with Democrat Andrew Johnson on the National Union ticket. In both cases, the death of the president and the succession of a politician from the other party led to governmental gridlock and worse: Tyler was censured and Johnson impeached and almost removed from office.

Prospects that a president and his vice president will serve two terms together are dim. Of the fifty-two presidential elections held between 1789 and 1992, only seven resulted in the reelection of the entire ticket. Presidents who kept their running mates through a second term were Washington, Monroe, Wilson, Franklin Roosevelt (who then ditched Garner for his third term), Eisenhower (after an abortive attempt to dump Nixon), Nixon (whose vice president, Spiro Agnew, resigned in 1973), and Reagan. George Bush was renominated with Vice President Dan Quayle, but the ticket was defeated in 1992.

When forming a ticket, the object, as Senator Barry Goldwater, the Republican nominee in 1964, succinctly put it, "is to get more votes." The presidential nominee usually balances the ticket by region and sometimes by religion: in 1960 John Kennedy, a northern Catholic, ran with Lyndon Johnson, a southern Protestant. In 1964 the Republicans nominated a Catholic vice presidential nominee, as did the Democrats in 1968, 1972, and 1984. The Democrats in 1984 had the first (and through 1992 the only) gender-balanced ticket when they nominated New York Representative Geraldine Ferraro. Occasionally a liberal will choose a conservative, or vice versa, but ideological balancing is rare. Most presidential nominees choose running mates whose ideas are compatible with their own. Often a governor or former governor or other "outsider" running for president will choose a senator or other Washington insider as running mate (Eisenhower and Nixon, Carter and Mondale, Reagan and Bush, Clinton and Gore) or vice versa (Nixon and Agnew).

In boss-dominated conventions, the vice presidency was often a coalition prize given to the defeated wing of the party. Coalition-building deals, however, often produced mediocre men for the vice presidency; in the nineteenth century, six could not even win renomination for the next election. Since World War II the quality of nominees has improved. Truman, Johnson, Mondale, and Bush all had impressive credentials when they joined the ticket. In fact, between 1952 and 1992, thirteen vice presidential nominees had more experience in public life than their running mates.[33] In 1992 the pattern was repeated: Bill Clinton had served 13 years in public office, all in his home state of Arkansas, and his running mate Al Gore had served sixteen years in Congress—eight in the House of Representatives and eight in the Senate.

The major problem with the selection process is that it comes at the end of the convention, when the candidate and campaign advisors are exhausted, and they may not devote sufficient time to their choice. A hurried decision resulted in George McGovern's selection of Tom Eagleton in 1972; a distinguished liberal senator from Missouri, his history of shock treatments for depression surfaced after his nomination, forcing him to withdraw from the ticket. Yet it is not all that clear that unhurried consideration, lengthy interviewing of contenders, or extensive consultation within the party always produces a better nomination than a rushed effort. Last-minute vice presidential nominees have included Lyndon Johnson, Edmund Muskie, Robert Dole, and George Bush, all of whom had extensive national government experience and were well qualified for the presidency. More leisurely consideration gave us Spiro Agnew, a mediocre and corrupt politician who ultimately resigned from the vice presidency in disgrace after pleading no contest to charges of corruption (taking bribes) when he was county executive and Maryland governor. Although Walter Mondale used a lengthy interviewing process, his staff failed to uncover any of the allegations about the alleged improprieties of Geraldine Ferraro's husband in his businesses—allegations that hurt the Mondale campaign.

Nancy Reagan turns to wave to her husband's image after addressing the 1984 Republican National Convention. Ronald Reagan was watching from his hotel suite. Such scripted video gimmicks did nothing to attract viewers, and audiences for the national conventions diminished in the 1980s.

Convention Media Coverage

With the suspense drained out of conventions, they have lost their audience: Prime-time convention coverage in 1976 by the three networks consisted of 142 hours; by 1992 it was down to less than thirty, with each network averaging two hours of programming nightly. The networks reduced coverage (dropping gavel-to-gavel coverage in 1984) because viewership had diminished: In 1968 each network averaged a 9.5 rating, while by 1992 each received approximately a 5.3 rating, and for each network that equaled approximately 4.9 million households. To make these figures more meaningful, consider this: In 1988 in New York City, more viewers watched *each* of the channels showing the Humphrey Bogart/Katherine Hepburn movie *The African Queen,* a Yankees baseball game, and Charles Bronson's movie *Death Wish* than watched the Democratic convention nominate Michael Dukakis. Because convention managers have managed to transform an exciting spectacle of real politics into a dull, stage-managed exercise of party propaganda, they have no one to blame but themselves for alienating and then losing their audience.

NOMINATIONS AND GOVERNANCE

Every few years a small cottage industry of political scientists, media commentators, and professional campaign experts tries to reform the system of presidential nominations. Critics argue that the self-selected field emphasizes the wrong kind of experience and downgrades real expertise based on a long apprenticeship in national government, that the need for a large campaign organization provides influence-peddlers with the opportunity to finance the costly nominating campaign, that the staffers who surround candidates are schooled in arts of media manipulation, and that nominations are now settled on the basis of media manipulation of an unrepresentative primary electorate.

Although some of these criticisms are exaggerated, it is clear that nominating politics divides the presidential candidate and his campaign organization from the state party organizations. Primaries promote an individualistic, media-centered approach to presidential politics, rather than a collegial party spirit. If candidates can win the nomination by going over the heads of party leaders and communicating directly to voters, they may decide they owe nothing to party leaders or workers—and the feelings will be reciprocated. To the extent that incompetent, inexperienced, egocentric, and unscrupulous candidates and their campaign staffers attempt to use the media to fool voters, the authority of the presidency is diminished—especially when the "hook" used by journalists to report on the nominating campaign emphasizes candidate success at media manipulation. One reform often called for by critics is a return of party politics at the conventions: as many as half of each state's convention delegation should consist of uncommitted delegates chosen by the state party professionals. The primary and caucus contests could winnow down contenders, but the politicians would make the final choice, and that in turn would force contenders to forge close links with the party organizations.

Defenders of the current system claim that the media exposes phonies. They point out that peer review and the politicking that goes with it has often led to mediocre nominees; the better candidates were nominated by bosses only after the advent of primaries in the early 1900s forced some element of accountability to party rank-and-file voters. They say that the constraints that bosses placed on presidents hardly served the public interest, and that we are better off without the horse-trading and corruption that attended convention politics. Today presidents are constrained, but in different ways: They can bypass the bosses, it is true, but they no longer can ignore the interests of the party rank and file, because they will have to run the primary gauntlet for renomination. Peer review could easily return us to the times in which popular contenders were denied nomination in favor of candidates backed by party bosses—making a mockery of intraparty democracy.

The argument between proponents and opponents of the modern nominating system has raged for more than two decades. In that time, the effects of divisive intraparty battles, negative ad campaigns, and negative media coverage have had an effect: the appeal of the nominees to voters has sharply declined, and incumbent presidents have become vulnerable to intraparty challengers. There may be a tradeoff between intraparty democracy and accountability and presidential power. Critics may ask if we really want a president to be distracted for the whole final year of his or her first term by renomination politics, and if the values of intraparty democracy are so important that we are prepared to see presidents devote much of their time to fending off opponents within their own party.

The current nominating game has significant consequences for governance. The way candidates are nominated does nothing to enhance their power once in office. Presidents become beholden to special interests and unrepresentative coalitions, they engage in endurance and popularity contests that are exhausting and demeaning, and they are encouraged to deal with issues tactically rather than substantively. They surround themselves with spinmeisters and pollsters who will eventually become part of their White House staff, and who act as if "politics is war" once involved in governance. Divisive intraparty contests often split the nominee's party and exacerbate tensions, making it difficult to put together enduring voter coalitions. The nominee's character, program, and private life are subject to media scrutiny, and rumor and innuendo cheapen and demean the nomination process. The authority of a newly elected president who has spent two years being picked apart by the media is bound to be reduced. Columnist David Broder once propounded Broder's Law: Any candidate willing to do what it now takes to win the nomination and election is not safely to be trusted with the office. As the general election campaign begins, many voters probably think that about sums it up.

FURTHER READING

Books

John Aldrich, *Before the Convention,* Chicago: University of Chicago Press, 1980.

Larry Bartels, *Presidential Primaries and the Dynamics of Public Choice,* Princeton, NJ: Princeton University Press, 1988.

James Ceasar, *Reforming the Reforms,* Cambridge, MA: Ballinger, 1992.

James Chase, *Emergence of the Presidential Nominating Convention, 1789–1832,* Urbana, IL: University of Illinois Press, 1973.

Alexander Heard and Michael Nelson, eds., *Presidential Selection,* Durham, NC: Duke University Press, 1987.

Kathleen Hall Jamieson and David Birdsell, *Presidential Debates,* New York: Oxford University Press, 1988.

Gary L. Rose, ed., *Controversial Issues in Presidential Selection,* 2nd ed., Albany, NY: State University Press of New York, 1994.

Byron Shafer, *Quiet Revolution: The Struggle for the Democratic Party and the Shaping of Post Reform Politics,* New York: Russell Sage, 1983.

Larry Smith and Dan Nimmo, *Orchestrating National Party Conventions in the Telepolitical Age,* Westport, CT: Praeger, 1991.

Peverell Squire, ed., *The Iowa Caucuses and the Presidential Nominating Process,* Boulder, CO: Westview Press, 1989.

Frank Sorauf, *Inside Campaign Finance: Myths and Realities,* New Haven, CT: Yale University Press, 1992.

Documentary Sources

Richard Bain and Judith Parris, *Convention Decisions and Voting Records,* 2nd ed., Washington, DC: Brookings Institution, 1973.

Commission on Party Structure and Delegate Selection, *Mandate for Reform,* Washington, DC, 1970.

Commission on Presidential Nomination and Party Structure, *Openness, Participation and Party Building: Reforms for a Stronger Democratic Party,* Washington, DC, 1979.

Kirk H. Porter and Donald Bruce Johnson, *National Party Platforms, 1840–1976,* rev. ed., Urbana, IL: University of Illinois Press, 1978 (supplements available for later elections).

National Party Conventions, 1831–1984, Washington, DC: Congressional Quarterly Press, 1987.

NOTES

1. Eugene McCarthy, *The Year of the People,* Garden City, NY: Doubleday, 1969, p. 69.

2. Ibid., p. 85.

3. Larry Sabato, *Feeding Frenzy,* New York: Free Press, 1991.

4. William Keech and David Matthews, *The Party's Choice,* Washington, DC: Brookings Institution, 1976, pp. 14–19; Arthur Hadley, *The Invisible Primary,* Englewood Cliffs, NJ: Prentice-Hall, 1976.

5. Howard Reiter, *Selecting the President,* Philadelphia: University of Pennsylvania Press, 1985, p. 35.

6. *Buckley v. Valeo,* 424 U.S. 1, 1976.

7. Michael Robinson, Clyde Wilcox, and Paul Marshall, "The Presidency: Not for Sale," *Public Opinion,* March/April, 1989, p. 51.

8. As of 1992 only ten states and the District of Columbia used proportional representation in caucuses and primaries held by the Republican Party. Democratic rules required proportional allocation of delegates in all contests.

9. *Congressional Quarterly Weekly Reports,* July 4, 1992, p. 70; Austin Ranney, "Participation in Precinct Caucuses," in James I. Lengle and Byron E. Shafer, *Presidential Politics,* 2nd ed., New York: St. Martin's Press, 1983, p. 175.

10. State election laws establish the rules for primaries: in *closed* primaries only Democrats vote in the Democratic primary and Republicans in the Republican primary; in *open* primaries independents may also vote in one party's primary; in *crossover* primaries voters from any party as well as independents may participate.

11. John Geer, *Nominating Presidents,* Westport, CT: Greenwood, 1989, p. 2.

12. Barbara Norrander, "Turnout in Super Tuesday Primaries: The Composition of the Electorate," Paper delivered at annual meeting of the *American Political Science Association,* Atlanta, GA, August 30–September 2, 1989, p. 10.

13. William H. Lucy, "Polls, Primaries and Presidential Nominations," *Journal of Politics,* Vol. 35, no. 4, November, 1973, p. 837; later calculations by author.

14. Gary Orren and Nelson Polsby, *Media and Momentum,* Chatham, NJ: Chatham House, 1987.

15. Barbara Norrander, *Super Tuesday,* Lexington, KY: University of Kentucky Press, 1992.

16. John A. Aldrich, *Before the Convention,* Chicago: University of Chicago Press, 1980, p. 161.

17. James Beniger, "Winning the Presidential Nomination: National Polls and State Primary Elections," *Public Opinion Quarterly,* Vol. 10, no. 1, Spring, 1976, pp. 22–29; Harvey Zeidenstein, "Presidential Primaries—Reflections of 'The People's Choice,' " *Journal of Politics,* Vol. 32, no. 2, November, 1970, pp. 836–874.

18. Robert S. Lichter, "How the Press Covered the Primaries," *Public Opinion,* Vol. 11, July/August, 1988, pp. 45–49.

19. Steven J. Brams, *The Presidential Election Game,* New Haven, CT: Yale University Press, 1978, p. 46.

20. Moisei Ostrogorski, *Democracy and the Organization of Political Parties, Vol. 2: The United States,* Garden City, NY: Anchor Books, 1964, p. 143.

21. Ibid.

22. Ed Flynn, *You're the Boss,* New York: Collier Books, 1962, p. 111.

23. Howard Reiter, op. cit., p. 74.

24. James Bryce, *The American Commonwealth,* "Why Great Men Are Not Chosen President," New York: G. P. Putnam's Sons, 1959, pp. 27–34.

25. Moisei Ostrogorski, op. cit., p. 137.

26. As of 1992, Democrats retained a rule stating that delegates "in all good conscience should reflect the sentiments of those who elected them."

27. Howard Reiter, op. cit., p. 74.

28. For Democrats see *New York Times,* July 13, 1992, p. B-6; for Republicans see *Washington Post,* August 16, 1992, p. A19.

29. Michael Goldstein, op. cit., p. 26.

30. *New York Times,* July 20, 1984, p. A-10.

31. Walter J. Stone, "The Carryover Effect in Presidential Elections," *American Political Science Review,* Vol. 80, no. 1, March, 1986, pp. 271–279.

32. John Aldrich, "A Downsian Spatial Model with Party Activism," *American Political Science Review,* Vol. 77, no. 4, December, 1983, pp. 974–990.

33. Joel K. Goldstein, *The Modern American Vice Presidency,* Princeton, NJ: Princeton University Press, 1982, p. 85.

CHAPTER 6

Presidential Elections

I run for the Presidency of the United States because it is the center of action, and in a free society, the chief responsibility of the President is to set before the American people the unfinished public business of our country.

—John F. Kennedy

INTRODUCTORY CASE: "GIVE 'EM HELL, HARRY!"

Harry Truman did not have a chance to win the 1948 presidential election, or so all the pollsters said. Elmo Roper gave up polling in early September, announcing that Republican candidate Thomas Dewey was sure to win. Journalists believed the pollsters, and a survey reported that only one member of the National Press Club thought Truman would win. All forty-seven reporters covering Dewey's campaign for the *New York Times* told their editors he would win, and the paper forecast a Republican landslide. *Newsweek*'s survey of fifty political pundits was unanimous: Dewey by a landslide. Bookies gave eighteen-to-one odds on Dewey.

"I'm going to make a common sense, intellectually honest campaign," Truman wrote in his diary. "It will be novelty—and it will win." Truman rode 31,000 miles to deliver 271 speeches on the *Ferdinand Magellan,* his campaign train. Republican Senator Robert Taft complained that "at every whistlestop in the West" Truman was attacking him and the rest of the Republicans in the "Do-Nothing Eightieth Congress." The press began referring to Truman's "whistlestop campaign." "Give 'em hell Harry," cried a supporter in Seattle. "I'm going to give them hell," Truman responded. Soon Democrats all across the country were talking about "Give 'Em Hell" Harry's speeches.

Dewey rode 16,000 miles and made thirteen speeches and forty-seven rear platform appearances on his campaign train, the Victory Special. Ahead in all the polls, Dewey took what the *New York Daily News* referred to as "the high road of rich baritone homilies." His inspiring message in Arizona: "Our future lies before us." To New Yorkers: "We need a rudder to our ship of state." He promised programs to "join us together in a more perfect union." "GOP with Dewey leading it means Grand Old Platitudes," not Grand Old Party, the Democrats joked.

At 11:30 PM on election night, Dewey's campaign manager, Herbert Brownell, claimed Pennsylvania and the election. At 1:45 AM Brownell claimed New York and once again proclaimed victory, but Dewey himself stayed in his suite at the Hotel

Plaza in Manhattan, listening intently to the returns. Meanwhile in Excelsior Springs, Missouri, Truman told his aides around midnight that he would carry Ohio, Illinois, and California, and win the election. Then he went to bed. He awoke the next morning at 10:30 AM to receive Dewey's concession telegram.

Truman was in high spirits, mimicking the radio commentator Herbert V. Kaltenborn, who had proclaimed confidently the night before that "when the farm votes are in, Thomas Dewey will be the next President of the United States." When he returned to Washington, DC, a sign on the *Washington Post*'s building greeted him, proclaiming, "Mr. President, we are ready to eat crow whenever you are ready to serve it." For waiting reporters at the train station, Truman held up a copy of the election-night *Chicago Tribune* with its headline "Dewey Defeats Truman." And he roared and roared with laughter.

Only one pollster got the election right. Leslie Biffle, the secretary of the United States Senate, had conducted his own nonscientific poll at Truman's request. Biffle went around disguised as a chicken peddler and asked people how they would vote. "Listen, Harry, you don't have to worry," he had telephoned Truman after his grass-roots interviewing. Perhaps that was why *Truman* was the only member of the National Press Club to predict correctly the outcome of the 1948 elections.[1]

Truman's come-from-behind victory in 1948 shows that almost anything can happen on the road to the White House. Journalists are often criticized, especially by political scientists, for emphasizing the "horse race" aspects of presidential campaigns, but in fact campaigns *are* horse races, in which skill at running counts for much more than initial advantages, issues mean less than the projection of character, luck plays a large role, and almost anything can happen.

The ways in which presidents reach the White House have profound effects on how they govern, and, once in office, their calculations about what it takes to get reelected affect every aspect of Oval Office decision making. Do presidents obtain the political authority and resources necessary to govern by virtue of their election by "the people"? Unfortunately, in the past thirty years their authority has been diminished by the campaign tactics used by candidates and the increasingly negative coverage of general election campaigns by the media. Presidents make commitments in campaigns that are not possible for them to meet, and that contributes to voter disillusionment, cynicism, or apathy, all of which makes it difficult for incumbents to govern.

COMPETING FOR ELECTORAL COLLEGE VOTES

Everyone knows that the president and vice president are the only two officials elected by all the American people—but everyone is wrong. They are the only elected officials in American government who are *not* elected directly by the voters. The Constitution provides for their selection by an electoral college. Each state chooses its electors (equal to its Senate and House representation in Congress) by any method its state legislature prescribes. In the early 1800s many state legislatures chose electors; all states but South Carolina switched to popular election by 1832, and South Carolina switched in 1856.

Mechanics of the Electoral College Vote

On the first Tuesday after the first Monday in November, voters in each state choose the presidential electors. In each state the party's candidates for electors run on a "slate" chosen by the presidential candidate. Voters may think they are voting for president when they enter the voting booth, but actually they are voting for one party's entire slate of electors, even though their names do not appear. A plurality of the popular vote in each state except Maine is enough to elect all the members of the slate, and other candidates receive nothing. (Maine chooses two of its four electors in congressional district contests.)

Many people believe that the entire electoral college meets, but that too is incorrect: electors meet in each separate state capitol and cast secret ballots on the first Monday after the second Wednesday in December after the election.[2] These ballots are then sent to the speaker of the House of Representatives, and they are opened at the Capitol early in January by the incumbent (and possibly outgoing) vice president of the United States in the presence of the newly elected Congress. In 1960, Vice President Nixon announced that John Kennedy had defeated him for the presidency, and in 1968 Vice President Hubert Humphrey had to announce that Nixon had beaten him!

Popular versus Electoral Votes

Surprisingly, the candidate with the most popular votes can lose. In 1824 Andrew Jackson had a plurality of popular votes, but no one received a majority in the electoral college, and John Quincy Adams won the subsequent House contingency election. In 1876 Rutherford Hayes defeated the more popular Samuel J. Tilden, after a

Contingency Elections

If the electoral college does not produce a majority for president—270 of the 538 votes cast—the Constitution specifies that Congress must conduct a contingency election. The newly elected House chooses from amongst the three candidates who received the most electoral college votes. Each state's House delegation casts a single vote (determined by a majority of its representatives). A majority is necessary to elect the president. The District of Columbia has no vote in the contingency election, because it does not have voting members of the House.

If the electoral college does not produce a majority for vice president, the Constitution specifies that the Senate chooses between the two candidates who received the most electoral college votes. Each senator casts one vote. A majority is necessary to elect the vice president.

If the House deadlocks, the newly elected vice president serves as acting president until the House resolves the deadlock and elects a new president.

special commission appointed by Congress awarded disputed electoral college votes to Hayes. In 1888 Benjamin Harrison defeated Grover Cleveland, though the latter had more popular votes.

Slight shifts in other elections might have produced similar results: in 1976 a shift of less than 10,000 votes in Hawaii and Ohio would have reelected Gerald Ford, even though Carter still would have had more popular votes. Even in 1988, when George Bush won a comfortable 54–46 percent popular vote victory over Michael Dukakis, shifts of 0.6 percent of the total popular vote (in the right eleven states) would have shifted the results to the Democrat.[3] Mathematicians claim that the discrepancy between the popular and electoral college vote should occur in one of every three elections in which the popular margin is less than 300,000.[4] The American people and Congress seem willing to live with the possibility of a discrepancy rather than reform the system.

The Electoral College and Campaign Strategy

The contest for presidential electors is won or lost on a winner-take-all statewide basis, and therefore campaign strategy must deal in winning states, not simply in demonstrating strength amongst demographic and ideological groups of voters. Nothing in the Constitution requires this system of winner-take-all elections. State legislatures can apportion electors as they wish, and some have done so by holding contests in congressional districts (South Carolina until 1856, Michigan in 1892, Maine since 1972). But all other states opted for the winner-take-all system because as soon as some did so, they provided more incentives for candidates to campaign there than in states still using a system that permitted split results.[5]

Candidates concentrate on states that constitute their geographic base, those with a large number of electoral votes, and those in which the contest is close. They cede the opposition most of its geographic base, as well as states that they have little chance of winning. The most effective strategy for candidates is to spend time and resources on the campaign trail according to the 3/2s rule: take the square root of a state's electoral college vote and then cube that number. In comparing New Jersey with Montana, the rule gives New Jersey a weight of 64 to Montana's 8, which means that a candidate should spend eight times the effort in the former as in the latter, even though New Jersey has only four times as many electoral college votes.[6]

Because campaign trails such as Truman's whistlestop campaign or Kennedy's motorcades are no longer essential in an age of high technology, these "rules" don't require candidates to be in the states in person, but are better used as guides to allocating resources for television commercials and other media efforts. These are concentrated on the "Big Eight" states with the most electoral votes: California (54), New York (33), Texas (32), Florida (25), Pennsylvania (23), Illinois (22), Ohio (21), and Michigan (18). These states in and of themselves accounted for 43 percent of the electoral college vote in the 1990s.

Between 1932 and 1944 Democrats won all four national elections handily by relying on their strength in the "Solid South" (which after the Civil War had become a one-party Democratic region) and on votes from the industrial north. In the post–New Deal period, 1948 through 1960, competition for electoral votes was more balanced. The Democrat's strength in the South splintered, and it eroded in New England, the upper Midwest, the Great Plains, and the Rocky Mountain states. Through the 1992 elections the Republicans consolidated their strength west of the Mississippi and made the South highly competitive. Democratic strength eroded throughout the nation, so that by the late 1980s their base consisted of the District of Columbia, Minnesota, Hawaii, Massachusetts, Rhode Island, and West Virginia. Some commentators began referring to a "Republican Lock" on the electoral college, though the election of Bill Clinton in 1992 put at least a temporary halt to that line of analysis.

To win the presidency, Democrats in 1976 and 1992 nominated "sunbelt" candidates who could compete in the industrial states, win a share of southern and border states, and carry California (to offset Republican advantages in other western states). No Democrat has ever won the presidency without winning a majority of southern states, and (Clinton excepted) without winning Texas. Democrats often *nominate* northern liberals, but they rarely *elect* them: Since 1944 the Democrats have not won a national election without a border- or southern-state politician on the ticket, and in four of their six victories, the ticket was headed by that candidate.

Republican candidates do best when they have a southern or western base, capitalizing on sunbelt politics. They go after Illinois, Michigan, Florida, Texas, and Virginia, and especially California. The Republican nominating process is weighted toward candidates who have strength in these states, so that Republicans usually start out with their most viable candidates—which may explain their record of success since 1968.

FINANCING THE CAMPAIGN

There are two campaigns, one for money and the other for votes. Money buys the organization that creates a message and an image, purchases the air time to deliver the message, and enables the candidate to create an organization to harvest the votes.

Traditional Financing

When voters were mobilized primarily by party organizations, campaigns were much less expensive. Candidates needed funds for transportation, salaries for staffers, preparation of campaign materials at rallies, and "walking around money" for state and local party workers who would "pull" voters in the precincts on election day—and sometimes pay them to vote! As late as 1960, the parties spent only $30 million on the campaigns (about fifty cents for each of the 68.8 million votes cast).

Campaign finance laws passed in 1907, 1925, and 1943 were supposed to prohibit corporate, banking, and union contributions to campaigns, and in the 1940s the Hatch Acts prohibited civil servants from making donations. Yet these laws were easily evaded. Corporations could funnel cash to firms or suppliers that provided them with services or goods, by accepting overbilling, with the understanding that the money would go to campaigns. Employees of corporations and trade associations could be given high salaries and bonuses, with the understanding that some of the money would be "laundered" into campaigns. Unions could provide campaigns with field workers and not be prosecuted for violating laws. Campaigns kept haphazard records, and no one thought of prosecuting anyone for violations. When a law was passed supposedly limiting campaign committees in a presidential election to $3 million in expenditures, the loophole was obvious: just set up additional committees. Campaign finance laws were a farce.

Reforming Campaign Financing

By the 1970s skyrocketing media costs led to a dramatic increase in expenditures: in 1972 the Republicans spent $61 million and the Democrats $30 million.[7] The abuses that year by the Nixon campaign—especially soliciting illegal corporate campaign contributions—became part of the Watergate scandal, and sent a number of people to jail (some protesting they had done nothing that had not been done in prior campaigns). Congress passed the Federal Campaign Amendments of 1974, providing public funds for presidential elections ($20 million plus an inflation adjustment) for candidates who did not accept private donations to their campaigns. Each taxpayer could allocate a dollar from income taxes to the Treasury's Presidential Campaign Fund, which then distributed the money to the presidential candidates. (The allocation did not increase a taxpayer's tax liability.) The percentage of taxpayers designating money to the Fund has declined, from 28.7 percent in 1980 to less than 20 percent by 1992. That year the Federal Elections Commission projected that the Fund would not have sufficient money for the 1996 election cycle unless the allowable taxpayer contribution were increased to keep up with inflation or the fund were permitted to tap into general revenues. Congress then raised the amount to $3 in 1994.

Beginning with the 1976 election, candidates have been eligible for full funding by the U.S. Treasury, up to an amount set by law ($55.2 million for each major-party candidate in 1992), provided they do not accept any private contributions. All major-party candidates have accepted public funding.[8]

Election Law Loopholes

Loopholes in campaign finance laws have allowed wealthy contributors and political action committees (PACs) to obtain influence with candidates. For every dollar spent under the federal finance provisions designed to limit expenditures, close to another dollar is spent by the wealthy or corporations and unions exploiting these loopholes. First, each national party may expend 2 cents per voter for their presidential nominee, and these parties accept large contributions (up to $20,000 under federal law) from private contributors. Second, raising or spending money by state and local parties is not covered by federal law, and contributions to their party committees, known as "soft money," has no limits except those passed by individual state legislatures. In 1988 more than 400 contributors made large contributions of more than $100,000 to the national and state parties, negating the attempt to keep "big pocket" contributors out of campaign finance.[9] Third, in twenty-eight states corporations may make campaign contributions, and in forty-one states unions may do so. These "party-building" donations allow party organizations to buy computers, pay staff, conduct voter registration drives, and do other things that help the presidential campaign.

In an election year supposedly nonpartisan organizations may be established by a candidate's supporters to conduct voter registration drives. Party organizers can then steer their own wealthy contributors to these groups, which use the money to fund grassroots efforts to register voters supporting their candidate. Corporate executives often use this method on behalf of Republican candidates; Democrats usually benefit from grassroots voter registration drives conducted by union officials.

Unaffiliated Funding

Political action committees (PACs) may make unlimited expenditures on behalf of presidential candidates, provided the expenditures are "noncoordinated" with the candidate's campaign. The Supreme Court has ruled that establishing spending limits on these groups would violate their freedom of speech under the First Amendment.[10] These unaffiliated committees (Americans for Reagan, Citizens for Reagan, Ronald Reagan Victory Fund, Americans for an Effective Presidency, Americans for Change) spent millions of dollars on campaign commercials on behalf of Ronald Reagan in 1980 and 1984. The infamous "Willie Horton" commercials in 1988 (focusing on Governor Michael Dukakis' furlough of Horton, a convicted felon, and Horton's subsequent murder of a housewife) were funded by an independent committee working on behalf of George Bush. Such committees not only spend additional funds to exceed the campaign limits, they also enable candidates to distance themselves from the dirtiest aspects of the campaign. In 1992, for the first time since the laws were passed, committees supporting the Democratic candidate actually outspent committees supporting the Republicans by a reported $40 million to $25 million.[11]

Soaring Costs

By 1988 total nomination and general election campaign expenditures for all contenders had soared to more than $500 million ($129.7 million in 1960 dollars). Put another way, parties spent $1.42 on each of the 91.6 million voters who cast ballots in 1988.[12]

Candidates now spend more than three-fifths of the funds they raise on television and radio advertisements and direct mail. Does this mean that the candidate with more money to spend has the advantage? Put more crudely, does money buy the election? Between 1860 and 1972, before campaign finance reform, the winner outspent the loser in twenty-five of twenty-nine contests.[13] In the elections of 1980, 1984, and 1988, Republicans outspent Democrats (in soft money and independent expenditures) and won the White House. In 1976 and 1992, Democrats outspent Republicans, and won the elections. It is not clear, however, which is the cause and which the effect. In recent elections, other things being equal, Republicans are likely to have more financial resources than Democrats. But when Republicans are in political trouble (as Ford and Bush were), then contributions may dry up, and Democrats may benefit as "deep-pocket" contributors put their money on the Democratic candidate. In short, success in fund-raising may reflect political odds rather than make them.

ON THE CAMPAIGN TRAIL

The history of presidential campaigning is the continuous adaptation by candidates to new transportation and communication technologies that allow them to reach the voters with their message.

Standing for Office

Initially candidates "stood" for election and did not "run" for the office, so they would not be accused of being too ambitious for power. In 1789 and 1792 George Washington was selected unanimously by the electoral college without campaigning, though Alexander Hamilton did organize massive demonstrations in his honor to demonstrate support for him. Beginning in 1796, party managers campaigned while the candidates remained at home. In 1840 William Henry Harrison took a short "tour" but did not discuss issues or seek votes. In 1844 Polk began the custom of sending "letters" to his supporters on issues such as the tariff, and these letters were printed in party newspapers, an early form of direct "speech making" through the press. Winfield Scott was the first candidate to campaign in 1852. By 1860 it was understood that the president did not campaign, but a challenger who trailed could take to the stump: Stephen Douglas campaigned throughout the South and Midwest, while Abraham Lincoln stayed home in Springfield, Illinois.

In 1876 Rutherford Hayes began the practice of responding to the party nomination with an "acceptance letter," which outlined his position on the issues: the letter was reprinted in newspapers throughout the nation. He also originated the "front-porch" campaign: his supporters would visit him, and his discussions with them would then be reported by the wire services and appear in newspapers. In 1892 Grover Cleveland held a "notification" ceremony before thousands of his supporters in Madison Square Garden, in which the convention decision offering him the nomination was relayed to him, following which he accepted in a speech, but he did not take to the campaign trail.

Running for Office

Usually there was no need for a popular presidential candidate to campaign: in 1896 Democrat challenger William Jennings Bryan went to twenty-seven states and made six hundred speeches to five million people, then got crushed by Republican William McKinley, who ran a front-porch campaign. Theodore Roosevelt in 1904, like his predecessors, thought it improper for an incumbent president to go on the campaign trail. Instead, he exhorted his cabinet to "attack Parker!" and wrote hundreds of letters to party leaders, making patronage appointments to secure their support. He defeated his opponent, Alton B. Parker, by the greatest landslide since 1832, yet hardly ever left his home in Oyster Bay, New York.

The first incumbent president to stump for votes was William Howard Taft in the election of 1912. In deep trouble because of a split in his party, Taft made an 18,000 mile, four hundred speech tour, designed primarily to counter Theodore Roosevelt's speeches. Democrat Woodrow Wilson also toured the nation, making this the first election in which both major-party candidates campaigned.

Yet even as candidates began to take to the campaign trail, political advertising began to eclipse their personal efforts at communicating with voters. In 1916 Wilson used newspapers and magazines, billboards, and motion pictures in his campaign for reelection. Because newspaper coverage was so important, candidates began to add press agents and speechwriters to their campaign staffs. In 1924 Calvin Coolidge campaigned on radio to more than one million radio listeners. By 1928 Alfred E. Smith used the radio to reach eight million people, though his strident speeches and heavy New York accent probably cost him votes. In 1932 President Hoover was defeated by Franklin D. Roosevelt, who made a series of radio "chats" to the voters from his Hyde Park home. Republicans responded in the 1944 and 1948 elections by using pollsters, public relations experts, and advertising executives to develop media campaigns—though they failed to dislodge the Democrats, who had a great advantage in traditional grassroots party organization.

MEDIA CAMPAIGNING

Although Harry Truman had made one television commercial in 1948 that reached fewer than one million Americans who owned television sets, Dwight Eisenhower pioneered the use of television commercials in 1952 and reached a mass audience (though there were only one hundred stations in operation). "Eisenhower Answers Mr. and Mrs. America" was a series in which the candidate answered questions from a moderator. "To think that an old soldier should come to this," Ike commented between "takes" for these spots, believing that media campaigning was beneath the dignity of the office. In 1956 expenditures for radio and television advertising amounted to only 6 percent of campaign budgets; by 1988 they accounted for 57 percent of major-party spending in the presidential general election.[14] Today presidential candidates make billions of "gross impressions" (calculated by each time a viewer sees a television commercial) during a campaign: each household may see up to thirty or more commercials. To conduct the media campaign, each candidate establishes an advertising group (consisting of advertising agency executives and campaign professionals) to create and produce campaign spots. "Nothing's real anymore unless it's on television," explained Michael Deaver, a Reagan campaign operator.[15]

Mass versus Segmented Marketing

Until the 1950s communications strategy for presidential candidates was dominated by party politicians with a feel for "the man in the street." These professionals were then displaced by advertising executives who worked to "sell" candidates to the voters: they took whatever positions the candidates and party had adopted at the Convention, and attempted to make the candidate and the party platform attractive to voters. By the late 1960s candidates themselves, rather than the party, created "candidate-centered" presidential campaigns that downplayed party identifications and party platforms and emphasized candidate traits. Campaign commercials were aired to a mass audience, mostly on network television.

In the 1970s and 1980s candidates marketed themselves to the voters like soft drinks, sneakers, automobiles, and other consumer goods.[16] They segmented the voters by party, ideology and values, and lifestyle, interviewing "focus groups" to find out what each of these segments thought. Then they targeted groups of voters and projected an image offering each of these "voter segments" different reasons to go to the polls and back them. The candidates developed their issues through an interactive process: The campaigning for voter support itself determined much of the content of the candidate's campaign, much as companies try to "stay close to the customer."

The network campaign commercials of the 1960s gave way to commercials geared to specific states in the 1970s. Broadcasters divided the nation into 60 ADIs (areas of dominant influence) that could be reached by commercial television stations, and subdivided these into two hundred DMAs (designated market areas), each with its own demographic characteristics. Then messages were designed for each separate ethnic and racial audience in the 1980s. Segmented marketing accounted for almost half the advertising expenditures in the 1992 campaign.[17]

Thematic Campaigning

Candidates use their polls to find positions on issues that would demonstrate their leadership qualities to the electorate. John Kennedy, for example, used surveys conducted at the state level by Louis Harris in his 1960 campaign to emphasize issues that would enhance his image as a leader ready to move the nation forward.[18] "Issues are only a means to establish personal qualities with voters," Republican media adviser Robert Teeter later observed. By the 1970s, focus groups were being used by candidates to pre-test campaign commercials. Groups of voters, gathered in small settings, would preview speeches and commercials: themes that appealed to them would be retained by candidates, and those that fell flat would be dropped.

Thematic campaigning ("You Never Had It So Good," "Life Is Better," "America Is Back," "It's Morning in America") or personalized campaigning ("I Like Ike") can substitute for spatial positioning, which is the attempt to convince voters that a candidate has the same positions they have on issues. In the 1980s thirty-second attack commercials and quick "sound-bites" were combined with sentimental ads designed to cause an emotional rather than an intellectual response. The Reagan campaign offered a nostalgic background for an America that once was and that yet might be in its "Morning in America" commercials, identifying Reagan with the timeless values of middle America. It went on the attack with an advertisement showing a grizzly bear (representing the Soviet Union) in an encounter with native Americans—symbolic of a need to reelect Reagan and ensure our national defense.

Another ad showed several American workers talking about Democratic candidate Walter Mondale's proposal to raise taxes. The Republicans used these two ads to erode Mondale's initial advantages with voters in domestic issues and to turn Reagan's "Cold Warrior" and warmongering image into a more reassuring image of Reagan as the architect of deterrence.[19]

Themes must be unified, coherent, and easy to follow. Complex arguments do more to confuse than to enlighten voters. A campaign is no place to change voters' minds: commercials play to and reinforce existing emotions.

Image Making

"The picture is everything," says campaign expert Michael Deaver.[20] An overstatement perhaps, but candidate image is a major determinant of voter choice. Candidates get coached in speech and body movement, learn how to "love the camera," and hone their presentation skills in front of the "imagemeisters" of the campaign. Richard Nixon's 1968 campaign shows the importance of improving the presentation skills of the candidate. The producer of Richard Nixon's campaign commercials in 1968 admitted that they started out with a problem:

> Let's face it, a lot of people think Nixon is dull. Think he's a bore, a pain in the a–. They look at him as the kind of kid who always carried a bookbag. Who was forty-two years old the day he was born. They figure other kids got footballs for Christmas, Nixon got a briefcase and he loved it. He'd always have his homework done and he'd never let you copy.[21]

According to speechwriter Ray Price, the answer was simple: "It's not the man we have to change, but rather the received impression. And this impression often depends more on the medium and its uses than it does on the candidate himself."[22] A media blitz converted Nixon's image from that of a partisan streetfighter into a mature, experienced statesman—into what columnists began referring to approvingly as "the New Nixon."

Influencing Media Coverage

Candidates and their managers prefer controlled media that they create and disseminate to the press. Reporter Jules Witcover, after trying to cover Nixon one day, recalled, "No soap. Couldn't get to him. They hustled him off. Just the idea of your going up there and confronting the candidate—the guys around him were startled. They couldn't believe their eyes that you were doing this. And they learned very quickly, and it didn't happen much after that."[23] Ronald Reagan used a similar strategy for the same reasons in 1984: his campaign provided reporters with one set of pictures and one story a day out of the White House. With only one story, networks could not "step on the message" of the day by highlighting other White House events or decisions. President Reagan held no news conferences the summer and fall he was running for reelection, par for the course for many presidents. As newsman Dan Rather observed, "The Reagan people saw the whole campaign as a movie. They saw it that way. And they thought as movie directors do, of shooting sequences—we have our star, this is our sequence, now how do we want the shot framed?"[24]

Reporters are the enemy: that is the received wisdom of campaigners who studied the lesson of the Humphrey, McGovern, Carter, and Dukakis campaigns. These campaigns thought there was more mileage to be gained by being open and accessible, and their staffs went out of their way to be accommodating to journalists. The result? Stories about staff disagreements, candidate temper tantrums, conflicts over strategy and tactics—and even stories about attempts by the campaign to manipulate press coverage. Reporters have a field day covering an open campaign critically, while doing little to uncover what goes on in a totally controlled one. As a consequence, media coverage is much more critical of open than of closed campaigns.[25]

Media stories about presidential campaigns portray the campaign as a race: who is ahead, who is behind, who has momentum in the polls—what television producer Av Westin called "here he comes, there he goes" stories.[26] Some reporters give the latest gossip about campaign personalities; others are "assistant district attorneys" reporting on campaign finance infractions, potential conflicts of interest, and the medical or sexual history of the candidates. Still others become "assistant campaign managers," offering the candidates advice.[27]

News reporting has changed over time. In the 1940s over half the campaign stories were concerned with issues of policy and leadership—substantive reporting on the content of a campaign. Media reporting emphasized the game of politics rather than its content by a two-to-one margin in the 1970s, and by more than a four-to-one margin in 1988 and 1992.[28] Since the early 1960s more voters have relied on television than on newspapers for information about politics, and those who rely on television newscasts to make up their minds are likely to get a sum total of less than an hour of reporting on issues during the general election. Some studies have shown that television viewers are more likely to get substantive information from candidate advertisements than from newscasts—a truly frightening thought.[29]

News reporting has gotten more negative over the decades. In 1960 three-quarters of the stories contained "good news" and one-quarter or so bad; by 1992 close to 60 percent involved bad news and 40 percent good.[30] Candidates find it increasingly difficult to get their words across on television or in the press. In 1960, two-thirds of the coverage in the press focused on what the candidate had actually said on the campaign trail; in 1992 more than 80 percent of the stories focused on the reporter's reactions, analysis, and evaluations.[31] Even worse, television news clips of candidate speeches have gone from thirty seconds of the candidate speaking to six or seven seconds: the candidate's voice is replaced by the commentator's providing an analysis of the strategy behind the speech, rather than the substance.[32] Candidates find it more and more difficult to get their message out to an audience that has been coached by the media to distrust what they say and to believe it is all a con job. Not only are the voters uninformed about candidate positions on issues, they are more likely to vote on the basis of candidate image and thematic appeals, or media evaluations of their political strategies and tactics.

Presidential Debates

Televised debates first were held between John Kennedy and Richard Nixon in 1960. After the Nixon–Kennedy debates of 1960, none were held in 1964, 1968, and 1972, because in each instance one of the candidates was ahead and felt he had nothing to gain. In 1976 debates resumed: President Ford wanted to debate because he was behind in the polls and had nothing to lose; Jimmy Carter wanted debates because his lead had begun to slip. Debates have become an established custom, and a candidate cannot avoid them without making it an issue. Originally sponsored by the League of Women Voters and the networks, presidential debates are now organized by the Commission on Presidential Debates, a bipartisan group created by Congress. Debates are also held between vice presidential candidates, but there is no evidence that these influence voters.

The debates attract huge audiences; usually more than 100 million people watch at least part of them. Usually a panel of reporters acceptable to both candidates questions them and they are given time to rebut their opponent's statements.

Vice President Richard Nixon (on the dais at right) and Senator John Kennedy (at left) just moments before the start of the first presidential debate in 1960. Radio listeners thought Nixon had done well, but his sickly TV image (he was recuperating from the flu) left a poor impression on the majority of viewers.

In 1992, Clinton and Bush agreed to three debates: In one, members of a randomly selected audience asked questions, a format that enabled Clinton, more articulate in these settings than President Bush, to gain ground with the voters. The reason? Because voters were more likely to ask "kitchen table" questions about the impact of governmental policies on their families, rather than the "inside the beltway" questions asked by Washington reporters, seemingly further from the concerns of average citizens.[33]

Debates raise voter interest and provide information about the candidates and their response under pressure. They help voters make up their minds. Usually two-fifths of the voters know which party they will vote for even before the primary season. Another one-fifth make up their mind during the primary season, and another tenth or so during the convention. The final thirty percent or so of the voters decide during the election campaign, and debates are crucial in reaching them.[34]

Debates can affect election results. In close contests many voters wait for the debates before deciding for whom to vote, especially independents and those without strong feelings for their parties. Those who watch debates tend to vote on the basis of the issues, whereas those who do not watch are more likely to vote on the basis of personality. The media report on the debates, replaying the most dramatic moments for several days on the evening news, which reinforces their influence on voters. Commentators announce the "winner," a verdict that may also affect voter behavior as people jump on the bandwagon.

Polls showed that 6 percent of the public—four million voters—based their votes in 1960 on the debates. John Kennedy received support of 72 percent of these voters, giving him his margin of victory. (A majority of those who listened to the debates on radio thought Nixon had won, which illustrates the impact of "watching" the candidates perform as well as listening to what they have to say.) In 1980 Ronald Reagan gained ground with undecided voters and political independents, helping him to defeat Jimmy Carter. The 1992 debates did for Clinton what the 1960 debates had done for Kennedy: neutralized his opponents' claim that he lacked enough experience or judgment to be president, though he lost some support to Ross Perot, who doubled his support, from 10 to 20 percent in their aftermath.[35] At other times debates are inconclusive: In 1984 Walter Mondale did well in his debates against Reagan, with 66 percent of the voters responding that Mondale had "won" to only 17 percent for Reagan, yet most voters said the debates had no effect on their opinion of Reagan.[36]

THE VOTERS DECIDE

The humorist Russell Baker once proposed a constitutional amendment that would bar an elected president from taking office. Pointing out that "skill at running for President has little relationship to the job of being President," he suggested that candidates should merely run on behalf of politicians capable of running the country, who, "because of low charisma, bad teeth and distaste for looking foolish, couldn't run successfully for a bus"—let alone for the White House.[37]

Presidential Term Limits

The Constitutional Convention of 1787 did not place any limits on the number of terms a president might serve, rejecting proposals for a single six-year term. The two-term tradition was begun by George Washington, but its principles were first expressed by Thomas Jefferson, who in 1809 announced that "rotation in office" was his reason for leaving the White House after two terms. Jefferson felt strongly that his precedent would prevent the danger of a president being reelected for life. The Democratic–Republican presidents who followed him (James Madison and James Monroe) also limited themselves to two terms, and their Democratic Party successors also bound themselves to the tradition. In the 1840s the Whig Party carried this one step further and in its platform stated that a president should serve only one term and not stand for reelection. Democratic President James Polk also pledged in his election campaign in 1844 that he would serve only one term, a tradition carried on until the Civil War, when Abraham Lincoln ran for reelection and won.

In 1940, Franklin Roosevelt, observing the outbreak of war in Europe, decided that the international crisis was too grave to leave office, and ran for a third term. Although his vice president and some other party leaders opposed his decision, and Postmaster General James Farley resigned in protest, Roosevelt was reelected to a third, and then a fourth term.

After Roosevelt's death a Republican-controlled Congress passed the Twenty-Second Amendment to limit presidents to two elected terms. Ratified on February 27, 1951, the amendment provides that no person may be elected president more than twice. It also provides that no vice president who succeeds to the office of President, or other person in the line of succession who acts as president, who then serves for more than two years of a presidential term to which someone else had been elected, could be elected to the presidency more than once. The first president to which this amendment applied was Dwight D. Eisenhower—a Republican.

Could a former president who had already served two terms become vice president and then succeed to the presidency? The answer is no. The Twelfth Amendment provides that "No person constitutionally ineligible to the office of President shall be eligible to that of Vice President of the United States." If a president is "ineligible to the office" after two terms under provisions of the Twenty-Second Amendment, he or she could not be elected vice president under provisions of the Twelfth Amendment. Nor could a former president who had served two terms be appointed under provisions of the Twenty-Fifth Amendment to the vice presidency. However, a former president who was named to the cabinet, or who became speaker of the House or president pro tempore of the Senate, would be in line of succession to become "acting president" in the event of a double vacancy (death or disability of both the president and vice president), and could serve until the next election. The chances of that ever happening are zero, because double vacancies are not likely, and in the twentieth century former presidents have not gone back to Congress or served in the cabinet.

The constitutional term limitation helps to allay our suspicion of excessive presidential power, yet it is actually an antidemocratic provision of the Constitution. There is little question that popular presidents such as Dwight Eisenhower and Ronald Reagan could have won third terms, yet the American people have been denied the opportunity to elect them again. Parliamentary systems have no such limitations, and some prime ministers, such as Margaret Thatcher in Great Britain, have served far longer than a U.S. president is constitutionally permitted. Prospects that the amendment will be eliminated, however, are nil. For one thing, term limitations for Congress and for state and local government are being passed at the state level because of anti-incumbency sentiment. For another, no president would want to face the wrath of the electorate by suggesting such a change, especially if it might benefit his own potential third-term candidacy.

Incumbent Advantage?

Conventional wisdom has it that presidents are supposed to win two terms. In all of the twentieth century, incumbents defeated challengers 75 percent of the time. Only Taft, Hoover, Ford, Carter, and Bush did not make it back, in several cases (Taft, Hoover, and Bush) losing by landslides. Special circumstances can explain each failure: Taft and Bush faced splits in their party with the introduction of a third candidate, Hoover was undone by a Depression, and Ford was an unelected president who had pardoned Richard Nixon. Overall the odds would seem to favor the incumbent. But consider the most recent period: Lyndon Johnson scared out of the nominating contest in 1968; Nixon resigning his office early in his second term; Ford defeated in 1976; Carter defeated in 1980; and Bush defeated in 1992. Since the end of World War II through 1992, only Dwight Eisenhower and Ronald Reagan have completed two terms, and Clinton was being talked of as a one-term president after the midterm elections of 1994.

There is no way to tell from a president's performance in office how he will do in the reelection campaign. Most presidents fall in the popularity polls during their first two years, including Eisenhower, Nixon, and Reagan, each of whom rallied to win impressive reelection landslides. In contrast, George Bush was riding high in the polls in 1991, with a 90 percent approval rating after the Persian Gulf War—and one year later he had been defeated for reelection. The size of midterm losses in Congress tell us nothing, because in almost all presidencies the party in the White House suffers a significant loss of seats in the House. Harry Truman's party had given up control of Congress in 1946; yet he rallied to win the election two years later.

Some data seem to count: when a president faces a recession or stagflation (no growth and high inflation), when the "misery index" (rates of inflation, interest, and unemployment) moves higher, and when the rate of growth of the gross national product (GNP) sinks below 3 percent, then an incumbent is in trouble. Other signs of an incumbent in distress include approval by less than half of the voters in an election year, significant primary opposition, a fractious convention, serious scandals, a third-party or independent candidate in the race, and U.S. forces bogged down in a major war.[38]

Declining Turnouts

Presidents may claim to represent the entire nation, but the turnout of those eligible to vote makes them the choice of a small minority of the electorate. In the nineteenth century, when suffrage was restricted first to white males over 21, and then to males over 21 (after the Fourteenth and Fifteenth Amendments gave African-American men the constitutional right to vote) turnout rates were close to 80 percent. Rates dropped about 20 points during the Progressive era, when "Americanization" laws requiring literacy in English and voter registration systems were introduced and discouraged high turnouts. In the 1920s the rates dropped to 40 percent because women were granted the right to vote by the nineteenth amendment and their initial turnout rates were low. During the New Deal period, however, turnout soared into the 60 percent range, and after a sharp dip in the 1940s during and after World War II, remained in the 60 percent range through the 1964 election. Since then candidates for president have not been very successful as vote mobilizers: turnout rates have fallen, dropping to 50 percent in 1988 before bouncing up to 55 percent in 1992.[39] Although students of the subject differ about causes, most seem to agree that the performance of presidents has played a significant role in the high dropout rate and the conversion of many from voters into nonvoters.[40]

Democratic candidates usually squeak into office. Only twice since 1944 have Democratic presidential nominees won 50 percent or more of the popular vote (Johnson with a 61 percent landslide in 1964 and Carter with 50 percent in 1976). They have averaged 43 percent of the vote since 1968—exactly the percentage Clinton received in his winning bid in a three-candidate race. Republicans have been more successful in winning a large majority of the vote (Eisenhower in both elections, Nixon in a landslide in 1972, Reagan in a landslide in 1984).

Because the percentage of voting-age population that actually turns out has been in the 50 to 60 percent range for the last forty years, the actual percentage of the electorate that voted for the winning candidate has oscillated between one-quarter (in a close election) and one-third (in a presidential landslide). Bill Clinton, for example, won 43 percent of the vote in an election in which only 55 percent of the eligible electorate voted: *his* mobilization of the electorate was 23.6 percent—the lowest since John Quincy Adams in 1824. Clinton's election demonstrated the truth of an observation by Ambrose Bierce, who in *The Devil's Dictionary* defined the term *president* as "the leading figure in a small group of men of whom—and of whom only—it is known that immense numbers of their countrymen did not want any of them for president."[41]

The Changing Determinants of Voter Choice

Over the course of several decades it is possible to trace the transformations in the way voters make up their minds. In the 1940s and 1950s the voters' identification with parties, and with social groups that were part of party coalitions, structured the competition between presidential candidates. The nominee could rely on a base of strong party supporters, would then solidify his position with weaker party identifiers, and finally would compete for the votes of independents and potential defectors by positioning himself on the issues and offering an assessment of the prior administration.[42]

Beginning in the 1960s, strong party identification declined in much of the electorate, more voters considered themselves weak or independent party members, and a larger number dropped party affiliations altogether and became independent, as voter attitudes toward parties turned increasingly negative.[43] Between 1964 and 1972, issues and ideology played a distinctly larger role in presidential elections than partisanship and personality, and it has retained considerable importance through the early 1990s.[44]

Since the Watergate scandal of 1974 issues of character and competence and honesty have become more significant in presidential elections than issues or ideology, especially among better educated and more affluent voters, and among independent voters or those with weak party affiliations. Candidate competence in recent elections has been twice as significant as any other factor: it includes integrity, reliability, and personal conduct. Voters seem to be especially sensitive to labels (big spender, liberal, dove) that personalize and characterize candidates.[45] The rule has become the following: whoever gets to define themselves and the other candidate wins. Responding to initial voter reactions, for example, the Clinton campaign in 1992 produced a fourteen-page game plan known as the General Election Project, which called on "Bill and Hillary" to revamp their image: from coldly intellectual yuppie-liberal policy wonks, they transformed themselves into down-home, family-oriented parents of Chelsea, and acted like "just folks."[46] They were able to define Bush as a remote, uncaring president who "just doesn't get it" and knows nothing of the lives of average Americans.

Two cues for voters have diminished in recent elections. First is the state of the economy. Most economic forecasting models that worked in predicting election outcomes in the 1970s and 1980s also predicted a victory for President Bush, some by a landslide, in 1992.[47] They failed because many voters, faced with possibilities of job layoffs and a fundamental restructuring of the economy that might dim their future employment prospects, were more concerned about the uncertain and perilous future than about past or even present economic performance. Second is foreign affairs. Between 1940 and 1988 winning candidates almost always seemed to voters to have more competence in foreign affairs and more credibility as commander in chief. With the end of the Cold War, foreign policy matters played almost no role in the 1992 presidential elections: voters gave Bush high marks in foreign affairs leadership and understood that Clinton had no experience whatsoever—and then turned Bush out.

Valence, Retrospective, and Reference Group Voting

Although Democratic and Republican candidates usually differ substantially, with Democrats drawing most of the liberal votes and Republicans drawing a majority of conservative votes, *spatial* campaigning—in which candidates position themselves as close as they can to the preferences of a majority of the voters on issues—has been overshadowed by other methods of winning votes better suited for the era of segmented marketing, brief thematic campaign commercials, and news "sound bites."

First, campaigns often use *valence* issues: those that involve values that command near-universal acceptance, such as fighting crime, improving education, and providing peace and prosperity. Candidates attempt to convince voters that they, rather than their opponents, are better suited to bring about these conditions, as Clinton did when he identified himself with the "courage to change," or Carter did when he called for "a government as good as the people." They make patriotic appeals, as George Bush did when he insisted that teachers in Massachusetts should have to salute the flag and faulted his opponent for arguing that such compulsion was unconstitutional. A valence campaign does nothing to provide a president with a mandate. A "Doonesbury" cartoon portrayed Bush describing his first day of office: "So far today I've said the Pledge and I haven't furloughed any murderers. I've delivered on my entire mandate, and it isn't even lunch yet." That was not far from the truth.

Campaigns attempt to drive up the opponent's "negatives" by running ads questioning the candidate's commitment to shared values: Republican George Bush ran a valence campaign when he showed commercials of pollution in Boston Harbor and then observed that "Michael Dukakis says he's going to do for America what he did for Massachusetts." The same line was less successful four years later in his commercials about the Arkansas economy, as Clinton countered with statistics showing job growth in the state was much higher than the national average.

Political commercials call on voters to make a "thumbs up or thumbs down" judgment about a particular candidate—is he up to the job or not?—rather than attempt to match the voter's position on a particular issue with the candidate's.[48] Each campaign hopes to exploit an error, gaffe, or scandal of the opposition, to develop a "defining moment" that portrays the opposition negatively. The "up or down" aspect parallels media reporting on sports and entertainment figures (not to mention people charged with criminal behavior), and therefore suits a public quick to make such judgments.

Second, candidates try to convince voters to cast their ballots *retrospectively,* on the basis of several calculations. The first, known as rough justice, asks the voters to reward good performance and punish bad performance in the White House. Has the party in power provided peace and prosperity? As President Reagan put it in the 1980 debates: "Are you better off now than you were four years ago?" A second set of calculations calls for a different comparison: Would the other party have done the job better had it controlled the White House for the past four years? Finally, voters can make "retrospective/prospective" judgments about this question: Based on the past four years, which party will do better in the next four?[49] Retrospective voting does not require much knowledge about specific issues: often a general sense of "goodness or badness of the times" is enough for a voter to cast an intelligent ballot.

Third, candidates appeal to voters by creating *reference groups* in their media campaigns: groups with which voters are invited to identify on the basis of shared values. Republicans appeal to union members, not by arguing that their party is better for the union movement (which would be an insult to the intelligence of union members), but rather by suggesting that union members are "Forgotten Americans," or a part of the "New American Majority" of taxpayers and law-abiding citizens, who should vote against the Democrats, a party Republicans describe as "radical-liberals" intent on overthrowing the American Way of Life. Campaigns try to marginalize the opposition by identifying their candidates with controversial groups: in Republican campaign rhetoric, Democrats become the party of "welfare cheats" "quota queens," and "gay rights activists" and "abortionists." Democrats respond by raising the specter of the radical and Christian right, claiming that Republicans would "end the separation of church and state" and trample on the Bill of Rights. By creating these reference group images, each party tries to cross-pressure the other's supporters, who may drop out and not vote or cross over and defect.

Presidential candidates have emphasized valence issues, retrospective voting, and the creation of emotionally charged reference groups so that they can maintain spatial positions on issues that appeal to their core partisan voters, while simultaneously broadening their appeal to undecided independent and opposition voters. They can appeal to these voters without necessarily moving their spatial positions to the center. Yet when presidents use these media techniques, it becomes highly unlikely that they can obtain a mandate on substantive issues, beyond a vague sense in the electorate that fundamental change is needed.

Winning Coalitions

When Republicans win the presidency, they are usually successful at breaking through the Democratic post–New Deal coalition and winning half or more of the votes of southerners, Catholics, union workers, and the elderly. The Democrats win when spatial positioning on issues retains voters from these groups, and when they successfully defend against character issues or creation of "reference groups" that would promote defections. A Democratic candidate from the South has a good chance of winning back defectors who have left the Democrats for the Republican Party, as Clinton did in 1992, when he won a majority of the southern vote (by combining huge margins from blacks with a respectable showing of white southerners).

Voter Dissatisfaction

The result of using these media techniques has been increased dissatisfaction with candidates—even by those who have voted for them. In some elections, as many as 40 percent of the voters said in postelection polls that they had supported candidates mainly to vote against the opposition—a tribute, in a way, to the persuasive power of negative campaign advertising. A newly elected president, even after triumphing over the opposition media campaign, does not have much of a mandate on substantive issues after these kinds of campaigns.

A PLEBISCITARY PRESIDENCY?

Presidential elections are at the heart of our democratic system. Even in the midst of the Civil War we held a national election. In July 1864, the troops of Confederate General George Breckenridge slipped behind Union lines and raided the District

Succession: Alternate Routes to the White House

Disability

The Constitution provides in Article 2, sec. 1, that in the event of the President's "inability to discharge the powers and duties of the said office, the same shall devolve on the Vice President," who serves "until a President shall be elected." One of every four presidents has been disabled while in office, several before their deaths. William Henry Harrison was bedridden for a week before dying of pneumonia, and Zachary Taylor was ill for five days before his death of an acute intestinal obstruction (or perhaps appendicitis). Abraham Lincoln was unconscious for nine hours, James Garfield was disabled for eighty days, and William McKinley lived for eight days, before each died of gunshot wounds. Warren Harding was incapacitated for four days before his death of food poisoning (and possibly a heart attack). Three other presidents recovered from major disabilities. Woodrow Wilson was incapacitated with a stroke for 280 days, during which time his wife communicated to government officials from his bedside. Dwight Eisenhower took 143 days to recover from his first heart attack and later convalesced for weeks from a stroke. He was also incapacitated briefly during an operation for ileitis. Ronald Reagan was incapacitated for twenty hours while undergoing surgery after suffering a gunshot wound, and later while undergoing surgery for the removal of polyps from his colon.

After Eisenhower's heart attack, he wrote a letter to Vice President Nixon stating that if he were again disabled, the vice president would serve as acting president until the president announced he was once again able to resume his duties. If Eisenhower could not communicate, then Nixon was to make the determination himself about taking over the duties of the office. Presidents Kennedy and Johnson continued this arrangement with their vice presidents.

The Twenty-Fifth Amendment (ratified in 1967) provided that if a president is disabled, the vice president acts as president. The president can declare disability, or the vice president, together with a majority of the cabinet, can find the president to be disabled. In either case the president determines when to resume the duties of the office. If the vice president and the cabinet do not believe that the president is fit to resume office, the final determination is made by Congress, with a two-thirds vote by each chamber required to permit the vice president to continue to act as president.

The Twenty-Fifth Amendment also provides for filling vacancies in the vice presidency. Six incumbents have died and two resigned from office and nine others succeeded to the presidency. There have been seventeen occasions through 1994 in which the vice presidential office was vacant. The president can nominate a vice president, who takes office on confirmation by a majority vote of both chambers of Congress. This provision was used in 1973, when Vice President Spiro Agnew resigned, and Gerald Ford was nominated by President Nixon and confirmed by Congress.

Vice Presidential Succession Procedures

The Constitution provides in Article 2, sec. 1, that in the event of a presidential death, disability, or resignation, "the same shall devolve on the Vice President" who serves "until a President shall be elected." It is not clear from the text whether the words "the same" refer to the office of president, or simply to the "powers and duties" of the office, which would make the vice president, on taking over, the "acting president." The wording of the Twenty-Fifth Amendment follows the precedent that Tyler and all other vice presidents who succeeded to the presidential office established: when a president dies or leaves office during his term, the vice president succeeds to the office and becomes president, rather than acting president.

Double Vacancy Succession

In the event that both the president and vice president were killed or incapacitated at the same time (which could happen through a terrorist attack or assassination), the Constitution in Article 2, sec. 1, provides that Congress shall determine "what officer shall then act as President, and such officer shall act accordingly." The language indicates that the person assumes the powers of the office, but as acting president rather than president. In 1792 Congress passed the first succession law, providing that the president pro tempore of the Senate (the presiding officer of the Senate in the absence of the vice president of the United States) would be next in line, and then the speaker of the House. It also provided for an interim election to choose a new president as soon as possible. In 1886 Congress passed a new law to handle double vacancies, establishing a line of succession beginning with cabinet secretaries in the order in which their departments had been created. It dropped any provision for an interim election. The most recent law, passed by Congress in 1947, provides that the speaker of the House is first in line, followed in turn by the president pro tempore of the Senate, and then the cabinet secretaries in the order in which their departments were created. The acting president would serve "until the expiration of the then current presidential term," an explicit rejection of the idea of an interim election. By dropping the interim election, Congress has emphasized that continuity of the administration, rather than a new mandate from the people, is the most important value to be reinforced in a double-vacancy situation.

Resignation

Article 2, sec. 1, paragraph 6, specifies that in case of resignation the Office of President devolves on the vice president. The Twenty-Fifth Amendment states that in case of resignation the vice president "shall become President." The

Continued

Succession: Alternate Routes to the White House *continued*

Constitution does not specify the procedures involved in a presidential resignation, and through 1994 there has been only one such instance: Richard M. Nixon resigned on August 9, 1974. Vice President Gerald Ford was notified by the secretary of state and took the oath of office at the designated time. In a parliamentary system it would probably be assumed that the resignation in disgrace of a president would be a reason to hold a new election. The U.S. Constitution instead chooses continuity rather than a new electoral mandate. The assumption of the convention delegates in 1787 was that the electoral college's second choice (the elected vice president) should succeed. This assumption makes much less sense since passage of the Twelfth Amendment before the election of 1804, for since then candidates for president and vice president run on a ticket, and the vice president is not the electoral college's second choice for the presidency, but rather an afterthought. A vice president chosen for second place on the party ticket might be the last person one would wish to succeed a disgraced president, because it is conceivable he or she might have participated in the actions that caused the presidential resignation. Moreover, if the vice president had previously been chosen by Congress under provisions of the Twenty-Fifth amendment, as Gerald Ford had been in 1974, he or she would have no democratic legitimacy, not having won election to the office.

of Columbia. Although General Grant regrouped his forces and kept the Capitol and White House from going up in flames, it was a jolting reminder that Union victory was still in doubt. After some politicians advised Lincoln that the elections should be postponed, or a referendum on the war substituted, he observed that "We cannot have free government without elections, and if the rebellion could force us to forego, or postpone a national election, it might fairly claim to have already conquered and ruined us." And so we held an election in the midst of a Civil War, so important was the democratic legitimacy involved for the exercise of presidential power.

Elections provide presidents not only with constitutional legitimacy, but also with the mantle of democratic leadership. In James Madison's words, they offer a "mark of confidence" from the people.[50] Presidents emphasize the personal victory they have achieved: the will of the people has been expressed, and the incumbent has reflected what Washington referred to as "the voice of my country."[51] Presidents fuse their prerogative powers, their statutory duties, and their political position through their electoral legitimacy. In retirement Harry Truman summed up his perspective on the office as follows:

> As the president came to be elected by the whole people, he became responsible to the whole people . . . Every hope and every fear of his fellow citizens, almost every aspect of their welfare and activity, falls within the scope of his concern—indeed, it falls within the scope of his duty.[52]

Yet elections are not true plebiscites and do not provide presidents with real mandates. Voters do not have much confidence in the leadership characteristics of the candidates, so their election is often a case of "the lesser of two evils" rather than a ringing endorsement of their potential for leadership.

There is no close connection between political and constitutional power and the margin of victory. Lincoln, Wilson, and Kennedy, elected to their first terms with less than half the popular vote, acted in office more decisively than did their predecessors, Grant, Harding, and Eisenhower, all elected by landslides. Conversely, the great victories of Roosevelt in 1936, Nixon in 1972, and Reagan in 1984 were all followed by spectacular collisions with Congress over the extent of presidential prerogatives, and stalemates or defeats in domestic policy making. Strong presidents may not even be elected, as the first-year performances of Theodore Roosevelt, Harry Truman, and Lyndon Johnson demonstrate.

Public dissatisfaction with presidential elections runs in cycles, and it reached another of its periodic peaks in the 1990s. The legitimacy of the campaign process itself has been challenged by political scientists and commentators in the media, who have found fault with the way campaigns are funded and the way "spin" artists have manipulated the voters. Some observers believe the presidential selection process is on the verge of fundamental change, much as it was transformed after 1824 and 1968.[53] What is clear is that the authority of the presidency has been challenged by media coverage of campaigns that focuses on character and gamesmanship and sexual behavior at the expense of substantive politics.

The president enters office with campaign aides, soon to become White House officials, who are inexperienced in governance and unfamiliar with the substance of issues, but who are skilled in the projection of images, in attack politics, in the use of a "war room" to defend against opposition attacks, and in cultivating good media relations.[54] "The very process of campaigning for the Presidency under the present system weakens the winner's ability to govern effectively," observed Theodore Sorensen, a former aide to President Kennedy, adding that "The special talents demanded by a Presidential campaign are for the most part not the skills needed in the White House."[55] Better put, they may be useful skills, but they are not the only skills a president and his staff should possess.

Prospects for effective presidential leadership are always chancy, even when presidents win landslide victories with high voter turnout. Yet it is ironic that as presidents have assumed the mantle of popular leaders, they have lost much of their moral and political authority with the voters. More than irony is involved, of course, because as presidents enter office, their prospects for effective party and public opinion leadership have been diminished by what voters think of their campaigns.

FURTHER READING

Books

Jeff Fishel, *Presidents and Promises,* Washington, DC: Congressional Quarterly Press, 1986.

Michael Goldstein, *Guide to the 1996 Presidential Election,* Washington, DC: Congressional Quarterly Press, 1995.

Kathleen Hall Jamieson, *Packaging the Presidency,* New York: Oxford University Press, 1984.
Matthew McCubbins, *Under the Watchful Eye,* Washington, DC: Congressional Quarterly Press, 1993.
Joe McGinnis, *The Selling of the President, 1968,* New York: Pocket Books, 1969.
Thomas Patterson, *Out of Order,* New York: Alfred A. Knopf, 1993.
Frank Sorauf, *Inside Campaign Finance, Myths and Realities,* New Haven, CT: Yale University Press, 1992.
Gil Troy, *See How They Ran,* New York: Free Press, 1991.
Martin Wattenberg, *The Rise of Candidate-Centered Politics.* Cambridge, MA: Harvard University Press, 1991.

Documentary Sources

Federal Elections Commission, *Presidential Campaign Summary Reports* (computerized index and data file on the financial activities of all presidential contenders).
Presidential Elections Since 1789, Washington, DC: Congressional Quarterly Press (updated after each election).
Richard Scammon, ed., *America Votes,* Vols. 1–20, Washington, DC: Congressional Quarterly Press (voting statistics).

NOTES

1. Louis Bean, a statistician in the Department of Agriculture, also predicted Truman's victory in his pre-election book, *How to Predict Elections,* New York: Alfred A. Knopf, 1948.

2. Since ratification of the Twenty-Third Amendment in 1961, electors are also chosen by the District of Columbia.

3. David Abbott and James Levine, *Wrong Winner: The Coming Debacle in the Electoral College,* Westport, CT: Praeger, 1991, p. 37.

4. Lawrence Longley and Alan Braun, *The Politics of Electoral College Reform,* New Haven, CN: Yale University Press, 1972, p. 3.

5. Lucius Wilmerding, *The Electoral College,* New Brunswick, NJ: Rutgers University Press, 1953, pp. 47–61.

6. Raymond Tatalovich, "Electoral Votes and Presidential Campaign Trails: 1932–1976," *American Politics Quarterly,* Vol. 7, no. 4, October, 1971, pp. 489–497; Steven Brams and Morton Davis, "The 3/2s Rule in Presidential Campaigning," *American Political Science Review,* Vol. 68, no. 1, March, 1974, pp. 113–134.

7. Herbert Alexander, *Financing Politics,* Washington, DC: Congressional Quarterly Press, 1980, pp. 5–10.

8. A major party is defined as one that has won more than 25 percent of the vote in the previous election. Minor parties (that have won more than 5 percent of the vote in the previous election) receive a lesser amount. A party that has not won 5 percent in the prior election may be eligible for reimbursement after the current election if it gains more than 5 percent of the vote.

9. Michael Goldstein, *Guide to the 1992 Presidential Election,* Washington, DC: Congressional Quarterly Press, 1991, p. 67.

10. *Federal Elections Commission v. National Conservative Political Action Committee,* 105 S. Ct. 1459, 1985.

11. F. Christopher Arterton, "Campaign '92: Strategies and Tactics of the Candidates," in Gerald Pomper, ed., *The Election of 1992,* Chatham, NJ: Chatham House, 1993, p. 107.

12. Data from Herbert E. Alexander and Monica Bauer, *Financing the 1988 Election,* Boulder, CO: Westview Press, 1991; *The People Speak: American Elections in Focus,* Washington, DC: Congressional Quarterly Press, 1990, as indicated in Table 1-3, "Presidential Spending and Votes," in Goldstein, op. cit., p. 13.

13. Stephen J. Wayne, *The Road to the White House, 1992,* 4th ed., New York: St. Martin's Press, 1992, pp. 50–51.

14. Michael Goldstein, op. cit., p. 7.

15. Quoted in Matthew McCubbins, *Under the Watchful Eye,* Washington, DC: Congressional Quarterly Press, 1992, p. ix.

16. Bruce I. Newman, *The Marketing of the President,* Thousand Oaks, CA: Sage Publications, 1994, pp. 12–15.

17. Ibid., p. 16.

18. Lawrence Jacobs and Robert Shapiro, "Issues, Candidate Image and Priming: The Use of Private Polls in Kennedy's 1960 Presidential Campaign," unpublished ms., September, 1992.

19. F. Christopher Arterton, "The Persuasive Art in Politics," in McCubbins, op. cit., pp. 100–101.

20. McCubbins, op. cit., p. 27.

21. Joe McGinnis, *The Selling of the President, 1968,* New York: Pocket Books, 1969, p. 54.

22. Ibid., p. 31.

23. Timothy Crouse, *The Boys on the Bus,* New York: Ballantine, 1973, p. 303.

24. Martin Schram, *The Great American Video Game,* New York: Morrow, 1987, p. 59.

25. McCubbins, op. cit., p. 143.

26. Av Westin, *Newswatch,* New York: Simon and Schuster, 1982, p. 93.

27. David Broder, "Political Reporters in Presidential Politics," in James Lengle and Byron Shafer, eds., *Presidential Politics,* New York: St. Martin's Press, 1980, p. 497.

28. Thomas Patterson and Robert McClure, *The Unseeing Eye,* New York: Putnam, 1976); *Report of the Commission on the Media and the Electorate: Key Findings,* New York: John and Mary R. Markle Foundation, 1990; Thomas Patterson, *Out of Order,* New York: Alfred A. Knopf, 1993.

29. Thomas Patterson and Robert McClure, *The Unseeing Eye,* New York: Putnam, 1976.

30. Thomas Patterson, *Out of Order,* New York: Alfred A. Knopf, 1993, pp. 114.

31. Ibid., p. 146.

32. Kiko Addato, "The Incredible Shrinking Soundbite," Cambridge, MA: Joan Shorenstein Barone Center, 1990; Daniel Hallin, "Soundbite News: Television Coverage of Elections, 1968–1988," Washington, DC: Woodrow Wilson International Center, 1991.

33. F. Christopher Arterton, "Campaign '92: Strategies and Tactics," in Gerald Pomper, ed., *The Election of 1992,* Chatham, NJ: Chatham House, 1993, p. 95.

34. Data from University of Michigan National Election Studies and *Los Angeles Times,* November 6, 1984.

35. Data from *CBS News/NYT polls,* as reported by Kathleen A. Frankovic, "Public Opinion in the 1992 Campaign," in Gerald Pomper, ed., *The Election of 1992,* Chatham, NJ: Chatham House, 1993, Fig. 4.2: "The Candidates' Changing Popularity," p. 115.

36. Michael Goldstein, op. cit., Table 4-7, "Impact of Presidential Debate on Public Opinion," p. 59.

37. Russell Baker, "Observer: Separation of State and Race," *New York Times,* April 12, 1980, p. 23.

38. See Allen Lichtman and Ken DeCell, *The Thirteen Keys to the Presidency,* Lanham, MD: Madison Books, 1990.

39. Richard Boyd, "Decline of U.S. Voter Turnout," *American Politics Quarterly,* Vol. 9, no. 2, April, 1981, pp. 133–136; John R. Petrocik, "Voter Turnout and Electoral Oscillation," *American Politics Quarterly,* Vol. 9, no. 2, April, 1981, pp. 161–180.

40. Lee Sigelman, "The Nonvoting Voter in Voting Research," *American Journal of Political Science,* Vol. 26, no. 1, February, 1982, pp. 47–55; Howard L. Reiter, "Why Is Turnout Down?" *Public Opinion Quarterly,* Vol. 43, no. 3, Fall, 1979, pp. 297–311; Stephen D. Shaeffer, "A Multivariate Explanation of Decreasing Turnout in Presidential Elections, 1960–1976," *American Journal of Political Science,* Vol. 25, no. 1, February, 1981, pp. 68–93.

41. Ambrose Bierce, *The Enlarged Devil's Dictionary,* New York: Doubleday, 1967, p. 226.

42. Angus Campbell, et al., *The American Voter,* New York: John Wiley, 1960, pp. 67–144.

43. Martin Wattenberg, "The Reagan Polarization Phenomenon and the Continuing Downward Slide in Presidential Candidate Popularity," *American Politics Quarterly,* Vol. 14, no. 3, September, 1986, pp. 219–245.

44. Norman H. Nie, Sidney Verba, Don Petrocik, et al., *The Changing American Voter,* Cambridge, MA: Harvard University Press, 1976, pp. 43–73; Jon Krosnick, "Americans' Perceptions of Presidential Candidates," *Journal of Social Issues,* Vol. 46, no. 2, Summer, 1990, pp. 159–181.

45. Arthur H. Miller, Martin Wattenberg, Oksana Melanchuk, et al., "Schematic Assessments of Presidential Candidates," *American Political Science Review,* Vol. 80, no. 2, June, 1986, pp. 521–540.

46. Donald E. Stokes and John J. DiLulio, Jr., "The Setting: Valence Politics in Modern Elections," in Michael Nelson, ed., *The Elections of 1992,* Washington, DC: Congressional Quarterly Press, 1993, p. 13.

47. Nathaniel Beck, "Forecasting the 1992 Presidential Election," *Public Perspective,* Vol. 3, September/October, 1992, pp. 32–34.

48. Ibid., pp. 1–20.

49. Morris Fiorina, *Retrospective Voting,* New Haven, CT: Yale University Press, 1981, pp. 3–64.

50. *Inaugural Addresses of the Presidents of the United States, 1789–1965,* Washington, DC: Government Printing Office, 1965, p. 14.

51. Ibid., p. 1.

52. *New York Times,* May 9, 1954, p. 54.

53. Gary L. Rose, *Controversial Issues in Presidential Selection,* 1st ed., Albany, NY: State University of New York Press, 1991, p. 11.

54. John Aldrich, "Presidential Campaigns in Party and Candidate-Centered Eras," in McCubbins, op. cit., pp. 59–82.

55. Theodore Sorensen, *A Different Kind of Presidency,* New York: Harper and Row, 1984, p. 45.

CHAPTER 7

President and Party

The longer I am President the less of a party man I seem to become.

—William Howard Taft

INTRODUCTORY CASE: PRESIDENT ROOSEVELT TRIES A PURGE

President Franklin D. Roosevelt sat in the Oval Office giving a "fireside chat" to the American people. He was frustrated, he told his radio audience, because the 75th Congress, controlled by his own Democratic Party, had not followed the platform. He drew a distinction between liberals like himself, who wanted fundamental change, and conservatives who did not. He did not want to take part in primary contests for Congress and state offices, but warned, "I feel that I have every right to speak in those few instances where there may be a clear issue between candidates for a Democratic nomination. . . ."[1]

Roosevelt organized "an elimination committee" in the White House that targeted nine senators and three members of the House. Roosevelt campaigned in the summer and fall of 1938 for Democratic candidates of his choice, but he snubbed and ignored other Democrats who had failed to support his programs in a dozen states, especially Georgia, Kentucky, Maryland, Oklahoma, and South Carolina. In Georgia, Roosevelt took on the senior Democratic senator, Walter George. Although he called him "my personal friend," he told an audience that George had not supported the party and did not believe in New Deal objectives, and endorsed challenger Lawrence Camp. "Mr. President," George replied, shaking his hand, "I want you to know that I accept the challenge."[2] Roosevelt went on to South Carolina and undercut Senator "Cotton Ed" Smith. In Maryland he supported an opponent of Senator Millard Tydings. In Texas he endorsed liberal Maury Maverick.

Roosevelt's purge efforts failed: George, Smith, and Tydings all won renomination. Liberals were trounced in Texas and in the mountain states. Only in New York City did he succeed, as John O'Connor, the anti–New Deal chairman of the powerful House Rules Committee, was defeated. Rank-and-file Democrats in a 1938 poll opposed his intervention in the primaries by a margin of 34 percent to 43 percent.[3] FDR had managed to divide his own party in the primary season, with lower-income Democrats who had benefited the most from his programs tending to support him, and upper-income and more conservative Democrats in opposition, leaving his party polarized, weakened, and in disarray during the general elections.[4] Precisely where the president wished to purge members, the local electorate in his party opposed his efforts the most. In the general elections Republican strength in the House rose from 88 to 170 seats, as the opposition picked up eight Senate seats (without losing any), and won thirteen gubernatorial contests. The worst defeats fell on many of the Democratic liberals Roosevelt was trying to help. "In pursuing his course of vengeance," Roosevelt's national party leader Jim Farley was later to write, "Roosevelt violated a cardinal political creed which demanded that he keep out of local matters."[5]

Roosevelt was one of a long line of presidents who found it difficult to exercise party leadership. Two of Roosevelt's predecessors, Taft and Wilson, had also tried to weaken party factions opposed to their programs, also without much success.[6] Roosevelt's successors, from Truman through Clinton, would learn the same lesson over and over again, though none would repeat FDR's mistake of openly intervening in the primaries against incumbents.

In the most fundamental sense the existing national and state party organizations are *anti-presidential:* They keep the White House from dominating Congress and they decentralize power from the national to the state and local levels. Yet if presidents do not control their parties, neither can it be said that their parties control them. No party mechanisms constrain presidents in the exercise of their power or influence.

TITULAR PARTY LEADERSHIP

Presidents have *always* had trouble leading their parties, and it is not far from the truth to suggest that the success or failures of their administration have far more to do with how well they deal with opponents in their own ranks than how successful they are in confronting the opposition party. A few presidents have managed to lead their parties for some time: yet eventually almost all have alienated some of their followers, split their party over controversial issues, and lost the support of congressional party leaders.

Party Leadership in American History

"The greatest political evil under our Constitution," John Adams proclaimed, was the division of the nation into two political parties.[7] Yet he was the first president to lead a political party when he became head of the Federalists in 1797. His presidency was wrecked because of the maneuvers and intrigues of Alexander Hamilton, leader of a "High Federalist" faction that conspired against him. His successor, Thomas Jefferson, founder of the Democratic–Republicans, had many legislative successes in his first term, but could not keep his party united in the Senate after he provoked the House's impeachment of Federalist Justice Chase, nor was he successful with his neutrality policy in the Napoleonic Wars, which eventually was repudiated by Congress. Andrew Jackson, founder of the Democrats, provoked a split in his party over his exercise of prerogative powers, and the Democrats abandoned his conception of the strong presidency as soon as he was out of office. Of all the nineteenth-century Democratic Presidents, only Jefferson, Jackson, and Polk were effective in using patronage to build up their party organizations or carry out party principles in their platforms.

Republican presidents in the nineteenth century fared no better than Democrats in handling divisions within their party. Radical Republicans pushed Lincoln to take a tougher policy against the South at the end of the war, and only his assassination prevented an open rupture between Lincoln and Congress. Grant was manipulated by corrupt members of his cabinet and congressional party who conspired in one financial scandal after another. Presidents Hayes and Garfield were plagued by a split between the Stalwart and Half-Breed Republicans, a feud that led to Garfield's assassination by a deranged office seeker from the Stalwarts.

Twentieth-century Democratic and Republican presidents have also had their problems. Theodore Roosevelt never dominated his party, even with all his energy and enthusiasm. He shared power with conservative congressional leaders. After two years as a successful party leader, Woodrow Wilson was unable to hold his congressional party together in the years prior to U.S. entry into World War I, as the Democratic Speaker Oscar Underwood actively opposed the possibility of U.S. involvement, undercutting his efforts to deter German submarine aggression. By 1918 he lost control of Congress to the Republicans. Franklin Roosevelt lost his bid to "pack" the Supreme Court in 1937 because of the defection of some Democrats, who then buried much of his remaining New Deal program.

After World War II the president may have become "Leader of the Free World," but that usually did not translate into party leader. A group of state party bosses unsuccessfully tried to drop Truman and get Dwight Eisenhower to run as a Democrat in 1948; two Democratic Party factions, the progressives and southern "Dixiecrats," fielded their own candidates against Truman in the general election. Eisenhower ran and won as a Republican in 1952; he was soon so enraged by the opposition of the Republican "Old Guard" to his "Modern Republican" (centrist) legislative proposals that he threatened to form a new party. John Kennedy was constantly conciliating northern liberals and southern conservatives, and neither faction completely trusted him. Opposition to the Vietnam War split the Democratic Party by 1966 and led to Johnson's decision to withdraw from the nomination contest in 1968. Moderate Republicans frustrated Richard Nixon's attempts to gut social programs and the Voting Rights Act, while conservative Republicans eventually pulled the plug on his presidency in 1974 during the Watergate scandal. Gerald Ford's foreign policy was repudiated by the Republican National Convention in 1976, which almost nominated his conservative challenger Ronald Reagan, paving the way for Ford's defeat by Jimmy Carter.

Congressional Democrats split with Jimmy Carter in his first months in office when he announced that rivers and harbors projects would be evaluated on cost–benefit grounds and vetoed if economically wasteful, and when he called for a balanced budget. By 1980 the Ted Kennedy wing of the party almost denied Carter renomination, and the split in the party cost Carter a second term. Ronald Reagan's conservative agenda was subverted by moderate Republican Senators, several of them chairs of important committees, on issues such as environmental protection, civil rights enforcement, and development of the "Star Wars" anti-ballistic missile system. Even conservative Republican Senator Barry Goldwater opposed certain covert activities of Reagan's CIA. Moderate Republicans such as Senator Bill Cohen of Maine forged a bipartisan coalition during the Iran–contra affair that reined in Reagan's national security advisors and forced many resignations at the top level of government. Throughout his term of office, George Bush had problems with conservative Republicans, who were as suspicious of him as the moderate Republicans had been of Ronald Reagan. The most vitriolic attacks against Bush came, not from Democrats, but from members of his own party such as House Republican Newt Gingrich, who in 1990 accused Bush of abandoning his "Read my lips, no new taxes" pledge to the Republican nominating convention in 1988, and torpedoed a budget agreement Bush had forged with the Democratic leadership.

Bill Clinton: A "New Democrat"

Bill Clinton campaigned for the presidency as a "New Democrat," who would move his party from extreme liberal positions that had cost it the White House so often, into the "mainstream" of American politics. Clinton found it was difficult to bridge the gap between liberals and his centrist and conservative followers. After two years, Democrats were divided on issues of international trade, fragmented on health care reform (with the major alternatives to his own plan sponsored by two Southern Democrats from his own wing of the party), and dubious about his foreign policies and his ten-year plan to balance the budget.

Why did Clinton have so much trouble with his fellow Democrats? Like most Presidents, Clinton was trying to lead a party consisting of disparate ideological, demographic, and geographic wings, and he found it impossible to hold these wings together. Traditional liberals viewed Clinton's victory as an opportunity to pass programs to compensate the "losers" in the economic marketplace—the groups referred to by one-time Democratic presidential contender Jesse Jackson as "the desperate, damned, disinherited, disrespected, and despised."

Clinton had problems with other influential Democrats. In New York, Governor Mario Cuomo said the health care plan would shortchange the state. After Clinton aides warned that if Senator Daniel Patrick Moynihan did not advance their program they would "roll right over him if we have to," Moynihan responded by criticizing the president's health initiative, and threatened to hold it "hostage" if the president did not support Moynihan's own welfare reform proposals. He was also the first Democrat to call for an investigation into the Whitewater banking scandal, an investigation that might touch the Clintons.[8] In October 1993, 77 moderate Democrats sent a letter to Clinton in which they called for a two-year limit for welfare benefits. Their letter promoted a response by 89 liberal Democrats, who claimed it would hurt needy families.

Clinton's support for the North American Free Trade Agreement (NAFTA) (a pact with Canada and Mexico negotiated by George Bush) cost him union support. Clinton put together a bipartisan coalition to win NAFTA, with 40 percent of his party joining 75 percent of the Republicans. After the vote, AFL-CIO leader Lane Kirkland would not even meet with Clinton for almost a month, and union members vowed reprisal against Democrats who had supported the President. Clinton had gone against representatives from his core constituencies in pushing for NAFTA. In congressional districts where Clinton had won a majority in the 1992 presidential election, the House vote was 61 against NAFTA to 37 in favor. In districts where Clinton had won a plurality of the vote, it was 86 for and 72 against. However, in districts in which Clinton had lost to Bush, NAFTA prevailed, 125 to 53.[9]

Clinton belonged to the southern wing of his party, dominated by centrists and conservatives. They argued that the old New Deal core of the party—religious and racial minorities, the elderly, and union workers—could not provide the party with enough votes to win presidential elections. To compete against the Republicans, the party would need younger voters and the white middle class. Clinton had helped found the Democratic Leadership Council (DLC) to reorient the party to the center. (The DLC was facetiously called the "Democratic Leisure Class" by its liberal opponents.) Yet even the DLC had its problems with Clinton's program. It thought too many appointments had gone to liberals. Clinton tried to heal a growing rift with the centrist Democrats. Speaking to a DLC annual meeting in December, 1993, he complimented them for their ideas. He also told them, though, "We don't want to be in the position that some of our predecessors were in the other party, where they were willing from time to time to exalt political rhetoric and where they were willing from time to time to let the perfect become the enemy of the good."[10] The following day, DLC Chairman Dave McCurdy responded that "it is our job to fight those who would water down our agenda," adding that "the Clinton administration is a bridge to a new Democratic Party. And we are on that bridge. But we have not crossed it. Making sure we do is the work of the DLC."[11]

Two years into his presidency Clinton seemed progressively weaker as a party leader. His party lost nine important off-year elections: Republicans won two governorships (New Jersey and Virginia), several big-city mayoralties (including Los Angeles and New York City), and two senate seats (Georgia and Texas). They even won the lieutenant governorship in Clinton's home state of Arkansas. Republicans took control of Congress after the midterm elections, winning 7 Senate seats (and obtaining the defection of one Democrat), 54 House seats, and 11 governorships from the Democrats, as well as 460 state legislative seats. As a result of that debacle, Clinton was viewed in many Democratic quarters, particularly in the DLC he helped to found, as an albatross rather than a leader.

CONTROLLING PARTY MACHINERY

Once in office the president takes control over the party's national committee, an organization with only limited power to influence the congressional, state, and local parties.

The National Committee

The sovereign bodies of the parties are the national conventions, but because they meet for less than one week every four years, they delegate their authority to the national committees (established by Democrats in 1848 and Republicans in 1856).

Each is composed of delegates from state parties, making the national party a league of semi-sovereign state organizations.[12] Until the 1930s, each committee ran and financed its party's presidential campaigns, and once in office, the president relied on the committee to conduct his political business with state and local parties.

Franklin Roosevelt established an independent White House operation to supersede the national committee. Until the end of his first term, Roosevelt attempted to build up the party, primarily by encouraging the establishment of special divisions to deal with African-Americans, women, and labor unions. In his second term, however, his used his own White House staff to deal with these and other elements of the New Deal coalition, bypassing the national committee completely.[13] Since Roosevelt's time, the White House political operation has supervised the national party, and key campaigners and political aides work out of the White House Office rather than party headquarters.

The National Party Staff

Woodrow Wilson began the practice of the president choosing the national chairperson. By custom the Democratic nominee may name a new party chair for the campaign, a practice the Republicans abandoned after 1964. Since 1980 the Republican party chair has served a fixed two-year term that runs from January to January through the nominating and election campaigns.

In both parties the nominees may appoint the director and deputy director of the national committee's political operations, or put in an unofficial "agent" at party headquarters who can communicate directly with their own campaign staffs. They may also select other national party staff, who serve at their pleasure. Often presidents select people who have helped them win their nominations. In the era of boss-dominated conventions, that usually meant state party leaders, and until the 1980s, chairpersons were usually seasoned professional politicians with close ties to the state parties, such as Mark Hanna, Jim Farley, Larry O'Brien, Ray Bliss, and Robert Strauss. Some, like Mark Hanna and Bob Dole, ran the committee while serving in the Senate. Others, like Jim Farley, were named postmaster general and served in the cabinet, though since 1947 no party chairman has served concurrently as a cabinet secretary. Because these chairmen were important political figures, some of them had presidential ambitions themselves, such as Hanna and Farley. In 1964 William Miller, running for vice president on the Republican ticket, was the first sitting chairman to run in a presidential election. After his stint, Robert Dole ran unsuccessfully for the Republican nomination. George Bush was the first former chairman to become president.[14]

Presidents usually do not want a strong national chairperson. Lyndon Johnson tolerated the ineffective John Bailey because he had no intention of revitalizing the Democratic party organization, which he thought might interfere with his own prerogative to conduct White House patronage politics.[15] Ronald Reagan set up his friend Senator Paul Laxalt as "general chairman" to supervise the work of the national party chair. Clinton's first chairman, David Wilhelm (his former campaign manager), worked under Harold Ickes, deputy chief of staff, and later was subordinated to unpaid "consultant" Tony Coelho, who worked out of the West Wing of the White House. In 1995 Clinton named Senator Christopher Dodd to head the DNC, hoping he would function more as an articulate spokesperson for the Democrats than as a nuts and bolts organizer. Dodd was immediately criticized by many state party leaders, who thought he was too liberal and would not be effective running the DNC while serving in the Senate.

In the era of media politics the chairman is usually a campaign operative skilled in image projection and media relations.[16] The position has become a way station toward more important jobs, because as Robert Strauss, former Democratic chair, observed, "If you're Democratic party chairman when a Democrat is president, you're a goddamn clerk."[17] After Carter was elected, Strauss resigned, went to work at the White House, and handled legislative liaison and trade negotiations with other nations. Similarly, after Bill Clinton was elected, Democratic National Chairman Ron Brown resigned, took a position as commerce secretary, and also played an important role in international trade issues. Both men, seasoned politicians, understood that political influence comes from being in the White House inner circle, and not from running the national party.

The job of the chairperson is to elect as many members of the party to public office as possible. Yet this may directly conflict with the White House tactics of accommodating important members of the opposition party. There is an inevitable tension between the adversarial stance taken by the political operation in the White House and the party national committees and the more conciliatory approach of the legislative liaison staffers within the White House. When Democratic Chairman David Wilhelm made a tough speech against Republican congressional leaders, Speaker of the House Thomas Foley appeared on a network television talk show, "This Week with David Brinkley," the following day to disavow personal attacks on members of Congress, saying, "I don't do that and I don't approve of it."[18] President Clinton maintained a studious neutrality.

With improved fund-raising capabilities, the national committee staffs swell during presidential election years. Several presidents, however, including Franklin Roosevelt, Lyndon Johnson, Jimmy Carter, and Bill Clinton, pressured the national committee to cut back on staffing after the election, either to reduce party deficits or (in Clinton's case) to hoard funds for midterm congressional campaigns. Clinton cut the staff from 240 to 200 to hire some Democratic media strategists and pollsters, to fund state contests, and to spend money on a public relations campaign for his health care reforms. In some ways the party staffers are better off when their party does not control the White House. They then are free to explore ideas, take new positions, change their methods of operation, employ new technologies, and develop their own initiatives; meanwhile the party that controls the White House often seems to falter under the burden of defending the President's political position and accepting White House supervision.[19] To some extent the parties have rebuilt, transformed, and revitalized themselves to a greater extent when seeking the White House than when they actually possess it.

Presidential Patronage

Party officials want to be dealt in on patronage (presidential appointments or other political favors) given to members of Congress or state and local parties. Thomas Jefferson began the practice of using federal appointments to build up his new state parties. Andrew Jackson made appointments of postal routes to independent contractors and postmasterships to local politicians. The collectors of the port, collectors of fees, Indian agents, and other federal officials were usually well connected to state parties or Jackson's congressional supporters. Lincoln relied on patronage to secure passage of the Thirteenth Amendment. Harrison and McKinley used patronage to pass tariffs, and McKinley used it to win Senate approval of the Treaty of Paris ending the Spanish–American War.

Presidents sometimes ignore the patronage demands of their party. Taft denied patronage to members of his party who refused to support his program, which infuriated them and led to a split within the Republican Party. Woodrow Wilson came into office prepared to ignore his regular party organizations in favor of his Progressive movement followers. Albert Burleson, his postmaster general, told Woodrow Wilson when he became president that "these little offices mean a great deal to the Senators and Representatives in Congress. . . . If they are turned down, they will hate you and will not vote for anything you want." Wilson came up with enough patronage to keep the bosses happy. "The pity is that Wilson appointed some who wouldn't recognize a Progressive principle if he met it in the road," complained Wilson's secretary of the navy, Josephus Daniel, many years later.[20]

Franklin Roosevelt attempted to build up his own national campaign organization rather than use patronage simply to build up the machines of local bosses. When Congress exempted his New Deal agencies from the merit system of the civil service, the result was more than 200,000 positions exempt from competitive examination, and White House patronage was dispensed after 1938 without reference to the national committee, in an effort to build up a "presidential party" within the Democratic Party. By 1939, Congress passed the Hatch Act, which forbade civil servants from contributing money to political campaigns or working in political activities (or even attending nominating conventions as delegates), and that put an end to FDR's use of the civil service to build up his own "presidential machine." Since then presidents have used their limited patronage to seal agreements with legislators to win their votes.

Presidents resent the pressure to dole out patronage. They view the national committee as a nuisance in these matters, and keep their distance from it and the state parties if they can. The White House uses the committee as a buffer against patronage requests. During the Kennedy administration White House assistant Lawrence O'Brien made sure that the President received credit for all patronage requests that were honored, while shifting the blame to the national chairman John Bailey for all requests that were denied.[21] Sometimes tensions boil over: in 1977 the Democratic National Committee unanimously passed a resolution condemning the Carter administration for neglecting state party patronage and fund-raising. To kick off the 1978 congressional campaign season, President Carter felt compelled to apologize publicly to the national committee for his neglect in his first year in office, and he promised to do better in working with it, creating an office of political coordination to channel party patronage requests to the departments.

The White House Political Operation

Since Franklin Roosevelt's presidency the White House staff has played a dominant role in presidential political business. Harry Truman put the "research division" of the DNC under the control of Clark Clifford, the White House counsel. Eisenhower relied on his chief of staff Sherman Adams and congressional liaison Bryce Harlow. Kennedy used the "Irish Mafia "consisting of his brother Robert, Kenneth O'Donnell, and Larry O'Brien. Nixon established a political section in the White House Office and installed Harry Dent, a southerner with close ties to congressional conservatives: After the Watergate fiasco he sent Dent to the Republican National Committee as deputy counsel and turned responsibility for party affairs back to national chairman George Bush—who was quick to distance the party from the scandal, pointing out that it had been a White House operation. Jimmy Carter relied on a principal aide, Hamilton Jordan, as well as on staff assistants from Vice President Mondale's office to remain in contact with "The Network," the hundreds of political operatives at the state level who had worked in the Carter campaign. Bill Clinton dismantled the political operation of the Democratic National Committee after his election and reestablished it in the White House under the direction of Deputy Chief of Staff Harold Ickes. Clinton also moved several veteran members of the Democratic Congressional Campaign Committee over to the White House to handle his legislative liaison with the House and Senate.[22]

Presidential Fund-Raising

When presidential campaigns were funded by "fat cat" contributors, huge contributions given to presidential candidates might mean less for wealthier state parties but might help those in poorer states. In the late nineteenth century, Republican Party Chair Mark Hanna even attempted to "tithe" the richer state parties so that funds sent by them to the national committee would go to party committees in the poorer states. Hanna had seven hundred "party agents" of the national committees systematically solicit funds from corporations and banks as an "investment" in the Republican Party. He got top party leaders to ask wealthy "friends of the party" to donate, and canvassed elite men's clubs. Even the patronage appointments in the administration were systematically canvassed by party agents, with "assessments" (disguised as voluntary contributions) calculated as a percentage of their salaries.

With the advent of media politics in the 1960s, the need for campaign funds increased, and competition between national and state parties for donations intensified. Between 1960 and 1980 the presidential elections drained national and state party resources. When John Kennedy was nominated in 1960, the Democratic Party debt stood at $70,000; by the time he was elected, it had climbed to over $4 million. The party retired much of the debt by establishing a "President's Club" for wealthy donors, but in doing so it alienated Senate and House Democrats who found out that some funds from their committees were used to retire the DNC debt. After the 1968 campaign the DNC took it on itself to retire a $9.3 million debt from the losing Humphrey campaign; after the McGovern defeat in 1972 it had a $2.4 million debt. Each presidential election seemed to put the national party into a financial hole.

Since the campaign finance reforms of 1974 the national parties have found it much easier to raise funds from individuals and political action committees (PACs): the national parties may receive up to $20,000 annually from individuals, up to $15,000 annually from PACs, and an unlimited amount from state and local party committees. The parties have retired their own crushing debts, built new headquarters, professionalized their staffs, bought technologically advanced communications equipment, and established "campaign schools" for candidates and for campaign managers to learn the latest technologies. Presidents put a lot of effort into expanding the base of large contributors to the party: Bill Clinton helped the Democratic National Committee raise $31.2 million in 1993, up from $16.2 million in 1991 when the party was in opposition. With a Democrat in the White House, the Democratic National Committee's Business Leadership Forum (an association of businesses and trade organizations that contributes at least $15,000) expanded its membership from one hundred to more than six hundred in Clinton's first year in office.

The national parties are now able to raise enough money to help congressional candidates and provide them with "coordinated party expenditures": For Senate nominees the ceiling is 2 cents times the voting age population, and in 1994 ranged up to $1,325,415 in California. In House races the limit was $58,600 in states with only one Representative, and $29,300 for nominees in all other states.[23] The national committees can provide funding to state and local parties for equipment (i.e., computers), headquarters buildings and maintenance, and staffers. It can finance polls, research, and schools of campaign management, and can beef up their direct mail fund-raising operations. Presidents raise a lot of money for their congressional parties: Ronald Reagan raised millions of dollars for the Republican

Actor Charlton Heston applauds President Reagan and Nancy Reagan as the president addresses contributors to the Republican congressional campaign committee in Los Angeles, August 17, 1981.

"Stay the Course" congressional advertisements in 1982, and helped the party raise $12 million for a media campaign in 1984 attacking the Democratic-controlled House and defending the fairness of his tax and spending cuts.[24] Clinton raised millions for the Democratic congressional and senatorial campaign committees in the 1994 elections.

Since 1979 "party-building" contributions to state parties (known as "soft money") have been exempt from federal campaign contribution limits. Funds have flowed into state and local parties and campaign organizations from wealthy individuals, corporations and unions, and PACs. The president can help state parties raise money by appearing at state or local party dinners. His own fund-raisers can fill a hall anywhere in the country with contributors—especially if they want access to the White House. Ronald Reagan's "unity dinners" raised almost $17 million for state parties in 1984. In 1994 Bill Clinton raised $2.5 million in a single evening at two fund-raising events in New York City, with the proceeds divided between the national and state parties, the latter using its share for direct mail and get-out-the-vote drives.[25] In three other events he raised more than $1.2 million for New York Governor Mario Cuomo's reelection campaign. In the two years between the national convention of 1992 and summer of 1994, the Democrats raised $40.5 million in "soft money," contributions to state parties, primarily from corporate contributors—almost twice the $21.5 million raised by the Republicans.[26]

Even with all this fund-raising, a president may still be a drain on his party, because the national committee spends most of its money on presidential politicking. Polls for the White House are paid for by the national committee. The president's campaign appearances and partisan speeches are also paid for by the committee—including the bills for Air Force One when used to transport the president to partisan appearances. In the Clinton era, the national committee, while raising a considerable amount of money, spent almost all of it. "We're not meant to sit here on top of piles of money," explained committee staffer Catherine Moor. "We had the responsibility of supporting the White House. It's a burden we're happy to bear."[27]

THE CONGRESSIONAL AND STATE PARTIES

The congressional and state parties welcome presidential fund-raising efforts on their behalf, but often distance themselves from the White House, especially during the campaign season.

Autonomous Congressional Parties

With the exception of Franklin Roosevelt, presidents have not taken sides in more than one or two congressional primary contests. Woodrow Wilson unsuccessfully opposed a few southern conservatives; Harry Truman intervened twice in House primaries in his home state of Missouri; John Kennedy helped a few incumbents, including a key committee chairman. When Dan Rostenkowski, senior Democrat on the House Ways and Means Committee, got into trouble for alleged corruption in his office, President Clinton helped him eke out a narrow victory against a primary opponent. Similarly, the White House went all out in successful bids to defeat challengers against Representatives Mel Reynolds and David Mann, Democrats from Illinois and Ohio who had risked labor's wrath by voting for NAFTA. Even so, White House director of political affairs Joan Baggett cautioned that "we try strenuously to avoid an endorsement in a primary."[28]

On the Republican side, Dwight Eisenhower expressed the standard rule of noninvolvement when he stated, "I have always refused in advance of any primary or of any selection of Republican candidate for any office to intervene in any way."[29] Richard Nixon did not intervene in primaries with open endorsements, but he allowed Vice President Spiro Agnew to undercut a liberal Republican senator from New York in favor of a nominee from New York's minor Conservative Party. Ronald Reagan broke his own "11th Commandment" (never speak ill of another Republican) and intervened in a primary contest, but only *after* he left office, when he criticized Oliver North and unsuccessfully threw his support behind a rival in a Virginia Senatorial primary in 1994.

Between 1913 and 1960 there were approximately twelve thousand nominations to Congress, and by one count presidents made only thirty-nine endorsements in contested primaries. In most the incumbent won the endorsement. In ten cases the opponent of the incumbent was endorsed, and in only five of those cases was the incumbent defeated.[30] The pattern has remained the same through the early 1990s.

Although the president remains neutral in primaries, he may help the party recruit candidates for public office. He may suggest to his followers that they run for the House or Senate. He may give them an advance "buildup" by appointing them to visible executive positions in advance of their expected run for elective office. Most important, he may get candidates to run for office by offering to raise money and campaign for them, and promising to appoint them to office if they lose. Richard Nixon recruited a very strong group of senatorial candidates in 1970 and 1972 and helped rejuvenate his Senate party. Most presidents devote little time or attention to such party-building activities. In 1994, for example, Clinton did not even try to recruit Democratic governors to make Senate races.

Presidents have little influence in shaping campaign strategy in congressional elections. In the summer of 1990 President Bush acquiesced in a budget deal with the Democratic congressional leadership that left him vulnerable to the charge of raising taxes. During the fall midterm congressional election campaign, the director of the Republican Congressional Campaign Committee, Edward Rollins, circulated a memo urging Republican candidates for House seats to keep their distance from the White House and to repudiate Bush's promise of a tax increase.[31] "I have to give the best political advice I can and in this case, it is to run away from the budget package," he explained.[32] Bush went ballistic when he found out, and early in 1991 Rollins resigned under White House pressure.

Congressional candidates need not adhere to the party platform. Members take their own records to the voters. Since the 1870s there have been Senate and House campaign committees that work under the same roof as the national party committee but are under the control of legislative leaders, not the White House. "The history of White House relationships with the Senate and House campaign committees more closely resembles a blood feud than a bond of partisan kinship," according to one close observer.[33] Members of Congress even oppose the national party's attempt to define the issues in their districts: Democratic senators lambasted the party's national committee for running television advertisements touting Clinton's health care plan without first consulting them.[34]

Vanishing Presidential Coattails

Presidential coattails might once have provided an incentive for legislators to work closely with the president, for his reelection effort would have a direct bearing on their own prospects.[35] But coattails have vanished in most House contests and are weak in most Senate races.[36] In a number of contests presidents win and their party winds up with fewer House seats: in 1956 Eisenhower won a landslide reelection and his party lost two; in 1960 John Kennedy won while his party lost twenty; in 1988 George Bush won while his party lost three; in 1992 Bill Clinton defeated Bush but his party lost nine. The situation is similar in the Senate: between 1940 and 1992, of fourteen presidential contests, seven involved a party winning the White House and losing an average of two Senate seats. In states carried by Bill Clinton in 1992 Republicans won six Senate contests.

Although there is some "presidential effect" on the congressional vote, the major determinants of voter choice in congressional elections are party identification (giving Democrats the advantage), the state of the economy, and incumbency.[37] In presidential election years, between two-thirds and four-fifths of the defections from the "party line" have been toward the incumbent congressional candidate.[38] Voters are comfortable splitting their ballots: Ticket-splitting by voters in federal elections in presidential years rose from less than 15 percent in the 1950s to more than 25 percent in the 1970s and 1980s.[39] The percentage of congressional districts carried by a president from one party that elect a member of the opposite party to the House (split-party results) rose from 19.3 percent in 1952 to 44.1 percent in 1972, a figure reached again in 1984. In 1988 it was 34 percent.[40]

Most congressional districts are not highly competitive. There are small coattails on the Republican side, especially when a popular candidate like Eisenhower or Reagan runs, but they are usually not enough to overcome the Democratic incumbent advantages. In 1972, when Nixon won by a landslide, thirteen additional House Republicans were elected, though Senate representation declined by two. The better Nixon did in a congressional district, the better the House Republican candidate performed, but most could not overcome the Democratic advantages and actually win the seat.[41] Goldwater, Nixon, Ford, Reagan, and Bush all wrote off the possibility of electing a Republican House, a strategy that did not bring them any closer to their congressional parties. "Here the son-of-a-buck ended up with 59 percent and you bring in fifteen seats," complained House minority leader Bob Michel after Reagan won his landslide in 1984 while House Republicans made only small gains.[42] In 1988 George Bush ran behind 85 percent of the winning Republican candidates in House elections.[43]

In Senate elections Republican coattails are longer. In 1952 Eisenhower brought in enough Republican senators to obtain a majority, though he lost it within two years. In 1972 when Nixon won a smashing victory over McGovern, seventeen Republicans were elected or returned to the Senate. In only six of these races did the Republican senatorial candidate have a greater margin of victory than Nixon, and in only six did the candidate receive more votes than Nixon, a good indication that Nixon's coattails helped in many cases. Although Democrats retained control of the Senate, Nixon claimed a "working majority" by virtue of the right of center ideological balance in the Senate. When Ronald Reagan was elected in 1980, his coattails not only provided the margin of victory for a number of senatorial candidates, they also enabled the Republicans to win a Senate majority for the first time since the elections of 1952—a majority they held through 1986.[44] Yet in 1988, when George Bush won the White House, his party lost seats in both the House and Senate—for the first time since 1916 when the same thing had happened to Woodrow Wilson.

Democratic presidents usually have no coattails: they usually receive a lower percentage of the two-party vote than their congressional colleagues. Most members of the Democratic congressional party do not consider the president responsible for their own election victories. As Democratic House Whip Percy Priest said in 1949 after Truman squeaked into office, "More than 100 of our 263 Democrats got more votes in their districts than Truman, and they felt they didn't owe him a damn thing."[45] Almost all Democrats elected with Kennedy, Carter, and Clinton could have said the same thing. In fact, when Kennedy entered the Democrats actually lost more than a score of seats, and many blamed him for it. Kennedy, Carter, and Clinton all found that House candidates (winners and losers) won more votes on the Democratic column than they did. The situation is similar in the Senate contests: in 1976 twenty-one Democrats were elected or returned to the Senate. In twenty of these contests, the Democratic candidate had a greater margin of victory than Carter, and in sixteen the Democrat received more votes than Carter. In the three-candidate race in 1992, Clinton did not outpoll a single Democrat elected to Congress.

In recent elections, many Democratic incumbents, though returned to office, find their margins of victory shrinking from landslide (over 60 percent) proportions into the more competitive range. The anti-incumbent mood in the 1992 and 1994 campaigns has been reflected by lowered "deserves re-election" responses in polls taken in incumbent districts: the average positive response for House incumbents went from 46 percent in 1990 to 40 percent in 1992 and into the mid-30s in 1994.[46] Incumbents who run scared may also run from the White House. So the president is in a no-win situation: a congressional party with comfortable margins can disregard him, and a congressional party on the ropes may distance itself from him.

Off-Year Contests and Midterm Congressional Elections

Legislative elections are constitutionally disassociated from presidential elections. The entire House is elected in the presidential year, but all members must run again two years later in the midterm elections; similarly members of the Senate elected in a presidential year will run six years later in an off year. Each member must consider how he or she can win in an off year election when turnout will be much lower (dropping from about 55 percent in a presidential year to about 35 or 40 percent in an off year), and no presidential campaign will distract those who do vote from assessing congressional performance.

Although constitutionally separate, congressional midterm elections usually are negatively affected by presidential politics.[47] In every midterm election since 1866 except three (1902, 1906, and 1934), the president's party has lost seats in the House of Representatives. Since 1945 these losses have averaged 15 seats in the first midterm election and about 45 seats in the midterm election that occurs in a president's second term (Figure 7.1). How do we explain these results? A huge victory for the president and his party may be followed by a subsequent large loss in the midterm elections, a phenomenon known as "surge and decline." It occurs when enough voters who have been drawn into the presidential elections and voted a "straight ticket" drop out two years later in the midterm election.[48] The larger the president's victory margin, the greater the loss in subsequent midterm contests. Another reason seems to be that the president and his congressional party are viewed as less able to solve national problems the longer they remain in office.[49] Other factors in midterm voting include economic conditions, a desire to "balance" one party's control of the White House with support for the other party, and the possibility that strong potential House candidates prefer to "sit out" a tough midterm election (when the president has taken unpopular actions and his party is on the defensive) and run in the presidential election year when the party's fortunes may have improved.[50]

Assessments of presidential performance in some midterm contests are crucial.[51] One study found that a change in presidential popularity of 10 percent in the Gallup polls is associated with a national change of 1.3 percent in the midterm vote for members of the president's party. In all cases studied, the president's popularity declined, and the voting change was negative.[52] Another study suggests that disapproval of the President's performance causes more defections from his party in midterm congressional elections than approval of his performance brings voters from the opposing camp to vote for his party, a situation that occurred to Bill Clinton in 1994.[53] President Clinton hurt his congressional party in the 1994 midterm elections because of a "negative valence" effect involving his character. As Terry

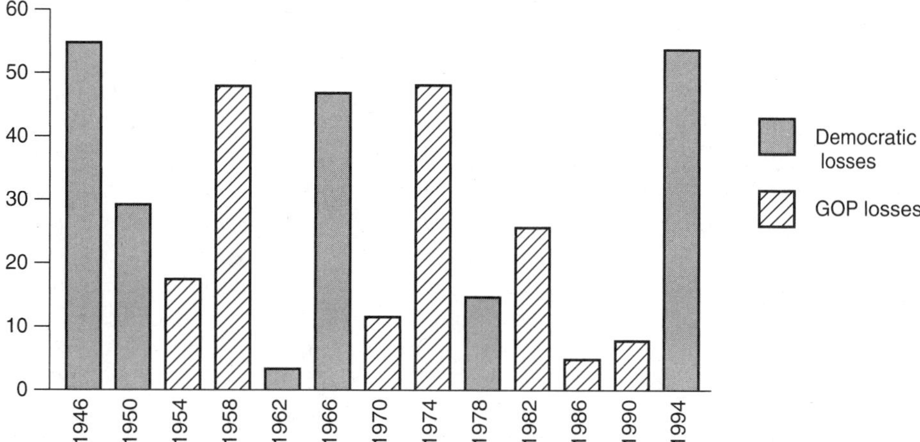

Figure 7.1 Number of seats lost by the president's party in midterm House elections, 1946–1994.

Michael, a former communications director for the Democratic National Committee, put it, "Clinton, on a personal level, embodies the concerns people have about politicians being self-serving and slick," and therefore he recommended that Democratic candidates identify with Clinton's proposals but not with the president himself.[54] A president who does well in office does not help his congressional candidates much, but an unpopular president or one who has stumbled into a domestic or foreign policy crisis, is involved in a scandal, or presiding over a recession, will hurt his party badly. The Nixon–Ford combination of Watergate crimes and a presidential pardon led to disastrous Republican midterm losses in the 1974 elections.[55]

Since Woodrow Wilson began the practice in 1918, presidents have campaigned for House and Senate candidates in midterm elections, yet their efforts at best stem large losses: even after campaigning Wilson's party lost control of both houses of Congress. Presidents are damned if they do and damned if they do not campaign: Lyndon Johnson did not campaign in 1966, and his party took heavy losses anyway in the House and in governorship races. Donald Sweitzer, political director of the Democratic National Committee, admitted that "there are clearly some areas of the country where it is not going to benefit a candidate to associate himself with Bill Clinton, and if you want us to stay away, we'll stay away."[56] Although Sweitzer was immediately repudiated by DNC chairman David Wilhelm, by early fall some Democratic candidates for the House were avoiding all mention of the president in their campaigns—in part based on the advice of the president's own pollster, Stanley Greenberg, whose memo, "Strategic Guide to the 1994 Elections," urged them to focus on their own agendas. There is some evidence that a popular president who campaigns strategically for Senate candidates will provide an additional 3 to 4 percent of the vote for them, sometimes enough to ensure a margin of victory in a close race.[57]

For Democrats there is no correlation between midterm losses of House seats and results in the next presidential elections. Between 1940 and 1992, when Democrats controlled the White House, there were three midterm elections (1950, 1966, 1978) followed by Republican presidential victories (1952, 1968, 1980): on average the Democrats lost 6.9 percent of the House in the midterm elections, and dropped 10.5 percent in subsequent presidential voting. There were three other midterm elections (1942, 1946, 1962) that were followed by Democratic presidential election victories (1944, 1948, 1964): in the midterm contests the Democrats lost 7.9 percent of the House on average, yet they gained 2.9 percent in the two-party vote in the subsequent presidential elections.

For Republicans there does seem to be some correlation between loss of seats in the House and subsequent elections. Since 1940, there have been three midterm elections (1958, 1974, 1990) that were followed by a Republican loss of the White House (1960, 1976, 1992): In the midterm elections the Republicans lost an average of 7.9 percent of the seats in the House, followed by a decline of 7 percent in their share of the two-party vote for president. Four other midterm contests (1954, 1970, 1982, 1986) were followed by Republican presidential victories (1956, 1972, 1984, 1988), and in these midterm elections the average seat loss was 3.5 percent of total House seats, followed by a 7 percent gain in the two-party presidential vote.

Autonomous State Parties

In 1936 Progressive Ray Stannard Baker wrote to Franklin Roosevelt to complain of the corruption of the Curley machine in Boston, calling on the president to "clean out the Democratic organization" in the state. "There is much, I fear, in what you say," Roosevelt wrote back, "but what is a poor fellow to do about it: I wish I knew."[58] The president does not control state or local parties: they recruit their own candidates, hold primaries without White House interference, finance their own campaigns, and develop their own campaign strategy. Elections for most state offices are held in nonpresidential election years to insulate them from national trends and issues: in the 1990s only about one-fifth of the gubernatorial races were held in the presidential year. Often a party will win the White House and lose governorships: In 1988 the Republicans suffered a net loss of one; in 1992 the Democrats had a net loss of two. And often the president will win in an important industrial state, only to find within one or two years the statehouse has gone to the opposition party, as happened in New Jersey in 1993 with the election of Republican Governor Christie Whitman.

Presidential candidates gain strength from strong state parties, not vice versa, especially on the Democratic side, where a correlation exists between Democratic strength in the state legislature and the percentage of the two-party vote for the presidential nominee. Jimmy Carter won 18 of 21 states in 1976 in which Democrats had 70 percent or more of the legislative seats. He won only five states in which the Democrats had lower percentages. In 1992 Clinton won states in which Democrats on average held 62 percent of the seats in the lower chambers of state legislatures; in contrast Bush won in states in which Democrats held on average 56 percent.

When a party wins the presidency it does not always translate into gains at the state level. While Ford was winning Kansas, North Dakota, and Vermont in 1976, Democrats were taking control of their legislatures. In 1988 Bush won the White House but Republicans lost several hundred seats in state legislatures, winding up with fewer seats than they had held in 1981. While Clinton was winning the presidency in 1992, the Republican Party was making strong inroads into his own southern base in several state legislatures, and chipping away at Democratic margins in many other states.

The White House and State Parties

State party leaders are kept at a distance by the president once the campaign ends. One study reported that these leaders work closely with members of Congress and with their delegations on the party national committee, but that there are few contacts with the White House staff and hardly any with the president.[59] Party leaders often take positions that conflict with the president's. Kennedy was opposed by southern state parties who were against his civil rights efforts. Johnson faced a coalition of Democratic mayors opposed to community control of his "War on Poverty" Community Action Program. Carter was unable to persuade the Florida and North

Carolina legislatures to pass the Equal Rights Amendment, and his proposals for a national system of election-day registration met with resistance from many Democratic governors and attorneys general. Moderate Republican mayors and governors fought against Reagan's plans for drastic cuts in community development programs and public housing. Clinton's health care proposals for "alliances" to manage competition among health insurers faced strong opposition from many Democratic governors, who recognized that it spelled electoral disaster for them in the midterm contests.

Presidents use patronage to try to cement relations with state parties, but in modern times it has had little impact. These parties do not help fill cabinet positions or senior posts within the White House. Only a small fraction of the subcabinet-level positions are filled through their recommendations. During the New Deal, Roosevelt and Truman did maintain some connection with the Democratic National Committee in filling "exempted" (nonmerit) positions in the civil service. During the Eisenhower administration the Republican National Committee proposed the "Willis Plan," which would have linked the departments, the committee, the state parties, and the congressional parties, but it was scuttled by White House aides. Instead, interest groups and careerists filled most political positions, and state party leaders were bypassed. After two years only 274 officials (of 10,000 appointed) had come from state party recommendations. As Eisenhower's chief of staff Sherman Adams recalled, Eisenhower "insisted on making the final decision on his own appointees and carefully avoided giving the Republican National Committee any responsibility in the selection of government officials, a duty the committee would have been happy to assume."[60]

Starting with John Kennedy the White House has bypassed state parties almost entirely, making appointments from universities and foundations, media, public interest watchdog groups, business and trade groups, the professions, and the career civil service at the state and national levels. Most presidents, like Bill Clinton, place their own loyalists, often from their own state parties, in sensitive positions, particularly in the Justice Department and White House Counsel's Office, where they can monitor politically sensitive (i.e., potentially embarrassing) law enforcement issues. While the president believes he is appointing "the best and the brightest" for his administration, he is doing little or nothing to build other state parties through federal appointments.

PARTY COMPETITION

To be an effective party leader, the president must lead his party to a dominating position over the opposition. Yet many presidents, by their policies, exercise of prerogative powers, or personal conduct, have repelled rather than attracted voters to their parties, and left their parties weaker after their term in office.

The Parties in the Electorate

In the past thirty years Democrats have lost their overwhelming advantage in party identification in the electorate, in large measure because of dissatisfaction with Democratic presidents and candidates. Between 1936 and 1977, Democrats averaged a three-to-two advantage in party identification over Republicans. With large numbers of white Southern Democrats switching to the Republican Party in the 1980s, and with younger voters choosing the Republican party in the Reagan era, the Democrats wound up almost neck-and-neck with Republicans by the late 1980s.

Coalition-Building

The Democrats have also lost their advantages in group identification. The New Deal coalition won support from labor, African-Americans, Hispanics, Roman Catholics, Jews, and the Solid South. Since the 1930s labor union membership has declined by half, and many workers now vote Republican on social issues. Although African-American and Jewish support remains high, Catholic support for Democratic candidates has dropped in many elections from the 60 percent range to less than 50 percent. Hispanic voters remain heavily Democratic, but in Florida they vote Republican and can often put that state in the GOP column. Republicans not only win the male vote in most elections, they would have won the presidency even if the race had been decided only by women. In 1980 Reagan won the male vote, 57 to 36, but he also won narrowly among women, 47 to 45 percent (remaining votes went to John Anderson). In 1984 Reagan also won a landslide among men (62 to 38 percent) and this time did almost as well among women, winning 58 to 42 percent. Although one wag commented that "George Bush reminds every woman of her first husband," Bush not only won the male vote in 1988, 57 to 41 percent, he also won the female vote, 50 to 49 percent. The most important defection from the Democratic coalition involves white southerners. In 1952 Democrats held a commanding lead of 78 to 9 percent in party identification among white southerners. By 1986 the Republicans held a slight lead, and by 1995 that had turned into a more than 2–1 advantage in party identification. Many working-class white southerners had moved from the racial voting of the 1950s (the so-called "redneck" vote) to the cultural and family values voting of the 1990s (the so-called "Christian" vote).

When Democrats win the presidency, they do so by winning narrowly, barely resuscitating their New Deal coalition, and then combining it with independent voters and some Republican defections. Their coalition has antithetical components, as it has since the New Deal era. When Republicans win the presidency, they do so through "deviating" elections: they win personal rather than party victories. Eisenhower, Nixon, and Reagan won landslide victories, but they were not able to make their party dominant.

REGIME FORMATION AND POLITICAL TIME

In seeking to explain the success or failure of presidents, some political scientists have developed a cyclical theory of presidential party politics, which relates electoral success to governance.[61] According to one theory presidents can be located in "political time" rather than chronological time. Political time involves the sequence of regime creation, regime maintenance, and regime disintegration.[62] A president may create a new regime (i.e., a set of stable relationships between the government and significant interest groups such as corporations, unions, trade associations, nonprofit organizations, which are mediated by a dominant political party), he or she may continue a regime created by a predecessor with only minor modifications or may preside over an administration that fails to preserve the regime.

Transformative Presidents

Some presidents have done nothing less than transform American politics by appealing to mass public opinion, changing the party system (either by creating a new party or else by reorienting an existing one), creating new coalitions of interest groups to back their party and its program, and expanding the formal powers of the presidency to change the scope and responsibilities of the government.[63] They have made their party and its coalition of interests the dominant political force in the nation for a generation or more.

The transformative presidents are those we erect statues and monuments to, whose graves and homes we visit, whose images are engraved on our currency as well as our collective national memory: George Washington, Thomas Jefferson, Andrew Jackson, Abraham Lincoln, and Franklin Roosevelt. Presidents are transformational leaders only in certain circumstances: during great depressions or times or rapid economic change; in domestic crises when the president can form a consensus about fundamental political reforms; or when the nation assumes a new role in world affairs. Even then they usually cannot accomplish a permanent change: Washington's attempt (through Hamilton) to promote an active role for the national government in economic development was soon overturned by Jefferson; in turn his conception of limited national government was eroded by his successors. Jackson renewed Jefferson's ideas, but his successor Van Buren was incapable of carrying on his legacy, and the Whigs renewed efforts at national direction of the economy. In the Gettysburg Address, Lincoln stated that "all men are created equal" as a fundamental constitutional creed, and after prosecuting the Civil War called for "charity for all, malice towards none" in victory. Yet after his death congressional Republicans initially imposed a harsh Reconstruction policy on the white south, then a decade later abandoned blacks to state-sanctioned inferiority and segregation. Of all transformative presidents, only Franklin Roosevelt managed to leave a legacy (in his case, the start of the social welfare state) that lasted a political generation without repudiation—Democratic presidents continued his efforts while Republicans consolidated and trimmed without making fundamental alterations until 1995.

Although transformative presidents have had some successes, complete regime construction does not take place. Presidents cannot fully reorient their parties because the congressional and state parties are autonomous. Some succeed in rallying the nation in a moral crusade and inaugurate an era of reform and innovation, but the American liberal tradition and preference for incremental changes sets limits on how much they can accomplish.

Maintaining Presidents

Maintaining presidents succeed a transformative president, and their policies reinforce his coalition of interests and his political principles. Examples include Madison and Monroe after Jefferson; Van Buren and Polk after Jackson; Grant, Hayes, Garfield, Arthur, Harrison, and McKinley after Lincoln; and Truman, Kennedy, and Johnson after Franklin Roosevelt. These presidents kept faith with the regime and did not disappoint their followers' expectations. They tried to complete the unfinished business of their predecessors and innovated without repudiating or abandoning the principles of the regime. They proceeded incrementally, but even so, they were usually beset by party factionalism.

Most maintaining presidents do not have impressive rhetorical skills: like Jimmy Carter, they mumble and fumble in their attempts to address the people; like George Bush, they lack "the vision thing," the intangible quality of leadership that enables some people to inspire others with their vision of the future. Their attempt to use inflated rhetoric and force a sense of urgency onto a nation content with existing conditions leads merely to grandiloquent gestures that fail to connect with the public mood. When President Ford unveiled his "WIN" program (for "Whip Inflation Now"), the public ridiculed him and it. When Jimmy Carter summoned the American people to support his "New Foundation" domestic proposals, comedians joked that it sounded like a new line of lingerie. When George Bush spoke of a "New World Order," the American people shrugged and turned their attention back to domestic affairs.

Minority-Party Presidents

Not all presidents come from the dominant political coalition. A candidate of the minority party may win without converting his party into majority status: examples include Grover Cleveland and Woodrow Wilson on the Democratic side, and Dwight Eisenhower, Richard Nixon, Ronald Reagan, and George Bush on the Republican side. Because they cannot rely on a majority political base, they may be tempted to rely on their prerogative powers to block or bypass Congress and on their rhetorical skills to intimidate it.

Unless minority-party presidents can convert their party into the majority through a realigning election in their first or second term, they seem doomed to a politics of constitutional confrontation and policy stalemates—or else, like Eisenhower, they must engage in constructive compromises with the majority party that gives them some illusion of success, but negates the principles of their party and weakens its electoral prospects. If they use prerogative powers they may suffer dramatic defeats, involving either the backlash or overshoot and collapse effects.[64] These presidents may be dangerous to their parties. Their "high-wire" act, use of controversial prerogatives, may result in a "crash and burn" presidency, that not only brings them down, but leads their party into terrible defeat. Richard Nixon not only was compelled to resign the presidency, but left his party in shambles after the 1976 election, when commentators began to refer to a "one and a half" party system to denote overwhelming Democratic dominance.

Failed Presidents

A regime may continue with an ideology or program that cannot solve national problems, and eventually it may face a crisis.[65] Then a president locked into existing commitments, policies, and politics may not be able to manage it successfully: he may block action, take half-measures, fashion a compromise that satisfies no one, or else become paralyzed by indecision. At some point the regime is so enervated it threatens to disintegrate. While there is nothing inevitable about the collapse of a regime, the intersection of a president who has poor leadership qualities and a historical moment at which leadership is absolutely imperative will lead to the collapse of the governing coalition and its replacement by a new majority party that is capable of constructing a new regime. Presidents whose regimes disintegrated include John Quincy Adams, James Buchanan, and Herbert Hoover. If we assume that the New Deal regime collapsed after 1968, we might also include Lyndon Johnson. If we assume that the Reagan presidency involved creation of a new regime—which is debatable, because the party system did not realign—then George Bush should be included.

How does a regime collapse? Contradictory elements within the party and administration can no longer reconcile the irreconcilable conflicts. There is no longer a pretense of ruling for the national interest, as each part of the coalition collapses into the rhetoric of special constituency and group demands, as happened with Jimmy Carter. The leaders lose their authority with the people, and lapse into irrelevance as new issues, for which they have no mandate or vision, become salient. Although George Bush presided over a victory over Saddam Hussein in Operation Desert Storm, his presidency (and party leadership) collapsed in the aftermath, as the nation's attention turned to domestic issues—and the nation saw that Bush had his own "attention deficit" in dealing with them.

The concept of political time is helpful, because it enables us to make comparisons across chronological time. We can see that opportunities for leadership and regime formation occur in pretty much the same way, even though a century or more separates the presidents we are comparing. We can see Carter and Kennedy struggle to hold their party factions together in much the way Van Buren and Polk did. We can see both John Quincy Adams and George Bush lose their authority with the people.

Above all, the placement of presidents in political time helps us focus on the key questions of party leadership: Is the president creating, affirming, or repudiating a regime? Is he developing new principles to guide the relationships between government, parties, and interest groups? Or is he presiding haplessly while the legitimacy of existing arrangements is challenged and ultimately repudiated by others? The answers to these questions help us understand not only specific questions about presidential party leadership, but also issues involving the transformation of the presidency itself.

A Critique of Cyclical Theories

Like all theories, the concept of political time must be used with care. It can explain some aspects of party leadership, but it may raise as many questions as it answers. For one thing, presidents do not create entirely new regimes, and most, even energetic party leaders, do not attempt a complete reorientation of their parties. Wilson moderated his progressive stance after a few years, and his party was as diverse when he left the presidency as when he entered it. Franklin Roosevelt made up to his enemies after the failure of the 1938 purge, and by the end of his presidency northern liberals confronted southern conservatives for more than three decades. Reagan may have tried to create a post–New Deal conservative regime but was unable to win enough electoral support to move his party to the majority.

It is difficult to know where to place some presidents in political time. After Reagan's victory, it seemed that Carter had been an enervated president presiding over the end of the New Deal regime. If that were so, however, then Reagan and Bush would have had to create a new regime. In light of Clinton's 1992 victory, the Reagan–Bush regime seems somewhat flimsy and transitory. Moreover, Clinton's presidency would also have marked the beginning of a new regime, a characterization which (in spite of his rhetoric about "New Democrats") seems to offer little in the way of an explanation for the policy zig-zags and competing ideological tendencies of his first years in office. If anything, his behavior appeared congruent with that of most Democratic "maintaining" presidents, and by 1995 the "regime" seemed short-lived.

The concept of regime outsider (the minority president) also makes little sense. The dominant regime until the 1960s was the New Deal. Supposedly Republican presidents Eisenhower and Nixon were regime-outsiders, whereas Truman and Kennedy and Johnson were regime-insiders. It does not make much sense, however, to consider Eisenhower an "outsider" given his military career and his connections with world leaders and important financiers and executives, unless we are using regime simply as a shorthand way of saying dominant party coalition. More can be understood about Eisenhower by viewing him as a part of an American establishment than can be gained by viewing him as somehow in "opposition" to a dominant political regime.

Conversely, it is hard to conceive of Kennedy as an insider: In party affairs and in the Senate he was a minor figure, and he had chilly relations with the business community and the military and intelligence communities. As for Lyndon Johnson, his power in the Senate did little to overcome his feelings of inferiority as a Texan from the southern wing of the party, who believed he would never be accepted by the "Eastern liberal establishment" that he thought dominated the party and the media.

Finally, the notion of a regime implies a stable electoral coalition. Yet almost everything we know about party identification, electoral voting coalitions, and relations of groups to parties indicates little stability, and a great play for "dynamic" factors such as personality, image making, and media manipulation in campaigns. To attempt to create a stable regime in current conditions may be as futile as building castles in the sand.

THE ANTI-PARTY PRESIDENCY

The changes in nominating and electing presidents and in organizing the Oval Office in the past half century have weakened the relationship between presidents and their parties. To make a president a strong party leader would require major changes in political practices. A greater proportion of campaign contributions would have to be channeled through the national party committees rather than through the candidates' campaigns. Presidential and congressional nominations would have to be controlled (or at least more strongly influenced) by party organizations and the White House, rather than left to the party voters in nominating primaries. Party rules would have to be changed to require all candidates to adhere to the national party platform. These and other reforms are well known to presidency scholars and political practitioners, but there is no incentive for presidents, members of Congress, or those party workers beholden to them to carry the reforms into effect. Everyone prefers maximum autonomy and freedom of maneuver to party discipline.

If the president does not dominate the party, neither does the party dominate the president. A president is free to strike a nonpartisan pose, to sell the party out, to rely on the opposition for votes on key issues (Bush on the budget, Clinton on international trade). In the final analysis the president is of the party—but also above it and sometimes in opposition to it. He or she does not find it of any great use to attempt to be a strong party leader. If the president finds it necessary to transcend party interests, he or she may do so without damage to personal principles or interests. The president may choose bipartisan consultation and accommodation for interests in routine situations, nonpartisan emergency prerogatives for crises. He or she may rally the party for a domestic program, but build liberal and conservative coalitions that cross party lines for other purposes. The president may shift from one day to the next; consistency may be the virtue of a party man or woman, but it is a presidential vice. The party, too, is free of presidential constraints: an anti-presidential party matches the anti-party presidency. After two centuries of party politics, American practices remain remarkably in tune with original constitutional principles of checks and balances and partial separation of powers, and therefore with the intentions of those who framed a system of limited constitutional government.

FURTHER READING

Books

James W. Davis, *The President as Party Leader,* New York: Greenwood Press, 1992.

Ralph Goldman, *The National Party Chairman and Committees,* Armonk, NY: M. E. Sharpe, 1990.

Robert Harmel, ed., *Presidents and Their Parties,* New York: Praeger, 1984.

John Kessel, *Presidential Parties,* Homewood, IL: Dorsey Press, 1984.

Ralph Ketcham, *Presidents above Party: The First American Presidency, 1789–1829,* Chapel Hill, NC: University of North Carolina Press, 1984.

Sidney Milkis, *The Presidents and the Parties: The Transformation of the American Party System Since the New Deal,* New York: Oxford University Press, 1993.

Stephen Skowronek, *The Politics Presidents Make,* Cambridge, MA: Harvard University Press, 1993.

Documentary Sources

Committee on the Constitutional System, *Reforming American Government,* Boulder, CO: Westview Press, 1985.

"Toward a More Responsible Two Party System," *American Political Science Review,* Vol. 44, September, 1950, supplement.

NOTES

1. Sidney Milkis, *The President and the Parties,* New York: Oxford University Press, 1993, p. 3.

2. James MacGregor Burns, *The Lion and the Fox,* New York: Harcourt, Brace and World, 1956, p. 363.

3. Charles M. Price and Joseph Boskin, "The Roosevelt Purge: A Reappraisal," *Journal of Politics,* Vol. 28, no. 3, August, 1966, p. 663.

4. Ibid., pp. 666–667.

5. James Farley, *Jim Farley's Story,* New York: Whittlesley House, 1948, pp. 146–147.

6. Sidney M. Milkis, "President's and Party Purges: With Special Emphasis on the Lessons of 1938," in Robert Harmel, ed., *Presidents and Their Parties,* New York: Praeger, 1984, pp. 151–175.

7. Robert V. Remini, "The Emergence of Political Parties and Their Effect on the Presidency," in Philip Dolce and George Skau, eds., *Power and the Presidency,* New York: Scribner's, 1976, p. 25.

8. Todd Purdum, "The Newest Moynihan," *New York Times Magazine,* August 7, 1994, p. 27.

9. David Broder, "Winning Strategy," *Washington Post National Weekly Edition,* November 29–December 5, 1993, p. 4.

10. *New York Times,* December 4, 1993, p. 10.

11. *New York Times,* December 5, 1993, p. 43.

12. James W. Davis, *The President as National Party Leader,* New York: Greenwood Press, 1992, pp. 97–118.

13. Milkis, op. cit., pp. 62–66, 134–135.

14. James W. Davis, *The President as Party Leader,* New York: Greenwood Press, 1994, p. 111.

15. Milkis, op. cit., p. 190.

16. Harold F. Bass, "The President and the National Party Organization," in Robert Harmel, ed., *Presidents and Their Parties,* New York: Praeger, 1984, pp. 63–65.

17. Joseph Califano, *A Presidential Nation,* New York: W. W. Norton, 1975, p. 153.

18. Lloyd Grove, "If You Can't Stand the Heat, Get Out of the DNC," *Washington Post National Weekly Edition,* May 9–15, 1994, p. 12.

19. John Bibby, "Party Renewal in the National Republican Party," in Gerald Pomper, ed., *Party Renewal: Theory and Practice,* New York: Praeger, 1980, pp. 102–115.

20. Quoted in Milkis, op. cit., p. 33.

21. Lawrence O'Brien, *No Final Victories,* New York: Doubleday, 1974, p. 108.

22. James Barnes, "Clinton's 1994 Political Machine . . . Gets an Oil Change and Tune-Up," *National Journal,* February 12, 1994, p. 381.

23. *Federal Election Commission Record,* March, 1994, Tables 1, 2, 3, pp. 2–3.

24. Dan Nimmo, "Teleparty Politics," *Campaigns and Elections,* Winter, 1986, pp. 75–77.

25. *New York Times,* June 28, 1994, p. B-2.

26. Michael Wines, "Givers' Largesse Is Putting Heat on Clinton," *New York Times,* June 21, 1994, p. 1.

27. Charles Babcock, "Winning or Losing Is like Money in the Bank," *Washington Post National Weekly Edition,* March 21–27, 1994, p. 8.

28. *Congressional Quarterly Weekly Reports,* March 19, 1994, p. 684.

29. Ibid.

30. William Riker and William Best, "Presidential Action in Congressional Nominations," in Aaron Wildavsky, ed., *The Presidency,* Boston: Little, Brown, 1969, pp. 250–267.

31. Milkis, op. cit., p. 293.

32. Andrew Rosenthal, "Bush Mounts Effort to Quell G.O.P. Rebellion over Taxes," *New York Times,* October 26, 1990, pp. A-1, A-2.

33. Roger G. Brown, "Presidents as Midterm Campaigners," in Robert Harmel, ed., *Presidents and Their Parties,* New York: Praeger, 1984, p. 139.

34. Dan Balz, "They Were Behind Him 1,000 Percent," *Washington Post National Weekly Edition,* August 15–21, 1994, p. 15.

35. Warren E. Miller, "Presidential Coattails: A Study in Political Myth and Methodology," *Public Opinion Quarterly,* Vol. 19, no. 4, Winter, 1956, pp. 353–368; Randall Calvert and John A. Ferejohn, "Presidential Coattails in Historical Perspective," *American Journal of Political Science,* Vol. 28, no. 1, February, 1984, pp. 126–146.

36. James A. Campbell and Joe A. Sumners, "Presidential Coattails in Senate Elections," *American Political Science Review,* Vol. 84, no. 2, June, 1990, pp. 516–524.

37. Richard Born, "Reassessing the Decline of Presidential Coattails: U.S. House Elections from 1952–1980," *Journal of Politics,* Vol. 46, no. 1, February, 1984, pp. 60–79; Robert Erikson, "The Advantage of Incumbency in Congressional Elections," *Polity,* Vol. 3, no. 3, Spring, 1971, pp. 345–405; Warren Kostroski, "Party and Incumbency in Postwar Senate Elections," *The American Political Science Review,* Vol. 67, no. 4, December, 1973, pp. 1213–1234.

38. Albert Cover and Donald Mayhew, "Congressional Dynamics and the Decline of Competitive Congressional Elections," in Lawrence Dodd and Bruce Oppenheimer, eds., *Congress Reconsidered,* New York: Praeger, 1977.

39. Ibid., Fig. 2: "House-President Ticket-Splitting," p. 393.

40. Morris P. Fiorina, "An Era of Divided Government," *Political Science Quarterly,* Vol. 107, no. 3, Fall, 1992, Table 4: "Congressional Districts Carried by House and Presidential Candidates of Different Parties," p. 392.

41. Gary Jacobson, "Presidential Coattails in 1972," *Public Opinion Quarterly,* Vol. 40, no. 2, Summer, 1976, p. 196.

42. *New York Times,* November 12, 1984, p. 8.

43. Richard Cohen, "Congress: Lonely Runner," *National Journal,* April 29, 1989, p. 1048.

44. Randall Calvert and John A. Ferejohn, "Coattail Voting in Recent Presidential Elections," *American Political Science Review,* Vol. 77, no. 2, June, 1983, pp. 407–419; James E. Campbell and Joe A. Sumners, "Presidential Coattail Voting in Senate Elections," *American Political Science Review,* Vol. 84, no. 2, June, 1990, pp. 513–524.

45. Alfred Steinberg, *Sam Rayburn,* New York: Hawthorn, 1975, p. 252.

46. Data compiled by Geoff Garin, in Dan Balz, "On the Inside Looking Out," *Washington Post National Weekly Edition,* April 4–10, 1994, p. 12.

47. Alan Abramowitz, Albert Cover, and Helmut Norpoth, "The President's Party in Midterm Elections: Going from Bad to Worse," *American Journal of Political Science,* Vol. 30, no. 3, August, 1986, pp. 562–576.

48. Angus Campbell, "Surge and Decline: A Study of Electoral Change," *Public Opinion Quarterly,* Vol. 24, no. 3, Fall, 1960, pp. 397–418.

49. Abramowitz, Cover, and Norpoth, op. cit.

50. Gary Jacobson and Samuel Kernell, *Strategy and Choice in Congressional Elections,* New Haven, CT: Yale University Press, 1981.

51. James E. Campbell, "The Presidential Surge and Its Midterm Decline in Congressional Elections, 1868–1988," *Journal of Politics,* Vol. 53, no. 2, May, 1991, pp. 477–487.

52. Edward Tufte, "Determinants of Outcomes of Midterm Congressional Elections," *American Political Science Review,* Vol. 71, no. 1, March, 1977, p. 817.

53. Samuel Kernell, "Presidential Popularity and Negative Voting," *American Political Science Review,* Vol. 71, no. 1, March, 1977, pp. 46–59.

54. *New York Times,* June 9, 1994, p. A-12.

55. Eric M. Uslaner and Margaret M. Conway, "The Responsible Congressional Electorate: Watergate, the Economy, and Vote Choice in 1974," *American Political Science Review,* Vol. 79, no. 3, September, 1985, pp. 788–803.

56. *New York Times,* June 9, 1994, p. 10.

57. Jeffrey Cohen et al., "The Impact of Presidential Campaigning on Midterm U.S. Senate Elections," *American Political Science Review,* Vol. 85, no. 1, March, 1991, pp. 165–178.

58. Quoted in Milkis, op. cit., p. 48.

59. Robert Huckshorn, *Party Leadership in the States,* Cambridge, MA: University of Massachusetts Press, 1976, p. 207.

60. Sherman Adams, *Firsthand Report,* Westport, CT: Greenwood Press, 1961, p. 57.

61. Stephen Skowronek, *The Politics Presidents Make,* Cambridge, MA: Harvard University Press, 1993.

62. Stephen Skowronek, "The Presidency in Political Time," in Michael Nelson, ed., *The Presidency in the Political System,* Washington, DC: Congressional Quarterly Press, 1990, pp. 117–163.

63. James MacGregor Burns, *Leadership,* New York: Harper and Row, 1978, pp. 385–397.

64. Stephen Skowronek, *The Politics Presidents Make,* op. cit., p. 44.

65. Ibid., pp. 39–41.

CHAPTER 8

National Agenda Politics

I tried to do so many things at once that I didn't take time to do one of the president's most important jobs, and that is to consistently explain to the American people what we were doing and why.

—Bill Clinton

INTRODUCTORY CASE: FRANKLIN ROOSEVELT'S HUNDRED DAYS

March 4, 1933, was a gray day, matching the mood of the American people. Thirteen million Americans, one-quarter of the labor force, were out of work. National income was half of what it had been in 1929 when the stock market crashed. Depositors and foreign governments were withdrawing their deposits from banks, threatening their solvency. As the crisis caused by the run on the banks spun out of control, outgoing President Herbert Hoover confided to his friends, "we are at the end of our string."

The American people had elected Franklin D. Roosevelt in the 1932 elections. Only a few thousand people could hear his inaugural address in person, but radio brought him into the living rooms of nearly half a million people, and millions more saw him in movie theater newsreels. "We must act, and act quickly," Roosevelt proclaimed. "The only thing we have to fear is fear itself."[1]

And so Roosevelt began the Hundred Days of the New Deal. He delivered radio "fireside chats" to the American people. "I want to talk for a few minutes with the people of the United States about banking," he began, referring to the "bank holiday" he had declared to stop a run on deposits. "I want to tell you what has been done in the last few days, why it was done, and what the next steps are going to be." Roosevelt was the first president to speak to the people in plain language. He spoke, neighbor to neighbor, about practical solutions to everyday "kitchen table" issues. After his talk, more deposits flowed into the system than were withdrawn. "In one week, the nation, which had lost the confidence in everything and everybody, has regained confidence in the government and in itself," newspaper columnist Walter Lippmann concluded. In the first hundred days, Roosevelt sent fifteen messages to Congress, made ten speeches, and held twenty-five press conferences, turning them from the strained formal affairs of his predecessors into biweekly, free-wheeling exchanges with two dozen or so reporters who crammed into the Oval Office.

Roosevelt was the first president to use public opinion polls.[2] Initially they were conducted by the Department of Agriculture and other agencies to measure support for New Deal programs. In 1935, Emil Hurja, an official of the Democratic National Committee, polled two samples of voters (employed and unemployed workers) to gauge Roosevelt's reelection prospects. Alarmed by findings that Roosevelt might lose if maverick Louisiana Governor Huey Long were to enter the race, the administration inaugurated a "second New Deal" and sponsored the Social Security Program and other measures to head off Long.[3] Later polls were conducted for Roosevelt by Hadley Cantril of Princeton University. By the president's third term, his polls had supplanted informal methods as well as the tabulating of letters in the White House mail room.[4] Before U.S. entry into World War II, Cantril conducted polls to measure public support for military assistance to Great Britain.[5]

"The average opinion of mankind is in the long run superior to the dictates of the self-chosen," Roosevelt once said—but it helped him enormously to mold and shape public opinion to support the New Deal.[6] To do so he created a White House unit run by assistant press secretary Steve Early, who hired six journalists to publicize presidential activities. A newly created White House Division of Press Intelligence summarized newspaper editorials and columns to determine what the press was reporting about Roosevelt's New Deal programs. The White House coordinated the work of more than three hundred press agents located in department publicity bureaus, charged with getting the word to newspapers about the accomplishments of their agencies. These agents created their own news magazines, such as the *NRA Blue Eagle* (to report on industrial recovery) and the *AAA News Digest* (on agricultural recovery). Department officials made documentary movies and newsreels for the growing movie audiences. They wrote radio scripts, press releases, and articles and editorials for newspapers. The White House Office of Government Reports provided the media with government documents and statistics.[7] First Lady Eleanor Roosevelt was also a tireless promoter of her husband's program. She held three hundred press conferences, open only to women reporters (numbering more than 130 by the 1940s). She also wrote a widely syndicated newspaper column titled "My Day."[8]

Roosevelt's "public presidency" demonstrates how American presidents not only respond to public opinion but also try to lead it. Yet, as the stakes of public opinion leadership have risen, most presidents have faltered: they have not been comfortable using the media and have failed to master its techniques.

PRESIDENTIAL OPINION LEADERSHIP IN AMERICAN HISTORY

The framers of the Constitution did not want the president to become "a favorite of the people," in the words of James Madison, and through the nineteenth century incumbents were inhibited in trying to lead public opinion. That changed in the twentieth century with new developments in communication technologies.

The Constitutional Understandings

At the Constitutional Convention the framers understood the need for "popular government" resting on the consent of the governed, but they put barriers between the president and public opinion leadership. Delegates wanted to inhibit the "hard demagogue" who pits people against each other. Alexander Hamilton argued that to avoid "tumult and disorder" elections should be few and far between, and they should be staggered to avoid "every sudden seizure of passion." Appeals to the public, James Madison believed, could only stir up these passions, and therefore the decisions of the government "could never be expected to turn on the true merits of the question."[9] The delegates also intended to safeguard against a "soft demagogue," who flatters the people and pretends to defer to their wisdom. Madison defended the complex mechanisms of separation of powers and checks and balances by arguing that they would defend the people against "their own temporary errors and delusions."[10] To insulate the president from a direct relationship with the people, the Constitution provided for indirect election by the electoral college and a fixed term so that the president would not be able to call elections at the height of his popularity.

Custom under Washington reinforced these constitutional provisions: the president was not to lead a faction or political party, and was not to appeal directly to the people for support in conducting his administration. The people, in turn, were not to try to influence the president directly; their influence on presidential politics would be indirect, exercised primarily by the state legislatures they elected, because in most states the legislatures chose the presidential electors to the electoral college.

Nineteenth-Century Rhetoric

These constitutional and political understandings were modified in the nineteenth century as parties organized and presidents were elected by a mass electorate. Yet the constraints against public opinion leadership remained. Starting with Jefferson in 1801, nineteenth-century presidents did not address Congress in person, but sent messages annually describing the state of the Union. With the exception of Jefferson and Jackson, none promoted their own legislative agenda, and none rallied their followers on pending issues before Congress. The fear of demagoguery remained strong: just after Jackson left office, writer James Fenimore Cooper complained of those who would "put the people before the Constitution and the laws, in the face of the obvious truth that the people have placed the Constitution and the laws before themselves," while French commentator Alexis de Tocqueville warned in his study of American government of the "tyranny of the majority."[11]

Presidents often spoke to the public—in the nineteenth century they made approximately one thousand public addresses—but were constrained in what they said.[12] They could tour the nation to gauge the temper of the people and reduce sectional tensions, but according to custom they could not appeal to their followers to back their requests to Congress. They gave patriotic orations and constitutional analyses of government powers, or dealt with the conduct of past wars. They made speeches about "civic republicanism." Their addresses were calm and deliberate rather than emotional; they did not make partisan addresses or campaign for office. Only four presidents defended or attacked specific legislation. Only two made speeches aligning themselves with their party on an issue. Only nine discussed the general direction of their policies in speaking before the public. None of the nineteenth century presidents held press conferences or allowed interviews by newspapers and magazine reporters (though Jackson and his successors funded party newspapers into the 1850s).

Andrew Johnson was the only nineteenth-century president to violate these conventions. He made speeches in the South and Midwest asking voters to support his lenient Reconstruction policies in the aftermath of the Civil War. He delivered sixty speeches on a nineteen-day railroad tour ("the swing around the circle"). In response, the tenth article of impeachment by the House of Representatives charged that Johnson, "unmindful of the high duties of his office and the dignity and propriety thereof," did "make and deliver with a loud voice certain intemperate, inflammatory, and scandalous harangues, and did therein utter loud threats and bitter menaces as well against Congress," all of which "are peculiarly indecent and unbecoming in the Chief Magistrate of the United States," bringing "the high office of the President of the United States into contempt, ridicule, and disgrace, to the great scandal of all good citizens."[13]

Twentieth-Century Rhetoric

Beginning with Theodore Roosevelt in 1901, the presidency became a "bully good pulpit." Roosevelt went over the heads of congressional leaders of his own party by arguing that his program represented "the public interest," as the partisan presidency shifted to a "public presidency." He held occasional press conferences, gave interviews to his favorites in the press, and encouraged the "muckraking" journalists and writers in weekly and monthly magazines to uncover scandalous conditions in American industry, so that the public outrage would lead to congressional support for his reform proposals. But Roosevelt too remained somewhat constrained: Once Congress took up a bill, Roosevelt believed it should debate without public pressure, and he made his case on rational principle rather than appealing to emotions.[14]

Theodore Roosevelt debates a point with a heckler in the crowd. Roosevelt described the presidency as "the bully good pulpit," and he took his case to the people in order to put pressure on conservatives in his own party in Congress.

"Policy—where there is no absolute or arbitrary ruler to do the choosing for the whole people—means massed opinion," Woodrow Wilson argued, "and the forming of the mass is the whole art and mastery of politics."[15] Beginning in 1913 Wilson gave an annual State of the Union Address to Congress, reversing Jefferson's century-long precedent of written messages. He presented a comprehensive program (the New Freedom) and held regular presidential news conferences for several years, until he became upset with the press coverage of his family.

Woodrow Wilson and Franklin Roosevelt transformed the presidency into an instrument of mass democracy by emphasizing White House responsiveness to public preferences. The opinions of the majority were to be given greater weight and legitimacy than any competing source of authority. To gain that legitimacy presidents were expected to address the nation: In the nineteenth century only 7 percent of presidential speeches were addressed to the public, and 85 percent were delivered to Congress; in the twentieth century almost half the speeches a president gave were addressed to the American people, and 20 percent were delivered to Congress.[16] Presidents became the focal point for newspaper and television coverage of the national government.[17]

The main function of the president in a modern mass democracy is to seek out public opinion and be responsive to it. The invention of the radio and television and airplane made it easier in the post–World War II period for presidents to communicate directly to the people. By the late 1930s most Americans had radios in their homes, and by the mid-1950s most had television. Presidents from Truman through Carter dramatically increased their prime-time addresses to the nation.[18] They also increased their domestic and foreign travel: Between the early 1960s and mid-1980s there was a fivefold increase in routine presidential media and public appearances.[19]

"Governing with public approval requires a continuing political campaign," Jimmy Carter was advised by pollster Patrick Caddell after he took office.[20] To run the "public presidency," presidents have used their White House staff. Fully one-quarter of President Reagan's top staff was involved in press and public relations, while the departments had more than 20,000 people involved in some form of public communication. Half of the top-level officials spent more than five hours a week on press relations.[21] In President Clinton's first two years in office, most of the top-level appointments, reshuffling, and reorganizing of the staff involved efforts to improve the staff's ability to communicate the president's message.

Clinton and the "New Media"

"You know why I can stiff you on press conferences?" President Clinton asked journalists at an annual dinner of Washington radio and television correspondents. "Because [talk-show host] Larry King liberated me by giving me to the American people directly."[22] Clinton could bypass the Washington press corps and either communicate directly with the public or rely on local news outlets.

Direct communications involved organizing televised town meetings, creating e-mail bulletin boards (which get 800,000 messages and requests for information from the White House annually), and distributing thousands of White House documents on the Internet. Officials participated in late-night television and morning talk-show radio programs. Presidents Reagan and Clinton both broadcast weekly five-minute radio addresses to the nation most Saturday mornings.

The White House television studios in the Old Executive Office Building enable the President and other officials to reach out to local media. The White House sets up "one-on-one" interviews between local reporters or television news anchors and cabinet secretaries, the vice president, and the president. Reporters around the nation can participate in the half-dozen or so "satellite press conferences" the president holds each year, bypassing the Washington press corps. Local papers and stations receive White House faxes, e-mail, audio and video clips, and press releases they can use as "news."

The news coverage gained from local television and radio stations is more favorable than from the skeptical Washington press corps.[23] Yet presidents like Clinton who seek to bypass the traditional print and broadcast media soon learn their lesson; within a year Clinton sought to repair relationships with traditional media, because it commanded larger audiences and was far more authoritative than any of the new communication media.

Success and Failure in Going Public

The essence of modern presidential political leadership consists of a two-stage strategy: win public approval for a significant policy change by selling the proposal to the American people through the media; then pressure Congress into passing most or all

On-Line to the White House

You no longer need to write a letter to the White House, send a telegram, or call the White House switchboard to let the president know what you think. In 1993 President Clinton's White House media director (Jeff Eller) and his director of public access, electronic mail, and electronic publishing (Jock Gill) established several on-line computer links to the White House, as well as bulletin boards for those interested in reading presidential press releases, speech transcripts, proposed legislation, executive orders, and transcripts of press conferences. By 1994 E-mail buffs could communicate directly with the White House and receive information they requested on specific topics such as foreign policy, the economy, and crime.

President Clinton signed the Government Printing Office Electronic Access bill (S.564) into law in 1993; it required that the Government Printing Office make available government documents to on-line services. The federal government operates many bulletin board services (BBSs), including FedWorld, on the Internet, a gateway to 120 government BBSs. E-mail commercial services that connect to the White House include the following (e-mail addresses are in parentheses): America Online (Clinton PZ); CompuServe (75300,3115); GEnie (Whitehouse); MCI Mail (White House); Prodigy (Write Washington). Bulletin boards from commercial services include the following (addresses in parentheses): America Online (Whitehouse); CompuServe (Go Whitehouse); GEnie (move 1600;1); MCI Mail (View White House); Prodigy (Politics). The White House is on the Internet at the following address: president@whitehouse.gov.

of the proposal in spite of the misgivings of legislators or the opposition of interest groups. Traditional "closed door" bargaining between the president and legislative leaders may be transformed on important measures into a plebiscitary system.[24] He or she may also combine plebiscitary politics with prerogative powers, by vetoing congressional bills or bypassing Congress by issuing executive orders.

At times the plebiscitary strategy works. Theodore Roosevelt, Woodrow Wilson, and Franklin Roosevelt all dominated Congress for a few years with the power of public opinion behind them. John Kennedy and Lyndon Johnson mobilized the American people around the moral imperative of ending racial segregation of public accommodations and providing legal protection for all Americans to vote in the 1960s. Ronald Reagan pressured Congress into passing his supply-side economic program in 1981 because of his ability to rally the American people.

Often, however, national agenda politics fails, sometimes disastrously. Since Woodrow Wilson's ill-fated speaking tour on behalf of the Treaty of Versailles in 1919, most presidents have done poorly in national agenda politics. Harry Truman lost the battle for public opinion when he called for a program of national health care for all Americans and the American Medical Association fought it by calling it "socialistic." Richard Nixon gradually lost the battle for public opinion during the Watergate crisis and was finally reduced to defensively claiming "Your president is not a crook" at a press conference. Jimmy Carter made four prime-time addresses about his energy program, with confidence in his program falling after each address. His advisors eventually dissuaded him from giving a fifth address on the subject. He ended a national television address by blaming the American people for a loss of spirit and confidence—hardly the way to rally the public. Although Ronald Reagan used public opinion successfully to win passage of his tax measures in 1981 and 1985, these victories should be put in some perspective: How hard is it, after all, to win public support for tax cuts? Often in Reagan's presidency when things were going poorly, he evaded the press and refused to hold news conferences, though sometimes he would shout out brief responses to reporters' questions as he boarded a helicopter on the White House lawn.

CONTROLLING THE NATIONAL AGENDA

The national agenda consists of issues on which the public concentrates at any given time that affect the distribution of power in Washington and may determine future elections. In 1981 the agenda involved tax and budget cuts, in 1990 a budget agreement and tax hikes, and in 1994 crime and health care reform. Presidents go public on only a handful of the thousands of issues with which their administration is concerned, and they do so when they calculate that "closed door" politics, involving persuasion, negotiation, and coalition-building, will fail. They then follow the advice of tennis star Bill Tilden, who once said "never change a winning game, but always change a losing one." Or as Lyndon Johnson put it:

> When traditional methods fail, a President must be willing to bypass the Congress and take the issue to the people. By instinct and experience, I preferred to work from

within, knowing that good legislation is the product not of public rhetoric but of private negotiations and compromise. But sometimes a President has to put Congress' feet to the fire.[25]

Public appeals are one of the few credible threats a president can make to get Congress to move on his program—sometimes the threat alone gives the president influence. Eisenhower threatened Republican Party leaders who were stalling on his measures in 1953 that he would take his case to the people; only then did his program begin to move.[26] When Jimmy Carter threatened to go to the public, though, he was cautioned by House Speaker Tip O'Neill that it would be the dumbest thing he could do. Carter's insistence on bypassing congressional leaders led to friction with House Democrats from the start of his presidency.

Sometimes a president who "goes public" *will* win big: Bill Clinton's most important economic measures, such as his first-year deficit-reduction program and NAFTA, were in maximum peril in Congress until he could demonstrate public support for them, after which they passed. When he could not gain public support, as with his economic stimulus, public works, and health care reform programs, Congress had no difficulty defeating or stalling him. Yet even when a president goes public, it is rarely a substitute for politics as usual. Most of the time it is a resource a president can use within the traditional Washington game. After Clinton started to move public opinion toward the crime bill, he still had to engage in a large number of horse-trades with individual members of Congress to round up the votes needed for passage.

The January Messages

A presidential decision to put his program on the national agenda galvanizes the White House pollsters, speechwriters, and media experts into action. Much of their effort follows an annual cycle based on the January Messages, which include:

- The State of the Union Address, which is delivered in person to a joint televised session of Congress. The speech is followed by a brief rebuttal by opposition party or congressional leaders;
- The Economic Message, which accompanies the annual *Report of the Council of Economic Advisers,* and which sets out the President's economic game plan for the coming year;
- The Budget Message, which accompanies the annual *Budget of the United States,* and which justifies spending requests to Congress for presidential priorities, as well as the policy in dealing with the deficit.

The president gets a chance at agenda-setting each year by using his January Messages. Indeed, much of the work of the government is geared to an annual cycle of innovation. Departments and agencies jockey to get their proposals in the president's State of the Union Address as a major new initiative.

Presidential Television

Presidents use television to influence the national agenda. They may address a joint session of Congress, either during a crisis or when they introduce the most important bills of their administration. They may travel around the country "barnstorming" on behalf of a particular measure and get coverage on the evening news. After presenting his health care plan in a televised speech, President Clinton participated in a town meeting moderated by ABCNews's Ted Koppel, who gave Clinton the results of an ABCNews/Washington Post poll, describing the initial public response to Clinton's proposal. Clinton then commented on parts of the plan that had left his television audience skeptical.[27]

Some observers have claimed that presidents can overwhelm their opposition because of their access to television, and proposals have been made to give the opposition party a formal "right of reply" and to provide for regular "national debates" between the two parties.[28] Through the early 1990s there was no government regulation regarding presidential access to television. The White House staff informs television-network Washington news bureaus that the White House is scheduling an address and asks for coverage. Each network's senior news executives decide whether the network will provide access—a costly decision when the speech interferes with prime-time programming. Occasionally a request for time will be denied if it is for partisan purposes, or if there seems to be nothing newsworthy, as happened to Clinton in 1995. There are some regulations and traditions regarding the "right of reply" for the opposition party, which receives network television time after the president's State of the Union Address and other major televised speeches. The Federal Communications Commission (FCC) has ruled that if presidential speechmaking has created an "imbalance" in the public debate, the opposition party has a right to respond on the major networks.

Between 1960 and the early 1990s, presidents increased their prime-time televised addresses but they gradually lost some of their viewing audience (Figure 8.1). John Kennedy in his first year and a half in office made only four speeches, each about thirty minutes in length. Ronald Reagan in his first eighteen months made twelve speeches, each averaging forty-five minutes in length. [29] Presidents such as Bill Clinton find that taking to the airwaves too often results in lessened ratings and lessened impact, so their use of television networks in prime-time is self-regulating. Since the American public discovered cable programming and video rentals, the audience for presidential prime-time television addresses has diminished from somewhat over half the viewing audience to around one-third.[30]

Pseudo-Events

Presidents rely on pseudo-events staged for the cameras to make their points on network prime-time news. When President Clinton went to the beaches of Normandy to commemorate the allied D-Day landings of World War II, his staff planned a "commemorative moment" to be captured by the cameras: Clinton walked alone at sunset down the beach, with warships behind him, then crouched in the sand, arranging stones (left there by his staffers) into a cross. Then he bent his head in prayer. The supposed "moment of solitude" was captured for television viewers by three television camera crews and a dozen news photographers, brought there for

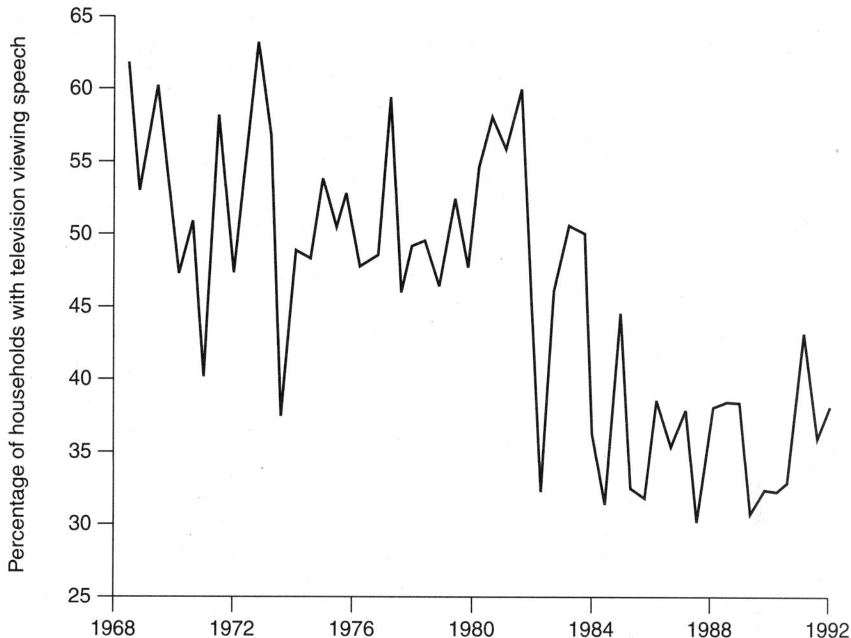

Figure 8.1 The declining presidential audience for television speeches, 1968–1992.
Source: Reprinted with permission from Nielsen Media Research.

the occasion by the White House staff.[31] Clinton, for all his effort, gained hardly any ground in the next set of presidential approval polls.

The main limit to the effectiveness of pseudo-events, especially when the President makes a speech, is the network news practice of using only brief snippets of the president's speech in its news reports or critically dissecting the staged event. The result often is a story that emphasizes a presidential attempt to manipulate the public, rather than a story focusing on the president's message.

News Releases

To stay "on message," by focusing on a single theme, the White House usually plans one event a day, held early so that it will make the evening news. It is planned to provide good "visuals." Often "photo opportunities" are arranged by the White House, but usually White House aides try to ensure that there is no opportunity for reporters to question the president on any other issues and divert public attention from presidential priorities. The White House distributes video and audio tapes of presidential statements, and the White House News

Service offers presidential speeches and announcements through on-line services and the Internet as well.

Daily News Briefings

Each morning or noon hour the White House press secretary holds a news briefing. About 60 reporters from the wire services, networks, and major newspapers and weekly magazines have assigned seats in the briefing room, which is located in the West Wing just off the Rose Garden. The daily briefing allows the White House to present the "theme" for the day, put its own spin on events, and knock down rumors. Live televised briefings do not work well, however: in the early stages of the Clinton presidency they turned into a small public relations disaster, because much of the briefing involved the press secretary informing reporters that information was not yet available or would not be forthcoming. The overall impression to the television audience was that the White House had something to hide, and the practice was soon abandoned.

Staffers use briefings to explain away misstatements from the president or White House aides. The Clinton White House initially claimed that it fired some staffers in the travel office because of mismanagement. It later developed that the Clinton's wished to put in their own people. The press office claimed Hillary Clinton studied up on the commodities market when she made a $100,000 profit; it later admitted her trades were handled by a commodities trader. The White House claimed that the President turned over papers involving the Whitewater probe voluntarily to the special prosecutor; it eventually admitted the papers were about to be subpoenaed when the president's lawyers struck a deal to turn them over. It claimed that papers in the office of Vincent Foster (a White House aide who committed suicide) were turned over to other officials and Foster's family lawyer; it later turned out that some papers were given to the Clintons in the White House residence before being turned over to the White House Counsel. Usually the misstatements were made by senior White House officials, and later when the more accurate version came out, the Press office had to scramble to repair the damage at a daily briefing. "Nineteen months of repeated falsehoods and half-truths have corroded the relationship between this White House and the reporters who cover it," concluded Ruth Marcus, the reporter who covered the Clinton White House for the *Washington Post.*[32] The damage that was done to the Clinton presidency by its carelessness or its contempt for facts was enormous, and avoidable.

Interviews

At the end of the nineteenth century, William McKinley permitted reporters to station themselves in an anteroom so they could interview officials waiting to see him. Theodore Roosevelt and Woodrow Wilson held interviews with their favorites. Franklin Roosevelt ended the practice of providing interviews to the Washington bureau chiefs of major newspapers, but when reporters tried to get Truman to adhere to that custom, he responded angrily, "I'll give interviews to anybody I damn please."[33] John Kennedy also gave interviews to his favorite columnists in small groups and had his newspaper friends to dinner. Beginning with Reagan, presidents have offered interviews to reporters for the Washington bureaus of radio and television stations. They target specific states or regions, which get exclusive interviews, videos, and news releases about local issues that are not designed for a national audience.[34]

News Conferences

Theodore Roosevelt began the practice of holding news conferences, but did so irregularly. Woodrow Wilson held them regularly for two years, but refused to allow reporters to quote him directly.[35] Herbert Hoover insisted, as his predecessors Harding and Coolidge had done, that written questions be submitted in advance, and that responses could not be attributed to the White House. Franklin Roosevelt changed the format completely.[36] He spoke "on the record" and provided hard news for the press corps. He would have twenty or thirty White House reporters crowd into the Oval Office periodically for interviews. Roosevelt would sit at his desk, and reporters would fire away. His first conference was described by correspondent Leo Rosten:

> Mr. Roosevelt was introduced to each correspondent. Many of them he already knew and greeted by name—first name. For each he had a handshake and the Roosevelt smile. When the questioning began, the full virtuosity of the new Chief Executive was demonstrated. . . . His answers were swift, positive, illuminating. He had exact information at his fingertips. He showed an impressive understanding of public problems and administrative methods. He was lavish in his confidences and "background information." He was informal, communicative, gay. When he evaded a question it was done frankly. He was thoroughly at ease. He made no effort to conceal his pleasure in the give and take of the situation.[37]

Roosevelt established several groundrules. With written authorization from the White House he could be quoted directly. All other comments could be attributed to the president without direct quotations, unless designated "background information," which was to be used *without* attributing it to the White House. "Off-the-record" remarks were not to be used in stories at all, but were given for the reporters' information.

Harry Truman moved the press conference to the Executive Office Building (then occupied by the State Department), where 200 or more reporters questioned the President, ending the intimacy of the Roosevelt era.[38] After the invention of fast camera film in 1955, Dwight Eisenhower permitted filming by television crews. At that point Roosevelt's rules gave way: everything the president said at a news conference was considered "on the record."[39] John Kennedy moved his news conferences into a large State Department auditorium and permitted live television coverage. His first conference was covered by 418 correspondents, and 65 million Americans viewed it on television, making live coverage the norm, though viewership soon declined.[40]

Presidents use the news conference to advance their agendas, stake out their positions, deal with criticism, or signal changes in government policy. The president makes a brief opening statement, which is followed by questions from reporters that may raise issues that the president prefers to ignore; instead of keeping the focus on his own agenda, he may "make news" that steps on his own priorities.[41] Because nothing is off the record, presidents no longer use press conferences to influence and educate reporters, or try to influence their coverage. Instead, they view their questioners as "props" in the White House attempt to go over their heads and reach the American people directly.

Press conferences are not regularly scheduled, but are held at the discretion of the White House. They were held much less frequently between the 1950s and the 1990s than during the Roosevelt era. News conferences declined by two-thirds, from Roosevelt's 6.9 per month to Lyndon Johnson's 2.2, then dropped to 1.2 by Carter's term.[42] Presidents duck conferences when they are on the defensive or when their administration is in the midst of a scandal such as Watergate or the Iran–contra affair—until their evasion itself becomes an issue. Nixon and Reagan held 0.5 and 0.3 conferences per month, respectively. Reagan held some on short notice so reporters would not have time to prepare, and during the Iran–contra affair held none at all.[43] Bush held some mini-conferences in the late mornings, which reduced attendance and made them more manageable for a president ill at ease with the media. Some presidents are more accessible than others, but the overall trend is for presidents to substitute media imagery that they can control for the chancy format of the news conference.[44]

Packaging Issues

The president will "package" his program to make it—and him—attractive to the public. Ever since the Kennedy administration's use of pollsters in its health care deliberations, even decisions about the substance of public policy may be affected by "how it will play in Peoria" (i.e., with the public).[45] Above all, the president needs a theme and a gimmick for a national agenda proposal, such as the following:

- *Make it an issue of national security.* Dwight Eisenhower claimed that federal aid to education was a way to defeat the Soviet Union in the Cold War. He called his proposal the National Defense in Education Act. Similarly his program of federal aid to build Interstate highways was called the Interstate Highway Defense System. Forty years later educational and job training programs were billed as a way to restore U.S. competitiveness against economic enemies.
- *Give people a card.* Franklin Roosevelt called his 1935 program of pensions for the elderly "Social Security Insurance." Everyone would receive a social security card with a number, indicating a specific account in which payroll contributions had been placed. By simulating programs of private insurance, Roosevelt led pensioners to believe that their contributions were their own. By giving them a card, Roosevelt told advisers, he was making sure that when "the Republicans get back in they won't dare try to take it away."
- *Declare war.* Lyndon Johnson called his grab bag of community action, public works, job training programs, and legal and health services a "War on Poverty." Other presidents have declared "war" on crime, drugs, disease, and illiteracy.
- *Establish a deadline.* John Kennedy sold the nation on high expenditures for space exploration in 1961 by calling for a manned lunar landing by the end of the decade. Bill Clinton's educational initiatives called for the United States to be first in the world in scientific education by the year 2000.

A conservative president may put a liberal program in conservative wrappings, and vice versa. Revenue sharing (which provided $5 billion in federal tax revenues to states and localities each year) was billed by Nixon as a return to "states rights" and "grassroots control" of domestic programs, themes calculated to win conservative support. Expensive job training and public works employment measures were promoted by Bill Clinton as a way to get the "able bodied" off welfare and onto tax rolls.

Defining Issues

National agenda politics is like campaign politics: the side that controls the definitions wins. Health care is a good example. When Democrats were pressing Richard Nixon for tens of billions in expenditures for national health insurance in the early 1970s, Nixon redefined the issue by saying that "an ounce of prevention was worth a pound of cure," and he proposed hundreds of millions of dollars "to find a cure for cancer by the end of the decade." Nixon not only forestalled the Democratic initiative, but was able to avoid spending any additional funds for his "war on cancer," merely shifting funds from one institute to another at the National Institutes of Health.

Presidents must know how to take or shift responsibility on a national agenda issue. When Democrats made "excellence in education" a major theme of the 1984 presidential campaign, Reagan took control of the issue. Instead of agreeing that new federal funding was needed for schools, Reagan proposed "merit pay" for excellent teachers, more local control of schools, and a "back to basics" approach in the classroom—none of which would involve increased federal funding. Reagan claimed that the major responsibility for education rested with state and local authorities, effectively shifting the focus from his administration.

Presidents may take symbolic actions to retain control of the national agenda, at times by getting personally involved. They may preempt the opposition. President Reagan and his wife Nancy joined hundreds of thousands of other citizens in a "Hands Across America" day to provide food for the hungry and homeless in America—even though his administration had made major cuts in eligibility for food stamps and had cut funding for public housing.

Presidents often use props in their speeches, but often to poor effect. In his first prime-time television address, George Bush called on Congress to pass his anti-drug program. He held up a bag of crack that he claimed had been seized by federal agents across the street from the White House in Lafayette Park. But the prop backfired: a federal agent had lured a drug dealer to the park to make the sale: the park was not a notorious outdoor drug supermarket. Bush was said to have been infuriated at the manipulation by the Drug Enforcement Administration (DEA) agents, which after being revealed by the media cast some doubt on his own credibility.[46]

Controlling Timing

Presidents want to keep control of the timing of national agenda issues but cannot always do so. Consider what happened to John Kennedy. In 1961 John Kennedy shelved plans to introduce civil rights legislation in Congress and sign an executive order banning racial discrimination in federal housing. He wanted a delay in these initiatives, even though he promised them during his campaign, because he wanted to gain southern congressional support for his economic program and military buildup. He planned on taking the initiative in civil rights after he was reelected, when he was willing to expend political capital on measures that would be unpopular among most white Southern Democrats. Faced with Kennedy's delay, Martin Luther King, Jr. and other black leaders took their followers into the streets in nonviolent demonstrations for civil rights. By 1963 the violent counterreaction of some white sheriffs in southern communities was being broadcast into American living rooms, and extensive media coverage of the violence against black civil rights demonstrators put public opinion on their side. Kennedy made an appeal to the nation for calm, adding that he would introduce civil rights legislation. After his death, Lyndon Johnson introduced a civil rights bill and lobbied for it heavily, ensuring its passage. Johnson had no intention of introducing more legislation, preferring a brief cooling-off period, but civil rights leaders again took to the streets, and the violence committed against their nonviolent protests by law-enforcement officials in Selma, Alabama, again focused public attention on their cause. Johnson then introduced a voting rights bill, which became law in 1965.

President Johnson gives the pen he used to sign the Civil Rights Act of 1964 to Dr. Martin Luther King, Jr., whose peaceful demonstrations in southern cities had been met with police brutality. After public opinion turned against racial segregation, Johnson was able to forge a majority in Congress to pass the law.

THE SELLING OF HEALTH CARE PLANS

National health care costs rose by 20 percent annually in the late 1980s and early 1990s. The number of people who (at any given time) were uninsured increased from 27 million to 40 million, with 120 million covered by insurance subject to lifetime limits on payments. One million people had problems obtaining insurance because of previous medical conditions. President Clinton claimed these facts constituted a national health care crisis, and he and Hillary Rodham Clinton were determined to make overhaul of health insurance their main domestic priority, on which much of the success or failure of the Clinton presidency would rest.

Misreading the Public Opinion Polls

As Clinton entered office, polls showed that although Americans were generally satisfied with their own coverage, they no longer believed that health care should be left completely to the private sector, favored some form of universal coverage, and were willing to pay more in taxes to get a better health care system. The nation was clearly ready for major new initiatives in health care, with a national consensus that the existing system no longer worked.[47] The stage seemed set for a national agenda initiative and a major overhaul of the health care system. Yet the Clintons misread public opinion polls: people were concerned more about improving their own health care benefits and paying less than they were about extending benefits to others. Polls did not indicate the "stop signs"—the choices that people would oppose once they became aware of them. Nor did polls indicate the sentiment that would soon emerge against "big government" running health care programs.

The National Agenda Campaign for Health Care Reform

Clinton established a "war room" on the main floor of the Old Executive Office Building next to the White House to handle the media campaign. It consisted of more than 30 staffers for congressional and party liaison, instant response to news stories, speech scheduling for Hillary Clinton and cabinet members, publicity events, liaison with friendly interest groups (such as unions and hospital workers), and coordination with the Department of Health and Human Services. The Democratic National Committee assigned twenty staffers to coordinate mailings to party members.

The Clinton national agenda strategy emphasized *security:* the title of the bill, the American Health Security Act, evoked the Social Security Act, and Clinton brandished a "health security" card similar to the social security card. Clinton wanted the average American to fear what might happen to family savings without the new plan. He explained how specific individuals had been bankrupted by medical expenses. His speeches emphasized security, quality, choice, simplicity, responsibility, and insurance "that can never be taken away."

The Interest Group Response

The Clintons misjudged the response of organized interest groups to their plans. They thought the business community really wanted a plan that would lower medical costs by allowing consumers and companies to pressure the health care providers in a "regulated market" system of "managed competition." But the providers struck back: the Federation of American Health Systems, representing more than 1,400 private (for profit) hospitals, and the Healthcare Leadership Council spearheaded the health industry's opposition to Clinton's plan. Their employees were mobilized with "informational sessions" and encouraged to voice their opposition to members of Congress. Large corporations and small businesses, after analyzing the Clinton plan, also came out against it.

Interest groups went on the offensive in a public relations campaign against Clinton's bill. The Health Insurance Association of America (HIAA), representing 270 small and medium-sized health insurance companies, attacked Clinton's bill because it would, in their view, favor larger insurance companies. They sponsored a $12 million "Harry and Louise" television campaign, featuring a middle American working class couple reacting negatively to the Clinton plan. HIAA spent 10 million in 1993 and an equivalent amount in 1994. There is little evidence that the ads by themselves changed the minds of many people, because they were as complicated as the Clinton plan itself, but extensive news coverage of the advertising campaign itself by the media left the impression that the health insurers were influencing the public, and gave its lobbyists some clout with members of Congress.[48] After the Harry-and-Louise ads, the administration was on the defensive. The terms of the debate had been changed, and the public was more skeptical. Congress began work on more modest plans.[49]

More was to come, a total of at least $120 million in media and direct mail opposition. The Republican National Committee spent $500,000 on advertisements promoting its own approach, though it protested a policy by the three networks that banned "advocacy" advertising, a policy that prevented it from reaching a national audience in a $2 million campaign to be paid for by Ross Perot. Radio spots produced by Americans for Tax Reform implied that Clinton's plan would require people to call a government "health care representative" before visiting doctor or rushing to a hospital emergency room. A National Right-to-Life ad warned that "the Clinton Plan equals involuntary euthanasia" requiring "your child or grandmother to die against her will." Citizen's for a Sound Economy ran radio ads in which a mother trying to visit "Dr. Murray," her regular doctor, was told that she could not; the ads warned that a government "gatekeeper" would decide "who, when, or even if you need to see a doctor." The American Council for Health Care Reform mailed brochures to millions of people warning that if they bought additional care, above and beyond the choices from the health care alliance, they would face 5 years in jail. In fact, criminal penalties in Clinton's bill referred only to bribing a doctor, and under the plan people would still have had the right to purchase any health care services they wished.[50] A study by the Annenberg School of Communications at the University of Pennsylvania found that more than one-quarter of the print advertisements and more than half of the broadcast spots were "unfair, misleading, or false."[51] As Congress began to take up the issue, most Americans remained confused and skeptical, believed Clinton's plan had too many bureaucratic layers, and were unconvinced that their health care options would be improved and their costs contained.[52]

Clinton tried to respond to his critics. At town meetings Clinton talked about his proposals, but was often distracted by questions about his character and the Whitewater scandal. "What's really going on in the heartland of America gets lost in a cloud of hot air" in Washington, Clinton told studio audiences, imploring voters to tell Congress "to deal with this issue and not fool with it anymore."[53]

The Media Endgames

In the summer of 1994, after Congressional committees reported heavily amended versions of his plan to the full House and Senate, the White House went on a second national agenda campaign. The Democratic National Committee ran a $250,000 ad campaign featuring their own "Harry and Louise" characters. They lay in bed, Louise with a broken arm, and Harry with a cast from head to toe. Because Harry had lost his job, they didn't have any health insurance: "You said universal coverage was too complicated," Louise says to Harry. "You said you'd never lose your job so we'd always be covered." The narrator then told the viewers to ask members of Congress "for what *they* already have: the security of affordable, universal health care." Ads were targeted to run in states with wavering Democratic lawmakers, such as Nebraska's Bob Kerrey—who responded negatively to the pressure.[54]

Cabinet officials spoke at "health care forums," emphasizing the universal coverage part of the Clinton plan, timed to coincide with a congressional recess. The idea was to shift public opinion so that members who were sympathetic toward it would not commit political suicide by voting for it. Once Congress resumed its deliberations, the administration organized a "Health Security Express": these consisted of "bus caravans" of Clinton supporters, joined at various stops by cabinet secretaries. Clinton told crowds that the only way to be assured of health care if his plan did not pass was to "go on welfare, go to jail, get elected to Congress, or get rich."[55] Most of the cabinet, the first lady, and the vice president were enlisted in August for radio and television appearances and newspaper and newsmagazine interviews.

It was too late: Clinton had lost the battle for public opinion. Overall support for Clinton's proposals dropped 22 points from the time he announced it at a joint session of Congress through April 1994. Democrats divided their support among his plan, a "single-payer" system (more liberal than his plan and backed by one-third of the Democrats in the House) and the Cooper Plan (more conservative than his plan, and backed by some Southern Democrats and the Business Roundtable consisting of executives of the largest 200 corporations). Clinton had barely increased the proportion of the public that believed health care was the most important problem facing the nation, from 15 to 20 percent. Slightly less than a majority of the public wanted an "employer mandate" to pay part of health care insurance, though a large majority favored "universal coverage." More than half believed that Clinton should compromise if 95 percent would be covered.[56]

Democratic congressional leader Steny Hoyer said one of the hardest parts of rounding up enough votes was convincing Southern Democrats that "this is not the Clinton plan." House Minority Whip Newt Gingrich taunted the Democrats, "We're told by pollsters you lose 20 to 30 points automatically if you put Clinton's name in front of the term 'plan.'"[57] At the end of July, by a two-to-one margin, Americans agreed with the statement that Congress should "start over next year."[58] This and other polls gave momentum to Clinton's opponents. As Congress recessed in late August, the Clinton plan was dead, legislators had given up on any comprehensive plan, and the prospect of Republican gains in the midterm elections meant that Clinton's best chance in his term to pass a comprehensive reform had passed.

On any given issue, as Clinton's health care fiasco demonstrates, a president that lives by the media may well also die by the media. A White House attempt to reach the people directly will call forth a reaction by opponents who often have more media resources than the president.

MEDIA COVERAGE OF THE WHITE HOUSE

Since the Watergate crisis in the 1970s, the media has taken on an adversarial tone that has made it difficult for a president to lead public opinion.

The Presidential Focus

Most Americans find it easier to understand news from Washington if it is given a "presidential" focus: the president, after all, is one person, whom everyone recognizes, and whom many people assume "runs the government." Congress by contrast seems to consist of a jumble of committees and hapless legislators who talk a lot but cannot do anything, most of whom are unknowns except to their own constituents. Presidents get much more coverage in network news than senators or members of the House, and stories involving the president are usually placed "at the top" of network news or on the front pages of newspapers. To provide the nation with news about presidents and their top aides, the Washington press corps has expanded dramatically in the past twenty years (with more than 2,000 accredited to the White House), as has the number of reporters specifically assigned to the White House beat, which now numbers in the hundreds.

All this coverage has made it harder for presidents to control the national agenda. Until the 1970s, presidents could count on a honeymoon with the media, followed by a period of adjustment and accommodation.[59] During the Vietnam War and Watergate, an investigatory and adversarial press corps emerged, interested in digging up information that would discredit abuses of power and presidential deception. The White House responded with attempts at news management and "spin," which in the Reagan years seemed to work quite well. The president received favorable treatment at the hands of the media, at least until the Iran–contra affair revived charges of presidential deceit. In the 1990s, an accusatory media style has emerged: the media takes an adversarial stance on almost every story, prints rumor and innuendo without cross-checking or investigation of facts, and makes "the controversy it has whipped up" the story rather than the substance of what the president is trying to achieve.[60] When a president wheels and deals, negotiates, and compromises on his positions, the media no longer reports the results as a successful political outcome for the White House. Instead, in an era of anti-politics, it views such activities by the president as a character flaw, a sign of insincerity, a sign that the president is (gasp!) a politician—as if he should or could be anything else. As columnist Russell Baker observes:

> A country dying for and of entertainment can't stand for dullness, doesn't want incomprehensible realities, doesn't want hundreds of Congresspeople, thousands of lawyers, hundreds of thousands of mind-glazing complications. It wants entertainment. That is why almost all media coverage of government centers on the President, his wife, his family and his entourage. These provide a manageably small cast for a national sitcom, or soap opera, or docudrama, making it easy for media people to persuade themselves they are covering the news while mostly just entertaining us.[61]

Rushing to Judgment and Feeding Frenzies

The media rushes to judgment on the president. Just two days after Clinton was sworn in, Lisa Myers of NBC said the White House looked like the "Not Ready for Prime Time Players" of the show "Saturday Night Live." "He hit the ground back-pedaling," said Fred Barnes on the syndicated show "The McLaughlin Group."[62] Reporting has come to emphasize the politics, the spin, the manipulation, at the expense of any reporting about the substance of the president's policies. "When everything the President does is covered as 'how is he doing?' rather than 'what does it mean?' you lose your ability to evaluate governance," observes Kathleen Hall Jamieson, dean of the Annenberg School of Communications.[63] Clinton himself described a Washington insider culture that was "too dominated by what happens to the politicians instead of what happens to the people and too much into the day-to-day gamesmanship of politics."[64] Traditionally two of three news stories on a president are "positive," but during the Clinton presidency that changed: in his first year two of three news stories were negative.[65]

In the midst of the Whitewater controversy, President Clinton remarked that he thought it was "unreal," and explained that he felt he was living some kind of nightmare, as events from a dozen or more years in his past were exhumed by the national media for evidence of ethical lapses or violations of criminal law. Every president since Nixon has faced one or more "media frenzies" in which a pack of journalists compete to see who can come up with the president's scalp. Media scandal-mongering has become a permanent fixture on the Washington scene, making it increasingly difficult for presidents to conduct their political business, explain their policies, or gain the support of the people. Not only are they subject to intense scrutiny, but their appointees are as well. Matters as trivial as failure to adhere to Internal Revenue Service regulations involving domestic employees, or a brief experimentation with drugs a decade ago, or writings in academic journals, become headline matters. Presidents spend an increasing amount of time on "defensive" national agenda maneuvers and have less ability to dominate the national agenda for their substantive agenda.

The "New" News Media

In recent years radio talk-show hosts have attracted a huge audience—by some counts more than 40 million Americans—and a staple of their commentary involves fierce attacks on the White House. Michael Harrison, the editor of *Talkers*, the magazine for the talk show industry, observes that "there is no question Bill Clinton is the most criticized individual in the history of the medium."[66] As conservative commentator Pat Buchanan boasted, the cumulative effect of conservative commentary on broadcast and cable television, talk-show radio, direct mail, and electronic mail, and in conservative Christian books and magazines, many of them "desktop published" by small publishers, was to keep the public focused on Clinton's alleged failings of character.[67]

Clinton remained on the defensive through the 1994 midterm elections. "I don't suppose there's any public figure that's ever been subject to any more violent personal attacks than I have, at least in modern history, anybody who's been President," Clinton complained during a 23-minute attack on the talk-radio commentators, broadcast on St. Louis KMOX radio station as he was flying on Air Force One. "The Republicans and the far right in this country have their own media networks," Clinton complained. "We don't have anything like that."[68]

PRESIDENTIAL POPULARITY AND ISSUE SUPPORT

Popular presidents can shift public opinion by their force of argument, as much as 5–10 percent in a few months, while unpopular presidents have little or no impact.[69] The president can "soften up" legislators and bureaucrats by brandishing his high approval ratings, or will suffer consequences if he stands low in the polls. "He may not be left helpless," concludes political scientist Richard Neustadt, "but his options are reduced, his opportunities diminished, his freedom of maneuver checked in the degree that Washington conceives him unimpressive to the public."[70]

The Continuous Referendum

Since the late 1960s, the increased frequency of poll taking by news organizations and commercial pollsters have created what amounts to a continuous referendum on presidential leadership. The president, evaluated daily by the Washington community, is like a company on the stock market or a baseball superstar in the middle of a pennant race, whose statistics—and therefore standing—changes daily. When a president is riding high, he will brandish his high poll ratings, and the White House will try to get favorable news media coverage of them. When his ratings fall, the White House will do all it can to minimize the damage, by undercutting their validity or even the legitimacy of "running a government by public opinion." According to some political scientists, Presidents Johnson and Nixon cultivated influential pollsters, getting their poll results about the presidency before publication, giving them time to prepare for adverse results.[71]

Presidents have problems trying to maintain their approval ratings. Every president since Eisenhower has begun his term with lower ratings than the last president of his own party, and overall ratings for presidents since Carter have suffered in comparison with their predecessors. Popularity is volatile: Even presidents riding high in the polls may suffer a precipitous decline. Nixon's involvement in Watergate dropped him forty points, from the mid-60s to mid-20s; Ford's pardon of Nixon triggered a collapse of thirty points, from the seventies into the forties, in a matter of days; Carter's handling of the Iran hostage crisis took him on a roller-coaster decline of thirty points, then a rise of fifteen, and then another decline; Ronald Reagan's popularity dropped sharply in 1982 during the recession, picked up in 1984, then dropped twenty points in 1986 during the Iran–contra affair, and then rose near the end of his term. George Bush went up in the early part of his term because of the end of the Cold War, then after a decline picked up again by invading Panama, then after another decline shot up to 91 percent approval after the Persian Gulf War—the highest approval rating ever recorded—and finally suffered a free-fall drop in the polls during the election into the 30 percent range. Bill Clinton rode a roller coaster in the first two years of his term of office as well: in his case foreign policy issues and questions of character undercut his achievements in providing for economic growth without inflation.

Determinants of Presidential Approval Ratings

The disparate experiences of Bush and Clinton raise the question: what accounts for changes in presidential approval or disapproval rates?[72] Initially presidents start with a high level of public support, doing best with members of their own party, then independents, and worst with voters from the opposing party. But they benefit from the honeymoon effect: the tendency of most Americans to wish a new president well.

The honeymoon does not last long. Presidential approval ratings fall during first terms as normal partisan patterns reemerge after the honeymoon. If the president wins a second term, they start high again, and once again plateau.[73] For one thing, the president has stitched together a coalition of voters with campaign promises, not all of which can be achieved. Some of his or her supporters are bound to be disappointed as rhetoric gives way to governance, and the president must make hard choices with tradeoffs.[74]

Presidential popularity is sometimes closely correlated with economic conditions. Some studies have shown that a one-point increase in the "misery index" (inflation, unemployment, decline in gross national product) can be correlated with a one-point decline in presidential popularity.[75] During Reagan's first term, a close correlation existed between changes in unemployment and a decline in his popularity through the midterm elections: as the economy rebounded, so did Reagan's approval ratings. But the correlations do not always work. John Kennedy's approval ratings increased even while unemployment rose, as voters gave him credit for trying to stimulate the economy. Conversely, President Clinton's approval ratings slid from 57 percent in spring 1994 to 40 percent at the end of the summer, with fewer than half of the respondents approving of his economic management; yet the deficit was cut sharply, inflation was under control, unemployment was down, and growth was strong. The public seemingly did not wish to give Clinton credit for these conditions.[76]

Divisive policies, decisions that contain more costs than benefits, scandals, policies that go against the grain of deep-seated values, and sometimes plain bad luck also hurt presidents. On average, such negative events drop a president 2 points in the polls, though some events result in major drops.[77]

"Valence issues" such as peace and prosperity have a strong impact on popularity. The public evaluates presidents in large measure in terms of the values the president uses to justify his or her position—sometimes this is more important than actual success or failure. When the public agrees with both the values and the outcomes, the president's popularity will increase; when it repudiates the values or is skeptical about the success of the policy, presidential popularity will decline.[78]

Presidential popularity is also affected strongly by international crises and wars. A president in the midst of a major crisis, especially during the Cold War, usually benefited from the "rally round the flag" effect—the tendency of Americans to support the commander in chief against foreign enemies.[79] A rally effect on average provides a 4 or 5 percent boost in the polls.[80] In short and victorious wars and other military engagements, presidential popularity soars, as it did when Reagan invaded Grenada and rescued American medical students, and when Bush waged war against Iraq and forced it to withdraw from Kuwait. After the crisis ends, presidential popularity is likely to decline, as voters from the opposition party return to traditional patterns of partisanship.[81]

Not all international events produce rally effects. In hostilities with many U.S. casualties presidential popularity declines, as it did for Truman in the Korean War and Lyndon Johnson and Richard Nixon with Vietnam. A botched covert action may hurt the president: Carter sank in popularity after the failure of a military effort to free U.S. hostages in Iran; Ronald Reagan's popularity went from 63 to 43 percent as a result of the Iran–contra affair, then stayed in the 50 percent range until it slowly climbed over 60 percent near the end of his second term.

Presidents may be caught between their international commitments and domestic public opinion. They may want lower barriers to international trade while the public believes that other nations are discriminating against the United States. The public may want the president to keep U.S. troops out of foreign conflicts or civil wars, while a president may feel the need to project U.S. power to maintain its superpower status and meet existing treaty and regional security commitments. Declines in popularity are often associated with a president's decision to send a treaty to the Senate, such as the Panama Canal Treaty restoring sovereignty over the Canal Zone to Panama. Other drops of popularity occurred when presidents seemed to be losing control of the borders, as happened to both Carter and Clinton when Cuban dictator Fidel Castro permitted exoduses of thousands of people in small boats in spite of U.S. opposition.

Nevertheless, foreign affairs provides the president with a way to restore his or her domestic image. Parlaying with foreign leaders, going abroad for summits or hosting them in the United States, mediating foreign conflicts, making major addresses at the United Nations or at international conferences—all these portray the president as chief diplomat and commander in chief, and are usually associated with temporary increases in presidential popularity.

Finally, presidential popularity usually increases near the end of the term, though generally not to the initial honeymoon levels.[82] Party identifiers continue to support the president long after opposition identifiers and some independents have begun to fall away. As the harsh economic recovery measures take hold, many presidents benefit from a third- and fourth-year economic improvement that translates into increased popularity. The fact that this rebound occurs comes as cold comfort to the many recent presidents elected to only one term, such as Johnson, Ford, Carter, and Bush.

Approval Ratings and Congressional Support

High approval ratings allow the president to go on the offensive. A president is much more likely to hold news conferences, make speeches on important issues, and hold court in Washington when his or her popularity is high. A popular Democratic president will take on a bigger agenda confident that he or she can persuade some of the uncommitted public to shift toward his position. A popular Republican president can bargain with a Democratic Congress, because the veto is a more credible threat, or institute the "administrative presidency" and ignore the legislature entirely.

Congress will give more support to the White House when a president is standing high in the polls. One study indicated that for every ten-point decrease in public approval, the president's rate of roll-call victories will drop by 3 percentage points.[83] Another suggests that a 10 percent increase in approval yields a 7.5 percent increase in legislative victories for bills on which the president has taken a favorable position.[84] A third study found a 1-point rise in approval ratings translated into a 1 percent increase in support scores for presidential bills in Congress.[85] But these correlations do not appear in all circumstances.[86] For one thing, a popular Democratic president who submits a large agenda may risk defeats on a larger number of marginal issues than presidents with more modest agendas, thus lowering his or her overall support score.[87] For another, Republican presidents facing a Democratic Congress may find popularity disassociated with success in passing bills. During his first two years George Bush had high popularity, especially after the Persian Gulf War, when his ratings set a record for the presidency, at 91 percent. Yet his legislative success scores were poor to begin with, and remained low—he asked for little and got even less, setting the record in the other direction.

When presidents are low in the polls, they are less likely to hold news conferences or make speeches. They are also less apt to propose major new initiatives. Congress picks up the slack with its own legislative initiatives. The less popular the president, the more likely Congress will move to limit presidential powers and enact laws requiring collaboration with Congress in decision making. Perhaps most important, the less popular a president, the more likely Congress will act on its own priorities, and the more likely the president will veto bills passed by Congress against his or her wishes—and the more likely Congress will override those vetoes.

Determinants of Public Support for the President's Program

The support and opposition for a presidential proposal almost always follows the same pattern: the highest support comes from members of the same party, followed by independents and then opposing partisans. Democrats win more support from a coalition of middle- and working-class voters, and Republican presidents gain support from upper-middle- and upper-class voters. Democratic presidents usually get more support from liberals and moderates and less from conservatives, and Republican presidents get more support from conservatives and moderates than liberals. Usually voters who believe that resolution of a problem is "urgent" are more likely to support the president than those who believe that there is no crisis. Presidents hope that knowledgeable voters will back them at higher rates than those who confess ignorance; a telltale sign that a president is losing the battle for public opinion occurs when voters who have learned about the issue move away from the president's position. The president hopes that voters not only will identify their own well-being with adoption of his or her plan, but also will view it as workable, likely to improve the situation, and in the national interest.

Spatial Positioning versus Valence Politics

Presidents Lyndon Johnson and Bill Clinton often complained that they were giving the American people what they wanted, but they were not getting credit or support for it. Some presidents may be masters at spatial positioning (as indicated by their successes in the primaries and the general election), yet they may lose much of their support because they come out on the wrong side on "valence" issues, or because they fail a "character test" in their public or private conduct.

There is considerable congruence between public preferences and public policy. One study of 248 national government decisions between 1960 and 1974 found that about two-thirds were consistent with public opinion (including 92 percent involving foreign policy). When the public favored change, the government responded in three-fifths of the cases; when the public favored the status quo, the government maintained it three-quarters of the time. Other studies have also shown that shifts in public policy follow shifts in public opinion, especially on issues involving crises or on which the public feels strongly.[88]

The president's spatial positioning on important issues is one determinant of his or her popularity: Liberals tend to vote for and approve of Democratic presidents who propose liberal programs; conservatives tend to vote for and prefer Republican presidents with conservative agendas. But a "New Democrat" such as Clinton faces a spatial problem if much of his program is perceived as "right of center." He runs the risk of alienating or confusing a majority of his congressional party and his strongest party identifiers. A similar problem faces a moderate Republican such as George Bush.

The way to finesse problems with spatial positioning involves the "valence" issues that involve deeply held values. Eisenhower was a "middle-of-the-road" Republican who won the support of party conservatives because of his character and personality and obvious leadership qualities. Presidents may confuse spatial positioning and valence politics: when President Clinton signed an executive order ending a ban on gays serving in the military, he may have thought he was engaging in spatial positioning to benefit part of his electoral coalition with a "liberal" position, but he left himself open to a partisan attack on his "values" that wound up splitting his own party and putting him on the defensive for months.

Defining Events

Defining events or decisions may shed light on the president's character and judgment and affect his standing with voters. When President Reagan decided to pay his respects to German war dead at the Bitburg cemetery, where German SS troops were also buried, in an effort to signal a new era of U.S.–German relations, it was converted by his opponents into a defining issue about Reagan's insensitivity to Nazi war crimes.

Accusations involving abuse of power, criminal behavior, sexual harassment, or ethical issues may hurt presidents badly. Presidents often face an "up or down" vote on their character—a vote that is reflected in their approval ratings. They "sink or swim" throughout their administration, irrespective of how well they have succeeded in their spatial positioning on the issues. As the media increasingly focuses on the finances, ethics, and "private" lives of presidents and their families, the potential for character definitions to dominate the national agenda has increased.

Reagan: Creating Defining Moments

Despite Bitburg, Ronald Reagan provides an example of a Republican president who understood the use of defining moments and character projection. He was adept at gaining and maintaining political support in spite of poor spatial positioning. Reagan never moved into the middle on issues. Instead, he relied on "valence issues" (balance the budget, cut the fat, end welfare fraud, "just say no" to drugs, "get back to basics" in education) and themes of patriotism to win public support. Reagan's public addresses were light on details of programs, but heavy on imagery, anecdotes, letters from voters, emotional images, and metaphors and allegories. Reagan's popularity increased sharply in his third and fourth year of his first term even though a majority of voters disapproved of many of his specific policies: sending troops into Lebanon, conducting a covert war against the government of Nicaragua, loosening environmental and civil rights protection, cutting the "safety net" for the poor, and opposing gun control legislation. "Such a strong upward trend on the part of an incumbent president seeking reelection is without precedent in Gallup's 50 years of polling experience," pollster George Gallup noted.[89]

Critics marveled at how Reagan could do it. Democratic representative Patricia Schroeder charged in a speech to the House that Reagan was "perfecting the Teflon-coated presidency." Nothing stuck to him, and voters refused to hold him personally responsible for his policies. "When Reagan talks, the government is never 'we'—it's always 'them,' " observed Democratic pollster Peter Hart. "Things never become his problem, they're always 'the government's' problem."[90]

Clinton: Defending against Defining Moments

"Maybe I'm just not as good a talker as you folks thought I was when I got elected President," responded President Clinton at a White House press conference when asked to explain why his standing in the polls had declined.[91] But Clinton was a good talker: other reasons accounted for his failure to win the confidence of the American people.

Bill Clinton had good spatial positioning for his programs. He sometimes won public support when he kept the focus on his proposals, especially when he proposed redistributive programs that imposed costs narrowly (in the form of higher taxes on the wealthy) and benefits broadly. He also preempted conservative valence issues with themes such as "workfare" (requiring welfare recipients to "go off welfare and get to work" within two years), and "three strikes and you're out" (lifetime sentencing for three-time offenders against federal criminal law). Yet, by doing so, he ran the danger of alienating supporters on the left: Shortly after the crime bill passed, Jesse Jackson announced that he might run in the Democratic primaries against Clinton in 1996 because the president had not delivered on policies that would benefit African Americans.

Republicans sometimes defeated Clinton by substituting valence issues for substantive debate. They went after programs that had not been administered well and charged corruption or poor management. They questioned whether government or the private sector had more expertise in dealing with social problems, often comparing any new federal initiative to "the post office." They raised the "states rights" issue, suggesting that local and state government were more suited than national government to handle the issue. They used the fiscal crisis to claim that the government could not afford to deal with every social problem. As Democrats do when a Republican president is in office, they demonized presidential appointees (claiming they were radicals and "out of the mainstream"), especially women and members of minority groups.

Republicans were able to keep Clinton pinned down and on the defensive for the first few months of his term by attacking and defeating several of his nominees for positions in the Justice Department. Law professor Lani Guinier, for example, was caricatured as the "quota queen" (by distorting her views about changing state election laws to encourage greater minority group representation). Through much of Clinton's second year, questions surrounding the Whitewater case raised further questions about his character, and the character of his appointees. The news photos of a line of presidential aides and cabinet secretaries "raising their right hands to swear to tell the truth" in front of a congressional investigating committee was not quite the image the Clintonites had hoped to project shortly before the midterm elections. The media did not focus on Clinton's program and his successes in passing it through Congress, but rather on the Clinton presidency and whether it could get off the ground.

THE PUBLIC PRESIDENCY

"I'd rather give up the veto than the bully pulpit," Vice President Walter Mondale argued, in assessing the power of the president as opinion leader.[92] Presidents need not obtain public approval for all, or even most, of their policies, because the public has not the time or the interest to concern itself with more than a small percentage. But no president can sustain the most important policies for long in the face of severe public disapproval. Nor can a president remain successful within the Washington community of policymakers without maintaining a high approval rating from the people.

For the public presidency to work successfully, the president must be adept at packaging an issue and "selling" it to the public. He or she must get the media to transmit the message accurately and to keep the *substance* of proposals rather than their *packaging* as the key story. The message must be understood by the public, and the president must be able to withstand opposition attacks. A significant part of the public must move toward the president's position, while defections within his or her own party must be minimal. The consequent movement in public opinion polls must be strong enough to impress members of Congress and others within the Washington community, so that followers stay loyal and opponents have an incentive to negotiate.

Most presidents are not successful at national agenda politics. Since the 1960s, the trend has been toward each successive president giving more speeches, conducting more interviews, making more trips around the nation, and receiving more media coverage than predecessors. Pollsters have been used to help calibrate rhetoric to meet public expectations, and presidents have become ever more adept at spatial positioning on issues. Presidents Kennedy, Johnson, and Nixon institutionalized White House polling operations, relying on poll data not only to track public opinion, but also to influence their own policy making. They assigned specific staff members to supervise pollsters, who by Nixon's presidency were using the most advanced methods and who worked under contract for the White House or the party national committee. These presidents commissioned polls with questions involving public preferences on policy issues; and they used these polls not only to discover trends that might help them position themselves on controversial issues, but also to provide themselves with political ammunition, allowing them to claim they represented the people better than their opponents did. By Nixon's first term in office, the number of private surveys had gone up to 233, from only sixteen in the Kennedy years, and costs had gone from almost nothing to several hundred thousand dollars (not counting election polling).[93]

Yet, during this time, public cynicism about their character and intentions has increased, fed by an inquisitorial, adversarial, and prurient press. Their attempts to speak to the people directly, over the heads of the Washington press corps, has been counterbalanced by hypercritical ideological talk-show hosts who engage in character assassination with a vengeance.

In 1941 British Prime Minister Winston Churchill responded to advice that he should keep his "ears to the ground" to know grassroots sentiment by remarking, "All I can say is that the British nation will find it very hard to look up to leaders who are detected in that somewhat ungainly posture." The danger for a president is that he or she will slavishly follow public opinion and watch his or her authority as a world leader erode.

Presidents who fail to retain their authority often find their legislative programs stalled, their renomination or reelection in doubt, and their political strength diminished. Most presidents do not have a clear mandate from the voters, support from most of their party, or strong public support for drastic change. They sometimes can use national agenda politics to get some of what they want. But they lose more often than they win.

Is this a bad thing? Is there something "wrong" with our system because presidents are so often frustrated? Because they have such a contentious relationship with the media? Do we really want a president who can always dominate the national agenda and use high approval ratings to get a program through Congress? Certainly the framers of the Constitution did not, because they did not want majorities to form around a single politician who might then unite separated institutions and dominate the government. In our mass democracy, presidents can claim that by virtue of their election and high approval ratings, their policies alone are authoritative, and they may further claim that opposition is not only not in the national interest, but is somehow illegitimate as well. The president may come to view—and to get the people to view—opposition as misguided, undemocratic, and (in the worst case) unpatriotic.

For the most part the framers fear of a plebiscitary presidency are unfounded. More often then not, presidents remain on the defensive, even after going public, because of the adversarial stance of traditional media, the inquisitorial tack of the new media, and the millions of dollars of paid advertisements that interest groups can use to influence public opinion. Media and interest group checks and balances complement the original constitutional mechanism and keep the president from dominating the national agenda. Perhaps that is why one of President Clinton's favorite White House paintings hangs in the Blue Room: it shows President John Tyler angrily crumpling up some newspapers.

FURTHER READING

Books

Paul Brace and Barbara Hinkley, *Follow the Leader,* New York: Basic Books, 1992.

Richard Brody, *Assessing the President,* Stanford, CA: Stanford University Press, 1991.

Robert Denton, *The Primetime Presidency of Ronald Reagan,* New York: Praeger, 1988.

Richard Ellis, *Presidential Lightning Rods: The Politics of Blame Avoidance,* Lawrence, KS: University Press of Kansas, 1994.

Joe Foote, *Television Access and Political Power: The Networks, the Presidency, and the "Loyal Opposition,"* New York: Praeger, 1990.

Michael Grossman and Martha Kumar, *Portraying the President: The White House and the News Media,* Baltimore, MD: Johns Hopkins University Press, 1981.

Mark Hertsgaard, *On Bended Knee: The Press and the Reagan Presidency,* New York: Farrar, Straus and Giroux, 1989.

Samuel Kernell, *Going Public,* 2nd ed., Washington, DC: Congressional Quarterly Press, 1994.

Marilyn Lashner, *The Chilling Effect in TV News: Intimidation by the Nixon White House,* New York: Praeger, 1984.

John Maltese, *Spin Control: The White House Office of Communications and the Management of Presidential News,* Chapel Hill, NC: University of North Carolina Press, 1992.

Mark Rozell, *The Press and the Carter Presidency,* Boulder, CO: Westview Press, 1989.

Carolyn Smith, *Presidential Press Conferences,* New York: Praeger, 1990.

Frederic Smoller, *The Six O'Clock Presidency: A Theory of Presidential Press Relations in the Age of Television,* New York: Praeger, 1990.

Richard Steele, *Propaganda in an Open Society: The Roosevelt Adminstration and the Media, 1933–41,* Westport, CT: Greenwood Press, 1985.

Mary Stuckey, *Playing the Game: The Presidential Rhetoric of Ronald Reagan,* New York: Praeger, 1990.

Jeffrey Tulis, *The Rhetorical Presidency,* Princeton, NJ: Princeton University Press, 1987.

Documentary and Data Source

George C. Edwards III with Alec M. Gallup, *Presidential Approval: A Sourcebook,* Baltimore, MD: Johns Hopkins University Press, 1990.

NOTES

1. *Inaugural Addresses of the Presidents of the United States,* Washington, DC: Government Printing Office, 1965, p. 238.

2. Richard W. Steele, "The Pulse of the People: Franklin D. Roosevelt and the Gauging of American Public Opinion," *Journal of Contemporary History,* Vol. 9, October, 1974, pp. 195–216.

3. Edwin Amenta, Kathleen Dunleavy, and Mary Bernstein, "Huey Long, Share the Wealth, and the New Deal," *American Sociological Review,* Vol. 59, no. 5, October, 1994, pp. 678–702.

4. Leila A. Sussman, "FDR and the White House Mail," *Public Opinion Quarterly,* Vol. 20, no. 1, Spring, 1956, pp. 5–15.

5. Richard W. Steele, "News of the Good War: World War II News Management," *Journalism Quarterly,* Winter, 1985, pp. 707–716.

6. Richard Jensen, "Democracy by the Numbers," *Public Opinion, February/March, 1980, p. 59;* George Gallup and Saul Rae, *The Pulse of Democracy,* New York: Simon and Schuster, 1940, p. 283.

7. A. Betty Winfield, "The New Deal Publicity Operation: Foundation for the Modern Presidency," *Journalism Quarterly,* Vol. 61, no. 1, Winter, 1984, pp. 40–48, 218.

8. C. Maurine Beasley, "Eleanor Roosevelt's Press Conferences," *Journalism Quarterly,* Vol. 61, no. 2, Spring, 1984, pp. 274–279.

9. James Madison, *The Federalist Papers,* no. 49.

10. James Madison, *The Federalist Papers,* no. 63.

11. James Fenimore Cooper, *The American Democrat,* New York: Vintage Press, 1956, p. 38; Alexis de Tocqueville, *Democracy in America,* Vol. I, Chapter XV: "Unlimited Power of the Majority," New York: Alfred A. Knopf, 1945, pp. 254–270.

12. Jeffrey Tulis, *The Rhetorical Presidency,* Princeton, NJ: Princeton University Press, 1987, p. 63.

13. Tulis, op. cit., p. 27.

14. Elmer Cornwell, *Presidential Leadership of Public Opinion,* Bloomington, IN: Indiana University Press, 1965, pp. 24–25.

15. Ray Stannard Baker and William E. Dodd, eds., *College and State,* New York: Harper and Brothers, 1925, p. 339.

16. Tulis, op. cit., p. 138.

17. Elmer Cornwell, Jr., "Presidential News: The Expanding Public Image," *Journalism Quarterly,* Vol. 36, no. 2, Summer, 1959, pp. 275–283.

18. Lyn Ragsdale, "The Politics of Presidential Speechmaking: 1949–1980," *American Political Science Review,* Vol. 78, no. 4, December, 1984, pp. 971–984.

19. Samuel Kernell, "The Presidency and the People," in Michael Nelson, ed., *The Presidency in the Political System,* Washington, DC: Congressional Quarterly Press, 1984, pp. 233–263.

20. Quoted in Richard A. Watson and Norman Thomas, *The Politics of the Presidency,* New York: John Wiley, 1983, p. 165.

21. Martin Linsky, *Impact,* New York: W. W. Norton, 1986, p. 46.

22. Quoted in Stephen Hess, "President Clinton and the White House Press Corps—Year One," *Media Studies Journal,* Vol. 8, no. 2, Spring, 1994, p. 5

23. Robert Locander, "Modern Presidential In-Office Communication," *Presidential Studies Quarterly,* Vol. 13, no. 2, Spring, 1983, pp. 243–254.

24. Samuel Kernell, op. cit., p. 3.

25. Lyndon Johnson, *The Vantage Point,* New York: Holt, Rinehart and Winston, p. 450.

26. Robert Donovan, *Eisenhower: The Inside Story,* New York: Harper and Row, 1956, p. 320.

27. Lawrence Jacobs and Robert Shapiro, "Public Opinion in President Clinton's First Year," unpublished paper, October 27, 1993, p. 11.

28. Newton Minow, *Presidential Television,* New York: Basic Books, 1973.

29. Data from Kernell, op. cit., Table 4–2, "Presidential Television from Kennedy to Bush, First 19 Months in Office," p. 98.

30. Data from Kernell, op. cit., Figure 4–5, "The Declining Presidential Audience, 1969–1992," p. 114.

31. Maureen Dowd, "Beached," *New York Times Magazine,* June 19, 1994, p. 18.

32. Ruth Marcus, "The White House Isn't Telling Us the Truth," *Washington Post National Weekly Edition,* August 29-September 4, 1994, p. 28.

33. Kernell, op. cit., p. 68.

34. Kernell, ibid., p. 77.

35. Elmer E. Cornwell, Jr., "The Press Conferences of Woodrow Wilson," *Journalism Quarterly,* Vol. 39, no. 2, Summer, 1962, pp. 292–300.

36. Betty Winfield, "Roosevelt's Efforts to Influence the News During His First Term Press Conferences," *Presidential Studies Quarterly,* Vol. 11, no. 2, Spring, 1981, pp. 189–199.

37. Leo C. Rosten, "President Roosevelt and the Washington Correspondents," *Public Opinion Quarterly,* Vol. 1, no. 1, January, 1937, pp. 36–52.

38. A. L. Lorenz, Jr., "Truman and the Press Conference," *Journalism Quarterly,* Vol. 43, no. 4, Winter, 1966, pp. 671–679.

39. Elmer E. Cornwell, Jr., "The Presidential Press Conference: A Study in Institutionalization," *Midwest Journal of Political Science,* Vol. 4, no. 4, November, 1960, pp. 370–389.

40. Harry Sharp, Jr., "Live from Washington: The Telecasting of President Kennedy's News Conferences," *Journal of Broadcasting,* Vol. 13, no. 1, Winter, 1968–69, pp. 23–32.

41. Jarol B. Manheim and William W. Lammers, "The News Conference and Presidential Leadership: Does the Tail Wag the Dog?" *Presidential Studies Quarterly,* Vol. 11, no. 2, Spring, 1981, pp. 177–188.

42. Michael Baruch Grossman and Martha Joynt Kumar, *Portraying the President,* Baltimore, MD: Johns Hopkins University Press, 1981, p. 245.

43. Elliott King and Michael Schudson, "The Myth of the Great Communicator," *Columbia Journalism Review,* Nov/Dec, 1987, pp. 37–39.

44. William Lammers, "Presidential Press Conference Schedules: Who Hides When?" *Political Science Quarterly,* Vol. 96, no. 2, Summer, 1981, pp. 261–270.

45. Lawrence Jacobs and Robert Shapiro, "Issues, Candidate Image and Priming: The Use of Private Polls in Kennedy's 1960 Presidential Campaign," unpublished paper, September 1992.

46. Terry Eastland, *Energy in the Executive,* New York: Free Press, 1992, p. 39.

47. Lawrence Jacobs and Robert Shapiro, "Questioning the Conventional Wisdom on Public Opinion toward Health Reform," *PS,* Vol. 27, no. 2, June, 1994, pp. 208–214.

48. Kathleen Hall Jamieson, "When Harry Met Louise," *Washington Post National Weekly Edition,* August 22–28, 1994, p. 20.

49. Sasha Soreff, "Selling the Clinton Health Care Plan," Department of Political Science, Barnard College, Senior Essay, May 1, 1994.

50. Rick Wartzman, "Truth Lands in Intensive Care Unit as New Ads Seek to Demonize Clinton's Health-Reform Plan, *Wall Street Journal,* April 29, 1994, p. A-14.

51. Adam Clymer, "The Overview," *New York Times,* July 26, 1994, p. A-16.

52. Richard Morin, "Don't Know Much about Health Care Reform," *Washington Post National Weekly Edition,* March 14–20, 1994, p. 37.

53. *New York Times,* April 6, 1994, p. A-18.

54. Joe Klein, "The Religious Left," *Newsweek,* July 25, 1994, p. 23.

55. Adam Clymer, "Clinton Opens Drive to Push Health Care Plan," *New York Times,* July 19, 1994, p. A-8.

56. New York Times/CBS Poll, July 14–17, 1994, *New York Times,* July 20, 1994, p. A-12.

57. Katharine Q. Seelye, "Some House Democrats Like Plan but Not Political Risks," *New York Times,* July 30, 1994, p. A-8.

58. *Newsweek* poll, August 1, 1994.

59. Michael Grossman and Martha Kumar, op. cit., pp. 13–16.

60. Thomas Patterson, "Legitimate Beef—The Presidency and a Carnivorous Press," *Media Studies Journal,* Vol. 8, no. 2, Spring, 1994, pp. 21–26.

61. Russell Baker, "Mired in Stardom," *New York Times,* March 15, 1994, p. A-23.

62. Elizabeth Kolbert, "The News Media's Rush to Judgment on Clinton," *New York Times,* January 31, 1993, sec. 1, p. 20.

63. William Glaberson, "The Capital Press and the President: Fair Coverage or Unreined Adversity," *New York Times,* June 17, 1993, p. A-22.

64. David Broder and Dan Balz, "Changing Directions Is Harder Than It Looks," *Washington Post Weekly Edition,* May 24–30, 1993, p. 10.

65. Thomas Patterson, "Legitimate Beef—The Presidency and a Carnivorous Press," *Media Studies Journal,* Vol. 8, no. 2, Spring, 1994, op. cit., p. 21.

66. Ann Devroy, "At Least He Isn't Boring," *Washington Post National Weekly Edition,* May 30–June 5, 1994, p. 13.

67. Pat Buchanan, "Silent No Longer," *New York Post,* June 29, 1994, p. 12.

68. KMOX St. Louis, Radio Interview with President Clinton, June 24, 1994.

69. Benjamin Page, Robert Shapiro and Glenn Dempsey, "What Moves Public Opinion?" *American Political Science Review,* Vol. 81, no. 1, March, 1987, pp. 23–43.

70. Richard Neustadt, *Presidential Power,* New York: John Wiley, 1960, p. 90.

71. Lawrence Jacobs and Robert Shapiro, "Disorganized Democracy: The Institutionalization of Polling and Public Opinion Analysis during the Kennedy, Johnson and Nixon Presidencies," Paper presented at annual meeting of the American Political Science Association, New York, September 1–4, 1994, p. 29.

72. See Charles Ostrom and Dennis Simon, "Promise and Performance: A Dynamic Model of Presidential Popularity," *American Political Science Review,* Vol. 79, no. 2, June, 1985, pp. 334–372; Charles W. Ostrom and Dennis M. Simon, "The President's Public," *American Journal of Political Science,* Vol. 32, no. 4, November, 1988, pp. 1096–1119.

73. Richard Brody, *Assessing the President,* Stanford, CA: Stanford University Press, 1991, pp. 36–37.

74. John E. Mueller, "Presidential Popularity from Truman to Johnson," *American Political Science Review,* Vol. 64, no. 1, March, 1970, pp. 18–34; James Stimson, "Public Support for American Presidents: A Cyclical Model," *Public Opinion Quarterly,* Vol. 40, no. 1, Spring, 1976, pp. 1–21.

75. Paul Brace and Barbara Hinkley, *Follow the Leader,* New York: Basic Books, 1992, p. 12.

76. Richard Morin, "Clinton Just Can't Win for Losing," *Washington Post National Weekly Edition,* August 15–21, 1994, p. 37.

77. Paul Brace and Barbara Hinkley, op. cit., p. 32.

78. Richard Brody, op. cit., p. 121.

79. Ibid., pp. 45–80.

80. Charles Ostrom and Dennis Simon, "Promise and Performance," pp. 334–358.

81. L. Hugick and A. M. Gallup, "'Rally Events' and Presidential Approval," *Gallup Poll Monthly,* Vol. 309, 1991, pp. 15–31.

82. Paul Brace and Barbara Hinkley, op. cit., pp. 33, 43.

83. Charles Ostrom and Dennis Simon, "Promise and Performance," pp. 334–358.

84. Paul Brace and Barbara Hinkley, op. cit., p. 81.

85. Douglas Rivers and Nancy Rose, "Passing the President's Program: Public Opinion and Presidential Influence in Congress," *American Journal of Political Science,* Vol 29, no. 2, May, 1985, pp. 183–196.

86. Jon R. Bond and Richard Fleisher, "Presidential Popularity and Congressional Voting," *Western Political Quarterly,* Vol. 37, no. 2, June, 1984, pp. 291–306.

87. Douglas Rivers and Nancy Rose, op. cit., p. 186.

88. Alan D. Monroe, "Consistency Between Public Preferences and National Policy Decisions," *American Politics Quarterly,* Vol. 7, no. 1, January, 1979, pp. 3–19; Benjamin Page and Robert Shapiro, "Changes in Americans' Policy Preferences, 1935–1979," *Public Opinion Quarterly,* vol. 46, no. 1, Spring, 1982, pp. 24–42.

89. Lou Cannon, "They Don't Call Reagan the Teflon President for Nothing," *Washington Post National Weekly Edition,* April 30, 1984, p. 8.

90. Ibid., p. 8.

91. *Newsweek,* August 15, 1994, p. 17.

92. *National Journal,* October 16, 1984, p. 1870.

93. Lawrence Jacobs and Robert Shapiro, "The Rise of Presidential Polling: The Nixon White House in Historical Perspective," *Public Opinion Quarterly,* Vol. 59, no. 2, Summer, 1995.

CHAPTER 9

The President and Congress

Oh, if I could be President and Congress too for just ten minutes.

—Theodore Roosevelt

INTRODUCTORY CASE: CONGRESS PASSES THE MARSHALL PLAN

At Harvard University's 1947 commencement, Secretary of State George Marshall announced that the United States would help Europe recover from the devastation of World War II. In March 1948, Congress passed the Marshall Plan, funding it with $13.2 billion for a four-year period. It was one of the great successes of postwar American foreign policy: By 1950 European industrial production was higher than it had been before World War II.

It was a miracle that the plan passed. President Harry Truman had not yet been elected to the White House in his own right and had no popular mandate. Republicans had won control of both houses of Congress in the 1946 midterm elections, had blocked Truman's domestic program, and were passing their own measures, sometimes over his veto. Most people in Washington viewed Truman as a one-term president about to be turned out of office. Yet Truman managed to win the support of Congress and the American people for a massive program of foreign aid (an amount equivalent to $75 billion in 1995 dollars) destined to go to the same European nations that had defaulted in the 1930s on their World War I loans. Given his political weakness, how could Truman possibly have succeeded?

First, the plan was known as the *Marshall* and not the *Truman* plan. Marshall had been a five-star general of the army (there were only three in World War II, the others being Dwight Eisenhower and Douglas MacArthur) and its chief of staff, and had more authority in foreign affairs than anyone else in America. Second, Truman sold the Marshall Plan to the American people as a way to ensure European and American security against communism. Third, the president needed Republican support, and that meant making the proposal bipartisan and sharing credit. He courted Republicans, particularly Arthur Vandenberg from Michigan, the chairman of the Senate Foreign Relations Committee, and on Vandenberg's suggestion, Truman appointed Paul Hoffman, president of the Studebaker Motors Corporation, to be the first administrator of the program. Finally, there was something in the Marshall Plan for everyone: for American business leaders and workers, there would be billions of dollars in orders for industrial goods (railroad cars, steel, machine tools, trucks, ships, and the like), stimulating production in U.S. industrial and defense plants that were in danger of being idled after the war. The business community organized a committee to support the program that rallied Republican lawmakers.

Truman's success illustrates the potential power of the president as a lawmaker, yet in many respects a case like the Marshall Plan is atypical: More often than not, Congress innovates, and the White House preempts the initiative; then its proposals are modified extensively as Congress does its work. Because presidents are often weak party and public leaders and lack a mandate from the voters on most issues, their legislative proposals often languish, and they must scramble to build winning coalitions for their programs.

THE CONSTITUTIONAL FRAMEWORK

Congress is granted all legislative powers in Article 1 of the Constitution, as well as the power "to make all laws which shall be necessary and proper for carrying into execution the foregoing Powers, and all other Powers vested by this Constitution in the Government of the United States, or any Department or Officer thereof." This "elastic clause" enables Congress not only to put its own powers into effect, but also to legislate on the constitutional powers of the president and the judiciary. It allows Congress to establish the White House Office and the Executive Office of the President, and to delegate vast powers to the president.

Congress has other powers that do not involve legislation, powers that it is crucial for a president to influence: the Senate consents to or rejects presidential treaties and nominations; Congress proposes constitutional amendments to the states; it has the power to declare war; it conducts oversight over the workings of the bureaucracy, and it has the impeachment power.

The President's Constitutional Role

The Constitution gives the president a limited role in the legislative process. Article 2, section 3 provides that the president "shall from time to time give to the Congress information of the state of the Union and recommend to their consideration such measures as he shall judge necessary and expedient." The language complements the president's responsibility to see that laws are faithfully executed, by allowing him to recommend improvements in laws already passed by Congress. This Recommendation Clause is an affirmative duty placed on the president: the Constitutional Convention rejected language providing that "he may recommend" measures in favor of the language "shall."[1] The president can veto bills passed by Congress, but his veto can be overridden by a two-thirds vote of members present.

The president can dismiss Congress if it cannot agree on an adjournment date, a function that has no practical significance. In contrast, the presidential power to call Congress into special session was once quite meaningful. The Constitution originally provided that Congress convened in its first session the December after the president's March inauguration—fourteen months after its election. Many presidents convened Congress in special session shortly after their inauguration, and much of their legislative priorities were passed in these sessions, including the 100 days of the New Deal. Beginning in 1936 (after passage of the Twentieth Amendment), the president and Congress both began their terms in January after their November elections, and special sessions have been held rarely. One famous special session was held in the summer of 1948, when Harry Truman called the Republican-dominated Congress back to take action on his legislative program. When the Republicans refused to pass his proposals, it gave Truman the campaign issues he used to defeat them. President Clinton called Congress back into special session in 1994 after the midterm elections to consider the GATT trade agreement, over Republican objections that the legislation should be considered in 1995 by a Congress in which Republicans would be in the majority.

A literal reading of the Constitution will misinform us about presidential–congressional relations. There is no neat division between powers exercised by president and Congress: each institution shares in, and competes for, legislative and executive power. When the president proposes laws, for example, he does so after widespread consultation within his administration, and the White House agencies and government departments act as a "quasi-legislature" because of all the interests and constituencies they represent. Congress then exercises a "veto" over presidential program formulation when it either accepts or rejects his program—a reversal of the constitutional roles.[2]

Concurrent Legislative Powers

The president can sometimes "legislate" independently of Congress. Since Washington's administration, presidents have asserted an "ordinance-making" power, exercised by proclamation and executive order.[3] Presidents can promulgate rules and regulations (some providing for fines and sanctions) even in the absence of an underlying statute. In 1902 Theodore Roosevelt prohibited bureaucrats from attempting to influence legislation, and anyone violating the order was subject to dismissal. In 1942 Franklin Roosevelt issued orders requiring the relocation of Japanese-Americans from the West Coast into internment camps, an order enforced by the military. In 1965 Lyndon Johnson issued an order barring discrimination by government contractors. In 1979 Jimmy Carter issued an order denying federal contracts to violators of his wage and price guidelines.

Sometimes an order can even supersede congressional legislation.[4] In 1897 Congress permitted public lands to be explored for oil without fee; if oil were discovered it could be exploited for nominal royalties. President Taft withdrew these privileges by issuing an executive order.[5] In *U.S. v. Midwest Oil Co.,* the Supreme Court upheld Taft's order, in spite of the fact that it overrode a congressional statute.[6] Congress can, however, pass legislation to override an executive order. When President Clinton planned to issue an executive order to permit homosexuals to serve in the military, Congress threatened to legislate to maintain existing policy (calling for discharge of homosexuals). Eventually Clinton and Congress compromised on a "don't ask, don't tell," policy—a sharp setback for the White House.

Delegation of Powers

When presidents send a bill to Congress, they usually frame their request for power broadly.[7] They want the law to specify general goals rather than specific procedures officials must follow. They want power delegated by Congress to them, so they can then subdelegate it to lower-level officials, ensuring a chain of command from the White House to departments.[8] They want indefinite or long-term authorizations from Congress, couched in broad language. Courts have traditionally permitted presidents or executive officials to "fill in the details" of vaguely worded statutes.[9]

At times the federal courts have struck down broad delegations of power, ruling that Congress must set specific standards for laws to be constitutional. Since the mid-1930s, however, broad delegations of power to the president have been held constitutional by the Supreme Court.[10] How much power Congress should delegate to the president is no longer a constitutional question but a political one. When it wishes, Congress will provide narrow statutory authority for officials, include detailed descriptions of authorized activities, include specific limitations and prohibitions on agency activities, and require annual authorization. Congress can delegate authority directly to subcabinet level officials, some at the career level, and limit presidential authority to set policy for agencies. It can require detailed reporting to committees or the full chamber. In 1988, for example, the Defense Department was required to submit a total of 718 reports to Congress.[11] A president who can lead Congress effectively will receive broad rather than narrow delegations of power.

Presidential versus Parliamentary Systems

The Congress of the United States is almost unique among legislatures because its vast powers are exercised autonomously and are not constitutionally subordinated to executive leadership. In parliamentary systems the legislatures not only make the laws, but also choose the executive leadership. The majority party (or coalition of parties) determines who becomes prime minister. The prime minister and cabinet ministers dominate the parliament, and government bills have priority. Once the debate is concluded, the function of the parliamentary majority that created the government is to pass the government's bill intact. The purpose of Parliament is not to check and balance the government, or prevent its abuse of power, or modify its initiatives, but rather to engage in a broad national debate, and then to allow the majority party to facilitate the government's exercise of power.

If the majority party (or coalition of parties) cannot pass important laws, that is taken as a "vote of no confidence" in the cabinet and the government "falls." The parliament must then select a new prime minister and cabinet, by either reshuffling the existing cabinet, modifying the existing coalition of parties, or permitting a new coalition to try to form a government. Alternatively, the monarch or president who serves as head of state may call for new elections to break the deadlock. In the U.S. system, divided government may continue for years with the president coming from one party and congressional majorities from another.

PRESIDENTIAL PROGRAM INNOVATION

In 1891, James Bryce, a British observer of American politics, could summarize the role of the nineteenth-century president as an initiator of legislation as follows:

> The expression of his wishes conveyed in a message has not necessarily any more effect on Congress than an article in a prominent party newspaper. No duty lies on Congress to take up a subject to which he has called attention as needing legislation, and in fact, the suggestions which he makes, year after year, are usually neglected, even when his party has a majority in both Houses.[12]

Things have changed since Bryce wrote: The modern presidency is well situated to propose comprehensive programs, articulate a conception of the national interest, and educate the public to the dimensions of national problems. Each year the president submits several hundred legislative requests (of which a few will form the core of his program). Congress has come to expect a presidential program and will criticize a president who does not offer one. As the chairman of the House Foreign Affairs Committee told an Eisenhower administration official in 1953: "Don't expect us to start from scratch on what you people want. That's not the way we do things here. *You* draft the bills and *we* work them over."[13]

Congress by law has required the president to present proposals: the Budget and Accounting Act of 1921 requires him to submit an executive budget; the Employment Act of 1946 requires an economic report and policy recommendations for maximum employment consistent with price stability. Congress may establish agencies in the bureaucracy that are required to develop new policy initiatives and submit reports to Congress on them, such as the Agency for Health Care Policy and Research, created in 1989. Or it can insist that initiatives be developed when certain conditions exist: when President Clinton's health care reforms were being debated by Congress in the summer of 1994, several versions specified that in the event less than 95 percent of the population had medical insurance, the president would be required to submit a report that would trigger further congressional action.

Sources of Innovation

Presidential legislative leadership is a characteristic of the modern presidency. Between the turn of the century and the 1930s Congress originated more than half of all major laws, while slightly less than one-fifth were initiated by the president, a bit more than one-fifth jointly developed, and one-tenth originated from interest groups. During the New Deal the pattern changed: more than one-third of new programs were presidential, only one-tenth were congressional, about half were joint initiatives, and almost none were developed by interest groups. By the end of the Kennedy years in the 1960s, more than half of major initiatives were presidential, and a bit less than half were jointly developed by Congress and the White House. Few were developed solely by Congress.[14]

Even so, many of the most important bills Congress has passed do not initiate with the White House.[15] These include the National Labor Relations Act, the Taft-Hartley Act, and the Landrum-Griffin Act, which establish the framework for labor–management negotiations. During the Nixon administration food stamps for the poor, national pension legislation, an environmental protection act, and consumer safety measures all originated in Congress. During the Reagan and Bush presidencies Democratic legislators expanded some social welfare programs (such as new day care initiatives) and provided increased civil rights protections for minorities and women, and took the initiative in such foreign affairs measures as sanctions against South Africa.

Most legislation does not involve major bills, is not proposed by the White House, and on only a small proportion of congressional business is the White House influential.[16] In many policy areas, White House indifference creates "policy gaps" that members of Congress can fill with their own proposals.[17] Bursts of congressional activism on an issue are associated with a public demand for governmental problem solving rather than with public support for a president as "chief legislator."[18]

Congress often considers legislation for a long period, sponsoring research, holding hearings, and preparing reports. Eventually a president may pick up these bills and make them part of his own program. Much of Kennedy's New Frontier program, including the Peace Corps, area redevelopment (to provide public works in depressed parts of the nation), and job training initiatives, had been considered by congressional Democrats in the four years preceding his term. Similarly Reagan's supply-side tax cuts and his tax reform measures had been originated in Congress by Republicans before his election.[19] Clinton found that Congress had been working for years on job retraining, infrastructure development, and welfare and health care reform, and legislators had their own ideas about these and many other Clinton proposals. Clinton introduced a welfare reform bill only after his hand had been forced by the Mainstream Forum, a group of conservative Democrats insistent that Clinton live up to his campaign pledge to "end welfare as we know it." In 1993, as part of the compromises the president made in getting his economic program through Congress, he agreed to the establishment of a Bipartisan Commission on Entitlement and Tax Reform, which then became a source of congressional proposals from both parties for modification of the Medicare program in 1995.

Program Innovation and the Presidential Transition

White House legislative initiatives come from many different sources. The presidential transition usually brings together ideas from the campaign, promises made in the party platform, and the suggestions from interest groups that backed and partly financed the President's campaign. Transition task forces, composed of academics, members of the campaign organization, former officials, and potential choices for the new administration, help shape the first presidential program. Clinton convened a large number of campaign advisors and policy innovators from state and local government, private foundations, and academia, at a conference he held in Little Rock during his transition. The meeting become a job audition, with some participants brought into high levels of the administration and others either banished to the outer perimeter or dropped from consideration altogether, depending on their "chemistry" with Bill and Hillary.

Presidential appointees bring their ideas with them. Frances Perkins, Franklin Roosevelt's secretary of labor, developed a program of comprehensive labor legislation, then sold it to her boss. Nixon's appointment of Daniel Patrick Moynihan as a White House counselor for urban affairs led to plans to reorganize training for workers—something Moynihan had worked on as assistant secretary of labor in the Kennedy administration. Robert Reich, Clinton's appointee as secretary of labor, brought his ideas about retraining workers and improving the transition from "school to work" for students not planning to go to college—ideas that were embodied in new vocational and educational laws passed in 1994.

Legislative Clearance

A president develops a large part of his or her program through "legislative clearance," by examining the requests for new laws that departments and agencies intend to submit to Congress.[20] The president has several options after agencies' proposals have been analyzed by the Office of Management and Budget, the Domestic Policy Office, and his or her political advisors. He or she may

- Submit the proposal to Congress as a White House measure;
- Identify the proposal to Congress as a departmental request "in accordance with the program of the president";
- Permit the department to submit the proposal to Congress without any presidential endorsement;
- Prohibit the department from submitting the proposal to Congress.

Legislative clearance is the responsibility of the Office of Management and Budget (OMB). The practice began in 1921 during the Harding administration: the Bureau of the Budget (OMB's predecessor) occasionally helped the president decide if a departmental proposal should become part of Harding's program, and President Coolidge institutionalized the practice.[21] Harding and Coolidge also used clearance on spending measures.[22] After 1947 the budget agency's Legislative Reference Division had the responsibility of creating much of the presidential program out of agency submissions.[23] In the 1960s and 1970s the budget agency competed with the White House staff and various policy councils for control of clearance: the more important the issue, the more likely it would have to defer to "higher authority" in the White House.

Task Forces and National Commissions

To develop programs that cross department lines, that rely on new technological developments, and that shake up the status quo, a president must go outside the bureaucracy. The president will rely on task forces that combine outside experts with career bureaucrats, and establish national commissions composed of leading citizens to recommend major new initiatives (especially on controversial subjects such as race relations, drugs and crime, and social security pensions).

The possibilities and pitfalls of using a task force are illustrated by health care reform in the Clinton administration. Five days after taking office, President Clinton established the President's Task Force on National Health Care Reform. He appointed his wife, Hillary Rodham Clinton, to chair the task force, directing her to submit proposals within one hundred days to Congress. "She's better at organizing and leading people from a complex beginning to a certain end than anybody I've ever worked with in my life," the president said about his appointee, who had chaired an Arkansas education task force and a southern task force on infant mortality.[24] The task force not only included executive officials, but also a variety of outside experts (primarily academic) and several governors. More than one hundred congressional staffers were invited to participate, as a way of getting congressional input. About 500 government employees formed its thirty-four "working groups," which were also attended by experts in the private sector.

The proceedings of the task force and its various subcommittees were closed to the public and to interest group lobbyists as they deliberated on various policy options. This approach was a public relations disaster and it gave Clinton's opponents some ammunition. Republicans on the House Government Operations Committee claimed that the Federal Advisory Committee Act (FACA) had been violated: it provided that any task force not entirely composed of government employees must hold all meetings in public after a fourteen-day advance announcement. They argued that Hillary Rodham Clinton (along with other participants) was not a public employee. The White House responded that Hillary was exempt from the provisions of FACA. The issue went to federal court, taken there by interest groups that Mrs. Clinton had excluded: the American Council for Health Care Reform, the American Association of Physicians and Surgeons, and the National Legal and Policy Center. The court decided that the task force would have to comply with FACA and hold public sessions.[25] (The working groups could continue closed-door meetings because they consisted of government employees and were not making recommendations to the president.)

When the Clinton administration appealed the decision, the original plaintiffs were joined by many news organizations. The Clintons had committed the error of getting much of the health care industry against her task force, and then compounded it by getting much of the media riled up as well. A court of appeals reversed the lower court and found that the Task Force could conduct its meetings in secret, because "Hillary Clinton was a 'de facto' [federal] officer or employee." But it also found that some of the working groups had permitted representatives of health care organizations to attend meetings (later the number of such people was put at more than 300), and therefore the task forces might have to open their proceedings and release their papers.[26]

The task force produced a long, complex and (for most people) incomprehensible set of recommendations, and it lost support even within the White House, where it was criticized by the Treasury Department for unrealistic cost estimates and by the National Economic Council for failing to tailor the plan to win business support. The 1,342-page draft bill and report from the task force that Clinton presented to Congress put the president in a hole, because his process of program formulation had alienated potential supporters, roused up the health care industry in opposition, ensured critical media coverage, and thoroughly confused the American people. It had also frozen out many of the cabinet secretaries, including the secretary of the treasury, and other fiscal advisers, limiting the support the plan had even within the administration.

The Cycle of Presidential Initiation

Democratic presidents usually propose more to Congress than Republican presidents: Kennedy submitted an average of 350 and Johnson an average of 380 requests annually; corresponding figures for Nixon and Ford were 178 and 87 proposals. By

1990 Bush's chief of staff John Sununu wisecracked that the administration's limited agenda had been completed, and Congress could go home and not come back until after the 1992 elections.

Presidents ask more of Congress at the start of their term than in later years. They average twenty requests in their initial State of the Union Addresses. Presidents often get a lot in their first year if they ask for it. Wilson's New Freedom, Roosevelt's Hundred Days, Lyndon Johnson's Great Society, and Ronald Reagan's supply-side program—all were instituted in the first year after the elections. Yet not all presidents succeed: Carter made 43 recommendations to Congress, which passed 21, rejected 4 outright, and delayed passing the remainder. The public never got over the impression that most of his "New Foundation" program had stalled in Congress, even though his overall legislative record was quite respectable. Some have faulted Carter for having a "shotgun" approach, not specifying his priorities, presenting Congress with too many confusing programs, and not showing willingness to bargain with Congress for them.[27] Nevertheless Carter did better with Congress than most critics are willing to concede.

Bill Clinton also had a kind of "shotgun" approach, piling more and more programs onto a Congress that quickly became exhausted by his requests. Nevertheless, Clinton achieved an extraordinarily high level of support from Congress in his first two years, winning passage of the largest domestic program since Johnson's Great Society (though, in Clinton's second year, Congress stalled on his health care plan, welfare reform, pension reform, public housing, water pollution, and regulation of telecommunications, pesticides, and toxic waste cleanups). There is something to be said for shotgun legislating, because as Lyndon Johnson pointed out on numerous occasions, when an opportunity to pass bills appears, a president should exploit the opening and drive everything he can through before it closes up.

After the first year, the number of new presidential proposals diminishes, falling to less than ten new requests in fourth-year State of the Union Address, and repeat requests go from zero to more than ten. In an election year many presidential initiatives are designed more for the campaign than for enactment. Harry Truman in 1948 proposed civil rights programs based on the recommendations of the President's Committee on Civil Rights. Although he knew the program hadn't a chance of passing Congress, he presented it to win the support of northern black voters. Before the 1956 election Dwight Eisenhower introduced a watered-down civil rights bill as a ploy to try to split Southern Democrats from their northern colleagues, and to maintain the tradition of the Republicans as "the party of Lincoln." Presidents have more success proposing a large number of distributive and pork barrel projects in a presidential election year: these get passed because Congress has as much of an interest in giving voters these goodies as they do.[28]

After the elections, a lame-duck president may try to embarrass his or her successor if the opposition party has won the White House. The president will again propose a balanced budget to be achieved within three or four years and a rosy scenario for coming economic prosperity. The outgoing president may also propose measures that are politically unpopular, because he or she can no longer suffer electoral consequences: Gerald Ford's proposed pay increase for the vice president, members of Congress, members of the cabinet, and federal judges falls into this category.

THE LEGISLATIVE STRUGGLE

The framers of the Constitution did not anticipate that members of Congress would subordinate themselves to the executive—or vice versa. James Madison, in *Federalist* no. 51, foresaw constant friction between the two institutions:

> . . . the great security against gradual concentration of the several powers in the same department consists in giving to those who administer each department the necessary constitutional means and personal motives to resist the encroachments of the others. . . . Ambition must be made to counteract ambition. The interests of the man must be connected with the constitutional rights of the place.[29]

To gain support in Congress a president must negotiate and bargain, compromise and persuade, and transact political business. In most respects his or her influence on legislation is marginal, but sometimes that marginal influence means the difference between passage or defeat.

Legislative Party Leaders

No president controls his or her legislative party. The president neither chooses its leaders nor do they serve at the pleasure of the White House. Each is elected by the caucus of the legislative party. The president does not intervene because it would interfere with the autonomy of the party. It is to the legislative party that the loyalty of the leaders run. They are not the president's lieutenants, but at best allies, sometimes adversaries: President Clinton, for example, found in 1994 that four of the top Democratic congressional leaders were sponsoring a bill to overturn his decision to retain China's favorable trade privileges with the United States. His House leader, Richard Gephardt, passed the word to reporters after the 1994 midterm losses that he and other Democratic congressional leaders would not look to the White House for their legislative agenda in the next congress.

The movement of bills out of committees and their eventual passage depend on the decisions of party leaders and committee chairs. Therefore the president consults with them about the content and timing of proposals. They sense the mood of the chamber and advise the president when to move ahead and when to lay back, when to make a dramatic gesture and when to adopt a low profile. Party leaders can advise the president on the choice of a sponsor for a bill and the choice of a committee and floor manager to move it along.

In the event that Senators invoke the tradition of unlimited debate and filibuster a bill the president favors, the president's party leader must round up the necessary sixty votes to invoke Rule XXII (cloture) and end debate, something that increasingly requires a bipartisan approach. Anytime forty-one senators wish to "veto" a presidential initiative, they can filibuster to do it, in effect a form of "congressional veto" of the will of the majority of Congress. (The filibuster was used only 16 times in the entire nineteenth century, yet it was used twenty times in the 1960s, fifty-two times in the1970s, ninety times in the 1980s, and more than one hundred times between 1990 and 1995, especially near the end of the session.) The president may help end a filibuster: this was the case in passage of several civil rights laws in the 1950s and 1960s. A president who fails to lead the procedural fight is likely to suffer a major defeat: Although Democrats had more than fifty votes for a pro-union Worker Fairness Act in 1994, they were unable to round up sixty votes to end a threatened filibuster by Republicans, and the bill died. The president supported the measure, but when push came to shove, he did not attempt to break the filibuster.

Senate Rule 22, some have argued, is unconstitutional, because it forces the Senate to round up sixty votes for passage when Constitution specifies only a simple majority is required. Nevertheless, the Senate constitutionally must remain free to make its own rules, and it is not likely the courts will intervene. In any event, presidents have not tried to force the issue. A president may benefit from the filibuster: In 1995 President Clinton's executive order banning replacement workers in most strikes was saved from a Republican effort to nullify it as a result of a successful filibuster in the Senate by the Democrats.

Party leaders play their most significant role after each chamber has passed a bill. They choose the members of the "conference committee" that reconciles the versions passed by the two chambers and may even add new provisions to the bill. They can pick people who can move a bill toward or away from the president's position.

Legislative Liaison

"I want to be especially sure," Lyndon Johnson told his cabinet secretaries after the 1964 elections, "that each of you selects a top man to serve as your legislative liaison. Next to the cabinet officer himself, I consider this the most important position in the department."[30] The Office of Congressional Relations handles liaison with Congress: it tracks progress of bills, communicates White House interests as subcommittees and committees move bills along, and gathers information about intentions of members. It also helps legislators facilitate constituency requests for service from the bureaucracy, and helps them get access to departmental secretaries and to the president. Alternatively, it serves as a buffer for the president, keeping members of Congress at bay while the White House is concerned with foreign crises or other issues. It can give Congress an input as the president formulates a program. It helps develop the White House legislative strategy.[31]

Before World War II presidents used cabinet secretaries and subcabinet officials, especially those with prior legislative service, to communicate with Congress. Wilson relied on his attorney general and also instituted the "Common Council Club," a group of thirty subcabinet officials (including Assistant Secretary of the Navy Franklin Roosevelt) to round up support on Capitol Hill. Roosevelt used his postmaster general Jim Farley, and the assistant secretary of commerce was the position designated for White House lobbying of Capitol Hill. During World War II the War Department performed liaison for the president, with more than two hundred officers assigned to its Legislation and Liaison Division. Several White House aides and the Bureau of the Budget's Legislative Reference Division also lobbied Congress. After the war the Department of Defense created an assistant secretary for congressional liaison, the Department of State named an assistant secretary for congressional relations, and between 1949 and 1963 the other departments followed suit, assigning more than 500 officials to these units.

Departmental liaison offices were supervised by the White House. Truman assigned oversight to two aides, and Eisenhower created the first formal office. Johnson occasionally attended its staff meetings to regale liaison officers with anecdotes and give them advice based on his experience as Senate majority leader.[32] Under Nixon the Office of Congressional Relations was enlarged and divided into Senate staff, House staff, a group to service requests by legislators to the departments, and a group that circulated a "reporter" of committee and chamber schedules for hearings, markups, floor debates, and votes.

Reagan established a Legislative Strategy Group, consisting of senior White House aides. These included the chief of staff, head of the Congressional Liaison Office, as well as the heads of the Public Liaison Office, the Political Office (which dealt with favors for legislators and party leaders), the Office of Intergovernmental Relations (to obtain support from governors and mayors), and the OMB. Bush operated somewhat more informally: he assigned senior White House aides to deal with Congress, and his Legislative Liaison Office played a smaller role than in any postwar administration: the OMB handled liaison on budgetary and management issues, the State Department handled foreign policy liaison with Congress, and the Defense Department and the Joint Chiefs dealt with Congress directly on defense issues. Such a system can only work when a president is interested in a small number of bills, and when his primary stake is to keep Congress from ignoring presidential interests on its own legislation. Clinton relied on his senior White House aides to develop congressional strategy, relegating his congressional liaison staff to housekeeping work (counting potential supporters on close votes). He created a "war room" to coordinate his national agenda strategy, run by former campaign aides. Clinton himself did a lot of his own liaison work, talking to members of Congress on the phone late at night and early in the mornings just before final votes on his trade, budget, and crime bills, all of which passed by narrow margins after his personal efforts.

Limits to Legislative Liaison

Congressional liaison staffers have backgrounds as legislators, legislative aides, lobbyists, public relations experts, or campaign staffers. Some move from departmental liaison to the White House. Ralph Huitt, a political scientist who served as a departmental liaison in the Johnson administration, pointed out that expertise can go a long way:

> The most effective tool . . . is knowledge, expertise, a command of the business at hand. The member wants to do his job well and succeed as a congressman. The person who can help him do that, who knows how to solve a problem—especially if he can offer a "little language," i.e., a well-drafted provision that can go into a bill—never has trouble getting access and a thoughtful hearing.[33]

The institutionalization of legislative liaison provides an object lesson for anyone who would equate a large White House staff with effective use of presidential power. An aide who is dealing with legislators needs immediate access to the president and authority to speak for him, and even make commitments in his name. Bryce Harlow observed that "for real effectiveness" a White House congressional aide must be known as a confidant of the president: he or she must be "in the know" and must be able to get in touch with the president when necessary.[34] Aides like Harlow and O'Brien recount the times they have spoken for the president during sensitive transactions with congressional leaders, and how impressed these leaders were with their access. But the president can give such authority to only a handful of top aides. No matter how large the office, only a few can gain the stature to transact business as equals with legislators. Low-ranking aides can neither deal for the president nor bring him or her accurate information, for as Lyndon Johnson cautioned, "the key to accurate head counts is personal knowledge or trust, and the ability to probe beneath the surface to see what individuals are really thinking and feeling."[35] No Office of Congressional Relations can substitute for intimate and sustained presidential involvement in legislation. The incumbent must know the mood in each chamber and demonstrate some ability to wheel and deal. The president must know the details not only of the bill, but also of the particular rules and procedures that govern its consideration. By mastering the details, like Lyndon Johnson, the president impresses supporters with his personal commitment and opponents with his skills. The president must have a tightly focused operation. One of the complaints about the Clinton White House lobbying effort on health care was expressed by a Democratic congressional leader, who explained, "They have so many people tripping over each other claiming they can make decisions that it's hard to get a straight answer on anything."[36]

There are even times when White House involvement is nonproductive. Over the summer of 1994, as five congressional committees worked on the Clinton health care proposal, the White House developed a "softball" strategy. It was more important to get bills out of committee—any bill at all—than to press for the president's ideas. "We will not say whether one option is better than another," White House Deputy Chief of Staff Harold Ickes said.[37] The White House kept its cabinet and subcabinet officials on a tight leash, not permitting them to lobby Congress. The Clintons stayed away from the details of the proposals coming out from Congress, and instead "went public" to drum up support for their bottom line—universal coverage.

Interest Group Liaison

The White House tries to reach outside constituencies that might be helpful in influencing legislators. When Kennedy submitted an aid-to-education measure, construction company lobbyists were dispatched to work on Republican members of Congress. In support of Johnson's aid-to-education bill in 1965, Commissioner of Education Francis Keppel won support from Catholic lay organizations, while White House aides Jack Valenti maintained communication with the Vatican apostolic delegate, Lee White consulted with Jewish organizations, and Douglass Cater drummed up support from the National Education Association.[38] Campaigning to raise the debt ceiling, Richard Nixon mobilized defense contractors, who called conservative Republicans and urged them to support the bill on national security grounds. The Clinton administration lobbied with law enforcement organizations representing police officers for its "Brady Bill" regulating handgun sales, and for its anti-crime package calling for federal funding of 100,000 community police.

Often interest groups will mobilize to oppose a presidential initiative. In 1994, for example, Clinton's health care proposals were opposed by the health care industry, small business (opposed to employer-mandated provisions), and the Business Roundtable, representing the one hundred largest corporations. The National Association of Manufacturers and the Chamber of Commerce also opposed the plan. Approximately one hundred lobbying firms, with eighty former members of Congress, as well as some prominent "friends of Bill," were hired by them to lobby against the measure.[39] The Federal Election Commission reported more than $46 million given by health care industry PACs to members of Congress, targeted on five congressional committees working on health care bills. Lobbyists invited more than one hundred legislators to attend seminars and conferences at which the industry point of view could be pressed. The National Federation of Independent Businesses mobilized hundreds of thousands of small entrepreneurs, who communicated their opposition to members of Congress.

Transactional Politics

James Madison, in *Federalist* no. 46, predicted that bills would be decided "not on the national prosperity and happiness, but on the prejudices, interests, and pursuits of the governments and the people of the individual states."[40] Congress represents the "scuffle of local interests" as journalist Henry Jones Ford put it at the turn of the nineteenth century. Although on many votes members may rise above their local constituent interests, the decentralized party structure and the lack of national party discipline means that the president must offer members inducements to vote on the basis of national policy. As one member of Congress described how Eisenhower sought to win passage of a law regulating labor union activities, "If a man goes along, he gets money for his campaign. If he doesn't go along, he gets nothing. It's that simple."[41] Former White House assistant Doris Kearns Goodwin wrote that during the Johnson administration, Senate Minority Leader Everett Dirksen "would blatantly and without hesitation send long memos to the White House detailing his requests for that week: a judgeship in the fifth district, a post office in Peoria, a presidential speech in Springfield, a tax exemption for peanuts."[42]

Granting favors is useful for low visibility yet crucial support from members, such as voting for a measure in committee, or voting for favorable rules, or voting to kill an unfavorable amendment on the floor. Legislators sometimes vote against the president on final passage when their constituents oppose a bill, yet vote for the president's position up until that time, confident that their constituents won't know the difference. Lyndon Johnson won key procedural votes and important amendments for the Voting Rights Act of 1965 from some members of southern states (especially Texas), even though the members voted against the measure on final passage. Similarly President Clinton won support from several African-American legislators for a House rule to debate a criminal justice bill in 1994, although these representatives could not, as a matter of conscience, vote for final passage because the bill contained the death penalty.

A president may use his or her control over the bureaucracy to trade policy implementation for legislative influence. President Kennedy kept open unneeded military bases in the South and made sure defense contracts were disproportionately placed there; he approved a manned space center for Houston (home of the committee chairman with jurisdiction); he channeled intergovernmental grants to depressed rural areas, many of them in the South; he proposed a farm program with high price supports for cotton and other crops grown in the South. In return for his solicitude, Kennedy won support from southerners for his defense buildup, new foreign aid programs, and tax cut proposals.

A president must know when to bargain and when to draw the line. A strong president like Wilson or Franklin Roosevelt may pass the word that all patronage and distributions will be given out near the end of the congressional session once loyalty to the administration has been demonstrated. Lyndon Johnson let it be known that he would reward legislators who generally supported him rather than deal with individuals on each issue in quid pro quo arrangements. With few exceptions (such as Dirksen), favors were "generally delivered by the White House staff after the fact, and on the basis of a pattern of voting, not by the President personally in exchange for a specific vote."[43]

Transactions whet the appetites of lawmakers. "I could not trade patronage for votes in any direct exchange," Lyndon Johnson recalled. "If word spread that I was trading, everyone would want to trade and all other efforts at persuasion would automatically fail."[44] But a president who announces a "no deals" policy commits political suicide. President Carter decided to cut out funding for 19 water development projects in his fiscal year 1978 budget. He announced he would review the economic feasibility of 320 more projects. Both the Senate and House responded by voting to require the president to spend funding for these projects. After the firestorm of protest the president backed down. He released 307 projects from his review, and restored funding to three of the nineteen he had dropped. A year later, after the defection of 101 Democrats on his consumer protection bill, Carter met with twenty-six party whips and agreed to facilitate their requests for patronage, grants, and contracts. The anti-politics president had finally come around, but by that time he had irreparably damaged his relationship with Congress. Similarly, Clinton had to back down on efforts to reform the way western lands were managed for the benefit of ranchers, after a group of Western Democratic senators indicated that if he did not drop his proposal they would vote against his economic program.

Clinton on NAFTA and GATT

President Clinton demonstrated how personal involvement and shrewd horsetrading can make the difference between victory and defeat on crucial legislation. He pulled out a victory on the NAFTA international trade agreement with Mexico and Canada by offering specific sweeteners to wavering members. For several California representatives, he offered a North American Development Bank to assist workers hurt by the NAFTA agreement. Florida growers of citrus fruits and vegetables, and sugar growers from other southern states were offered protection from Mexican imports. As word spread that Clinton was willing to bargain, farmers growing tomatoes, sweet peppers, cucumbers, and peanuts got protection. Legislators from Philadelphia protected cream cheese producers. Appliance makers, flat glass producers, and those making bed frames got special breaks. To gain the vote of Floyd Flake, representing a poor district in Queens, New York, an "economic empowerment" zone was guaranteed for his district, meaning new government grants and jobs for his constituents.[45] To seal Republican support, Clinton promised to repudiate any Democratic challenger that used a pro-NAFTA vote by a Republican member of Congress in the next midterm elections.[46] Similarly, in trying to round up support for the General Agreement on Tariff and Trade (GATT) implementation bill in Congress in late 1994, Clinton offered tariff protection or compensating favors to companies making cellular telephones, automobiles, steel, ball bearings, and airplanes, as well as wheat farmers and lumber and cement producers.[47]

Some political scientists argue that a president's legislative skills are only marginally useful in winning support for their program.[48] Nevertheless, what seems a marginal shift of support to a political scientist charting overall support scores looks quite different from the perspective of the White House, where a shift of a few votes does not change the overall pattern and percentages, but makes the difference between victory or defeat.

Hardball Politics

At times presidents play rough against members who cross them. After Kennedy lost a crucial vote in the Senate, he ordered the Bureau of the Budget to drop a project sponsored by Senator Jennings Randolph, who had cast the deciding vote against. Yet as White House aide Ted Sorensen recounted, conservative Democratic senators helped Randolph by channeling new projects to his state in other legislation.[49] Two Maine Republicans, William Cohen and David Emery, were told by White House aides that if they did not vote to sustain a veto by President Ford, a former Maine governor would not be reappointed as chairman of the National Transportation Board. They did not, he was not, and they leaked the threat to the press, which prompted Ford, after the public outcry, to send his liaison officials over to the Capitol to apologize to Cohen and Emery. When Democratic Senator Richard Shelby led the opposition to Clinton's first-year economic package, the White House announced it was moving a contract for building the space shuttle out of Alabama, and cut him off from White House social functions. Late in 1994 Shelby got his revenge, hitting Clinton when he was already down, by announcing immediately after the midterm elections that he was switching to the Republican Party. Most of the time, it is fair to say, hardball tactics create more problems for the president than they solve. There is more political profit to be made by revealing the White House pressure and standing up to it than there is to knuckling under.

THE WHITE HOUSE AND THE "NEW CONGRESS"

Beginning in the 1970s, Congress has gone through three waves of procedural reforms, each of which has adversely affected the prospects that the president can be an effective legislative leader.

The Changing Role of Congressional Committees in the 1970s

Under most circumstances the key to presidential success in Congress has been to influence its committees, because that was where most of the work was done. A sympathetic majority could speed consideration of presidential proposals, arrange for "friendly" hearings, and "mark up" the bill to reflect White House priorities. Committee leaders would control the floor debate and work with party leaders to create a coalition for passage. A hostile committee would pigeonhole a bill by refusing to report it out, delay hearings, hold hostile hearings, or revise the president's measure so thoroughly in "mark-up" sessions he might wish he had never introduced it. When a committee bottled up a measure it was almost impossible for a president to win its release.

Reforms in the 1970s sponsored by House Democrats decentralized power from committees to subcommittees, by establishing a "subcommittee bill of rights" granting them powers over bills similar to full committees. It also reduced the power and influence of committee leaders, and modified the "seniority rules" so that party caucuses would have the final word on committee chairmanships. Power moved from a small group of committee leaders to a larger group of middle-level legislators in charge of subcommittees as well as to party caucuses and party leaders. The president had to negotiate with a wider range of leaders and had to pay more attention to rank-and-file party members. No longer could he work out a deal with one or two committee leaders.

The Post-Reform Congress of the 1980s

In the 1980s, a quiet revolution in the way Congress did business occurred. Presidents asked less of Congress, and members of Congress asked less of their colleagues. Fewer bills were introduced, and fewer were referred to committees. The number of hearings declined, as did the number of bills reported to the chambers. Yet in some ways the White House was asking more: legislation increasingly required complicated trade-offs involving cutbacks of some programs and expansion of others. Most new programs were incorporated into "mega-bills," such as the Carter Energy Plan of 1978, the Reagan budget proposals of 1981, or the Clinton health care proposals of 1993, that required work by several different committees acting sequentially. Legislation was often developed outside of the formal committees by party caucus task forces. This complicated work was coordinated by party leaders, acting as "traffic cops" for the committees, determining which committees got jurisdiction over what policies, and when or whether their reported bills (or parts of bills) would be taken up by the chamber.[50]

Presidents worked with party leaders to create "fast-track" procedures, sometimes specified in laws and sometimes in informal agreements, for important measures.[51] The "fast track" might embody one or more of the following provisions:

- A measure must be considered within a specified time period after being submitted to Congress by the executive (as with international trade agreements);
- Caucus or party task forces mark up bills instead of congressional committees (as with energy legislation in the late 1970s);

- No amendments to the bill reported to the chamber may be considered or voted on (as with NAFTA);
- Committees report legislation without holding hearings (as with laws barring the railroad strike in 1987);
- A large conference substitutes for several different committees in considering a "global" bill that cuts across many committee jurisdictions (as with international trade, energy, or health care).

The fast-track approach has been used by party leaders and the White House to avoid committee "choke points" that otherwise would kill or delay legislation, and to prevent floating coalitions of opponents within the committees or the full chamber from amending a bill to death, a situation likely to occur unless unfriendly amendments are prohibited. Sometimes, as with international trade legislation to implement the 1994 GATT agreement, the president does not submit a formal bill for "fast-track" consideration until the Senate and House committees have separately and then jointly deliberated on his proposals. After getting the sense of what the members are prepared to accept, the president then sends a proposal for "fast-track" consideration.

The fast-track provisions themselves can be a subject of negotiation when a bill is being considered by Congress. In 1994 as Congress considered implementing legislation for GATT, Clinton offered to drop the fast-track provision from the bill, so that when he submitted to Congress controversial legislation under the GATT accords, members would be able to offer amendments. His offer was crucial in obtaining bipartisan support for the GATT measure.

Incoming Speaker Newt Gingrich holds a copy of the "Contract with America" as Republicans assume control of the House of Representatives for the first time in forty years. Their 1994 midterm victory put an end to President Clinton's legislative agenda; he would now have to threaten vetoes in order to influence Congress.

The Republican Reforms in the 1990s

With the ouster of the Democrats from House and Senate leadership in the mid-1990s, the stage was set for radical reform of congressional procedures that would increase the congressional role in program initiation and public opinion leadership. Under new Speaker of the House Newt Gingrich, congressional party and House rules were changed to provide for expedited consideration of party proposals: the leadership was strengthened as committees were weakened. Party leaders played a greater role in setting agendas with national visibility, such as Gingrich's controversial "Contract with America." Republicans in both chambers voted with a high degree of party unity on most of the Contract. Instead of Congress being preoccupied with passage of a presidential program, in the mid-1990s it was more accurate to state that the president was preoccupied with the passage of a congressional program.

PASSING THE PRESIDENT'S PROGRAM

"I learned the hard way that there was no party loyalty or discipline when a complicated or controversial issue was at stake," Jimmy Carter observed.[52] The president must create a separate coalition for each proposal he sends to Congress.

Party-Based Coalitions

Presidents can count on support from their own party. Since 1945 a Democratic president gets on average close to 80 percent of the votes of House Democrats and 75 percent of the votes of Senate Democrats, and this percentage has been increasing into the high 80s in domestic measures in the 1990s. Republican presidents on average receive 70 percent support from House Republicans and 75 percent from Senate Republicans. Members of the president's party almost always provide greater support than the opposition: Republican presidents get on average support from 40 percent of House Democrats and 45 percent of Senate Democrats; Democratic presidents on average have received support of 40 percent of House Republicans and 50 percent of Senate Republicans, though this figure declined into the 30 percent range during the Clinton presidency. (One reason for seemingly high support scores from the opposition is that a large number of roll-call votes in the House and Senate are bipartisan, with majorities of both parties supporting a measure while minorities from both parties oppose it.)

Between 1981 and 1992, with a conservative president facing off against a liberal Congress, party unity scores (in which a majority of one party is pitted against a majority of the other) increased markedly compared with the period between 1967 and 1981. The percentage of votes on which members cast ballots in accord with a majority of their own party then reached new highs during the first two years of the Clinton administration, as Democrats voted with their party on average 85 percent of the time, and Republicans did likewise on average 84 percent of the time.[53] Fueling the increased polarization was the shifting regional composition of the Republican Party, which had fewer moderates from the Northeast and urban Midwest, and more conservatives in its ranks from the South—12 Southern Republicans in 1960 had increased to 61 by 1994, almost all highly ideological and partisan. Meanwhile Southern Democrats were more likely to vote with a majority of their party: By the 1970s rural Southern Democrats were more likely to support urban legislation from their party than urban northern moderate Republicans.[54] As some conservative white Democrats were replaced by liberal African-American representatives after southern redistricting in 1992, the Southern Democratic Party became even more liberal, whereas Southern conservatives increased their opposition to Democratic presidential initiatives.

With partisan voting patterns increasing, presidents could count on even higher support from their own party but found it more difficult than ever before to win support from the opposition. A president's success in Congress increasingly has been determined by the number of seats his party controls.[55] Most important measures, including the budget, defense, and foreign policy issues, will involve partisan patterns. The influence of party is stronger than the influence of ideology, of the local constituency, or of any other factor.

Party members support the president for several reasons. They are more likely to have the same position on issues because they come from similar electoral constituencies and rely on similar electoral coalitions. They may share similar ideologies and have made similar campaign commitments. They have an incentive not to embarrass or weaken their president, to deny the opposition an opening that may hurt them as well as the White House. Different factions in the party have an incentive to logroll and compromise with each other and with the president, to get together on a measure they can support, rather than defect to the opposition. Democrats especially have a political style that encourages compromises to benefit each faction in turn, and this style of "facilitative" leadership results in high party cohesion.[56]

These patterns do not always hold: In 1994 the Clinton anti-crime program was initially defeated in the House when fifty-eight Democrats deserted the president; of these, ten were members of the Congressional Black Caucus, most from safe seats, who had backed the president strongly on most issues. Yet on this one they voted against him because they believed new death penalties would be applied disproportionately against African-Americans. On the centerpiece of the Clinton program, health reform, the Democrats splintered, with many abandoning the president to support the most liberal "single-payer plan," and others supporting a more conservative incremental proposal put forth by several Southern Democrats. For Clinton, the problem of party loyalty was compounded because Democrats in Congress were not used to presidential leadership: in his first Congress (1993–1994) only 28 percent of the House Democrats had ever served with a Democratic president, and only 6.6 percent had served with a Democratic president other than Clinton or Carter.[57] In his second Congress, some Democrats deserted Clinton's liberal agenda and voted for the Republican "Contract with America" because of his low public approval ratings, especially in the South and West, as they girded themselves for renewed Republican attacks in 1996.

Conservative versus Liberal Coalitions

"Some Democrats support us better than some Republicans do," Richard Nixon once reminded his assistants at a White House meeting.[58] Tactics to encourage defections vary. Sometimes members can be detached from their party when the issue is highly ideological. Since the mid-1930s a conservative coalition consisting primarily of Southern Democrats and Republicans has formed one-sixth to one-quarter of the roll-call votes. It was able to block meaningful civil rights legislation through the 1950s.[59] Between 1961 and 1976, the coalition appeared on approximately one-quarter of the roll-call votes, winning as little as 35 percent of them in 1965 (when the House contained a large number of liberal Democrats and a small number of Republicans) and as much as 83 percent when it appeared in 1971 (when a Republican president was in the White House and could help them).[60] Liberal proposals were often defeated or substantially modified from the Roosevelt through the Carter presidency.[61] By the early 1980s the coalition consisted of a shrinking number of Southern Democrats organized in the House as the Conservative Democratic Forum and known as the Boll Weevils, a few Northern Democrats, and most Republicans. President Reagan's tax and spending programs and his military buildup were strongly and successfully supported by the coalition. During the Bush presidency and the first two years of the Clinton presidency, the coalition appeared on less than 10 percent of the votes, primarily on budget and defense issues and on "lifestyle issues" (against civil rights for homosexuals), though it won on 90 percent of the votes it contested.[62] After Republicans won control of Congress in 1995, the conservative coalition dominated for the first time since the 1920s.

Democratic presidents often put together a "lib-lab" coalition—a group of mostly Democratic liberals (members of the Democratic Study Group in the House), including those elected with labor union support, combined with moderate Republicans. This coalition does best when a Democratic president such as Lyndon Johnson wins a landslide election and brings in an unusually large number of liberal Democrats in the House to overcome the strength of the conservative coalition. Then major measures of the liberal agenda can be enacted until midterm losses reduce the size of the lib-lab majority.[63] When Republicans win control of Congress, as they did in 1994, the lib-lab coalition's prospects for enactment of a liberal agenda are nil.

Bipartisan Coalition-Building

The "hunting" is often quite good when a president looks for votes across the aisles, especially when he works with influential members of the opposition. President Johnson won key votes from Republicans by working with Senate Minority Leader Everett Dirksen, enabling him to break a filibuster against the civil rights bill in the Senate in 1964. President Reagan won 43 votes from Boll Weevil Democrats to get his comprehensive supply-side economic program passed in 1981. President Bush won a large number of votes from a Democratic group led by Stephen Solarz in the House to provide a bipartisan authorization for his war policy against Iraq in 1991. In 1993 President Clinton got the NAFTA legislation through Congress only because a majority of Republicans, led by their congressional leaders, joined a minority from his own party. He got the Brady gun control measure through Congress in 1994 by lobbying for thirty-eight Republican votes in the House in a late-night and early-morning phone-a-thon, votes needed because seventy-seven members of his own party defected. In 1994, after an initial procedural defeat on his crime bill, Clinton adopted a bipartisan strategy and won votes of forty-six Republican moderates for his crime bill by offering them some cuts in its funding; in doing so Clinton rejected an alternative strategy of dropping a ban on assault weapons to unify the Democrats that had been proposed by House Speaker Thomas Foley—and lost some Democrats in the second round of voting that finally passed the bill. A president who overlooks the fertile ground of the opposition party would be foolish indeed, especially on the most important "valence" issues involved in his or her legislative program.

Presidential Support and Programmatic Politics

Some political scientists have argued that the type of policy dealt with by Congress can explain the pattern of presidential–congressional relations.[64] There are four general types of policies:

- *Constituent:* policies related to the running of government, including administrative reorganization proposals; management reforms; civil service personnel reform; salaries and pensions; campaign finance and electoral reform; and changes in the budget process;
- *Redistributive:* policies that enable the government to shift income, benefits, or services from one region or class of people to another through a mix of taxing and spending. These involve tax laws, Social Security, unemployment insurance, health care programs, and other social welfare programs;
- *Distributive:* policies that provide benefits to a small group of people, corporations, state or local governments, or other public and private sector organizations. These include intergovernmental grant-in-aid programs to build airports, hospitals, and roads; grant programs for job training; capital construction projects; research and development contracts; and government procurement contracts;
- *Regulatory:* policies that involve formulation of general rules for particular industries, such as transportation, communication, banking, and finance. There are also general regulatory policies, such as those that regulate labor–management disputes, ban discrimination, or require affirmative action.

Several studies have found differences in the level of presidential success with Congress, depending on the policies the White House proposed. One study of presidential programs between 1954 and 1974 found that the president was most successful in constituent issues, in large measure because there is less disagreement with Congress on these issues; legislators seem to have a small stake in them, and are willing to concede dominance to the president. Presidents also were successful in many redistributive issues; because they could use their electoral mandates early in their terms, engage in national agenda politics successfully, and parlay a favorable public response to their initiatives. Both Reagan and Clinton were successful in their first year with comprehensive economic game plans: in Reagan's case, it was a major tax and spending cut that redistributed income upward; in Clinton's case, it was a large tax increase that redistributed income away from the wealthy and (with an earned income credit) toward the working poor. In contrast, presidential influence is weakest in regulatory issues, because there the president faces strong opposition from congressional committees and interest groups intent on maintaining their own influence over bureaucracies.[65]

Presidential Success Scores

How successful are presidents with Congress? If we look at bills on which the president took a position, we find on average that Congress passes four-fifths when a

Democratic president deals with a Democratic Congress and three-fifths when a Republican president confronts a Democratic Congress (with the Republican percentages declining steadily from Eisenhower's almost 70 percent to Bush's barely 50 percent). President Clinton, for example, had a "success score" of 86.4 percent in his first year—the third highest rating any president has ever achieved, just behind Eisenhower's 89 percent and Lyndon Johnson's 88 percent.[66] Yet these statistics are misleading: the president often endorses minor bills he or she really does not care about, he or she supports bills that have been modified from the original proposals, and the support scores include bipartisan bills passed with no controversy—in recent years Congress has passed a large number of resolutions embodying values as part of the reelection strategies of the members. So the "president's success" score inflates presidential influence—no one in his or her right mind could believe that Clinton was nearly as successful as the scores suggest.

A better measurement, compiled by *Congressional Quarterly* between 1954 and 1975, was the "presidential boxscore" of support for the president's own proposals. It showed that presidents were less successful with Congress when it came to their own initiatives. In only four years between 1961 and 1975 did more than half of presidential proposals pass. The overall percentages were: Eisenhower, 45 percent; Kennedy, 39 percent; Johnson, 57 percent; Nixon, 34 percent; and Ford, 30 percent.

The best measurement of presidential success involves the fate of major bills—those that the Office of Management and Budget (OMB) indicates are "in accord with the program of the President" and that also are mentioned in the State of the Union Address. On the most important measures presidents sought from Congress between 1961 and 1975, Democratic presidents actually did somewhat better than on their overall program: Kennedy, 53 percent; Johnson, 59 percent; Nixon, 35 percent; and Ford, 31 percent.[67] A Congress controlled by the president's party is more likely to give the president what he wants than a legislature dominated by the opposition. Carter, for example, won 49 percent on key bills between 1977 and 1981. Although the OMB stopped indicating presidential success on priority bills after 1980, these percentages were in all likelihood comparable or even lower for Reagan and Bush than for Nixon and Ford.

Cautions on Quantitative Measurement of Presidential Support

The entire "boxscore" approach is somewhat misleading. At times the proposal a president submits has already been modified in anticipation of the reactions of Congress, so even if passed intact, it may still incorporate a "congressional" rather than a White House viewpoint. Lyndon Johnson modified a program to provide urban development funds to a few large cities into a program to provide funds to most midsize cities, to ensure congressional passage. A measure that is passed may actually represent a defeat for the president because its content has been changed substantially, even though the president continues to support it as the best he might achieve. The boxscore does not include bills that a president decided not to propose because he or she knew there would not be the votes to pass it. Some bills are "inherited" from prior administrations: a president may support them, but they do not represent his or her own priorities. Sometimes a president may pass many minor bills, boosting boxscore percentage, but a defeat on a single measure—such as Clinton's health care plan in 1994—may signal the president's political demise for much of the remainder of the term.

Most quantitative studies implicitly assume that the larger the percentage of votes in support of the president's program, the better for the White House. But this is not always the case. Sometimes there is a tradeoff between the percentage of votes the president gets and his or her spatial positioning on a bill: the more the president seeks to win by getting a bill that corresponds closely to his or her own position, the more likely some votes will be lost. Yet a president may prefer the tradeoff: a smaller vote margin may yield a more satisfying victory. Bill Clinton's first-year economic package was played according to such a tradeoff; in the end, he won by only a handful of votes, but his margin of victory was irrelevant—provided he won. In his second year, Clinton rejected a compromise with the House Republican leadership on his crime bill that would have forced him to gut key provisions to win broad bipartisan support: he preferred to struggle for a narrower victory with fewer compromises on a measure he preferred.[68] So the data on presidential support scores are far less useful than a roundup of the number of key bills he managed to get passed that reflected effective positioning, i.e., an ability to get most of what he wanted without making crippling compromises that would weaken him for subsequent political struggles and diminish his reputation as a "winner."

One final caution on quantitative scores: neither the president nor the party leaders in Congress want to round up every last possible vote on every measure. They merely need to ensure the majority that passes the bill. "To get along, go along" was the advice given to new members of the House in the 1950s by Speaker Sam Rayburn. But Rayburn would never ask a member to put his career in jeopardy or violate his conscience for a vote. A corollary of the Rayburn rule was developed by Larry O'Brien. "I never expected any member to commit political suicide to help the President, no matter how noble our cause" he claimed, adding, "I expected politicians to be concerned with their own interests. I only hoped to convince them that our interests were often the same."[69] A president who can win without the votes from some members of his party on controversial measures may be saving them from electoral defeat, and helping himself on later legislative struggles.

ARE THERE "TWO PRESIDENCIES"?

Some political scientists have argued that the president is much more likely to be successful with Congress in foreign affairs than in domestic matters. When the security of the nation is at stake, Congress and the president are likely to drop partisan politics because "politics stops at the water's edge." Is this true?

The Initial Findings

"In the realm of foreign policy," political scientist Aaron Wildavsky concluded in the 1960s, "there has not been a single major issue on which Presidents, when they were serious and determined, have failed."[70] For Truman, Eisenhower, Kennedy, and Johnson, the average "Congressional Quarterly Boxscore" on presidential domestic proposals was 40.2 percent approved; for foreign policy it was 58.5 percent, and for defense policy 73.3 percent. Wildavsky argued that bipartisanship in foreign policy accounted for the phenomenon.

The Refutation

Other political scientists challenged these findings. Some argued that in the post-Vietnam era the differences in support levels were narrower.[71] Higher congressional support rates for presidential foreign policy initiatives reported for the 1950s and 1960s dropped in the 1970s and 1980s to rates similar to those for approval of domestic programs in the House.[72] Only among Senate Republicans was there a significant difference for most presidents, and only for the Reagan presidency was there a significant difference in the House.[73] The drop in support for the White House may have been attributable to the fears of an "imperial presidency" in the Vietnam War era. Another possibility was that it marked the reassertion of traditional patterns, which had been obscured by the unusual success of Dwight Eisenhower in the 1950s. Conservative Republican presidents after Eisenhower were unable to duplicate his bipartisan success, because liberal Democrats were able to modify or block their more extreme proposals.[74]

In analyzing the data some political scientists argued that Eisenhower was simply an exception to general patterns, and that the "two-presidency" phenomena existed only for his presidency.[75] Others argued that it only appeared for Republican presidents.[76] Still another analysis indicated that much of the "two-presidency" phenomenon really involved split-government: the opposition majority party may give the benefit of the doubt to a minority president in foreign affairs.[77] Wildavsky eventually changed his mind, after seeing congressional opposition to the Vietnam War and much of presidential foreign policy in the late 1960s and early 1970s, with consequent lower presidential support scores for defense and foreign policy.[78] He then argued that the parties were increasingly polarized on foreign policy issues, so that "foreign policy has become more like domestic policy—a realm marked by serious partisan divisions in which the President cannot count on a free ride."[79]

The Pattern in the 1990s

The "two-presidency" pattern does seem to exist in the 1990s at times. Presidents do seem to be more likely to succeed with Congress in "intermestic" affairs: those matters, such as environmental and trade issues, that straddle the supposed boundaries between domestic and foreign policy. President Bush fashioned a bipartisan coalition to authorize war with Iraq in 1991. President Clinton won over more than 80 percent of the Republicans for key votes on the NAFTA and the GATT trade agreements in the same year that party-line voting in domestic matters reached an all-time high. In the same month when his health care and crime legislation was being stalled and gutted in the House, he won an overwhelming vote against restricting trade with China as a means of punishing it for human rights violations, and beat off congressional restrictions on aid to Russia. On the most significant foreign policy issues a president brings to Congress, he is often able to win. Yet the important point since the early 1980s is this: to the extent that any residual "two-presidency" phenomenon continues to show up in the data, it is because some presidents (Reagan and Bush) were much weaker in passing domestic legislation, not because they were so strong in passing foreign policy bills.[80]

No quantitative roll-call analysis can capture the dynamics of presidential successes or failures in leading Congress in foreign policy. Most roll-call measures are routine, and even those rated "major" are not as significant as the one or two crucial bills or treaties that make or break a presidency in foreign affairs. Presidents have often been challenged by Congress and their most important policies repudiated. Into the 1930s, the Senate routinely used to defeat or postpone treaties, the most significant example being Woodrow Wilson's defeat on the Treaty of Versailles in 1919. In the 1930s neutrality legislation handcuffed Franklin Roosevelt before World War II. In the 1970s anti-war sentiment in Congress ended the bombing of Cambodia, led to passage of the War Powers Resolution, and resulted in significant cuts in foreign aid programs, limits to U.S. contributions to the UN and multilateral lending agencies, and modification of military assistance programs. In the 1980s Congress refused to grant President Reagan's request for aid to the Nicaraguan contra guerrillas in their attempt to overthrow the leftist Sandinista government, instead restricting aid entirely by passing the Boland Amendments.[81] Clinton had to implement a $20 billion bailout for Mexico in 1995 by an executive order that directed the Treasury to use its Exchange Stabilization Fund to back peso-denominated bonds issued by the Mexican government. He did so only after rank-and-file legislators from both parties defied their leaders and indicated they would defeat the loan guarantee bill backed by the president.

VETOING BILLS

The framers of the Constitution were aware of state constitutions that entrusted the veto power over laws passed by state legislatures to governors and judges acting together in "councils of revision." Nevertheless, they entrusted the veto power to the president alone.[82] Article 1, sec. 7, clause 2 provides that:

> Every Bill which shall have passed the House of Representatives and Senate shall, before it become a law, be presented to the President of the United States; if he approve he shall sign it, but if not he shall return it, with his objections to that House in which it shall have originated, who shall enter the objections at large on their journal and proceed to reconsider it.

The president has ten days (not including Sunday) to sign the bill. If he or she opposes the measure, it may be returned to Congress, or nothing may be done, in which case it becomes law without a signature. The president is required to give reasons for returning the bill in a veto message, explaining why the legislative will was blocked.

The presidential veto power is not absolute. Congress has until the end of its session to override the veto by a two-thirds vote of each chamber. In fact, the Constitution does not use the term *veto* (Latin for "I forbid") because the framers did not want to confuse this suspensory power with the absolute negative that British monarchs had asserted over legislative enactments. The Constitution refers to the president's right to "return" a bill to Congress.[83]

The veto applies to "every order, resolution or vote to which the concurrence of the Senate and House may be necessary." But the courts have construed this check more narrowly. Presidents cannot veto constitutional amendments proposed by both houses of Congress.[84] They do not veto concurrent resolutions of both chambers (such as a budget resolution). They cannot veto measures of the House or Senate that deal with internal organization, such as election of officers, assignments of members to committees, or establishment of rules, because each chamber operates without the concurrence of the other. It is unclear whether the president can veto a declaration of war.

Through 1994 the president did not have a line-item veto, though forty-three governors have it, and one of the first orders of business for the Congress in 1995 was to redeem a Republican pledge to give the president such a veto over spending bills. Absent such a veto, the president must veto the whole bill or nothing, even if Congress puts on riders to evade the veto. Presidents have often signed bills with legislative vetoes on foreign aid and other programs because they want authority and funds to continue these programs. In 1990 President Bush signed a statute imposing trade sanctions on China and denouncing it for human rights violations. He issued a signing statement claiming that nine provisions were unconstitutional and reserved the right to interpret and administer them in ways inconsistent with congressional intent.[85] In effect, this statement was a form of line-item veto exercised through the "take-care clause."

The framers believed that a president should protect the Constitution with the veto power. They granted presidents a veto because they wanted them to check any congressional usurpation of their own powers. As Madison put it, each department must have "the necessary constitutional means and personal motives to resist encroachments [by] the others."[86] Hamilton argued that granting the president the veto was done "to enable him to defend himself" against a congressional attack on his powers, adding "one ought not to be left at the mercy of the other, but ought to possess a constitutional and effectual power of self-defense."[87] "Six times in my presidency," Bush proclaimed, "I have vetoed bills that would have weakened presidential powers," adding that when Congress "tries to manage the Executive Branch . . . by writing too specific directions for carrying out a particular law," he would continue to use the veto.[88]

The Pocket Veto

There is one circumstance in which the veto is absolute. If Congress has adjourned within ten days of sending a bill to the president, and the president does not sign the measure, it is pocket vetoed. The president cannot return the bill to either chamber (because Congress is no longer in session). He or she need not provide reasons for the pocket veto and need not send a message to Congress. Congress cannot later convene, override the veto, and enact the measure into law. It must start from scratch, pass the bill in its next session, even if identical to the one that had been pocket vetoed, and present it to the president after it reconvenes from adjournment.[89] Somewhat fewer than half of all vetoes have been pocket vetoes.

The pocket veto has been misused by several presidents. Both Nixon and Ford used it during interim adjournments of Congress, Nixon to kill a health care bill and Ford to kill vocational rehabilitation, farm labor, and wildlife refuge measures. Congress responded by recessing rather than adjourning for vacations, and by designating officers in each chamber to receive suspensory veto messages from the president, thus attempting to inhibit the president from exercising the pocket veto.[90] In August 1974 a Court of Appeals decided that the president could not use the pocket veto during congressional recesses, provided an officer was appointed to receive veto messages.[91] In 1976 President Ford's attorney general announced that the pocket veto would be used only for the final adjournment of Congress at the end of its second session, and not during vacation adjournments or for the period between the first and second congressional session.[92] After President Reagan revived the practice of using the pocket veto during congressional recesses, a federal court in 1984 also ruled against Reagan, noting that a congressional recess is not the same as an adjournment.[93]

The Bush administration used the pocket veto expansively. Bush pocket vetoed a bill *within* a session of Congress in 1989 (the first time this had been done since Nixon), claiming that it was constitutional whenever Congress recessed for more than three days.[94] Later, when Congress passed a measure that would have allowed Chinese students to remain in the United States after their visas expired (to protect them after they had protested the massacres of students by the Chinese communist regime in Tienanmen Square), Bush exercised a pocket veto of the measure. He did, however, issue an executive order to departments to establish rules protecting the students, claiming that he had pocket vetoed the bill to prevent "micro-management" of United States–Chinese relations by Congress.

Review of Enrolled Bills

To decide whether to exercise the veto or the pocket veto, the president reviews all enrolled bills sent to him by Congress. Bills are received by the OMB's Legislative Reference Division, then sent to departments and agencies for comment, who submit recommendations back to the OMB. White House aides, advisory councils and departments, legislative leaders, and lobbyists all offer advice to the president. The OMB makes its recommendation within five days of receiving the enrolled bill.[95] White House aides then make a final recommendation, transmitting it along with the OMB and departmental papers to the president within eight days of congressional passage for a final decision.

Presidents rely heavily on OMB recommendations. In almost all cases that the OMB favors a bill signing, they go along with it, regardless of whether the department agrees. Between 1953 and 1960, Eisenhower approved all but 1 percent of the bills recommended for signature by the Bureau of the Budget. The figure was similar for subsequent presidents.[96] However, when the Bureau wanted a veto, and the department wanted the bill signed, Eisenhower followed the recommendation three-quarters of the time, and Lyndon Johnson sided with the departments more than two-thirds of the time.[97] In the Nixon and Ford administrations, in contrast, two out of three times the president sided with the department rather than go along with OMB.[98] In the Reagan and Bush presidencies, the OMB was upheld more often, especially on spending measures.

Functions of the Veto

Woodrow Wilson referred to the president in the 1880s as "the third branch of the legislature" when he threatened to use his veto, because it gave him influence in shaping legislation as it went through Congress, and because he could use the veto to control legislative outcomes, especially those with budget implications.[99] Timely warnings by the White House may induce committees to compromise on the details of the committee markups, an approach referred to as "veto bargaining."[100] Negotiations involve calculations on the part of all participants about the likelihood that the president is not bluffing. It is said that Franklin Roosevelt occasionally asked his aides to find him "something I can veto" just to impress on legislators that he had the power. The threat of a veto may itself derail a measure so that it never passes Congress at all. President Bush was able to use his veto threat to modify Democratic bills involving child care, the minimum wage, civil rights, pollution control, and the extension of unemployment benefits.[101]

The veto only gives the president influence in certain situations. He cannot use it to get more from Congress than it wants to give him. For example, if he wants more funding for foreign aid or defense budgets, the veto is absolutely useless in bargaining with a Congress that wants to provide less money for these purposes. If he wants a new program and Congress balks, the veto is also useless. When he wants to spend less and Congress wants to spend more, his veto can block Congress; and when Congress wishes to take action and the president is opposed, his veto is most successful. Like most presidential prerogatives, the use of the veto is not a demonstration of presidential power, but an indication that White House influence in Congress has eroded, and the system of bargaining and accommodation has broken down.

The veto is often used to cement the support of electoral or interest group coalitions that have supported the president. Bush, for example, vetoed bills authorizing spending on abortion and birth-control counseling and providing for family leave (after working women gave birth), to consolidate his support among religious conservatives favoring a "pro-family" and "pro-life" set of social policies. Clinton in 1995 threatened to veto bills cutting too deeply into programs for the poor, children, and the elderly.

Veto Patterns

Political scientists have attempted to specify conditions under which the veto is likely to be exercised. One study tracing the use of the veto from Washington through Nixon found that Democratic presidents had been more likely to wield the veto than Republicans, and that presidents with prior service in Congress were least likely to veto bills.[102] The key variable was not partisanship, but as the research pointed out, seemed to be whether the president has a Congress dominated by his or her party—or is facing split government. Democrats Kennedy and Johnson vetoed far fewer bills than Republicans Eisenhower, Nixon, and Ford, all of whom faced a Democratic Congress, as Table 9.1 indicates.

Presidents veto all types of bills: economic, tax, natural resources, and appropriations tend to be disproportionately represented, though farm bills seem to escape vetoes. Highly important and minor measures seem to get vetoed with equal likelihood. Presidents veto bills primarily on the grounds of unwise policy, or because they break the president's budget priorities. The veto is most likely when presidents and Congress are controlled by different parties; when Congress has passed a measure that is a direct challenge to the president's ideology; during election years; and when the president is losing popularity. Congress then is more likely to pass bills that invite a veto, and also more likely to challenge the president and override the veto.[103]

Strategic Choices

Not all presidents seek to cooperate with Congress, especially when it is controlled by the opposition party. Truman in 1947–1948, Nixon in 1970–1971, and Ford in 1975–1976 all confronted Congress rather than capitulate to opposition majorities. Truman's strategy in 1947–1948 is quite instructive. Republicans held a majority in Congress, and Truman perceived that their main interest was in preparing for the next presidential election by raising issues that might embarrass him. Truman decided to preempt the Republican attack. He vetoed key measures passed by the Republicans, then he called Congress into special session and presented Republicans with proposals they found unacceptable. When they balked at passing his measures, he went on the campaign trail and savagely attacked the "do nothing Congress." The strategy worked: the electorate blamed Congress rather than Truman for gridlock. Truman may not have been a legislative leader that year, but he won the election against long odds. In late 1994, Clinton's key domestic advisors

Table 9.1 **Presidential Suspensory Vetoes and Pocket Vetoes, 1953–1994**

Years	Presidents	Vetoes	Overridden	Pocket Vetoes	Total Vetoes
1953–1961	Eisenhower	73	2	108	181
1961–1963	Kennedy	12	0	9	21
1963–1969	Johnson	16	0	14	30
1969–1974	Nixon	26	7	17	43
1974–1977	Ford	48	12	18	66
1977–1981	Carter	13	2	18	31
1981–1989	Reagan	39	9	39	78
1989–1993	Bush	39	1	5	44
1993–1994	Clinton	0	0	0	0

were sharply split on the strategy that the president should employ: should he follow the Truman example of 1947–1948 and confront Congress with a veto? Or should he compromise in an effort to avoid gridlock? Typically, Clinton did some of both.

Not all confrontations end successfully for the White House. President Bush used the veto effectively as a negotiating tool with Congress. But although the veto gave him influence at a time when his party had a small number of seats in the House, he couldn't get his own programs through. His failure led to the perception that government was deadlocked, paralyzed, and stalemated. Voter antipathy to "gridlock" gave Democrats an opening in the next presidential election.[104]

When a president threatens to use a veto as a bill is going through Congress, there are several possible outcomes: Congress backs down, the president retreats, a compromise is reached, or the president makes good on the threat. In one study of veto threats from Nixon through Reagan, vetoes were not often useful in getting Congress to compromise when it was controlled by the opposition. Nixon's five public threats led Congress to pass bills, leading to a presidential veto, a sign that the veto was not useful for negotiation. Ford made ten threats: twice Congress gave ground, and eight times it passed the initial bill and incurred the veto, again demonstrating that the veto could not influence Congress. Under Carter the pattern changed because of party government. He made twelve threats: five were compromised, three times Congress conceded, twice the president backed off, and there were only two vetoes. With Reagan, through 1986 when his party controlled the Senate, there were forty-eight threats: nineteen resulted in compromises, nine times Congress gave way, four times Reagan signed the bills, and sixteen times there were vetoes.[105]

Overriding the Veto

The veto is a credible weapon if a president is willing to use it. The president must obtain the votes of only one-third of a *quorum* of a single chamber to defeat an override attempt.[106] Only about 4 percent of presidential vetoes have been overridden, a figure that is artificially low because it includes a large number of private bills whose vetoes were upheld. If these are eliminated, then a little over 80 percent of the vetoes of public bills have been sustained, including almost all vetoes of appropriations measures.[107] Sometimes Congress overrides on the most important issues: Truman was overridden on the Taft-Hartley Act (a Republican measure on labor–management relations) and on the McCarran-Walter Immigration Act of 1952. Nixon's veto of the War Powers Act of 1973 was overridden in spite of his vehement protest that it would infringe on the president's constitutional powers as commander in chief.

On many vetoes Congress will not even attempt to override. When challenges to the White House do occur, it is because opponents calculate that they have some chance of success, especially when the opposition party controls one or both chambers of Congress. Nixon, Ford, and Reagan lost several significant battles, and the average percentage of votes against them on all override challenges was above the two-thirds necessary to win.

Alternatives to the Veto

A president is not always in a position to veto a bill, but he or she may have other ways to indicate disapproval or take action to minimize the effect of the law. The president can do one or more of the following:

- *Withhold signature.* If a president does not sign the bill, it becomes law. He or she may then issue a statement outlining objections and indicating reasons for refusing to sign. The president may take this action if a favored bill has a rider attached that he or she opposes, or if he or she opposes a measure but thinks a veto might cause political damage.
- *Refuse to enforce an objectionable provision.* The president may allow a bill to become law but indicate that he or she will not enforce a provision he or she believes to be unconstitutional.[108] The president may, alternatively, enforce a provision in a way not contemplated by its supporters.[109] Federal courts have the last word on the constitutionality of the measure.
- *Limit the effect of the measure.* The president may issue regulations or take actions just before a bill becomes law that limit its effect. Theodore Roosevelt established much of the National Forest system by executive order in the ten-day period before signing a bill that had a provision restricting the use of federal lands.
- *Issue a signing statement.* The president may issue a statement used to signal policy difference with Congress, to indicate that a provision of the law is unconstitutional and "has no legal force or effect" or will be treated only as advisory, to express a concern to Congress that it has acted irresponsibly, or to recommend legislation to Congress for future consideration.[110]
- *Affect the legislative history of the bill.* The president may claim that the signing statement is part of the "Legislative History" of the measure, and that White House interpretation of its provisions should take precedence over the "Congressional intent," because the president's signature on the bill was the final act permitting it to become law.[111]

Signing statements were used by President Reagan on five important measures between 1984 and 1987. In *Lear Siegler, Inc. v. Lehman,* a federal court of appeals denied the government's claim that the power to "take care that the laws be faithfully executed" could be read to mean that the president could disregard laws believed to be unconstitutional, calling it a "violation of our system of separation of powers and checks and balances," because the power of judicial review over the constitutionality of legislation belonged to the judiciary.[112] President Bush used the signing statement even more extensively, on defense and foreign aid bills, as well as on an important civil rights bill. He also used it to block a congressional attempt to end "leveraging," a practice by which the administration can get a foreign nation to undertake activities that Congress has prohibited.[113] The approach developed by his White House Counsel Boyden Gray involved getting Republicans in Congress to engage in a dialogue on the floor of the House or Senate to establish a "legislative history" about the bill: then the administration could go into court and cite those speeches as a justification for the court to uphold the presidential interpretation of the law. Bush also indicated that dozens of specific provisions of bills would not be enforced, in effect establishing his own "item veto" on legislative authorizations.[114]

Veto Reform Proposals

Conflict between president and Congress has led to proposals for constitutional amendments to strengthen or weaken the veto power. After Andrew Jackson frustrated the Whig economic program with his bank veto, the Whigs proposed to abolish the veto by constitutional amendment. After Tyler vetoed their bank bill the Whigs proposed a new tack: an amendment that would permit a majority in each house to override, in effect making the veto simply an advisory and dilatory tactic for the president. In the era of "congressional government" after the Civil War, President Rutherford B. Hayes, beset by "riders" attached to appropriations bills, recommended a constitutional amendment that would give him an item veto on appropriations. Between 1877 and 1888 several such amendments were introduced in Congress but never passed. President Eisenhower revived the request in his 1959 budget message, and it was supported by Nixon, Ford, Carter, Reagan, and Bush.

The item veto, passed by House and Senate Republicans as part of their "Contract with America" in 1995, strikes at the heart of the system of transactions and deals that form the core of the legislative process. A president who can strike out any specific provision from a law or appropriation has great influence in the legislative process: no one in Congress can then be sure that deals made in committees or the caucus will be honored—especially if the president has not been party to the arrangements.

THE LEGISLATIVE PRESIDENCY

Presidents are not the "chief legislators" of American government. Although they often take the initiative, dominate the national agenda, and pressure Congress to act, it remains the case that while presidents propose, Congress disposes of the national agenda—often in ways opposed by the White House. Even the veto power does not provide the president with sufficient power to control Congress, because he cannot use it to get most of what he wants, but only to keep others from getting too much of what they want. As presidents have taken increasingly more responsibility for passing laws, their use of the veto to temporarily deadlock or paralyze government has hurt them politically. In the last half of the twentieth-century presidents often confronted Congresses controlled by the opposition party. In many respects the "legislative presidency" of the first half of the century has therefore given way to an "administrative presidency"—an institution prepared to use its influence and formal controls over the departments and agencies to govern—if necessary without the cooperation of Congress.

FURTHER READING

Books

Jon Bond and Richard Fleisher, *The President in the Legislative Arena,* Chicago: University of Chicago Press, 1990.

George Edwards, *At the Margins,* New Haven, CT: Yale University Press, 1989.

Louis Fisher, *The Politics of Shared Power,* 3rd ed., Washington, DC: Congressional Quarterly Press, 1993.

Charles Jones, *The Presidency in a Separated System,* Washington, DC: Brookings Institution, 1994.
David Mayhew, *Divided We Govern,* New Haven, CT: Yale University Press, 1993.
Mark Peterson, *Legislating Together,* Cambridge, MA: Harvard University Press, 1990.
Steven Shull, ed., *The Two Presidencies,* Chicago: Nelson-Hall, 1991.
Robert Spitzer, *The Presidential Veto,* Albany, NY: State University of New York Press, 1988.

Documentary Sources

Congressional Quarterly, Inc., *Congressional Quarterly Weekly Reports; Congress and the Nation,* Vols. 1–8 (narrative summaries of congressional activities).
Congressional Information Service, *Congressional Committee Prints Index* and *Congressional Committee Hearings Index.* Indexes all committee documents published during each congressional session. CIS also publishes annual volumes of legislative histories.
Government Printing Office, Washington, DC, *The Congressional Record.* The revised and extended speeches of the members of Congress on the floor of the House and Senate.
West Publishing Co., *U.S. Code Congressional and Administrative News.* Committee reports on selected bills and the text of all laws passed by Congress.
Robert Goehlert, *Congress and Law-Making: Researching the Legislative Process,* Santa Barbara, CA: ABC-CLIO, 1979. How to compile the legislative history of a bill.

NOTES

1. J. Gregory Sidak, "The Recommendation Clause," *Georgetown Law Journal,* Vol. 77, no. 6, August, 1989.

2. Samuel Huntington, "Congressional Responses to the Twentieth Century," in David Truman, ed., *Congress and America's Future,* New York: American Assembly, 1964, pp. 5–31.

3. James Hart, "Ordinance Making Power of the President," *North American Review,* Vol. 218, July, 1923, pp. 59–66.

4. Louis Fisher, "Laws Congress Never Made," *Constitution Magazine,* Fall, 1993, pp. 59–66.

5. A. L. Weil, "Has the President of the United States the Power to Suspend the Operation of an Act of Congress?" *California Law Review,* Vol. 1, March, 1913, pp. 230–250.

6. *U.S. v. Midwest Oil Co.,* 236 U.S. 459, 1915.

7. Louis Fisher, "Delegating Power to the President," *Journal of Public Law,* Vol. 19, no. 2, Spring, 1970, pp. 251–282.

8. Glendon A. Schubert, Jr., "The Presidential Subdelegation Act of 1950," *Journal of Politics,* Vol. 13, no. 4, November, 1951, pp. 647–674.

9. *The Brig Aurora,* 11 U.S. 382, 1813; *Field v. Clark,* 143 U.S., 1892; *U.S. v. Grimaud,* 220 U.S. 506, 1911.

10. *National Labor Relations Board v. Jones and Laughlin Steel Corp.* 301 U.S. 1, 1937.

11. Barry Blechman, *The Politics of National Security,* New York: Oxford University Press, 1990, p. 41.

12. James Bryce, *The American Commonwealth,* New York: Macmillan, 1891, Vol. I, p. 206.

13. Richard Neustadt, "The Presidency and Legislation: Planning the President's Program," *American Political Science Review,* Vol. 49, no. 4, December, 1955, p. 1015.

14. Lawrence Chamberlain, *President, Congress and Legislation,* New York: Columbia University Press, 1946; William Goldsmith, *The Growth of Presidential Powers,* New York: Chelsea, 1974, pp. 1139–1189.

15. Ronald C. Moe and Steven Teel, "Congress as Policy-Maker: A Necessary Reappraisal," *Political Science Quarterly,* Vol. 85, no. 3, Summer, 1970, pp. 443–470; John R. Johannes, "Where Does the Buck Stop?—Congress, President, and the Responsibility for Legislative Initiation," *Western Political Quarterly,* Vol. 25, no. 3, September, 1972, pp. 396–415.

16. Jean Reith Schroedel, *Congress, the President and Policymaking,* Armonk, NY: M. E. Sharpe, 1994, p. 12.

17. David Price, *Who Makes the Laws? Creativity and Power in Senate Committees,* Cambridge, MA: Schenkman, 1972, p. 332.

18. E. Scott Adler and Charles M. Cameron, "The Macro-Politics of Congress," unpublished paper, Version 2.0, July 29, 1994, p. 27.

19. David R. Beam, Timothy Conlan, and Margaret Wrightson, "Solving the Riddle of Tax Reform: Party Competition and the Politics of Ideas," *Political Science Quarterly,* Vol. 105, no. 2, Summer, 1990, pp. 193–217.

20. Norman Thomas and Harold Wolman, "The Presidency and Policy Formulation: The Task Force Device," *Public Administration Review,* Vol. 29, no. 5, September/October, 1969, pp. 459–471; Margaret J. Wyzomirski, "A Domestic Policy Office: Presidential Agency in Search of a Role," *Policy Studies Journal,* Vol. 12, no. 4, June, 1984, pp. 705–718.

21. Bureau of the Budget Circular No. 44.

22. Bureau of the Budget Circular No. 49.

23. Arthur Maass, "In Accord with the Program of the President?" in Carl J. Friedrich and J. Kenneth Galbraith, eds., *Public Policy,* Vol. 4, 1953, pp. 77–93; Richard Neustadt, "The Presidency and Legislation: The Growth of Central Clearance" *American Political Science Review,* Vol. 48, no. 3, September, 1954, pp. 641–670; Richard Neustadt, "The Presidency and Legislation: Planning the President's Program," *American Political Science Review,* Vol. 49, no. 4, December, 1955, pp. 980–1018; Robert Gilmour, "Central Legislative Clearance: A Revised Perspective," *Public Administration Review,* Vol. 31, no. 2, March/April, 1971, pp. 150–158.

24. *New York Times,* January 26, 1993, p. A-1.

25. *Association of American Physicians and Surgeons, Inc., v. Clinton,* 813 F. Supp. 82, D.D.C. 1993.

26. *Association of American Physicians and Surgeons, Inc., v. Clinton,* 997 F. 2nd. 898, D.C. Cir., 1993.

27. Randall Ripley, "Carter and Congress" in Steven Shull and Lance LeLoup, eds., *The Presidency: Studies in Policymaking,* New Brunswick, NJ: Kings Court Communications, 1979, pp. 65–82.

28. Robert J. Spitzer, *The Presidency and Public Policy,* University, AL: University of Alabama Press, 1983, pp. 98–100.

29. James Madison, *The Federalist Papers,* no. 51.

30. Abraham Holtzman, *Legislative Liaison,* Indianapolis, IN: Bobbs-Merrill, 1973, p. 1.

31. John Manley, "Presidential Power and White House Lobbying," *Political Science Quarterly,* Vol. 93, no. 2, Summer, 1978, pp. 255–275.

32. Lawrence F. O'Brien, Jr., "The Invisible Bridge," Harvard College senior thesis, 1967; G. Russell Pipe, "Congressional Liaison: The Executive Branch Consolidates Its Relations with Congress," *Public Administration Review,* Vol. 26, no. 1, March, 1966, pp. 14–24.

33. Ralph Huitt, op. cit., p. 83.

34. "Text of Bryce Harlow Keynote Address at Nashville Symposium," in *Center House Bulletin,* Vol. 4, no. 1, Winter, 1974.

35. Lyndon Johnson, *The Vantage Point,* New York: Rinehart and Winston, 1971, p. 447.

36. Michael Wines, "Lobbying on Health Care," *New York Times,* August 14, 1994, p. A-22.

37. Robert Pear, "Key Voice Missing on Health," *New York Times,* June 27, 1994, p. A-12.

38. Holtzman, op. cit., pp. 251–254.

39. Charles Lewis, "Balm for the Well-Healed: Money Still Talks in Washington," *Washington Post National Weekly Edition,* August 29–September 4, 1994, p. 24.

40. James Madison, *The Federalist Papers,* no. 46.

41. Charles Clapp, *The Congressman,* Washington, DC: Brookings Institution, 1963, p. 182.

42. Doris Kearns, *Lyndon Johnson and the American Dream,* New York: Harper and Row, 1976, p. 182.

43. Lyndon Johnson, op. cit., p. 458.

44. Ibid., p. 457.

45. Michael Wines, "A Bazaar Method of Dealing for Votes," *New York Times,* November 11, 1993, p. A-23.

46. Gwen Ifill, "Clinton Would Protect Republicans Who Vote for Trade Pact," *New York Times,* November 13, 1994, p. A-10.

47. Keith Bradsher, "Plenty of Favors Made for Industry Backing," *New York Times,* September 30, 1994, p. D-4.

48. George Edwards, *At the Margins,* New Haven, CT: Yale University Press, 1989, pp. 167–224.

49. Theodore Sorensen, *Kennedy,* New York: Harper and Row, 1965, p. 344.

50. Roger Davidson, "The Emergence of the Postreform Congress," in Roger Davidson, ed., *The Postreform Congress,* New York: St. Martin's Press, 1992, pp. 3–25.

51. John F. Hoadley, "Easy Riders: Gramm-Rudman-Hollings and the Legislative Fast Track," *PS,* Winter, 1986, pp. 30–36.

52. Jimmy Carter, *Keeping Faith,* New York: Bantam, 1982, p. 80.

53. Kitty Cunningham, "With Democrat in the White House, Partisanship Hits New High," *Congressional Quarterly Weekly Report,* December 18, 1993, p. 3432; *Congressional Quarterly Almanac,* 1993, Washington, DC: Congressional Quarterly Press, 1994, p. 17-C.

54. Demetrios Caraley, "Congressional Politics and Urban Aid," *Political Science Quarterly,* Vol. 91, no. 1, Spring, 1976, pp. 19–47.

55. Jon Bond and Richard Fleisher, *The President in the Legislative Arena,* Chicago: University of Chicago Press, 1990.

56. David Mayhew, *Party Loyalty among Congressmen,* Cambridge, MA: Harvard University Press, 1966, pp. 148–168.

57. Norman Ornstein, "Too Many Lone Rangers," *Washington Post National Weekly Edition,* September 12–18, 1994, p. 28.

58. William Safire, *Before the Fall,* Garden City, NY: Doubleday, 1975, p. 685.

59. Ira Katznelson, Kim Geiger, and Daniel Kryder, "Limiting Liberalism: The Southern Veto in Congress, 1933–1950," *Political Science Quarterly,* Vol. 108, no. 2, April, 1993, pp. 283–306.

60. *Congressional Quarterly Almanac,* Vol. 32, 1976, p. 1008.

61. Mack C. Shelley, II, "Presidents and the Conservative Coalition in the U.S. Congress," *Legislative Studies Quarterly,* Vol. 8, no. 1, February, 1983, pp. 79–96.

62. "Conservative Coalition History," *Congressional Quarterly Almanac,* Vol. 49, 1993, Congressional Quarterly Press, 1994, p. 26-C.

63. David Brady and Barbara Sinclair, "Building Majorities for Policy Change in the House of Representatives," *Journal of Politics,* Vol. 46, no. 4, November, 1984, pp. 1033–1060.

64. Theodore J. Lowi, "Four Systems of Policy, Politics and Choice," *Public Administration Review,* Vol. 32, no. 2, July–August, 1972, pp. 298–310.

65. Robert J. Spitzer, *The Presidency and Public Policy,* University, AL: University of Alabama Press, 1983, pp. 36–104.

66. "Presidential Success History," *Congressional Quarterly Almanac,* 1993, Washington, DC: Congressional Quarterly Press, 1994, p. 4-C.

67. Paul C. Light, "The Focusing Skill and Presidential Influence in Congress," in Christopher J. Deering, ed., *Congressional Politics,* Chicago: Dorsey Press, 1989, p. 247.

68. Douglas Jehl, "White House Sees a Compromise Met on the Crime Bill," *New York Times,* August 19, 1994, p. A-1.

69. Lawrence O'Brien, *No Final Victories,* Garden City, NY: Doubleday, 1974, p. 118.

70. Aaron Wildavsky, "The Two Presidencies," *Trans-Action,* Vol. 4, December, 1966, pp. 7–14.

71. Lance LeLoup and Steven A. Shull, "Congress vs. the Executive: The 'Two Presidencies' Reconsidered," *Social Science Quarterly,* Vol. 59, March, 1979, pp. 704–719.

72. Steven A. Shull, ed., *The Two Presidencies: A Quarter Century Assessment,* Chicago: Nelson-Hall, 1991; Mark Kesselman, "Presidential Leadership in Congress on Foreign Policy: A Replication of a Hypothesis," *Midwest Journal of Political Science,* Vol. 9, no. 4, November, 1965, pp. 401–406.

73. Richard Fleisher and Jon Bond, "Are There Two Presidencies? Yes, But Only for Republicans," *Journal of Politics,* Vol. 50, no. 3, August, 1988, pp. 747–767.

74. George Edwards III, *At the Margins: Presidential Leadership of Congress,* New Haven, CT: Yale University Press, 1989, pp. 65–69.

75. George Edwards III, p. 69; see evidence that the phenomena existed in the early part of the Truman administration in Karen Tombs Parsons, "Exploring the 'Two Presidencies' Phenomenon: New Evidence from the Truman Administration," *Presidency Studies Quarterly,* Vol. 24, no. 3, Summer, 1994, pp. 495–514.

76. Richard Fleisher and Jon Bond, "Are There Two Presidencies?"

77. Russell D. Renka and Bradford S. Jones, "The 'Two Presidencies' and the Reagan Administration," *Congress and the Presidency,* Vol. 18, no. 1, Spring, 1991, pp. 17–35.

78. Duane M. Oldfield and Aaron Wildavsky, "Reconsidering the Two Presidencies," *Society,* Vol. 26, no. 5, July/August, 1989, pp. 54–59.

79. Ibid., p. 58.

80. Russell Renka and Bradford Jones, op. cit., pp. 27–36.

81. Judith D. Hoover, "Ronald Reagan's Failure to Secure Contra-Aid: A Post-Vietnam Shift in Foreign Policy Rhetoric," *Presidential Studies Quarterly,* Vol. 24, no. 3, Summer, 1994, pp. 531–543.

82. Ronald C. Moe, "The Founders and Their Experience with the Executive Veto," *Presidential Studies Quarterly,* Vol. 17, no. 2, Spring, 1987, pp. 413–432; Richard Watson, "Origins and Early Development of the Veto Power," *Presidential Studies Quarterly,* Vol. 17, no. 2, Spring, 1987, pp. 401–412.

83. Similarly in the *Federalist Papers* the word "veto" appears only once in the four essays in which the power is discussed. *Federalist* nos. 51, 66, 69, and 73; discussion in Terry Eastland, *Energy in the Executive,* New York: Free Press, 1992, p. 65.

84. *Hollingsworth v. Virginia,* 3 Dallas 378, 1798.

85. *Congressional Quarterly Almanac,* 1989, Washington, DC: Congressional Quarterly Press, 1990, p. 526.

86. James Madison, *The Federalist Papers,* no. 51.

87. Alexander Hamilton, *The Federalist Papers,* no. 73.

88. George Bush, "Remarks by the President in Honorary Degree Ceremony, Princeton University," *Weekly Compilation of Presidential Documents,* Vol. 27, no. 19, May 10, 1991, p. 590.

89. *The Pocket Veto Case,* 279 U.S. 644, 1929.

90. Arthur S. Miller, "Congressional Power to Defuse the Presidential Pocket Veto Power," *Vanderbilt Law Review,* Vol. 25, no. 2, April, 1972, pp. 557–572.

91. *Kennedy v. Sampson,* 511 Fed. Reporter 2nd series, 430, 1974.

92. Edward Kennedy, "Congress, the President and the Pocket Veto," *Virginia Law Review,* Vol. 63, no. 2, April, 1977, pp. 355–382.

93. *Barnes v. Kline,* 759 F. 2nd 21, D.C. Cir., 1985.

94. Robert Spitzer, "Presidential Prerogative Power: The Case of the Bush Administration and Legislative Power," *PS,* Vol. 24, no. 1, March, 1991, pp. 38–42; Nancy Kassop, "The Arrogant Presidency II: The Bush Administration Confronts Separation of Powers," paper delivered at the Western Political Science Association Annual Meeting, Albuquerque, NM, March 10–12, 1994, pp. 6–10.

95. Clement Vose, "The Memorandum Pocket Veto," *Journal of Politics,* Vol. 26, no. 2, May, 1964, pp. 397–405.

96. Stephen Wayne, *The Legislative Presidency,* New York: Harper and Row, 1978, p. 76.

97. Stephen Wayne, ibid., p. 81.

98. Stephen Wayne, Richard Cole, and James Hyde, "Advising the President on Enrolled Legislation," *Political Science Quarterly,* Vol. 94, no. 2, Summer, 1979, p. 310.

99. Woodrow Wilson, *Congressional Government,* p. 53.

100. Charles Tiefer, *The Semi-Sovereign President,* Boulder, CO: Westview Press, 1994, p. 26.

101. Barbara Sinclair, "Governing Unheroically (and Sometimes Unappetizingly): Bush and the 101st Congress," in Colin Cambell, S. J., and Bert Rockman, eds., *The Bush Presidency: First Appraisals,* Chatham, NJ: Chatham House, 1991, pp. 155–184.

102. Jong R. Lee, "Presidential Vetoes from Washington to Nixon," *Journal of Politics,* Vol. 37, no. 2, May, 1975, pp. 526–540.

103. Gary Copeland, "When Congress and the President Collide: Why Presidents Veto Legislation," *Journal of Politics,* Vol. 45, no. 3, August, 1983, pp. 696–710; David Rohde and Dennis Simon, "Presidential Vetoes and Congressional Response: A Study of Institutional Conflict," *American Journal of Political Science,* Vol. 29, no. 3, August, 1985, pp. 397–427; David McKay, "Presidential Strategy and the Veto Power: A Reappraisal," *Political Science Quarterly,* Vol. 104, no. 3, Summer, 1989, pp. 447–461.

104. Robert Spitzer, *The Presidential Veto,* Albany, NY: State University of New York Press, 1988, p. 75.

105. Ibid., p. 103.

106. *Northern Pacific Railway Co. v. Kansas,* 248 U.S. 276, 1919.

107. Robert Spitzer, op. cit., 1988, pp. 81–83.

108. Arthur Miller and Jeffrey Bowman, "Presidential Attacks on the Constitutionality of Federal Statutes: A New Separation of Powers Problem," *Ohio State Law Journal,* Vol. 40, no. 1, Winter, 1979, pp. 51–80.

109. Arthur Miller, "The President and the Faithful Execution of the Laws," *Vanderbilt Law Review,* Vol. 40, no. 2, March, 1987, pp. 389–406.

110. M. N. Garber and K. A. Wummer, "Presidential Signing Statements as Interpretations of Legislative Intent: An Executive Aggrandizement of Powers," *Harvard Journal of Legislation,* Vol. 24, no. 1, Summer, 1987, pp. 154–164; for a contrary view, see Terry Eastland, *Energy in the Executive,* New York: Free Press, 1992, p. 74.

111. William D. Popkin, "Judicial Use of Presidential Legislative History: A Critique," *Indiana Law Journal,* Vol. 66, no. 3, Summer, 1991, pp. 699–722.

112. *Lear Siegler, Inc. v. Lehman,* 842 F. 2nd 1102, 9th Cir., 1988.

113. Charles Tiefer, op. cit., p. 38.

114. Charles Tiefer, ibid., pp. 31–59.

CHAPTER 10

The President and the Bureaucracy

The Treasury is so large and far-flung and ingrained in its practices that I find it is almost impossible to get the action and results that I want. . . . But the Treasury is not to be compared with the State Department. You should go through the experience of trying to get any changes in the thinking, policy and action of the career diplomats, and then you'd know what a real problem was. But the Treasury and the State Department put together are nothing compared with the Na-a-vy. . . . To change something in the Na-a-vy is like punching a feather bed. You punch it with your right and you punch it with your left until you are finally exhausted, and then you find the damn bed just as it was before you started punching.

—Franklin Roosevelt

INTRODUCTORY CASE: SECRETARY BABBITT'S "YEAR OF DECISION"

"I don't often feel this good about the people I am introducing," California Representative George Miller told the crowd of environmentalist activists gathered among the redwoods at the John Muir Historic Site in June 1993. Speaking of President Clinton's new secretary of the interior, he observed that "Bruce Babbitt has captured the imagination of Congress and the country." Before an admiring audience, Babbitt pledged "a year of decision" about the 500 million acres of public lands that would resolve disputes over old-growth forests, grazing, logging, and mining in favor of environmental protection. Babbitt, a third-generation Arizonan from a ranching family, had become an avid naturalist and president of the League of Conservation Voters. As governor of Arizona, he had doubled the size of the state park system, fought against overgrazing by ranchers, and organized a groundwater protection program. He favored wildlife management and recreational use of public land over ranching.

But Babbitt ran into trouble. Western Democratic senators informed the White House that any attempt to change the low grazing fees on federal lands would force them to vote against Clinton's economic program. Clinton responded by removing Interior's proposed new grazing fees from his first budget requests to Congress, and only minor increases were implemented. Instead of instituting tough new national regulations for rangeland practices, Babbitt retreated and established 50 "multiple resource advisory councils" filled with local ranchers and businesspeople to institute local regulations. Babbitt tried unsuccessfully to get Congress to overhaul an 1872 mining law permitting companies (most of them foreign-owned) to take billions in gold and silver from public lands without paying royalties to the national government. His attempts to get an agreement with Florida sugar growers to restore the Everglades (by limiting phosphorous runoff from their lands) first led to a compromise that environmentalists denounced, then fell apart as the growers backed away from a tentative agreement. Instead of fully protecting the old-growth Northwest forests, Babbitt produced yet another compromise: Under White House pressure to save lumbering jobs, Interior did not put any of the forests off limits to loggers. By 1995, testifying before oversight committees in Congress controlled by Republicans, Babbitt offered to cooperate "as the sun rises on an entirely new era," and he pledged to speed up logging in the Pacific Northwest in an effort to avoid deep cuts in Interior's budget.

Why did Babbitt have to compromise so much? Like many cabinet secretaries, he set too-high expectations with his overheated rhetoric. The inability of environmentalists to forge a bipartisan congressional coalition and win over most state and local officials in the West left Babbitt politically vulnerable. President Clinton was ultimately responsible for Babbitt's compromises. Assessing his own political situation, he understood that a strong environmental position—if it cost jobs—would also cost him states such as California and Montana in the next presidential election.[1]

Babbitt's years in office illustrate some of the issues involved in relations between presidents and the bureaucracy. A president may appoint someone with an ambitious agenda to institute fundamental reform in government programs, but the appointee must win the support of Congress and interest groups as well.

EXECUTIVE POWER IN THE CONSTITUTION

Article 2 of the Constitution assigns the president "The Executive Power" of the United States, allows him to appoint by and with the advice and consent of the Senate the "officers of the United States," permits him to request reports in writing from the heads of departments, and requires him to "take care that the laws be faithfully executed." But the Constitution specifies no removal power, budget authority, or management functions for the president, and though we often refer to the president as "the chief executive," the Constitution provides him with few explicit executive powers.

Presidential Interpretation of "Executive Power"

Presidents construe the "Executive Power" and the duty to take care that the laws be faithfully executed to mean that department officials are their subordinates. Presidents have assumed the responsibility for controlling the departments, as they abrogated to themselves the title of "chief executive" supervising an "executive branch" of national government—terms that nowhere appear in the Constitution. Franklin Roosevelt argued that "the Presidency was established as a single strong Chief Executive Office in which was vested the entire executive power of the National Government."[2] Harry Truman observed that "it is not the business of Congress to run the agencies of government for the President."[3] Yet much of the nineteenth-century legacy of congressional government still remains in place. The departments and agencies are not part of the president's "executive branch," but rather function as a separate administrative establishment—a "fourth branch" of government—that is supervised concurrently by the legislature, the executive, and the judiciary.[4]

Executive Orders

The president formally directs officials by issuing an executive order. Between 1789 and 1908 presidents issued approximately 2,400 such orders. Since 1908 more than 13,000 have been issued. The first executive order, promulgated by George Washington on June 8, 1789, instructed the heads of departments to make a "clear account" of matters in their departments. Since then executive orders have been used to regulate the civil service, to determine holidays for federal workers, to recognize federal employee unions, to fire employees in an illegal strike, to institute security programs, to classify government documents, to regulate the environment, to organize federal disaster assistance efforts, to organize the intelligence agencies at the beginning of every president's term in office, and for internal White House organization.

Executive orders once were used to create government agencies: President Franklin Roosevelt used executive orders to create New Deal and wartime agencies without going through Congress, until in 1944 Congress prohibited funding of such agencies. John Kennedy established the Peace Corps in 1961 by executive order. In 1968 Congress passed a law prohibiting creation of presidential commissions, councils, or study groups that were not authorized by Congress.

Since the Civil War, executive orders have been used to assert presidential war powers. Franklin Roosevelt seized defense plants during strikes to ensure aircraft production during World War II and issued an order to prevent racial discrimination in defense plants; Harry Truman banned racial segregation in the armed forces. Executive orders have also been used in domestic matters such as civil rights enforcement: John Kennedy prohibited racial discrimination in public housing and pay discrimination against women by federal contractors; and Richard Nixon required government contractors to institute "affirmative action" hiring programs for women and members of minority groups.

Limits to the Executive Power

One might think that executive orders would enable the president to control the bureaucracy, but these orders, as well as oral presidential commands and directives, run up against constitutional and legal limits. Provided that it is based either on a president's constitutional powers or laws passed by Congress, an executive order has the force of law and will be enforced by the courts. An order that conflicts with existing law, however, will not be judicially enforced: When President Nixon tried to dismantle several agencies by executive order, his actions were blocked by federal courts, because Congress had not abolished them.[5] An executive order that carries out a law may later be revoked by new legislation. An executive order that is unconstitutional, such as President Truman's seizure of steel mills during the Korean War, can be nullified by the Supreme Court or lower federal courts.[6]

When an executive order or other command issued by the president conflicts with a law passed by Congress, officials are duty bound to execute the laws, and if they do not, the federal courts will require them to do so. In the 1830s, for example, the Supreme Court required Postmaster General Amos Kendall to pay private postal carriers an amount determined by the solicitor of the treasury, despite an order issued by President Andrew Jackson to pay these postal carriers less money.[7] Moreover, rules and regulations promulgated by the bureaucracy itself have the force of law and will be upheld by the courts if the president has issued orders that conflict with them. In 1974, for example, the federal courts ruled that the firing of special prosecutor Archibald Cox during the Watergate crisis was illegal, because the firing violated regulations about the independence of the prosecutor that had been promulgated previously by the attorney general.[8] Finally, the officials appointed by the president do not take an oath to obey him or her, but rather take an oath to obey the Constitution and the laws of the land. This oath is no formality: Officials have multiple responsibilities, and enforcing presidential priorities does not take precedence over enforcing the law.

Anti-Bureaucratic Politics

Americans have always been mistrustful of officials and scornful of "bureaucracy." One of the complaints against the king in the Declaration of Independence in 1776 was that "he has enacted a multitude of new offices, and sent hither swarms of officers to harass our people and eat out their substance." Presidents have always been in the forefront of those calling for reform of the bureaucracy. In the early nineteenth century, politicians gained power by attacking an aristocratic careerist bureaucracy and called instead for "rotation in office" as a democratic reform. After the Civil War, reformers called for the merit system and tenure in office to end the evils of party patronage, and the civil service was created by President Arthur. In modern times the public has complained of overregulation, lack of accountability, and unresponsiveness. Anti-bureaucratic politics has become a "valence issue" that has been exploited by every winning presidential candidate since Richard Nixon. President Clinton's pollster Stan Greenberg reported that those who voted for independent candidate Ross Perot in 1992 wanted a president who would "cut waste and bureaucracy, search for efficiencies" and do nothing less than "reinvent government."[9] Mismanagement, corruption, and ethical issues may put a president on the defensive, as political opponents demonize his or her nominees or officials to personify the larger issue of "big government." It is no accident that the only three presidents who won two terms after 1945—Eisenhower, Nixon, and Reagan—were adept at aligning themselves against the Washington bureaucrats.

APPOINTING AND REMOVING OFFICIALS

The president nominates—and by and with the advice and consent of the Senate, appoints—14 cabinet secretaries, 50 or so directors of other nondepartmental agencies, and 90 or so commissioners of independent regulatory agencies, as well as 600 to 700 subordinate political executives in the departments (with titles such as deputy secretary, undersecretary, assistant secretary, and deputy assistant secretary). The president also appoints the 200 or so U.S. attorneys and marshals; more than 200 ambassadors, and approximately 200 members of the boards of directors of government quasi-independent corporations. Without the advice or consent of the Senate, the president appoints over 400 aides in the WHO and 1,800 officials in the Executive Office of the President, about 700 senior managers of the federal civil service, and about 1,700 of its lower-level managers.[10]

These White House and departmental and agency appointees are the officials who constitute "the administration" and who are responsible for implementing presidential policies. Each year about one-quarter of these positions open up, so the president has regular opportunities to make policy through appointments. The other million or so federal civilian employees are considered "inferior officers," and almost all of them are appointed by heads of departments under civil service regulations, based on laws passed by Congress.

The White House Talent Search

Recruitment of appointees for the administration begins during the campaign and then continues with a personnel recruitment operation during the transition. Professional headhunters (from firms that recruit executives) are hired to compile lists of thousands of potential employees from the tens of thousands of resumes that are submitted. The chief "headhunter" is an assistant to the president in charge of the Office of Presidential Personnel (OPP), a unit of the White House Office. When the personnel operation is going full blast between 100 and 150 staffers will be assigned to the OPP. They cull resumes looking for past work in campaigns of their party, political connections, a personal connection with the president, ideological and partisan compatibility, and career experience that might be useful in a high-level governmental position. Exhaustive background investigations are required, and candidates must comply with ethics guidelines. The recruitment process takes a long time: Kennedy filled his positions on average in about two months, while President Bush took eight months and President Clinton even longer.[11]

When a potential nominee is being considered, the White House personnel office submits his or her name to the "Special Inquiries Unit" (SPIN) of the Criminal Investigation Division of the Federal Bureau of Investigation (FBI). Agents check a potential nominee's character, reputation, and loyalty. They consider personal history, education (checking resumes for exaggerated achievement or falsification), and financial data (with the consent of the nominee). The Internal Revenue Service reports on whether the nominee has filed taxes, whether there are tax delinquencies or liens outstanding, and whether civil or criminal penalties have been assessed.[12]

Senate Advice

Although it may seem that the Constitution assigns the president the dominant role in making departmental appointments, both constitutional law and political tradition often suggest otherwise. Senate committee leaders often propose nominees to the president. "I regret I have but one staff to give to my department," Senator Orrin

Hatch once joked after getting three of his aides jobs in the Department of Health and Human Services. Senators routinely "nominate" officials for positions affecting their states: regional and district personnel, U.S. attorneys, and federal marshals. Often they are given a "veto" by the administration over appointments. All these practices invert the appointment process: Senators (and sometimes House members) "nominate" by suggesting names to the White House, while the president has the power to "consent" to or reject the suggestion.

Senatorial courtesy allows a senator from a state affected by a presidential nomination subject to Senate confirmation to declare that the prospective appointee is "personally obnoxious," in which case the Senate committee considering the nomination will put it on hold until the president or the nominee provides assurances that lead the senator to withdraw the objection. Sometimes the committee will cast a negative vote and refuse to send the nomination to the Senate. Or the entire Senate may pass a resolution requesting the president to withdraw a nomination. If necessary, the Senate will defeat the nomination on the floor.

Senate Consent

The Senate consents to presidential nominees by majority vote of those present. The Senate may not attach conditions to its assent, nor can it require a nominee to promise to take or abstain from certain actions. But it usually gains reassurances from a nominee about the concerns of key members when the nominee makes the rounds of the offices of senators on the committee with jurisdiction.

The Senate blocks few presidential appointments. Before the 1960s, only eight cabinet nominations had been turned down by Senate vote; since then George Bush's nomination of John Tower for secretary of defense in 1989 was defeated. In 1962 Congress refused to create a Department of Urban Affairs because President Kennedy made it known that he intended to appoint Robert Weaver to head it—he would have been the first African-American in the cabinet. By 1967 President Johnson won congressional approval for the department, and then for Weaver's appointment. Other cabinet-level nominees have withdrawn before a Senate vote if the president sensed they would be defeated: President Carter withdrew the nomination of Theodore Sorensen for the position of director of Central Intelligence in 1977, and two of Clinton's nominees for attorney general, Zöe Baird and Kimba Wood, withdrew in 1993.

If the Senate blocks the promotion of an official already in a department, the president or cabinet secretary may unofficially use the person in the job anyway, even though he or she has been denied the title and the pay. After Assistant Attorney General William Bradford Reynolds was blocked from the position of deputy attorney general in 1985, Attorney General Edwin Meese gave him the title of "counselor" to the attorney general, putting him at the top level in the department. Democratic Senator Edward Kennedy accused Meese of making an "end run" around the Senate.

Nominees get in trouble over character, conflicts of interest, or ideology. The Senate usually agrees that presidents are entitled to have whom they want in their administration. But a nominee involved in racial or gender discrimination is in for rough sledding (as is a nominee who refuses to resign from a private club that discriminates). Those who lack the background or skills necessary for a position may withdraw after criticism. Anyone forced from one office is not likely to get Senate consent to another.

The Senate is likely to block nominations when partisan and ideological issues are at stake. President Reagan made twenty-five nominations to the Legal Services Corporation's 11-member board of directors, and was unable to get a single appointment past the Senate in his first term, because of Democratic fears that he would use control of the board to dismember the corporation. Clinton could not win consent to the appointment of Lani Guinier to head the civil rights division of Justice, because of conservative criticism that her law review articles were too "radical" in proposing changes in voting procedures to benefit minorities. In the face of mounting negative publicity referring to her as a "quota queen" the White House convinced her to drop her nomination bid. Consent can be delayed by objecting to expedited committee proceedings and then submitting hundreds of questions to the nominee—which happened to Sam Brown, Clinton's nominee to head the U.S. delegation to the Conference on Security and Cooperation in Europe.

University of Pennsylvania law professor Lani Guinier, whose nomination to head the Office of Civil Rights in the Department of Justice was withdrawn by President Clinton. She told reporters she could have won Senate confirmation if she had been allowed to speak out in defense of her views on voting rights for minorities.

In recent years the appointment of presidential nominees has become so entangled in partisan and ideological politics that it threatens to undermine the recruitment of capable people into government service. More than one-third of the nominees to office found the process hostile, slow, politicized, or humiliating in a survey conducted by the National Academy of Public Administration.[13] It takes much too long to get nominees through the Senate: from seven weeks in the 1960s to fourteen weeks in the 1980s (though in the Bush presidency the time was cut back to 6.3 weeks).[14] Innuendo about personal lives and the leaking of FBI summaries of field investigations to the media discourages people from the public service. Senators put indefinite "holds" on nominees for ideological reasons, or threaten to filibuster a nomination that reaches the floor of the Senate, to extort policy concessions from the president or favors from the White House, further deterring potential nominees from agreeing to go through this demeaning process.

Congressional Regulation of Appointments

The Constitution provides that Congress by law may vest the appointment of "inferior Officers" in the president alone, in the Courts of Law, or in the heads of departments. It specifically excludes Congress from making its own appointments. When Congress established the Federal Elections Commission in 1974, however, it provided that two members of the Commission would be appointed by the president, and two each by the Speaker of the House and president pro tempore of the Senate. The Supreme Court, in *Buckley v. Valeo,* held that if the commission's rule-making powers were to be enforced by federal courts, the commissioners must be "officers of the United States," and then held that if they were to be "officers of the United States," they must be appointed by the president. Congress promptly rewrote the law to provide for presidential appointment of all commissioners.[15]

Congress by law determines whether each subcabinet position it creates will require Senate consent. It may stipulate the qualifications to hold a particular office: In the nineteenth century, Congress sometimes stipulated age, sex, race, and property qualifications, practices it later abandoned; in modern times it has required technical skills, specialized training or education, or membership in a particular professional organization. It requires that the director of the Fish and Wildlife Service and the director of the Soil Conservation Service have the scientific backgrounds necessary for their jobs, and that the surgeon general be a medical doctor. It may specify partisan requirements: members of regulatory agencies must be evenly divided between the two major parties.

Recess, Temporary, and Interim Appointments

When the Senate is in recess and unable to vote on a nominee, the Constitution provides that the president may unilaterally make a recess appointment. When the Senate returns, the president has forty days to submit the nomination to it. Congress has provided for temporary and acting appointments that do not require Senate consent and which are made while the Senate is in session. Within thirty days of such appointments the Senate must give its consent or the appointee leaves office. When a new agency is created, Congress has provided an interim appointment system: it allows the transfer of officials to run the new agency without Senate consent, provided they had already obtained Senate consent for their prior position.

The Removal Power

Article 2 of the Constitution does not mention a presidential removal power. In *Federalist* no. 77, Alexander Hamilton argued that the Senate's "advice and consent" to presidential nominations also extended to removals unless Congress legislated otherwise. But James Madison, in the congressional debates in 1789 over a removal clause in the law creating the Department of Foreign Affairs (later the State Department), argued for an unrestricted presidential removal power. He pointed out that no president could be held responsible for the actions of the departments without having the corresponding power to remove officials for failing to execute their duties and the laws. In creating the Foreign Affairs, War, and Treasury Departments, Congress accepted Madison's argument and acknowledged a presidential removal power.

At first, presidents pressured officials to resign. George Washington secured the resignation of Edmund Randolph as secretary of state in 1795. An intercepted letter implied that Randolph would pursue a pro-French policy in exchange for a bribe; when Washington showed the letter to Randolph, he promptly sent back his resignation. All told Washington used this method to remove seventeen officials whose appointments had been consented to by the Senate, including three foreign ministers, two consuls, eight collectors of customs, and four surveyors of internal revenue. John Adams was the first president to remove a cabinet secretary without the formalities of a resignation. Incensed at Secretary of State Timothy Pickering's interference with his French policy, and his failure to support Adams's nomination of his son-in-law for adjutant general, Adams wrote to Pickering asking for his resignation on grounds of maladministration, and when Pickering did not respond he fired him.

Andrew Jackson was the first president to claim the power to remove cabinet officials simply for disagreeing with presidential policy. Secretary of the Treasury William J. Duane was entrusted by Congress to deposit the funds of the United States in such banks as he saw fit. Jackson ordered Duane to remove the funds from the Bank of the United States and deposit them in state banks. "Congress confers discretionary power," Duane argued. Jackson responded that "a secretary, sir, is merely an executive agent, a subordinate." When Duane refused, Jackson fired him. The opposition Whigs argued against an unrestricted presidential right of removal. Henry Clay offered a resolution in 1834, stating that "The Constitution of the United States does not vest in the President the power to remove, at his pleasure, officers under the Government of the United States, whose officers have been established by law." Instead, Congress would legislate their tenure. Clay further proposed that a law be passed that the power of removal be exercised only "in concurrence with the Senate," but Jackson managed to keep this and other proposals from becoming law. The Whig-dominated Senate did pass a Resolution of Censure against Jackson, who sent a "Response" claiming that he possessed the right of "removing those officers who are to aid him in the execution of the laws."[16] The Whigs then put in their 1836 party platform the principle that Congress possessed the removal power.

During the Civil War, Congress infringed on the presidential removal power. It gave the Comptroller of the Currency a five-year term, authorizing his removal only with the consent of the Senate. In 1864 Congress passed a statute requiring the president to submit to Congress the reasons for removal of consular clerks. In 1865 a law gave military officers dismissed by the president a right to apply for a trial. In the aftermath of the Civil War, Congress passed two measures to protect its reconstruction policies from President Andrew Johnson. The Command of the Army Act, passed March 2, 1867, provided that "the General of the Army shall not be removed, suspended, or relieved from command, or assigned to duty elsewhere than at said headquarters, except at his own request, without the previous approval of the Senate." The Tenure of Office Act, passed the same day, provided that "every person holding any civil office to which he has been appointed by and with the advice and consent of the Senate . . . shall be entitled to hold such office until a successor shall have been in like manner appointed and duly qualified." During a

Senate recess the president could suspend an official for reason of misconduct in office, criminal activity, incapacity, or legal disqualification, but he would be restored to his office if the Senate refused to endorse the president's action. Both acts were passed over President Johnson's veto.

After Congress adjourned Johnson asked Secretary of War Edwin Stanton to resign. When he was refused, the president, in August 1867, seemingly acting in accordance with the laws, suspended him and authorized General Grant to act as secretary of war. Johnson had outmaneuvered Congress, for he used a provision in the law that permitted him to suspend a department secretary until the Senate reconvened. But when the Senate did so, it reinstated Stanton. Now Johnson acted for the first time in apparent violation of the Tenure of Office Act. He removed Stanton while the Senate was in session and appointed General Lorenzo Thomas as his secretary of war. The House thereupon voted articles of impeachment in February 1868.

At his Senate trial, Johnson argued that the law was unconstitutional. He also argued that even if it was constitutional, his removal of Stanton did not violate it. Stanton had been appointed by Lincoln; Johnson argued that the law could not prevent a president from removing an official nominated by his predecessor, but covered only those nominations he himself had made. Johnson was acquitted by one vote. Congress did not repeal the last provisions of the law until 1887. Nevertheless, several other Tenure of Office Acts remained on the books.

The Courts and the Removal Power

Eventually the Supreme Court recognized a constitutional removal power exercisable by the president. In *Shurtleff v. U.S.*, the court indicated that although Congress could legislate about removals, in the absence of legislation the president could remove an official.[17] The issue was again considered by the courts when President Wilson acceded to requests by Democratic Party officials in Oregon to remove a party insurgent named Myers from his position as fourth-class postmaster. Wilson acted in spite of provisions of the 1876 Postmaster Act that guaranteed Myers a term of four years. In *Myers v. U.S.*, Chief Justice William Howard Taft recognized the removal power as a presidential prerogative and struck down all congressional efforts to legislate about it or exercise a congressional power in its place.[18] Taft concluded that the framers of the Constitution intended to grant the power exclusively to the president—a conclusion some historians have found debatable. The executive must be assigned that power, Taft believed, to fulfill his executive responsibilities and take care that the laws be faithfully executed. Justice Oliver Wendell Holmes, in dissent, argued that if Congress could organize departments and fund them, it could also regulate the appointment and removal process as part of its "necessary and proper" clause.

In 1935, in *Humphrey's Executor v. U.S.*, the Court retreated somewhat from *Myers*. It distinguished between officials doing executive tasks and those engaged in "quasi-legislative" and "quasi-judicial" duties, such as members of independent regulatory commissions.[19] Congress could insulate these officials from the removal power to ensure their independence. Then in 1958, in *Wiener v. U.S.*, the Supreme

Court held that even when Congress had not legislated their independence, the president could not remove them.[20] The nature of their responsibilities, not laws passed by Congress, protected them from the president's removal power.

Since these Court decisions, Congress has often protected officials with executive responsibilities from presidential removal by establishing them in independent agencies and quasi-governmental corporations. In 1994, for example, it detached the Social Security Administration from the Department of Health and Human Services and made it an independent agency. Its commissioner would henceforth serve a six-year term, and would be removable by the president only for wrongdoing.

Courts and Congress have protected special prosecutors and independent counsel, officials who investigate wrongdoing at the highest levels of a president's administration. The Ethics in Government Act of 1978 prohibits the removal of an independent counsel except for extraordinary impropriety, physical disability, mental incapacity, or "any other condition that substantially impairs the performance of such special prosecutor's duties."[21] Sometimes protecting an official against a presidential removal power can backfire against Congress. In *Bowsher v. Synar,* the Supreme Court determined that because the comptroller general of the General Accounting Office could not be removed by the president alone (but only with the concurrence of both houses of Congress), the comptroller general was not an "officer of the United States" and therefore could not exercise deficit reduction duties assigned by Congress.[22]

PRESIDENTIAL CONTROL OF ADMINISTRATION

There are several thousand national government programs. No president is interested in running all of them, nor would have the time or energy to do so. The president is not a "hands-on" administrator: He or she wants to promote the impression of economy, efficiency, and accountability and wants the bureaucracy to be technologically up to date. The White House wants to avoid scandals and mismanagement or at least avoid the blame for scandals when they occur. The president wants to use the bureaucracy to reward his or her electoral coalition and to provide favors to members of Congress. Moreover, the president wants agencies to be responsive to the party platform and White House priorities. Presidents, in sum, want to influence the work of departments, and each has a different managerial style for doing so.

Franklin Roosevelt: Fostering Competition

Franklin Roosevelt dealt directly with all the top officials in his administration. He created New Deal agencies that reported directly to him, bypassing cabinet secretaries, and many were set up outside the structure of the traditional departments. He staffed them with the "New Dealers," young lawyers committed to the public interest. He fostered rivalries, established agencies with overlapping functions, and then played off one official against another, as each reported to him the shortcoming's of the other's agency. Officials were usually correct in assuming he knew as much about their agencies as they did—especially when his wife Eleanor Roosevelt took an interest in them. All disputes eventually wound up in the Oval Office for Roosevelt to arbitrate, which put him at the center of the New Deal. As historian Arthur Schlesinger, Jr. put it:

> His favorite technique was to keep grants of authority incomplete, jurisdictions uncertain, charters overlapping. The result of this competitive theory of administration was often confusion and exasperation on the operating level, but no other method could so reliably ensure that in a large bureaucracy filled with ambitious men eager for power, the decisions, and the power to make them, would remain with the President.[23]

Roosevelt would give several different staffers the same assignment, or ask them to write the same speech. He had a political method to this administrative madness: his aides and cabinet secretaries had to compete for his time, attention, and favor. To do so they not only had to show him complete loyalty, they also had to provide him with more information than their rivals. They tried to discredit each other in Roosevelt's eyes by providing him with information about each other. Roosevelt was the most informed person in his administration, because everyone had an incentive to tell him everything. Had he given an official a monopoly on a policy area, that official would have had an incentive to build his or her own bureaucratic empire, cut Roosevelt out of information, and spoonfeed him pablum about how wonderfully things were going.

The disadvantages of Roosevelt's approach are twofold: First, it is quite an inefficient and wasteful way to run the government, since duplication of effort costs money; second, it puts an enormous burden on a president, who must manage the rivalries and stroke the egos of many White House aides. By the middle of World War II, Roosevelt had fifty agencies reporting directly to him in theory; in practice, that meant that many administrators were left unsupervised by anyone guarding presidential interests.

Dwight Eisenhower: Building Up the Presidential Staff

President Eisenhower abandoned the competitive approach in favor of a staff system that borrowed much from his military experience. The White House was run by a chief of staff, who controlled access to the president and organized the flow of information to him. Aides developed options for the president to consider by using interagency committees and White House councils such as the National Security Council and Council of Economic Advisers, and nothing was presented to the president for consideration unless it had gone through the committee gauntlet and been thoroughly reviewed by all affected agencies and officials.[24] No one (at least in theory) could make an "end run" around the system to lobby with the president personally for a preferred policy. After Eisenhower made decisions, they moved down the bureaucracy in a similar fashion: Cabinet secretaries were required to report to a cabinet secretariat as to how decisions were being implemented. An operations coordinating board handled implementation for military and foreign policy decisions. Nixon, Ford, Reagan and Bush all used variants of the Eisenhower staff system, with Bush permitting his chief of staff John Sununu and budget director

Richard Darman to oversee every significant White House decision, usually intervening even before the various councils and staff agencies within the White House had finished their policy reviews.[25]

John Kennedy: Collegial Decision Making

The staff approach has not appealed to Democratic presidents. Kennedy and Johnson functioned as their own chiefs of staff. As political scientist Richard Neustadt advised John Kennedy during the transition, "You would oversee, coordinate, and interfere with virtually everything your staff was doing. A collegial staff has to be managed; competition has to be audited."[26] Kennedy was energetic, restless, and impatient with formal processes. He acted as the "hub of the wheel," consulting widely with officials at all levels of government, as well as with task forces, outside advisors, and friends, and using his advisors as "spokes" to facilitate communication with those at the rim. Explained his speechwriter Theodore Sorensen: "Each person has a special relationship to the president and does what the president needs done. . . ."[27] The collegial system permits new ideas to move to the top quickly, and allows a president to take charge and put his or her own stamp on all levels of government. The president can communicate directly (or through White House aides) with lower-level officials, bypassing the department secretaries and their staffs, to see that presidential orders are precisely carried out in areas of greatest concern. But the complexity of the White House staffing system and the huge size of the government has made such a personalized approach impossible except for the most important presidential priorities.

Bill Clinton: From Ad Hocracy to the Staff System

President Clinton initially started with an inexperienced White House chief of staff, boyhood friend Mack McClarty, who served primarily as an advisor. Clinton served as his own chief of staff, which meant little or no organization to his White House operations. Clinton used White House aides to handle ad hoc tasks. Different circles of aides (the lawyers, the businesspeople, the campaign workers, the old Washington hands) all networked furiously within the White House to gain influence. Officials who were not in the inner circle, or who lacked standing with the president, were frozen out when decisions were made, even though they might have a useful perspective or important information. "The lines of authority seem to resemble a plate of spaghetti," one White House news reporter concluded. "Everyone seems to be in charge of everyone so that no one is held accountable, there is little hierarchy, and there are loops of influence and access that collide, coincide or work in blissful ignorance of one another until some fiasco looms."[28]

The ad hoc approach to executive leadership was time-consuming, draining, and often led to foul-ups, delays, and snafus. Clinton lagged in making appointments because he insisted on reviewing each proposed nomination personally; his nonpriority business lagged because officials were loath to act until they could gain his attention.[29] Worst of all, the image promoted in the media was of a poorly managed and chaotic White House. Eighteen months into his presidency Clinton appointed as White House chief of staff his first budget director, Leon Panetta, a former member of Congress with great credibility in Washington, signaling that "ad hocracy" was to be scrapped and Clinton was introducing a staffing system to focus the president's attention on important issues.

Presidential Assistants

To influence the bureaucracy the president needs help, and he has had it since the creation of the White House Office (WHO) and the Executive Office of the President (EOP) in 1939. The Brownlow commission envisioned a limited administrative role for presidential assistants:

> These aides would have no power to make decisions or issue instructions in their own right. They would not be interposed between the president and the heads of his departments. They would not be assistant presidents in any sense. . . . They would remain in the background, issue no orders, make no decisions, emit no public statements. . . . [30]

In fact, White House aides soon began doing all these things, and the number of staff members grew (Figure 10.1). White House agencies were established specifically to influence personnel, administrative, and budgetary matters in departments and protect some presidential stakes in bureaucratic performance. It is not too much of an exaggeration to say that the Brownlow "rules" are precisely what White House aides do *not* follow. Instead of aides with Brownlow's "passion for anonymity," consider the description of staffers offered by journalist Patrick Anderson: "They tend to be young, highly intelligent, and unashamedly on the make. They take chances, they cut corners, and unlike most politicians they sometimes have a little spontaneity and irreverence left in them. This accounts for much of their charm and most of their problems."[31] White House staffers are more likely to have campaign experience and much less likely to have significant experience in national government. Their principal qualification is a demonstrated personal political loyalty to the president.[32]

Office of Management and Budget (OMB)

Of all the presidential staff agencies, the most important in helping the president influence the work of the departments is the Office of Management and Budget (OMB). The Budget and Accounting Act of 1921 created its predecessor, the Bureau of the Budget (BOB) to prepare the *Budget of the United States,* the president's annual budget requests to Congress. Originally located in the Treasury Department, the BOB was moved to the Executive Office of the President in 1939, and renamed the Office of Management and Budget in 1970. Its director serves as one of the president's key advisors, since 1968 has had a West Wing office, and since 1973 has had the title "assistant to the President."

The OMB's General Management Division, established in 1970, suggested efficiencies to department secretaries. Over the years it promoted everything from "cost–benefit" and "systems" analysis (using sophisticated quantitative tools to

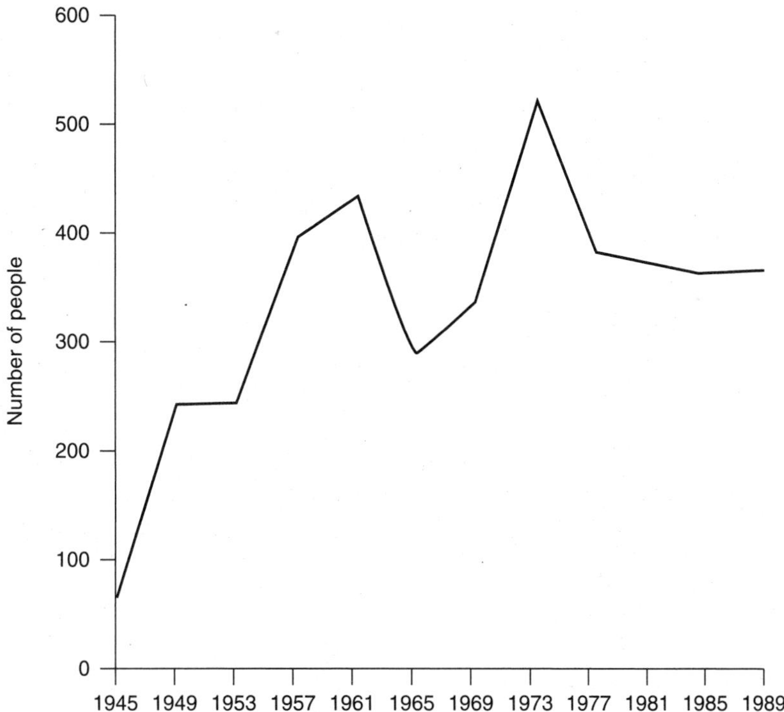

Figure 10.1 White House staff, 1945–1989.
Source: Data from Harold W. Stanley and Richard F. Niemi, *Vital Statistics on American Politics,* 3rd ed., Washington, DC: Congressional Quarterly Press, 1992, pp. 265–267.

weigh costs against benefits in current and proposed programs) through "zero-based budgeting" (in which all activities are to be reviewed annually) and "total quality management" (an approach to improving operations taken from the corporate sector). Often its recommendations fell on deaf ears in the departments, though OMB did provide some tangible budget incentives to go along with its recommendations for management improvements. In 1994 the management division was reintegrated into the budget division, and the two major units were then reorganized into six Resource Management Offices (Natural Resources, Energy and Science, National Security and International Affairs, Health and Personnel, Human Resources, General Government) each headed by a political appointee (program associate director).

The OMB's Division of Federal Procurement Policy recommends ways of cutting procurement costs, which are higher than in the private sector. In 1994 it participated in drafting the Federal Acquisition Streamlining Act, which made major savings in the cost of procurement in federal agencies, repealing or modifying more than 225 onerous contracting regulations that had formerly been imposed by Congress, promoting "electronic procurement" via e-mail (Federal Acquisitions Network, or FACNET), and promoting use of "off the shelf" commercial products rather than those made according to government specifications.

The OMB's Office of Information and Regulatory Affairs (OIRA) reviews all regulations proposed by departments to see if they should go into effect, a function known as *regulatory clearance.* The OMB develops reorganization plans: President Carter created the President's Reorganization Project within OMB and it formulated ten plans designed to give the administration greater control over departments; Reagan established an OMB Reform Task Force to implement "Reform '88," a special effort to establish more "businesslike" procedures in departments, to be implemented through the President's Council on Management Improvement.

Presidential Commissions

Presidents often appoint outside experts to national commissions and task forces assigned to recommend changes in the way the government works. Establishing such commissions is always good politics, given the anti-bureaucratic mood of the voters. Yet most commissions have not had a major impact. President Taft's Commission on Economy and Efficiency proposed that the president be given vast budgetary powers and called for reorganizing agencies by function—its recommendations were ignored. President Franklin Roosevelt appointed the Brownlow Commission, a group of three academic experts on public administration, who made recommendations to strengthen the president's grip on government agencies: it recommended that independent regulatory and New Deal agencies be brought into the departments to establish a unified chain of command, a recommendation that was disregarded. Presidents Truman and Eisenhower appointed the First and Second Hoover Commissions (chaired by former president Herbert Hoover), which in 1949 and 1955 recommended sweeping changes in the departments to reduce costs and increase efficiency. Nixon appointed the Ash Council in 1970, which concentrated on improving the federal system by promoting revenue sharing and block grants to state and local governments to replace grants earmarked for particular programs (which were adopted in part by Congress), and which recommended the consolidation of several cabinet departments along functional lines—recommendations that Congress also ignored.

Recent presidents have fared no better. In the Reagan administration, the President's Private Sector Survey on Cost Control, headed by business executive J. Peter Grace, along with 161 Chief Executive Officers of major U.S. corporations, organized 36 task forces with 2,000 staffers to study every aspect of the U.S. government. The Grace Commission issued a 47-volume report in 1984. It made close to 2,500 recommendations about putting government on a more "businesslike" basis by emulating the practices of large corporations, and promised hundreds of billions of dollars in savings. But the commission made policy recommendations about reducing or eliminating many government programs—issues not of efficiency but of political direction. Most of its major recommendations about cutbacks were not implemented. The Reagan White House refused to sponsor the ceremony at which the report was announced, and it was held in an auditorium in the Commerce Department, because, as one White House staffer remarked, "we couldn't book a place in Siberia."[33] Grace kept his criticisms of Reagan to himself, but he did claim later that two-thirds of the members of Congress were "clowns" for not considering his proposal seriously.[34]

Similarly, in 1988 a Presidential Commission on Privatization issued eighteen recommendations to turn over mail delivery, air traffic control, and other functions to private companies, to sell off Amtrak, and provide educational vouchers to help pay private school tuitions—recommendations that went nowhere. During the Bush years the Volcker Commission proposed that the merit system be extended upward and the number of political appointees in the departments be reduced. President Bush made no recommendations to Congress.

"Reinventing Government"

During the Clinton administration the main reform effect was made by Vice President Gore and a task force under his direction to "reinvent government."[35] The idea was to get government agencies to be more flexible, entrepreneurial, and technologically adept—to do more with less funding and fewer personnel. Between 1993 and 1999, Congress required the government to shed 272,900 jobs from the 2.1 million government employees—160,000 of those positions to come from the Pentagon. The report also called on each department and agency to appoint a "chief operating officer" (CEO) responsible for "transforming the agencies' day-to-day management cultures," and "re-engineering administrative processes" by cutting the steps required to take action and making it easier for the public to deal with government officials. The CEO would be responsible for "ensuring that the President's and agency head's priorities are implemented." The recommendations bowed to political realities by assuming that deputy secretaries would become the CEOs—although most are political appointees and many lack managerial experience. It called for drastic reductions in "the structures of over-control and micromanagement that now bind the federal government: supervisors, headquarters staffs, personnel specialists, budget analysts, procurement specialists, accountants and auditors." It made no mention, however, of cuts in the number of political appointees.

Some of its recommendations were adopted, especially when department secretaries adopted them as their own. In some departments the entrepreneurial spirit seemed to be taking hold. Hazel O'Leary at Energy talked about "Total Quality Management" reforms, and Jack Siegel, an assistant secretary, suggested, "We've got to be more customer-oriented, we've got to utilize our people better than we have in the past, we've got to become more efficient. If we don't, we're going to find ourselves outmoded and outdated, and I think people are going to find out they don't need us anymore."[36] The department soon announced it would put up for competitive bidding the management of its nuclear energy and research complexes to save billions of dollars.

Other reforms were instituted when the budget process required the president to propose massive cuts.[37] Clinton's National Performance Review, sent to Congress in the fall of 1993, specified agency by agency cutbacks to save $11 billion by closing field offices and research facilities, authorizing the sale of assets to private industry, opening up government jobs to private bidders, combating fraud, merging duplicative programs, increasing fees for government services, freezing many programs, reforming federal procurement, and providing incentives for early retirement. Although overall cuts over a five-year period in "reinventing government" were projected at $108 billion by Clinton, the estimate of the House Budget Committee indicated only $37 billion would be saved. Congressional Republicans in 1995 intended far deeper cuts, possibly eliminating entire departments and agencies.

Presidential Rewards and Punishments

Presidents are involved in setting pay and determining benefits in the civil service. The Pay Comparability Act requires them to submit a report to Congress recommending pay scales comparable to the private sector. In practice, presidents submit reports specifying why they believe that pay comparability would be fiscally irresponsible, and they have let pay in the public sector deteriorate significantly. The Office of Personnel Management develops benefit packages for congressional consideration, and since the late 1970s these too have involved cutbacks in benefits. However, presidents since Kennedy have recognized the right of federal employees to join unions, though they have maintained a firm line against strikes by public sector employees. President Reagan dismissed striking air traffic controllers in 1981 and replaced them permanently with non-union workers because they had broken federal law, prohibiting strikes by federal employees.

Presidents can reorganize agencies into larger units, give them more responsibility and prestige, and even propose cabinet status, as President Carter did with the Office of Education, when he honored a campaign promise to make it into a cabinet department. They may designate a "lead agency" in interdepartmental task forces: the State Department always wishes such a designation in any matter involving foreign affairs, but the president may turn a foreign issue over to Treasury, Commerce, Labor, or Agriculture rather than State. The White House may identify so strongly with the work of a particular agency that it coordinates its public and media relations and congressional relations.

Conversely, an agency may be marked for retrenchment or even extinction. It may be scapegoated for its failures and used by the White House to score political points against a preceding administration of the other party. Reagan went after the Occupational Safety and Health Administration. He appointed officials hostile to the agency's mission, and they in turn assigned Senior Executive Service (SES) managers who cut back on the agency's enforcement of laws. Vulnerable agencies like OSHA find their budgets slashed, existing quarterly allotments of funds reduced by OMB, personnel ceilings lowered by the Office of Personnel Management (OPM), and reductions in force (personnel cutbacks) ordered. Good people leave, realizing there is little future in working for an agency that is being targeted by the White House.

POLITICAL EXECUTIVES AND CAREERISTS

Presidents find it difficult to get good help. John Kennedy once remarked that after years of campaigning for the Oval Office, he knew the people who could help him win the presidency, but not those who could help him govern. Most presidents are in the same situation.

The Cabinet

The cabinet consists of the secretaries of the departments and other invited officials. At the Constitutional Convention delegates assumed that the president might convene the heads of departments for advice, but the cabinet was not mentioned in the original Constitution.[38] George Washington created the cabinet in 1789, when he invited the secretaries of state, treasury, war, and the attorney general to meet informally with him. At first these officials met the president with other advisors, such as the chief justice of the United States, and it was not until 1791 that the cabinet met separately with the president.

Through the 1930s there are only a handful of examples of presidents taking major decisions without prior consultation with the cabinet. These include the Emancipation Proclamation issued by President Lincoln, who gathered his cabinet and said, "I do not wish your advice about the main matter. That, I have determined for myself." When Woodrow Wilson decided to enter World War I, he did not call his cabinet together and did not read them the message to Congress asking for a declaration of war. In the 1930s the cabinet lost its importance as a policy-making body. President Franklin Roosevelt would meet with one or two secretaries to thrash out policy, but did not rely on the full cabinet, though it often met for discussions about Democratic Party business. "My principal reason for not having a great deal to say at cabinet meetings," Roosevelt's secretary of commerce Jesse Jones admitted, "was that there was no one at the table who could be of help to me except the president, and when I needed to consult him, I did not choose a cabinet meeting to do so."[39] The real action occurred after cabinet meetings, when secretaries would see FDR for individual appointments—if they could get them. Since then presidents have convened their cabinets irregularly, one or two times a month at best. John Kennedy thought the cabinet meetings were a waste of time, asking "Why should the Postmaster sit there and listen to a discussion of the problems of Laos?"[40] Kennedy held only six meetings in three years. Subsequent presidents tended to begin their terms with regular cabinet meetings, but these tapered off, especially if information was leaked to the media. "No [president] in his right mind submits anything to his cabinet," Nixon concluded.[41]

Today, infrequent cabinet sessions provide the president with political advice, serve as sounding boards for his or her ideas, and enable secretaries to coordinate their public statements on administration policy. Presidents also use cabinet meetings for symbolic purposes: Jimmy Carter used his first meeting to order that high officials use fewer limousines, a "decision" reported widely by the media. Presidents only pay lip service to governing through the cabinet, because they cannot expect the secretaries, individually or collectively, to be in tune with White House priorities. Their responsibilities, outlook, and constituencies differ (as does their tenure, which averages 3.3 years).[42] They must execute specific laws and run particular programs effectively, while serving Congress and gaining support from interest groups. The president sees the "big picture," and his priorities may be difficult for cabinet secretaries to accept.[43]

The Inner and Outer Cabinets

The "inner cabinet" consists of the secretaries of State, Defense, Treasury, and the attorney general, and these officials are usually the most prestigious and their opinions carry the most weight with the president.[44] The president sees these officials often, together or individually. Although some may be chosen because of their personal loyalty and political connections to the president, many appointees for secretary of state and defense are completely unknown to the president. The "outer cabinet" consists of clientele agencies such as Agriculture, Commerce, Interior, Labor, and Veterans Affairs, whose secretaries mediate between constituencies such as union workers, farmers, and business executives. Most secretaries represent the administration to their constituencies, and their constituencies to the president, serving in effect as an "honest broker" between the two.[45]

Once having appointed these people who have worked previously for and with the constituencies they now represent in the department, a president often sloughs them off to his White House staff and EOP agencies, having as little to do with them as possible. That, in turn, will alienate the very constituencies he was originally attempting to appease. There is some evidence that the newest of these departments—Education, Energy, Health and Human Services, Housing and Urban Development, and Transportation—may be less likely to be captured by interest groups.[46] This will be the case when presidents appoint secretaries who are not from constituencies served by the departments: Kennedy, Carter, and Clinton did not choose their secretaries of labor from unions, although the union movement is a mainstay of the Democratic coalition. Secretaries of defense sometimes come from the world of defense contracting, but often do not. Secretaries of Health and Human Services and Education may be academics or former governors who have an interest in the policies of their agencies, but they do not directly represent their educators.[47] Since the Kennedy administration's "best and brightest," it seems that broad-based administrative, managerial, or technical experience has become more important than partisan or interest-group support. When cabinet secretaries leave they tend to be replaced either by their subordinates or by other Washington "insiders," with either managerial experience or personal loyalty to the president.[48]

Cabinet Councils

Presidents sometimes establish cabinet councils to deal with issues that cross departmental lines, often designating a White House aide or departmental secretary as a "double-hatter" to coordinate the work across departmental lines. The Reagan administration established cabinet councils dealing with Economic Affairs, Commerce and Trade, Human Resources, Natural Resources and the Environment; Food and Agriculture; Legal Policy; and Management and Administration. Although Reagan formally was designated the chair of all councils, a cabinet secretary usually chaired meetings. Work was coordinated by the Office of Policy Development and Office of Cabinet Affairs, which viewed each council as a "chokepoint" or "funnel": all policy initiatives would have to move through the councils, enabling the White House senior aides to monitor departmental initiatives and either support or eliminate them. The president attended few meetings and by most accounts took little or no part in meetings. Half the councils were failures, with few meetings and little to show for them, while others, especially the Legal Policy and Economic Affairs, took major roles.

The council mechanism need not always fail, provided the people running the council can work effectively with the department secretaries. President Clinton's National Economic Council played a major role in coordinating economic policy on deficits, taxes, and foreign trade, and getting the most important of the president's programs through Congress, in large measure because of the self-effacing work of its chairman, Robert Rubin. He was able to cooperate closely with Treasury Secretary Lloyd Bentsen, probably because both men—highly successful and independently wealthy—had nothing to prove to the other or to anyone else in Washington, and neither let ego get in the way of effectiveness.

Subcabinet Appointees

The president appoints (by and with the advice and consent of the Senate) approximately 600 political appointees in the departments (up from 71 in 1933 and 152 in 1965).[49] Many of them come from constituencies that helped the president to get elected. More than half are recruited from outside the national government, and one-quarter do not have any prior government experience.[50] "Presidents seldom know more than a few of their appointees," observed Paul Craig Roberts, a Treasury official under Reagan, "and have no idea who they are relying on."[51] Not only does the president not know them; they do not know the president. The personnel operation can provide people who are nominally members of the party, who come from constituencies that the White House favors, and who have supported the president. But what the appointees need, and often cannot get from the president without personal contact, is a sense of the "big picture." They do not know the president's priorities or political strategy, and they do not know whether the White House will back them when they start to make policy. Presidents may also find that while they and their appointees agree on partisan principles and overall philosophy, they disagree about specifics.[52]

As soon as most subcabinet officials have accepted their jobs, they are cut adrift by the White House. No one is in charge of seeing to it that new officials are properly oriented and that their transition to life in Washington is smooth. They and their families have a rough time getting settled, and they complain of overwork, stress in their personal life, salaries that are not adequate (purchasing power of executive level salaries declined 39 percent between 1969 and 1985), and above all, isolation from the president.[53]

Turnover is high: About one-third leave within eighteen months, another third last it out for three years, and less than one-third remain beyond that. Most political appointees supervise officials who have far more expertise and experience than they do.[54] The Federal Aviation Administration, for example, had four directors between 1987 and 1994, making it almost impossible for any president to reform the agency. Bob Carr, one-time chair of the House Appropriations Subcommittee on Transportation, observed of careerists that "They figure that the administrators can come and go: 'If I don't like what this administrator is asking me to do, I'll just wait another six months and there will be another one, and by the time he learns that I'm even here, I'll be able to assert what I want to have happen.' "[55] The more savvy of these officials will build their own power bases and constituencies. They abandon presidential priorities and develop their own support by currying favor with career officials, lobbyists, reporters, and congressional committees.[56] Political executives, inexperienced in the ways of Washington and lacking knowledge about the agencies they are to supervise, have, in the words of one political scientist, "enough time to make mistakes but not enough time to learn from them."[57]

The Career Service

Political appointees must rely on career civil servants to make government work, yet presidents are often deeply suspicious of a "Washington establishment," especially when they have campaigned against bureaucrats to get into the White House. President Nixon warned his cabinet secretaries that "if they did not act quickly, they would become captives of the bureaucracy they were trying to change," and he added "We can't depend on people who believe in another philosophy of government to give us their undivided loyalty or their best work."[58]

The top-level career officials consist of approximately 7,000 career officials of the Senior Executive Service (SES) and most of the 1,500 high-level officials of the Foreign Service. The SES was created by President Carter after Congress passed the Civil Service Reform Act of 1978: the purpose of the law was to make top-level civil servants more responsive to the White House. Members are given greater responsibility and can get pay increases and bonuses on the basis of superior performance. But they give up some of the protections of the civil service system: it is easier for their political superiors to transfer them, demote them back to the civil service, or even remove them (after a 120-day waiting period at the start of a new administration). The president also may appoint people to the SES from outside the career service, not exceeding 10 percent of the total SES.

"What is at issue between career and noncareer executives is *control,*" explained one bureaucrat in the Federal Emergency Management Agency.[59] Presidents, with their discretionary appointment power, can now select people who share their party or ideological orientation, or are independent and "neutral," and therefore willing to do the president's bidding and work harmoniously with the noncareer officials of his administration. President Reagan filled about 850 SES positions with his own political appointees. Because 40 percent of the SES officials left their posts in the first three years of the Reagan administration, the White House had the opportunity to promote to the SES some careerists who were ideologically more in sympathy with the new administration.[60] Officials who have been promoted into the SES or appointed to it from the outside now operate within the bureaucracy at lower levels than ever before, and the president can cluster them in key agencies that deal with his or her priorities. The president can remove or transfer officials whose attitudes makes them liabilities. Personnel decisions can be made by the White House and its top appointees to maximize administrative control. This may mean transferring people, giving them low-priority assignments and encouraging them to retire.[61] It may also mean not filling career slots when vacancies arise, leaving noncareerist SES appointees in full control of a particular program targeted for White House influence.

Critics of the SES contend that it fosters favoritism, party politics, and slavish adherence to the administration by civil servants angling for more pay. They claim that the SES system has eroded the neutrality of the Civil Service.[62] A 1984 report issued by the Merit System Protection Board (MSPB), the agency assigned by Congress to preserve the integrity of the civil service system and prevent political reprisals against careerists, indicated that 40 percent of officials thought the SES was not free of improper political influence, and more than half felt unprotected from arbitrary action by political superiors.[63] Supporters say that SES creates a more responsive bureaucracy that is better able and willing to carry out the policies of elected officials, that it gives the president more flexibility, and that it makes for better relations between political executives and career officials. They point out that studies by the General Accounting Office, the Office of Personnel Management, and the MSPB have not found widespread abuse.[64] Others have found some evidence that SES officials who share the president's party and ideology receive preferential treatment, and that other officials are more likely to be subject to transfers or reductions in rank. These may not involve favoritism, however, but more likely reflect the fact that a Republican administration is likely to cut back on bureaucracies that harbor liberal Democratic careerists—especially domestic social welfare agencies.[65] The Senior Executive Association, a group representing senior careerists, defends the SES system but opposes political appointments to SES ranks, arguing that it introduces partisan politics in the bureaucracy.

Top-level careerists at the SES level (which runs from GS 16 through Executive Level IV), and at the managerial ranks slightly below the SES (the 1,500 or so Schedule C positions, ranked at GS 15 and below) that require political discretion and confidentiality, usually begin and end their careers in government, working for only one or two agencies. They average about twenty years of service by the time they attain SES rank and are put in charge of programs or bureaus. They identify strongly with the goals and missions of their units. They may fight to maintain programs that the president wants to modify or eliminate. Because the political executives above them hardly have time to learn their jobs before they move on, it is difficult for the administration to win the allegiance of career officials or translate administration policy into program. Often lower-level officials simply outlast them, putting career or agencies' interests ahead of the president's. They tend to discount the "two-year wonders," the revolving-door assistant secretaries. They do not take kindly to directives instructing them that, for the good of a president who may serve for only four years, they should sacrifice programs on which they have worked all their professional lives.[66]

Republican political executives tend to get along well with conservative careerists and those whose mission the Republican president supports—such as the Department of Defense. They have more difficult relations with liberals and careerists in social welfare and regulatory agencies. Democratic political executives have a much more difficult time with conservative careerists and those in the Defense Department.[67]

In dealing with political executives, senior civil servants try to engage in "education from below." Instead of refusing to carry out orders, they present their superiors with unpleasant alternatives: They may claim that proposed budget cuts would mean the elimination of popular programs. They may inform their superiors that proposed policies cannot be implemented without first obtaining new statutory authorization from Congress. In doing so, they often delay or block presidential priorities. Officials may refuse to carry out orders from political appointees that they believe violate laws or ethical guidelines. In 1994, for example, Roger Altman, deputy secretary of the Treasury and head of the Resolution Trust Corporation (an agency created to handle bankruptcy of savings and loan institutions), asked RTC officials to set up an "early warning system" to let him know about politically sensitive actions they were about to take. Agency officials rejected his proposals and refused to implement such a system.[68]

Political scientists talk of a "cycle of accommodation," in which initial distrust between political appointees and SES careerists gradually gives way to mutual respect, accommodation, and teamwork in carrying out the policies of the administration.[69] To some extent such accommodation does occur: surveys show that most noncareerists wind up with a great deal of respect for the professionalism and competence of career officials. But even more significant seem to be personnel policies that provide accommodation on the noncareerist's terms: by requiring careerists either to subordinate their own goals to that of the administration, or else find some other agency in which to work.

PUBLIC SERVICE ETHICS

The president must develop ethical standards for the administration and for careerists in the public service and deal with alleged violations of these standards.[70]

Ethical Violations

The most common ethical violations committed by appointees in the White House or in departments include the following:

- *Self-dealing:* profiting from insider information on government decisions; accepting stock or other interests in companies benefiting from governmental actions (stock jobbery); obtaining loans at favorable rates or conditions; obtaining preferential treatment in making investments; providing benefits to family members (nepotism);
- *Careerism:* moving from a governmental position to the private sector after making decisions or rendering improper assistance, or disclosing information, that benefited the future employer (revolving door);
- *Corruption:* accepting graft, or extorting payments from contractors and others in a position to benefit from a favorable decision;
- *Salary supplementation:* accepting honoraria, fees, gifts, and hospitality from those in a position to benefit from one's decisions;
- *Misuse of benefits:* padding expenses, accepting the use of government services when off duty or for private uses;

- *Interference:* attempting to exert political pressure in quasi-judicial proceedings of regulatory agencies, for the benefit of a party involved;
- *Obstruction of justice:* shielding the White House or administration officials from investigations of wrongdoing. Actions include destroying evidence, committing perjury, misleading investigators, providing misleading information or making false statements to Congress, or conspiring with others in cover-ups.

Codes of Ethics

In 1965 President Lyndon Johnson issued Executive Order 11222, which ordered officials to avoid actions that gave the appearance of using their offices for private gain, or giving preferential treatment to any individual or organization, or "affecting adversely the confidence of the public in the integrity of government," or making decisions outside of official channels. President Jimmy Carter established stricter standards for appointees, including disclosure of assets, divestiture of assets that might create conflicts of interest, and restrictions on private employment after officials left government, including a one-year prohibition on lobbying. These provisions were incorporated by Congress into the Ethics in Government Act of 1978.

The Presidential Transition Effectiveness Act of 1988 covers ethics issues during presidential transitions. It provides that transition aides who make conduct investigations and make recommendations about policy in government departments and agencies must fill out disclosure forms, so that the public will know the names, recent employment history, and "sources of funding" (if not paid for by transition funds) of such transition officials. During the Clinton transition, additional rules for transition staff included a six-month ban on subsequent lobbying of government agencies by staffers involved with these agencies. There was also a prohibition against using any information gathered during the transition for personal gain.

Clinton developed the strictest code of ethics for political appointees. His executive order prohibited officials from lobbying their former departments for five years after leaving government service. Top-level officials in many departments would also be banned for life from representing the interests of foreign governments and political parties, though they would be free to represent foreign corporations and interest groups after five years. Nevertheless, a number of incidents involving White House aides improperly misusing the perks of office (such as using the White House helicopters for a golf outing), the investigations into possible ethical and legal lapses by three cabinet secretaries, and claims that White House staffers were impeding an investigation into President Clinton's financial affairs before his assuming the presidency, cast an ethical shadow on the Clinton administration.

Presidents must balance their desire for an ethically "pure" administration with the need to recruit people into government. Instead of a "pure" merit system going almost all the way to the top, as in some parliamentary systems, the United States has a "mixed" system that permits a large number of "in-and-outers" to move into government from the private sector and then move out again. Not only political appointees at the top, but also some officials in the SES, and technical and scientific officials at lower levels, may be "in and outers." The president may make "130-day appointees," such as Clinton's former White House counsel Lloyd Cutler, who are then exempted from conflict of interest laws that otherwise would forbid them from representing their clients when they left the government for a year or more. Instead of requiring a full disclosure of financial assets, presidential regulations (and laws passed by Congress) must balance disclosure against privacy requirements needed to recruit people into office. A complete ban on postgovernment employment in the same field in the private sector would certainly end "revolving-door" abuses, but how would a president get talented people to take jobs in the administration in the first place, if they knew they were cutting themselves off from all further employment in their professions thereafter? A near-exodus took place from the Carter administration in 1979 after the Ethics in Government Act was passed with strict postemployment bans, and the following year it had to be amended to exempt officials leaving to work in universities, research institutes, and state and local governments.

Ethics Enforcement

The Office of Government Ethics (OGE), created by the Ethics in Government Act of 1978, implements ethical standards. The director is appointed by the president with the advice and consent of the Senate for a five-year term and supervises a staff of about twenty-two. The director submits to Congress a biennial report about implementation of ethics laws. The office develops rules and regulations regarding standards of conduct, identification of conflicts of interest, and financial disclosures of appointees, in consultation with the attorney general and the Office of Personnel Management, which are then promulgated by the president. The office then supervises compliance by providing government officials with advisory letters and formal advisory opinions that deal with their particular situations. It trains departmental ethical officials to enforce the rules and deal with violations, including disciplinary action, dismissal from the service, or recommendation to the Justice Department for prosecution and criminal penalties.

In the 1980s the OGE was criticized by Democrats for being lax in enforcing regulations, and the agency admitted that it did not play a watchdog in dealing with the White House or cabinet. One member of Congress, Democrat Gerry Sikorski, called it "a toothless terrier on Valium."[71] Then, in 1994, Republicans criticized its conclusion that President Clinton's aides committed no violations of laws or ethical standards in the Whitewater case, despite the fact that the office was headed by a Republican appointee.[72]

Cover-Ups

What gets an administration into more trouble than almost anything else is a cover-up of official misconduct. Had President Nixon come clean at the beginning about the Watergate affair and admitted low-level White House involvement, the issue probably would not have taken on the great significance that it did. It was his role in the conspiracy to conceal White House involvement in the burglary that formed the basis of the impeachment charges against him. The Clinton administration fell into the same trap. High-level White House aides and subcabinet officials misled (either deliberately or inadvertently) Congress about briefings that had occurred between officials of the Resolution Trust Corporation (RTC), the Treasury, and the White House. These meetings dealt with the question of whether a recommendation for a criminal referral (indictment) against business associates of the Clintons would be referred to the Department of Justice. (The indictment involved a failed savings and loan in Arkansas that might have benefited from decisions made by Clinton while he was governor.) Republicans pressed for congressional hearings, then exploited the inconsistencies in testimony of top Clinton officials, charging a cover-up, though there was no credible evidence that the Clintons or their appointees had done anything to prevent other officials from making such a criminal referral.

Whatever the extent of Clinton's involvement in events in Arkansas, the White House was put on the defensive on national television at the specter of its officials providing inconsistent testimony, apologizing for gaps in prior testimony, admitting "misstatements" about how files involved in the case had been handled. Their conduct and demeanor led the public and Congress to conclude that *something* fishy must have been going on, and several of these officials resigned from the administration. The lessons of these and other cover-ups ought to be clear: The attempt at "damage control" in these cases will be uncovered by the media, exploited by the opposition, and will itself only compound the ultimate damage to the White House. As for Clinton administration officials, they would have been better off operating ethically from the start without considering the political stakes of the White House. "Do what you think is the right thing early," was one of the lessons learned by Treasury Chief of Staff Joshua Steiner about the Whitewater mess; another was "don't let the White House get involved in any way."[73] Ignoring the White House's immediate political interest in containing the damage involved in a scandal probably will turn out to be the best way for officials to guard the president's long-term interests.

As a result of the questions raised in the Whitewater case, White House Counsel Lloyd Cutler announced that new regulations would be in place involving any "heads up" (advance notice) given by officials to the White House about pending criminal investigations or referrals. Although Iowa Republican Representative Jim Leach suggested that officials give no notice to the White House about pending investigations, Cutler (and his predecessor Bernard Nussbaum) rejected that argument, because the White House needs to know about investigations to respond to media inquiries. In addition, because the president is chief law enforcement officer, the White House has a constitutional right to inquire about the status of criminal investigations, even those that involve a sitting president.[74] Since 1994 such contacts can only involve the legal counsel of the agency reporting to the White House counsel. Officials were also expected to recuse (disqualify) themselves from dealing with any criminal investigations involving the president, and do so without prior consultation with the White House.

Independent Counsel

Under certain circumstances the prosecutions for wrongdoing in the government pass from the Justice Department to an independent counsel. Title VI of the Ethics in Government Act of 1978 provides for the appointment of an independent counsel to investigate and prosecute the president, vice president, members of the cabinet, or other political executives appointed by the president, if the attorney general receives "specific information" about their possible violation of federal criminal law. The attorney general conducts a preliminary investigation and then may request appointment of independent counsel by the Special Division of the Court of Appeals for the District of Columbia circuit. The panel is appointed by the chief justice of the United States. The Judiciary Committee may also request the attorney general to conduct a "threshold inquiry": If the attorney general fails to apply for an independent counsel, he or she must explain the decision to Congress within thirty days, and a majority of either party on either the House or Senate Judiciary Committees may request the Special Division to appoint an independent counsel. The law provides that he or she may not be dismissed by the president, or by the attorney general except on the grounds of "extraordinary impropriety," thus ensuring the independence of the counsel, and the integrity of the investigation and prosecution.

An independent counsel investigated President Carter's chief of staff, Hamilton Jordan, on charges that he used cocaine, but did not prosecute. President Reagan's attorney general, Edwin Meese, was subject to two investigations, but was not prosecuted. Another official in the Reagan Justice Department, Theodore Olson, was prosecuted on charges of giving false information to Congress. Reagan's secretary of labor, Ray Donovan, was investigated for business activities that had occurred before he joined the administration. Reagan's secretary of defense, Caspar Weinberger, was indicted by an independent counsel in 1992 for giving false statements to Congress about the Iran–contra affair.[75] President Clinton's secretary of agriculture, Mike Espy, was investigated for allegedly taking several hundred dollars' worth of entertainment tickets, food, and lodging from a poultry company—which if true would be a violation of the Pure Food and Drug Act—and Clinton's secretary of housing and urban development, Henry Cisneros, was investigated for making false statements to the FBI during the background check for his nomination.

Clinton and the Counsel

When President Clinton faced allegations of financial irregularities in the Whitewater scandal, the provision for an independent counsel had temporarily lapsed. Attorney General Janet Reno therefore appointed a special prosecutor in 1993 within the Justice Department to handle the investigation, choosing a Republican, Robert Fiske, to ensure impartiality. The counsel's independence was ensured by Justice Department regulations, which provided that the appointee could be removed only for good cause, physical disability, mental incapacity, or other circumstances that impaired the performance of his duties.[76]

After the independent counsel law was renewed by Congress, the three-judge panel made its own appointment to ensure impartiality; ironically, its own actions gave the appearance of partisan politics. Democrats attacked the appointment of Kenneth Starr, a former solicitor general in the Bush administration, arguing that he had already prejudiced himself by working on a legal brief for a woman's organization in a case involving President Clinton. Starr had gone on record stating that Clinton, as an incumbent president, did not have immunity from civil suit while in office. President Clinton's personal lawyer, Robert Bennett, called on Starr to withdraw. The *New York Times,* as well as five past presidents of the American Bar Association, argued that his impartiality had been called into question because Judge David Sentelle, head of the special panel who had appointed him, had lunched with several senators who were the most critical of Clinton while the question of appointing a new independent counsel was being considered by the panel.[77] Congressional Democrats, such as Ohio Senator Howard Metzenbaum, said the appointment "reeks of politics," and Democratic House Speaker Tom Foley referred to it as "rather strange."[78] However, it could be argued that by appointing someone who served in high positions with the opposition party to investigate the administration, the special panel had left no doubt that a full investigation would take place.

To guard his reputation for impartiality, Starr hired an ethics counsel to his staff, choosing Samuel Dash, former chief counsel of the Senate committee that had investigated the Watergate scandal two decades before. Federal Appeals Judge Harry T. Edwards then ruled that no ethics rules had been violated by Judge Sentelle in naming Starr to the position, because there was no reason for the judges to refrain "from consulting with others in the exercise of their appointment authority."

The legality of the independent counsel provisions of the law has come under attack. The Reagan administration, through its Department of Justice, argued that the statute was unconstitutional because it infringed on the presidential removal power (although Reagan himself had not vetoed its extension in 1987).[79] The law was upheld by the Supreme Court in *Morrison v. Olson* in 1988, by a 7–1 vote.[80] The act, according to Chief Justice William Rehnquist, did not violate the appointments clause, did not expand the role of federal courts beyond that contemplated by the Constitution, and did not infringe on the presidential power to remove executive officials.

Critics of the independent counsel provision such as Terry Eastland, former director of public affairs in the Justice Department under President Reagan, argue that there is a "culture of scandal" in Washington, in which members of an administration find themselves under constant scrutiny and suspicion for ethical violations. President Clinton's counsel Lloyd Cutler warned of "the growing cynicism in Washington about people who serve in government," claiming that the investigative media's notion that government officials are "presumptively crooked, dishonest liars" will discourage capable people from serving.[81] Others respond that given the frequency with which conflicts of interest and conspiracies to cover up violations of laws seem to surface in the Capitol, what the nation needs is more investigation of the administration, not less. If there is a culture of scandal, perhaps it has been "cultured" by presidents and their appointees.

CONGRESS AND THE BUREAUCRACY

"The Constitution sets up no such thing as an executive branch," argues political scientist Don K. Price, and "we should acknowledge that in all major issues of management and policy the Congress and the President are jointly involved in the direction and control of the departments and agencies."[82] On many issues of public policy, intermittent White House supervision may be less significant than congressional oversight, especially in periods of split-government when the party controlling Congress has a great incentive to block the White House efforts to control the bureaucracy.

Congressional Statutory Controls

The Constitution grants Congress most powers over the administrative establishment. Congress passes laws establishing departments, their subordinate bureaus, and independent agencies. It establishes their table of organization and endows their bureaus with powers (known as the statutory base). Congress has the power to reorganize departments, but it has passed Reorganization Acts that allow the president to submit reorganization plans himself, which are then approved or vetoed by Congress. Any time a new department is created or an old one abolished, it must be done by legislation. Congress has reduced two cabinet-level departments in rank (the Army and Navy Departments, which were subordinated to the Defense Department in 1949), and split a third (Health, Education, and Welfare, divided in 1978 into the Departments of Education, and Health and Human Services). Congress has rarely eliminated bureaus, even when presidents have made considerable efforts to have it do so.[83] When Reagan proposed to eliminate 45 government agencies in 1986, Congress responded by eliminating only two minor ones.

Congress has created the permanent career civil service, monitored by the Merit Systems Protection Board, and has established alternate ways to enter the civil service for noncareerists. It passed the Ramspeck Act in 1940 to permit its own congressional staffers to bypass civil service process and enter the career civil service without competitive examination. Congress has acted against executive nepotism: A 1968 law prohibits the president from appointing a close family member to a paid federal office—it passed in reaction to President Kennedy's appointment of his brother Robert Kennedy as attorney general.

Congress delegates power to the president to determine all grades and pay scales (based on quadrennial recommendations of the Commission on Executive, Legislative, and Judicial Salaries), and determines which officials are eligible for bonuses (it bars bonuses to political employees during an election year). It determines travel allowances, expense accounts, office facilities and furnishings, and other "perks" and fringe benefits. It legislates on the up-front sums the administration can offer workers as "buyouts" to induce voluntary early retirements.

Congress often establishes roadblocks in the way of administrative actions. By law it may require officials to report to it and then wait a specified period before acting, just in case Congress wishes to block action by passing a law. It may require "clearances" that officials must obtain from governors, local officials, or private interest groups. It establishes review procedures that officials must follow before acting, that require them to obtain "impact statements" or other factual data. Congress may require the General Accounting Office (GAO) to conduct field or headquarters audits of agencies to see that funds appropriated by Congress are properly spent. It may disallow unlawful expenditures and punish officials involved. It investigates irregularities in government bidding under the Competition in Contracting Act of 1984. It conducts policy analyses of agency operations: After its study of the Civil Rights Commission in 1986, Congress cut funding for the agency by one-third and insisted that the remaining funds be spent according to GAO recommendations.

The Legislative Veto

One of the most useful tools Congress has is the legislative veto: a statutory provision whereby Congress delegates power to the president or other executive officials, but reserves to itself a "veto" over its execution—in effect making a conditional and provisional grant of power. One type of legislative veto requires officials to "report and wait" until Congress or its committees decides whether to allow them to proceed. Another permits officials to act, but both houses of Congress can subsequently pass a joint resolution that blocks it.

Before 1932, legislative veto mechanisms were used by Congress primarily to control agencies such as the Government Printing Office that provided services to legislators. Only about eighteen such vetoes were put into law during the New Deal (including a provision dealing with proposed government reorganizations) and only thirty-six existed through Lyndon Johnson's presidency, primarily to influence the distribution of government contracts or construction of military bases or post offices. During the Nixon and Ford administrations they were used as a check on a Republican president by a Democratic Congress. They dealt with such significant presidential decisions as the use of military force, the withholding of funds appropriated by Congress, the transfer of nuclear technology to other nations, and the sale of weapons to foreign nations—all presidential decisions that were now subject to checks by Congress. Even after Jimmy Carter became president, the Democratic Congress continued to add vetoes, with more than 245 provisions in 196 laws by the end of his presidency. Congress actually used the veto only 85 times through 1981, but its very presence served as a deterrent on the executive. The fact that it might be employed gave Congress leverage in dealing with the president and other officials. It provided an incentive for officials to consult in advance with members of Congress and gain their concurrence to proposed policies.

Presidents oppose legislative vetoes as an infringement on their executive powers. But at times they acquiesce in them, especially when Congress couples them with broad delegations of power. President Franklin Roosevelt was able to implement a "lend-lease" program of foreign aid to our military allies during World War II; while Congress nominally gave itself a legislative veto over these arrangements, in fact the delegation of power to the White House was enormous. Similarly, aid to Greece and Turkey at the beginning of the Cold War in 1947 was accompanied by a legislative veto provision, to which Truman did not object. When Congress permitted the president to put U.S. military observers into the Sinai Peacekeeping Force in the 1970s, it gave itself a "veto" so that it could insist that the observers be withdrawn in the event of renewed hostilities between Israel and Egypt. Sometimes a president will sign a bill with a legislative veto provision because he or she wants the legal authority or funding for programs—as is often the case with foreign aid and military authorization bills.

The Supreme Court has ruled on the constitutionality of the legislative veto provision. The Immigration and Naturalization Service (INS) was about to deport Jagdish Chadha from the United States. He and his lawyers managed to get the attorney general to give him a "parole"—a decision that allowed him to remain in the United States. The parole was overturned by the House of Representatives, under a legislative veto provision. Chadha, facing deportation by the INS, sued in federal court, arguing that the House legislative veto was an unconstitutional infringement on the parole power of the attorney general. By extension, his argument put in jeopardy about 400 other legislative veto provisions.

In *Chadha v. INS,* Chief Justice Warren Burger held that legislative vetoes are "acts of Congress," and as such require both chambers to assent. Furthermore, according to the "presentment clause," all acts of Congress must be presented to the president for signature or veto. Yet, in this instance, only one branch of the legislature had acted, and President Reagan had not had any chance to "veto" the "legislative veto" because it had never been presented to him. Burger also held that if Congress gives itself a legislative veto, it is making a conditional delegation of power to executive agencies. Burger held that a congressional delegation must be final, or else it would violate the separation of powers by giving Congress the final say on administrative actions. This not only violates the separation of powers, Burger held, but also the provision that it is the president, not Congress, who must take care that the laws be faithfully executed.

Burger rejected the argument that not all legislative acts require both chambers. The House votes on impeachment and the Senate tries impeachments, the Senate alone consents to nominations, and the Senate alone consents to treaties. For Burger, these were clearly stated exceptions in the Constitution to the general principles of bicameralism, and therefore were the only exceptions permitted. Nor did he accept the congressional argument that not all acts of Congress must be presented to the president. The Constitution must specify any exceptions to the presentment clause. Finally, Burger denied the congressional assertion that not all laws involve unconditional delegations of power. After all, some laws require clearances by state and local governments, or private groups. Cannot Congress provide itself with a "veto" when it can and does give "veto" powers to others? This is not, legislators claimed, an infringement on the executive power, but rather legislative oversight of administration. The Supreme Court disagreed.

Chadha v. INS put in jeopardy hundreds of legislative vetoes. Yet, after that case was decided, Congress continued to use the legislative veto: In the next three years Congress put 102 more legislative veto provisions into 24 laws, and then another 100 provisions between 1986 and 1990.[84] To meet the bicameral and presentation requirements, it specified that a legislative veto be exercised by a joint resolution of both houses (which is then presented to the president) rather than by concurrent resolution (which is not presented to the president). Congress might ultimately have to muster two-third majorities to repass its original legislative veto in the event the president struck the joint resolution down with his suspensory veto.

Congress also used other devices that worked like legislative vetoes. It passed laws requiring a joint resolution of approval before a president could take or complete certain actions. It used "report and wait" provisions so that it might have time to disapprove of pending executive actions by regular legislation. It put more agencies outside presidential control by establishing independent boards, commissions, and agencies that would be susceptive to informal congressional committee clearances. It indicated in its committee reports accompanying new legislation that it expected officials to seek concurrences before taking action. For example, the National Aeronautics and Space Agency (NASA) came to an agreement with the House Appropriations Committee: a legislative veto provision would be dropped, provided NASA followed committee "recommendations" about spending for projects on a voluntary basis. In another example, Bush's Secretary of State James A. Baker and Congress struck a deal involving a "gentleman's agreement legislative veto": Congress appropriated $50 million in humanitarian aid for the Nicaraguan contras, but half of the funds would be withheld for six months and would be released thereafter only with the concurrence of key committee and congressional leaders.[85] The agreement itself was not put into law.

Congressional committees even created a complicated mechanism to restore the single-chamber resolution that *Chadha* had ruled unconstitutional. A committee or the entire chamber could pass a resolution against an action of an agency, which could then be followed by a point of order raised against the appropriation to fund such an action. One instance involved the Environmental Protection Agency: If it spent funds for the national flood insurance fund beyond a specified amount, additional spending would be subject to "point of order" objections, and the appropriations committee would honor the objections and refuse to authorize the spending.

IRON TRIANGLES AND ISSUE NETWORKS

Bureaucrats, legislators, and lobbyists have developed alliances over the years to make public policy. Often they work together to impede the president's efforts to control the bureaucracy.

Iron Triangles

Presidents and their political appointees sometimes confront an "iron triangle" of career officials, powerful legislators on congressional committees, and lobbyists representing constituencies served by these officials.[86] There are hundreds of iron triangles controlling government programs. The Department of the Interior, for example, works with ranchers, farmers who need irrigation on arid lands, and forestry and mining companies.

The most important of the transactions that go on among the participants of an iron triangle are as follows:

- *Interest groups and bureau chiefs.* Lobbyists want to write guidelines for the administration of programs, gain formal access by participating in "national advisory committees" established by the agency, and win formal or informal vetoes of agency decisions. They want influence over personnel decisions by top managers of agencies. The bureau chiefs want these lobbyists to testify favorably at congressional committee hearings and to lobby at the departmental and White House levels for more funds for the bureau's programs. They want help in developing reorganization plans within the department that give their bureaus more authority.

- *Bureau chiefs and committee leaders.* Bureau chiefs want statutory language giving them maximum authority and discretion, expanding their jurisdiction, and funding more programs. They want better facilities, more personnel, and "grade creep" (promotions for career personnel and a greater percentage of positions allocated at high civil service categories). Committee members want special treatment for their constituencies. They want to influence the distribution of goods, services, and contracts.
- *Committee leaders and interest group lobbyists.* Committee leaders want campaign contributions from the PACs organized by interest groups. They rely on the expertise of lobbyists in writing laws. Interest groups want statutory language that gives their representatives formal access to advisory committees that write guidelines detailing how agencies will operate. They also want language that allocates some of the funds given to bureaus to activities organized or controlled by their groups at the state and local levels. They want congressional help in lobbying the president to appoint members of their groups to executive-level positions in the departments overseeing the agencies.

The iron triangles maintain themselves because of the close professional relations among participants: lobbyists and bureaucrats may work together for twenty years or more. Retired members of Congress and bureaucrats often become lobbyists. Iron triangles have expertise and technical skills that recently appointed political executives cannot match. They frustrate presidential appointees and delay or block presidential priorities. They pressure the president to expand bureaucracy, provide new services to special interests, spend more money, and add personnel. They take away the presidential ability to determine priorities and budget for them. They prevent coordination of policy and elimination of "red tape," and promote needless duplication of activities.[87]

Iron triangles are created to get things from the government, or to get government out of their business, or to get government regulations that will reduce their risks of doing business. Iron triangles are heavily involved in "corporate" welfare: They reinforce private-sector dependence on government subsidies, below-market loans or loan guarantees, tax breaks, and government insurance, which in turn prevents the free market from disciplining inefficient businesses. They substitute political influence for the discipline of the free market in allocating investment capital. They wheedle contracts for goods and services, research and development, employer training, and capital construction—expenditures that might not be economically justifiable. They get regulations that freeze out competitors and substitute connections and influence for the operations of the free market.

Issue Networks

Sometimes iron triangles face challenges for control of the bureaucracy from issue networks. These consist of political executives, career bureaucrats, management and policy consultants, academic researchers, journalists, foundation officers, and White House aides, all of whom want fundamental change in the way a bureau operates its programs. They think about the issues in a broader context than do members of iron triangles, and they are interested primarily in rational problem solving, efficient allocation of resources, and better techniques of management and decision making. They are more interested in changing policy to conform to the public interest than they are in bureaucratic empire building, lobbying for the benefit of a particular industry, or personal economic gain.

Examples of issue networks include conservationists who challenge water allocation rules for western farmers and grazing permits for western ranchers; activists who claim that nuclear safety rules are lax and might lead to a disaster near populated areas; and public health experts who believe that inefficient veteran's hospitals might be consolidated or shut down, and the money saved used on other medical priorities. A network may consist of career employees in several agencies, such as the Public Employees for Environmental Responsibility, a group of several thousand federal officials in the Forest Service, Environmental Protection Agency, and the Departments of Agriculture, Energy, and the Interior.

The issue network challenges an iron triangle by conducting research on a problem or investigating an ethical abuse or criminal violation. It then "goes public" and attempts to forge a broad coalition of public-spirited groups together to force fundamental changes. Well-timed op-ed pieces in the newspapers, research reports, magazine articles, and appearances on talk shows may put opponents off balance. The issue network wants the president to side with it and give it a mandate to control the resolution of the issue by appointing someone from the network to the top policy-making position. He or she can in turn bring others in to the bureau management. Karen Nussbaum, for example, the former director of "9 to 5," a working women's advocacy organization, was named to head the Women's Bureau of the Labor Department when the Clinton administration decided to upgrade it. Agency advisory committees also can be shaken up by putting within them representatives from groups within the issue network.

Presidents often find themselves caught in the midst of conflicts between issue networks. Presidents can then can act as magistrates, listening to the arguments of each group, weighing their options, and then tipping the scales toward one or the other. The danger is that media coverage, fueled by leaks from competing issue networks, will give the impression of a White House in disarray. Moreover, there may be trouble with issue network activists the president has appointed or is trying to appoint. Either the White House must accept their views, or, if they are too extreme politically, the administration can try to moderate them, back away from them, or if necessary disavow them. Appointees may themselves become a major issue, making them a political liability.

Competition among issue networks, and between them and iron triangles, is good for the White House and good for the country. It brings more participants, with a wide range of views, before the president. It allows the White House to launch trial balloons, enabling the president and Congress to gauge public opinion. Issue networks can "get out in front" on an issue, bring the public and Congress around, and then get presidential support—tactics used by public health officials coping with the AIDs epidemic in the last years of the Reagan presidency. It enables groups that are not well entrenched in the bureaucracy to win over the White House through the force of their ideas. It serves as an antidote for entrenched bureaucratic interests and political privilege. It enables outside policy entrepreneurs to gain access and compete with the iron triangles.

THE NEW ADMINISTRATIVE PRESIDENCY

The president does not function effectively as "chief executive" over the departments and agencies of American government. Since the New Deal the institutionalized presidency has been created to allow him to be just that, but its agencies cut against the grain of the American political system, which is antibureaucratic to its core. The large presidential staff provides capabilities for managerial control, but it also raises expectations and responsibility that go far beyond what the Constitution supports. Moreover, the dysfunctions of "palace guard" politics, which include staff friction, incompetence, ethical violations, and leaks to the media, keep the president on the political defensive. There is a limit to what presidential staffing can accomplish in "running the government"—especially when there is open resistance to White House interference by cabinet secretaries on down the line.

In almost every modern organization, managers who emphasize command and control, replete with extensive staff work, are giving way to those who rely on lateral coordination, networking, teamwork, and initiatives from the grassroots—with far fewer staffers. The presidency seems one of the last institutions to adapt, still relying too much on ineffectual attempts at command and control. Perhaps what is needed is a "downsized" and "reengineered" presidency, equipped with a much leaner staff that does not attempt to run a nonexistent "executive branch," but instead focuses on collaborative management with department secretaries, congressional committees, and issue networks, to solve national problems.

FURTHER READING

Books

Peri Arnold, *Making the Managerial Presidency,* Princeton, NJ: Princeton University Press, 1986.

Larry Berman, *The Office of Management and Budget and the Presidency, 1921–1979,* Princeton, NJ: Princeton University Press, 1979.

Hugh Heclo, *A Government of Strangers,* Washington, DC: Brookings Institution, 1977.

Stephen Hess, *Organizing the Presidency,* 2nd ed., Washington, DC: Brookings Institution, 1988.

Samuel Kernell and Samuel L. Popkin, eds., *Chief of Staff,* Berkeley, CA: University of California Press, 1986.

Donald F. Kettl and John J. Dilulio, eds., *Inside the Reinvention Machine,* Washington, DC: Brookings Institution, 1994.

Paul Light, *Thickening Government,* Washington, DC: Brookings Institution, 1995.

Robert Maranto, *Politics and Bureaucracy in the Modern Presidency,* Westport, CT: Greenwood Press, 1993.

G. Calvin Mackenzie, *The Politics of Presidential Appointments,* New York: Free Press, 1981.
Richard Nathan, *The Administrative Presidency,* New York: John Wiley, 1983.
James Pfiffner, *The Strategic Presidency,* Chicago: Dorsey Press, 1988.
Harold Seidman and Robert Gilmour, *Politics, Position and Power,* New York: Oxford University Press, 1986.
Richard Waterman, *Presidential Influence and the Administrative State,* Knoxville, TN: University of Tennessee Press, 1989.
Thomas J. Wekon, *The Politicizing Presidency,* Lawrence, KS: University Press of Kansas, 1995.

Documentary Sources

Beyond Distrust, Report of the National Academy of Public Administration, Washington, DC, 1992.
Commission on the Organization of the Executive Branch of Government, *General Management of the Executive Branch,* Washington, DC: Government Printing Office, 1949.
National Commission on the Public Service, *Leadership in America: Rebuilding the Public Service,* Washington, DC: Government Printing Office, 1989.
The National Performance Review, Washington, DC: Government Printing Office, 1993.
President's Committee on Administrative Management, *Report with Special Studies,* Washington, DC: Government Printing Office, 1937.
President's Reorganization Project, *Report: The Reorganization of the Executive Office of the President,* Washington, DC: Government Printing Office, 1977.
The President's Task Force on Government Reorganization, *Report: The President and the Executive Office,* Washington, DC: Government Printing Office, 1967.

NOTES

1. Joan Hamilton, "Babbitt's Retreat," *Sierra,* Vol. 79, no. 4, July/August, 1994, pp. 53–57, 73–78; Timothy Egan, "Interior Secretary Endures Storms from All Directions," *New York Times,* August 26, 1994, p. 3.

2. President's Committee on Administrative Management, *Report with Special Studies,* Washington, DC: Government Printing Office, 1937, p. v.

3. *New York Times,* May 9, 1954, p. 54.

4. Peter Woll and Rochelle Jones, "The Bureaucracy as a Check upon the President," *Bureaucrat,* Vol. 3, April, 1974, p. 18; Lawrence Lessig and Cass R. Sunstein, "The President and Administration," *Columbia University Law Review,* Vol. 94, no. 1, January, 1994, pp. 1–123.

5. *Local 2677, The American Federation of Government Employees v. Phillips,* 358 F. Supp. 60, D.D.C., 1973; *Gaudamuz v. Ash,* 368 F. Supp. 1233, 1973.

6. *Youngstown Sheet and Tube Co. v. Sawyer,* 343 U.S. 79, 1952.

7. *Kendall v. U.S.,* 37 U.S. 524, 1838.

8. *Nader v. Bork,* 366 F. Supp. 104, D.D.C. 1973.

9. *Newsweek,* June 20, 1994, p. 43.

10. For a listing of most of these positions, see *Policy and Supporting Positions* (informally known as the Plum Book), published alternately by the House and Senate Post Office and Civil Service Committees at the beginning of each administration.

11. G. Calvin Mackenzie, "Appointing Mr. (or Ms.) Right," *Government Executive,* April, 1990, pp. 30–36.

12. *The Presidential Appointees' Handbook,* Washington, DC: National Academy of Public Administration, 1985, p. 8.

13. *Leadership in Jeopardy: The Fraying of the Presidential Appointments System,* Washington, DC: National Academy of Public Administration, 1985, p. 17.

14. Christopher Deering, "Damned if You Do and Damned if You Don't," in G. Calvin Mackenzie, ed., *The In-and-Outers,* Baltimore, MD: Johns Hopkins University Press, 1987; Janet Martin, "George Bush and the Executive Branch," in Ryan J. Barilleaux and Mary E. Stuckey, eds., *Leadership and the Bush Presidency,* Westport, CT: Praeger, 1992, p. 41.

15. *Buckley v. Valeo,* 424 U.S. 1, 1976.

16. James D. Richardson, ed., *Compilation of the Messages and Papers of the Presidents, 1789–1897,* Vol. 2, New York: Johnson Reprint, 1969, pp. 79–80.

17. *Shurtleff v. U.S.,* 189 U.S. 311, 1903.

18. *Myers v. U.S.,* 272 U.S. 52, 1926.

19. *Humphreys Executor v. U.S.,* 295 U.S. 602, 1935.

20. *Wiener v. U.S.,* 357 U.S. 349, 1958.

21. Title VI, *Ethics in Government Act of 1978,* 28 U.S.C. sec. 591, passim.

22. *Bowsher v. Synar,* 478 U.S. 714, 1986.

23. Arthur Schlesinger, Jr., *The Coming of the New Deal,* Boston: Houghton Mifflin, 1958, pp. 527–528.

24. Bradley H. Patterson, Jr., "Teams and Staff: Dwight Eisenhower's Innovations in the Structure and Operations of the Modern White House," *Presidential Studies Quarterly,* Vol. 24, no. 2, Spring, 1994, pp. 277–298.

25. Colin Campbell, "The White House and Cabinet Under the 'Let's Deal' Presidency," in Colin Campbell and Bert Rockman, eds., *The Bush Presidency: First Assessments,* Chatham, NJ: Chatham House, 1991, pp. 210–211.

26. Richard E. Neustadt, "Staffing the President-Elect," unpublished memorandum, October 30, 1960, pp. 3–4.

27. Emmette Redford and Richard McCulley, *White House Operations: The Johnson Presidency,* Austin, TX: University of Texas Press, 1986, p. 52.

28. Ann Devroy, "The Shakedown Cruise: Year Two," *Washington Post National Weekly Edition,* April 11–17, 1994, p. 11.

29. Jack Watson, "The Clinton White House," *Presidential Studies Quarterly,* Vol. 23, no. 2, Summer, 1993, pp. 429–436.

30. Brownlow Commission, President's Committee on Administrative Management, *Reorganization of the Executive Departments, Final Report,* Washington, DC: Government Printing Office, 1937, p. 5.

31. Patrick Anderson, *The President's Men,* Garden City, NY: Doubleday, 1969, p. 114.

32. James W. Riddlesperger, Jr. and James D. King, "Presidential Appointments to the Cabinet, Executive Office, and White House Staff," *Presidential Studies Quarterly,* Vol. 16, no. 4, Fall, 1986, pp. 691–699.

33. *New York Times,* April 6, 1983, p. D-7.

34. Robert Rothman, "Few Grace Commission Suggestions Adopted," *Congressional Quarterly Weekly Reports,* November 24, 1984, p. 2990.

35. *National Performance Review,* Washington, DC: Government Printing Office, 1993.

36. *National Journal,* December 11, 1993, p. 2930.

37. After one year, according to the General Accounting Office, 11 recommendations were fully adopted, 95 were partially adopted, and 261 were not implemented. See Stephen Barr, "Report Tallies Progress of Gore's 'Reinventing,' " *Washington Post,* September 7, 1994, p. A-19.

38. The Twenty-Fifth Amendment gives the cabinet certain duties regarding succession to the presidency in cases of disability.

39. Michael Nelson, ed., *Congressional Quarterly Guide to the Presidency,* Washington, DC: Congressional Quarterly Press, 1989, p. 980.

40. Arthur Schlesinger, Jr., *A Thousand Days,* Boston: Houghton Mifflin, 1965, p. 688.

41. Joan Hoff-Wilson, "Richard M. Nixon: The Corporate Presidency," in Fred I. Greenstein, ed., *Leadership in the Modern Presidency,* Cambridge, MA: Harvard University Press, 1988, p. 170.

42. Stanley Mann Doig, *Men Who Govern,* Washington, DC: Brookings Institution, 1967, p. 152.

43. James Pfiffner, "White House Staff versus the Cabinet: Centripetal and Centrifugal Roles," *Presidential Studies Quarterly,* Vol. 16, no. 3, Fall, 1986, pp. 673–674.

44. Thomas Cronin, *The State of the Presidency,* 2nd ed., Boston: Little, Brown, 1980, pp. 276–282.

45. Graham K. Wilson, "Are Department Secretaries Really a President's Natural Enemies?" *British Journal of Political Science,* Vol. 7, no. 3, July, 1977, p. 292.

46. Jeffrey Cohen, *The Politics of the U.S. Cabinet,* Pittsburgh, PA: University of Pittsburgh Press, 1988, p. 144.

47. Graham K. Wilson, op. cit., pp. 273–299.

48. Nelson W. Polsby, "Presidential Cabinet Making: Lessons for the Political System," *Political Science Quarterly,* Vol. 93, no. 1, Spring, 1978, pp. 15–25.

49. James Pfiffner, "Political Appointees and Career Executives," *Public Administration Review,* Vol. 47, no. 1, January/February, 1987, p. 58.

50. "Leadership in Action," op. cit., p. 19.

51. Paul Craig Roberts, *The Supply-Side Revolution,* Cambridge, MA: Harvard University Press, 1984, p. 125.

52. Francis E. Rourke, "Executive Responsiveness to Presidential Politics: The Reagan Presidency," *Congress and the Presidency,* Vol. 17, no. 1, Spring, 1990, p. 4.

53. National Academy of Public Administration, Presidential Appointee Project," *Leadership in Question,* pp. 19–21.

54. Carolyn Ban and Patricia Ingraham, "Short-Timers: Political Appointee Mobility and Its Impact on Political Career Relations in the Reagan Administration," *Administration and Society,* Vol. 22, no. 1, May, 1990, pp. 106–124.

55. Kirk Victor, "Air Waves," *National Journal,* February 19, 1994, p. 418.

56. Patricia Ingraham, "Building Bridges or Burning Them? The President, the Appointees, and the Bureaucracy," *Public Administration Review,* Vol. 47, no. 5, September/October, 1987, p. 430; James Pfiffner, "Political Appointees and Career Executives," *Public Administration Review,* Vol. 47, no. 1, January/February, 1987, p. 61.

57. James Pfiffner, "Political Appointees," p. 63.

58. Carl Brauer, *President Transitions,* New York: Oxford University Press, 1986, p. 150.

59. Ibid., p. 1.

60. Joel Aberbach, Bert Rockman, Robert Copeland, et al., "From Nixon's Problem to Reagan's Achievement: The Federal Executive Reexamined," in Larry Berman, ed., *Looking Back on the Reagan Presidency,* Baltimore, MD: Johns Hopkins University Press, 1990, pp. 175–194.

61. *White House Personnel Manual,* November, 1972.

62. Patricia Ingraham, "Building Bridges or Burning Them? The President, the Appointees, and the Bureaucracy," *Public Administration Review,* Vol. 47, no. 5, September/October, 1987, p. 431.

63. Robert Maranto, op. cit., p. 55.

64. Chester Newland, "A Mid-Term Appraisal—The Reagan Presidency: Limited Government and Political Administration," *Public Administration Review,* Vol. 43, no. 1, January/February, 1983, pp. 1–21.

65. Robert Maranto, op. cit., pp. 110–113.

66. Joel Aberbach and Bert Rockman, "Mandates or Mandarins? Control and Discretion in the Modern Administrative State," *Public Administration Review,* Vol. 48, no. 2, March/April, 1988, pp. 606–612.

67. Maranto, op. cit., pp. 3, 5.

68. Jeff Gerth, "Treasury Department Scolded Regulator in Navy Chief's Case," *New York Times,* July 26, 1994, p. A-13.

69. James Pfiffner, "Political Appointees," pp. 57–65.

70. Robert N. Roberts, *White House Ethics: The History of the Politics of Conflict of Interest Regulation,* Westport, CT: Greenwood Press, 1988.

71. *New York Times,* July 8, 1987, p. B-6

72. The OGE suggested that "misconceptions on the part of Treasury employees" may have contributed to the fact that certain "troubling" discussions between the White House and these officials occurred, rather than concluding that officials consciously attempted to impede a potential criminal investigation—a conclusion that Republicans found unlikely.

73. Maureen Dowd, "Bentsen Aide's Lessons, Penned in Diaries, Emerge Painfully in Public," *New York Times,* p. A-16.

74. Terry Eastland, "Cutler's Lessons for Mikva," *Wall Street Journal,* August 17, 1994, p. A-13.

75. Katy J. Harriger, *Independent Justice: The Federal Special Prosecutor in American Politics,* Lawrence, KS: University Press of Kansas, 1991.

76. Department of Justice Regulations, Section 600.1.

77. "Mr. Starr's Duty to Resign," *New York Times,* August 18, 1994, p. A-22.

78. Stephen Labaton, "Democrats Intensify Push to Oust New Prosecutor," *New York Times,* August 9, 1994, p. 10.

79. Terry Eastland, *Energy in the Executive,* New York: Free Press, 1992, pp. 90–95.

80. *Morrison v. Olson,* 487 U.S. 654, 1988.

81. Terry Eastland, "Cutler's Lessons for Mikva," *Wall Street Journal,* August 17, 1994, p. A-13.

82. Don K. Price, *America's Unwritten Constitution,* Baton Rouge, LA: Louisiana State University Press, 1983, p. 86.

83. Herbert Kaufman, *Are Government Agencies Immortal?* Washington, DC: Brookings Institution, 1976.

84. Daniel P. Franklin, "Why the Legislative Veto Isn't Dead," *Presidential Studies Quarterly,* Vol. 16, no. 3, Summer, 1986, pp. 491–502.

85. Louis Fisher, "The Legislative Veto: Invalidated, It Survives," *Law and Contemporary Problems,* Vol. 56, no. 4, Autumn, 1993, pp. 288–290.

86. The concept was first developed by J. Lieper Freeman, *The Political Process,* New York: Random House, 1955; for a review of the literature on it, see Daniel McCool, "Subgovernments as Determinants of Political Viability," *Political Science Quarterly,* Vol. 105, no. 2, Summer, 1990, pp. 269–293.

87. McCool, op. cit., p. 274.

CHAPTER 11

The President and the Courts

Whenever you put a man on the Supreme Court he ceases to be your friend.

—*Harry Truman*

INTRODUCTORY CASE: ROOSEVELT'S COURT-PACKING PLAN

Franklin Roosevelt's New Deal program was in trouble. On May 27, 1935, the Supreme Court ruled against the president in three cases. In *Schechter v. U.S.,* it invalidated a plan for industry and government cooperation in setting production targets and price levels by ruling that Congress had unconstitutionally delegated its powers over the economy to the president. In *Humphrey's Executor v. U.S.* it ruled that the president did not have the power to dismiss a member of an independent regulatory agency, limiting the presidential removal power. In *Louisville Bank v. Radford,* it invalidated a bill providing relief for farm mortgagors, putting in jeopardy rural banks and farm households.[1] Later, on January 6, 1936, the Court struck twice more at the administration. In *U.S. v. Butler,* the High Court struck down a processing tax used to pay subsidies to farmers who accepted acreage controls or production quotas set by the Department of Agriculture, a decision that ended the government's efforts to stabilize farm production and support farm prices.[2] In *Carter v. Carter Coal Co.,* it struck down a federal tax on coal producers who had not accepted an industry-wide production and conservation code sponsored by the government.[3] Between 1935 and 1937 the Court struck down a total of thirteen major New Deal laws.

Four justices, Willis Van Devanter, James McReynolds, George Sutherland, and Pierce Butler, were ardent opponents of the New Deal. Justices Louis Brandeis, Harlan Stone, and Benjamin Cardozo voted regularly to uphold Roosevelt's program. That left the ultimate decision with two moderates: Chief Justice Charles Evans Hughes and Associate Justice Owen Roberts. None of these justices had been appointed by Roosevelt, who was the first president since James Monroe to serve a term without making an appointment. At times Roosevelt grumbled that McReynolds and his anti-New Deal colleagues would "serve until they're 101."

Yet in the spring of 1937, after Roosevelt's landslide reelection, the Court reversed itself. Hughes and Roberts voted with the three pro–New Deal justices, establishing a 5–4 majority that upheld a major law regulating labor–management relations in *NLRB v. Jones and Laughlin Steel Co.,* and then upheld New Deal unemployment insurance and social security programs.[4] Why had the High Court reversed field? The answer involved presidential pressure on the judiciary. On February 5, 1937, President Roosevelt had introduced a "court-packing" measure to Congress, calling for the appointment of an additional justice to match each justice who had not retired within six months of reaching the age of 70.[5] The maximum number of justices would be set at fifteen, giving Roosevelt six additional appointments.

FDR took his case to the people in a speech at the Democratic Victory Dinner on March 4, and then in a fireside chat on the radio on March 9, in which he accused the Supreme Court of "improperly setting itself up as a third house of Congress—a superlegislature," and of "reading into the Constitution words and implications which are not there, and which were never intended to be there." He called for appointment of younger men with "a present-day sense of the Constitution," who would not "undertake to override the judgment of Congress on legislative policy."[6] Faced with this threat to the independence of the judiciary, the Chief Justice fought back. Hughes sent a letter to the Senate Judiciary Committee indicating that the Court was abreast of its caseload and was operating efficiently. Congress passed a measure offering retiring justices full salary, which prompted Justice Van Devanter on May 18th to announce his forthcoming retirement, eliminating the necessity for FDR to pack the court to obtain a pro–New Deal majority.[7]

Support for court-packing eroded. Roosevelt had not informed members of Congress nor his cabinet (except for Attorney General Homer Cummings, who had suggested the idea to FDR) before introducing his plan, nor had he asked their opinions. Vice President John Garner was infuriated, went down to his ranch in Texas, and remained there on a sit-down strike. "Boys, here's where I cash in," said House Judiciary Committee Chair Hatton Sumners of Texas.[8] Midwestern progressives were opposed, as well as influential liberal governors such as New York's Herbert Lehman. Media coverage was more negative than positive.[9] Public opinion had initially moved toward the president's position after his speeches, but the change in the Court's direction, combined with the criticism of FDR's plan in the newspapers and the announced resignation of Van Devanter, resulted in a majority opposing the plan.[10]

The Senate Judiciary Committee reported negatively, noting that the older judges were the most effective in keeping abreast of their business.[11] It recommended that the plan "should be so emphatically rejected that its parallel will never again be presented to the free representatives of the free people of America."[12] Roosevelt agreed to a compromise: the president would make one additional appointment each year for every justice age 75 or older. But it was too late. On July 20 Vice President Garner gleefully reported to Roosevelt: "You are beat. You haven't got the votes."[13] On July 22, 1937, the court-packing plan was voted down by the Senate, 70 to 20. A combination of Republicans and anti–New Deal Democrats defeated the measure, and even some staunch pro–New Deal legislators defected.

The High Court had not only outmaneuvered the president—the backlash in Congress against his plan made it one of the most costly attempts ever made to try to dominate the judiciary. Nevertheless, Roosevelt ultimately won judicial approval for the New Deal, just as most presidents win their fights with the Court when it comes to issues of public policy backed by a majority. Within thirty months after the court-packing fight FDR had appointed five justices to what would become known as the "Roosevelt Court." The High Court as reconstituted by Roosevelt not only validated Roosevelt's New Deal program, but in the next half-century it almost never struck down economic legislation proposed by a president and passed by Congress. Years after the dust had settled on the court-packing fight, Justice Robert Jackson (a Roosevelt appointee) summed up the irony of the struggle: "In politics the black-robed reactionary Justices had won over the master liberal politician of our day. In law the President defeated the recalcitrant Justices in their own Court."[14]

THE CONSTITUTIONAL DIMENSION

The Constitution, in Article 3, vests all judicial power in the Supreme Court and the lower federal courts. The partial separation of powers and checks and balances, however, give the president responsibilities in law enforcement as well. Moreover, the courts themselves have legislative and executive functions: they interpret the meaning of statutes, executive orders, and administrative regulations. Through their decisions they execute and implement the law in much the same way that the president does when issuing executive orders or directives to the departments.[15] No president can achieve legislative or administrative goals without judicial acceptance or acquiescence.

Presidential Law Enforcement

Presidents claim the mantle of "Chief Law Enforcement Officer." They take an oath to preserve, protect, and defend the Constitution, and execute the duties of their office. They have a constitutional duty to see that the laws are faithfully executed: not only laws passed by Congress, but also federal court decisions. They preserve the "peace of the United States," giving to themselves a "protective power" to defend the institutions of government from mobs or from terrrorist attacks.[16] If the U.S. marshals under the Department of Justice are unable to enforce the laws and decisions of the federal courts, presidents may use federal troops or call the National Guard to federal service, or both, as Dwight Eisenhower did in desegregating Little Rock's Central High School in Arkansas in 1957, and as President Kennedy did in 1961 to enforce a federal court order desegregating the University of Mississippi.

Amnesties and Pardons

Presidents can control the ultimate disposition of any criminal case brought by the government because the Constitution in Article 2, section 2, gives them the power "to grant reprieves and pardons for offenses against the United States except in cases of impeachment." A reprieve is a temporary postponement of a court's sentence, designed to give the president time to consider a request for a pardon. A pardon stops the civil or criminal judicial process from proceeding, and in effect makes a "new person" of the offender. In *Ex Parte Garland,* the Supreme Court held that when a person accepts a pardon, "in the eye of the law the offender is as innocent

In September, 1957, President Eisenhower sent federal troops to guard African-American students enrolled in Little Rock's Central High School, after white mobs prevented federal marshals from enforcing a district court order that the school be racially desegregated.

as if he had never committed the offense." A pardon restores to the offender all civil and political rights.[17]

The framers of the Constitution gave the president the pardon power to prevent miscarriages of justice, and also to provide the president with a way to end treasonous activities such as rebellion. Therefore the power may even be exercised before a criminal indictment has been brought. The pardon power may not be used to nullify the impeachment process; moreover, a presidential pardon used to prevent the execution of the laws would itself constitute an impeachable offense, according to Chief Justice Taft in *Ex Parte Grossman.*[18]

The attorney general provides the president with recommendations about pardons. The attorney general, in turn, relies on the Office of Pardon Attorney, created by Congress in 1891, which supervises consideration of possible pardons and handles the paperwork when a president issues one.

President Washington issued an amnesty to all participants in the Whiskey Rebellion (a struggle by farmers in Pennsylvania against paying federal excise taxes). Jefferson ended prosecutions based on the Alien and Sedition Acts that the Federalists had instituted during the naval war with France, and pardoned those already convicted. During the Civil War President Lincoln issued a proclamation offering a full pardon to Confederate rebels, on condition that they take an oath to support the Constitution, laws, decisions of the Supreme Court, and presidential proclamations. At war's end President Andrew Johnson issued a proclamation excluding certain groups of rebel leaders from amnesty, but pardoning most other secessionists, including Jefferson Davis, president of the Confederate States of America, and members of his cabinet. President Warren Harding issued a pardon to labor organizer and Socialist Party leader Eugene V. Debs for anti-war organizing after World War I, with only one condition: Debs had to travel to Washington and meet Harding in person. President Truman issued amnesty covering 1,500 draft resisters in World War II, and later he issued amnesty to 9,000 individuals who had deserted from the military during the Korean War. Amnesty was also granted by Presidents Ford and Carter for more than 10,000 persons who had resisted the draft during the Vietnam War.

The most unpopular pardon was issued by Gerald Ford to his predecessor, Richard Nixon, for all offenses against the United States in the Watergate scandal. Ford's popularity dropped from 71 to 49 percent within a week after he issued the pardon, and his press secretary resigned in protest. By a 55 to 24 vote, the Senate passed a resolution opposing pardons for other Watergate conspirators.

President Reagan did not offer pardons to any of those accused of violating federal laws in the Iran–contra affair, including Lt. Colonel Oliver North, Rear Admiral John Poindexter, Colonel Robert McFarlane, or the various arms dealers who sold weapons to Iran. President Bush did pardon former defense secretary Caspar Weinberger and several others about to be tried. Lawrence Walsh, the independent counsel investigating the matter, charged that Bush did so to prevent trial proceedings in which he might have faced "searching questions" about his own conduct.[19] Walsh accused the president of showing "disdain for the law" by disregarding the guidelines of the Justice Department that strongly discouraged pardoning before trial.

Military Courts and Martial Rule

Under certain circumstances presidents exercise judicial or quasi-judicial functions, sometimes without sanction of federal courts. During the Mexican-American War, President Polk established military courts to handle the disposition of ships that had been seized for trading with the enemy. During the Civil War, President Lincoln established courts of martial law in several border states, even though the regular federal district courts remained open. These courts tried civilians who had been arrested by military authorities for treasonous activities. In the case of *Ex Parte Milligan,* the Supreme Court ruled that President Lincoln had acted unconstitutionally in establishing such courts when the regular courts of the United States were in operation.[20] But this was not quite the great confrontation between president and court: Lincoln had successfully defied the Court throughout the war; the Civil War had ended when the Court made its decision—and Lincoln himself was already dead.

During World War II, President Roosevelt established a military tribunal to try several German saboteurs who had been caught on Long Island. Because some of them had dual citizenship, their attorneys sought to have the cases transferred to the civilian courts. Roosevelt went ahead with the execution. The Supreme Court, in the case of *Ex Parte Quirin,* decided shortly before the executions that the president had the authority to act, no doubt in recognition of the fact that the president intended to execute the spies with or without civilian judicial acquiescence.[21] Roosevelt also used his executive authority to round up Japanese and Japanese-Americans on the West Coast and transport them to "relocation centers" (i.e., concentration camps) in the deserts. The Supreme Court in several cases upheld the curfews, exclusions, and relocations of Japanese-Americans.[22] It did, however, insist that the individuals in these camps had a right to individual hearings to determine the grounds for their detention.[23] Rather than provide these hearings, Roosevelt ended the detentions. Three decades later, Congress provided partial compensation for the damages they had suffered.

Checks and Balances

Alexander Hamilton observed that the judiciary "is in continual jeopardy of being overpowered, awed, or influenced by its coordinate branches." Presidents and Congress can influence the federal courts through checks and balances. In concert with the Senate, the presidential appointment power changes the personnel of the lower courts and the Supreme Court, and a president can therefore influence Court decisions. In the 1860s the Supreme Court decided that currency issued by the government during the Civil War was not legal tender; several new appointees quickly led to a reversal of that decision. In modern times, liberal justices appointed by Roosevelt, Truman, Eisenhower, Kennedy, and Johnson expanded civil rights and liberties. Conservative justices appointed by Presidents Nixon, Reagan, and Bush implemented a conservative line in matters involving criminal procedure and abortion rights. Overall, three of four justices make decisions that embody the expectations of the presidents who appointed them.[24]

There are other checks and balances. The size of the Supreme Court is determined by statute, and at times presidents have induced Congress to increase or decrease its size. Federalists decreased the size of the Court from six to five members (effective on the next vacancy) to deny Jefferson the chance to make an appointment. Jefferson promptly had the law repealed, and by 1807 had increased the Court to seven members. Nevertheless, the Court under Chief Justice John Marshall retained its independence. The Court expanded to nine justices in 1837 to give the Jacksonians the opportunity to make additional appointments. During the Civil War Congress increased the number from seven to ten to give Lincoln a pro-Union majority. It then decreased the permanent size to seven (by not having vacancies filled as they occurred) when Andrew Johnson became president. Congress passed a law to deny Johnson the opportunity to appoint justices to vacancies—the law even forced Johnson to withdraw a nomination he had already made. When General Grant was elected president, Congress increased the number back to nine. Since then the Court size has remained the same, and after the court-packing controversy of 1937, any attempt by a president to alter it would bring renewed charges of tampering with judicial independence.

Congress may by law overturn federal court decisions that have interpreted laws, but that congressional check in turn may be checked by a presidential veto. In 1988 the Department of Health and Human Services issued a regulation prohibiting counseling about abortion as a means of family planning at clinics accepting federal funds. The Supreme Court, in *Rust v. Sullivan,* upheld the regulation against claims that it violated First Amendment rights.[25] When Congress then passed a law to prevent implementation of these regulations, President Bush vetoed the bill.

The House has impeached eleven federal judges and one associate justice of the Supreme Court. The Senate has convicted and removed five federal judges but has never convicted and removed a member of the Supreme Court. Ever since Jefferson's time, when the Senate refused to convict Justice Samuel Chase, Congress has rebuffed any presidential attempt to instigate legislators to use impeachment powers to reduce the independence of the courts. In 1986 the House Judiciary Committee decided that it would not impeach a federal judge for a judicial decision, because no decision could be considered a "high crime or misdemeanor" under the Constitution.

Enforcing Judicial Decisions

Most presidents pay considerable deference to the opinions of the Court. Charged with seeing that the laws are faithfully enforced, they interpret their duty to mean enforcement of Supreme Court decisions as part of the Supreme Law of the Land. Jimmy Carter, when asked his opinion of the Supreme Court's *Roe v. Wade* decision permitting abortions, indicated that although he was a born-again Christian, "as President I have taken an oath to uphold the laws of the United States as interpreted by the Supreme Court of the United States. So, if the Supreme Court should rule as they have, on abortion and other sensitive issues contrary to my own personal beliefs, I have to carry out in accordance with my solemn oath and duties as President, the ruling of the Supreme Court."[26] Yet Carter, like many presidents, did not always pay such deference to Court rulings. He supported legislation to overturn Supreme Court decisions he did not agree with, such as the decision that permitted searches of newsrooms, because he believed that the searches violated the First Amendment.[27]

Most presidents agree with Thomas Jefferson that they have a right to interpret the Constitution, and that each branch of government has "an equal right to decide for itself what is the meaning of the Constitution in the cases submitted for its action." They sometimes go so far as to argue that Supreme Court decisions can be confined solely to the case at hand, and need not be taken as general principles in guiding or limiting Congress or the White House in future decisions.

Some presidents have intimated that they would not carry out a decision or other order of the High Court or other federal courts, or have actually not done so.[28] Jefferson refused to answer a judicial "subpoena duces tecum" ("come and bring with you") issued by a federal trial judge (in this case, Chief Justice John Marshall on circuit court duty), requiring him to go to Richmond and testify at the trial of his former Vice President Aaron Burr, whom Jefferson had arrested for treason.[29] Jefferson refused to appear, though he sent a letter promising to turn over to the Court an intercepted "cipher letter" (which Burr had written in code), which the government claimed would detail Burr's plans to use a 2,000-man military force he had raised to attack Spanish territories in the Western Hemisphere and seize control of western territories of the United States. In spite of this evidence, Burr was acquitted, which prompted Jefferson to call for Marshall's impeachment.[30] Madison refused a subpoena from a federal court to testify and sent a written response instead. Jackson observed of a Supreme Court decision declaring that Georgia had no jurisdiction over an Indian reservation and requiring the state to release several missionaries it had arrested: "[Chief Justice] John Marshall has made his decision, now let him enforce it." In fact Jackson did not actually refuse to enforce the Court's order, because Marshall's decision was directed at the governor of Georgia and not the national government.[31]

President Lincoln's military commanders refused on many occasions to obey writs of habeas corpus issued by federal courts requiring them to turn over prisoners in their custody to federal marshals.[32] Lincoln even prevented one District of Columbia circuit court judge from issuing such writs by placing him in "protective custody" until he could get Congress to abolish the court. His attorney general made the following observation: "No court or judge can take cognizance of the political acts of the president or undertake to revise and reverse his political decisions."[33] Lincoln also threatened to disobey any federal court order requiring him to return emancipated slaves to their owners, a confrontation that never occurred because the courts did not rule his Emancipation Proclamation unconstitutional. During the arguments over the government's seizure of steel mills in 1952, Truman intimated in a talk with reporters that he might not enforce a decision requiring him to return the mills to the owners, but quickly retreated from that position. In the Watergate controversy Nixon's lawyer James St. Clair argued before the justices that "This matter is being submitted to this Court for its guidance and judgment with respect to the law. The president, on the other hand, has his obligations under the Constitution."[34] The Court ruled unanimously that Nixon had to turn over the evidence; recognizing that his failure to do so would lead to his impeachment, the president complied.

The Reagan administration used an indirect variation. Court decisions, according to its Department of Justice, would be enforced in the particular case at hand, but would not always be taken as the supreme law of the land, binding everyone else. In 1981 the Reagan administration dropped close to 500,000 disabled people from the Social Security program. More than 200,000 were reinstated through appeals to federal courts. To limit the impact of Court rulings, the Social Security Administration, following Reagan directives, announced a policy of "nonacquiescence." It would obey rulings only in the particular cases in which the courts had ruled, rather than apply them to similar situations. Subsequently, the House voted 410 to 1 to instruct the agency to use court rulings as guidance for eligibility. In

1985 a federal judge ordered the administration to abandon the nonacquiescence policy.[35]

Presidents do not accept past cases as binding precedent. They point out that the Court itself has reversed or overruled its own precedents more than 260 times.[36] Although the Supreme Court ruled that Congress could create a national bank in 1819, for example, President Andrew Jackson later vetoed a bill rechartering the bank on the grounds that he believed a national bank chartered by Congress to be unconstitutional. In his message to Congress he argued that "the opinions of the judges have no more authority over Congress than the opinion of Congress has over the judges, and on that point the President is independent of both."[37] Martin Van Buren, long after leaving the White House, argued that a president could not execute a law he believed to be unconstitutional, because he would be violating his oath and opening himself up to impeachment. To carry the logic one step further, Van Buren argued that a president could also continue enforcing a law he believed to be constitutional, even in the face of a judicial decision declaring it unconstitutional.[38]

Presidential Immunity

In most monarchies the king or queen, as the sovereign of the nation, may not be prosecuted or sued in law courts. Presidents are not monarchs and they are not above the law, yet there are sound reasons why the jurisdiction of the courts over the president may be limited, either by the principles of the Constitution or by specific statutory or case law. A president might be distracted by frivolous lawsuits brought by political enemies. If the president commits a crime or damages someone, though, shouldn't he or she have to answer in court? Competing values must be balanced, and in practice that has proven extremely difficult.

The Constitution says nothing about presidential immunity from civil or criminal actions. The Supreme Court ruled that the president has absolute civil immunity, extending to the outer limits of official duties, in *Nixon v. Fitzgerald,* a case involving a Pentagon official who had "blown the whistle" on cost overruns and had later been fired improperly by President Nixon.[39] In the same case, however, the Court also ruled that presidential aides and White House officials had more limited immunity.[40]

Article 1, sec. 3, of the Constitution specifies that impeachment extends only to removal from office, but permits officials to be prosecuted thereafter in the courts. The clause provides a guarantee that an impeachment trial, which might not have due process guarantees, cannot be used for criminal sanctions against a president, and also protects the president from double jeopardy. This has sometimes been asserted to mean that impeachment and removal must precede a criminal prosecution. At the Constitutional Convention there was no discussion of criminal immunity for the president, although limited immunity exists for members of Congress in Article 1 (who may not be arrested going to or from the Capitol or when they are attending its session, or held answerable for anything they say within the Capitol). A federal court of appeals, in *U.S. v. Isaacs,* ruled that a federal judge could be indicted and tried before impeachment proceedings, good grounds to believe a criminal indictment could also be brought against a president before impeachment.[41] The Supreme Court has not ruled on the issue and has sidestepped it on at least one occasion.[42] No sitting president has ever been indicted for a criminal offense, although President Nixon was named an "unindicted co-conspirator" by the grand jury investigating the Watergate scandal.[43]

Can a president be taken to civil court for something done before assuming the office? President John Kennedy was sued in California after his limousine was involved in a traffic accident during the 1960 Democratic Convention. Because he was in the White House when the suit was filed, his lawyers claimed that he was immune from suit. A Los Angeles judge ruled otherwise, and the case was then settled before trial.[44] The issue was presented again in 1994 when a former Arkansas civil servant, Paula Jones, charged that Bill Clinton, while governor of Arkansas, had propositioned and sexually harassed her in a motel room. She sued in federal district court three years later, while Clinton was in the White House, claiming that Clinton had violated her civil rights. President Clinton's personal lawyers, supported by a brief filed by the Department of Justice, argued in *Jones v. Clinton* that a sitting president should have immunity against lawsuits relating to private matters that occurred before his term, or alternatively that the case should be postponed until he was out of office.[45] In a Solomon-like decision, Federal Judge Susan Wright held that the trial would be postponed until Clinton left office, but that pretrial proceedings (depositions of witnesses and discovery of evidence by opposing counsel) could commence while he was in office. Her decision did not grant any immunity to Clinton, as the White House had called for, but was based on Rule 40 of the Federal Rules of Civil Procedure, which permits a federal judge broad discretion "as the courts deem expedient" in arranging trial dates. Clinton then appealed to prevent pretrial fact-finding during his term. Even if his argument were rejected, the lengthy court proceedings ensured that any trial would be delayed until he left office. Meanwhile, to pay the mounting legal fees for his defense, the Clintons established a legal defense fund (a first for a sitting president) that would accept contributions from individuals (with a contribution ceiling of $1,000).

Providing Evidence

Most presidents provide evidence to courts voluntarily. Presidents Ford and Carter provided videotaped testimony in criminal trials (not their own). President Reagan responded to written questions from Lawrence Walsh, independent counsel in the Iran–contra probe. He gave a videotaped deposition in the trial of his former national security advisor John Poindexter. President Bush turned over some of his diary to the Iran–contra counsel. President Clinton and Hillary Rodham Clinton gave depositions to the Whitewater Special Prosecutor about the circumstances surrounding the death of White House staffer Vincent Foster. A president may be compelled by the courts to produce evidence even if he or she claims "executive privilege": President Nixon refused to turn over evidence to the Watergate special prosecutor, but was eventually compelled to do so by the Supreme Court in *U.S. v. Nixon*.[46]

JUDICIAL NOMINATIONS

The Constitution provides that the president nominates and the Senate consents to the appointment of the Supreme Court justices and the federal district and appeals court judges. Few decisions a president makes can have as significant or as long-term an impact on the power and authority of his or her presidency.

Lower Court Nominations

Each year the president nominates approximately fifty judges for district and appeals courts. A two-term president such as Ronald Reagan can fill close to half of all 800-plus (as of 1995) lower-court positions. Nominations are made after the White House and Justice Department consult with members of the president's party in Congress. Since 1840, according to the practice of senatorial courtesy, senators of the president's party from states in which there are vacancies for federal district judgeships have been able to block a Senate vote on a nomination, giving each senator a veto over the nomination of judges from his or her state. Senators suggest nominees to the White House (in consultation with state party leaders) and the president exercises a veto over their choice—a reversal of constitutional expectations. "It's a senatorial appointment with the advice and consent of the President," according to former Senator Robert F. Kennedy.[47] Presidents Reagan and Bush changed that practice and required senators to make three "nominations" for each district judgeship, leaving the final choice up to the White House.[48] When a senator is from the opposition party, he or she is usually given one-quarter of the state's judicial nominations to the federal bench.

Nominations for the U.S. Court of Appeals in each circuit are usually made by the president after consulting with the senators from the circuit's states for a "clearance," but without conceding them the veto power. Because each circuit comprises several states, no one senator can dictate nominations. Yet informally, nominations in the circuit courts are "assigned" to the states, and when a vacancy exists, the senator from that state has a say in filling it. When a "New York" vacancy opened up in the 2nd circuit, for example, New York Senator Daniel Patrick Moynihan was emphatic in seeking the appointment of Jose Cabranes even though Cabranes lived in New Haven, Connecticut. Moynihan referred to him as a "native son" New Yorker for the purpose of pushing through the nomination.

"Becoming a federal judge wasn't very difficult," recalls Griffin Bell. "I managed John F. Kennedy's presidential campaign in Georgia. Two of my oldest friends were the senators from Georgia. And I was campaign manager and special unpaid counsel for the governor."[49] Although a majority of federal judges have been politically active and many have worked for candidates in campaigns, the majority do not come from elective office, and few come from Congress. Republicans are more likely to choose lawyers who have had extensive experience in private practice, while Democrats are more likely to choose legal aid and anti-poverty lawyers, county prosecutors, state judges, and U.S. attorneys. About half the appeals court judges are chosen from the ranks of district judges. The candidates for these nominations are recruited by the attorney general and deputy attorney general, along with input from the White House Counsel's Office, other federal judges, political party leaders, and state and local bar associations.

Judicial nominees are subject to intensive scrutiny. Since 1978 about half the senators have established their own screening committees to ensure that their choices are qualified. The FBI then runs a background check. The Standing Committee on the Federal Judiciary of the American Bar Association (ABA) rates all nominees as follows: extremely well qualified, well qualified, qualified, or not qualified. Eisenhower's attorneys general referred potential nominees to it for prescreening. The practice was discontinued by President Kennedy, though the ABA continued rating nominees once announced. In the 1970s Nixon, Ford, and Carter permitted the ABA once again to engage in prescreening of potential nominees, then Reagan discontinued the practice and permitted screening only of announced nominees. George Bush once again allowed ABA prescreening, as did Clinton. The ABA rating of "well qualified" went to 57 percent of Carter's nominees, 53 percent of Reagan's, 52 percent of Bush's, and 63 percent of Clinton's (in his first two years).[50] Poor ABA ratings do not constitute a roadblock, however: Kennedy got eight "not qualified" nominees through the Senate, Ford one, and Carter three.[51]

Presidents respond to their electoral coalitions: Republicans nominate mostly white males while Democrats look for women and minorities. Republicans nominate more Protestants (around 70 percent) and Catholics (25 percent); Democrats nominate more Jews (around 10 percent).[52] To ensure diversity, President Carter created a United States Circuit Court Nominating Commission and established thirteen nominating panels, one for each appeals circuit, to recommend five candidates for each vacancy. Carter appointed nine blacks and eleven women to the appeals courts. Reagan abolished the panels and gave his Justice Department the responsibility, in consultation with senators: In consequence he appointed only one black and one woman in his first term.[53] Senator Patrick Leahy, a Democrat from Vermont, took the Reagan administration to task for making only five African-American and twelve Hispanic appointments to fill 300 vacancies. He argued that the White House had a "shameful record" in turning the courts into "an enclave of white male exclusivity."[54] Yet his ire was misplaced: It was his own Senate Republican colleagues who had failed to propose minority and women candidates to Reagan. President Clinton reversed the Republican approach: Of his first 143 appointments, 44 were women, 31 were African-American, 12 were Hispanic, one Native American, and one Asian-American.[55]

Presidents nominate members of their own party at better than a ninety-percent rate because the candidates have been selected by their fellow partisans in the Senate. This is important because party affiliation is correlated with judicial decisions. Judges selected by Democratic presidents are more likely to favor defendants in criminal cases, regulatory agencies in conflict with corporations, minorities and women in affirmative action cases, and individuals in civil liberties cases. Judges selected by Republican presidents are more likely to rule for the government in criminal and civil liberties cases, and for corporations in regulatory matters. The Reagan and Bush judges were also more conservative on affirmative action issues and upheld the government more on First Amendment issues.[56]

Presidents choose nominees who share their conservative or liberal ideologies. Ronald Reagan established an Office of Legal Policy (with a staff of twenty) within the Justice Department to screen candidates. It had more than one thousand potential nominees fill out exhaustive questionnaires about their judicial philosophies, and made a litmus test of their views on abortion. Every potential nominee went to Washington for a personal interview. A state judge recommended for the federal bench complained, "I guess most of us have accepted that we're not going to get these judgeships unless we're willing to commit to a particular position, which we think would be improper."[57] The President's Committee on Federal Judicial Selection, consisting of the White House counsel, the attorney general, and the White House chief of staff, went over the results, eliminating some candidates and proposing others, mostly on ideological grounds.[58] By Reagan's second term, moderate Republican senators found many of their choices for judgeships sidetracked, not by Democrats in the Senate, but by Reagan appointees in the Justice Department.[59]

Republican interest groups active in the search for conservative judges included the Federalist Society, the Free Congress Foundation, the Center for Judicial Studies, and the Washington Legal Foundation. The most conservative nominees were opposed by a coalition of liberal groups led by People for the American Way and the Alliance for Justice. It occasionally succeeded in derailing a nomination in the Senate, which had less enthusiasm for Reagan's method of selecting judges because it excluded their participation when it came time to filling vacancies on the courts of appeals. Yet, except for the abortion issue, on which a strong anti-abortion position was required, the practical consequences of requiring ideological tests seemed minimal: Reagan judges, once on the bench, rendered decisions that were only slightly more conservative than decisions by those appointed by other Republican presidents such as Richard Nixon—and their decisions were slightly *less* conservative than judges appointed by President Ford.[60] Clinton's judicial nominees for the most part were experienced former judges and prosecutors, whose lack of strong ideological commitments and centrist positions seemed to match the president who had nominated them.

Supreme Court Nominations

The Constitutional Convention initially intended the Senate to make appointments to the Supreme Court, but the Committee on Style eventually divided the appointment power, giving the president the power to nominate, and appoint "by and with the advice and consent of the Senate." The Constitution also provides that a sitting Supreme Court justice nominated to be chief justice must go through a new confirmation procedure.

Presidents on average make two appointments to the Supreme Court. Half of the nominees have been personally known to the presidents who appointed them. Harry Truman elevated Sherman Minton, a senator who had a desk next to Truman's during World War II. Earl Warren helped Eisenhower win the Republican nomination in 1952. Byron White headed up a "Citizens for Kennedy" operation in the 1960 campaign. Thurgood Marshall served as Lyndon Johnson's solicitor general before receiving the High Court nomination, and Abe Fortas, a Washington lawyer, handled Johnson's personal legal matters and was influential in the circles of power in the capital. In recent years the percentage of nominees known by the president has diminished as fewer "politicians" and more lower-court judges have won appointment to the High Court.[61]

Supreme Court justices themselves sometimes try to influence presidential nominations: on at least sixty-six occasions through 1976 they had made suggestions for filling vacancies.[62] William Howard Taft played a major role in getting Pierce Butler on the Court in 1922.[63] Chief Justice Warren Burger recommended his Minnesota colleague Harry Blackmun to President Nixon, and William Rehnquist lobbied President Reagan on behalf of Sandra Day O'Connor, one of his classmates at Stanford Law School. Presidents are also influenced by their chiefs of staff and other top aides, their attorneys general, and their White House counsels, who are sometimes present when the president conducts his final interviews with those on his "short list."

Presidential appointment, according to Gouverneur Morris, would provide accountability, while Senate consent would provide security against a "monarchical" president conspiring with the judiciary, and would guarantee diversity, because senators would insist that justices come from all parts of the union and represent a variety of interests.[64] Until 1891 geographical representation was ensured by the practice of nominating a new justice from the same geographical circuit to which his predecessor had been assigned. When the circuit-riding of Supreme Court justices ended that year, geographic criteria diminished: in the 1930s there were three New Yorkers on the Court at the same time.

Presidents tend to choose their Supreme Court justices from the lower courts and from political life, as well as from large law firms at the pinnacle of the legal profession. Occasionally they choose a lawyer who has represented labor, the poor or minorities (such as Woodrow Wilson's choice of labor lawyer Louis Brandeis, or Lyndon Johnson's selection of civil rights advocate Thurgood Marshall). The immediate prior appointments of the 108 justices who served through 1994 include twenty-two from state courts and twenty-six from federal courts. Twenty-one had served in the cabinet (including eight attorneys general). Eighteen came directly from private law practice, two from law professorships, and three had been governors. All told, twenty-eight justices had served in Congress, though only six were appointed directly from the Senate and only two directly from the House.

Of the sixteen chief justices of the United States through 1994, five had served as associate justices, one came from the Court of Appeals, five came from the cabinet, two from state government, one from the Senate, and two (including former President Taft) from private life. Republican presidents are likely to choose former state or federal judges or corporate lawyers (they have done so in twenty-nine of thirty-two appointments). Democratic presidents are more likely to lean toward politicians who have served in high executive positions: Since the 1880s they have made seventeen of their thirty appointments outside the judiciary.

Since the late 1940s some presidents have given the ABA Standing Committee on the Judiciary a role in screening potential Supreme Court nominees. Their ratings for Supreme Court justices are "well qualified," "qualified," or "not qualified." Truman and Eisenhower allowed the ABA committee to screen some potential nominees. Presidents Kennedy and Johnson discontinued the practice. After losing two nomination fights in the Senate, Nixon allowed the committee to screen his next nominees, but in 1971 when the ABA deliberations on a nominee deemed "unqualified" were leaked to the press, Nixon discontinued the arrangement. President Ford allowed the committee to screen 15 potential nominees for his one vacancy, but Reagan, Bush, and Clinton discontinued the practice of ABA prescreening for the High Court (while permitting it for lower-court appointments).

Politics often plays a role in nominations. Learned Hand, one of the finest lower-court judges, was denied a seat on the Supreme Court because in 1912 he had supported Theodore Roosevelt's new Bull Moose Party against President William Howard Taft. Chief Justice Taft returned the favor and lobbied against Hand with the White House whenever his name came up as a potential nominee. When Oliver Wendell Holmes retired from the Court in 1932, it was understood that the next vacancy was to go to a westerner to ensure geographic balance. President Hoover, however, considered Benjamin Cardozo, the chief judge of the New York State Court of Appeals, to be the best qualified. He was not only an easterner, but also Jewish, and Hoover was not sure how a second Jewish justice (Brandeis was already on the Court) would be received. However, Cardozo was a Democrat, and the Senate majority was Democratic. Hoover consulted with the Senate's senior westerner, William E. Borah of Idaho. Borah wrote to Hoover that the interests of the people of Idaho would be served by putting the most qualified person on the Court, a signal that he had no objections to Cardozo, whom Hoover then felt free to appoint.

Clinton's Choice

Sometimes presidents are pressured and maneuvered into their choices. Consider the problem facing President Clinton in 1994. With the retirement of Justice Harry Blackmun, Clinton had his second vacancy to fill. His first choice was Senate Majority Leader George Mitchell, who took himself out of consideration (many thought so that he might become Major League Baseball commissioner). Then Clinton wanted his friend from Arkansas, Judge Richard Arnold. There were two problems: First, Arnold was open to a charge of "cronyism"; second, he was suffering from lymphoma (a form of cancer) and his health was open to question. Clinton's next choice was Bruce Babbitt, his secretary of the interior. This would give Clinton the chance to choose a "public servant" rather than a legal scholar, something he wanted for balance on the Court. Again, there were difficulties: Babbitt would be opposed by many western senators antagonistic to his environmentalist views, requiring Clinton to use political capital in trying to get the nomination through; Clinton would also have to replace Babbitt with a new interior secretary, reopening the divisive fight in the Democratic Party between western ranching and grazing interests and environmentalists. At the top of the list of potential nominees for Interior was Bill Richardson, a Hispanic member of the House of Representatives; he would raise the ire of the environmentalists, but if he were passed over, Hispanics would be slighted. Reluctantly, Clinton left Babbitt at Interior.

Once his first three choices had been eliminated, Clinton explored several options. One was to choose Jose Cabranes, the highest-ranking Hispanic jurist in the nation. But Cabranes had little High Court experience, and Clinton had already nominated him for the U.S. Court of Appeals. He had the backing of the Hispanic

Congressional Caucus and the Hispanic Bar Association. The nomination would please Hispanic groups but would expose Clinton to charges that he was choosing an "affirmative action" candidate with less judicial experience than others he might select. Amalya Kearse, an African-American judge on the court of appeals in New York, was open to the same criticism.

Eventually Clinton nominated Stephen Breyer, a federal appeals court judge from Boston. Breyer had met with Clinton when the president was choosing his first nominee, and media accounts suggested they had lacked rapport. He seemed too scholarly, and Clinton had passed him over in favor of Ruth Bader Ginsburg. Now a consensus was forming behind Breyer: He was the choice of Massachusetts senator Edward Kennedy, ranking majority member of the Senate Judiciary Committee, and others in the Northeast, including the majority leader from Maine, George Mitchell. Republican conservatives, impressed with his moderate record on business regulation, informed the president that he would have no problem with the nomination. The ranking Republican on the Judiciary Committee, Orrin Hatch, pledged his support; years before, Breyer had been a staffer on the committee. Senate Minority Leader Robert Dole predicted "smooth sailing" for the nomination. (In a replay of the nomination of Cardozo, the fact that Breyer would be the second Jew on the High Court was irrelevant to these western Republicans.) By selecting Breyer, Clinton avoided controversy and risk, and named a fine jurist, albeit one without the political experience he had wanted in a nominee.

Race, Religion, and Gender

Like their counterparts in the lower courts, until recently the Supreme Court justices have been almost exclusively Protestant white males (ninety-two) from "high-status" backgrounds.[65] Only two women (Sandra Day O'Connor, appointed by Reagan, and Ruth Bader Ginsburg, appointed by Clinton) and two African-Americans (Thurgood Marshall, appointed by Johnson, and Clarence Thomas, appointed by Bush) had served through 1994. Presidents in the nineteenth century began to take religion into account through the choice of the Catholic Roger Taney as chief justice. Dwight Eisenhower's nomination of William Brennan was a recognition of the legitimacy of a "Catholic seat". The custom of a "Jewish seat" began with Woodrow Wilson's nomination of Louis Brandeis in 1916. Thereafter Hoover's nomination of Cardozo and Roosevelt's nomination of Frankfurter to replace Brandeis seemed to ensure continuous Jewish representation: Frankfurter in turn was replaced by Kennedy appointee Arthur Goldberg, who in turn was replaced by Johnson appointee Abe Fortas. Nixon, however, ended the tradition of the "Jewish seat" when he replaced Abe Fortas with southern Protestant Lewis Powell as part of his "southern strategy." Through 1994, seven justices have been Jewish.

Party and Ideology

Since the 1860s, Republican presidents have nominated only eight Democrats and Democratic presidents have nominated only one Republican. Harry Truman nominated Republican Harold Burton, who had served with him on the "Truman Committee" during World War II, when they investigated abuses in the defense industries. A cross-party nomination occasionally is made for a political advantage: Dwight Eisenhower chose liberal Democrat William Brennan to win support among northern Catholics, while Richard Nixon chose conservative Democrat Lewis Powell of Virginia as part of his southern strategy.

Presidents care about the policy orientation and ideology of potential justices. "I should hold myself as guilty of an irreparable wrong to the nation if I should put any man on who was not absolutely sane and sound on the great national policies for which we stand in public life," said Theodore Roosevelt. In justifying the nomination of Democrat Horace Lurton, Roosevelt pointed out that although Lurton was from the other party, "He is right on the Negro question; he is right on the power of the federal government; he is right about corporations; and he is right about labor."[66] Justices do not slavishly follow the policies of the presidents who appointed them. Salmon Chase, who had been treasury secretary during the Civil War, was put on the High Court to uphold the government's wartime currency, yet he wrote the opinion holding the paper "greenback" currency unconstitutional. Oliver Wendell Holmes so outraged President Theodore Roosevelt in a case involving antitrust laws that he told his friends, "I could carve a judge with more backbone than that out of a banana." James McReynolds, one of the most conservative, probusiness justices, had been the choice of Progressive President Woodrow Wilson. Harry Truman, when asked about the biggest mistake he ever made as president, said that it was his appointment of Justice Tom Clark. After Chief Justice Earl Warren marshaled the Court for the decision overturning racial segregation in public schools, President Eisenhower was said to have remarked that appointing Warren was "the biggest damnfool mistake I ever made."[67] One of Chief Justice Warren Burger's earliest decisions upheld lower-court orders to bus students to overcome prior effects of racial segregation—a ruling denounced by the president who appointed him, Richard Nixon. Justices Souter, Blackmun, and Stevens, all appointed by conservative Republican presidents, formed a moderate bloc on the high court in the early 1990s.[68] Justices Kennedy, O'Connor, and Souter all voted to uphold the controversial *Roe v. Wade* right to abortion in subsequent cases, even though they had been appointed by presidents who had gone on record in opposition to such a constitutional right.

Justices want to demonstrate to the legal community and the public that they are independent, and no justice wants a reputation as a presidential flunky. Even the arch-conservative Justice Antonin Scalia voted against Justice Department positions on cases involving the Voting Rights Act, jury selection, and job protection for pregnant workers, thus establishing himself as an independent jurist.

Presidents who choose lower-court judges for the Supreme Court are least likely to be disappointed, because these justices usually continue along the same path they followed in their lower-court rulings.[69] Sandra Day O'Connor, for example, wrote an article for a law review the summer before her nomination in which she argued that in certain criminal cases state judges should be given more leeway and subject to less oversight by federal courts. On the Supreme Court she figured in several major decisions in which the High Court instructed its lower-court judges to do just that.

SENATE ADVICE AND CONSENT

The Constitution requires not only the consent of the Senate to presidential nominations to the High Court, but also its advice. Almost 20 percent of nominations have failed, so Senate consent is no certainty. Candidates who are too extreme ideologically, who are considered mediocre jurists, whose prior career on the bench has created controversy and opposition from important interest groups (such as labor and civil rights organizations), whose personal lives raise questions about their values, and whose conflicts of interest are exposed may face tough going or be defeated.

Informal Consultations

The president consults informally with members of the Senate before making his choice or faces the consequences. President Grover Cleveland nominated a New Yorker without talking to New York Senator David B. Hill, who rallied enough senators to defeat the nomination as a breach of "senatorial courtesy." Cleveland tried again with another New Yorker, again did not consult Hill, and again was defeated. He finally got a nominee through the Senate by choosing Edward White, the Senate Democratic majority leader, who was consented to the day the Senate received his name. Sometimes the President does not accept advice and pays the consequences. In 1987, before nominating Robert Bork, Reagan's attorney general Edwin Meese met separately with Republican and Democratic leaders of the Senate. Senator Joe Biden, chair of the Judiciary Committee, called the meeting "blunt but friendly," but expressed grave reservations to Meese about a Bork nomination.[70] Nevertheless, Reagan went ahead, willing to have a contentious nominee and a floor fight—which he lost.

Confirmation Battles

The first great confirmation battle fought over ideology involved President Wilson's nomination of Louis D. Brandeis in 1916. He was a Boston lawyer who had fought against interlocking corporate directorships and bank control of companies (finance capitalism), and he had championed minimum-wage and maximum-hour laws and the right of unions to collective bargaining. He had been one of Wilson's advisors in developing the New Freedom program of industrial regulation. Unions supported Brandeis. Corporate leaders, the president and several former presidents of the American Bar Association, and former President Taft opposed him. In those days nominees did not appear in person at congressional hearings, but Brandeis's law partner went to Washington and worked with the attorney general to defend Brandeis against the attacks of his critics. The Judiciary Committee waived its rules at President Wilson's request, and a subcommittee held open hearings. Democrats eventually voted on party lines to confirm the appointment in the subcommittee and then in the full Senate. In the 1930s, the tables were turned, as liberal and labor groups opposed the nomination of Charles Evans Hughes to be chief justice, while corporations supported it. This time Republicans had the votes, and Hughes was confirmed.[71]

The Brandeis and Hughes nomination struggles presaged the modern-day ideological battles in the Senate, which culminated with the defeat of conservative Judge Robert Bork after a media campaign by liberal opponents that turned the confirmation process into the equivalent of an election campaign. On the court of appeals since becoming a federal judge in 1981, Bork had compiled the most conservative record of all Reagan appointees. The chair of the Senate Judiciary Committee, Joseph Biden, declared that he would try to defeat Judge Bork's nomination on the grounds that it would push the Supreme Court too far to the right. Critics called for ideological "balance" on the Court.

At the Judiciary Committee Hearings Democrats portrayed Bork as an unprincipled opportunist—an attack on his reputation as a principled conservative jurist. He had testified that he believed in the precedents established by the Court; Senator Edward Kennedy played a tape of a Bork speech at Canisius College in which Bork had said, "I don't think that in the field of constitutional law, precedent is all that important." Bork had testified in his 1982 confirmation hearing for appeals court judge that, when he had been solicitor general in the Justice Department, he had taken steps to ensure the independence of the special prosecutor's staff "to go to court to get White House tapes" after he had fired Archibald Cox. Several of these lawyers, however, testified at the 1987 Supreme Court hearings that Bork had given them no such assurances—again, an attack on his credibility.[72]

During the Bork nomination, public opinion polls made it clear that the public had far more confidence in the Senate than in the president to "make the right decision" on Supreme Court nominees. Seventy percent of the public chose the Senate, compared with 23 percent who trusted the president more.[73] After a week of hearings, public opinion began to swing against Bork. He answered questions about his philosophy and made clear his opposition to Supreme Court opinions on abortion rights, privacy, the poll tax, and "one person, one vote." As public opinion against Bork increased, so did the coalition of liberal groups coming out against him, and, as that coalition grew, so too the number of Senators opposed to Bork. Meanwhile pro-Bork conservative and anti-abortion groups mobilized in his defense.

The nomination battle increasingly resembled a modern political campaign, with various interest groups contributing funding and engaging in grassroots mobilization of supporters. More than $10 million was spent on a media campaign by various groups against Bork, and an equal amount was spent on his behalf to influence public opinion. Radio spots and material for editorials were distributed by Bork's opponents. Each day, immediately after Bork's testimony his opponents distributed critical commentary to reporters covering the hearings. Ultimately, with public opinion turning against him, Bork was rejected by the Judiciary Committee, 9–5, and by the full Senate, 58–42.

In response, President Reagan chose Anthony Kennedy despite his initial vow to choose "another Bork, or worse" as his nominee. Reagan noted that Kennedy "seems to be popular with many senators of varying political persuasion." In a reference to the bruising battles over Bork, he added ruefully, "the experience of the last several months has made all of us a bit wiser."[74]

That experience led President Bush to choose David Souter, an obscure but brilliant state judge from New Hampshire, acceptable to conservatives such as Bush's chief of staff John Sununu, but sufficiently respectful of Court precedents to win Bush's own respect, and sufficiently open-minded on the abortion issue to get by in the Senate without a fight from liberals.[75] President Clinton chose Ruth Bader Ginsburg and Steven Breyer as his first two nominees. They were nominees whose legal skills and centrist positions on most issues would eliminate ideological battles in the Senate. "It's just the way we want it," a White House aide told a reporter, commenting about how dull the Breyer hearings had turned out.[76] No president comes out of a confirmation battle unscathed: His party may split and be put on the defensive, as happened in the Bork case, or his party may stick together and forge a winning coalition but then face the wrath of disaffected voters in subsequent presidential and congressional elections. Most presidents know enough to shy away from those fights.

In spite of some publicized battles, most nominees have smooth sailing and win Senate confirmation by large bipartisan margins. Even in the period of divided government (1953–1993), Republican presidents made thirteen nominations when Democrats controlled the Senate, and most of them were confirmed, including several conservatives. The Senate does not require that the president choose centrist nominees, though some critics have argued that the result is a "one-sided partisanship" in which the president makes ideological and partisan choices while the Senate—its constitutional equal in the nomination process—stands idly by.[77]

The Judiciary Committee and Valence Politics

Between 1791 and 1929 the Senate considered nominations in closed executive session. The only exceptions involved Louis Brandeis and Harlan Fiske Stone, when the Senate suspended its own rules for public debate. The Judiciary Committee began calling nominees to appear before it beginning with Judge Parker in 1930. He declined to testify and was rejected, in large measure for his anti-labor rulings. Beginning with Felix Frankfurter in 1939, all nominees have testified with the exception of Harold Minton in 1949, who declined to testify (and nevertheless was confirmed). Since the 1981 nomination of Sandra Day O'Connor, the first woman nominated to the High Court, the Judiciary Committee's hearings have been broadcast on radio and television.

The media coverage has transformed the hearings from a relatively low-key "insider" process into national agenda politics: the nation is interested in the character and values of the nominees. Candidates polish their image and describe their early lives to resonate with traditional values: Clarence Thomas described his poverty-stricken life in Pinpoint, Georgia; David Souter talked about how he once counseled a friend of his about whether to get an abortion; Ruth Bader Ginsburg talked of her teenage years in Brooklyn; Stephen Breyer discussed his teenage job as a ditch-digger to establish his "just-folks common touch," although he came from an upper-middle-class background and had married a wealthy woman.[78] A president can suffer political damage if a nominee receives a "thumbs down" from the public; conversely, there are few things that can add more to a president's authority than a well-received nomination.

Those opposed to a nomination prepare for hearings by trying to find controversial past decisions (if the nominee is a judge), or "far-out" statements of judicial philosophy, or "gaffes" from speeches, all designed to show that the nominee is an ideologue, a "kook," or someone with a questionable personal life. If the nominee counters with a moderate presentation, opponents will attempt to demonstrate that the nominee has shifted views in a "nomination conversion" and is an unprincipled opportunist. For the nominee, preparations for hearings consist of rehearsals conducted by the Department of Justice and White House counsel in the Old Executive Office Building.

The Judiciary Committee since 1959 has asked nominees their views about specific cases and their judicial philosophy. A controversial nominee, such as liberal Abe Fortas, will find his ideology and judicial philosophy fair game for the opposition. In 1968 Republicans successfully filibustered against the nomination of sitting justice Abe Fortas to be the new chief justice, preventing a vote on his nomination. They hoped to derail the nomination so that Richard Nixon, then running for president, might have the chance to make the nominations if he won. Republican Senator Howard Baker argued that "the Senate must consider . . . their social, economic and legal philosophies." Senator Strom Thurmond agreed that "a man's philosophy, both his philosophy of life and his judicial interpretation, are extremely relevant."[79] Some nominees are willing to talk about past cases, and others, such as Rehnquist and Scalia and Souter, steer clear of discussing cases that involved issues that they might have to deal with on the High Court. Often senators are frustrated when nominees decline to discuss their views on issues such as abortion.

The Committee takes into account the ratings by the American Bar Association's (ABA) Standing Committee on the Judiciary.[80] The ABA committee was first used to evaluate President Eisenhower's nomination of William J. Brennan in 1956. In almost all modern cases, it has given nominees its highest rating, "well qualified." It has never rated a nominee unqualified, even in the case of G. Harrold Carswell, who was defeated by the Senate on precisely those grounds. In the case of Robert Bork, however, four voted "not qualified" and one voted "not opposed." The number of low rankings was unusual, and gave ammunition to Bork's Senate critics.

Most of the time nominees breeze through the Judiciary Committee, which subjects them to little scrutiny. But a nominee need not receive favorable action from it. Clarence Thomas's nomination was forwarded to the full Senate on a 13–1 vote denying him the committee recommendation, yet he managed to win confirmation from the full Senate.

The Odds on Senate Consent

Through 1994 there were 146 nominations (some of the 108 justices received a second nomination for chief justice), and of these, 120 have been approved (of these 3 declined to serve), 11 have been rejected in a Senate vote, and of the others, 6 were withdrawn before a vote, 4 had action postponed by the Senate, and 5 had no Senate action taken.[81] Eight were rejected for lack of qualifications or ethical problems, 15 for partisan reasons, and 3 on the grounds of policy differences with the Senate majority. In the twentieth century only 6 of 61 nominations have been rejected or withdrawn: John Parker (1932); Abe Fortas for chief justice (1968) (which then prevented the nomination of Homer Thornberry for associate justice, also in 1968); Clement Haynsworth and G. Harrold Carswell (1970); Robert Bork and Douglas

Ginsburg (1987). Parker was turned down because of his antilabor decision in lower courts; a vote on Fortas was delayed by a Senate Republican filibuster and he later resigned because of revelations about conflicts of interest (he had received payments from a foundation while on the bench); Haynsworth was defeated because of his segregationist views and the possibility of a conflict of interest (he had not recused himself from cases in which his decisions might have given him a gain in his financial portfolio); Carswell lost because many senators considered him a mediocre legal talent; Bork, because moderate and liberal senators thought he was too partisan and too ideologically conservative; and Ginsburg withdrew his nomination after admitting to casual drug experimentation while in college and while teaching at Harvard Law School. Only one nomination for chief justice, that of Abe Fortas, has ever been turned down, of the seventeen nominations through Rehnquist.

Although Senate consent is no certainty, the odds favor the president. Even after charges of sexual harassment leveled against Clarence Thomas by his co-worker Anita Hill, a full-court press by the Bush administration, including efforts by White House staffers to discredit Anita Hill and her testimony against Thomas, managed to win Senate consent, though the Senate was controlled by the Democrats. Thomas got through in part because a majority of the American public believed him and disbelieved the charges of his accuser, and in part because the Bush White House skillfully brought along conservative and moderate Southern Democrats to join their Senate coalition.

President Bush's achievement with the Thomas nomination is even more impressive considering that when the president's party controls the Senate, better than 90 percent of the nominations are approved; when the opposition controls the Senate, the approval rate drops to 46 percent. Presidential nominations are also more vulnerable in an election year or in the lame-duck period before a change of party in the White House: At such times the opposition party has defeated 11 of 15 nominations, hoping that it might win the White House, or believing that the president-elect of its own party should fill the vacancy.[82] Presidents who are not eligible to be reelected, those not likely to be reelected, and those who succeeded to the office and had not yet been elected in their own right all suffer higher "rejection rates" than elected presidents who were later to win reelection. Presidential popularity is also a factor: more than two-fifths of the nominations of unpopular presidents have been rejected.[83]

Recess Appointments

Under Article 2, sec. 2, clause 3, of the Constitution the president has the power to make recess appointments when the Senate is not in session. When a president does so his appointee serves until the end of the next session. President Eisenhower made recess appointments of Earl Warren, William J. Brennan, Jr., and Potter Stewart. The Senate Democrats, by a 48 to 37 vote, passed a resolution in 1960 stating that recess appointments should not be made "except under unusual circumstances and for the purpose of preventing or ending a demonstrable breakdown in the administration of the Court's business." There is some question about the constitutionality of recess appointments of federal judges and justices: The Constitution states that federal judges serve "on good behavior," a clause that preserves their independence from other branches. Yet a recess appointment is for a limited term that ends with the end of the congressional session. The appointee wants the president to make a new nomination at that point and the Senate to consent—which might lead the recess appointee to compromise his or her judicial independence. Since 1960, no president has made a recess appointment to the Supreme Court.[84]

PRESIDENTIAL POWERS AND THE COURTS

Presidents win more than 70 percent of the time in lower federal courts and almost all the time in the Supreme Court in cases involving national security, diplomatic powers, and presidential war-making. Yet the situation is quite different in domestic matters, in cases involving statutes passed by Congress and presidential determination to evade the intent of Congress. The judicial response more than half the time is to uphold the law and insist that the president (or more likely, his appointees) obey it. As with presidents and Congress, it is not an exaggeration to claim that there are "two presidencies" in the courts.[85]

Political Factors

Federal judges do not make decisions in a vacuum. Their party affiliations and ideologies and experiences may influence them, no matter how dispassionate they wish to be on the bench. Public opinion and outside events also may shape their views, just as it does other decision makers. Political scientists who have studied these factors have concluded that, other things being equal, popular presidents do better in federal court than unpopular presidents, and that judges that they have appointed are more likely to uphold their claims than other judges. Furthermore, Republican judges are more likely to rule for the government in cases involving the exercise of presidential power than are Democratic judges.[86]

Justice Jackson's Threefold Test

In 1952, after President Harry Truman had seized the steel mills, the Supreme Court ruled his action unconstitutional. In a concurring opinion, Associate Justice Robert Jackson set out a threefold test for federal courts to apply in evaluating presidential actions:

- When the president acts pursuant to law, presidential authority is at a maximum and the Court should give the president maximum deference;
- When the president acts without congressional authorization, the Court should scrutinize the action carefully, but "there is a zone of twilight in which he and Congress may have concurrent authority, or in which its distribution is uncertain," and therefore the courts may well uphold the action;
- When the president acts in ways that are incompatible with the express or implied will of Congress, "his power is at its lowest ebb, for then he can rely only upon his own constitutional power, minus any constitutional powers of Congress over the matter."[87]

Marbury v. Madison: The Judiciary versus the President

The Constitution did not explicitly give the Supreme Court the power to overturn laws of Congress and actions of executive officials. The debates at the Constitutional Convention shed little light on the subject. Gouverneur Morris argued that courts "could not be bound to say that a direct violation of the Constitution was law," but others demurred, and Article 3 was silent.

The issue came to the Supreme Court itself in the case of *Marbury v. Madison.* Before surrendering power in 1801, the outgoing Federalist Congress passed a judiciary act increasing the number of federal judges. President John Adams nominated, and the Federalist Senate confirmed, Federalists for these positions. But when Republicans took office, 17 of the commissions remained to be delivered. Secretary of State James Madison refused to deliver them to the appointees, arguing that their delivery (which would allow them to act as judges) was a political act within the discretion of the new administration. The Republican-dominated Congress passed a law that revoked the new judgeships and provided that the Supreme Court was not to meet for a year. It also impeached and convicted a Federalist judge as a warning to the judiciary not to oppose the Federalist program.

One of the Federalist appointees, William Marbury, went to the Supreme Court when it reconvened in 1803 and asked it to rule that Madison had acted illegally and unconstitutionally. He asked the Court for a writ of mandamus, a judicial order compelling Madison to deliver him his commission. Issuing such writs was a power that Congress had granted the Supreme Court in section 13 of the Judiciary Act of 1789. The Supreme Court, dominated by Federalists, was headed by John Marshall, who now had a golden opportunity: he could declare Madison's actions unconstitutional and establish the principle of judicial review of unconstitutional executive actions.

Suppose, though, that Marshall had issued the writ ordering Madison to release the commission to Marbury. Madison would probably have disobeyed it, because the Republicans were looking for an opportunity to discredit and weaken the Federalist-dominated Supreme Court. Marshall would play into their hands if he had come down with a ruling that Madison and Jefferson could flout. If Marshall ruled in favor of the Republicans, however, he would be sanctioning Madison's action.

Marshall avoided both suicidal confrontation or humiliating capitulation through a decision that permitted the Republicans to gain the political victory, but that also established the principle of judicial review. The genius of his decision was that it could not be disobeyed by the president. Marshall used the procedural rules of the Court: Marbury had brought his case directly to the Supreme Court, according to section 13 of the Judiciary Act of 1789, that gave the Court original jurisdiction and empowered it to issue writs of mandamus against national officials. Marshall seized on the jurisdictional question: was Marbury entitled to bring his case in the Supreme Court?

To answer that question, the Supreme Court had to determine if the statute itself was constitutional. Article 3 specifies the original jurisdiction for the Supreme Court and does not mention the kind of case that Marbury brought. Could an act of Congress add to the original jurisdiction of the Supreme Court? Marshall answered no, and held that the congressional act had unconstitutionally added to the original jurisdiction of the High Court. He concluded that section 13 was unconstitutional, stating the principle that "a law repugnant to the Constitution is void." The Supreme Court would not issue the writ against Madison. The beauty of the case, from Marshall's point of view, was that the decision was self-executing: it was enforceable by the justices themselves when they refused to grant Marbury the writ. Marshall had avoided a test with the Jeffersonians but had established the principle that the federal judiciary could strike down laws passed by Congress—a principle much more important to the Federalist judges as they contemplated the possibility of checking and balancing Jefferson's Congress. And there was nothing Madison or Jefferson could do about it.

The Supreme Court must always consider its power problem. How does it maintain its legitimacy and authority against elected politicians who might be tempted to disobey its decisions? In this case Marshall acted strategically for long-range institutional goals and gave up short-term partisan advantage. He knew he could not get Madison to release the commissions, so he gave up the power to issue writs against executive officials (writs that would never be obeyed). He gave up nothing that the Court might reasonably have ever possessed. By doing so, he was able to establish the precedent of judicial review of legislative acts, a power of much greater value to the Court.

The strategy for a president is clear: Any claim of power should be placed in the first category, by arguing that the Congress has explicitly or implicitly collaborated in its exercise and that there is a statutory basis for it; if necessary in the second category, by arguing that Congress has acquiesced in the matter or even invited the president to act. If possible, presidents should avoid the third situation, in which they act against the express or implied will of Congress. And, by all means, presidents must avoid making arguments that seem to diminish the powers of the judiciary itself.

Judicial Responses to Claims of Presidential Prerogative

The federal courts have three choices in dealing with claims of presidential prerogative when a case is presented to them: They can use procedural rules to evade the issue, they can check and balance the president and deny the constitutionality of his or her use of power, or they can affirm the constitutionality of the prerogative.

Federal courts may evade the issue by denying jurisdiction (as Marshall did in *Marbury v. Madison*). They can throw the plaintiff out of court because of lack of standing to bring suit, as judges have sometimes done when individual members of Congress have brought suit against a presidential use of force. Federal courts may insist that the entire House or Senate, not just individual members, must bring the case.[88] They may decide that the issue is not yet "ripe" for judicial consideration, as one judge did when members of Congress brought suit against President Bush before hostilities began in the Persian Gulf.[89] Alternatively, they may decide the issue has already been settled and is "moot," or that Congress has not put itself on record in opposition to the presidential action.[90] In certain national security and military matters, the courts may decide that the issue is a "political question" that is not suited for resolution by the courts, and must be confided to the "political" branches, that is, the president and Congress, to settle. Sometimes, after a lower court has ruled in favor of the president, the high court evades the issues simply by a denial of the petition for certiorari—the petition asking the High Court to review the case already decided by the lower court, leaving the lower-court decision to stand. And sometimes it dismisses a case already decided by the lower courts, without rendering a decision at all, leaving the entire issue without any judicial precedent at all—in which case a presidential prerogative action stands, but without judicial approval.[91]

Federal courts can check the president or other officials acting under White House direction. They can issue a temporary restraining order that prevents a policy from going into effect until the courts can consider it. They can issue permanent injunctions requiring executive officials to desist, though most of the time, as part of their "respect for a coordinate branch," they issue a declaratory judgment that states the law and that gives the president time to comply without judicial order.[92] Alternatively, they can issue writs or judicial orders requiring officials to take actions that the president has ordered them not to do. They can use their power of statutory interpretation to require or forbid actions by executive officials. They may also use their power of judicial review to strike down a presidential action—done only thirteen times by the Supreme Court through 1994. In doing so, they may decide that the president had no authority at all, or had narrower powers than those exercised; or that the powers were not exercised properly.

Most of the time, the federal courts refuse to check the president. Their decisions can be arrayed along a continuum. The weakest decision occurs when the High Court "affirms per curium" a lower-court decision favoring the president. The High Court issues no decision itself, merely affirming what a lower court has ruled. When issuing an opinion, the High Court may say that it finds "no constitutional or legal violation," nor has it found any objection by Congress, and therefore it concludes that it is not prepared to say that what the president has done is unconstitutional. This form of tepid endorsement has been used in situations in which the president managed an issue that had to be resolved, but where the Court did not wish to provide a ringing endorsement, because of the controversial nature of the power.[93] A somewhat stronger endorsement occurs when the Court finds historical precedents for the exercise of power, or when it finds explicit congressional intent to allow the president to act. In a number of cases the High Court upheld presidential power because president and Congress were acting "in concert." Provided both institutions favored the policy and had supported it (by appropriations or legislation), the Court was not prepared to go against their judgment.[94] The best form of endorsement, of course, is when the Court finds an explicit constitutional provision that can be read to uphold the exercise of presidential power, as it finally did in 1926 in *Myers v. U.S.*, when it ruled that the president had the power to remove executive officials.[95]

The federal courts will rule against a president who raises a claim of national security in cases that are clearly domestic conflicts. In *Youngstown Sheet and Tube Co.*, the Supreme Court denied President Truman's contention that a steel strike was a national security matter, when it really involved a domestic dispute between management and labor.[96] In *U.S. v. Nixon*, the High Court ruled that President Nixon had to provide audiotapes and transcripts to the Watergate special prosecutor, because the jury was entitled to every person's evidence—even a president's. It rejected his claim that only the president could decide what materials were to be made available, and ruled that if national security matters were at stake, the presiding judge would determine what, if any, materials, the administration could withhold from the grand jury.[97]

Guarding Judicial Powers

One of the worst mistakes the president or administration lawyers can make when arguing in federal court is to imply or state that the courts lack jurisdiction or competence to judge the constitutionality or legality of a presidential action involving domestic matters. In the steel seizure case, for example, the solicitor general argued that the definition of the emergency provided the justification for the exercise of any powers needed to handle it: In other words, there was no need, or room, for judicial examination of the constitutionality of the president's power as commander in chief. This provoked a sharp exchange with the federal judges, who were unimpressed with the argument that they had no role to play. Similarly, when President Nixon argued in several cases that he was faced with conflicting laws, and that it was his job in seeing that the laws were faithfully executed to decide which ones to execute and which to dispense with, a federal district court responded that Nixon was attempting to usurp the power of the judiciary to make those decisions.[98] In the Watergate scandal, when President Nixon argued that he, and he alone, could decide on the scope of executive privilege, the High Court overruled him and decided that, even if a president did have a valid claim of executive privilege, it would be decided by the courts.[99]

THE COURTS AND THE NATIONAL SECURITY PRESIDENCY

With a few well-publicized exceptions such as the steel seizure and the Watergate cases, the judiciary almost always legitimates the vast role of the president in foreign policy or stays out of the way of its exercise.

Judicial Legitimation

The vast powers of the presidency in foreign affairs were acknowledged by the Supreme Court in *U.S. v. Curtiss-Wright,* decided in 1936, which recognized the "delicate and plenary" powers of the president as sole organ of the American government in foreign affairs. The Curtiss-Wright Corporation was accused by the government of violating an arms embargo imposed by President Franklin Roosevelt on two warring Latin American nations. Roosevelt had imposed the embargo pursuant to a law passed by Congress, but the company argued in its defense that Congress did not have the right to make a broad delegation of embargo authority to the president.

In the course of his decision (upholding the conviction of the company for selling bombers in violation of the embargo), Justice Arthur Sutherland had to find a way to distinguish the broad delegation of power to the president in this case from the delegations of power the court had previously struck down in the New Deal cases. He did so by arguing that the powers of the United States in external affairs derived from the sovereignty of the United States, not just from the written provisions of the Constitution. These sovereign powers, Sutherland went on to say, could be exercised by the president, who had plenary (full) powers over foreign affairs, with only such exceptions (treaty power, regulation of commerce) specified in Article 1 of the Constitution. Sutherland combined the Article 1 powers of Congress to embargo goods with the responsibilities of the president in foreign affairs to uphold a broad delegation of power granted the president by Congress in a foreign affairs issue, even though such a delegation would not have been upheld if the law had dealt with domestic matters.[100] Since then the courts have given the president great leeway in interpreting laws dealing with foreign affairs.

Judicial Restraint

Sometimes the courts simply refrain from deciding an issue involving presidential diplomatic or war powers. In 1978 President Carter terminated a mutual defense treaty with Taiwan, a condition insisted on by the People's Republic of China before it would agree to an exchange of ambassadors. Although the treaty permitted the United States to give Taiwan a year's notice and then abrogate it, the question of who within the U.S. government could exercise that power was open, because the Constitution does not specify how a treaty is to be terminated. There are several possibilities:

- The president has the power to terminate a treaty unilaterally as part of his or her "executive power" and his various diplomatic powers;
- The president can only terminate a treaty with the consent of the Senate, since the treaty must be consented to by the Senate before it may go into force;
- The president has no termination power, but Congress can terminate a treaty by concurrent or joint resolution or by passing subsequent legislation inconsistent with the treaty.[101]

Opponents of the treaty termination in the Senate protested that Carter had usurped its powers. Senator Barry Goldwater sued the president in federal court, which ruled that Carter did not have a unilateral power to terminate treaties. The court held that either Senate or congressional consent to treaty termination was required.[102] The federal court viewed treaty abrogation as a process, which Congress or the Senate should participate in. From that perspective, unilateral presidential abrogation can be considered usurpation of a congressional prerogative.

In contrast, the Federal Appeals Court upheld the right of the president to abrogate the treaty.[103] It compared abrogation to the removal power: although the Senate consents to presidential nominees to office, the president may remove them without the consent of the Senate.[104] The court did not view Senate consent to a treaty as a process, but rather as a hurdle in the checks-and-balances system. Therefore getting out of a treaty would not require consultation either. As a practical matter, a president might need to make a quick decision on national security grounds.

The case finally went to the Supreme Court, which threw it out. One justice said it was not "ripe" for a court to decide, because the Senate had not passed its resolution condemning Carter's action. Four others thought the issue involved a "political question" better left to the Senate and president to sort out. These five justices agreed to dismiss the case, but no majority agreed on the grounds. The practical effect of the Court's ruling, however, was to leave Carter with the authority he claimed to abrogate the treaty.[105]

Judicial Expedience

In 1981, just as it was leaving office, the Carter administration concluded an executive agreement with the Islamic revolutionary government in Iran. The agreement provided for the return of American diplomatic hostages, in return for establishment of an international claims tribunal that would settle Iranian claims against the United States and U.S. claims against Iran.[106] As part of the agreement, the United States agreed that cases pending in U.S. courts would be transferred to the tribunal. The United States and Iran agreed to terminate all legal proceedings in U.S. courts involving claims of U.S. persons and institutions against Iran and its state enterprises, to nullify all attachments and judgments obtained therein, to prohibit all further litigation based on such claims, and to bring about the termination of such claims through binding arbitration. Dames and Moore, a construction company that had done work for Iran and had not been paid, sued President Reagan's treasury secretary Donald Regan, claiming among other things that the executive agreement exceeded the authority of the president because it blocked Dames and Moore from getting justice in U.S. courts.

The Supreme Court determined that the constitutional authority of the president, combined with the International Economic Emergency Powers Act, was sufficient to make the executive agreement constitutional. It reached that conclusion despite the fact that the statute had said nothing about terminating access to U.S. courts. To legitimize the agreement, the court read it to mean that claims were being transferred from district courts in the United States to the claims tribunal, but that ultimate jurisdiction was retained by the federal courts. Therefore, the Supreme Court held, the agreement did not change the jurisdiction of the federal courts (which can only be done by Congress under the Constitution), but merely "the procedural rules" by which the courts would resolve the cases. To reach this astonishing conclusion, Rehnquist had to ignore the plain language of the agreement that specified the jurisdiction of the international tribunal. Yet what choice did he have? The hostages could not have been freed without such an agreement, and having concluded it, the United States was bound to honor its part of the bargain—or else what good would its word be in future situations in which agreement might be necessary?

Rehnquist himself signaled his distaste for his own decision. He noted that the executive acted according to congressional intent and the "general tenor of laws" if not according to a specific statute. He held that congressional legislation in a matter might invite an executive to act to perfect the congressional policy, even without a specific authorization, and pointed to other occasions in which presidents had done so. He noted that Congress had acquiesced in this executive agreement and was raising no challenge to it. Most important, Rehnquist at the end of his decision noted "the necessity to rest decision on the narrowest possible ground capable of deciding the case": He pointed out that the decision dealt only with this case and did not give the president general power to make agreements with other nations and settle claims; that such a power might be recognized by the Court only if it solved a major dispute between the United States and another nation; that the Court would agree only if Congress acquiesced; and that if all those circumstances were present, the Court "was not prepared to say that the President lacked the power to settle such claims."[107] In other words, for reasons of state, the Court would rule an illegal agreement to be legal.

Rehnquist also observed that Dames and Moore could argue in the court of claims that the U.S. government had engaged in an "unlawful taking" of property prohibited by the Fifth Amendment after the proceedings in an international tribunal had been concluded. "The Government must pay just compensation when it furthers the Nation's foreign policy goals by using as a 'bargaining chip' claims lawfully held by a relatively few persons and subject to the jurisdiction of our courts," Rehnquist held.[108]

PRESIDENTIAL WAR POWERS AND THE COURTS

The courts have always acquiesced in the power of the president as commander in chief to use the military as he sees fit. They do so either by directly affirming presidential powers, or by using the doctrine of political questions to excuse itself from settling the issues.

The Supreme Court, in the case of *Johnson v. Eisentrager,* upheld the power of the president as commander in chief to order troops to Europe to meet NATO obligations, even though Congress had not specifically authorized the commitment.[109] In the Vietnam War case of *Massachusetts v. Laird,* it denied a request by the State of Massachusetts for an injunction against the secretary of defense that would have prevented him from sending draftees to Vietnam. Massachusetts argued that the war had been unconstitutionally prosecuted because Congress had not declared war, and it claimed damages because its citizens were being killed and injured in the war (and it would lose tax revenues because of these casualties). The state legislature had even passed a law forbidding its citizens from fighting in a war unless it had been declared by Congress, though of course it had no power to prevent the U.S. government from drafting its young men. The federal district court rejected Massachusetts's claim, arguing that the president had not, as a matter of fact, unilaterally gotten the United States into war in Vietnam: Congress not only had passed the Gulf of Tonkin Resolution, it had also passed legislation for drafting young men into the meliorate, and it had provided appropriations for the war, more than $110 billion at the time the court made its decision.[110] Given the "joint concord" of Congress and the president in prosecuting the war, the court felt no need to decide a "boundary question" of whether Congress should have declared war.

The issue of "joint concord" came up in a second Vietnam War case. In *Mitchell v. Laird,* 13 members of the House of Representatives argued that their power to declare war had been infringed on by the president.[111] The appeals court suggested that "joint concord" might not be so easy to establish. Judges John Wyszanski and David Bazelon argued that Congress might support appropriations for a war even while opposing it, because members would not want to deny U.S. forces the supplies they needed while engaged with the enemy. Congress might vote an initial resolution in support of a president, but might not have the facts at that time to decide on war policy. Nevertheless, the appeals court threw the case out as a political question best left to Congress and the president to resolve.

Several cases have dealt with the power of the President as commander in chief to make battlefield decisions. In *Da Costa v. Laird,* the bombing of North Vietnam had been challenged. An appeals court found that it was a political question, beyond the competence of the courts, because the president as commander in chief had to make a judgment about the need to escalate or de-escalate a war based on conditions on the battlefield.[112] Near the end of the Vietnam War, Representative Liz Holtzman and other members of Congress sued Secretary of Defense James Schlesinger, arguing that the Nixon administration's bombing of Cambodia was illegal and unconstitutional. District Judge Orrin Judd agreed with Holtzman, and had issued a declaratory judgment and an injunction forbidding the government from continuing the war. The government immediately appealed (enabling it to continue bombing Cambodia), and the case went to the court of appeals. In *Holtzman v. Schlesinger* that court relied on the doctrine of political question, holding that bombing of Cambodia was a decision for the commander in chief and Congress to make, not the courts.[113]

THE COURTS AND THE ADMINISTRATIVE PRESIDENCY

In domestic cases presidents and their subordinates are often checked by the courts, primarily because they have not implemented laws according to the intent of Congress.

Checks and Balances

Two cases involving the Nixon presidency demonstrate how the federal courts are able to block presidential actions. The first involved federal workers in the National Treasury Employees Union (NTEU). The NTEU took President Nixon to court to compel him to comply with the provisions of the Pay Comparability Act of 1970. According to this law, the president was required either to submit to Congress a pay increase for federal workers equal to the increase in the private sector for that year, or else to submit a report proposing a lower increase. The president did neither. Instead, relying on provisions of the Economic Stabilization Act of 1971, Nixon argued that his primary obligation was to control inflation, and to do so he would not request any pay increase for federal workers at all. The federal court that heard the case rejected Nixon's contention that the president, and the president alone, had the power to determine the relationship between his obligations under the two statutes. Instead, the court held that it was up to the federal courts to work out Nixon's obligations under the laws, and then to state these obligations according to the Declaratory Judgment Act—a law giving federal courts the power to determine the meaning or applicability of any law at issue in a federal case. The federal court determined that Nixon's obligation was to submit a pay request to Congress, and that nothing in the Economic Stabilization Act passed by Congress could be taken to interfere with that duty.

A second case involved the failure of the Nixon administration to spend funds appropriated by Congress. In the early 1970s the Nixon administration argued that the president had a constitutional power to spend less funds in programs than Congress had appropriated. The Supreme Court, in *Train v. New York,* ruled against Nixon, but did so in a way that did not address Nixon's constitutional claims.[114] The Supreme Court simply ruled that lower-level officials had no choice but to spend all funds Congress had appropriated, unless Congress had put permissive language in the statute. By recasting the issue as one of statutory interpretation, involving lower-level officials dealing with congressional instructions, the Court was able to sidestep the constitutional issue involving presidential power completely.

Although the federal courts sometimes check and balance the president, for the most part they prefer to do it indirectly, by addressing judicial orders to lower officials. The precedent was established, when the court voided an executive order issued by John Adams, that the courts could void an executive order that conflicted with an act of Congress.[115] Similarly, a presidential order to a subordinate involving political discretion must bow to a law passed by Congress requiring officials to perform "ministerial" duties, and if there is a conflict between the two duties, the courts insist that the will of Congress prevail.[116] Yet these powers are rarely used directly against a president: between 1789 and 1956 the Supreme Court declared only fourteen presidential executive orders to be unconstitutional, and even at the height of the "imperial presidency," through 1975, it declared only eight more unconstitutional.[117] Most of these involved cases in which the president made a national security claim in matters that really involved partisan domestic politics, and in which Congress and at least one of the parties strongly opposed the president; in which the president had made a sweeping claim of power and denied that the courts had a right to interfere; and in which the courts believed that the integrity of the constitutional system had been undermined by a presidential action.

Judicial Subgovernment

Day in and day out, federal courts limit the impact of a president on the bureaucracy. They uphold statutory requirements, "ministerial duties," and even agency regulations over and above presidential directives. They prevent presidents and their subordinates from impounding funds or transferring them from accounts without congressional statutory authorization or acquiescence. Congress has detailed prescriptions for administrative officials and has legislated various rights or "mandated requirements" for officials, going so far as to require agencies to expend their resources to comply—even without specific budget authority. These reduce presidential discretion and political direction. The federal courts become part of an "iron quadrangle" that combines with the iron triangle system to further erode presidential power.[118] Congress by law or the courts by their own decisions may give interest groups standing to bring cases, and courts often expand on the statutory entitlements due to members of these groups. A great deal of the administrative law that fleshes out the framework of legislation is written year by year by the federal courts in their decisions.

Presidents try to break through this judicial subgovernment in two ways: First, they appoint federal judges and Supreme Court justices who concede the executive a large role in statute-making and interpretation. Second, their solicitor general in the Justice Department controls the flow of agency litigation in the federal courts: by reviewing initial federal court decisions and preventing agency appeals from lower-court decisions that may have limited the reach of the subgovernment in regulatory matters, the White House can ensure that the decisions of their appointees to the federal bench will stand.[119]

THE LEAST DANGEROUS BRANCH

Both our political culture and our constitutional system make conflict between the president and the federal courts inevitable. The courts ensure that we remain a nation under the rule of law. As Justice Felix Frankfurter once put it, "The Court's authority—possessed of neither the purse nor the sword—ultimately rests on sustained public confidence in its moral sanction."[120] The president, instrument of a national majority, argues that he (and by extension those who voted for him) should have his way in public policy, and when a presidential mandate involves "valence" issues, the stage is set for confrontation.

In national security matters presidents may feel the necessity to act outside the framework of established constitutional and statutory law. When they do, our fear of concentrated power is usually reflected in public support for the Supreme Court when it checks and balances the president. When the Supreme Court ruled against President Nixon in the Watergate scandal, for example, it was reflected in a large increase in public confidence in the Supreme Court—a more than 10-percentage-point rise in public approval.[121] In constitutional collisions, the high court benefits from a reservoir of public respect for its role as constitutional arbiter. A larger proportion of the American public expresses "a great deal of confidence" in the Supreme Court than it does in the presidency.[122]

Even so, presidents usually are upheld by the federal courts in constitutional litigation, especially in national security matters.[123] The federal courts sometimes check and sometimes balance the president, but by and large the checks and balances run the other way: The federal judiciary is shaped by presidents and tends to acquiesce in their priorities.

FURTHER READING

Books

Henry Abraham, *Justices and Presidents: A Political History of Appointments to the Supreme Court*, 3rd ed., New York: Oxford University Press, 1992.

Susan Bloch and Thomas Krattenmaker, *Supreme Court Politics*, St. Paul, MN: West Publishing, 1994.

Cornell Clayton, ed., *Government Lawyers*, Lawrence, KS: University Press of Kansas, 1995.

Louis Fisher, *Constitutional Dialogues*, Princeton, NJ: Princeton University Press, 1988.

Michael Genovese, *The Supreme Court, the Constitution, and Presidential Power*, Lanham, MD: University Press of America, 1980.

Christopher Pyle and Richard Pious, eds., *The President, Congress and the Constitution*, New York: Free Press, 1984.

Robert Scigliano, *The Supreme Court and the Presidency*, New York: Free Press, 1971.

Mark Silverstein, *Judicious Choices: The New Politics of Supreme Court Nominations*, New York: W. W. Norton, 1994.

Reference and Documentary Sources

Paul Freund, ed., *History of the Supreme Court of the United States*, New York: Macmillan, 1969–1974.

Leon Friedman and Fred. L. Israel, eds., *The Justices of the United States Supreme Court, 1789–1971*, 5 vols., New York: Bowker, 1978.

Philip Kurland and Gerhard Casper, eds., *Landmark Briefs and Arguments of the Supreme Court of the United States: Constitutional Law*, Washington, DC: University Publications of America, 1975.

NOTES

1. *Schechter v. U.S.*, 295 U.S. 495, 1935; *Humphrey's Executor v. U.S.*, 295 U.S. 602, 1935; *Louisville Bank v. Radford*, 295 U.S. 555, 1935.

2. *U.S. v. Butler*, 297 U.S. 1, 1936.

3. *Carter v. Carter Coal Co.*, 298 U.S. 238, 1936.

4. *NLRB v. Jones and Laughlin*, 301 U.S. 1, 1937; *Seward Machine Co. v. Davis*, 301 U.S. 548, 1937; *Helvering v. Davis*, 301 U.S. 619, 1937.

5. James MacGregor Burns, *The Lion and the Fox,* New York: Harcourt Brace and World, 1956, pp. 291–315; William Leuchtenburg, "The Origins of Franklin D. Roosevelt's 'Court-Packing' Plan," *Supreme Court Review,* 1966, pp. 347–400.

6. *New York Times,* March 10, 1937, p. 15.

7. Louis Fisher, *Constitutional Dialogues,* Princeton, NJ: Princeton University Press, 1988, p. 215.

8. Burns, op. cit., p. 294.

9. Gregory A. Caldeira, "Public Opinion and the U.S. Supreme Court: FDR's Court-Packing Plan," *American Political Science Review,* Vol. 81, no. 4, December, 1987, pp. 1139–1153.

10. Caldeira, ibid., p. 1147.

11. U.S. Senate, Report no. 711, 75th Congress, 1st sess., 1937.

12. Ibid., p. 23.

13. Burns, op. cit., p. 308.

14. Robert Jackson, *The Struggle for Judicial Supremacy,* New York: Alfred A. Knopf, 1941, p. 196.

15. Max Farrand, ed., *The Records of the Federal Convention of 1787,* New Haven, CT: Yale University Press, 1937, Vol. 2, p. 34.

16. Henry P. Monaghan, "The Protective Power of the Presidency," *Columbia University Law Review,* Vol. 93, no. 1, January, 1993, pp. 1–74.

17. *Ex Parte Garland,* 4 Wall 333, 1867; *Klein v. United States,* 80 U.S. 128, 1872; David Gray Adler, "The President's Pardon Power" in Thomas Cronin, ed., *Inventing the American Presidency,* Lawrence, KS: University Press of Kansas, 1989, pp. 209–235.

18. *Ex Parte Grossman,* 267 U.S. 87, 1925.

19. Lawrence E. Walsh, Independent Counsel for Iran/Contra Matters, *Fourth Interim Report to Congress,* February 8, 1993, p. 22.

20. *Ex Parte Milligan,* 71 U.S. 2, 1866.

21. *Ex Parte Quirin,* 317 U.S. 1, 1942.

22. *Hirabayashi v. U.S.,* 320 U.S. 81, 1943; *Korematsu v. U.S.,* 323 U.S. 214, 1944.

23. *Ex Parte Endo,* 323 U.S. 283, 1944.

24. Robert Scigliano, *The Supreme Court and the Presidency,* New York: Free Press, 1971, p. 147.

25. *Rust v. Sullivan,* 111 S. Ct. 1759, 1991.

26. *The Public Papers of the Presidents,* Washington, DC: Government Printing Office, 1981, President Carter, Vol. 4, p. 2354.

27. Louis Fisher, op. cit. p. 27.

28. Robert Scigliano, "The Presidency and the Judiciary," in Michael Nelson, ed., *The Presidential System,* op. cit., pp. 454–455.

29. *U.S. v. Burr,* 25 Fed. Cas. 187, 1807.

30. Thomas Fleming, "The Trial of Aaron Burr," *Constitution,* Vol. 6, No. 2, Fall, 1994, p. 16.

31. *Worcester v. Georgia,* 6 Peters 515, 1832.

32. *Ex Parte Merryman,* 17 F. Cas. 144, 1861.

33. Scigliano, in Nelson, op. cit., p. 456.

34. *U.S. Law Week,* July 16, 1974.

35. Mark Silverstein and Benjamin Ginsberg, "The Supreme Court and the New Politics of Judicial Power," *Political Science Quarterly,* Vol. 102, no. 3, Fall, 1987, pp. 385–386.

36. Terry Eastland, *Energy in the Executive,* New York: Free Press, 1992, p. 175.

37. Henry Richardson, ed., *Messages and Papers of the Presidents,* Washington, DC: Bureau of National Literature and Art, 1900, Vol. 2, pp. 576–591.

38. Martin Van Buren, *Inquiry into the Origin and Course of Political Parties in the United States,* New York: Hurd & Houghton, 1867, pp. 342–343.

39. *Nixon v. Fitzgerald,* 102 S. Ct. 2690, 1982.

40. Kathryn Lindbeck, "Presidential Immunity—Supreme Court Attaches Absolute Immunity to the Presidential Office, *Nixon v. Fitzgerald,* 102 S. Ct. 2690," *Southern Illinois University Law Journal,* 1983, no. 1, pp. 109–126.

41. *U.S v. Isaacs,* 493 F. 2d 1124, 1974.

42. *Mississippi v. Johnson,* 71 U.S. 475, 1867, pp. 500–501.

43. George E. Danielson, "Presidential Immunity from Criminal Prosecution," *Georgetown Law Review,* Vol. 63, no. 5, May, 1975, pp. 1065–1069.

44. *Bailey v. Kennedy,* July 19, 1962, Superior Court, Los Angeles County, Los Angeles, CA.

45. Robert Bennett, Counsel for William Jefferson Clinton, brief filed August 10, 1994; Drew S. Days 3rd, Solicitor General, Department of Justice, "Statement of Interest," filed with Federal District Court, August 18, 1994.

46. *U.S. v. Nixon,* 428 U.S. 683, 1974.

47. David M. O'Brien, op. cit., p. 52.

48. Edwin Meese, *With Reagan,* Washington, DC: Regnery Gateway, 1992, p. 317.

49. O'Brien, ibid., p. 52.

50. Al Kamen, "Building Up The Bench, Finally," *Washington Post National Weekly Edition,* September 12–18, 1994, p. 15.

51. Robert G. Scigliano, *The Supreme Court and the Presidency,* New York: Free Press, 1971, pp. 109–123.

52. Sheldon Goldman and Thomas Jahinge, *The Federal Courts as a Political System,* 3rd ed., New York: Harper and Row, 1985, p. 54.

53. W. Gary Fowler, "Judicial Selection under Reagan and Carter: A Comparison of Their Initial Recommendations Procedures," *Judicature,* Vol. 67, December, 1983–January, 1984, pp. 265–283.

54. *New York Times,* February 13, 1987, p. A-17.

55. Stephen Labaton, "President's Judicial Appointments: Diverse, but Well in the Mainstream," *New York Times,* October 17, 1994, p. A-15.

56. Jon Gottschall, "Reagan Appointments to the United States Court of Appeals," *Judicature,* June/July, 1986, pp. 48–54; Robert Carp, Donald Songer, C. K. Rowland, et al., "The Voting Behavior of Judges Appointed by President Bush," *Judicature,* Vol. 76, April–May, 1993, pp. 298–302.

57. Lincoln Caplan, "Annals of Law—The Tenth Justice," *The New Yorker,* August 10, 1987, p. 31.

58. Sheldon Goldman, "Reorganizing the Judiciary: The First Term Appointments," *Judicature,* April–May, 1985, pp. 315–317.

59. Howard Kurtz, "The Wheels of Judgeships Grind Slowly," *Washington Post National Weekly Edition,* June 8, 1987, p. 34.

60. David Whitman, "Reagan's Conservative Judges Are Singing a Different Tune Now," *Washington Post National Weekly Edition,* August 24, 1987, p. 23.

61. Robert Scigliano estimated it at 60 percent as of 1973; Scigliano, *The Supreme Court and the Presidency,* op. cit., p. 95.

62. Henry J. Abraham and Bruce A. Murphy, "The Influence of Sitting and Retired Justices on Presidential Supreme Court Nominations," *Hastings Law Quarterly,* Vol. 3, no. 1, Winter, 1976, pp. 37–63.

63. David Danelski, *A Supreme Court Justice Is Appointed,* New York: Random House, 1964.

64. David Strauss and Cass Sunstein, "The Senate, the Constitution and the Confirmation Process," *Yale Law Journal,* Vol. 101, no. 7, May, 1992, pp. 1491–1524.

65. Thomas Halper, "Supreme Court Appointments: Criteria and Consequences," *New York Law Forum,* Vol. 21, 1976, pp. 563–584.

66. Ibid., p. 196.

67. Steve Neal, *The Eisenhowers,* Wichita, KS: University Press of Kansas, 1984, p. 382.

68. "Voting Patterns," compiled by William Casey and Lucy Shackelford, in *Washington Post National Weekly Edition,* July 11–17, 1994, p. 31.

69. David W. Rohde and Harold J. Spaeth, *Supreme Court Decisionmaking,* San Francisco, CA: W. H. Freeman, 1976, pp. 107–109.

70. Linda Greenhouse, "White House Involves Senate in Powell Succession," *New York Times,* July 1, 1987, p. A-16.

71. Paul A. Freund, "Appointments of Justices: Some Historical Perspectives," *Harvard Law Review,* Vol. 101, no. 5, March, 1988, pp. 1146–1163.

72. Nina Totenberg, "The Confirmation Process and the Public: To Know or Not to Know," *Harvard Law Review,* Vol. 101, no. 5, March, 1988, pp. 1213–1229.

73. New York Times/CBS Poll, *New York Times,* September 15, 1987, p. A-27.

74. *New York Times,* November 11, 1987, p. B-10.

75. David J. Garrow, "Justice Souter: A Surprising Kind of Conservative," *New York Times Magazine,* September 25, 1994, p. 64.

76. Linda Greenhouse, "Why Breyer's Hearing Was Meant to Be Dull," *New York Times,* July 17, 1994, p. E-4.

77. David Strauss and Cass Sunstein, op. cit., pp. 1491–1524.

78. Neil Lewis, "For This Court Choice, Policy Is Passion," *New York Times,* July 11, 1994, p. A-13.

79. Quoted in Joseph A. Califano, Jr., "The '68 Version of the Bork Debate," *New York Times,* September 14, 1987, p. A-19.

80. Henry J. Abraham, *Justices and the Presidents: A Political History of Appointments to the Supreme Court,* 3rd ed., New York: Oxford University Press, 1992, pp. 36–37.

81. A complete listing of nominees and actions taken by the Senate through 1988 is contained in Appendix I of John Massaro, *Supremely Political,* Albany, NY: State University of New York Press, 1990, pp. 199–203.

82. Lawrence Baum, *The Supreme Court,* Washington, DC: Congressional Quarterly Press, 1981, p. 45.

83. Thomas Halper, "Senate Rejection of Supreme Court Nominees," *Drake Law Review,* Vol. 102, no. 1, September, 1972, pp. 102–113.

84. Louis Fisher, op. cit., p. 142.

85. Craig R. Ducat and Robert L. Dudley, "Federal District Judges and Presidential Power during the Postwar Era," *Journal of Politics,* Vol. 51, no. 1, February, 1989, pp. 98–118.

86. Ibid., p. 111.

87. *Youngstown Sheet and Tube Co. v. Sawyer,* 343 U.S. 579, 1952.

88. *Lowry v. Reagan,* 676 F. Supp. 333, D.D.C. 1987.

89. *Dellums v. Bush,* 752 F. Supp. 1141, D.D.C. 1990.

90. *Crockett v. Reagan,* 558 F. Supp. 893, D.D.C. 1982.

91. *Goldwater v. Carter,* 481 F. Supp. 949; 617 F. 2d 697; 444 U.S. 996, 1979.

92. *National Treasury Employees Union v. Nixon,* 492 F. 2d. 587, 1974.

93. *Dames and Moore v. Regan,* 452 U.S. 654, 1981.

94. *Hirabayashi v. U.S.,* 320 U.S. 81, 1943; *Korematsu v. U.S.,* 323 U.S. 214, 1944.

95. *Myers v. U.S.,* 272 U.S. 52, 1926.

96. *Youngstown Sheet and Tube v. Sawyer,* 343 U.S. 579, 1952.

97. *U.S. v. Nixon,* 418 U.S. 683, 1974.

98. *National Treasury Employees Union v. Nixon,* 492 F. 2d 587, 1974.

99. *U.S. v. Nixon,* 418 U.S. 683, 1974.

100. *U.S. v. Curtiss-Wright,* 399 U.S. 304, 1936.

101. *La Abra Silver Mining Co. v. U.S.,* 175 U.S. 423, 1899.

102. *Goldwater v. Carter,* 481 F. supp. 949, 1979.

103. *Goldwater v. Carter,* 617 F. 2nd 697, 1979.

104. *Myers v. U.S.,* 272 U.S. 52, 1926.

105. *Goldwater v. Carter,* 444 U.S. 996, 1979.

106. "Declaration of the Government of the Democratic and Popular Republic of Algeria Concerning the Settlement of Claims by the Government of the United States of America and the Government of the Islamic Republic of Iran."

107. *Dames and Moore v. Regan,* 452 U.S. 654, 1981.

108. Arthur S. Miller, "Dames and Moore v. Regan: A Political Decision by a Political Court," *UCLA Law Review,* Vol. 29, nos. 5–6, June-August, 1982, pp. 1104–1128.

109. *Johnson v. Eisentrager,* 339 U.S. 763, 1951.

110. *Massachusetts v. Laird,* 451 F. 2nd 26, 1971.

111. *Mitchell v. Laird,* 488 F. 2nd 611, D.C. Cir., 1973.

112. *Da Costa v. Laird,* 448 F. 2nd 1368, 2nd Cir., 1971.

113. *Holtzman v. Schlesinger,* 484 F. 2nd 1307, D.C. Cir., 1973.

114. *Train v. New York,* 420 U.S. 25, 1973.

115. *Little v. Bareme,* 2 Cranch 170, 1804.

116. *Kendall v. U.S.,* 37 U.S. 524, 1838.

117. Robert Scigliano, "The President and the Judiciary," in Michael Nelson, ed., *The Presidency and the Political System,* Washington, DC: Congressional Quarterly Press, 1984, p. 408.

118. Martin Shapiro, "The Presidency and the Federal Courts," in Arnold J. Meltsner, ed., *Politics and the Oval Office,* San Francisco, CA: Institute for Contemporary Studies, 1981, pp. 141–157.

119. Cornell Clayton, "Separate Branches—Separate Politics: The Case for Judicial Enforcement of Congressional Intent," *Political Science Quarterly* (in press).

120. *Baker v. Carr,* 369 U.S. 186, 1962.

121. Gregory A. Caldeira, "Neither the Purse Nor the Sword: Dynamics of Public Confidence in the Supreme Court," *American Political Science Review,* Vol. 80, no. 4, December, 1986, p. 1213.

122. In 1981, for example, 29 percent expressed confidence in the Supreme Court, and only 24 percent in the presidency, down from 51 percent for the Court and 41 percent for the presidency in 1966. See Seymour Martin Lipset and William Schneider, *The Confidence Gap,* New York: Free Press, 1983, pp. 48–49.

123. Craig R. Ducat and Robert L. Dudley, "Federal District Judges and Presidential Power during the Postwar Era," *Journal of Politics,* Vol. 51, no. 1, February, 1989, pp. 98–118.

CHAPTER 12

Presidential Budgeting

You don't need more taxes to balance the budget. Congress needs the discipline to stop spending more, and that can be done with the passage of a constitutional amendment to balance the budget.

—Ronald Reagan

INTRODUCTORY CASE: PRESIDENT REAGAN UPENDS THE BUDGET PROCESS

Republicans in Congress were ecstatic. Newly elected President Ronald Reagan, addressing Congress in January, 1981, proposed cuts of $41.3 billion from former President Carter's final budget, and a total of $130 billion in cuts for his first three years in office. Democrats, controlling the House of Representatives, mapped a defensive strategy. Reagan might have big plans, Democratic House leaders thought, but sooner or later he would have to compromise.

If Reagan had worked within the existing budget process the Democrats would have been right. Since 1974, Congress had usually passed a First Budget Resolution in the spring with overall goals for spending, followed by thirteen separate spending bills, then a Second Budget Resolution in the fall, and finally a Reconciliation Bill just before the start of next fiscal year to keep spending under the ceilings of the Second Budget Resolution or adjust the ceiling upward. Such a lengthy budget process, with its piecemeal approach to spending bills, guaranteed that Reagan's proposals would be stalled, gutted, or modified.

Instead of playing by the existing rules of the game, Reagan decided to change them.[1] He put his entire program into an "early reconciliation bill" that, if passed, would bind congressional committees to make his proposed spending cuts.[2] All his cuts would be considered at one time through a single bill that he could make the focus of national agenda politics. By simplifying the budget process, he felt he could get public opinion to support him on its substance.

Reagan's early reconciliation bill passed the Republican-controlled Senate with ease. In the House, the Democratic leadership proposed that the bill be split into six separate measures. Instead of allowing members to cast a single vote for or against Reagan's entire program, they wanted a separate vote on different categories (i.e., defense, social welfare) that would make legislators susceptible to constituency and interest group pressures. The issue would turn from cutting the deficit (Reagan's issue) to maintaining popular programs (the Democrats' issue). With his high standing in the polls and with public concern about mounting deficits, however, Reagan was able to put together a bipartisan coalition of Republicans and conservative Southern Democrats to support him on rules changes. He held sixty-nine meetings in the Oval Office with members of both parties, and more than sixty Democrats met with him in the three weeks preceding the vote. Southern Democrats were brought into the fold by Reagan's promise that if they voted his way, the White House would not campaign against them in the 1982 midterm elections. "I could not in good conscience campaign against any of you," Reagan told a group of them.[3] To keep moderate Republicans in line the national committee warned them that unless they voted for Reagan's plan, they would receive no campaign funds from the party.[4] All 190 Republicans and 63 Democrats voted with Reagan.

President Reagan capitalized on his election mandate, exploited Democratic divisions, and kept his own party unified. His budget proposals were highly visible and dramatic—and therefore newsworthy. His domination of the national agenda raised the stakes for his party: Reagan created the equivalent of a parliamentary "vote of confidence," because no member of his party could afford to undercut the president so early in his first term on such an important bill.[5] In doing so he had also reversed the role of the president from chief innovator of new programs into "Curtailer in Chief." Reagan was able to dominate budget politics because he had created a new coalition more interested in cutting back on spending than in providing new government benefits. When the House and Senate Conference reported a final bill, it repealed or amended 436 laws and affected 266 of the 1,310 spending accounts in the federal budget, and was projected to cut $35.2 billion from that year's anticipated deficit.

Although Reagan's early reconciliation is a case study of presidential success, subsequent Reagan budget proposals were usually dead on arrival on Capitol Hill. The coalition was temporary: by the fall of 1981 even the Republicans deserted Reagan when he called for additional cuts in Social Security programs. After 1982, Republican defeats in the House gave the Democrats greater party control and ended the influence of the conservative coalition. In the Senate, moderate Republicans followed their own spending priorities and distanced themselves from Reagan's proposals. For the rest of Reagan's presidency he never again enjoyed nearly the influence he had in budget politics in his first year. Reagan was later to complain that Congress paid no attention to his recommendations. In truth, he is not the only president ever to have felt that way. Presidential control of the budget process requires a rare combination of public support, coalition building in Congress, and inventiveness.

THE EXECUTIVE BUDGET

To budget is to govern. To determine what goes into a budget, and the process by which a budget becomes law, is to answer the key question of politics: "Who gets what, when, and how." A budget determines government activities for the coming year, specifies when they will take place, and puts a price tag on them; above all, it decides among alternatives and among claims for scarce resources. Perhaps because the stakes are so high, presidents are granted so few budget powers.

Constitutional Powers

Presidents have no specified budget powers granted in Article 2 of the Constitution. Their influence is felt through "the executive power" that enables them to set general lines of policy, and the veto power, which allows them to negotiate with Congress about spending bills. The constitutional powers to tax and spend are assigned to Congress in Article 1, which specifies that "No money shall be drawn from the Treasury, but in consequences of appropriations made by law." What formal budget powers the president possesses are granted by Congress—and what Congress gives, it can also take away.

The Premodern Budget Process

Until 1921 budget politics were dominated by cabinet secretaries and congressional committee leaders. As part of his duty to report to Congress on the State of the Union, the president would annually submit to Congress a *Book of Estimates* consisting of spending requests compiled by each department after consultation with its bureaus. Congress was uninterested in seeing presidential budget requests, and even refused to look at a budget compiled by President Taft in 1912. Congress would ask for the opinion of the treasury secretary (but not of the president) about agency requests. It would then pass separate appropriations bills, prepared by appropriations committees in the House and Senate, and other bills providing budget authority reported to it by standing legislative committees. A few presidents, such as Hayes and Cleveland, acted as "Guardians of the Treasury" by vetoing excessive appropriations, but most went along with the system and signed the appropriations into law.

The premodern budget process was wasteful and corrupt. It was dominated by interest groups with influence in both the departments and the committees. It provided the "pork" for congressional logrolling and favor trading. Nowhere in the national government was there any attempt to set priorities, make tradeoffs among competing claims on public funds, or match up the need for revenues with anticipated expenditures. In short, the system had budget outcomes, but not budget policies.

The Modern Budget Process

In response to mounting deficits and the Progressive movement's call for "businesslike" practices in government, Congress in 1921 superimposed a more coherent system of budgeting over the department-committee nexus. It passed the Budget and Accounting Act of 1921, which allowed the president (assisted by a newly created Bureau of the Budget located in the Treasury Department) to "assemble, correlate, revise, reduce, or increase the estimates of the several departments or establishments."[6] The president was required to prepare an Executive Budget and transmit it to Congress within fourteen days after it convened for its annual legislative session. Department secretaries were expected to defend the president's requests when they testified before appropriations committees.

After passage of this law, bureau and agency heads no longer had direct access to congressional committees. Only rarely would Congress pass a law requiring particular agencies to submit their estimates to Congress as well as to the president, or requiring the president to include the original agency requests in his budget.[7] In 1994, for example, the Social Security Administration was authorized to submit its budget requests directly to Congress rather than go through the presidential budget agency.

Perhaps the most important impact of the 1921 reforms was the path not taken: Congress rejected parliamentary-style budgeting. President Wilson's secretary of the treasury David Houston had recommended that an extraordinary two-thirds majority be required to modify a presidential budget request—and got nowhere with his idea. Congress retained the final say about budgeting; its appropriations committees were assigned most money bills through other reforms in the 1920s. Their modifications to the president's budget were given great weight by Congress when it passed spending measures.

Assisting the President with Budgeting

The 1921 law created an agency to prepare the budget estimates for the president. Known as the Bureau of the Budget (since 1971 it has been called the Office of Management and Budget, or OMB), it was located within the Treasury Department until 1939, but functioned as a presidential agency from the start.[8] President Harding's first budget director, Charles Dawes, instructed all departments to submit their budget requests to the bureau (rather than to Congress) for inclusion in the Executive Budget.[9] It reviewed each agency request, line by line, then revised the initial figures in line with presidential priorities. It also reviewed and revised the testimony of department secretaries when they appeared before the appropriations committees, and coordinated White House efforts to influence the decisions of these committees, including threats to veto appropriations bills if they exceeded presidential requests.[10] Once funds had been appropriated by Congress, it controlled departmental spending through quarterly allotments. It could order the reprogramming of funds (transferring money from one activity to another) within an agency or across agency lines with the concurrence of Congress. In the 1970s President Nixon made the budget bureau one of the most important presidential agencies in setting overall policy. Its directors spent as much time cultivating legislators and negotiating budget agreements with Congress as they did creating the president's budget.[11]

Budgeters versus Bureaucrats

Two years before the president's budget is sent to Congress, the OMB sends departments a budget call, which instructs them to plan on expansion or contraction of their programs on the basis of overall forecasts about revenues and presidential priorities. The OMB has a number of options in dealing with each department: It may suggest small increases, it may limit increases to adjustments for inflation (the current services budget), it may freeze expenditures (the zero-base option) along with a freeze on new activities and new hiring, it may require targeted or across the board cutbacks, or it may require a reduction in nonessential activities.

Bureaus estimate what it would cost to maintain programs at existing levels by factoring inflation into their new budget—these figures constitute their *current services budget.* They then request a fair share of any projected increases in spending for their programs, or try to ward off any cuts or minimize their impact. Most agencies budget incrementally, rarely asking for more than 10 percent more than their previous budget, and hardly any suggest cuts on their own initiative.[12] After coming up with valid estimates, agencies often pad their requests in anticipation of OMB cuts. They include programs and services for key committee leaders so they can build a congressional and interest group coalition that can help them withstand OMB austerity pressures. If they are forced to accept OMB spending reductions, they may leak to the media proposed plans to cut popular programs. The Coast Guard and Border Patrol claim they will not be able to stop illegal immigrants. The Postal Service suggests it will eliminate Saturday mail deliveries. The Park Service announces shorter hours at tourist sites and less police protection in national parks. The strategy is to get the public to protest against the cutbacks and pressure OMB to drop them.

Departmental officials review agency requests. Most departments make significant changes, adding to some programs and cutting others, even though most overall departmental budgets do not change much from year to year.[13] When the national government expands its role, as it did from the 1930s through the 1970s, agencies that asked for major increases were likely to get them approved in the president's budget.[14] When overall expenditures for programs are capped or cut, agencies that disregard the prevailing budgetary winds and ask for large increases may be penalized, and officials may be reprimanded by the White House.

Departments submit their proposed budgets to OMB for review. These traditionally included *language sheets,* which estimated spending authority requested from Congress, and *green sheets,* which estimated annual outlays (a combination of past and present spending authority). Today agencies transmit computerized equivalents (spreadsheets) to the OMB. Examiners from OMB's Budget Review Division then make recommendations for every agency and program. They look for the padding and suggest management reforms, or even consolidation of agencies and functions. Their recommendations and a tentative agency budget prepared by OMB examiners are sent to the OMB Program Associate Directors, political appointees who make sure the recommendations are acceptable to the White House.

The OMB creates its own budget for each department. The budget director and top White House aides then hold "review sessions" so every cabinet secretary can make final arguments to restore cuts. Sometimes secretaries are given one last chance to appeal directly to the president. Truman, Ford, Carter, and Clinton listened to these appeals carefully, acting like judges deciding cases. Other presidents, like Nixon, Reagan, and Bush, used an intermediate "appellate division" consisting of the OMB director and the White House chief of staff to screen appeals. Presidents rarely reverse decisions of their budget directors: to do so would simply invite more appeals.

The final OMB product, submitted to Congress each year by the president along with a special message, is the Executive Budget, more formally known as the *Budget of the United States Government,* though in fact it is nothing of the sort. It is actually the set of requests the president makes to Congress for budget authority. It provides current and projected budget figures for every agency and activity of the national government (secret intelligence activities excepted).[15]

Valence Politics

"I like those numbers," Lyndon Johnson is reported to have told his budget director, indicating increased spending for programs that he knew would be politically popular; "but I hate those," he added, pointing to the overall spending for his budget, which for the first time exceeded $100 billion—a symbolic number Republicans could use against him. The White House focuses primarily on the overall size of the budget, particularly on the rate of spending increases and the projected deficit, so that the president can avoid the label "Big Spender."

The increased size of deficits (Figure 12.1) and the overall national debt have left presidents politically vulnerable. Postwar presidents through Lyndon Johnson were fortunate to govern in periods of economic expansion. During their terms, tax receipts often outpaced expenditures, and there was money for new domestic programs. Since then Presidents have had to budget in leaner times, with recessions, stagflation (high inflation combined with low economic growth), and weak recoveries or massive restructuring of the economy limiting the increase in tax receipts. Democratic and Republican presidents since Carter have found that budget politics have been transformed into "no fun, no win" situations. "He was puzzled and irritated by the fact that the choices were so brutal," OMB official W. Bowman Cutter observed about Carter, adding that "he grew to hate the budget process."[16]

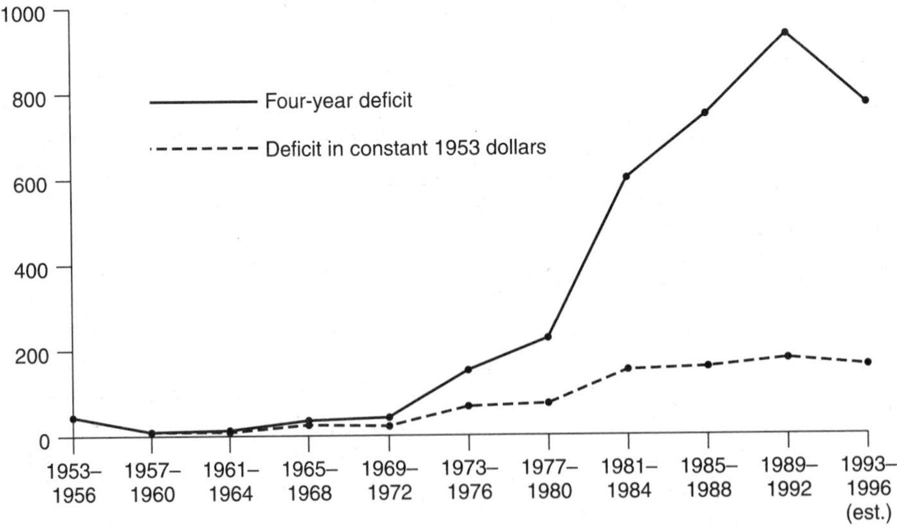

Figure 12.1 Deficits by presidential term, 1953–1996, in billions of dollars.
Source: Council of Economic Advisers, *Economic Report of the President, 1993,* Washington, DC: Government Printing Office, 1993, p. 435.

President Clinton's meetings with advisors during budget preparation degenerated into tirades in which he railed against congressionally imposed spending caps, and sarcastically commented on how he had been forced to submit a "Republican budget." Clinton got only 60 percent of his "investment" initiatives for job training, national service program, and educational reforms. Tradeoffs were required: to free up money for new initiatives for young people and welfare reform, Clinton had to ask for cuts in programs providing reimbursement to the elderly poor for heating bills, and cuts in mass transit subsidies for big cities—and even then Congress rejected some of these proposed transfers. In the 1994 midterm elections, House Republicans proposed massive spending cuts and major reforms in the budget process in their "Contract with America," and public opinion polls indicated that many voters, believing that Clinton and the Democrats were "Big Spenders," cast their ballots for the Republicans. House Republicans then proposed cuts of $185 billion over five years to pay for their promised tax cuts, ending all possibility that Clinton could find funding for new domestic initiatives.

Presidents sometimes use accounting tricks to avoid passing crucial milestones: Johnson postponed some expenditures into the next fiscal year to avoid spending more than $100 billion in 1964 (with an election approaching); Reagan did the same thing two decades later when the debt approached the $1 trillion mark. Clinton cemented negotiations on his first budget cuts by agreeing to a "Budget Reduction Trust Fund," no more than a gimmick to win votes with no real budget consequences, as well as a national commission to consider further cuts in entitlement programs (those involving payments to individuals, such as Social Security and Medicare). Presidents use current "buzzwords" with favorable valence when they propose spending increases. In the 1950s President Eisenhower supported the National *Defense* in Education Act and the National *Defense* Highway System to defuse conservative opposition to building classrooms and roads. In the 1990s, commented one Clinton administration official, "we use [the word] *investment* to describe everything we like."[17]

Presidents usually claim that if Congress follows their recommendations the budget will soon be in balance. These forecasts of balanced budgets (usually within five years) are reminiscent of the queen in Lewis Carroll's *Through the Looking Glass,* who promised her subjects "jam yesterday and jam tomorrow," though never jam today. Presidents promise fiscal discipline because it comports with deep-seated feelings of the electorate; but they do not propose spending measures that would actually achieve that goal because that same electorate also wants tax cuts and supports most of the programs run by the national government. The voters are ideologically conservative about deficits, but in most elections (1994 excepted) they have been operationally liberal about big government.[18] The result is that deficits climb even as presidential rhetoric promises restraint: in 1981 Reagan promised that the budget would be in balance by 1985; in 1985 he promised it would happen by the end of his second term; in 1988 he said it would balance in 1991. In fact, he ran up $1.5 trillion in additional debt over his two terms by increasing defense expenditures and lowering taxes. He did make cuts in some social welfare programs, but his own budget director, in a book entitled *The Triumph of Politics,* pointed out that he did not propose big cuts in politically popular social programs.[19] Bush forecast a balanced budget within five years after the 1990 budget summit. He ran up $930 billion in total debt, with deficits approaching $300 billion annually by the time he left office.

President Clinton departed somewhat from the pattern. A self-proclaimed "New Democrat," Clinton wanted credibility with financial markets, Congress, and the American people. He appointed Leon Panetta and Alice Rivlin as budget director and deputy director, respectively. Both of these "deficit hawks" had criticized his campaign program, "Putting People First," because it did not go far enough in promising budget reduction. These appointments gave Clinton some credibility when he submitted his budget deficit package with all the bad news up front. He promised lower deficits if his cuts were enacted, but even if Congress passed his plan in its entirety, he warned, deficits would only be cut to more manageable size, not eliminated entirely. In fact, he managed to cut the deficit three years in a row (moving it into the $150 billion annual range), the first time that had been accomplished since 1948. Yet even his plan anticipated deficits rising in the late 1990s to the $200 billion range because he could not bring himself to recommend enough cuts to stabilize the size of projected deficits. Clinton defended his budgets, arguing that his approach would reduce the deficit as a percentage of gross national product from the 4.9 percent ratio at the end of the Bush administration to 2.1 percent by the year 2000.

The Legacy of Split Government

In the 1980s Republicans abandoned their traditional stance on fiscal prudence and balanced budgets and instead proposed large tax cuts. Although they claimed that these cuts would produce additional revenues that would make up for the tax re-

President Clinton meeting with his advisors on ways to control health care costs. From left to right, Alice Rivlin from the Office of Management and Budget, Vice President Gore, President Clinton, and Treasury Secretary Robert Rubin.

ductions, in reality budget officials like David Stockman, OMB director, understood that deficits would increase greatly. Nevertheless, the Republicans found it good politics to advocate lower taxes. Meanwhile, in Congress, Democrats could not stave off Reagan's tax cuts and defense increases, but they were able to keep most domestic programs intact, even after a round of Reagan budget cutting succeeded in 1981.

Split government did not produce stalemate, but rather a set of contradictory and fiscally unsustainable policies. A Republican president could forge a coalition for tax cuts and defense spending increases while Democratic congressional leaders could forge a coalition for domestic program increases, enabling each party to get what it most wanted. Republican presidents from Nixon through Bush could criticize "Big Government" and promise cutbacks in spending, but most of the huge runup in deficits and the national debt occurred in their administrations—partly because of their own policies (tax cuts and defense increases) and partly because of actions of the Democratic Congresses. The steepest increases in domestic entitlements (welfare, food stamps, Medicare, and Social Security) and intergovernmental programs (federal grants to states in such areas as highways and hospitals) occurred in the Nixon–Ford presidencies; the largest increases in defense spending and health care in the Reagan–Bush presidencies. Between 1950 and 1980, Democratic presidents ran average deficits of $19.1 billion, and Republican presidents ran deficits averaging $24 billion (all figures in constant 1982 dollars).[20] Presidents Reagan and Bush presided over a huge increase in the size of the annual deficits, and an increase in the total national debt from under $1 trillion to more than $3.5 trillion. Total debt during the Reagan–Bush years rose from 32 percent of the annual gross national product to 60 percent. (This would be the equivalent of saying that, in a family that had an annual income of $50,000, their total debt went from $16,000 to $30,000.) Much of the blame for this situation can be traded to the dysfunctions of split government.[21]

When split government ended in 1993, the good news for the Democrats was that their party controlled the entire national government: the bad news was that voters could and did hold them responsible for not bringing down the deficit sharply enough and not redeeming a campaign pledge for middle income tax cuts. Split government returned in 1995, as Republicans gained control of Congress. At that point, it seemed clear that the party that could deliver on its budget proposals would have an excellent chance of dominating the national government through the remainder of the 1990s—and perhaps beyond.

CONGRESS AND THE EXECUTIVE BUDGET

Presidents and members of Congress found themselves on the defensive with voters because of mounting deficits and debt. To get themselves off the hook, legislators promoted comprehensive reform of the budget process in the 1980s and early 1990s—reforms that reduced the policy-making powers of both president and Congress.

A Budget Glossary

Fiscal Year. A twelve-month period beginning October 1 and ending September 30 (distinguished from the calendar year, which begins January 1). The fiscal year, abbreviated FY, is numbered according to the month in which it ends, so that FY 1995 ends September 30, 1995.

Receipts. The total income that the federal government raises in a fiscal year. Receipts come from the following sources: personal, corporate, and capital gains taxes; social security and unemployment insurance payroll taxes; excise taxes (e.g., on whiskey, tobacco, and gasoline); estate and gift taxes; customs duties; fees for services; sale of property; and borrowings by the Treasury.

Tax Expenditures. Receipts that the Treasury foregoes because of provisions in the Internal Revenue Code passed by Congress. These include "enterprise zones," which provide tax breaks to businesses who locate and hire people in inner-city depressed areas; deductibility for mortgage payments and property taxes; contributions to charitable organizations; and pension plans in which interest or capital gains are not taxed until benefits are paid on retirement.

Budget Authority. Permission granted by Congress to the U.S. Treasury to pay obligations incurred by government agencies. Budget authority includes the following:

- *Total obligational authority:* the sum that the government can spend in current and future fiscal years;
- *Prior year authority:* money allocated in previous years but not yet spent;
- *New obligational authority:* money requested in the president's budget for the coming fiscal year.

Outlays. The total expenditures paid in cash or check by government agencies in a fiscal year. Outlays include direct payments to individuals, such as social security or unemployment insurance or welfare checks; spending on government programs; grants to state and local governments; payments to private organizations for participating in programs; interest payments on the national debt. Outlays are a mixture of current and prior year obligational authority.

Controllable versus Uncontrollable Outlays. Controllable outlays involve discretionary spending by government agencies. Uncontrollable outlays involve legal claims by people to government payments or services, so that agency spending is mandated by law and not subject to discretionary cutbacks by agency officials. Uncontrollable outlays are required in entitlement programs such as Social Security, Medicare, Medicaid, welfare, veteran's benefits, food stamps, and military and civilian pensions. (Of course, Congress can always control the uncontrollables by changing the laws regarding entitlement to services or payments.) Approximately 75 percent of the national budget consists of uncontrollable expenditure outlays.

Deficit or Surplus. In any fiscal year the government runs a surplus when receipts are greater than outlays and a deficit when outlays exceed receipts.

National Debt. Not to be confused with a fiscal year deficit, the national debt is the sum total of money owed by the U.S. government to those who have loaned it money and hold obligations in the form of U.S. Treasury bonds, Treasury bills, Treasury notes, or other U.S. obligations. The national debt is serviced by paying interest on these obligations each fiscal year.

Impoundment. The power claimed by presidents to refuse to spend money appropriated by Congress.

Line-Item Veto. A provision that permits the president to veto individual budget items in an appropriations bill, rather than veto the entire measure.

Rescission. A cut in previously appropriated spending, requested by the president and approved by Congress. *Expedited rescission* is a rule that Congress be required to act on rescission requests made by the president.

Sequester. A mandatory across-the-board cut in budget authority for government programs if Congress approved budget authority in a fiscal year that exceeded specified budget-reduction targets.

Appropriations Committees

Presidential requests in the *Budget of the United States Government* are converted by Congress into budget authority, and executive officials as well as lobbyists for iron triangles and issue networks know that figures in the presidential budget are not written in cement—if the president proposes, it is Congress that disposes when it comes to spending. Revising the president's proposals has become the single most important congressional function. Since 1980 more than half the annual roll-call votes in the House and Senate have dealt with budget matters.[22]

Until the 1970s Congress dispersed power to many committees in a "bottom-up" system. Revenue bills were reported to Congress by the tax committees (House Ways and Means and Senate Finance), and spending measures were considered by the appropriations committees and some legislative committees. The appropriations committees would take the president's budget and "crosswalk" its numbers into thirteen appropriations bills, each considered by one of its subcommittees. Between the 1950s and the 1970s, members of the House Committee prided themselves on their role as "guardians of the Treasury." In the House, Republicans combined with border and Southern Democrats to fashion a conservative bipartisan majority. "No subcommittee of which I have ever been a member has ever reported out a bill without a cut in the budget," boasted one member.[23] The Senate would then restore many of these cuts, and its decisions would come closer to the final numbers passed by Congress.

Budgeting was "non-zero sum," with overall expenditures for domestic programs increasing incrementally each year. True, Congress often cut the numbers submitted in the president's budget, but this should be put in perspective: these "cuts" were made against the *increases* already proposed by the president from the preceding year's spending levels, so that even with Congressional "cuts," agency expenditures rose gradually, albeit at a lower rate than recommended by the White House.

In the 1970s the pattern changed. Presidents Nixon, Ford, and Carter recommended smaller increases and sometimes recommended significant cuts in agency budgets. The House Democratic committee majorities responded by championing many agency programs against proposed cutbacks. No longer functioning as "Guardians of the Treasury," the House appropriations committees saw the budget as a storehouse of goodies to be dispensed to other members of Congress, a trend that intensified in the 1980s. "When you handle money," observed House Appropriations Committee Chair Jamie Whitten, Democrat from Mississippi, "you're in the strongest position you can be in, in Congress."[24] Legislators got on subcommittees that had jurisdiction over programs that directly benefited their districts. Hardly anyone went onto the committee to cut spending.[25] One subcommittee with jurisdiction over the Department of the Interior, for example, received requests from 260 House members to include their pet projects in an appropriations bill in 1984. "There is no such thing as a fiscal conservative when it comes to his district or his subcommittee," Reagan's budget director David Stockman observed.[26]

Funding defense installations, highways, hospitals, airports, and public works projects have always helped members get reelected. But by the 1970s legislators also used job training, education, health, anti-crime, anti-drug, child care, and community development programs as a form of "human resources porkbarrel," creating their own political machines with the aid of community organizations that received federal grants. (The subcommittees would often put specific "directives" as to how funds should be spent into reports accompanying the spending bills, rather than in the laws themselves.) The Senate Appropriations Committee in the 1970s and 1980s continued to counterbalance the House, but the roles were reversed: a bipartisan coalition on the Senate committee often moderated the increases in domestic spending proposed by the House committee, dominated by liberal Democrats. After 1995 the pendulum shifted again, as the House appropriations subcommittees were dominated by conservative Republicans, who once again embraced deep cuts, while the Senate committee, more moderately inclined, became the forum for "appeals" from House actions.

The Standing Committees and "Backdoor" Financing

Power to budget was not only dispersed into subcommittees of the appropriations committees; half of the president's budget requests were considered by standing legislative committees. These committees might provide the following kinds of spending authority to agencies in their jurisdiction:

- *Contract authority:* permission for an agency to contract for goods or services with public agencies or private companies. Congress pledges its full faith and credit to provide funds as needed to meet contractual obligations incurred.

- *Loan or credit authority:* permission for an agency to make a loan or extend credit to individuals, corporations, cooperatives, and state, local, or foreign governments. Sometimes an agency may buy loans made by a bank to individuals, which makes more loan money available to the lending institution (i.e., the student loan program).
- *Loan guarantee authority:* an agency is permitted to guarantee bonds issued by, or a loan made to, a local government or corporation. The guarantee enables near-bankrupt institutions (Chrysler, Lockheed, and New York City in the 1970s) to borrow money, using the backing of the U.S. government.
- *Borrowing authority:* an agency may borrow funds from the Treasury or the private bond markets to finance its operations, with interest and principal to be repaid by fees collected. Certain government corporations, such as the Tennessee Valley Authority, are granted this borrowing power by Congress.

Granting Budget Authority

Appropriations and standing legislative committees that report bills granting budget authority to agencies have several options. They have the Current Services Estimate in the Executive Budget, a document that tells them what it would cost simply to continue funding agencies at existing levels. They have the president's budget requests. At their hearings they can find out what the agency or department really wants. They have policy alternatives prepared for them by congressional staff agencies such as the Congressional Budget Office, the General Accounting Office (GAO), or the Office of Technology Assessment. And they have recommendations of outside interest groups and issue networks.

Committees mark up the president's budget and usually substitute their own figures. In 1994, for example, a Congress controlled by his own party almost doubled Clinton's requests for the Immigration and Naturalization Service, ordering it to add border patrol agents and put them in "hot spots" along the border. It gave Clinton small increases in social programs such as Head Start, while vastly increasing funding for scientific and technological agencies such as the National Institute of Standards and Technology. Committees often attach restrictions, prohibitions, exemptions, and waivers, and other provisions that specify how funds may or may not be spent: these *limitation riders* generally start with the language "no funds appropriated may be used for the purpose of" and then specify the restriction. Committees mark up appropriations and other budget authority bills in ways that provide tangible benefits for members. Projects are funded by horse trading for votes and political benefits, rather than because of high benefit-to-cost ratios. Agencies shift from presidential priorities to respond to congressional pressures. They disperse their facilities into areas where costs are high and coordination is difficult, because by relocating into certain congressional districts they gain support from committee members.

Limiting Budget Authority

On the basis of its appropriations powers and its "necessary and proper" powers, Congress has passed measures regulating spending.[27] These include the *Miscellaneous Receipts Statute,* which prevents the President from raising funds privately and spending them on activities not authorized by Congress: The law requires that all funds in the possession of any official be turned over to the Treasury.[28] The *Anti-Deficiency Act* prohibits officials from spending more than Congress has authorized.[29] Even if the president believes that Congress has violated the Constitution or treaty obligations or other laws by failing to appropriate funds for critical activities, he has no constitutional power to spend money on his own prerogative to uphold the Constitution or enforce the laws.[30]

Congress enforces its spending laws through the GAO, an independent agency accountable to it. The comptroller general of the GAO audits the spending accounts of government agencies and may disapprove expenditures that have not been authorized by Congress. The GAO's informal discussions or formal rulings have an affect on presidential and departmental interpretation of laws. The judiciary usually backs up the GAO's interpretations.[31]

A president may rely on his own prerogative power to spend funds without an appropriation in an extreme emergency, as Lincoln did at the start of the Civil War, and throw himself later on the mercy of Congress and the people. Presidents have argued that in the event Congress failed to appropriate funds for a mandated constitutional function, the president could do so on his own prerogative, and have argued that it would constitute a "political question," presumably requiring the federal courts to abstain from any ruling on the legality or constitutionality of the president's actions.[32]

Presidential Vetoes of Spending Measures

Presidents may threaten to veto spending measures, claiming that they will bust the budget, a strategy employed by presidents since James Monroe vetoed public works bills in the 1820s. Although presidents threaten often, they rarely act: the veto was used against appropriations fewer than thirty times between 1945 and 1993. Although few vetoes cast against appropriations have been overridden, presidents rarely can mount a credible veto threat, and they accept many bills with numbers far above their original amounts. Their threats are not taken seriously because they have to accept or reject an entire spending measure, and a Congress intent on spending can craft controversial bills so that they contain many more items a president wants than items he opposes. When presidents do veto appropriations, it is because they know that one-third of the members of one chamber will uphold it. Sometimes more than one-third of the members of a chamber will pledge in advance to support a presidential veto, giving the president some bargaining chips in negotiations with a spending committee.

Presidents may win some veto battles, but often lose the political wars that follow. Gerald Ford successfully vetoed many spending bills in 1976, but they came back to haunt him in the presidential campaign, and a similar fate awaited George Bush after he brandished the veto. Congress often tries to maneuver the president of the opposition party into a veto just for campaign purposes. The veto is a defensive weapon. It can keep Congress from funding at higher levels than a president would like, but it is useless if Congress is intent on giving the president less than he wants—as Reagan found out with regard to defense programs and Clinton discovered with foreign aid.

Impoundment of Funds

After Congress grants budget authority and the fiscal year begins, the president may *impound* funds by ordering the OMB to direct Treasury officials to withhold some of the funds from agencies' "checking accounts" at the Treasury.[33] It is important to remember that Congress does not actually provide money to the bureaucracy: it simply authorizes the Treasury to honor checks written by the departments. Congress cannot physically prevent the OMB from directing an agency not to spend money or lowering an agency's quarterly allotment to reflect a lower spending rate, and it cannot physically prevent the Treasury from enforcing OMB directives.

Congress itself sometimes legislates an impoundment power to presidents, who have been granted the power to impound by Congress for managerial savings (e.g., if they can do the job without spending all the money) or to comply with across-the-board budget-cutting resolutions passed by Congress. They also may have statutory powers to impound funds in the intergovernmental grant system when state and local governments are not in compliance with antidiscrimination or environmental statutes.[34]

Impoundments become controversial when presidents exercise the power to make policy. Presidents have asserted their right to impound funds for unneeded weapons as part of their power as commander in chief, claims they have been successful in enforcing, but that caused Truman and Kennedy much trouble with the Armed Services Committees.[35] Domestic impoundments have been less successful. Faced with Democratic control of Congress in his first term, President Nixon impounded funds already appropriated by Congress on his own prerogative, going far beyond statutory powers granted by Congress.[36] Nixon impounded funds without any statutory authorization whatsoever, and his impoundments were selective, directed at programs he and his party opposed, such as rural electrification, public housing, urban renewal, environmental programs, and antipoverty activities.[37] As of 1973 he had impounded more than $20 billion, and his FY 1974 budget contained a listing of 109 reductions he intended to make, 101 of which he claimed would require no congressional action.[38]

Nixon claimed that he could impound funds because Congress had passed the *Economic Stabilization Act,* a law that permitted him to impose wage and price controls to combat inflation. Yet Congress in that law had not granted him any impoundment authority. He argued that because he was planning to dismantle some agencies, it was rational to impound funds for programs he no longer considered necessary. In doing so, he ignored the fact that it is Congress, and not the president, that determines when an agency has outlived its usefulness. Finally, he argued that all congressional appropriations were permissive (giving the president discretion not to spend) unless their language was mandatory—unless the law itself stated that the president lacked spending discretion.[40]

Nixon had pushed the impoundment power well beyond the frontiers established by Franklin Roosevelt, Harry Truman, John Kennedy, or Lyndon Johnson, all of whom impounded small amounts of money, for short periods, and usually after consulting congressional committees dominated by members of their own party. His *policy* impoundments struck at the heart of congressional politics. If the president could make them stick, he would control the favors, side-payments, pet projects, and logrolling that members use to conduct business. No committee could forge coalitions if its members believed that the White House could undo their deals. "He has no authority under the Constitution to decide which laws will be exercised, or to what extent they will be enforced," North Carolina Democratic Senator Sam Ervin fumed. "Yet by using the impounding technique, the President is able to do just that."[41]

To counter the impoundment prerogative, federal employee unions and state and local governments took Nixon to court, where his administration lost fifty cases and won none. In each instance, a federal judge ordered administration officials to continue funding programs at levels that Congress had set. The Supreme Court, in *Train v. New York,* issued a definitive opinion, although it did not deal directly with Nixon's assertion of constitutional impoundment prerogatives.[42] The Court simply ruled that when Congress appropriates funds for an activity using the language "sums," an official has no legal authority to spend less than "all sums" appropriated, even if directed to spend less by the president.

CONGRESSIONAL REFORMS

Between 1974 and 1994, Congress passed several laws drastically overhauling the budget process. At first it experimented with procedures that would permit the president and Congress to collaborate on a discretionary fiscal policy; its subsequent reforms took away almost all discretion from both the White House and Congress and substituted inflexible and ultimately unworkable deficit reduction targets or spending caps. By 1995 a Republican Congress was pledged and poised to implement the most far-reaching changes in the budget process since 1921, changes that would limit the flexibility of the president and Congress in making budget policy to an unprecedented extent.

The Budget and Impoundment Act of 1974

In 1974 Congress attempted a shift from a "bottom-up" system of fragmented committee decisions to a "top-down" system of comprehensive budgeting. Congress passed the Congressional Budget and Impoundment Act of 1974.[43] It had two goals: First, it aimed to replace the haphazard system of appropriating funds with a coordinated mechanism to make fiscal policy; second, to check-and-balance the presidential assertion of constitutional impoundment powers with a new statutory process requiring the consent of Congress.[44]

To develop fiscal policy Congress created the House and Senate Budget Committees and charged them with proposing a First Budget Resolution in the spring of a fiscal year. When passed by Congress in the form of a concurrent resolution (not subject to presidential veto), it would offer fiscal policy guidelines to taxing and spending committees. In September, after the committees had completed their work, Congress would pass a Second Budget Resolution, and if necessary, a Reconciliation Act that would have the force of law—it would change tax and spending laws to conform with the Second Resolution's fiscal policy. "Perhaps the most important aspect of the resolution" according to former House Budget Committee chair Brock Adams, "is the fact that it contains the budget of Congress and not that of the President."[45]

For a president to influence spending decisions he would have to influence the work of the Budget Committees. White House influence was limited: typically a conservative Republican president submitted a budget with large cuts in domestic programs; then the Democratic majority on the House Budget Committee came up with its own budget numbers; finally a bipartisan Senate coalition on the Budget Committee served as the "honest broker" between the two sides.

The new budget process worked poorly. Neither president nor Congress developed an effective fiscal policy. For one thing, participants practiced "escapist budgeting."[46] The OMB would issue a "rosy scenario" on the economy, projecting high tax revenues, and anticipating "management savings and other economies" to lower projected expenditures. The Budget Committees would play along, reporting similar high-revenue figures so that they could get enough support in the House and Senate to pass their resolutions. In just about every year the forecasts adopted by Congress were far too optimistic in forecasting revenues and greatly underestimated the size of the deficit.[47] In the 1980s, for example, congressional budget resolutions underestimated annual deficits by an average of $28 billion.[48]

The process was so complex that often it was not completed on time. Between 1975 and 1985, Congress managed to do so only once, in 1977. During that period on average it took 364 days for legislators to complete work on all appropriations bills, *twice* the amount of time contemplated by the process.[49] Funding for many agencies required continuing resolutions in a new fiscal year until delayed appropriations bills were passed. Until 1980 Congress did not even pass reconciliation bills, preferring to accept the "bottom-up" decisions of spending committees rather than the "top-down" fiscal policies of the budget committees.[50] Deficits ballooned after the new procedures were put into place, even though the law had been designed to promote fiscal restraint.

The Budget and Impoundment Act of 1974 put presidential impoundment powers on a statutory basis. It provided that a president might recommend policy impoundments but gave Congress the final say.The president could request *rescissions* (i.e., cuts) in agency funding, which would go into effect only if Congress passed a joint resolution. Approvals of such requests ranged from 80 percent in 1979 to none in 1980, and usually a president wound up with fewer than half of his requests approved.[51] (In a period of split government he will average one-quarter approval.) A president could also request *deferrals* of spending to a future fiscal year. The deferral would go into effect after forty-five legislative days unless either chamber of Congress disapproved—a form of legislative veto. Congress usually granted presidential deferral requests; in most years up to 90 percent of the requests were not vetoed.

In 1983, in the *Chadha v. INS* case, the Supreme Court invalidated the one-chamber legislative veto, ending the deferral mechanism of the budget law. Presidents continued to make deferrals ($25 billion requested by Reagan in fiscal year 1986), and thereafter Congress blocked them if it wished only by passing regular or supplemental appropriations bills that denied the deferrals.[52]

The Attempt to Lower the Deficit: Gramm-Rudman-Hollings

With deficits soaring in the early 1980s, Senators Warren Rudman and Ernest Hollings and Representative Phil Gramm proposed the Balanced Budget and Emergency Deficit Control Act (known as the Gramm-Rudman-Hollings Act, or GRH) in 1985. In the course of a five-year period it was supposed to reduce the deficit from $172 billion in FY 1986 to zero by FY 1991.[53]

Under the law the budget resolution would have mandatory reconciliation instructions to committees to meet the targets—no longer was "top-down" budgeting optional. If the legislature did not pass a reconciliation measure that met the targets (or if the president vetoed it because its spending did not correspond with his own priorities), the law mandated automatic cuts in proposed spending to comply with the targets. These cuts would be proposed by the OMB and Congressional Budget Office, but would then be submitted to the GAO, a quasi-independent agency whose Comptroller General is appointed by the president for a fourteen-year term but is removable only by congressional joint resolution.[54] GAO's statute refers to it as "an instrumentality of the United States Government independent of the executive departments." The GAO would revise the recommendations and then submit a final list of cuts to the president, who would then implement a "sequestration order" based on the GAO list—half of which would be in defense and half in non-defense spending. (Several exempted programs included Social Security and Medicare and unemployment insurance, welfare programs and food stamps for the poor, interest on the national debt, veterans' pensions and benefits; and only small cuts were permitted in Medicaid or cost-of-living increases for federal retirees.)

President Reagan endorsed the proposal, saying that "the United States government is not only going to pay its bills, but we're also going to take away the credit cards."[55] Targets would eliminate presidential fiscal discretion; no longer could fiscal policy be used to stimulate the economy through large deficits.[56] Although spending was not capped, it would certainly be constrained: the law required the president to enforce the strict deficit-reduction targets of the new law by making "sequesters" the equivalent of impoundments, in this case *legally* authorized by Congress. The president was to withhold funds in any category in which Congress exceeded its spending limits within fifteen days after Congress adjourned for the year. If Congress passed a supplemental appropriations measure, the president was to sequester funds within the category within fifteen days of its enactment. If Congress increased spending for mandated programs without increasing taxes, the president was to sequester funds in discretionary programs.

The bill passed with strong bipartisan support: most Republicans voted in favor, and in both the House and Senate only a small majority of Democrats opposed it. President Reagan signed the bill into law because of its conservative orientation, but thought it had "constitutionally suspect" provisions that violated the separation of powers: he objected to the provision that if Congress did not stay within the deficit targets, the final determination of sequesters would be made by the GAO and not by the president.

These provisions were soon tested in court. After the comptroller general ordered $11.7 billion in mandated cuts, a three-judge federal district court held that his power to do so was unconstitutional, because the comptroller general was not a part of the executive branch, was not removable by the president, and therefore the powers Congress had granted him to direct spending cuts violated the separation of powers.[57] The Supreme Court agreed with the lower court, 7–2, and knocked the spending cuts out.[58] A back-up provision of the law (passed in case the courts knocked out the sequestration provisions) went into effect, specifying that OMB-CBO projections would be brought to Congress, and a temporary Joint Committee on Deficit Reduction, composed of all members of both Budget Committees, would make cuts to comply with deficit-reduction targets. Congress would then vote to certify the size of a projected deficit to comply with the law.[59] In 1987 the law was amended to provide that sequesters be specified by the OMB, giving the power to meet mandated deficit-reduction targets back to the president.

Gramm-Rudman-Hollings in Operation: The Failure of Budgeting by Rule

The Gramm-Rudman-Hollings Act (GRH) accomplished none of its goals. The main problem was that it dealt only with *projections* about future deficits, not with actual *spending.* The president had to present a *plan* that reduced the deficit, and once Congress passed its version, both were in compliance with law. Actual deficits in the fiscal year could be much higher than the targets in the GRH law. This loophole provided everyone with incentives to prepare fantasy budgets: no one had an incentive to produce accurate estimates, because they would have required tax increases or unpopular spending cuts to stay on target. The White House presented Congress with unrealistic assumptions about a booming economy that would produce greater revenues and lower interest rates, requiring decreased interest payments on the national debt. It put in unspecified "management and efficiency" savings to lower projections on expenditures. Presidents relied on gimmicks, such as the one-time sale of government assets, slowdowns in government spending, and even postdating employee paydays into the next fiscal year, all to meet the deficit-reduction requirements.

Congress then compounded the problems. Although the Congressional Budget Office provided accurate estimates of the projected deficit, Congress refused to certify these high figures, because it would then have to make cuts. Instead, it relied on the lower presidential estimates. It "backdated" some spending into a prior fiscal year to meet the FY 1987 targets. That year both the president and Congress claimed to have passed a budget that would meet the deficit-reduction target of $144 billion—but the deficit actually turned out to be more than $170 billion, and deficit-reduction efforts stalled.

After the midterm elections were over, GRH targets for FY 1988 required a deficit projection of $108 billion. Reagan submitted a completely unrealistic budget calling for deep cuts in domestic programs. Democrats abandoned all hopes of meeting the GRH targets, passed a resolution $20 billion over the target, and offered President Reagan a choice: permit a tax increase or accept deep cuts in defense spending. Because Democratic liberals and conservative Republicans could not come to an agreement on cuts or taxes, both sides took the easy way out. Congress amended the law to push back the deficit reduction targets: The Balanced Budget and Emergency Deficit Control Reaffirmation Act of 1987 provided for a deficit of $144 billion—a target that was within reach—and did not call for a zero deficit until FY 1993. The amended law got everyone through the 1988 elections, but two years later President Bush found it impossible to present a budget that could meet the third-year target without deep defense and social spending cuts. At that point the president and Congress agreed to scrap deficit-reduction targets entirely.

The Budget Summit of 1990

By the summer of 1990 the budget process had stalemated. Deficits were zooming toward $300 billion. Nevertheless, a Democratic Congress and Republican president played high-stakes politics in the midst of the crisis. Republicans hoped to sucker Democrats into passing new taxes that the President could veto and thereby score points close to the elections. Democrats wanted to make Bush take responsibility for a tax increase.[60] White House Chief of Staff John Sununu and OMB Director Richard Darman met with six congressional leaders to seek a compromise at Andrews Air Force Base, away from the congressional appropriations and budget committees, the party caucuses, and the lobbyists for special interests on Capitol Hill.

The summit participants agreed on "tax revenue increases" to solve the crisis. They hoped that a bipartisan accord would insulate each from blame. They didn't figure on the responses within their own parties. Republican conservatives jumped on President Bush for breaking his "read my lips, no new taxes" election promise. Democratic liberals attacked their congressional leaders for accepting spending cuts and regressive taxes. Matters were not helped by the attitude of White House Chief of Staff John Sununu, who met with the House Republican conference to sell the compromise, and after hearing opposition, threatened Republicans thinking of breaking ranks with reprisals. Led by Party Whip Newt Gingrich, the House Republicans rose up and deserted the president, with only three Republican House ranking minority committee leaders supporting Bush's agreement. More than half the Republicans voted it down, 105 against to 71 in favor. On the Democratic side, the story was the same: More than half the Democratic chairs of standing committees and appropriations subcommittees voted against the plan, as did a majority of the House Democrats. It went down to defeat, 179–254.

Within the next two weeks the White House position completely unraveled. Democrats in Congress voted a continuing resolution (to provide funds for the new fiscal year), but Bush vetoed it, hoping to put pressure on Democrats to support the compromise in a new vote. Most Republicans joined the president to uphold his veto in the House, 138–260. Yet, three days later, with government activities at a standstill after most budget authority had expired, Bush allowed a new continuing resolution to go into effect, abandoning his original strategy because of the public reaction to allowing "the government to close down." He then hinted that, to break the deadlock, higher income taxes might be acceptable, provided Democrats agreed to back his proposal for lower capital gains taxes (on stocks and property). Then he quickly backed off his trial balloon, telling Republican senators to "take it off the table." On the campaign trail, with midterm elections less than a month away, he told reporters that it was a legislative matter, and said, "let Congress clean it up." Finally, he told a group of reporters to "read my hips" as he turned and began his morning jog, refusing to answer any questions. By October 11, back in the White House, the confusion reached its peak when Bush came out of a meeting with House leaders to reaffirm that he wanted a deal on income and capital gains taxes, shortly to be followed by White House press spokesperson Marlin Fitzwater, who told reporters a deal "would be a waste of time."

Eventually congressional leaders picked up the pieces, continued their negotiations with Bush's aides, and came up with a deficit reduction plan. They agreed on $150 billion in tax increases over five years, raised by increasing the top tax bracket from 28 to 31 percent, lowering tax deductions for the affluent, and increasing gas and whiskey taxes. The deficit would drop by $40 billion in the first year and supposedly by $460 billion in the following four years. The White House and Democratic leaders rounded up congressional votes for this version, and Bush signed the measure.

Expenditure Caps

The budget summit not only raised taxes, but also produced the Budget Enforcement Act of 1990.[61] This law abandoned the Gramm-Rudman-Hollings deficit-reduction targets. Instead, it provided that between 1991 and 1993 strict caps would be placed on all discretionary domestic, defense, and international affairs spending. Overspending in any fiscal year would be charged against the next fiscal year and lower the cap for that year. (Mandated spending for Social Security, Medicare and Medicaid, welfare and food stamps, federal pensions, and interest on the national debt would be exempted.) Between 1993 and 1995 separate spending limits for the three categories would be ended, and overall limits on federal discretionary spending would be in place. Throughout this entire period, no allowance for inflation would be made, thus reducing discretionary expenditures between 2 and 4 percent annually.

Although mandated spending was exempted from the ceilings, the new law required that changes in entitlement programs that would increase expenditures be paid for by increased taxes or offsetting spending cuts—known as the "paygo" rule. Moreover, any tax *decreases* enacted into law would have to be matched either by other offsetting tax *increases* or by spending cuts to match the anticipated loss in revenues. A similar rule applied to politically sensitive social security payroll taxes: any decreases in these taxes would require a decrease in benefits; correspondingly any benefit increases voted by Congress would require an increase in Social Security payroll taxes. The law would require the president and Congress to make zero-sum choices. They would have to trade increases in some programs for equivalent cuts in others.[62] The president would have the power to sequester funds if Congress exceeded the spending limits.

By removing as much discretion as possible from the budget process, proponents hoped that eventually an increase in revenues would catch up to the capped expenditures. The White House predicted (as it had with Gramm-Rudman-Hollings) that at last balanced budgets were in sight: it projected a $61 billion deficit in FY 1994 and $2.9 billion in FY 1995, with a surplus of $19.9 billion by FY 1996.

These predictions were preposterous, though they did provide political cover for Bush and members of both parties in Congress through the 1990 midterm elections and the 1992 presidential-year elections. By early 1993, when Bush left office, predictions for each of the 1993 and 1994 deficits ran to over $300 billion. The budget reforms of the 1980s had failed.

BUDGETING IN THE 1990s

President Clinton decided to try the "early reconciliation" device used by President Reagan in 1981. He proposed expenditure cuts of close to $500 billion (from projected amounts over a five-year period) in his first budget, and in a highly charged partisan atmosphere, won a very narrow victory in Congress. As a result, Clinton sliced the deficit by one-third in FY 1994 from original estimates. Nevertheless, the deficit was projected by his own budget officials to rise to $397 billion by FY 2004 without additional measures and budget reforms, and would further rise to $1.5 trillion annually by 2020, an unsustainable figure.[63] Throughout the Clinton presidency conservative "blue dog" Democrats and Republicans in Congress offered numerous ideas to reform the budget process. Much of budget politics in the mid-1990s involved White House maneuvers to derail or subvert these proposals, and while they were initially successful, Democrats paid the price in the 1994 midterm elections, as Republicans issued a "Contract with America," calling for a constitutional amendment requiring a balanced budget and other budget reforms.

Power to Congress: Fast Tracks, Caps, and Special Sessions

One set of reforms called for use of the fast-track legislative system. Fast-track proposals (such as the Penny–Kasich bill introduced in 1993, calling on Congress to trim $103 billion from the projected deficits) would not go through the appropriations or standing committees. They would go directly to the Rules Committee for consideration, in an effort to trump the budget cuts proposed by the president. Fast-track proposals were opposed by President Clinton and Democratic congressional leaders, who in 1993–1994 managed to defeat them.

Another budget idea was to designate funds for deficit reduction. The Crapo-Schumer "lockbox" measure was proposed by Democrats for political cover. It provided that whenever Congress made budget cuts, the funds saved would be applied solely to deficit-reduction efforts, rather than revert to the appropriations subcommittees, which under existing rules could spend any money "saved" on other programs, provided they remained under the overall spending caps. A much more serious Republican proposal in the "Contract" provided that taxpayers could designate as much as 10 percent of their taxes for deficit reduction; because many taxpayers might do so, enactment of this law would require either tax increases to sustain other programs or, more likely, significant cuts in domestic expenditures—exactly the outcome hoped for by proponents of the measure. In 1995, House Republicans and conservative Democrats agreed on "The Lockbox"—a proposal to target a specified amount of the spending cuts for deficit reduction (rather than for the tax cut favored by the Republicans).

In 1994 conservative Republicans and Democrats put pressure on Clinton to continue cutting the federal deficit by proposing automatic spending caps on nondiscretionary "entitlement" programs: Social Security, Medicare and Medicaid, food stamps, and welfare. These and other cash payment programs account for half of government expenditure and 12 percent of the gross national product. More federal and state government money in the 1990s was spent on these than on any other type of program.[64] If programs continued to grow at their current rates, payroll taxes would zoom, and still there would be no money for discretionary programs. In the 1990s it was projected that almost all of the growth in the federal budget would involve growth in these programs.[65] In the past, the effort to slow their growth has been politically explosive. These programs were exempted from budget reform laws that capped discretionary spending. Charles Stenholm, a Republican representative from Texas, proposed capping overall entitlement spending, limiting it to inflation offsets or increases in the number of recipients but preventing expansions in benefits. Representative John Kasich of Ohio proposed setting an overall limit and limits on individual entitlement programs annually. Payments would be cut back when the limits were breached. The Clinton White House and Democratic congressional leaders responded to these challenges before the 1994 election by writing a bill with "political cover." Legislators could vote for a watered-down measure sponsored by John Spratt of South Carolina: if total entitlement spending rose above targets, the president would have to propose ways to get under the target, and Congress would be required to approve or disapprove of the president's plan.

Another idea was a special session to cut spending "from A to Z." Proposed in 1993 by Democrat Robert Andrews and Republican Bill Zeliff (hence the "A to Z"), the special budget session would last a week. Any lawmaker could bypass committees and offer a proposal to cut government spending. Each measure would be guaranteed a House vote. "A to Z" was picked up by talk-show hosts in 1994 as part of anti-Congress bashing, because it pitted the new members who in 1992 had been elected on "cut-the-deficit" promises against the committee leaders. The A-to-Z sponsors forged an alliance of Republicans and Democrats; more than 230 representatives signed as cosponsors of a bill for such a session. The House Rules Committee refused to act. Supporters then signed a discharge petition: a majority of members could force the call for the A-to-Z session out of the Rules Committee for a floor vote. The Democrats' leadership and the White House headed the petition off with threats about reprisals and with promises of reforms; they pledged at least eight votes on budget issues during the summer of 1994, one or two days on proposals to cut entitlements, and promised to give members more chances to propose spending cuts on appropriations bills. Although the Democrats won the battle, they lost the war: the first three months of the Congressional session in 1995 was, in effect, the "special session" for budget cutting Republicans had been calling for.

Power to the President: Rescissions and the Line-Item Veto

Some of the Republican House proposals would give more power to the president as Curtailer-in-Chief. When presidents propose to rescind spending, Congress must approve by joint resolution. If Congress does nothing, the rescission request fails. President Bush proposed to change the procedure so that Congress would have to put itself on record if it opposed his rescission requests. On March 20, 1992, Bush proposed that Congress vote separately on each proposed rescission, provided that one-fifth of the House moved to discharge a rescission request from the House Appropriations Committee. Later Bush called for "expedited rescission" that would require a vote on each request without the formality of the discharge petition. The House passed the measure in 1992 and 1993 but the Senate blocked it. In 1994, to forestall a move in the House for deep spending cuts, the House once again voted an expedited rescission measure. It contained a proviso that the Appropriations Committee would submit its own recommendations first, and if that failed, the president's cuts would be considered. Congress passed this reform in 1995.

Another reform would provide that the president's proposed cuts would go into effect automatically within a fixed period unless both houses of Congress disapproved. Known as "enhanced rescission," it would completely reverse the Budget and Impoundment Act by putting the onus on the president's opponents to win a congressional majority to block cuts, rather than require the president to win a majority to approve his rescissions. The president could veto any resolution of disapproval, and his veto would stand unless Congress overrode it. Enhanced rescission would give one-third of a single chamber the ability to impose presidential spending cuts on the entire Congress, in effect transferring budget power from Congress to the president.

Six presidents, including Franklin Roosevelt, Ronald Reagan, and George Bush, have called for a line-item veto: the power to veto particular items in a spending measure rather than the entire bill. Governors of forty-three states have such power.[66] (President Reagan claimed that he had more budget power as governor of California than as president of the United States.) Every State of the Union Address by Reagan and Bush called for the line-item veto, either by law or constitutional amendment. Reagan argued that it would permit him to "reach into massive appropriations bills, pare away the waste, and enforce budget discipline," citing as examples research funds for "cranberry research, blueberry research, the study of crayfish, and the commercialization of wild flowers."[67] Bush, guided by White House Counsel C. Boyden Gray, suggested that the veto might be an inherent presidential power, but Attorney General William Barr contradicted Gray in an Opinion of the Attorney General, suggesting that such a view had no basis.[68]

In 1994 Senator Arlen Specter revived this theory in hearings on the proposal held by the Subcommittee on the Constitution of the Senate Judiciary Committee, but President Clinton argued that Congress would have to pass a constitutional amendment (which he opposed) or pass hundreds of separate appropriations bills, each referring to a single line in the budget, which would enable him to veto individual budget lines. Because of heated opposition from the Congressional Black Caucus, Democratic liberals, and committee chairs, House Speaker Thomas Foley pulled back on his plans to have the House of Representatives vote on the measure to provide a line-item veto to the president. Public opinion polls in the early 1990s showed an overwhelming majority in favor of such a presidential power. The House Republicans, in their "Contract with America," promised to pass a presidential line-item veto bill, and they did so in early 1995, as did the Senate. Clinton supported the measure, because, in this instance, Congress would be giving the president power rather than taking it away.

Power to No One: The Balanced Budget Amendment

Presidents hardly ever submit balanced budgets to Congress, and even if Congress stuck with the presidential requests rather than increase it, the amounts saved would be only a few billions each year.[69] Congress has balanced the budget only eight times since the end of World War II, the last time in FY 1969.[70] This track record forms the basis for a proposed constitutional amendment requiring a balanced budget. In most versions, including the one sponsored by House Republicans in their "Contract with America," the president would be required to submit a balanced budget to Congress. An increase in the national debt through an unbalanced budget would be permitted only if three-fifths of the members of Congress approved (or by majority vote if the nation were at war).

To deflect criticism away from his own failure to propose anything even approaching balanced budgets, President Reagan called on Congress in his 1985 State of the Union Address to pass a balanced budget amendment. Advocates of such an amendment had won resolutions from thirty-two states calling for Congress to call a constitutional convention, only two short of the number needed. Meanwhile, the Senate Judiciary Committee had drafted a constitutional convention implementation act to provide for the popular election of delegates to any such convention. Under the terms of the act, the convention would be limited to considering only the balanced budget amendment; it would not, as some critics claimed, be able to run amok and revise the entire constitution. After that approach failed, members of Congress drafted their own "balanced budget amendments."

In 1994 the Senate was just four votes shy of passing the amendment, with 63 members in favor and 37 against, in spite of the strong opposition of Senate Democratic leaders. The vote in the House fell twelve votes short (271 in favor, 153 against) as House leaders rounded up Democratic first-year members, 20 of whom voted in favor and 43 against. The Clinton White House, reversing the course of its Republican predecessors, played a major role in the amendment's defeat, not only by rounding up votes, but also by releasing budget figures forecasting a sharp drop in the deficit for FY 1995. "You don't need a constitutional amendment," observed Budget Director Leon Panetta. "What it takes is real leadership in this country, and that's what's being provided by this President."[71] Unfortunately for Clinton, voters did not agree in the midterm elections, and the proposal was revived in the next Congress. The House passed it by a large margin, but on March 2, 1995, it was defeated in the Senate by one vote, as Republican Mark Hatfield defected. Senator Bob Dole promised to bring it up for a vote again, while Speaker Newt Gingrich warned Democrats that they would lose additional Senate seats in 1996 because of their opposition, after which the Republicans would have the votes to pass the amendment.

The amendment has been criticized by many economists and political scientists as bad economics and bad public policy. Either it would put the government in a straitjacket, preventing emergency actions, contingency planning, and necessary capital investment in the nation's future, or else it would have loopholes, and be ignored like the various budget acts passed by Congress. One loophole, for example, provided that "debt of the United States held by the public" could not be increased without a three-fifths vote of each chamber. Aside from the fact that such a vote could then make a nullity of the amendment's purpose, the terminology itself excluded one-third of the national debt held by government trust funds (such as the Social Security trust fund), which could allow some increases in government debt. Another loophole occurs when quasi-governmental agencies are excluded, such as the Student Loan Marketing Association or other federally chartered financial institutions that are not "agencies of the United States Government."[72] An amendment containing these loopholes would not balance the budget and would further the cynicism of the American people about the way government (especially Congress) works.[73]

Finally, the amendment might alter the balance of fiscal power between president and Congress. If the experience of states is any guide, adoption of such an amendment might enable the president to claim and exercise impoundment powers. Conceivably the federal courts, in interpreting the new amendment, might agree that the president had to exercise such power to comply with the terms of the (amended) Constitution, powers not subject to any congressional override.

THE FAILURE OF PRESIDENTIAL BUDGETING

Since the mid-1960s the budget process has failed to control deficits, failed to develop coherent fiscal policies, and failed to provide the president with political resources or governing power.[74] The legacy of split government during the Reagan and Bush administrations was a ballooning deficit and debt, combined with so-called budget reforms that had all the integrity of a three-card monte game played by sidewalk hustlers. Presidents and Congress improvised, used creative accounting, and promoted an illusion of fiscal responsibility in desperate attempts to keep "the process" going—at least until they turned over the presidency to their successors. Although President Clinton brought more candor and honesty to the budget numbers, he too failed to match the rhetoric of deficit cutting with the reality—by the late 1990s deficits were expected to rise sharply without further cuts.

Presidents remain in a no-win situation. If they fail to dominate Congress or propose difficult choices, they will get blamed for the gridlock and paralysis and will be accused of government or political cowardice. Yet, when they do exert influence, it can only be in the direction of unpopular cuts. If they are effective at governance, it can only be in ways that may erode their political base. The president and the political party that can find a way out of this conundrum will have found the key to political dominance in the early part of the next century. If there is no answer, or if no president can find one, the prospects are for the continuation of a weakened presidency facing a resurgent Congressional leadership pledging new reforms of the budget process. For the nation, prospects are for weak and ineffective government until budget politics begins to correspond with fiscal realities.

FURTHER READING

Books

John Cogan, *The Budget Puzzle,* Stanford, CA: Stanford University Press, 1994.

Robert Eisner, *How Real Is the Federal Deficit?* New York: Free Press, 1986.

Louis Fisher, *The Presidential Spending Power,* Princeton, NJ: Princeton University Press, 1975.

Lawrence Haas, *Running on Empty: Bush, Congress and the Politics of a Bankrupt Government,* Homewood, IL: Business One Irwin, 1990.

Daniel Ippolito, *Uncertain Legacies: Federal Budget Policy from Roosevelt through Reagan,* Charlottesville, VA: University Press of Virginia, 1990.

Donald Kettl, *Deficit Politics,* New York: Macmillan, 1992.

James D. Savage, *Balanced Budgets and American Politics,* Ithaca, NY: Cornell University Press, 1988.

Allen Schick, *Congress and Money,* Washington, DC: Urban Institute, 1980.

Allen Schick, *The Federal Budget: Politics, Policy, Process,* Washington, DC: Brookings Institution, 1994.

David Stockman, *The Triumph of Politics,* New York: Harper and Row, 1986.

Aaron Wildavsky, *The New Politics of the Budgetary Process,* Glenview, IL: Scott, Foresman/Little, Brown, 1988.

Documentary Sources

An Analyis of the President's Budgetary Proposals for Fiscal Year—, Washington, DC: Congressional Budget Office, annually.

The Budget in Brief, Washington, DC: Government Printing Office, annually.

The Budget of the United States Government, Washington, DC: Government Printing Office, annually.

Setting National Priorities: The FY—Budget, Washington, DC: Brookings Institution, annually.

NOTES

1. Naomi Caiden,"The New Rules of the Federal Budget Game," *Public Administration Review,* Vol. 44, no. 2, March/April, 1984, pp. 109–118.

2. Congress had used early reconciliation for the first time in 1980 for a small $8.3 billion deficit reduction that it included in its first budget resolution (H. Con. Res. 307); see James Sundquist, *The Decline and Resurgence of Congress,* Washington, DC: Brookings Institution, 1981, pp. 227–230.

3. Peter Goldman, "Tax Cuts: Reagan Digs In," *Newsweek,* June 15, 1981, p. 27.

4. "How Reaganites Push Reluctant Republicans to Back Tax-Rise Bill,"*Wall Street Journal,* September 9, 1982, p. 1.

5. Lance T. LeLoup, "After the Blitz: Reagan and the U.S. Congressional Budget Process," *Legislative Studies Quarterly,* Vol. 7, no. 3, August, 1982, pp. 321–339; Allen Schick, "In Congress Reassembled: Reconciliation and the Legislative Process," *PS,* Vol. 14, pp. 748–752.

6. Louis Fisher, *The Presidential Spending Power,* Princeton, NJ: Princeton University Press, 1975, p. 35.

7. Louis Fisher, *Constitutional Conflicts Between Congress and the President,* 3rd rev. ed., Lawrence, KS: University Press of Kansas, 1991, pp. 228–231.

8. Harold D. Smith, "The Bureau of the Budget," *Public Administration Review,* Vol. 1, no. 2, Winter, 1940–41, pp. 106–115; Fritz Morstein Marx, "The Bureau of the Budget: Its Evolution and Present Role," *American Political Science Review,* Vol. 39, no. 4, August, 1945, pp. 653–684; Allen Schick, "The Budget Bureau That Was: Thoughts on the Rise, Decline, and Future of a Presidential Agency," *Law and Contemporary Problems,* Vol. 35, no. 3, Summer, 1970, pp. 519–539.

9. Bureau of the Budget, Circular 40.

10. D. Roderick Kiewet and Matthew D. McCubbins, "Presidential Influence on Congressional Appropriations Decisions," *American Journal of Political Science,* Vol. 32, no. 3, August, 1988, pp. 713–736.

11. James Thurber, "The Consequences of Budget Reform for Congressional-Presidential Relations," *The Annals of the American Academy of Political and Social Science,* Philadelphia: Academy of Political and Social Science, Vol. 499, September, 1988, p. 110; Larry Berman, "The Office of Management and Budget That Almost Wasn't," *Political Science Quarterly,* Vol. 92, no. 2, Summer, 1977, pp. 281–303; Bruce Johnson, "OMB's New Role," *Journal of Policy Analysis and Management,* Vol. 3, no. 4, 1983–1984, pp. 501–515.

12. Mark Kamlet and David Mowry, "The Budgetary Base in Federal Resource Allocation," *The American Journal of Political Science,* Vol. 24, no. 4, December, 1980, pp. 804–8; Otto Davis, M. A. Dempster, Aaron Wildavsky, et al., "A Theory of the Budgetary Process," *The American Political Science Review,* Vol. 60, no. 3, September, 1966, pp. 529–547.

13. Peter Natchez and Irving Bupp, "Policy and Priority in the Budget Process," *The American Political Science Review,* Vol. 67, no. 3, September, 1973, pp. 951–963.

14. Lance LeLoup, "Agency Policy Actions: Determinants of Non-Incremental Change," in Randall Ripley and Grace Franklin, eds., *Policy-Making in the Executive Branch,* New York: Free Press, 1975, pp. 65–90.

15. The overall intelligence budget of $26 billion, including approximately $3.5 billion for the Central Intelligence Agency, is "hidden" in other budget requests and is classified information. In 1994 the overall totals were revealed in a House Appropriations Subcommittee document by mistake.

16. W. Bowman Cutter, "The Battle of the Budget," *The Atlantic,* Vol. 261, March, 1981, p. 64.

17. Steven Pearlstein, "Clinton Puts His Stamp on a 'New Democrat' Budget," *Washington Post National Weekly Edition,* February 14–20, 1994, p. 31.

18. Lloyd A. Free and Hadley Cantril, *The Political Beliefs of Americans,* New York: Simon and Schuster, 1968, pp. 51–58.

19. David Stockman, *The Triumph of Politics,* New York: Harper and Row, 1986; John P. Frendreis and Raymond Tatalovich, *The Modern Presidency and Economic Policy,* Itasca, IL: F. E. Peacock, 1994, p. 95; Thomas M. Hollaway and Joseph C. Wakefield, "Sources of Change in the Federal Deficit, 1970–1986," *Survey of Current Business,* May, 1985, p. 29.

20. David Stockman, op. cit., pp. 576–577.

21. Matthew McCubbins, "Government on Lay-Away: Federal Spending and Deficits under Divided Government," in Samuel Kernell and Gary W. Cox, eds., *The Politics of Divided Government,* Boulder, CO: Westview Press, 1991, pp. 113–154.

22. Allen Schick, *Crisis in the Budget Process: Exercising Political Choice,* Washington, DC: American Enterprise Institute, 1986, pp. 42–43.

23. Richard E. Fenno, *The Power of the Purse,* Boston: Little, Brown, 1966, pp. 311–312.

24. *Congressional Quarterly Weekly Reports,* March 28, 1987, p. 552.

25. Bruce A. Ray, "Federal Spending and the Selection of Committee Assignments in the U.S. House of Representatives," *American Journal of Political Science,* Vol. 24, no. 3, August, 1980, p. 494.

26. Quoted in Kenneth Shepsle, "The Failure of Congressional Budgeting," *Society,* Vol. 20, May-June, 1983, p. 5.

27. Kate Stith, "Congress' Power of the Purse," *Yale Law Journal,* Vol. 97, no. 7, June, 1988, pp. 1343–1396.

28. 31 U.S.C. Sec. 3302(b), 1982.

29. 31 U.S.C. Sec. 1341(a)(1)(A), 1982.

30. Ibid., p. 1351.

31. Kate Stith, op. cit., p. 1390.

32. *Opinions of the Attorney General,* Vol. 41, Washington, DC: Government Printing Office, 1961, p. 507ff.

33. Ralph S. Abascal and John R. Kramer, "Presidential Impoundment: Historical Genesis and Constitutional Framework," *Georgetown Law Journal,* Vol. 62, no. 6, July, 1974, pp. 1549–1618.

34. Frank Church, "Impoundment of Appropriated Funds: The Decline of Congressional Control Over Discretion," *Stanford Law Review,* Vol. 22, no. 6, June, 1970, pp. 1240–1253.

35. John H. Stassen, "Separation of Power and the Uncommon Defense: The Case against Impounding of Weapons System Appropriations," *Georgetown Law Journal,* Vol. 57, no. 6, June, 1969, pp. 1159–1210.

36. Louis Fisher, "Impoundment of Funds: Uses and Abuses," *Buffalo Law Review,* Vol. 23, no. 1, Fall, 1973, pp. 141–200.

37. Louis Fisher, "The Politics of Impounded Funds," *Administrative Science Quarterly,* Vol. 15, no. 3, September, 1970, pp. 361–377; Louis Fisher, "Presidential Spending Discretion and Congressional Controls," *Law and Contemporary Problems,* Vol. 37, no. 1, Winter, 1972, pp. 135–172; James Pfiffner, *The President, the Budget and Congress: Impoundment and the 1974 Budget Act,* Boulder, CO: Westview Press, 1979, pp. 27–48.

38. James Sundquist, *The Decline and Resurgence of Congress,* Washington, DC: Brookings Institution, 1982, p. 205.

39. *Economic Stabilization Act Amendments of 1971,* P.L. 92–210, sec. 203, December 22, 1971.

40. "Note: Protecting the Fisc: Executive Impoundment and Congressional Power," *Yale Law Journal,* Vol. 82, no. 8, July, 1973, pp. 1636–1658; Abner V. Mikva and Michael F. Hertz, "Impoundment of Funds—The Courts, the Congress and the Presidents: A Constitutional Triangle," *Northwestern University Law Review,* Vol. 69, no. 3, July/August, 1974, pp. 335–389.

41. James Sundquist, *The Decline and Resurgence of Congress,* Washington, DC: Brookings Institution, 1981, p. 206.

42. *Train v. New York,* 420 U.S. 25, 1973.

43. P. L. 93–344, 1974.

44. Allen Schick, "Budget Reform Legislation: Reorganizing Congressional Centers of Fiscal Power," *Harvard Journal of Legislation,* Vol. 11, no. 2, February, 1974, pp. 303–350.

45. Lance LeLoup, op. cit., p. 126.

46. Louis Fisher, "Ten Years of the Budget Act: Still Searching for Controls," *Public Budgeting and Finance,* Vol. 5, no. 3, Autumn, 1985, pp. 3–28.

47. Rudolph G. Penner and Alan J. Abramson, *Broken Purse Strings: Congressional Budgeting, 1974–1988,* Washington, DC: Urban Institute, 1989, p. 99.

48. CBO, *The Economic and Budget Outlook, Fiscal Years 1991–95,* Washington, DC: Congressional Budget Office, 1990, as cited in Donald Kettl, *Deficit Politics,* New York: Macmillan, 1992, p. 115.

49. John Ellwood, "Budget Control in a Redistributive Environment," in Allen Schick, ed., *Making Economic Policy in Congress,* Washington, DC: American Enterprise Institute, pp. 74–81.

50. John P. Gilmour, *Reconcilable Differences? Congress, the Budget Process, and the Deficit,* Berkeley, CA: University of California Press, 1990, p. 107.

51. John Ellwood and James Thurber, "The Congressional Budget Process Re-Examined," in Lawrence G. Dodd and Bruce I. Oppenheimer, eds., *Congress Reconsidered,* 2nd ed., Washington, DC: Congressional Quarterly Press, 1981, Table 11–15, p. 266.

52. Louis Fisher, "The Impact of Chadha on the Budget Process," *CRS Review,* 1983, pp. 12–14.

53. The deficit ceilings under the law P.L. 99–177 (1986) were as follows (in billions): $144 in FY 1987; $108 in FY 1988; $72 in FY 1989; $36 in FY 1990; zero deficit by FY 1991; see James Thurber, "The Consequences of Budget Reform for Congressional-Presidential Relations," *The Annals of the American Academy of Political and Social Science,* Vol. 499, September, 1988, pp. 101–113.

54. GAO's statute refers to it as "an instrumentality of the United States Government independent of the executive departments."

55. *New York Times,* October 5, 1985, p. 1.

56. Kate Stith, "Rewriting the Fiscal Constitution: The Case of Gramm-Rudman-Hollings," *California Law Review,* Vol. 76, no. 3, May, 1988, pp. 595–668.

57. L. Harold Levinson, "Balancing Acts: Bowsher v. Synar, Gramm-Rudman-Hollings, and Beyond," *Cornell Law Review,* Vol. 72, no. 3, March, 1987, pp. 527–552.

58. *Bowsher v. Synar,* 478 U.S. 714, 1986.

59. L. Donald Elliott, "Regulating the Deficit after Bowsher v. Synar," *Yale Journal on Regulation,* Vol. 4, no. 3, Summer, 1986, pp. 317–362.

60. Donald Kettl, *Deficit Politics,* op. cit., p. 5.

61. Title XIII, *Omnibus Budget Reconciliation Act of 1990;* Edward Davis and Robert Keith, "Budget Enforcement Act of 1990: Brief Summary," Washington, DC: Congressional Research Service, November 5, 1990.

62. James A. Thurber, "New Rules for an Old Game: Zero Sum Budgeting in the Postreform Congress," in Roger Davidson, ed., *The Postreform Congress,* New York: St. Martin's Press, 1992, pp. 257–278.

63. Alice Rivlin, "Memorandum on Deficit," Office of Management and Budget, October 20, 1994.

64. Congressional Budget Office, *The Economic and Budget Outlook: Fiscal Years 1992–96,* Washington, DC: Government Printing Office, 1991, p. 151.

65. Congressional Budget Office, *The Economic and Budget Outlook: Fiscal Years 1992–96,* Washington, DC: Government Printing Office, 1991, p. 91.

66. Judith Best, "The Item Veto: Would the Founders Approve?" *Presidential Studies Quarterly,* Vol. 14, no. 1, Spring, 1984, pp. 183–188; Aaron Wildavsky, "Item Veto without a Global Spending Limit: Locking the Treasury after the Dollars Have Fled," *Notre Dame Journal of Law, Ethics and Public Policy,* Vol. 1, no. 2, June, 1985, pp. 165–176; Thomas Cronin and Jeffrey Weill, "An Item Veto for the President," *Congress and the Presidency,* Vol. 12, no. 2, Fall, 1985, pp. 127–152; Robert Spitzer, "The Item Veto Reconsidered," *Presidential Studies Quarterly,* Vol. 15, no. 2, Summer, 1985, pp. 611–617.

67. Ronald Reagan, "State of the Union Message" January 20, 1988.

68. Charles Tiefer, *The Semi-Sovereign Congress,* Boulder, CO: Westview Press, 1994, p. 16.

69. Paul E. Peterson, "The New Politics of Deficits," *Political Science Quarterly,* Vol. 100, no. 4, Winter, 1985/1986, p. 375.

70. Donald Kettl, op. cit., p. 13.

71. Douglas Jehl, "Forecasts New White House Weapon in Balanced Budget Debate," *New York Times,* January 28, 1994, p. A-18.

72. Louis Fisher, "The Effects of a Balanced Budget Amendment on Political Institutions," *Journal of Law and Politics,* Vol. 9, no. 1, Fall. 1992, p. 102.

73. "Statement by Louis Fisher: Congressional Research Service, Senate Committee on Appropriations, February 17, 1994, Balanced Budget Amendment."

74. Allen Schick, *The Capacity to Budget,* op. cit., p. 159; Louis Fisher, "Federal Budget Doldrums: The Vacuum in Presidential Leadership," *Public Administration Review,* Vol. 50, November/December, 1990, pp. 693–700.

CHAPTER 13

Presidential Economics

The business of America is business.

—Calvin Coolidge

INTRODUCTORY CASE: PRESIDENT REAGAN REFORMS THE TAX CODE

President Reagan, in the midst of his 1984 State of the Union Address, had just announced that he was asking the Treasury "to simplify the entire tax code so all taxpayers, big and small, are treated more fairly," when members of Congress on both sides of the aisle began laughing at what seemed to be a transparent election ploy for votes. No one in Congress thought Reagan was serious, and no one gave tax reform a chance. "I sort of like the tax code the way it is," said the Republican chairman of the Senate Finance Committee. At a party on the day after the election, Republican Senate Majority Leader Bob Dole waved a blank sheet of paper at some campaign workers and joked, "I've just obtained a copy of President Reagan's secret tax plan."[1]

But Reagan had been serious. He again proposed tax reform in his 1985 State of the Union Address. He called the existing tax code "un-American" and asked Congress to write a measure that would be "clear, simple, and fair for all." James Baker, his secretary of the Treasury, came up with a plan to cut personal income tax rates. With midterm elections looming, Congressional Democrats, led by House Ways and Means Chair Dan Rostenkowski, completely rewrote the measure so that their party could preempt the president and take the credit. Democrats kept taxes higher for the wealthy (at 38 percent) than the Republican plan (which had a top marginal rate of 35 percent.) Even though House Republicans had been frozen out of the deliberations, President Reagan urged them to vote for it. Nevertheless a Republican and conservative Democratic coalition defeated it, because the White House could get only 35 Republicans to vote for it. Speaker of the House Jim Wright then announced that unless fifty Republicans were found to support it on a new vote, tax reform was dead. Reagan went to Capitol Hill in person and appealed to his party caucus to support the measure. It passed with the fifty Republican votes.

The Republican-controlled Senate Finance Committee's bill proposed to end loopholes, lower the top marginal rate to 25 percent, and increase corporate taxes. The bill passed, as a coalition of liberal Democratic tax reformers who wanted an end to loopholes, and "supply-side" conservatives interested in tax reduction, prevailed over those favoring "business as usual." Eventually the House Democrats and Senate Republicans compromised on a bill with a top rate of 28 percent. On October 22, 1986, President Reagan signed the bill in a ceremony on the South Lawn of the White House.[2]

Tax reform succeeded because the Reagan administration used an effective political strategy. Treasury aide Richard Darman explained, "You force the political system to make an up-down choice . . . any time you can force a binary choice, politicians are very hard pressed not to choose tax reform."[3] Media coverage was extensive, the public was interested, and legislators were able to build records as tax reformers. House Democrats could vote for a bill that removed six million poor people from the tax rolls, gave relief to six million families of the working poor with children, and increased taxes on the rich. Senate Republicans could point to a drop in marginal tax rates on the wealthy and on corporations, and an end to inequitable loopholes, shifting $21 billion in tax liabilities to those who had formerly relied on tax shelters. The Treasury could point with pride to a tax system that it claimed would increase the gross national product by 1.2 percent annually. The Treasury was right: Voluntary tax compliance rose, there was less deferral of taxable income, and less cheating. President Reagan could wrap himself in the mantle of tax reformer and tax cutter—always good presidential politics. In fact, Reagan's own commitment to tax reform gave Congress a breathing space from the pressure of special interest groups, who were unwilling to take on a popular president.

"My job is to keep the growth going and keep jobs coming into the economy," President Clinton explained, when asked about the role of presidents as economic managers.[4] They use fiscal instruments such as tax and expenditure policies to try to moderate the booms and busts of the business cycle, maintain price stability, reduce unemployment, and promote growth. Although presidents can point to successes like the tax reform package of 1986, often their efforts are hampered by three factors: lack of adequate constitutional powers that leaves most formal powers to regulate the economy to Congress; the failure of their advisory system to formulate effective economic strategies, leaving a political vacuum that the opposition party in Congress is able to fill; and the limits of fiscal and monetary mechanisms that presidents rely on to influence an American economy that increasingly functions within a world economy.

THE PRESIDENT AS ECONOMIC MANAGER

Presidents have taken more and more responsibility for promoting prosperity, economic growth, and competitiveness in world markets. But there is a great mismatch between their political responsibilities and their constitutional powers.

Constitutional Powers

Article 2 grants the president no economic powers. He or she may recommend measures to Congress and report to Congress on the state of the union, but the president is given no budget powers, does not control the currency or monetary policy, does not have the power to levy taxes or tariffs, and does not have discretionary power to raise or lower them. In contrast, Article 1 assigns Congress plenary powers over interstate and foreign commerce, spending and taxation, the currency, and regulation of the economy. When Congress delegates its economic powers, it often does so to independent regulatory agencies or to entities independent of the White House, such as the Federal Reserve Board. It is Congress that has the final say on economic matters.

Political Responsibility: The Eroding American Dream

Since the 1970s the "American dream" has become more difficult for most Americans, particularly young people, to achieve. The workforce has shifted from manufacturing goods (31 percent of the workforce in 1960, down to 17 percent in 1994) to providing services. Between the late 1970s and early 1990s, the United States had a lower rate of economic growth than most other industrial nations, and its manufacturing and service industry wages remained stagnant or decreased.[5] Re-engineering and downsizing companies to cut costs, outsourcing to companies that pay less in wages and benefits, and using temporary professionals instead of in-house lawyers, accountants, and other professionals enabled large companies, which once kept workers for a lifetime, to lay off millions of employees. Between 1979 and 1994, the Fortune 500 companies laid off more than 4.5 million workers. Those who remained in full-time jobs had more work, labored under worse conditions, and received less compensation. The percentage of private-sector employees with pension plans and health benefits also declined. Unions lost membership (from 18 percent of the workforce in 1980 to 11 percent in 1994) and had less power in negotiations, often accepting wage and benefit "givebacks" required by employers.

In the new American economy, wages remained stagnant or declined. In the 1950s, real wages (adjusted for inflation) increased annually at a 2.5 percent rate, and in the 1960s at a 1.7 percent rate. In the 1970s wages stagnated, rising at a 0.2 percent rate. Then in the 1980s wages declined, so that overall, weekly wages fell (in constant 1993 dollars) from $315 in 1972 to $255 in 1993.[6] Between 1977 and 1992, average family income for the bottom 60 percent of the population declined (in inflation adjusted dollars) by 20 percent. It increased only slightly for the next 20 percent, rose 10 percent for the next 9 percent of the population, while the very top 1 percent of families more than doubled their family income.[7] By 1994 income inequality was greater than at any time since before World War II and also greater than in every other industrial nation. The top 20 percent of American families had 46.2 percent of the national income, but the bottom 20 percent enjoyed less than 5 percent of the national income earned each year. Wealth was even more concentrated than income. Between 1980 and 1990, the share of the nation's wealth owned by the richest 1 percent of the population went from 20 percent to 35 percent.

For young people the situation was particularly bleak: In constant 1984 dollars, the average 30-year-old earned $23,580 in 1973, a figure that declined to $17,520 by 1993.[8] The percentage of young males earning low wages (less than $12,195 in 1990 dollars) doubled from 18 to 40 percent between the 1970s and 1990s; for women the figures went from 29 to 48 percent.[9]

Both the restructuring of work in the United States because of changes in technology (such as the automation of industry) and the competition from low-wage and low-benefit nations (primarily in East Asia) caused a widening income gap between "knowledge worker professionals" and industrial, agricultural, and service workers. Although wages for industrial workers declined, workers with advanced graduate education increased their pay by 10.2 percent between 1979 and 1991.[10] Because of the growing income inequalities and job insecurities, white and blue collar workers were angry, alienated, afraid, and resentful. Some deserted their parties and voted for independent candidates, voted retrospectively in protest against the party in power, or dropped out of the electorate entirely, as more than twenty million voters did between 1968 and 1994.

"A society that lives with a very, very large gap between the well-educated and everybody else," Clinton's secretary of labor Robert Reich observed, is "an unstable society."[11] The "American dream," built in the aftermath of World War II, embodied a social contract between the people and their government based on opportunity to join the middle class and participate in the increased prosperity. By the 1990s, the dream of economic security for working- and middle-class people had been shattered. Underlying all the specific conflicts about economic policy was the fundamental truth that most Americans no longer believed that they and their children would share fully in the economic opportunities of the future. Hillary Clinton understood the political stakes for the White House in the new economic environment: she referred to the president's economic plan as first and foremost a "values document."[12] In the climate of the 1990s, she recognized that the president had to speak about economics with moral authority as well as with the knowledge of the economist.

PRESIDENTIAL POLITICAL STAKES

The stakes for the president in managing the economy are enormous, because absent economic prosperity the prospects of an incumbent winning reelection are small.

Electoral Stakes

"It's the economy, stupid!" was the slogan at the Clinton campaign headquarters in 1992—the reminder that presidential elections are often won or lost on the state of the economy. Since the 1940s, whenever economic growth has exceeded 3.5 percent in an election year, the party in power has retained the White House; below that level the opposition party has always won. The performance of the economy in an election year is critical.[13]

Presidents ride an economic roller coaster, with relatively minor changes in economic conditions leading to a rise or fall in presidential popularity and a gain or loss of seats in Congress in midterm elections. Most voters do not reward or punish presidential candidates based on their own personal economic circumstances,

President Bush confers with Secretary of State Jim Baker at the annual G-7 summit conference for the leaders of the major industrial nations (Munich, Germany, 1992).

but rather on the overall economic performance of the nation.[14] Although some voters decide retrospectively (punish a president for poor performance), other decide prospectively: If the economy is picking up, they assume things will be even better in the next four years.[15] The question, "under which candidate will I be better off in the years to come?" becomes a key determinant of who gets the swing voters. For Democratic voters in particular, rising or falling unemployment rates loom large in the decision about whether to support a Democratic presidential candidate or defect to a Republican or independent candidate.[16]

Incumbent presidents are most likely to be reelected when employment is increasing, inflation is held in check, and interest rates are low. Consider how economic performance has correlated with recent election results. The growth rate under President Carter was 2.96 percent over his first term, and employment shot up 12.5 percent. In his last year, however, growth declined slightly, employment declined slightly, and inflation and interest rates were high. The "misery index" (formed by adding the inflation, unemployment, and prime interest rates) stood at 40 percent. Carter was defeated handily by Ronald Reagan. In contrast, Reagan's overall first-term rate of economic growth was 3.02 percent, hardly better than Carter's, and in the 1982 recession voters took it out on Republican congressional candidates, while Reagan's own popularity plummeted into the 30 percent range. In Reagan's fourth year, however, there was a 6 percent increase in growth and a 5 percent gain in employment. Interest rates were far lower than in the Carter years, and the rate of inflation had declined greatly. The misery index had been cut almost in half, to approximately 24 percent. Reagan won a landslide reelection victory, even though overall job creation and economic growth at that point was no better than during the Carter years. Other things being equal, a president who presides over a growing economy with low unemployment and inflation will be far more popular than a president who presides over either a weak economy or one that is overheated.[17]

A president who tries to solve economic problems will be more popular than one who is perceived to be standpat; a president who takes dramatic actions and communicates a sense of urgency is more likely to win public support than a president who tries to soothe the public, pretend little is wrong, or who claims that the economic cycle is self-correcting.[18] Although Franklin Roosevelt was unable to end the Depression, he was reelected by large margins in 1936 and 1940 because he constantly proposed new measures to alleviate suffering and promote recovery. In the 1960s, even as unemployment rose, President Kennedy's popularity with voters increased because they could see he was making an effort to solve the problem. In 1992 George Bush pointed out that the misery index had remained low and that 1.3 million jobs had been created, but, as the economy lost steam, voter dissatisfaction with his presidency increased. The president was loath to take decisive action, claiming the economy was improving and that the problem was one of communicating that fact to the public. Although the economy *was* improving in George Bush's last year in office in 1992, most voters were upset by his stand-offish and passive approach and thought the economy was getting worse. (Over the summer of 1992 the economy actually grew by 3.9 percent, but these figures were not available until after the election.) Because voters thought Bush was passive and remote, he was unable to assuage middle-class voter insecurity about personal finances and job prospects; his standing in the polls continued its downward slide (a 43 percent drop from March 1991 to January 1992); media assessment went from highly positive to sharply negative; and subsequently he was defeated for reelection.[19]

After his election, Bill Clinton kept calling for more economic growth in 1993, even as unemployment fell with three-quarters of a million new jobs created, because he understood that any self-congratulatory rhetoric would only backfire with those still unemployed or afraid of losing their jobs. Initially his strategy paid off. By December of his first year, as his economic programs passed Congress, the economy picked up steam, and unemployment dipped, Clinton's popularity went up from 39 percent to over 50 percent for the first time since early spring.[20] Other things are not always equal, however. Although Clinton's economic performance in his twenty months involved creation of 4.7 million jobs (almost all in the private sector) while keeping inflation in check, his performance was not enough to keep his popularity from sagging and his party from suffering a crushing defeat in the midterm elections in 1994 because of noneconomic factors.

The Political–Business Cycle

In 1960 Richard Nixon thought that one reason he had lost his race for the White House was that the Republican administration of which he had been a part led by President Eisenhower had not done enough to get the economy out of a recession.[21]

Nixon vowed that if he were ever elected president, he would make sure the economy was on an upward path on a presidential election year. Presidents try to manipulate the business cycle so that downturns in the economy will occur in the first years and prosperity will return in the election year.[22] Between 1946 and 1984, for example, the gross national product rose 1.9 percent in nonelection years, 2.8 percent in congressional election years, and 3.7 percent in years in which the president was running for reelection. Presidents try to boost employment and raise incomes in an election year with infusions of federal spending. Many presidents have accepted large deficits and proposed tax cuts in the fourth year of their first term (including Johnson, Nixon, Ford, Reagan, and Bush). They sometimes propose "dipsy doodle" policies that provide benefits before an election and levy costs afterward: President Bush implemented a new withholding formula for income taxes that boosted workers' take-home pay before the elections, but resulted in lower refund checks the following spring.

Party Politics

Presidents pursue economic policies designed to unify their parties and reward the voters who elected them. Democratic presidents usually try to lower the unemployment rate with a high-growth strategy, because blue-collar and other unionized workers, women, and minorities, are most affected, and they are important elements of the Democratic coalition. Republican presidents concentrate on lowering inflation and interest rates, and reducing the capital gains tax, because their strongest party identifiers are disproportionately from higher-income groups. Democrats Kennedy, Johnson, Carter, and Clinton all lowered the unemployment rates substantially in their first terms (Figure 13.1). In contrast, under Republicans Eisenhower, Nixon, Ford, Reagan (in his first term), and Bush, unemployment rates all increased. Democratic presidents are also more likely to stimulate the economy to provide economic growth. Johnson, Kennedy, Carter, and Clinton all enjoyed economic growth rates in the 3 percent range, whereas Eisenhower, Nixon, Ford, and Bush all had growth rates of under 2 percent. Only Ronald Reagan in his second term presided over boom times involving high economic growth and low unemployment, and he did so by running budget and trade deficits unparalleled in American history. Inflation is almost always lower in a Republican administration, as are interest rates, in part because more sluggish economic performance means reduced demand for goods and for loans. (Figure 13.1, however, shows recent inflation levels that might be taken as exceptions to this trend.) Finally, income *equality* increases under Democratic presidents, while income *inequality* increases under Republicans, because the former raise taxes on the wealthy and the latter lower them.

Presidents cannot always count on their own party to support their economic programs. Eisenhower was badgered by conservative Republicans who pressed him for large budget cuts and reductions in business taxes. Kennedy had to delay proposals for a tax cut because of opposition of Democratic leaders. Lyndon Johnson could not get his tax surcharge bill out of the Ways and Means Committee (a measure needed to pay for the Vietnam War) until he agreed to the Democratic chair-

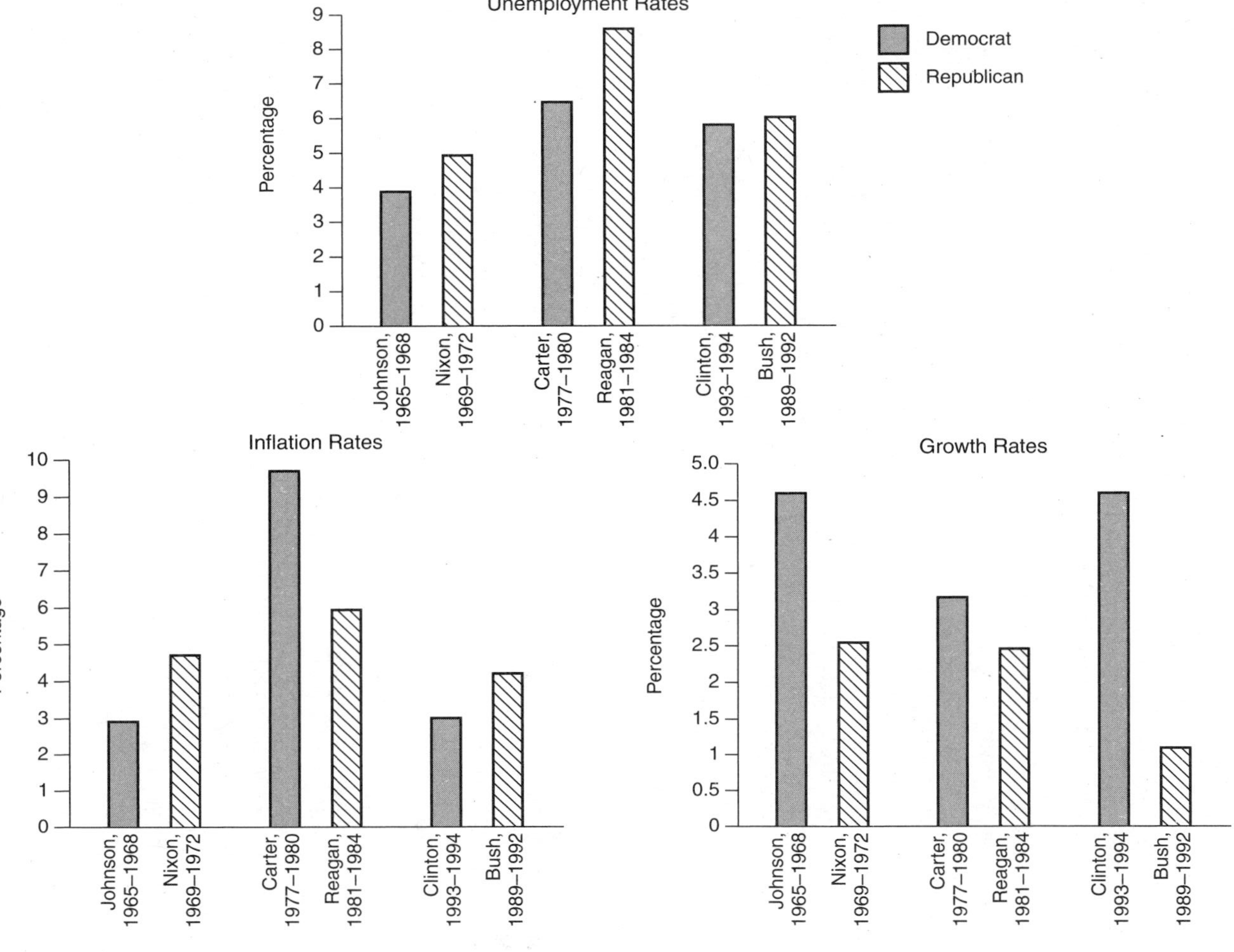

Figure 13.1 Economic measures: how Democratic and Republican presidents compare, 1965–1994.
Source: Data from John P. Frendreis and Raymond Tatalovich, *The Modern Presidency and Economic Policy,* Itasca, IL: F. E. Peacock, 1994), Table 12.1, pp. 308–309; data for Clinton from Council of Economic Advisers, *Annual Report, 1994.*

man's demand for expenditure cuts. Ford's tax cut proposals met with strong opposition from Republicans on the Senate Budget Committee. Carter's $31 billion counterrecessionary expenditure program was criticized by Democrats on the Joint Economic Committee as too little too late. Ronald Reagan's plans to cut Social Security benefits were unanimously rejected by Senate Republicans, and many of his proposals to cut expenditures were routinely defeated by bipartisan coalitions in congressional committees. George Bush's compromise with the Democrats on tax increases in 1990 was initially scuttled by House Republicans, and a second compromise had to be forged, which passed against the opposition of a majority of Bush's own party.

Bill Clinton won many significant victories in Congress on economic issues, but did so without a unified party. Over the summer of 1993 his economic program narrowly passed in the House of Representatives, 218 in favor to 216 against. Clinton gained the support of 98 percent of the Democratic members in House districts that he had carried by a majority in 1992; he received 85 percent of the Democrats whose districts he carried by a plurality; he won only 60 percent of the Democrats from districts he had lost in 1992. In the South, his own regional base, he lost significant support in both the House and Senate.[23] When his programs were consistent with a conservative (and Republican) agenda—deficit reduction, for example—they were likely to pass; when they followed an activist Democratic approach, they were likely to fail: Clinton's energy tax proposals were killed by Democrats on the tax-writing committees, and his economic stimulus package was blocked by conservative coalition.

THE WHITE HOUSE ECONOMIC ADVISORY SYSTEM

In their efforts to manage the economy, presidents are weakened by the frictions within their advisory system, the lack of adequate, accurate, and timely information about the economy, and the weakness of existing economic theories.

The Economic Advisory System

The president receives economic advice from the secretary of the treasury, who serves as his principal spokesperson before Congress, the chair of the Council of Economic Advisers (CEA), the director of the Office of Management and Budget (OMB), the secretaries of commerce and labor, and the U.S. trade negotiator. He may also create an economic policy board or council where his advisors (and their deputies) can debate policy options and provide him with recommendations.[24]

Economic advisors have different responsibilities and political roles. Most Treasury secretaries are former corporate executives or Wall Street financiers, appointed to reassure the business community. They bring a business perspective into the administration, calling for reductions in expenditures and balanced budgets. Some, like Lloyd Bentsen in the Clinton administration, come out of Congress, and serve as principal liaison between the White House and Capitol Hill. During the debate over NAFTA, Bentsen was an indefatigable lobbyist with his former colleagues, telephoning 64, meeting with 85 others, and talking with 233 reporters.[25]

The chair of the CEA uses economic theories to formulate advice. Some, like Edwin Nourse, the first chair of the CEA, thought that they should be neutral advocates, speaking for the economics profession to the president.[26] Truman fired Nourse because he did not like being lectured to; presidents usually want advisors who help advance the presidential program rather than condescending academic experts who talk down to them or become embroiled in public disputes with cabinet secretaries and members of Congress. CEA Chair Arthur Okun did better than Nourse because he offered advice framed to reflect the president's political problems.[27] Some CEA chairs become policy advocates before Congress; others work on the inside as problem-solvers, studying particular parts of the economy, such as Laura D'Andrea Tyson, whose own area of economic expertise involved analysis of domestic economic sectors and how they might become more successful in the world economy against foreign trade barriers.

The CEA is likely to square off against the Treasury on the question of the impact of high deficits: the Treasury almost always argues that deficits will "crowd out" private investment and result in a rise in interest rates that makes Treasury refinancing of debt more difficult. Similarly, the Treasury and the OMB differ about projected expenditures and revenues: The OMB forecasts lower expenditures and higher revenues than the more conservative Treasury. Sometimes these disputes get out of hand. Once, during a congressional hearing, Treasury Secretary Donald Regan was asked if OMB Director David Stockman had spoken for the president. "I'll let Mr. Stockman describe his point of view," Regan responded, undercutting the OMB director by adding, "I think the president expressed the administration's view." On another occasion, when asked if the *Annual Report of the Council of Economic Advisers* should be used by Congress, Regan responded, "As far as I'm concerned, you can throw it away."[28] Congress does not trust any administration forecasts, preferring to rely instead on those prepared by its own Congressional Budget Office, which have been considerably more accurate.[29]

Infighting among advisors can provide the president with better analysis of alternatives and a better range of viable choices.[30] But not always. Few presidents have had as much conflict among advisors as George Bush. None had Bush's full confidence, and none was designated chief spokesperson. His Economic Policy Council, an interagency group, did not provide him with memoranda setting forth his options, and he found the advice of key aides confusing and sometimes indecipherable. In 1991 Bush named Clayton Yeutter, former secretary of agriculture and GOP national chairman, to be his coordinator, but Treasury Secretary Nicholas Brady insisted on chairing all economic policy groups under the council, again splitting authority. OMB Director Richard Darman ignored Brady, according to some accounts.[31] He refused to concede that Brady spoke for the administration. CEA Director Michael Boskin also had problems with Brady, believing that his upbeat assessments of the economy were counterproductive; Boskin tried to get Bush to present a more balanced account of the sluggishness of the economy. Meanwhile Darman undercut Boskin, claiming he was "irrelevant" to policy formulation.[32]

To end conflict in the advisory system, Alice M. Rivlin (who served as director of the Congressional Budget Office and later as Clinton's budget director) proposed that the presidential advisory system be consolidated into a new Department of Economic Affairs, which would take over the CEA advisory function, the OMB budget preparation, and the fiscal duties of the Treasury. The president would no longer adjudicate amongst competing centers of power, and a "highly professional permanent staff" of trained economists would develop policy, somewhat removed from the "short-run political concerns of the White House."[33] Although the idea makes sense from the point of view of a professional economist, it would deprive the president of a range of advice and would professionalize what for the president remain primarily political issues.

The National Economic Council

President Clinton created a National Economic Council (NEC) to coordinate economic policy, headed by investment banker Robert Rubin. The members of the council were the secretaries of the Treasury, Commerce, and Labor Departments, the vice president, the budget director, and the chair of the Council of Economic Advisers. Rubin participated in deliberations of the National Security Council, in return for permitting the deputy national security advisor to sit in on the NEC. Rubin described his job as that of the "honest broker," claiming, "You have to make sure that you are dealing with the president—and with everybody else in the economic team and in the Administration—in a totally neutral way. That you express the pluses and the minuses, and then totally separate that from the expression of your opinion."[34]

Far from being neutral, Rubin was also an important advisor in his own right and was a decisive voice at times: Just before Clinton introduced his economic program, Rubin convinced Clinton to stick with some unpopular spending cuts, against the advice of several political advisors. He also campaigned against a generous health care plan that would have imposed heavy burdens on business (in this case joining with CEA Chairman Tyson), favored reducing business taxes, and proposed new incentives for business investment and programs in employee training.

The council prepared decision memoranda laying out options. President Clinton chose to make deeper cuts in the budget than some cabinet secretaries (notably Labor Secretary Robert Reich) favored after such memoranda and a series of debates within the NEC. The council took a major role in developing urban renewal proposals and debating international trade policies (with CEA Chair Tyson squaring off against Trade Representative Director Mickey Kantor). The council also helped coordinate the public stance that members of the president's economic team took about issues, so there were fewer contradictory statements from presidential advisors.

Some economists were worried that the NEC would eclipse the CEA and the secretary of the treasury. As Nobel laureates James Tobin and Robert Solow warned, "Any way you slice it, the new bureaucracy is a bad idea whose time has apparently come."[35] They were worried that the special assistant to the president would serve as a buffer between department secretaries and the CEA on the one hand, and the president on the other. They believed that council members were likely to become "special pleaders" with the president on routine matters with which he should not be concerned. Advocates argued that many problems transcend individual departments or presidential agencies, involve foreign and domestic matters simultaneously, and are best considered by bringing officials together and forging a consensus.

They saw the council as a mechanism that could break through departmental obstructionism and interagency rivalries and force decisions and implementation according to a presidential schedule.

Economic Forecasting and Estimating as a Presidential Problem

Ever since Herbert Hoover became a national joke during the Depression with his slogan "prosperity is just around the corner," presidents have had a hard time convincing the public that they can correctly forecast economic conditions. To influence the U.S. economy the president must know how it is performing and where is it headed, but his or her advisors will have great difficulty helping in this task. To begin with, most statistical information used within the advisory system comes from sample surveys (either data collected from companies or polling surveys). The initial information is often revised upward or downward substantially after further analysis, which often comes too late to influence policy. The 1990–1991 recession was far shallower than the government believed and the recovery far stronger, once analysts had further examined the data in 1993—two years after the initial description came out from the Commerce Department. The president may believe that the economy is moving in one direction, only to find out a few months later that the more complete and corrected data pointed to a different trend.

The data collection itself may suffer from distortions: In 1993, for example, Labor Department statisticians announced that their monthly surveys of sixty thousand households were undercounting the number of people unemployed or underemployed, because of the way they had been phrasing their questions. The categories may minimize problems. The "unemployed," according to the government, do not include those who do not hold a job and who have given up looking for work (perhaps calling themselves retired) because they are discouraged—a group that includes as many as 1.1 million former workers. Nor do they include former white-collar workers with good jobs who now work part-time in menial positions or are self-employed as "consultants" or providers of business services—at half their former pay and without their former benefits. The government has not properly counted many married women seeking jobs, who were called "homemakers" in the surveys and were not listed among the unemployed.[36] The government collects no data on the length of time discouraged workers who have dropped off its statistical charts remain without work. The Labor Department does compile a quarterly index of employment that factors in part-time workers and those who have dropped out of the workforce and stopped looking for work—by that measurement the unemployment rate is about 3.5 percent higher than the monthly unemployment rate commonly used by the government.[37] Labor Department officials themselves are cautious about using the data from the monthly survey, which Secretary Robert Reich admitted was "bouncing around a bit" in part because of the small number of households surveyed.[38] The Labor Department's survey of households and survey of employers do not gibe, especially when the economy is recovering: the latter estimates six times as much increase in employment as the former.

Because the economy is based on billions of individual decisions that are interconnected daily through increasingly complex financial markets, there is a contingent and chaotic quality to its performance. Almost any external event (war, scandal, assassination) can set off a change in market psychology, and alter a preexisting trend before it plays out. There is a very low level of probability that any scenario devised by a government or outside observer can take into account more than a small fraction of these external market-influencing events, and therefore forecasting becomes a roll of the dice, no matter how sophisticated the mathematical models and economic theories. For example, in December 1994 a group of "economic intelligence" experts from the State Department and the CIA gave a briefing at the State Department to business leaders about the Mexican economy. They forecast continued growth because of NAFTA. Three days later, the peso began to tumble, and within the next three months Mexico's economy required a $44 billion bailout. Mexico was in the grip of a deep recession and plagued by political instability, all of which put the value of the U.S. currency in jeopardy, and might put new pressures on interest rates if the Federal Reserve felt compelled to defend the dollar. None of this was anticipated by administration officials or their economic advisors, who minimized any need for currency coordination when NAFTA was signed—despite warnings from some leading students of the Mexican economy.

There is an old joke to the effect that economists have successfully forecast eight of the last two recessions. It is not enough to make correct forecasts; it is necessary to avoid incorrect forecasts as well. To be an expert forecaster, it is not sufficient to be right; it is necessary on most occasions not to be wrong. By that measure most presidential economists have failed the test. Between 1991 and 1993, economists in two administrations kept forecasting a strong economic recovery. Throughout that period, their forecasts were off the mark, as the recovery sputtered. Then in the fall of 1993, just when the CEA, the CBO, and private economic forecasters were scaling back their estimates, the economy started a strong upward push. Presidential economists are supposed to forecast four years out—an impossible task given all the contingencies that will occur within that time.

Presidents and their advisors often get their numbers wrong. They consistently overestimate revenues and underestimate expenditures. Their forecasts for deficit reduction are almost always wide of the mark. They overstate the impact of their deficit-cutting measures: Clinton's program in 1993 claimed $496 billion in deficit cuts over a five-year period, but only two months later it was revised downward to $433 billion.[39] They are slow in predicting recessionary conditions and often delay taking measures that might alleviate it, a circumstance that cost Bush the 1992 election. They claim that a recovery is imminent, even when conditions remain stagnant or are getting worse. President Clinton in 1993 boasted creating a million new jobs, when in fact 60 percent were part-time, real wages continued to fall, and layoffs ran higher than in the recession of 1991. He also claimed that the lower interest rates would add a $100 billion stimulus to the economy, only to back off and reduce the claim to $50 billion after being challenged by private economists.[40]

Perhaps the greatest technical problem facing the president is that there is no fully developed science to economics (though there is plenty of wisdom and good advice that savvy economists can impart). The president must choose not only an advisor, but also a school of advice. The advisors may well be talking past each other if they are an eclectic mix. Under those circumstances, a president must be pardoned for simplifying the decisional problem by going for an "election year fix" on taxes, deciding on spending policies that are popular with political constituencies, and putting the burden on the Federal Reserve System to counterbalance and correct any distortions the administration's policies might cause.

FISCAL POLICY

Fiscal policy relies on a combination of tax and spending decisions to reduce the excesses of the business cycle while putting the economy on an upward growth path. Presidents have used a variety of "decisional rules" in making fiscal policy, yet there is little or no evidence that fiscal policy has worked well. The average length of downturns between 1887 and 1917 was 9.7 months, before there was any economic science or fiscal policy; yet the average increased to 12.4 months after 1948, after creation of the Council of Economic Advisers.[41] Economists have not developed effective theories and the experts often disagree on policies and their consequences.

The Phillips Curve: The Illusion of Choice

According to some economists, increased growth and employment stimulate demand to such an extent that inflation occurs. To maintain price stability, they argue, it is necessary to keep demand lower than it would be at conditions of full employment. A tradeoff exists, according to this "Phillips Curve," between employment and price stability. The belief that such a tradeoff is necessary has often structured presidential economics. To the extent the curve is correct, it justifies the verdict that economics is "the dismal science" because presidents have to choose between growth and price stability. Presidents seem to accept the validity of the curve, in large measure to reassure financial and currency markets that they will be "firm" against inflation. They have tended to opt for price stability and moderate growth, and they have never made a sustained attempt to promote full employment in the United States.[42]

The Phillips Curve and its theory of tradeoffs is half-right and all wrong. It is *theoretically* true that when the economy is at full capacity and near-full employment, greater production will require more workers, and eventually a labor shortage will result in "wage-push" inflation, as occurred in the 1940s. Yet, in the real world, inflation is not so closely linked to the labor market: Sometimes "full-capacity" inflation occurs without wages increasing, as in the late 1970s and late 1980s; sometimes wages increase without inflation rising, as happened in the mid-1950s and early 1960s, because of other factors increasing productivity, a situation also found in Japan and Germany at times of great growth; sometimes businesses operate at near to full capacity, while wages fall or remain stagnant, as happened in the early 1990s. The Labor Department's Cost Index for the last quarter of 1994 rose only 3 percent, the smallest increase for salaries and benefits ever recorded during a period of economic growth, declining unemployment, and a high factory utilization.

Many economists reject the Phillips Curve. They argue that inflation will remain low because wages are being held down by the prospect that jobs may be moved "offshore" to low-wage countries. Even as the economy improves and U.S.

factories reach their capacity, there will be no price increases because production can be shifted abroad where factories have extra capacity. In addition, there is plenty of unused labor and productive capacity in the United States and around the world. A large number of part-time, consulting, and contract workers who are officially listed as "employed" are available to compete for the relatively few additional industrial jobs being added as the economy improves; therefore, there is no labor shortage to push labor costs up, even though unemployment is relatively low, a situation referred to as "disguised slack" by labor market economists. In short, U.S. labor and capital no longer function within a purely domestic economy, and theories that applied in the past cannot predict the behavior of prices in the present.[43]

Decisional Rules in Fiscal Policy

Through the 1930s, most presidents believed that the business cycle was self-regulating. As wages and prices fell in a depression, investment would become more attractive and would increase, eventually ending the slump. Presidents believed that, during a depression or recession, their role was simply to reduce government spending to match the reduction in revenues and wait for things to improve. Even Franklin Roosevelt campaigned for the presidency in 1932 on a platform calling for spending cuts and balanced budgets.

By the late 1930s, Roosevelt had come around to the view of economists in the Fiscal Division of the Bureau of the Budget, who argued that to end the Depression the government should "prime the pump" with massive injections of spending to stimulate demand, after which it might return to a more neutral role.[44] Other economists, known as Keynesians, believed that the private sector could never supply enough demand, so the government would have to make up the difference indefinitely. In the postwar period every president from Truman through Carter pursued a fiscal policy based on the Keynesian idea that when the nation was sliding into recession or depression the government should increase expenditures or lower tax rates to increase demand; conversely, when the economy became overheated, the government could raise taxes or decrease outlays, lessening demand and stabilizing prices.[45] Each president from Eisenhower through Carter had his own variant on the general Keynesian theme of providing stimulus to the economy:

- President Eisenhower called for a compensatory policy. In booms the government would run a surplus and in recessions a deficit, trying to balance the budget over an entire business cycle.
- President Kennedy called for a propulsive policy. He wanted to increase the growth rate so that we would be a better example than the Soviet Union to developing nations of the world.
- President Nixon proposed a full-employment balanced budget. He calculated the revenues that the government would have obtained had full employment already existed in a booming economy, and then set government expenditures to exactly match the hypothetical revenues. The budget was in deficit, but Nixon could still refer to a "balanced budget" to satisfy conservatives in his own party.
- President Carter proposed restrictive budgets in much of his presidency, to lower government demand and lower the high interest rates that plagued his presidency. By failing to embrace a stimulus model, he ensured himself a one-term presidency.

Supply-Side Economics

President Ronald Reagan abandoned the postwar consensus that stimulating *demand* was the best way to rev up the economy. Instead, he argued that growth could be achieved and inflation and unemployment reduced by providing new incentives to the *supply side* to increase production and provide new jobs. He would do this by lowering tax rates on income and capital gains and by deregulating the economy. His idea was that people would work harder if they could keep more of what they earned. Entrepreneurs would be encouraged to develop new products, and companies would invest more in new plants and equipment, all of which would add new jobs. Lower tax rates would encourage more saving, which would mean lower interest rates and even more investment. As the supply of goods increased relative to demand, prices would stabilize, bringing down inflation. Once inflation was licked, interest rates would decline even more, because lenders would no longer charge an "inflation premium" on their loans (an extra amount to compensate them for the risk of lending in a high-inflation period). The lower interest rates, in turn, would provide yet a further stimulus for business expansion.[46]

Supply-side "Reaganomics" had mixed results. Reagan got Congress to adopt most elements of his tax and spending and deregulation program. The tax reduction increased demand for goods and services, but savings decreased. Investment initially declined for two years, and in Reagan's first term only five million jobs were created—fewer than the ten million created in President Carter's one term. In his second term, however, the massive deficits fueled a classic "demand" boom: more than ten million new jobs were created, and economic growth zoomed. Meanwhile inflation was cut drastically, as were interest rates—and these remained low through Bush's presidency. Low interest rates, however, do not always stimulate the economy: studies have shown that company decisions to expand depend less on low rates and far more on cash flow and projections about sales and potential profits.[47] The Reagan and Bush legacy was a $4 trillion national debt, which resulted in new budgeting rules passed by Congress that made it impossible to run stimulative deficits in the event of a recession.

Clintonomics

When Bill Clinton ran for the presidency he had the advice of several Nobel Prize–winning economists (all Democratic liberals) who told him that he should propose a huge jump-start stimulus program for the economy. He promised a $60 billion job stimulus program. Once in office he proposed a more modest $19 billion. Clinton failed to convince the country that there was a need for a stimulus program to create 300,000 jobs. He found his own party unenthusiastic, Democratic first-year representatives openly hostile, and Republicans united in their opposition to the point where they mounted a successful filibuster in the Senate against Clinton's initial proposals and against his two compromise proposals of $15 and $12 billion. Congress cut each of his proposals to shreds, leaving only a small $500 million program for public works and summer jobs, while approving an extension of unemployment benefits. His longer-term "investment" programs were also cut out of the economic plan that Congress passed.

Clinton did propose and win a program to restore business confidence in fiscal policy making. It involved a five-year, $496 billion program of deficit reduction (which would have an $80 billion negative effect on the economy in the first year). He argued that lower interest rates (promoted by the Federal Reserve Board) would have an offsetting stimulative effect. An informal caucus of Democratic "deficit hawks" kept pressure on Clinton for more spending cuts throughout his first two years.

Clinton was unable to get his tax program passed as he had originally proposed it. As a candidate he made a speech at Georgetown University in which he said, "I will offer middle-income tax cuts. The average working family's tax bill will go down about 10 percent, a savings of about $300 a year, and I won't finance it with increasing the deficit."[48] He also proposed giving Americans making less than $80,000 annually a "middle-class" tax cut, raising taxes on the top 2 percent making over $200,000 per year, and imposing a 10 percent surtax on those with annual incomes of over $1 million. Clinton backed off his tax cut promises even before his inauguration. Faced with projections of ballooning deficits, he quickly turned his attention to ways to raise revenues. "Under my economic program," he told the nation, "we will build an America where even the most privileged pay their fair share, not because we want to soak the rich, but because we want to stop soaking the middle class and ask everybody to bear a fair share of the load."[49] These included proposals to lower the amount an estate could transfer to children from $600,000 to $200,000 without being taxed, an increase of income taxes to 36 percent, up 5 percent, on those making more than $140,000 annually (for individuals, $115,000), and a tax surcharge on those making over $250,000. To defend his tax increases, he claimed that he had never promised not to increase taxes; he only had promised not to increase taxes to pay for new government programs—*these* tax increases would be going for deficit reduction. He also called for new tax breaks on capital gains and a tax credit for business investments, all geared toward emerging small high-technology companies. Clinton's plans were attacked on the grounds that they violated the spirit of the 1986 reforms: they promoted tax breaks for favored groups at the expense of general rules for all, and they "soaked the rich" rather than treated everyone equitably. Critics called it a boon for accountants, tax lawyers, and lobbyists. Yet Clinton claimed his reforms were not geared to special interests. Resorting to populist rhetoric to win support from the public, he charged that special-interest opponents "have already lined the corridors of power with high-priced lobbyists."[50]

Although Clinton did get Congress to pass higher taxes on the wealthy, he failed to gain support for his capital gains cut. He failed to win support for special targeted investment breaks for high technology, including a two-year temporary $21 billion investment tax credit, after the heads of the two tax-writing committees in Congress failed to support it. Most economists thought it would have at best the effect of accelerating planned investment rather than stimulating new investment.

President Clinton also failed to get Congress to enact a $70 billion tax on energy sources, a tax that would have translated into higher prices for heating fuels and industrial goods. Clinton wanted to use the funds for a variety of public works and infrastructure investment projects in his budget (and 40 percent would have gone to poor people to help them cope with the higher prices). A broad-based coalition led by the National Association of Manufacturers organized to kill his proposal. More than 600 companies and Chambers of Commerce around the nation joined forces in the American Energy Alliance; 1,650 small businesses, corporations, and trade associations first won exemptions for most sectors of the economy, leaving only taxes on gasoline, diesel fuel, methanol and ethanol (used by farmers), and jet fuel. By passing out loopholes to gain support, Clinton committed a fatal error: the public saw the bill as unfair, violating principles of tax reform. Meanwhile key senators needed to pass Clinton's budget plan indicated that if a broad-based energy tax passed Congress they would not support the budget. To preserve his budget proposals, Clinton finally turned the tax issues over to the Senate Finance Committee, which voted to kill a broad-based tax and instead set a very small increase in the tax on gasoline, hardly noticeable as prices at the pump went down because of a glut of gasoline on world markets.

By 1995, Clinton's economic program had been rejected by the American voters. Republican congressional majorities were busy fashioning taxing and spending policies that were the antithesis of the Clinton approach, including capital gains tax reductions, tax credits to benefit families with children, and drastic deficit reductions that would reduce the government's role in stimulating the economy.

MONETARY POLICY

President Kennedy once told Federal Reserve Board Chairman McChesney Martin, "I know you've got a job to do, but I like my job, and I'd like to stick around here awhile." Kennedy knew that maintaining effective working relations with the Federal Reserve Board (known as the Fed) was one of the keys to an effective economic policy for any president. Borrowing a leaf from his predecessor, Clinton seated Chairman Alan Greenspan next to Hillary Rodham Clinton when he presented his first economic program to Congress, as a tangible sign to financial markets that he would work closely with the Fed.

Monetary Instruments

The Fed influences the economy by influencing the quantity and cost of money. Monetarists believe that controlling money is the key to managing investment and consumption decisions, and that monetary policy rather than fiscal policy is the key to controlling inflation and stimulating growth. A restrictive policy that contracts the money supply may damp down a boom and control inflation, but it also can plunge the nation into a recession or choke off a recovery—as happened in the 1930s. A permissive policy that expands the money supply rapidly may stimulate a boom, but it can also lead to runaway inflation and ultimately choke off growth as interest rates are forced up—as happened in the 1970s. A lowering of interest rates between 1992 and early 1994 helped stimulate the economy, even as taxes were rising and deficit spending was being brought under control—the first time the United States ended a recession since the 1930s without fiscal stimulus (in 1993 and 1994 deficits were headed down). The following year the Fed changed direction and raised short-term rates six times to keep a new inflationary spiral from starting. Most

To underscore his desire for close coordination of fiscal and monetary policies, President Clinton invited Federal Reserve Chairman Alan Greenspan to sit next to First Spouse Hillary Rodham Clinton as he unveiled his economic program to Congress, February 17, 1993. The administration worked closely with the Federal Reserve Board to restrain inflation during a period of sustained economic growth.

members of the Federal Reserve Board put the control of inflation as the primary goal, although Congress since 1978 has given the Fed statutory direction to stimulate the economy as well.

The Fed has several ways to influence the economy through its regulation of the banking system. These include the following:

- Setting the discount rate on its loans to member banks. A rate increase forces banks to raise interest rates.
- Setting a reserve requirement for member banks, which is a specified ratio between deposits and loans. Raising the requirement means banks will lend less, while lowering it eases credit.
- Buying and selling government securities in "open-market operations" from commercial banks. When it sells securities, the banks or their customers pay by check, draining money from the banking system and reducing funds available for loan. When the Fed buys securities, it pays the banks, and that injects money into the banking system.

Between the 1960s and the 1990s these instruments became weaker. Using the discount rate to increase interest rates did not necessarily dampen business activity; foreign investors might transfer funds into the United States to take advantage of higher rates, keeping funds available in the banking system for loan. Moreover, higher rates do not often correlate with investment decisions: if businesses think rates will go even higher in the future, an increase in the discount rate may become a signal to "lock in" a loan sooner rather than later. The reserve requirements became less important as a lower percentage of commercial banks were involved in the Federal Reserve System. Corporations could finance their investments by issuing stock or commercial paper, by obtaining loans from foreign banks and investment houses, or by selling their bonds to insurance companies and pension funds, all of which had money to lend.

Monetary Theories

One of the problems in making monetary policy is the lack of consensus among economists as to what effect interest rates or the money supply has on the economy. Some argue that every 1 percent increase in the money supply yields close to a 1 percent increase in the gross national product (GNP). Others claim that the increase is only temporary or that increased inflation washes out the benefits. Some say that decreasing the money supply will raise interest rates and slow inflation and growth. Others say that raising interest rates itself promotes inflation (as it did to 1995 costs for car leases and purchases) and may lead consumers and corporations to borrow (if they anticipate rates going even higher) rather than inhibiting borrowing. Conversely, lowering interest rates might increase the demand for money, but it might not do so if people and corporations think that rates will go even lower if they wait a bit longer before borrowing. And low rates do nothing if businesses have no confidence: In 1933 effective interest rates were close to zero, yet there was little investment, because businesses had no confidence that they could find consumers to buy goods produced. Between 1989 and 1993, with real interest rates at their lowest in two decades, a predicted economic boom did not materialize: lack of confidence among producers and consumers kept many from making new commitments (especially in buying a new house) even though "the numbers" seemed to be ideal. There is no credible evidence that low rates stimulate the economy in the absence of an underlying demand based on other factors.

Monetarists are divided into several different camps, so it is no coincidence that presidents may not be sure of what policy to promote with the Fed. Some believe in "fine-tuning" and continuous intervention, using the various instruments of the Fed. Yet even those promoting monetary intervention are divided as to which indicators they should use to signal the need for intervention. Should it be rates of interest charged by banks, the supply of money, the velocity of money (which indicates the level of business activity), international currency exchange rates (the value of the dollar against other major currencies), inflation rates, or unemployment rates? Matters are not helped by the fact that the Fed has only an imprecise idea of the quantity of money in circulation (there are seven definitions from which to choose), and as financial services companies develop new lending products (such as credit cards with large borrowing lines), definitions of "money" constantly change.

Decisional Rules in Monetary Policy

Some monetarists, among them Nobel Prize–winning economist Milton Friedman, have argued that monetary policy should involve an expansion of the money supply by a set amount each year, without any other intervention.[51] Such a policy would provide certainty about the Fed's policies for investors, and in their view such certainty would yield greater benefits than any attempt at government intervention. Indeed, some monetarists have argued that highly interventionist Federal Reserve policies, far from transforming booms into "soft landings," have been responsible for credit crunches that have brought about recessionary or "stagflation" conditions that have damaged the economy.

The Federal Reserve has no consistent decisional rules to use in regulating the money supply or preventing inflation. As the Council of Economic Advisers points out, the Fed operates on an incremental, "seat of the pants," approach, one that is often highly criticized by the Treasury and administration economists, especially when the policy becomes restrictive.[52] In the Clinton presidency, the Fed opened to the public the minutes of its heretofore private board discussions, and it became clear that it used no decisional rules at all in making policy, other than its desire to be "better safe than sorry" when it came to keeping inflation down.[53] Chairman Alan Greenspan pointed out that the Fed used anecdotal, case study, and experiential approaches rather than econometric models, which he suggested relied on outdated relationships and correlations that did not capture an economy in flux, and "need to be viewed skeptically when making policy for the future."[54]

In 1994 the Fed claimed that in setting interest rates, it would rely on a new approach: it would try to find the "equilibrium real interest rate," defined as a rate that would promote a maximum level of growth without an increase in inflation. Whether anyone could correctly find that single point remained an open question, especially because Greenspan admitted that economists had no precise measurement of the economy's maximum capacity, nor any consensus about how close the economy must come to that (unmeasurable) indicator for inflation to begin.[55] Even if these theoretical problems did not exist, the Fed would still have an implementation problem: some models of the economy suggest that actions taken by the Fed take 15 to 18 months to have a significant effect—time enough for conditions that originally precipitated the Fed's actions to change.[56]

White House–Fed Relations

The Federal Reserve Board consists of seven members appointed to fourteen-year terms by the president with the advice and consent of the Senate. They are joined by the presidents of the twelve Federal Reserve Banks, located in each region of the country, to form the Fed's Open Market Committee, the group that develops monetary policy and initiates changes in interest rates, subject to final approval of the Board. By law, the regional bank boards must make a recommendation about whether to maintain or to change interest rates every two weeks. The Chair of the Federal Reserve is appointed to a four-year term, which coincides with the midterm of the president, a system designed to preserve the independence of the Fed and act as a check on a new administration, because an incoming president "inherits" the existing Fed's chair and board.

Relations between the Federal Reserve System and the White House range from forced cordiality to open hostility. Presidents in economic trouble become "instant monetarists"—they blame the Fed for their problems (giving new meaning to the old term *buckpassing*). Lyndon Johnson called the chairman of the Federal Reserve down to his Texas ranch in 1965 after the Fed raised the discount rate, and dressed him down for leaving Johnson politically vulnerable. Later he blamed the Fed for the 1967–1968 inflation, even though it was caused by his own war policies.[57] Carter attacked the Fed in 1980 for policies that he claimed had driven interest rates sky-high. When the Fed pursued tight-money policies in 1981–1982, the Treasury accused it of sabotaging the supply-side program of Reaganomics. Treasury Undersecretary Beryl Sprinkel was given a go-ahead by Reagan to conduct a "study" of the structure of the Fed, and the Treasury created an Office of Domestic Monetary Policy to keep tabs on Fed operations. A visit to the Fed by White House staffers James Baker and Edwin Meese put pressure on the Fed to be more responsive to the administration program. Early in Reagan's second term the Treasury announced that it was considering proposing to Congress that the Fed be put in the Treasury or that the Treasury secretary serve as its chair: again, Reagan was pressuring the Fed to modify its policies. During the Bush administration the Fed was constantly pressured to lower interest rates to promote a recovery from the recession. Bush himself met with Greenspan three times early in 1992 seeking lower rates.

President Clinton continued the Reagan–Bush carrot-and-stick approach to the Fed. He and Greenspan agreed on a deficit reduction package through 1997. When the Fed began thinking of raising its Federal Funds rate (the rate at which banks borrow from each other and from the Fed) at the end of the year to make sure the economic recovery did not touch off inflation, Clinton "jawboned" it not to raise rates, claiming it would be a "big mistake" and that raising rates would "choke off an economy that has already had a false start or two."[58] He was concerned about the possibility of a "growth recession," a situation in which the economy would continue to grow, but not at a rate sufficient to absorb enough new entrants into the workforce to keep unemployment rates down. Many economists argued that the Fed was trying to whip an inflation that had not yet appeared, and that would not appear, given the continued weakness in wages and the strong price competition from foreign imports. In May of 1993, the Open Market Committee of the Federal Reserve voted to push rates higher at the slightest sign of inflation. Through the next eighteen months it raised interest rates six times, and banks responded by increasing the "prime rate" for their customers by 3 percent. Although Clinton's own appointees to the Fed voted for these increases, his undersecretary of the Treasury, Frank Newman, referred to the last increase as "a more marginal decision," a clear indication of White House concern that the Fed might not only choke off inflation, but economic growth critical to the administration's political future as well.[59] In fact, if economic models were correct, then the full effect of the Fed's "slowdown" policy would be felt just in time for the 1996 presidential primary and general election season!

Although Clinton claimed his administration had been "well served" by the independence of the Fed, he also let it be known that he was "deeply sympathetic" with the goals of some members of Congress to create mechanisms to provide for more coordination of policy between the Fed and the administration, without endorsing specific measures.[60] Clinton also endorsed a Treasury Department proposal to remove the Fed's regulatory role over state-chartered banks that are members of the Federal Reserve System.

Often the Fed and White House can come to an arrangement benefiting both. The chairman of the Fed may be included in the president's informal "quadriad" of economic advisors. The president appoints the chair of the Fed and other members of the board, which gives him or her some inducements to offer, as well as some leverage when he makes new appointments. The president may agree to keep the deficit below a certain figure if the Fed accommodates the White House on interest rates. Examples of these arrangements include the 1961–1965 expansion under Kennedy and Johnson, the 1970 accord between Nixon and Fed chairman Arthur Burns that ended a tight money policy, and the 1983–1984 Fed cooperation with the Treasury in financing huge Treasury borrowings caused by Reaganomics. In 1993 Federal Reserve chairman Greenspan endorsed the Clinton economic program. Testifying before the Senate Banking Committee, he called the plan a "serious" proposal based on "credible" economic assumptions, thus improving its chances of passage. The Fed agreed to keep rates low (helping the Treasury refinance debt), provided Clinton came up with large numbers for his deficit reduction package.

Much of the time the Fed delivers monetary policies favored by the administration. Often significant changes in monetary policy occur shortly after a new administration takes office, accommodating the fiscal policies it has introduced. The Fed often adopts White House goals with regard to employment, growth, and price stability.[61] But except for the 1972 elections, in most instances the Fed does not "pump up" the money supply in an election year. In 1980, for example, it actually pursued a deflationary policy that hurt Carter's reelection bid.[62] Its 1994 interest rate increases could not possibly help the Democratic White House in the 1996 presidential elections.

REGULATORY POLICY

Presidential policy making often involves decisions about when and under what circumstances the White House should try to persuade Congress and the American people that free-market outcomes should be modified by the government.

The Privileged Position of Business

Corporate executives, financiers, and entrepreneurs have a privileged position in dealing with the national government.[63] Since the Depression, Congress has passed laws requiring departments to sponsor industry associations and councils that guarantee business leaders access to government officials. These advisory committees formulate guidelines for government agencies, advise officials about the impact of proposed regulations, and propose new government programs to assist business. In sectors of the economy such as agriculture, advisory committees may even be given authority to help determine output and administer prices, substituting political for market allocations.[64] These advisory councils often talk to their opposite numbers in government. Many of the top government officials are recruited from corporations, banks and investment houses, and trade associations. This is true not only in conservative Republican pro-business administrations like Ronald Reagan's, but also in centrist and liberal Democratic administrations. Corporate leaders also talk directly to the president, treasury secretary, and other top-level officials making economic policy at sessions of the Business Roundtable and the Business Council, two corporate groups that hold quarterly meetings in or near Washington so that they can have an exchange of views with the administration.

When presidents want to mobilize the nation around a common purpose, they often seek help from business leaders. When President Truman sought to convince the American people to help with European reconstruction after World War II, he turned to business to form a committee to influence public opinion. When President Clinton needed to round up votes in Congress to support NAFTA with Mexico in 1993, he worked with a coalition of business groups that set up shop right in the Capitol Building to influence legislators.

The preferred status of business sometimes leads to abuses. Corporations heavily involved in politics may want government contracts, exemptions from regulations, subsidies, insured loans, and capital at below market terms, a system that critics such as Labor Secretary Robert Reich refer to as "corporate welfare."[65] In the 1980s the business community received more than $80 billion annually in government grants, loans, loan guarantees, and other subsidies—twice the amount given out in the 1970s. Presidents often recommend that Congress provide assistance to firms and industries (so called "bailouts") when it comes to protection against foreign competition, such as the low-interest loans to Chrysler Corporation in the 1970s. Presidents also recommend subsidizing exports with credits, and insuring business investment abroad: Clinton proposed a record $17 billion in Export-Import Bank funding to promote exports in FY 1994, mostly in deals that commercial lenders refused to back because of political instability in other nations.

The national government funds much of the research for aircraft, mass transit, solar power, metallurgy, communications, electronics, and scientific instrumentation. It has granted antitrust exemptions for research enterprises set up by the semiconductor and automobile industries. The White House often facilitates such arrangements, or accepts them when congressional committees place them in tax and spending bills. Even "free market" President Ronald Reagan found himself approving these subsidies: when presidential ideology clashes with a practical arrangement for an industry, often the ideology falls by the wayside. President Clinton, as "salesman in chief," worked the phones personally with the rulers of Saudi Arabia to land a $6 billion contract for Boeing Aircraft. "When I think it's appropriate," President Clinton observed, "I don't mind asking for the business." Conversely, the president may also ask, or even insist, that U.S. companies refrain from getting the business. In 1995 President Clinton issued an executive order barring American oil companies from making deals with Iran, to stop Conoco from a $1 billion oil exploration deal. He did so to punish Iran for continuing to harbor terrorists and sponsoring terrorist acts.

Regulating Markets

A completely free market is like an exotic hothouse plant: difficult to maintain and therefore extremely rare. Markets and government are inextricably intertwined. Contracts are enforced by courts established by government. The medium of exchange (currency) is provided by the government, which may decide to "defend" its value against other currencies or let it seek a pure market level. Regulatory agencies prohibit the monopolies that otherwise would form.

The president often becomes the political lightning rod for complaints about the way markets are working. Traders in financial markets want the government to establish fiscal and monetary policies that will reduce inflation and keep trade deficits low, thus maintaining the value of the dollar on currency markets. Small producers and those involved in new technologies want government protection against oligopolies or monopolies or cartels, and large producers sometimes want the government to legitimize their arrangements in the name of international competitiveness against large foreign enterprises. Labor wants guarantees about the right of association and a requirement that producers bargain collectively with unions. Consumers in the marketplace look to the White House for redress: they want protection against unsafe or faulty products. When inflation is rampant they may call for price controls.

In any free market neither producers nor consumers walk away from transactions completely satisfied, nor do they expect to. The problem for the White House begins when one side seems at the mercy of the other. Either business or labor or consumers call for presidential action, or at least some "jawboning" by the White House to moderate the effects of the market. Presidents always have a calculation to make: when is it in their and the nation's interest to substitute a political allocation for a free-market allocation of resources?

The president may regulate markets or even substitute a command economy in times of war or economic crisis provided he receives authority to do so from Congress. In 1971 President Nixon, acting after legislation was passed by a Democratic Congress, imposed a ninety-day freeze on wages, prices, rents, and interest rates in an effort to halt runaway inflation. Later wage and price boards considered applications for increases for several years. The results of the Nixon program are instructive for anyone who thinks that government controls can stop inflation. The program worked politically (prices were controlled through the 1972 election) but not economically: inflation zoomed, as if to make up for lost time, after the controls ended. It also led to inequities: wealthier people received income from stock dividends and capital gains that were not regulated, and executives were compensated through stock options that were not subject to controls. Meanwhile salaries of wage-earners were regulated and capped. The brunt of controlling inflation fell on middle- and lower-income people.

To regulate the economy in noncrisis situations presidents rely primarily on appointments (with the advice and consent of the Senate) to the regulatory commissions. By law, commissioners are appointed on a bipartisan basis (half are Democrats, and half Republicans), and the president can always find nominees from either party who share his perspectives. Often appointees are politically connected to the White House: they are personal friends or professional colleagues of the president and top White House officials, or they are recommended to him by the very sectors of the economy they are supposed to regulate. The president has no power to remove such officials, because the statutes insulate them from his removal power (except in specific cases of misconduct defined by Congress). Even though their terms of office are staggered and the president makes only a few appointments to each regulatory agency at a time, commissioners serve on average less than three years (of four-year terms) and so a two-term president can pack most agencies with appointees sympathetic to his goals. By law the White House is not supposed to intervene in particular regulatory matters before these commissions (known as ex parte proceedings).

The White House attempts to control regulatory policy through several mechanisms. In 1981 President Reagan issued an executive order requiring all departments to submit regulations to the Office of Management and Budget for Review. By 1985 the OMB had developed a formal "regulatory clearance" mechanism whereby it reviewed every agency's proposed regulations to see that they comported with administration policy. All drafts of proposed regulations were sent to the OMB, which met with industry representatives before returning regulations (sometimes with suggested revisions) back to the agencies. Beginning in 1986 the White House sent to Congress each year a volume entitled the *Regulatory Program of the U.S. Government,* which contained the proposed regulations for the following year, along with a cost–benefit analysis of their effectiveness. Only regulations that promised greater benefits than their costs would be proposed. Finally, the Bush administration by executive order created the Council on Competitiveness, headed by Vice President Dan Quayle. It reviewed all proposed rules and regulations (including those of independent agencies), using the OMB and its own staff to monitor them and get them adjusted to White House priorities. Congressional Democrats eventually cut off all government funding for the staff of the council, arguing that it had no statutory power delegated by Congress to conduct these reviews.[66]

These mechanisms were abolished by the Clinton administration, which set departments free to regulate industry. After the 1994 midterm elections, however, House Republicans, as part of their "Contract with America," proposed legislation that would require government regulators to use new "cost–benefit" rules that would inhibit their ability to impose costs on corporations, especially in environmental and consumer safety regulation. They would also require the national and state governments to compensate owners of property when they regulated (i.e., limited) their use to preserve the environment.

Deregulating Markets

Presidents Carter, Reagan, Bush, and Clinton favored selective deregulation of industries. In 1978 President Carter got Congress to deregulate the rail, trucking, and airline industries, resulting in fierce competition between existing companies and new upstarts, and a complete upheaval in the structure of each industry (leading some executives to ask for reregulation a few years later). The Reagan administration deregulated financial services, resulting in the excesses of the Savings and Loans industry that cost the taxpayers hundreds of billions of dollars. It also deregulated more successfully the telecommunications industries, cutting the total number of regulations by almost 50 percent from the Carter years and sparking a wave of new information services and technological innovations. Clinton supported a one-third cut in the budget of the Interstate Commerce Commission and spurred it to end many of its outdated regulations.

Industrial Policy

The Carter and Clinton administrations argued that we should replace our haphazard and scatter-gun support for politically connected businesses with a coordinated industrial policy that would get the government more directly involved in promoting particular sectors of the economy. In one approach the government would concentrate on restoring our manufacturing base to bring back some of the millions of jobs lost in the past two decades. The approach favored by the Clinton administration would have the government promote emerging high-tech "sunshine" industries and would let the "sunset" manufacturing industries move their operations to other nations if they could not compete with their U.S. factories against foreign producers. Tax incentives and government-funded research and development would help the high-tech industries. Clinton's National Competitiveness Act of 1993 proposed $1.5 billion for grants, loans, and technical aid programs for industry to make 250,000 small businesses more competitive in the global marketplace. Other proposals called for tax credits to be given to corporations that retrained displaced workers. The government would fund more university-based scientific and technical education and worker training. Health insurance would become "portable and universal," so workers would find it easier to move from job to job. President Clinton and Labor Secretary Robert Reich, architects of the "high-tech" approach, argued that the United States was losing international markets in many technologies. They argued for an industrial policy that could provide workers with high-wage, sophisticated work.

TRADE POLICY

The U.S. economy functions within the larger world economy, and the president must take into account the impact White House policies will have on other nations. In turn, the effectiveness of those policies may be influenced by other nations. Economists differ as to how much weight a president should put on making the United States "competitive" in world markets. Some argue that if the president can boost U.S. exports into new markets, and promote and protect U.S. investments in other nations, the American economy will expand, employment will increase, and our standard of living will rise. Others point out that the United States produces more than 90 percent of what it consumes, and consumes more than 90 percent of what it produces, so that the impact of international trade remains relatively minor.[67] Yet the U.S. position in world markets has become a "valence issue": the notion that others can outproduce or outsell us in world markets is galling to the public and puts a president at political risk. The question for the president is how to proceed: through the economic nationalism of industrial and trade policies coordinated by the government (as economists known as the New Trade theorists propose), through trade liberalization and the workings of the free market (as free traders suggest), or by confronting other nations and charging them with violations of trade agreements (as fair traders recommend).

Trade and Investment Strategies in a Changing World Economy

In the 1790s Treasury Secretary Alexander Hamilton and President Washington promoted British investment in American industry. They called for high tariffs to protect American industry and trade concessions to the British, policies embodied in the Jay Treaty. When Jefferson became president in 1801, he emphasized agricultural development rather than industrial, and he called for lower tariffs on manufactured imports and less reliance on foreign capital, a policy embraced by the

Democrats. After the Civil War the American economy expanded rapidly under a Republican high-tariff protectionist policy: Foreign technology and capital were welcome, and a liberal immigration policy met the demands of industry for workers. The United States became a net debtor nation to build its railroads, factories, and cities. During World War I the United States accumulated a capital surplus, and President Wilson proposed lower tariffs. He was a Democrat, but he argued that free markets and free trade were good for the United States—ideas that presidents from both parties have championed ever since.

As European and Asian nations recovered from World War II, the U.S. share of world production fell from 60 percent in the 1950s to 20 percent in the 1990s. Our technological edge was diminished, although U.S. productivity and total output remained the highest in the world. Some nations, notably Japan and other nations of the Pacific rim (Indonesia, Malaysia, South Korea, Taiwan, Thailand), relied on close cooperation and coordination between industry, labor, and government. The "Pacific Rim Model" involved purchase of U.S. and European technology, government subsidies to perfect low-cost manufacturing techniques, protection of the domestic market from outside competition, "dumping" goods at low prices to gain market share in other nations and thereby lower production costs, and reducing foreign competition in export markets through low prices.

These nations became formidable competitors and ran up large trade surpluses with the United States. In part, the trade imbalances were caused by U.S. corporations that used foreign plants to manufacture goods produced more cheaply with lower-paid foreign labor. Corporations owned primarily by U.S. interests held steady their share of markets, but the proportion of their output derived from foreign factories went from 25 percent in 1966 to more than 50 percent by the mid-1980s. In 1980 U.S. plants produced 6 percent more manufactured goods than the American people consumed; by 1986 they produced only 85 percent of the goods consumed in the United States. The resulting loss of manufacturing jobs caused a backlash against trade liberalization in the 1990s. "We have turned into a nation of people who sell one another foreign-built goods," claimed Andrew Grove, the President of Intel, one of the largest U.S. manufacturers of computer semiconductor chips.[68]

Trade Liberalization

The U.S. economy has become the largest importer and exporter of goods in the world. Those who favor a relatively open system (known as free trade), such as Presidents Reagan and Bush, believe that there should be no artificial barriers against trade or investment among nations, and that Americans must and can compete in such a world economy. "Free trade offers Americans the greatest hope for a prosperous future," President Reagan argued in the president's *Annual Economic Report* in 1986. Free-traders argue that imports have helped our economy grow without inflation because of price competition. Consumers obtain a greater variety of goods and more reliable and technologically advanced products. Free trade may provide a more efficient allocation of each nation's productive resources, when each nation invests scarce capital in what it can do best.

Ad Hoc Protectionism

Although, since the New Deal, Republican and Democratic Presidents have promoted some form of trade liberalization to lower tariff and nontariff barriers, in practice most have offered some protection to industries hard hit by foreign competition.[69] Some protectionist policies were supported by labor union leaders, who argued that in some industries, such as textiles, cheap labor enables foreigners to underprice American workers. Without protection U.S. workers would either lose their jobs or have to settle for working in sweatshop conditions for lower wages. The United States has negotiated trade restrictions (known as multifiber agreements) on textiles with a number of other nations to protect U.S. workers. The policy has not worked: When presidents have given industries protection, the results have been disastrous for exporters. President Reagan imposed tariffs on Canadian shingles, and Canada retaliated on American tea bags, books, semiconductors, and Christmas trees. When he put textile quotas on China, it responded by cutting purchases of food and chemicals.

Protectionists believe that some industries should receive protection indefinitely, because they cannot compete in the world market or maintain their share of the domestic market without such aid. This policy shifts the economic burden from the workers and managers and owners of noncompetitive industries to the consumers. Agreements involving dairy products, citrus fruits and sugar, lumber, and wheat cannot be justified on national security grounds, and do not involve high technology, but a president often gives ground to the producers and either asks Congress to provide protection (as Clinton did in 1993 on the NAFTA bill) or stands back while Congress does so itself (as Clinton did in 1994 on GATT-enabling legislation).

Much of the protection a president calls for does not involve tariffs, but rather involves regulations promulgated by executive agencies under authority granted by Congress.[70] The United States may require a certain amount of "domestic content" in products sold in the United States, such as automobiles. It may impose consumer safety requirements that foreign companies may find hard to meet without raising prices. It may even suggest "voluntary restraints" on foreign imports, as Reagan negotiated in 1981 on Japanese car imports and 1982 steel imports from Europe, or encourage other countries to build factories to produce their goods in the United States, as the United States has done with Asian car manufacturers. It may limit imports as a sanction against nations engaged in human rights violations (China and South Africa) or against companies that engage in actions detrimental to U.S. national security, such as the Norwegian and Japanese companies that sold propeller manufacturing technology to the Soviet Union, enabling the Soviets to manufacture quieter submarines that could avoid detection by U.S. ships.

Managed Trade

A completely liberalized system is impossible, because most nations try to protect certain industries or agricultural sectors. Some embrace an industrial policy or rely on low-wage workers to give their factories advantages. The reciprocal (fair trade) movement promoted by Presidents Eisenhower and Kennedy, and efforts at "managed trade" in the Clinton administration, are two attempts at finding a middle way: a strategy of using tariffs and other import barriers as bargaining chips to develop "we win, they win" agreements with other nations that lower barriers to trade, investment, and technology transfers.

In the 1890s the president was given power by Congress to negotiate with other nations to lower tariffs. In 1916 Congress created the U.S. Tariff Commission (since 1974 known as the U.S. International Trade Commission) to recommend changes in tariff rates. Since the late 1960s, presidents rely on the Office of Trade Representative (OTR), a unit of the Executive Office of the President, to conduct trade negotiations. It is aided by a National Advisory Council for International Monetary and Financial Policy. The office is headed by the U.S. trade representative, a cabinet-level official with the rank of ambassador, who reports directly to the president. Voluntary trade restriction agreements with other nations (involving steel, machine tools, and automobiles) are negotiated by the trade representative and implemented by the Department of Commerce (International Trade Commission) and the Foreign Agricultural Service of the Department of Agriculture. The trade representative is the chief negotiator for the United States at the General Agreement on Tariffs and Trade (GATT). There have been seven rounds of GATT negotiations, which have resulted in a 90 percent reduction in tariffs and an increase in world trade of 1,000 percent.

Presidential Trade Sanctions

Congress has granted the president several statutory powers he may deploy in the interests of fair trade. Since 1974 the president has had the authority to restrict imports from countries that discriminate against U.S. exports. Since 1979 he has had authority to order the U.S. Customs Service to impose duties equal to the monetary advantage foreign companies gain by selling their goods below cost in U.S. markets. The United States has a countervailing tariff it can impose to offset unfair advantages by nations involving unfair labor conditions. The trade representative annually issues a report listing barriers to American trade.

The trade representative negotiates with foreign nations under Section 301 of the Trade Act of 1974 to eliminate the most serious of these barriers. The Omnibus Trade and Competitiveness Act of 1988 gave the trade representative authority to implement section 301 sanctions against foreign nations that have not abided by the principles of free trade embodied in international trade agreements with the United States.[71] These 301 provisions put other nations on notice that we intend to be treated fairly.

Sometimes foreign governments prefer confrontation to the political costs of "giving in." Or they may retaliate: when the United States imposed punitive duties on Canadian lumber and roof shingles, Canada imposed a 67 percent punitive duty on U.S. corn. Section 301 often works in unimportant cases with low visibility and limited stakes, but for the most significant trade negotiations, presidents prefer high-level quiet diplomacy. In dealing with Japan, President Reagan in 1985 initiated talks to identify and remove impediments to market access. The so-called

MOSS talks (market-oriented, sector-selective) have been used by several U.S. presidents to reduce or eliminate barriers created by Japanese trade associations against American imports and services, such as the virtual ban against purchasing telecommunications equipment and the freezing out of U.S. construction companies bidding for contracts on a Japanese airport.

To further ensure U.S. interests in international trade, Senate Republican Leader Robert Dole cut a deal with President Clinton in late 1994: Congress would ratify GATT, but the legislation would provide for a U.S. panel that would review decisions of the new World Trade Organization. If the panel determined that three decisions were decided unfairly against the United States in any five-year period, it could recommend that Congress end U.S. participation in GATT. Dole proposed the provision to provide political cover for himself and other Republicans who intended to vote for the agreement against charges by protectionists that he was "selling out" American workers and businesses—political cover that was just as useful for President Clinton in an era of increasing skepticism about the benefits of trade liberalization.

THE LIMITS TO PRESIDENTIAL ECONOMICS

The president has only limited influence as an economic manager because the U.S. economy functions internally at three levels (national, regional, and state) and externally within a larger international system. Presidential policies have only a limited effect because of adjustments by Congress, state governments, foreign nations, and private markets. If the national government reduces expenditures on social welfare programs, for example, the fiscal effects may be counteracted if state and local governments increase theirs. An attempt to stimulate the national economy may be negated if state and local governments (required by law to balance their operating budgets) make cuts in expenditures. Similar situations can occur internationally: an effort by the U.S. Treasury, the Federal Reserve, and other central banks to "defend" the value of the dollar by buying several billions of dollars on the currency markets can be dwarfed by the more than $1 trillion in daily currency transactions.

A presidential policy may suffer from an intertemporal substitution effect: it has only a temporary effect that may be canceled out over time. President Nixon's wage and price controls, for example, only delayed price increases but could not prevent them from occurring after controls were lifted. A monetary stimulus from the Fed may lead to an initial boost in the economy, but in the perspective of a decade may have had little or no long-term effect. The same may hold true for a tax decrease or a stimulative budget deficit proposed by the president and instituted by Congress.

Finally, because tax and spending decisions require congressional approval, which may not be forthcoming for a considerable period, economic management is subject to lag and fishtail effects: a policy may kick in at exactly the wrong time in the economic cycle. A president may propose a stimulus package, but by the time Congress considers it, the economy is improving and the program is defeated as unnecessary—or worse, goes into effect and sends the economy into an unsustainable inflationary cycle.

Separation of powers, bicameralism, and periods of split government all combine to give a "stop–go" quality to presidential attempts at economic management, as occurred during the Clinton presidency. Because of the gap between the political responsibility taken by presidents to "manage the economy," and the inability of their advisory system to consistently deliver policies that have more than a marginal impact on private domestic and international markets, their efforts remain erratic and they remain politically vulnerable. Hobart Rowen, the dean of journalists reporting on presidential economics, summed up the White House performance by saying that it is "a story of blunder, mismanagement, stupidity, and irresponsibility by officials whose chief obligation to govern the nation was betrayed by their embrace of policies misconceived and ineptly applied."[72] That may be somewhat exaggerated. Periods of presidential ineffectiveness or support for dangerous economic nostrums sometimes give way to periods of decisive and constructive leadership in economic crises. On balance, however, presidents of both parties have yet to solve the problem of restoring the American dream.

FURTHER READING

Books

Herbert Stein, *Presidential Economics,* New York: Simon and Schuster, 1984.

John Frendreis and Raymond Tatalovich, *The Modern Presidency and Economic Policy,* Itasca, IL: F. E. Peacock Publishers, 1994.

Hobart Rowen, *Self-Inflicted Wounds: From LBJ's Guns and Butter to Reagan's Voodoo Economics,* New York: Times Books, 1994.

George Shultz and Kenneth Dam, *Economic Policy beyond the Headlines,* New York: W. W. Norton, 1977.

Joseph Stiglitz, *The Economic Role of the State,* Oxford, UK: Blackwell, 1989.

C. Eugene Steurle, *The Tax Decade,* New York: Urban Institute Press, 1992.

Documentary Sources

Annual Report of the Council of Economic Advisers, Washington, DC: Government Printing Office.

NOTES

1. Lou Cannon, *President Reagan: The Role of a Lifetime,* New York: Simon and Schuster, 1991, p. 554.

2. Jeffrey H. Birnbaum and Alan S. Murray, *Showdown at Gucci Gulch,* New York: Random House, 1987.

3. *New York Times,* October 26, 1986, p. D-8.

4. Presidential News Conference, August 3, 1994.

5. "The American Experience: Another View," *New York Times,* May 8, 1994, p. F-23.

6. Council of Economic Advisers, *Annual Economic Report of the President, 1993,* Washington, DC: Government Printing Office, 1993.

7. "Eroding Incomes for Working People," *New York Times*, June 4, 1994, p. F-21.

8. Bureau of Labor Statistics, Department of Labor.

9. Jack Beatty, "Who Speaks for the Middle Class?" *The Atlantic*, Vol. 273, no. 5, May, 1994, p. 66.

10. Lawrence Mishel and Jared Bernstein, Economic Policy Institute, analysis of data from Bureau of Labor Statistics, *New York Times*, December 13, 1993, p. D-1.

11. *New York Times*, December 13, 1993, p. D-3.

12. Bob Woodward, *The Agenda*, New York: Simon and Schuster, 1994, p. 255.

13. Gregory B. Markus, "The Impact of Personal and National Economic Conditions on the Presidential Vote: A Pooled Cross-sectional Analysis," *American Journal of Political Science*, Vol. 32, no. 1, February, 1988, pp. 137–154; Robert S. Erikson, "Economic Conditions and the Presidential Vote," *American Political Science Review*, Vol. 83, no. 2, June, 1989, pp. 567–573.

14. Don R. Kinder and Roderick P. Kiewet, "Sociotropic Politics: The American Case," *British Journal of Political Science*, Vol. 11, part 2, April, 1981, pp. 129–161.

15. Morris Fiorina, "Economic Retrospective Voting in American Elections: A Microanalysis," *American Journal of Political Science*, Vol. 22, no. 2, May, 1978, pp. 426–443.

16. Douglas Hibbs, Jr., *The American Political Economy*, Cambridge, MA: Harvard University Press, 1987.

17. Kirsten Monroe, "Economic Influences on Presidential Popularity," *Public Opinion Quarterly*, Vol. 42, no. 3, Fall, 1978, pp. 360–369; Robert Shapiro and Bruce Conforto, "Presidential Performance, the Economy, and the Public Evaluation of Economic Conditions," *Journal of Politics*, Vol. 42, no. 1, February, 1980, pp. 49–67; Donald R. Kinder, "Presidents, Prosperity and Public Opinion," *Public Opinion Quarterly*, Vol. 45, no. 1, Spring, 1981, pp. 1–21; Helmut Norpoth, "Economics, Politics and the Cycle of Presidential Popularity," *Political Behavior*, Vol. 6, no. 3, Fall, 1984, pp. 253–273.

18. Michael MacKuen, "Political Drama, Economic Conditions, and the Dynamics of Presidential Popularity," *American Journal of Political Science*, Vol. 27, no. 2, May, 1983, pp. 165–192.

19. Henry C. Kenski, "A Man for All Seasons? The Guardian President and His Public," in Ryan J. Barilleaux and Mary E. Stuckey, eds., *Leadership and the Bush Presidency*, Westport, CT: Praeger, 1992, pp. 91–114.

20. Los Angeles Times Poll, December 4–7, 1993.

21. Ann May, "President Eisenhower, Economic Policy, and the 1960 Presidential Election," *Journal of Economic History*, Vol. 50, no. 2, June, 1990, pp. 417–427.

22. M. Kalecki, "Political Aspects of Full Employment," *Review of Economic Studies*, Vol. 14, no. 4, October–December, 1943, pp. 322–341; William Nordhaus, "The Political Business Cycle," *Review of Economic Studies*, Vol. 42, no. 1, April, 1975, pp. 169–190; Asser Lindbeck, "Stabilization Policy in Open Economies with Endogenous Politicians," *American Economic Review*, Vol. 66, no. 2, May, 1976, pp. 1–19; Douglas Hibbs, "Political Parties and Macroeconomic Policy," *American Political Science Review*, Vol. 71, no. 4, December, 1977, pp. 1462–1487.

23. Data from *Congressional Quarterly Weekly Reports*, as reported in David Broder, "By the Numbers," *Washington Post National Weekly Edition*, September 6–12, 1993, p. 4.

24. Roger B. Porter, "Economic Advice to the President: From Eisenhower to Reagan," *Political Science Quarterly*, Vol. 98, no. 3, Fall, 1983, pp. 403–426; Alice Rivlin, "Economics and the Political Process," *American Economic Review*, Vol. 77, no. 1, March, 1987, pp. 1–10.

25. Steven Greenhouse, "Bentsen the Insider Insists He Still Is," *New York Times*, December 28, 1993, p. D-18.

26. Edwin G. Nourse and Bertram M. Gross, "The Role of the Council of Economic Advisers," *American Political Science Review,* Vol. 42, no. 2, April, 1948, pp. 283–295.

27. Arthur M. Okun, "The Economist and Presidential Leadership," in Joseph A. Pechman, ed., *Economics for Policy-Making,* Cambridge, MA: MIT Press, 1983, pp. 577–582.

28. *New York Times,* July 28, 1984, sec. 3, p. 2.

29. Mark S. Kamlet, David Mowery, and Tsai-Tsu-Su, "Whom Do You Trust? An Analysis of Executive and Congressional Economic Forecasts," *Journal of Policy Analysis and Management,* Vol. 8, Spring, 1987, pp. 365–384.

30. Gerhard Colm, "The Executive Office and Fiscal and Economic Policy," *Law and Contemporary Problems,* Vol. 21, no. 3, Autumn, 1956, pp. 710–723; Edward S. Flash, Jr., "The Broadening Scope of the President's Economic Advice," *George Washington Law Review,* Vol. 35, no. 2., December, 1966, pp. 286–298; Neil H. Jacoby, "The President, the Constitution and the Economist in Economic Stabilization," *History of Political Economy,* Vol. 3, no. 2, Fall, 1971, pp. 398–414; Leon Keyserling, "The Council of Economic Advisers Since 1946: Its Contributions and Failures," *Atlantic Economic Journal,* Vol. 6, no. 1, March, 1978, pp. 17–35.

31. Bob Woodward, "Bickering While Rome Burns," *Washington Post National Weekly Edition,* October, 19–25, 1992, p. 8.

32. Ibid., p. 9.

33. Alice M. Rivlin, "Taming the Economic Policy Monster," *New York Times,* January 18, 1987, p. B-2.

34. Gwen Ifill, "The Economic Czar behind the Economic Czars," *New York Times,* March 7, 1993, pp. 1, 22.

35. James Tobin and Robert Solow, "Clintonomics Doesn't Need a Czar," *New York Times,* December 10, 1993, p. A-27.

36. Robert D. Hershey, Jr., "Jobless Rate Underestimated, U.S. Says, Citing Survey Bias," *New York Times,* November 17, 1993, p. A-1.

37. Louis Uchitelle, "How the Job Count Is Off," *New York Times,* November 7, 1993, p. D-3.

38. *New York Times,* August 6, 1994, p. A-44.

39. Congressional Budget Office, September 8, 1993.

40. Hobart Rowen, "Backpedaling," *Washington Post National Weekly Edition,* August 23–29, 1993, p. 5.

41. Data compiled by Stanford University economist Christina Romer, published in *Business Week,* July 19, 1993, p. 85.

42. Margaret Weir, *Politics and Jobs: The Boundaries of Employment Policy in the United States,* Princeton, NJ: Princeton University Press, 1992.

43. Louis Uchitelle, "Inflation Specter," *New York Times,* March 28, 1994, p. D-1; research studies of James Medoff and Andrew F. Harliss, cited in Hobart Rowen, "The Fed's Time Warp," *Washington Post National Weekly Edition,* June 13–19, 1994, p. 5.

44. Alan Sweezy, "The Keynesians and Government Policy, 1933–1939," *American Economic Review,* Vol. 62, no. 2, May, 1972, pp. 116–125; E. Cary Brown, "Fiscal Policy in the 1930s: A Reappraisal," *American Economic Review,* Vol. 46, no. 5, December, 1956, pp. 851–879; Donald T. Critchlow, "The Political Control of the Economy: Deficit Spending as a Political Belief, 1932–1952, " *The Public Historian,* Vol. 3, no. 1, January, 1981, pp. 5–22.

45. Alonzo L. Hamby, "The Vital Center, the Fair Deal, and the Quest for a Liberal Political Economy," *American Historical Review,* Vol. 77, no. 3, June, 1972, pp. 653–678; Martin Bronfenbrenner, "Postwar Political Economy: The President's Responsibilities," *Journal of Political Economy,* Vol. 56, no. 5, October, 1948, pp. 373–391.

46. Paul Craig Roberts, "Supply-Side Economics—Theory and Results," *The Public Interest,* Vol. 93, Fall, 1989, pp. 16–36.

47. Studies by Steven Fazzari and Robert Chirinko, cited in Clay Chandler, "The Incredible Shrinking Deficit Issue," *Washington Post National Weekly Edition,* February 14–20, 1994, p. 20.

48. Michael Kelly, "Gambling That a Tax-Cut Promise Was Not Taken Seriously," *New York Times,* February 18, 1993, p. A-16.

49. *New York Times,* February 14, 1993, p. D-8.

50. Michael Wines, "Clinton Makes Lobbyists a Target in Opening Battle over Tax Rise," *New York Times,* February 17, 1993, p. A-1.

51. Milton Friedman, "A Monetary and Fiscal Framework for Economic Stability," *American Economic Review,* Vol. 38, no. 3, June, 1948, pp. 245–264; Milton Friedman, "Monetary Policy: Theory and Practice," *Journal of Money, Credit and Banking,* Vol. 14, no. 1, February, 1982, pp. 98–118.

52. John M. Berry, "The Fed's Seat of the Pants Approach Worries the White House," *Washington Post National Weekly Edition,* February 29, 1988, p. 20.

53. Hobart Rowen, *The Washington Post National Weekly Edition,* April 25–May 1, 1994, p. 5.

54. Keith Bradsher, "Greenspan Says the Fed Uses Anecdotal Guides," *New York Times,* August 11, 1994, p. D-4.

55. *New York Times,* August 15, 1994, p. D-8.

56. Peter Passell, "Fine Tuning with a Hammer," *New York Times,* November 20, 1994, p. E-6.

57. Donald F. Kettl, "The Economic Education of Lyndon Johnson: Guns, Butter and Taxes," in Robert A. Divine, ed., *The Johnson Years,* Vol. 2, Lawrence, KS: University Press of Kansas, 1988, pp. 54–78; John W. Sloane, "President Johnson, the Council of Economic Advisers, and the Failure to Raise Taxes in 1966 and 1967," *Presidential Studies Quarterly,* Vol. 15, no. 1, Winter, 1985, pp. 89–98.

58. *New York Times,* December 20, 1993, p. D-1.

59. Keith Bradsher, "White House Gets Nervous about the Fed," *New York Times,* November 20, 1994, p. A-12.

60. Hobart Rowen, "Reforming the Fed," *Washington Post National Weekly Edition,* December 20–26, 1993, p. 5.

61. Donald Kettl, *Leadership at the Fed,* New Haven, CT: Yale University Press, 1987; Robert Weintraub, "The Political Economy of Inflation," Joint Economic Committee, Washington, DC: Government Printing Office, 1981; Dudley Lockett and Glenn Potts, "Monetary Policy and Partisan Politics," *Journal of Money, Credit and Banking,* Vol. 12, no. 3, August, 1980, pp. 540–546.

62. Myles F. Wallace and John T. Warner, "Fed Policy and Presidential Elections," *Journal of Macroeconomics,* Vol. 6, no. 1, Winter, 1984, pp. 79–88; Nathaniel Beck, "Presidential Influence on the Federal Reserve in the 1970s," *American Journal of Political Science,* Vol. 26, no. 3, August, 1982, pp. 415–445; Stuart D. Allen, "The Federal Reserve and the Electoral Cycle," *Journal of Money, Credit and Banking,* Vol. 19, February, 1985, pp. 89–94; Nathaniel Beck, "Elections and the Fed: Is There a Political Monetary Cycle?," *American Journal of Political Science,* Vol. 31, no. 1, February, 1987, pp. 194–216; John T. Woolley, "Partisan Manipulation of the Economy: Another Look at Monetary Policy with Moving Regression," *Journal of Politics,* Vol. 50, no. 2, May, 1988, pp. 335–360.

63. Charles Lindblom, *Politics and Markets,* New York: Basic Books, 1977, pp. 170–189.

64. Grant McConnell, *Private Power and American Democracy,* New York: Alfred A. Knopf, 1967, pp. 230–243.

65. James P. Donohue, "The Corporate Welfare Kings," *Washington Post National Weekly Edition,* March 21–27, 1994, p. 24.

66. Joseph Cooper and William West, "Presidential Power and Republican Government: The Theory and Practice of OMB Review of Agency Rules," *Journal of Politics,* Vol. 50, no. 4, November, 1988, pp. 864–895; Alan B. Morrison, "OMB Interference with Agency Rulemaking: The Wrong Way to Write a Regulation," *Harvard Law Review,* Vol. 99, no. 5, March, 1986, pp. 1059–1074.

67. Paul Krugman, *Peddling Prosperity,* New York: W. W. Norton, 1994.

68. Andrew S. Grove, "Winning the Trade War," *New York Times,* December 13, 1987, p. 3.

69. Pietro Nivola, "The New Protectionism: U.S. Trade Policy in Historical Perspective," *Political Science Quarterly,* Vol. 101, no. 4, Winter, 1986, pp. 577–600.

70. Robert Pastor, "The Cry-and-Sight Syndrome: Congress and Trade Policy," in Allen Schick, ed., *Making Economic Policy in Congress,* Washington, DC: American Enterprise Institute, 1983, pp. 158–195; Roger Porter, "The President, Congress and Trade Policy," *Congress and the Presidency,* Vol. 15, no. 2, Autumn, 1988, pp. 165–184.

71. Pietro E. Nivola, "Trade Policy: Refereeing the Playing Field," in Thomas E. Mann, ed., *A Question of Balance,* Washington, DC: Brookings Institution, 1990, pp. 201–253.

72. Hobart Rowen, *Self-Inflicted Wounds,* New York: Times Books, 1994.

CHAPTER 14

Presidential Diplomacy

I know many people ask whether the United States plans to retreat or remain active in the world, and if active, to what end. Let me answer that question as clearly and plainly as I can. The United States plans to remain engaged and to lead.

—*Bill Clinton*

INTRODUCTORY CASE: PRESIDENT CARTER MEDIATES AT CAMP DAVID

There was a chill in the air of the Catoctin Mountains in September, 1978. President Jimmy Carter had invited Egyptian President Anwar Sadat and Israeli Prime Minister Menachem Begin to Camp David, the vacation retreat of U.S. presidents, to negotiate a Middle East peace accord. Progress was slow. Carter shuttled between their cabins, mediating between the delegations. His own position adhered to United Nations Resolution 242, which instructed Israel to withdraw from occupied Arab territory (whether that meant some territory or all occupied lands had not been specified by the resolution), and called on Arab nations to recognize Israel and make peace with it. Carter's proposals included an Israeli withdrawal from the Sinai Peninsula and Gaza strip, restoring the borders that existed before the 1967 war, an autonomous "homeland" for Palestinians in Gaza and the West Bank, a moratorium on new Israeli settlements in the West Bank, and a five-year transitional period in which the final status of the West Bank would be determined. In return, Egypt would recognize Israel, extend it full recognition, and give it navigation rights through the Suez Canal and Straits of Tiran.[1]

Egypt wanted reparations from Israel for the occupation of its territory and for oil it had taken from the Sinai. Israel insisted that the Sinai be demilitarized and wished to keep some settlements and military bases there. Israel wanted to retain the right to buy land and settle on the West Bank. The main disagreements were between Carter and Begin. Israel expressed interest in a mutual defense treaty with the United States—an idea Carter rejected. Carter argued that international borders could not be changed; Begin insisted that the 1967 war gave Israel the right to change its frontiers. Carter claimed that West Jerusalem was part of the West Bank; Begin insisted it was an integral part of Israel and that Jerusalem must remain a unified city. Carter wanted a freeze on Israeli settlements; Begin resisted. The Israeli leader insisted that Carter honor a pledge made by President Ford that the United States would coordinate with Israel any American proposal for a peace settlement before submitting it to the Arabs. Carter rejected this approach to the negotiations. After a week of discussions, Begin yielded to Carter and made a number of concessions. These included Egyptian sovereignty over the Sinai and complete withdrawal from all military facilities and all settlements.

Sadat and Carter were in substantial agreement on most issues, and they became close friends as the conference proceeded. Sadat's concessions to Carter alienated members of his own delegation, including his foreign minister (who resigned at the end of conference), two former foreign ministers, the leading general of his army, and the editor of the leading Egyptian newspaper. All believed that he had been outmaneuvered by the Israelis.

On September 17, with Carter presiding, the Israelis and Egyptians signed the Camp David accords. Israel withdrew from the Sinai peninsula and dismantled its settlements there. It recognized the principle that there were Palestinian rights to be negotiated in the future. Egypt made peace with Israel, recognized that nation, and agreed to limit Egyptian military presence in the Sinai. Egypt also recognized that Israel had legitimate security interests subject to further negotiation. Sadat and Begin came to Washington and signed a peace treaty on March 26, 1979. For their efforts, they shared the Nobel Peace Prize.

Sadat was later assassinated by Muslim fundamentalists opposed to the accord, but the peace between the two nations held. Egypt became a mediator between Israel and the Palestinian Liberation Organization (PLO), eventually getting Israel to recognize in 1992 that the time was ripe for negotiations with its adversary. President Clinton presided over two Rose Garden ceremonies: Israeli Prime Minister Yitzhak Rabin met with PLO Chairman Yasir Arafat to sign an autonomy accord in 1993, and with King Hussein of Jordan to sign a framework agreement for peace with Israel in 1994. By the end of that year Morocco had joined these nations in recognizing Israel, a sign that its isolation in the Middle East was coming to an end.

The events at Camp David and in the White House Rose Garden illustrate the potential for presidential diplomacy as well as its limitations. The president is the leader of the most powerful nation in the world. His efforts are indispensable in securing peace in many of the trouble spots around the world. Yet even the president of the world's only superpower cannot resolve conflicts unless the parties are ready to proceed. A 1992–1993 Middle East peace conference co-sponsored by the United States and Russia had gone nowhere, and was finally bypassed by Israel and the PLO, which held their own secret talks in Oslo under the auspices of Norway. The U.S. government had merely been "informed" that negotiations were taking place, and neither President Clinton nor his secretary of state Warren Christopher had played any role in shaping the agreements.[2] Similarly, when Israel and Jordan were ready to make peace, the main role of the American president was to assure Jordanian King Hussein that he would recommend to Congress that Jordanian debts to the United States be canceled.

There are four problems facing any president trying to be "diplomat-in-chief." His foreign affairs powers under the Constitution require him to compete with Congress for foreign affairs powers; the departments and agencies look to Congress as well as to the president for direction in foreign affairs; partisan divisions within Congress (and sometimes between president and Congress), and infighting between different executive officials, makes coordination and control by the White House very problematic. In addition to these three structural problems, presidents since the end of the Cold War have found it difficult to rally the American people to play a leadership role in world affairs, in large measure because they have not developed a convincing rationale for doing so.

THE CONSTITUTIONAL FRAMEWORK

"Politically, the President is the leader of the nation," argued President Truman's secretary of state Dean Acheson, and "constitutionally he is the director of American foreign policy."[3] The Constitution, however, does not provide the president with many explicit foreign affairs powers. The president makes, by and with the advice and consent of the Senate, treaties that are the supreme law of the land, receives envoys from foreign nations, and, with Senate consent, appoints ambassadors to foreign nations. These constitutional provisions, though, hardly add up to plenary powers in foreign affairs.[4]

Sole Organ of Foreign Relations

Presidents combine their powers and responsibilities to claim that they are the sole organ of the federal government in the field of international relations. "The President alone has the power to speak or listen as a representative of the nation," the Supreme Court agreed in 1936 in *U.S. v. Curtiss-Wright.*[5] The President is the sole organ of *communication* with other nations in foreign affairs; this does not necessarily make him or her the sole *policy maker.* Nevertheless, presidents argue that they have all the sovereign diplomatic powers of the nation except those the Constitution specifically assigned to Congress. They may do in foreign affairs anything that the general welfare of the nation requires, subject only to express constitutional limitations. "I took the Canal Zone and let Congress debate," Theodore Roosevelt boasted in 1904, expressing the "presidentialist" approach.

Presidents argue that once they have made foreign policy it is up to Congress to support them by law and appropriations. Members of Congress often agree. When Richard Russell, chair of the Senate Armed Services Committee in the 1950s, was informed that President Eisenhower might send military advisors to South Vietnam, he responded, "I think this is the greatest mistake this country's ever made. I could not be more opposed to it, but if he does it I will never raise my voice."[6] Since President Johnson got the United States into the Vietnam War, many members of Congress have reacted strongly against presidential prerogative power. "Unbridled presidential power in foreign affairs can be just as wrongheaded, just as destructive, and just as harmful to the nation as unbridled congressional power," claimed Clement Zablocki, chair of the House Foreign Affairs Committee in the 1970s, reflecting a post-Vietnam mood of skepticism about presidential management of foreign relations.[7]

By using constitutional prerogatives presidents have expanded their powers greatly: We can see this expansion by examining how the original "treaty power" providing for a balanced participation by the president and Senate has become a unilateral presidential power, and has itself been superseded by a presidential "commitment power" based on the executive agreement, an instrument of diplomacy not even mentioned in the Constitution.

Treaty Powers

The Constitution provides that the president "shall have the Power, by and with the Advice and Consent of the Senate, to make Treaties, provided two-thirds of the Senators present concur." The framers expected the Senate to play a major role in the treaty-making process: In fact, most drafts at the Constitutional Convention gave the Senate the power to make treaties, and it was not until ten days before the Convention adjourned that the president was given the major role.[8]

May the Senate advise the president while the administration is negotiating the treaty, or does the Senate's role begin only when the president submits the treaty to the Senate? The president "makes" the treaty with the advice and consent of the Senate, which seems to imply a role for the Senate in the negotiations. George Washington set the early precedents. While negotiating an Indian treaty, he suggested that "the business may possibly be referred to their deliberations in their legislative chamber." Washington met with the Senate on August 22, 1789, to obtain its advice. The senators decided they would not commit themselves to any treaty draft that Washington presented to them that day. Washington had to return two days later to obtain their consent, and the experience soured him; he did not consult with the Senate again in person, but only through written correspondence.[9] When he negotiated the Jay Treaty with Great Britain, he consulted with Senate leaders, but submitted the treaty to the Senate only after it was completed.

Since Washington's time, practices have varied. Until 1815 it was the custom for presidents to send a special message to Congress before starting negotiations and when treaty drafts had been concluded. Since then, some presidents have consulted informally with congressional leaders before negotiations, as President Chester Arthur did in 1884 concerning a treaty with the independent island of Hawaii. Many have given extensive briefings to senators while negotiations were in progress; Secretary of State Dean Acheson, on behalf of President Truman, briefed key senators on the North Atlantic Treaty negotiations in 1947.

The composition of the negotiating team may help the president secure Senate consent, as President McKinley found out after appointing three senators to the delegation that negotiated the Treaty of Paris ending the Spanish–American War—he won consent by one vote, due in part to senatorial participation. President Truman used a Republican, John Foster Dulles, as his chief negotiator for the Japanese Treaty at the end of World War II to give it bipartisan support. Some presidents have given key senators on the armed services committee an informal "veto" over members of their negotiating teams at strategic arms talks, or allowed senators to send staff members as observers to negotiations. President Carter named 26 senators as "official advisers" to his arms negotiating team at Geneva in 1977–1978.[10] Since 1962 legislators have been advisors on trade agreement negotiations.

In contrast, when President Woodrow Wilson negotiated the Treaty of Versailles in 1919, he did not include a single member of the Senate on his delegation, nor did he provide Congress with any information about negotiations. The Senate defeated the Treaty. President Carter almost committed the same error, failing to include senators on his negotiating team or provide them with briefings when he negotiated the Panama Canal Treaty in 1977. To save the treaty Carter acquiesced in "negotiations" conducted by several Senate leaders with the Panamanian government and agreed to several amendments to the treaty—as did the Panamanians.

Treaties are submitted after negotiations to the Senate for its advice and consent. If the president refuses to submit a draft of a treaty, the Senate may pass a nonbinding resolution requesting him to do so, as it did in 1982 when it asked President Reagan to submit two arms controls treaties negotiated with the Soviet Union. The president, of course, is free to disregard the request.

The two-thirds provision by which the Senate gives its formal consent has been interpreted since 1953 to mean two-thirds of a quorum (the minimum number necessary to transact business). Senate consent is no formality. Between 1789 and 1969, 23 of 195 treaties submitted by the president were defeated by the Senate. These included a treaty to annex Texas in 1844, other attempts to add territory (such as Santo Domingo in 1869) to the Union, arbitration treaties proposed by Roosevelt and Taft between 1905 and 1912, and Wilson's Treaty of Versailles in 1919. In the 1920s and 1930s the Senate prevented American entry into the Permanent Court of International Justice and blocked general arbitration treaties. Other treaties that failed to win consent or were withdrawn include the Genocide Convention of 1950, and the SALT II Treaty of 1979. Secretary of State John Hay at the turn of the nineteenth century concluded that "a treaty entering the Senate is like a bull going into the arena; no one can say just how or when the blow will fall—but one thing is certain—it will never leave the arena alive."[11]

The Senate may amend the treaty before giving its consent, in which case the new language must be accepted by the other party, but once the other side accepts there is no need for the treaty to be resubmitted to the Senate. The Senate may also express its "reservations" about the language whereby the United States limits its obligations under the terms of the treaty, a procedure which does not require any renegotiation with the other party. The Senate may also state its "understandings," which interpret provisions. After the Senate consents, the president may ratify the treaty by signifying to the other party that it is in effect; or the president may withhold ratification, deciding not to put the treaty into force.

Although the House of Representatives does not have a role in the approval of a treaty, it often must pass legislation that implements or funds treaty provisions, and the president must negotiate with the House leadership to get its agreement to implement treaty provisions.[12]

The president and Congress may come into conflict about treaty enforcement. The president is charged with seeing that "the laws be faithfully executed," and Article 6 refers to treaties as the "Supreme Law of the Land." The president defines the terms of treaties and sees to their enforcement as he or she sees fit. In the 1980s, for example, President Reagan interpreted a treaty with the Soviet Union banning the development or deployment of antiballistic missile systems in a "narrow" manner so that he could proceed with his intention to develop a "Star Wars" defensive system against Soviet missiles. The Soviets protested his interpretation, and there was considerable complaint from Democrats in Congress and many outside experts involved in arms control issues. These critics wanted a "broad" interpretation of the treaty that would bar almost all efforts to test prototype antimissile systems in outer space.[13]

Executive Agreements

Theodore Roosevelt once negotiated a pact with Santo Domingo to which the Senate refused approval: thereupon he informed the senators that he would put it into effect as an "executive agreement." He assured the outraged senators that if they ever decided to consent to the Sanchez-Dillingham Agreement, he would then ratify it and put it into effect as a treaty. They were not amused. "I do not much admire the Senate," Roosevelt concluded about the incident, "because it is such a helpless body when efficient work for good is to be done."[14] Since Roosevelt's day, executive agreements have become important instruments of unilateral presidential diplomacy.

An executive agreement is a written or verbal pact or understanding reached by the president or another authorized official with a foreign government.[15] It can be implemented solely on the president's constitutional authority, without any submission to the Senate. The first involved a postal agreement with Canada in 1792, negotiated by the American and Canadian postmasters general. Since that time the vast majority have involved agreements between departments of government and their foreign counterparts in agriculture, health, trade, communications, the environment, science, and defense.

Executive agreements have been crucial in settling some important diplomatic issues. They were used in 1817 in the Bagot-Rush agreement to limit American and British naval forces on the Great Lakes; in 1900 to participate in a coalition to crush the Boxer Rebellion in China; in a 1905 agreement with Japan recognizing its domination of Korea in return for its acknowledgment of U.S. control of the Philippines (an agreement kept secret for twenty years); in 1905 in the Gentlemen's Agreement to regulate Japanese immigration to the United States; in 1918 to conclude an armistice with Imperial Germany; in 1933 to normalize relations with the Soviet Union; in 1940 to exchange U.S. destroyers for British naval bases; in 1941 to defend Iceland from German attack; in 1945 to end the fighting in Germany and establish the status of Berlin; in 1953 to end the Korean War; in 1973 to end American involvement in the Vietnam War; in 1975 to establish an American observation force for the demilitarization of the Sinai Peninsula; in 1979 to implement a strategic arms limitation agreement with the Soviet Union; in 1981 to secure the release of American diplomats from Iran in exchange for establishing procedures to settle Iranian claims against the United States; in 1990 and 1991 to forge a coalition to defeat the Iraqi military in the Persian Gulf War.

There are close to ten times as many executive agreements as there are treaties: on average only thirty treaties and more than 250 executive agreements are concluded yearly. The majority involve routine matters, are authorized by Congress in advance, and require subsequent laws or funding by Congress to be implemented. About five percent of executive agreements, however, are implemented without any congressional participation. Some of these are American commitments to defend other nations or agreements to lease military bases in other countries, such as Kenya, Oman, and Israel. Some pacts have created de facto military alliances without any congressional participation, such as agreements with Spain in the 1950s.

In 1969 Congress passed the National Commitments Resolution, which stated that a national commitment of the United States could not be made by executive agreement, but only by "affirmative action taken by the executive and legislative branches of the U.S. Government by means of a treaty, statute, or concurrent resolution of both Houses of Congress specifically providing for such commitment." Presidents do not accept this interpretation of a national commitment, arguing that executive agreements are binding obligations of the United States.

Presidents have kept some executive agreements secret, especially those involving the Department of Defense and intelligence agencies. In 1972 Congress passed the Case Amendment, a law that provided that the secretary of state must transmit the text of any executive agreement to Congress within sixty days. Secret agreements must be submitted to the House Foreign Affairs and Senate Foreign Relations Committees; about 200 such agreements are submitted each year. In 1977 the time limit under the Case Amendment was reduced by Congress to twenty days. Although Congress was signaling its displeasure with presidential reliance on such agreements, it did not pass proposed legislation that would have prevented such agreements from coming into effect if Congress "vetoed" them by passing a resolution of disapproval. Nor did it pass a proposed bill requiring that Congress determine, by resolution, whether an international agreement must be submitted to the Senate in the form of a treaty.

The courts have imposed some limits on executive agreements: they cannot be inconsistent with prior congressional legislation; agreements that affect prior laws passed by Congress must be implemented by new congressional legislation; and they cannot impair the constitutional rights of American citizens.[16] In *Reid v. Covert,* for example, agreements with Great Britain and Japan that permitted the spouses of U.S. military personnel stationed in these nations to be tried by military courts (without juries) in murder cases violated the provision of the Bill of Rights giving U.S. citizens the right to trial by jury in capital offenses, and were struck down.[17]

Parallel Unilateral Policy Declarations (PUPD)

Presidents may issue a statement unilaterally declaring a U.S. commitment. If such a declaration is issued by two or more nations at the same time, committing them to parallel actions, it may serve as the functional equivalent of an executive agreement. Such declarations were used to extend the SALT I arms control agreement with the Soviet Union after it expired in 1977 and governed the SALT II agreement between 1980 and 1986.[18] Why use a parallel unilateral policy declaration (PUPD)? In arms control matters, it allows the president to bypass a provision of the Arms Control and Disarmament Act that required that any arms control actions be taken either by treaty or law—thus giving Congress the final say. The president argues that these are informal "undertakings" between two executives and not commitments under international law between two nations. The use of the PUPD enables the president to circumvent the treaty power and other congressional checks if it can find a willing partner in its negotiations.

PRESIDENT VERSUS CONGRESS

Congress has many more explicit powers than the president in foreign affairs. In Article 1 it is given power to regulate commerce with foreign nations and set tariffs, as well as authority over immigration and naturalization policies. It creates and organizes all departments of government, including the Department of State and other agencies that deal with foreign affairs. The Senate consents to nominations of ambassadors and to treaties. Given these and other foreign affairs powers, Congress is not likely to concede plenary authority to the president in diplomacy. Indeed, as the constitutional commentator Edward Corwin put it, the Constitution is an "invitation to struggle over the privilege of directing American foreign policy."[19]

Executive versus Legislative Functions

In the *Federalist Papers,* John Jay, a distinguished American diplomat, argued that a president could act with "unity, secrecy, efficiency and dispatch" in foreign affairs.[20] Congress, a deliberative body constructed as much to block as to facilitate action, is not suited to run foreign affairs. The framers constructed the legislative role in part as a facilitator (providing laws and funding for American diplomatic efforts) and in part as an instrument of checks and balances, to reject presidential initiatives if they did not command support in the country. "You can keep the President from doing bad things," Representative Barney Frank once explained, "but you can't make him do good things."[21]

The constitutional mechanisms create a situation in which each institution needs the other: The president needs the congressional power of the purse and statutory authority to act; Congress needs the instruments of diplomacy that the president controls to get the specific programs of interest to its constituencies implemented.

The president competes with Congress for the privilege of directing American foreign policy. Sometimes there is a role reversal: congressional leaders may use "alternative track" diplomacy, communicating directly with foreign leaders rather than working through the Department of State. In 1985, for example, after free elections in the Philippines had been aborted, Democratic Representative Stephen Solarz, chair of the subcommittee dealing with Asia in the House Foreign Relations Committee, engaged in his own diplomacy to encourage pro-democracy forces in the Philippines to topple the Marcos dictatorship. Shortly thereafter the dictatorship fell and was succeeded by the democratically elected leader Cory Aquino. Solarz's efforts were instrumental in a transition that was only reluctantly supported by the State Department and President Reagan. Similarly, Jim Wright, the speaker of the House, pursued his own diplomatic efforts with the government of Nicaragua in 1987, bypassing the secretary of state and other officials of the Reagan administration, who preferred covert action and pressure on the Nicaraguan government to a diplomatic solution proffered by Wright and many Central American nations.

Patterns of Presidential–Congressional Relations

Congress complains that the president acts too quickly, fails to consult it and keeps it in the dark, and relies on constitutional prerogatives rather than collaborative policy making. The president complains that Congress acts too slowly to take advantage of diplomatic openings or to protect American interests, and that it acts irresponsibly when it substitutes its judgment for the president's. After all, the White House argues, the president is privy to intelligence information that the average member of Congress does not have. The president argues that members of Congress may act for parochial constituency interests rather than in the national interest. Institutional differences are exacerbated by political and ideological differences. Republican presidents square off against Democratic majorities in Congress, and vice versa. Even when the White House and Congress are controlled by the same party, presidents face strong opposition to their foreign policies from leaders of the opposition party and dissidents in their own party.

The partisan divisions of the twenty-six years of split government between 1947 and 1997 have led to the following patterns of presidential–congressional relations in foreign affairs:[22]

- *Confrontation.* The president and Congress may deadlock over foreign policy, leading to paralysis or vacillation in making policy, or the institution of secret prerogative government by the president to bypass congressional obstructionism. In response, Congress uses oversight, checks and balances, and after-the-fact investigations to check the president. Examples include the neutrality policy of Congress before World War II, a policy that prevented Franklin Roosevelt from taking assertive measures against the Axis threats to peace; the congressional cutoff of aid to Turkey after its invasion of Cyprus in 1974; the cutoff of covert assistance to rebels in Angola in 1975; the prohibition of shipments of nuclear fuel to nations that detonate nuclear weapons in 1976; and the Boland Amendment of 1984, which prohibited aid to the Nicaraguan contras. In 1990, after the invasion of Panama, Congress insisted on attaching conditions to postwar reconstruction; President Bush threatened to spend funds unilaterally if Congress refused to give him broad authority.
- *Competition.* Congress and the president may offer alternative foreign policies. Congress passes laws to implement its policies, and these substantially modify the policies proposed by the president. Examples include Senator Jackson's insistence in the 1970s that trade with the Soviet Union be linked to that nation's increase in emigration visas for Soviet Jews; congressional sanctions against South Africa's apartheid government in the 1980s, penalties that went significantly beyond those favored by the Reagan administration; efforts to impose trade sanctions on China after the army's massacre of pro-democracy students in Tiananmen Square; and the Republican congressional proposals in 1995 that the United States end its arms embargo on Bosnia even if the embargo had not been lifted by the United Nations.
- *Compromise.* Congress and the president compromise on foreign policy after a period of confrontation or competition. Compromise usually involves a great deal of consul-

tation between executive officials and members of key congressional committees. The Clinton administration's package of aid to Russia, passed in early 1993, is an example of such compromise, because the final budget figures were somewhat smaller than those proposed by the president.

- *Cooperation.* Congress agrees to cooperate with and support a presidential initiative, by passing legislation and funding in substantially the form proposed by the administration. Congress may also give the president resolutions of support, legitimize presidential actions taken without prior authorization, and downplay legislative oversight or investigations of presidential operations. Members of the opposition party are likely to emphasize bipartisan cooperation with the president. Examples of such cooperation include the Greek and Turkish emergency aid in 1947, the Marshall Plan, passed in 1948, and funding of peacekeeping missions, such as the 1,200 U.S. soldiers in the Sinai Police Force that monitors the treaty between Israel and Egypt.

Presidents cannot always rely on members of their own party when they conduct their diplomacy. President Clinton was opposed by the Democratic Majority Leader and Whip in the House on the North American Free Trade Agreement (NAFTA). Presidents Reagan and Bush faced opposition from conservative Republicans when they negotiated agreements with communist nations. Republican senators distanced themselves from Ronald Reagan during the Iran–contra crisis. Jimmy Carter had difficulty with Democratic senators who forced him to modify his Panama Canal treaties before consenting to them. Gerald Ford's "detente" diplomacy with the Soviet Union was bitterly criticized by rightwing Republicans in the Senate.

Congressional and Bureaucratic Diplomacy

Other nations adjust to our system of divided powers and split government by lobbying Congress and administrative agencies as much as they conduct formal diplomacy with the president and the State Department. Foreign governments cannot assume that anything has been resolved in American government until Congress as well as the president have made a commitment, through laws and appropriations as well as presidential agreements. They may spend as much time monitoring the implementation of agreements within subgovernments as they do negotiating the original agreement. Foreign bureaucracies (military, economic, intelligence) often establish bilateral "horizontal" relationships with their opposites in the United States to implement policy: the U.S. and Israeli defense departments have worked out bilateral agreements for the U.S. Navy to use the Israeli port of Haifa; the U.S. and British intelligence agencies have bilateral agency agreements to share information; U.S. and Canadian and Mexican commerce, labor, and agricultural agencies have agreements to implement NAFTA.

Collaborative Foreign Policy Making

"Let us in on the takeoffs if you want us in on the crash landings," Senator Arthur Vandenberg once advised President Harry Truman.[23] Should the president try to manage foreign affairs unilaterally through executive prerogatives, or should the

White House collaborate with Congress? Every president and every secretary of state promises to cooperate with Congress, at least at the beginning. But it does not work out that way. Presidents impose a curtain of secrecy, present Congress with faits accomplis, and then give briefings on plans already made and decisions already taken. For a collaborative relationship to exist, it would be necessary to reconstitute the way the government makes decisions.[24] Information would have to be shared with Congress on a timely basis. Members of Congress would need to have access to intelligence reports, military assessments, and cable traffic from officials abroad.

Since the mid-1970s Congress has attempted to create a collaborative system of "interbranch policy codetermination" by passing laws providing for consultation. Instead of engaging in "after-the-fact" oversight of presidential decisions, Congress has passed "framework" laws that require one or more of the following from the White House:

- *Briefings, timely notice, and reports.* Officials may be required to brief congressional committees on proposed actions, give timely notice as decisions are made, and provide quarterly or annual reports on programs. The State Department is required to issue an annual report on human rights, used in making decisions about trade and foreign aid.
- *Certifications.* Officials may not take certain actions unless they certify to Congress that other nations are in compliance with certain U.S. policies. The president must certify that nations are making progress in human rights, or that they are in compliance with the Nuclear Non-Proliferation Treaty, to receive U.S. military aid. Nations that cannot be certified face mandatory cutoffs.
- *Waivers.* Officials may not act if certain circumstances exist unless the president waives the congressional restriction. Congress in the Arms Export Control Act of 1979 allows the president to send arms to allies without prior notification if he waives the requirement on national security grounds, as President Carter did in 1979 in sending arms to Southern Yemen. The Trade Act of 1974 permits the president to waive certain trade sanctions (denial of Most Favored Nation status) if by doing so freedom of emigration would be promoted. Trade sanctions imposed on China in 1989 could be lifted "in the national interest" by the president. When a president does issue a waiver, the administration is required to provide detailed written justification to Congress.
- *"Report and wait."* Officials must report to Congress and wait (usually thirty days) before implementing a decision. This gives Congress the opportunity to block the decision or modify it, as often happens with arms sales. The Nelson-Bingham Amendment passed in 1974 required the president to give Congress notice of any proposed military sales exceeding $25 million, a figure lowered to $7 million in 1981.

Legislative veto provisions have often been attached to foreign aid bills and measures dealing with transfers of nuclear technology and fuel, trade agreements, and other foreign policy issues. Although many such provisions have been adopted, no legislative veto has ever been used by Congress against a foreign policy decision made by a president or his subordinates. In the case of arms sales and some other decisions, the possibility that these formal "veto mechanisms" might be used created incentives for the president to negotiate agreements with members of Congress, and often arms sales were substantially modified to avoid a veto.[25] Since the Supreme Court's *Chadha* decision (invalidating a one-chamber legislative veto),

Congress has relied on "informal" veto mechanisms or the passage of legislation to block presidential initiatives.

Critics of collaborative mechanisms argue that Congress should not try to "micromanage" foreign policy. Its laws and appropriations should develop general principles, whereas diplomacy, covert actions, and military signaling involve specific cases best left to executive judgment and discretion. They argue that Congress is irresponsible, partisan, subject to pressure by interest groups and foreign governments, and that it cannot act quickly and decisively in collaborating with the president.[26]

Presidents cast their lot with the critics of framework laws: their response to these statutes often involves minimal compliance. Presidents may not report in a candid or timely fashion. They exploit loopholes, as Reagan did in the Iran–contra affair to avoid reporting at all. Instead of providing real consultation to members of Congress, they offer briefings after presidential fait accomplis. Members of Congress charge that presidents treat them like mushroom farmers treat their crop (keep them in the dark and cover them with manure). "Everybody in Congress is his own secretary of state," complained Assistant Secretary of State Elliot Abrams in 1986.[27] However, many Republican officials who had chafed under congressional restrictions gleefully began to "Carterize" President Clinton in 1994 (i.e., claim the president was irresolute and weak), because Clinton often attempted to work within the collaborative framework, even going so far as to solicit suggestions from Congress about his policies in Bosnia, Haiti, and Somalia.[28] Yet how else could a Democratic president respond in the post-Vietnam era to the wishes of a Democratic Congress for a role in foreign policy making?

Defenders of collaborative decision making argue that it comports well with the original constitutional understandings. Presidents are well advised either to persuade Congress to back them up or to drop their initiatives. If they cannot win congressional support, it probably means they do not have public support, and if they adhere to their policies, it is a prescription for disaster.

THE WHITE HOUSE FOREIGN POLICY ADVISORY SYSTEM

The president has three principal groups of officials to help him formulate foreign policy—the diplomatic, military, and intelligence communities—and each group of officials has its own views about the best combination of diplomatic talk, military pressure or force, and covert action needed to manage foreign affairs. Each provides the president with its own intelligence assessments and policy recommendations. "The real organization of government at higher echelons is not what you find in textbooks or organization charts," said Dean Rusk, secretary of state for Kennedy and Johnson. "It is how confidence flows down from the President."[29]

The president presides over advisors and agencies with competing missions and overlapping jurisdictions, and they often engage in "turf wars" to expand the missions of their organizations, or try to form coalitions to "surround" the president with a consensus.[30] Yet when the president brings advisors together in small groups, sometimes they forsake their organizational allegiances and function as advisors "without portfolio," so that military officers or intelligence officials urge diplomatic solutions and diplomats call for the use of force. In August of 1994, as the military regime in Haiti came under heavy U.S. pressure to cede power, Secretary of Defense William Perry argued strongly against an invasion, while Deputy Secretary of State Strobe Talbott argued equally forcefully for quick military action.[31]

The Secretary of State and the Diplomatic Community

The secretary of state is the principal spokesperson for the president on American foreign policy and the principal officer of the Department of State. The secretary serves as a statutory member of the National Security Council and as a member of the president's "inner-cabinet" of advisors. The secretary has the primary responsibility for preparing the budget for foreign affairs programs, including diplomatic missions, foreign aid to developing nations, and contributions to multilateral organizations such as the World Bank, the Inter-American Development Bank, and the International Monetary Fund. The secretary defends foreign affairs program before subcommittees of the House and Senate Appropriations Committees and is principal spokesperson for the administration before the House Foreign Affairs and Senate Foreign Relations Committees. The president may also make the secretary the envoy to communicate foreign policy to foreign heads of state, or principal diplomat at international conferences.

Some secretaries are highly influential advisors and policy makers, and others merely administer the State Department.[32] Although Thomas Jefferson, the first secretary of state, resigned from Washington's cabinet because his pro-French policies were not adopted, for the first two decades of the nineteenth century each secretary of state was an influential shaper of foreign policy, and each became the next president. In modern times, President Truman relied heavily on George Marshall, who proposed the "Marshall Plan" for economic recovery in Western Europe after World War II, and on Dean Acheson, the architect of the American policies of collective security and containment of communist aggression. President Nixon and Secretary of State Henry Kissinger worked so well together, bypassing almost all of the government in implementing foreign policy, that critics referred to them as the "two-man band" when they concluded arms control agreements with the Soviet Union. George Bush's secretary, James Baker, was his close political advisor and campaign manager: the two dominated foreign policy in much the way Nixon and Kissinger had done, bypassing most other officials at the end of the Cold War, as they encouraged the Soviet Union to withdraw from Eastern Europe, conclude arms reductions agreement with the United States and NATO, and join the allied coalition in the war against Iraq.

Three secretaries tried to control all aspects of foreign policy, but each was rebuffed by the president. William Seward wrote a memorandum to Lincoln in which he suggested that by controlling foreign policy he could unite the nation and avoid civil war between the North and South (by substituting a war with France or England instead), but Lincoln wrote back that as president he would retain final responsibility. Seward's main accomplishment was buying Alaska from the Russians. Henry Kissinger was secretary of state when Gerald Ford assumed the presidency;

at first, his knowledge and his control of the bureaucratic machinery was indispensable to Ford, but eventually Ford decided to appoint his own national security advisor, forcing Kissinger to give up one of his two posts; he also began to bypass Kissinger on some foreign policy issues and backed the Treasury's attempt to strip Kissinger of control of international economic policy making. As soon as he took office as secretary of state, Alexander Haig asked President Reagan to name him "vicar to the community of departments having an interest in the several dimensions of foreign policy," adding that he should become "the single manager to present views and choices."[33] He argued that the principal advisors to the president should be "those officials who have undergone the confirmation process with the legislature" rather than the national security advisor.[34] Reagan refused Haig's suggestions, and eventually he resigned in frustration.

The president can make the secretary of state the key White House advisor and the negotiator with foreign governments. He can put most of the responsibility for formulating foreign policy in State's Policy Planning Staff, as Truman did at the end of World War II. He can let State establish "interdepartmental" committees under assistant secretaries, to put State's imprint on the foreign activities of all agencies, as Nixon permitted Kissinger to do when he appointed Kissinger his secretary of state in 1973.

Alternatively, the president can bypass or downgrade the secretary and reduce the influence of the department. Franklin Roosevelt used presidential assistants to implement his policies, rather than Secretary of State Cordell Hull. Nixon's secretary of state William Rogers was overshadowed by National Security Advisor Henry Kissinger. Cyrus Vance, Jimmy Carter's secretary of state, resigned as a matter of honor after Carter ordered an American raid to free diplomats held hostage by Iran; Vance had been kept in the dark about the raid and had not been able to keep his promise to the Senate to brief it in advance of any military action against Iran. George Shultz opposed Ronald Reagan's plan to sell arms to Iran and was frozen out of policy making along with Secretary of Defense Caspar Weinberger. After the Iran–contra scandal erupted, Shultz became the dominant figure in the Reagan administration because he had the confidence of Congress. President Clinton's secretary, Warren Christopher, was bypassed when the United States came to an agreement with North Korea about ending its program of nuclear weapons development and was also bypassed in the final negotiations with Haiti's military rulers that permitted a peaceful U.S. intervention. In both cases President Clinton permitted former president Jimmy Carter to negotiate directly with the leaders of foreign nations and suggest compromise positions at variance with the approach of the State Department.

Presidents often are disappointed in the Department of State. They view it as hidebound, traditional, and slow to get moving on new White House initiatives. They may mistrust career diplomats and foreign service officers, who they claim fail to see the "big picture" and focus instead on their particular areas of specialization. They are suspicious of the bureaucracy because it is so responsive to Congressional committees. They believe that career diplomats are too interested in promoting the interests of foreign countries to the White House, rather than promoting U.S. national interests abroad. Most of all, in an era of mass communication, presidents want State Department officials to be able to win the confidence of the American people for their diplomatic efforts. President Clinton signaled his displeasure with the performance of Secretary of State Warren Christopher by sending one of his political aides, David Gergen, over to "Foggy Bottom" to provide some "image control" and focus for the department.

The negative feelings are often reciprocated by State Department careerists. They are upset when a secretary such as James Baker freezes them out of policy in favor of political appointees with little foreign policy experience, and they are equally upset when a secretary such as Warren Christopher finds it difficult to articulate a vision of what foreign policy is all about. They have little respect for presidential political appointees, especially diplomats who won their job by making campaign contributions and high-level officials who have made their mark in journalism, law, or politics. They resent the fact that their expertise is ignored by new appointees: Five career officials resigned in protest in the first two years of Clinton's presidency because they were excluded by political appointees from making policy regarding Bosnia.

There are tensions between the career foreign service officers and assistant secretaries of the State Department whenever the White House signals a sharp turn in foreign policy. It is not always easy to get the State Department or other civilian officials working in "country teams" in foreign nations to respond quickly and effectively to shifts in policy. The various flip-flops in policy toward Haiti from one week to the next (such as whether to take in Haitian refugees to the United States, confine them to Guantanamo base, or put them in other nations) were known as "the Lurch" at Foggy Bottom, as officials scrambled to keep up with political executives who themselves were whipsawed from one direction to the next by a combination of domestic and international pressures.[35]

The Secretary of Defense and the Defense Community

The secretary of defense is the principal civilian advisor to the president on military matters and administrator of the Department of Defense. The secretary serves as a statutory member of the National Security Council and as a member of the president's "inner-cabinet" of advisors. The secretary participates with the chair of the Joint Chiefs of Staff in the formulation of military strategy, reviews recommendations of the Pentagon's weapons acquisition committees, and recommends new weapons systems to the president. The secretary prepares the defense budget and defends it before military subcommittees of the House and Senate Appropriations Committees and serves as the principal spokesperson for the administration when testifying before the House and Senate Armed Services Committees.

Some secretaries of defense have been strong managers, instituting centralized controls over the departments of the army, navy, and air force, and asserting their authority over the Joint Chiefs of Staff. President Kennedy relied on Robert McNamara and his "whiz kids" to streamline Pentagon procurement and rationalize weapons system development and procurement. So great was Kennedy's faith in McNamara that he backed McNamara's budget requests against his own Office of Management and Budget. Others have been disappointments, failing to control the uniformed military officers and get them to adhere to administration policy, and failing to convince Congress of the soundness of defense policy.

The main point of contention between the secretary and the president may be whether and under what circumstances to use the military for diplomatic purposes. The president may be advised by his secretary of state and national security advisor that the threat of U.S. military force will induce a foreign government to modify its policies. Such threat may include holding maneuvers offshore with the Navy (as the United States does periodically in the Gulf of Sidra near Libya, the Persian Gulf near Iran and Iraq, and the Caribbean near Haiti). It may involve flying reconnaissance missions, sending military units or airplanes or aid to nations (as we did to help Chad in 1987 repel a Libyan invasion), providing training missions, or quarantining a nation (as we did with Haiti in 1993–1994).

The secretary of defense and Joint Chiefs are reluctant to use the military for such diplomatic signaling or for foreign peacekeeping operations. These officials argue that the military should only be used when the most important U.S. national interests are at stake. The military is usually opposed to sending units for peacekeeping and humanitarian operations, arguing that these divert the units from training for warfare, cost inordinate amounts of money that must come from Pentagon readiness accounts (for example, $1.2 billion to finance the Somalian relief operations in 1993–1994), and unbalance the force structure needed for other missions or for deterrence. The military opposed sending troops to Lebanon in 1982 for peacekeeping, as well as the mission in Somalia in 1992. During the Clinton administration the Joint Chiefs opposed proposals to bomb Serbian positions in Bosnia and were reluctant to use military force in Haiti, and they were joined by Clinton's secretary and deputy secretary of defense. They also opposed any thought of a "preemptive" strike on North Korean nuclear plants or facilities, arguing that such an attack would fail (the North Koreans would have hidden their nuclear weapons) and might lead to all-out war on the Korean peninsula.[36] At times it seems that "hell no, we won't go" is the motto not only of war resisters, but also of the defense secretary and the Joint Chiefs of Staff.

The Director of Central Intelligence (DCI) and the Intelligence Community

The Director of Central Intelligence (DCI) is the principal intelligence advisor to the President. He or she is also the director of the Central Intelligence Agency (CIA), and a statutory advisor to the National Security Council (NSC). The position of DCI was established by the National Security Act of 1947, to provide a coordinating mechanism for intelligence reporting to the president and to maintain civilian control over the compilation of national intelligence estimates (NIE) submitted to the president. The director advises the president on proposed covert operations and, according to the Intelligence Oversight Act of 1980, briefs the Intelligence Committees of Congress on such operations. The DCI is a member of the National Security Planning Group, a committee of the NSC that monitors, reviews, and oversees the implementation of national security policies, and also serves on the NSC crisis monitoring committee. The director coordinates all the intelligence reports from the CIA, the Defense Intelligence Agency, the National Security Agency (which deals with codes and electronic intelligence), the National Reconnaissance Office (spy satellites), and the State Department's Bureau of Intelligence.

The DCI provides the president with "The President's Daily Brief," a five- to seven-page summary of intelligence reports, which serves as background for the president's daily national security briefing, and is also distributed to the secretaries of state and defense, the national security advisor, and chairman of the Joint Chiefs of Staff. Transcripts of intercepted conversations of foreign leaders, or satellite photographs and other electronic intelligence, may also be included.[37] The DCI also oversees preparation of the National Intelligence Estimates dealing with military and diplomatic capabilities and intentions of foreign nations.

Some presidents include the intelligence director in their inner circle as a top advisor: Lyndon Johnson included his DCI in the "Tuesday Lunch" meetings, along with the secretaries of state and defense, the national security advisor, and the chair of the Joint Chiefs of Staff. Other presidents, such as Bill Clinton, neither attend the morning "hot spot" briefing (about world trouble-spots) given daily by the DCI, nor include the DCI in their inner circle or pay more than intermittent attention to the DCI's analysis of world events.[38]

Because the Central Intelligence Agency (CIA) has engaged in controversial activities, a director may be chosen to reform an agency and reassure Congress that the "spooks" are firmly under administration control. Gerald Ford chose George Bush to serve as DCI after revelations that the CIA had engaged in unauthorized activities, including attempted assassinations of foreign leaders. Bush made fifty-one appearances before Congress as it considered new legislation to supervise CIA activities. Jimmy Carter chose William Colby to reorganize the CIA and keep it from unauthorized actions; Colby dismissed a large number of agency officials and moved the agency away from covert operations toward intelligence collection and analysis. These reforms were overturned when Ronald Reagan picked William Casey, former head of the Securities and Exchange Commission and his campaign manager in 1980. Casey once again oriented the agency toward covert operations, including the resupply of anti-communist forces in Afghanistan and the funding of the anti-Sandinista guerrillas in Central America.

Intelligence directors are in a "damned if you do, damned if you don't" situation in dealing with the White House. The CIA and the DCI may provide unwelcome news to a president, as they did during the Vietnam War, when their pessimistic evaluation about the Pentagon's ability to win the war against communist guerrillas were rejected by Lyndon Johnson. If they provide conservative estimates, as they did in assessing the Iraqi nuclear program, they may be discredited by those favoring an interventionist policy. If they provide an alarmist estimate, as they did in assessing the North Korean program, they may be accused of trying to "cover themselves" with a "just in case" scenario.

The intelligence agencies compartmentalize operational and analytical units, so that neither group will contaminate the other, but the DCI sometimes becomes a policy advocate, and then slants recommendations and intelligence to the White House. George Shultz criticized Casey for doing that in the Iran arms sales: "If the two things are mixed together, it is too tempting to have . . . the selection of information that is presented favor the policy that you are advocating."[39] Casey told Reagan that Iraq was winning the war and that Iran had not engaged in terrorist activities, neither of which was the case, as Shultz unsuccessfully tried to point out to Reagan.

DCIs may lose the confidence of the White House because their intelligence estimates contradict official administration policy, because they cannot control "leaks" from their agencies that cast doubt on presidential decisions, because they oppose White House priorities, or because they cannot gain the confidence of the Intelligence Committees. R. James Woolsey, Jr., President Clinton's DCI, was passed over for secretary of defense because he had fought against Clinton's proposed cuts in his agency budget, because he alienated many congressional Democrats, and because the CIA sought to discredit exiled President Bertrand Aristide of Haiti (by calling his mental stability into question) just as the State Department was trying to broker a deal with Haiti's generals to permit Aristide to return to power.[40] Woolsey eventually resigned, having had no influence with the president.

The National Security Advisor (NSA) and the National Security Council (NSC)

The national security advisor (NSA), formally called assistant to the president for national security affairs, serves as the principal advisor to the president on national security matters, organizes meetings of the National Security Council (NSC), and supervises its staff. The advisor prepares initial drafts of National Security Decision Directives (NSDD) for NSC consideration and monitors implementation of national security decisions taken by the president. The advisor is a White House aide, with no statutory powers or duties, is not a member of the National Security Council, and is appointed to office by the president without Senate consent.

The advisor may play several different roles in presidential decision making. President Eisenhower used Robert Cutler, his special assistant for national security affairs, as a "custodian-manager" to see that all options were being considered, especially for long-range planning, and ensure that the elaborate staffing method he put in place (with 76 aides to the National Security Council) operated smoothly. President Reagan used Colin Powell in the same role in the 1980s: Powell sought consensus among agencies, and where it did not exist, tried to balance the views of others so the president would have a full range of options.

In contrast, President Kennedy used McGeorge Bundy as one of his key advisors and policy makers, less concerned with process and paperwork than with policy advocacy, especially in short-term crisis management. Similarly, President Johnson used Walt Rostow as a policy advocate for escalating the Vietnam War, and as a defender of the policy before Congress and the media.

Some presidents use their advisors to formulate overall principles for American foreign policy. President Nixon relied on Henry Kissinger as his principal agent as well as advisor in foreign policy and national security. Instead of using an ambassador, he sent him on top-secret diplomatic missions to the People's Republic of China, and entrusted him with negotiating arms control agreements with the Soviet Union. Kissinger used the NSC staff to dominate interdepartmental committees concerned with arms control negotiations with the Soviets (the Verification Committee) and defense budgeting. Similarly, President Carter used Zbigniew Brzezinski to formulate his foreign policy goals, and as a counterweight to his secretary of state Cyrus Vance, making him the first assistant with cabinet rank. Brzezinski presided over national security committees dealing with intelligence, arms control, and crisis management. President Clinton relied on Anthony Lake to conceptualize a U.S. role in the post–Cold War era: Lake developed a theory of "enlargement of democracy" to justify a U.S. role as a leader in world affairs.

The most controversial role for the advisor and other staffers is as implementors of foreign policy. During the Reagan administration, the two national security advisors with military backgrounds, former Marine Colonel Robert McFarlane and former Navy Admiral John Poindexter, used the NSC staff as an operational agency to implement policy, often relying on another NSC staffer, a Marine colonel named Oliver North. One successful operation involved capture of terrorists who had been responsible for the seizure of the cruise ship *Achille Lauro* and the death of a U.S. citizen. But, instead of developing policy proposals for the president, the national security advisor and the Political-Military Affairs Directorate within the NSC conducted covert operations and diplomatic negotiations with presidential concurrence, creating a "government within a government" not subject to customary congressional oversight.[41]

The president attempts to coordinate foreign policy making through the National Security Council (NSC), a unit of the Executive Office of the President established by the National Security Act of 1947.[42] Initially it consisted of the president, who chaired its meetings, the secretary of state, the secretary of defense, and the three service secretaries for the army, navy, and air force. The DCI was not a member but would serve as an advisor. In 1949 Congress amended the law to change the composition of the council: the three service secretaries were dropped, and the vice president was added. The chair of the Joint Chiefs of Staff became an advisor to the council and attended meetings. The president might "from time to time" designate other officials to sit on the council or attend its meetings, and twenty or more officials have often been invited. The council has a staff of forty or more aides, supervised by the assistant to the president for national security. The NSC has no powers of its own, takes no votes, and makes no decisions. Presidential decisions taken after NSC deliberations are embodied in National Security Decision Directives and are implemented by the departments.[43]

The NSC staff monitors national security communications in the Situation Room, located in the White House basement, and in a Crisis Management Center located in the Executive Office Building (equipped with computers and projection facilities for display of information). These include State Department instructions to American embassies and missions, Defense Department messages to military commands, and Joint Chiefs of Staff orders to the regional military commanders in chief. Data from the National Military Command Center can be simultaneously displayed in the Executive Office Situation Room.

Although Presidents Truman and Eisenhower convened the NSC frequently, most presidents rely on very small meetings with their key national security advisors much more than on meetings of the council itself. Presidents disregard the formal council because they prefer informal consultations without the cumbersome NSC machinery: a typical NSC meeting will have thirty to forty deputies in attendance, which will require considerable advance staff preparation.

Often presidents prefer much smaller and more informal settings. President Kennedy used the "Ex Comm," an executive committee of the council consisting of a dozen top national security officials from various agencies, to deliberate in situations such as the Berlin Crisis and the Cuban Missile Crisis. Lyndon Johnson relied on his "Tuesday Lunch" with the secretaries of state and defense, the director of central intelligence, chair of the Joint Chiefs, and his national security advisor, to plan strategy for the war in Vietnam. Jimmy Carter held "Friday Breakfasts" with his vice president, the secretaries of state and defense, and his national security advisor to deal with the Iran hostage crisis and relations with the Soviets. Ronald Reagan used the National Security Planning group, consisting of the members of the NSC, the director of central intelligence, the national security advisor, and three top White House political aides—the first president to include political advisors in national security decision making.

National security advisors often want a leading voice in formulating foreign policy. Consider the recommendations of Carter's advisor Zbigniew Brzezinski: "The definition of the strategic direction would originate from the assistant for National Security Affairs, who would then tightly coordinate and control the Secretary of State, the Secretary of Defense, the chairman of the Joint Chiefs, and the Director of Central Intelligence as a team, with them knowing that he was doing so on the President's behalf."[44] Carter refused to give Brzezinski such sweeping authority.

Presidents sometimes have more confidence in their national security advisors than in their secretaries of state. In that case the secretary may handle routine affairs of the department but be frozen out of presidential diplomacy. Like Henry Kissinger or Zbigniew Brzezinski, advisors may seek to establish NSC coordinating committees to control diplomatic missions and arms control negotiations, writing their "talking points" (negotiating instructions), and reviewing all cable traffic from State and Defense department officials in foreign countries. The advisor is likely to run into opposition from the State Department, which prefers to be the "lead agency" in all interagency committees dealing with foreign policy, and the Defense Department, which wants no interference with its budget recommendations to the president. A strong advisor, such as Henry Kissinger, will dominate the policy-making machinery provided he has the backing of the president, but often Washington is convulsed with epic battle royals or low-level sniping between the secretary of state and the national security advisor.

Presidential-Centered Foreign Policy

Activist presidents can set up a presidential-centered system.[45] Like Kennedy and Carter and Clinton, they can parcel out assignments and make senior officials de facto White House assistants, each in charge of a particular international issue. They can play off the NSA against the secretary of state, and both against the secretary of defense and Joint Chiefs. They may create interdepartmental groups chaired by a variety of different departments, dividing responsibility, in a way that provides themselves with multiple options. They can go outside the department and NSC machinery to establish their own informal advisory system, as Eisenhower did when he established an arms control group headed by Nelson Rockefeller during the 1950s. They may rely on special emissaries who are not even government officials to conduct their diplomacy. President Clinton sent a former diplomat, Michael Armacost, to discuss trade relations with China, helping to avert a serious rupture in diplomatic relations. He asked Jesse Jackson, a two-time candidate for the presidency, to go to Nigeria in an attempt to mediate a political crisis. These emissaries give the president greater flexibility in negotiating a settlement, but unofficial emissaries are not fully subject to his control: former President Carter, for example, went well beyond the intentions of the administration in negotiating with Haiti and North Korea.

The problem with presidential-centered foreign policy making is that it is chaotic, and if a president does not pay much attention, his subordinates may get the president into difficult situations precisely because of their free-wheeling efforts. Issues may fall through the cracks. Debate and discussion may not take place among all relevant agencies before a president makes a decision. Policy may be made haphazardly by lower-level officials because no systematic review at the highest level occurs until matters reach a crisis. As Zbigniew Brzezinski warns, "the basic danger is that the U.S. government then acts through fits and starts. Initiatives are launched suddenly without effective coordination, or alternatively there are long periods of policy paralysis."[46] When a president fails to manage the national security machinery personally, the question "Who's in charge here?" can resolve itself into the answer: "Whoever spoke to the President last."

Former president Jimmy Carter leaving the presidential palace in Port-au-Prince, Haiti, on September 18, 1994, after discussing with Haiti's military junta the terms of its departure. Carter's mission led to a peaceful occupation of Haiti by U.S. forces rather than an invasion, which would have resulted in substantial loss of life.

The danger of presidential inattentiveness was illustrated in the first year of the Clinton presidency. President Clinton scheduled only an hour a week with his national security advisor, and sometimes canceled meetings, leading to a stern rebuke from his secretary of state Warren Christopher late in 1993, when he told Clinton that he had to devote much more time to foreign policy. Policies toward Bosnia and Serbia were made and unmade in the space of weeks, without any coherence: the administration rejected the Vance-Owen peace plan for Bosnia, for example, without having anything to propose in its place other than an ill-conceived hope that European allies would back a more forceful policy. A systematic attempt at foreign policy making would have had the United States line up allied support before rejecting the mediators' peace plan. Clinton succeeded in those aspects of foreign policy that resembled most closely U.S. domestic policy, such as negotiating trade agreements and selling them to Congress. He was spotty when it came to statecraft and crisis management in the post–Cold War era, though his NSC staff played a key role in brokering an agreement between the British Government and the Catholic Sinn Fein party in Northern Ireland, as well as an agreement between Russia and Latvia leading to the withdrawal of Soviet troops from the Baltics.

KENNEDY AND THE CUBAN MISSILE CRISIS

President John Kennedy's decisions in the Cuban Missile Crisis demonstrate successful presidential decision making. On October 15, 1962, Kennedy received a briefing from intelligence advisors informing him that the Soviet Union was putting intermediate-range ballistic missiles, medium-range bombers, and more than 10,000 troops into Cuba. Kennedy's fourteen advisors in the Executive Committee of the National Security Council (ExComm), an informal group of senior officials and former government officials whom he had convened to give him advice, offered him four options: do nothing; use quiet diplomacy and not publicize the presence of the missiles; take the weapons out with an air strike; or impose a naval blockade against Cuba.

Weighing Options

The "do nothing" option was not feasible: Congress had already passed a joint resolution backing military action if offensive weapons were found in Cuba; Republicans were using the possibility of such weapons against Democrats in the upcoming midterm congressional elections; and Kennedy believed that if he did not take decisive action Congress might even act to impeach him.[47] Several members of the ExComm favored an air strike.[48] Kennedy decided against it because he thought Allied support would not be forthcoming until other alternatives had been tried. The State Department Legal Advisor argued that bombing would be a violation of international law.[49] The bombing could not be done by a single "surgical" strike: 500 or more missions would be required, destroying hundreds of targets to prevent missiles or aircraft from attacking the United States. The magnitude of the operation would lead to high casualties (provoking international outrage) and losses among the Soviet military, which might bring on military action by its forces against the United States. Because Soviet forces in Cuba were equipped with nuclear weapons (a fact we did not know at the time), Kennedy's caution may have prevented World War III and a nuclear holocaust.[50]

On October 17 Kennedy decided on a blockade (or "quarantine" as his advisors called it, because a blockade is prohibited under international law unless a nation is at war). It would begin only with further shipments of missiles, but if necessary could expand to cover civilian goods. Implementing it in stages would give the United States time for diplomacy to work. It would take place near American waters, where the United States had overwhelming naval superiority. On October 22 Kennedy gave a television speech to the nation, in which he called the presence of the missiles "a change in the status quo which cannot be accepted by this country if our courage and our commitments are ever to be trusted again, by friend or foe." He described the threat to the United States, saying that "the purpose of these bases can be none other than to provide a nuclear strike capability against the Western Hemisphere." He announced the quarantine and warned the Soviet Union that "it will be the policy of the United States Government to regard any missile launched from Cuba against any nation in the Western hemisphere as an attack upon the United States by the Soviet Union, requiring a full retaliatory response." Soviet ships attempting to enter Cuban waters would be subject to search in international waters and if they tried to run the blockade, Kennedy could order American ships to fire on them. The following day the Organization of American States unanimously backed Kennedy's quarantine. For several days Soviet ships headed toward the blockade line, and work on missile sites in Cuba accelerated. Then the ships stopped dead in the water; members of the ExComm thought the crisis was over. But one ship started again toward Cuba, and a Soviet air-de-

President Kennedy addressing the nation on October 22, 1962. He revealed that the Soviet Union had placed offensive missiles in Cuba, and he announced a quarantine on all shipments of military equipment to the island.

fense missile battery shot down an American U-2 reconnaissance plane flying over Cuba, heating the crisis up again, and leading Kennedy and his aides to think that war might not be averted.

White House Diplomacy

The crisis was resolved by presidential diplomacy. Soviet leader Nikita Khrushchev offered to remove the missiles if the president would pledge that the United States would not invade Cuba. Kennedy responded, through Attorney General Robert Kennedy, that if the Soviets ended the crisis, the United States would remove intermediate-range missiles from bases in Turkey. On October 28, the Soviets agreed to withdraw missiles (and accepted verification by United Nations observers), and the United States ended the quarantine and pledged not to invade Cuba.[51]

The Soviets withdrew 42 missiles and 42 long-range bombers, as well as 5,000 troops. They also removed weapons which the United States did not know were on the island: 9 short-range missiles equipped with nuclear warheads, which would have been used in case of an American invasion, and 36 nuclear warheads for use on the medium-range Soviet missiles. The short-range missiles could have been fired without authorization from Moscow, by local commanders, a possibility of which the American side was completely unaware. After the crisis ended, the Soviets maintained 37,000 Soviet troops in Cuba, as well as fighter planes and antimissile weapons.[52] In accord with the secret agreement, American intermediate-range Jupiter missiles were withdrawn from Turkey and Italy. Kennedy pledged not to invade Cuba, but on December 14, 1962, he wrote to Khrushchev that the United States would require "adequate assurances that all offensive weapons are removed from Cuba and are not reintroduced, and that Cuba itself commits no aggressive acts against any of the nations of the Western Hemisphere," leaving open the possibility that the United States might invade Cuba if that nation did commit aggressive acts.

Kennedy did not rely on the consensus of his advisors, nor did he cede his power to make decisions to the ExComm. He made the ultimate decisions himself. At various times a majority of the advisors counseled him to take military action against the Russians in Cuba, a path Kennedy always rejected. His decisions were not based on ExComm debates nor on position papers or advice from his national security advisor: rather, Kennedy understood his power stakes when he decided to confront Khrushchev (his credibility as a national leader was at stake). He tried to put himself in Khrushchev's position to understand his adversary. He used a combination of carrot (pledges to dismantle U.S. missiles and not invade Cuba) and stick (the quarantine) to get the Soviet leader to negotiate a settlement. His quid pro quo diplomacy was based on his constitutional prerogatives, but it also relied on power stakes, and it successfully avoided the pitfalls of irrational small group decision making.

REAGAN AND THE IRAN–CONTRA AFFAIR

The Iran–contra affair provides a case study of the pitfalls of presidential decision making, especially when the president is inattentive to details, and the national security advisors bypass the departments of State and Defense. The scandal involved the sale of weapons to Iran authorized by President Reagan: three shipments of American-made weapons from Israel in 1985, and four sales to Iran of Hawk anti-aircraft and TOW anti-tank missiles from the United States Defense Logistics Agency stockpiles between February and October, 1986. The weapons were sold by the CIA to arms dealers, who had raised $15.3 million from private investors. The dealers then sold the weapons to Iran and were paid $30 million. Some of the profits remained with the dealers, but $3.5 million was transferred by them to the Nicaraguan contras for use in a guerrilla war against the Sandinista government of Nicaragua. The arms sales and transfers, a covert intelligence operation, were kept secret from the American public and Congress until November 3, 1986, when *As-Shiraa,* a pro-Iranian newsmagazine in Beirut, Lebanon, broke the story.

Operationalizing the National Security Council

The arms sales were authorized by Reagan to strengthen a so-called "moderate" faction within its government. They were also part of a deal to trade arms for hostages held by a pro-Iranian group in Lebanon, including the CIA station chief in Lebanon, whom terrorists were torturing for information. The sales were coordinated by Lt. Col. Oliver North, a Marine officer who had been assigned to work on special projects in the NSC staff. They took place in spite of Operation Staunch, the official U.S. policy, which was to deny all arms to Iran as a terrorist nation. (The operation also violated the Iran Hostage Agreement, whose first clause specified that the United States would not interfere in the internal affairs of Iran.) President Reagan himself had said in 1985, about dealing with terrorists who take hostages, that "The United States gives terrorists no rewards. . . . We make no concessions. We make no deals."[53]

The operation was sponsored by the NSC staff, against the opposition of the Defense and State Departments. In August, 1985, Secretary of State George Shultz argued that "this is a very bad idea" because we were "just falling into an arms-for-hostages" business." Secretary of Defense Caspar Weinberger wrote on a draft presidential memorandum about the arms sales, "this is too absurd to comment on."[54] Unfortunately, Weinberger and Shultz did not combine to try to put a stop to the initiative because of their own personality differences, and they were excluded from subsequent meetings with Reagan by Admiral John Poindexter, the national security advisor, who favored the plan.

Once the story of the arms sales broke, the first reaction at the White House was to deny it. The next response was to suggest that it was an Israeli operation with minimal American involvement. President Reagan claimed that only a small amount of weapons had been transferred, hardly enough to fill a single plane. As new revelations emerged, President Reagan ordered Attorney General Edwin Meese to conduct an investigation. Meese uncovered the diversion of funds to the contras. Reagan thereupon fired Lt. Colonel North, and Admiral Poindexter chose to resign.

Reagan appointed a commission headed by Senator John Tower (the other members were former secretary of state Edmund Muskie and former national security advisor Brent Scowcroft) to investigate the scandal. The Tower Commission portrayed Reagan as remote, indifferent, and inattentive to national security decisions, and recommended changes in national security decision making.[55] President Reagan appointed Frank Carlucci and then Colin Powell to be his national security advisor. They implemented the recommendations of the Tower Commission. To end the NSC role in policy implementation, Reagan dissolved the Political-Military Affairs Directorate. To encourage full debate and discussion, Reagan allowed all departments involved in national security matters to present policy options directly to the president. He once again had his national security advisor serve as an impartial custodian-manager of the national security advisory process.

To keep himself from being manipulated by any single official or advisor, Reagan took other measures. On March 31, 1987, he announced a "double-safe" arrangement: when the national security advisor briefed Reagan, the White House chief of staff would be present; when the secretaries of state or defense met with the president, both the advisor and the White House chief of staff would attend.[56] (The system was later dropped by George Bush, whose extensive experience in foreign affairs left him with confidence that he could not be manipulated by any advisor.) He also removed his chief of staff, Donald Regan, and replaced him with former senator Howard Baker, a person who could command respect in Congress. Reagan's approval ratings plummeted more than twenty points, remaining low until his final year in office, and most of his legislative program was stalled. For the remainder of his term, he held almost no news conferences and made little attempt to lead the American public on important issues.[57]

Iran–Contra and Presidential Prerogative

The covert arms sales was a case study of prerogative power, including violations of a presidential executive order and several laws:

- Executive Order 12333 promulgated by President Reagan directed that "no agency except the CIA . . . may conduct any special activity [i.e., a covert operation] unless the President determines that another agency is more likely to achieve a particular objective." Admiral Poindexter testified that the "president never authorized the NSC to conduct covert actions."[58]
- The Arms Export Control Act requires that the U.S. government license private exporters and issue an end-user certificate. But no arms could be sold to Iran because that nation was on the list of nations sponsoring state terrorism, and under two executive orders previously signed by Presidents Carter and Reagan, sales were barred to nations on the list.
- Laws dealing with arms sales passed by Congress required that the Pentagon notify Congress in advance of arms sales and wait thirty days before consummating the transfer of weapons, which was not done in this case.
- Laws specifying that private funds raised by government officials or received by them must be transmitted to the Treasury, and may not be expended except in accordance with appropriations or other acts of Congress, were violated by the direct transfer to the contras. Further, no official may promise a diplomatic "quid pro quo" to a foreign government in return for that government expending its own funds to accomplish purposes not authorized by Congress, something that might have been done in the Iran–contra affair.[59]

To avoid complying with the executive order and the law, the sales and subsequent diversion of funds were designated intelligence operations. Yet even as intelligence operations they ran afoul of the law. The Intelligence Oversight Act of 1980 requires the president to issue a "finding" that an operation is in the national interest.[60] All three of the sales in 1985 took place before President Reagan signed such a "finding," raising the question of whether he could do so retroactively, because the original intent of the law was to require intelligence operations to obtain presidential approval *before* commencement. Once a finding has been signed by the president, the director of central intelligence is required to brief members of the House and Senate Select Committees on Intelligence before the operation begins. The president may bypass these committees and inform eight congressional leaders. The law provides that if such a briefing cannot be held before the operation commences, it must take place "in a timely fashion." Neither the DCI nor President Reagan ever informed Congress under the procedures of the law.

The diversion of funds to the contras occurred after Congress had passed several Boland Amendments (named after congressional sponsor Edward Boland, Democrat of Massachusetts), which prohibited funds available to the CIA, the Defense Department, or "any other agency or entity of the United States involved in intelligence activities" from being used to support the contras, either directly or indirectly.[61] Did the Boland Amendments, passed between 1982 and 1986, cover the staff of the National Security Council? Lt. Colonel North said they did not, basing his opinion on a legal memorandum prepared by the President's Intelligence Oversight Board. According to Reagan's Executive Order 12333, however, the NSC is "the highest executive branch entity that provides review of, guidance for, and direction to the conduct of all national foreign intelligence," making the NSC staff part of an intelligence entity, subject to the restrictions of the Boland Amendment in force at that time.[62]

Congress investigated the entire affair, but never focused on President Reagan's role and did not seriously consider impeachment. The Democrats realized if they managed to remove Reagan, they would be installing George Bush in the White House—a potential Republican presidential candidate in 1988. It would not make sense to allow Bush to run as an incumbent president.

President Reagan's Role

Did President Reagan authorize the diversion of funds to the contras? "Throughout the conduct of my entire tenure at the National Security Council," North testified, "I assumed that the President was aware of what I was doing and had, through my superiors, approved it."[63] But North could not recall specific presidential approval. National Security Advisor John Poindexter testified that President Reagan had *not* been briefed on the arms sales or contra diversion. Poindexter took responsibility for the decisions, saying he was sure it was what the president would have wanted. A large number of North's associates, including several arms dealers he worked with, believed that North was inaccurate in his recollections of Reagan's role in the affair.

North, Poindexter, and various arms dealers and other participants were charged with various violations of law by Independent Counsel Lawrence Walsh. All were convicted by federal district courts on several counts. North and Poindexter won reversals of their convictions by the Court of Appeals for the District of Columbia on technical grounds—they had already testified before Congress under a grant of immunity (none of the testimony could be used against them in court), and some of their congressional testimony may have tainted the federal trials.[64]

Independent Counsel Lawrence Walsh thought it highly unlikely that North and Poindexter, two military officers used to going through a chain of command, would have carried out the funding of the contras without Reagan's explicit approval. "I was told by Admiral Poindexter that not only was he pleased with the work I had been doing but the President was as well," arms dealer Richard Secord testified.[65] But neither the congressional hearings nor subsequent court cases established that Reagan knew in advance about the diversion of funds to the contras. Reagan may not have known, because he usually did not bother himself with "details." His advisors knew he wanted the hostages returned, and they knew he strongly supported efforts by private individuals to assist the contras. Perhaps they gave Reagan what they thought he wanted, without any direct presidential order.

The Iran–contra affair raises crucial issues about presidential power. If Reagan is to be believed and did not know about the diversion of funds, then what kind of system is it that allows the secretaries of state and defense to be edged out of key policy decisions by staffers on the National Security Council? That encourages staffers to deceive Congress and violate laws on their own volition? Is this a case, as Senator Paul Sarbanes put it, of a "junta within the White House" that had taken over? But if Reagan did authorize both the sales and the diversion, other questions are raised: May a president violate laws at will? Or decide not to implement the Intelligence Oversight Act because he does not want to follow its procedures?

Whatever President Reagan may have known, it is clear that officials in the Reagan administration tried to create a secret government, funded not from the Treasury but by its own sale of arms, with no congressional supervision, acting outside the framework of law, which could engage in top-secret operations. Such a secret government would not be subject to the Constitution, the rule of law, or democratic accountability.

Yet there is no need for a secret government in the conduct of intelligence operations. Congressional intelligence committees have fully supported many CIA operations and have provided hundreds of millions of dollars to fund covert operations such as the anti-Soviet war in Afghanistan in the 1980s. Between 1976 and 1986 they tripled the CIA budget, hardly a sign of general opposition to covert operations. Presidential covert operations usually obtain congressional support, especially if their goals are fully consistent with State Department diplomacy rather than running counter to it, and if proper procedures have been followed: full deliberation within the NSC; presidential authorization within the framework of the Intelligence Oversight Act of 1980; and congressional intelligence committee advance notification. In 1989 President Bush vetoed a measure that would have required advance notification; in 1991 he signed amendments to the law only after Congress and the president "agreed to disagree" on the definition of "timely notice" in the law.[66]

PRESIDENTIAL DIPLOMACY IN A CHANGING WORLD

American presidents face geopolitical problems as well as constitutional difficulties in conducting American foreign policy. The United States is thousands of miles away from most nations of the world, and it is difficult for us to project our power and influence in most regions except when other nations wish to ally with us to do so—usually for purposes of tilting a local balance of power in their favor. Although we think of our diplomacy and military might as a force for stability and "a new world order," in reality we are sometimes viewed by other nations as a "wild card" in world politics, capable of tipping the balance toward nations for whom we intervene.

Presidential Statecraft and Valence Politics

Presidents often conduct a foreign policy with contradictory values, in large measure because the American political culture is contradictory. Our values lead presidents and our secretaries of state to formulate an idealistic foreign policy. We have believed that ours was an "exceptional" nation, part of a "new world" free from the power politics of the old. "We are Americans; we have a unique responsibility to do the hard work of freedom," George Bush reminded us in his 1991 State of the Union Address. Our idealism has led us to attempt to export our political practices and beliefs to other countries. We want to make the world over in our image. "The most stable friends and allies of the United States," Secretary of State George Shultz pointed out, "are inevitably the democratic nations."[67]

The media sometimes play up the dissonance between the values in our political culture and the unfortunate circumstances in other parts of the world. Scenes of famine-stricken children or refugees fleeing from war and tribal genocide lead to calls for the White House to "do something." Thus President Bush dispatched a military mission to Somalia to provide relief during a famine, and President Clinton ordered an airlift of relief supplies for 500,000 Rwandan refugees. Yet there is little indication that presidents make most of their foreign policy decisions because of media pressure. President Clinton remained out of Bosnia despite nightly scenes of suffering in that nation; he resisted pressure for a year to invade Haiti, again despite intense media coverage. He invested considerable time in a successful effort to defuse a confrontation with North Korea over its nuclear energy program, although that issue was hardly covered by the media.

Despite their idealistic rhetoric, in practice, presidents usually take a realistic approach to international affairs: we must take the world for what it is, rather than try to make it over. Instead of trying to make the world "safe for democracy," we often concentrate on making it safe—period. "We have friends and allies who do not always live up to our standards of freedom and democratic government, yet we cannot abandon them," George Shultz observed.[68] At times presidents have allied the United States with repressive and dictatorial regimes, attempted to overthrow unfriendly governments, bribed foreign politicians or subsidized political parties, or engaged in other covert operations.

The president must manage the political conflict between those who would put the interests of the nation above all else, and those who would sacrifice some U.S. interests to build a larger structure of international cooperation. Nationalists see foreign relations as a zero-sum game among nations: to the extent that we win some others must lose, and if others gain then we must lose. The goal of our foreign policy must be to outwit or outmaneuver everyone else. Internationalists argue that we can make agreements in which everyone gains something: these are efficiency negotiations because benefits to all are greater than costs. Or we can make constructive exchanges, in which we come to agreements that enable winners to compensate those that must give up something. When the United States and Canada agreed to construct the St. Lawrence Seaway, for example, both nations gained. When to emphasize United States first and when to take the internationalist position remains a key problem for the White House.

The President as Chief Diplomat

American presidents are not well trained to deal with many foreign policy issues, at least when compared with their foreign contemporaries. Since the 1820s, hardly any have had extensive experience in foreign affairs. In the twentieth century, the exceptions were Taft (governor of the Philippines), Hoover (relief coordinator during and after World War I), Eisenhower (commander of allied forces in Europe during World War II and NATO commander), and Bush (director of central intelligence and head of the U.S. liaison office in China).

None of our presidents have had experience in dealing with the issues involving international economics or held positions in government involved with them. Most presidents tackle these issues at international summits without adequate knowledge or experience, though the quick studies among them may hold their own with their foreign counterparts. Many of their opposite numbers at summit conferences will have served in their national governments as ministers of trade or as chancellors of the exchequer (Treasury) or in similar positions; they often have years of experience conducting international economic negotiations, whereas our presidents start as a neophytes.

Given our nominating and electoral system, there is no way to ensure that in the future presidents have experience in international affairs. The advisory system itself might be improved, however, because the national security advisors tend to be uninformed and uneducated about international economic issues, with expertise for the most part confined to experts in the Treasury, the Commerce Department, and the Office of Trade Representative. Proposals including the following:

- Reorganize the NSC so that it deals with international economic issues as much as it deals with military and diplomatic matters;
- Equip the president with a high-level advisor on international economic security affairs, equal in rank to the national security advisor;
- Organize cabinet-level policy councils that integrate an "intermestic" perspective (i.e., a combination of domestic and international);
- Establish a Department of Trade and Commerce (by combining the trade representative with the Commerce Department).

The Post–Cold War World

During the Cold War, presidents were "leaders of the free world," and they led a coalition of allies against communist adversaries. International affairs consisted of a succession of "crises," any one of which might ultimately lead to a nuclear conflict. The image of the president was of the commander in chief with a finger on a nuclear button. The disposition of the American people and of Congress was to back up the president in crisis diplomacy.

With the end of the Cold War, the president no longer leads a unified alliance. His influence with allies and adversaries has lessened for several reasons: the United States lacks both the "will and wallet" to intervene militarily in most situations, or to use the threat of force to back up its diplomacy, and most other nations do not see threats sufficient to turn over their security to the U.S. president. In the emerging world economy, the United States is as much an adversary (albeit a friendly one) as an ally for many of our traditional friends in Western Europe and Asia.

The powers of the president are more open to dispute in the aftermath of the Vietnam War and the Iran–contra crisis. Framework legislation makes it more difficult for a president to act unilaterally and maintain his legitimacy and authority, and there is less bipartisanship after an era of split-party government. Absent the threat of all-out nuclear war, there is less inclination on the part of the public to "rally round the flag" and support the president in crises. The American public is less informed and less interested in foreign affairs, and a White House focus on foreign policy issues—in the absence of a compelling crisis—often leads to a decline in presidential poll standing, as President Clinton found out during his first months in office. The president must deal with the rest of the world because the U.S. economy is interdependent and many issues (the environment, drugs, and terrorism, to name three) require international cooperation. Yet the U.S. president has fewer financial inducements (with the sharp drop in foreign aid funding) and fewer military resources (with the sharp cut in U.S. armed forces) to use in conducting foreign policy. Presidential diplomacy will require more skill and professionalism than ever before to succeed in an era of high expectations and diminished resources.

FOREIGN POLICY MAKING AND AMERICAN DEMOCRACY

The president has overcome a weak constitutional position to assert primacy in conducting foreign affairs, and the White House has little to fear from the judiciary when it asserts prerogative powers. Nevertheless, Congress has established its own important role in the oversight of foreign affairs, and through alternative track diplomacy or collaborative mechanisms and framework legislation it has the ability to check and balance or strongly influence presidential initiatives. With the end of the Cold War, U.S. foreign relations are increasingly dominated by issues of international economics, areas in which presidents have little intellectual authority and in which Congress has traditionally played an important role. Presidents cannot dominate the international system because of the U.S. geo-strategic isolation; neither can they dominate the U.S. political system in international affairs in the absence of crisis.

FURTHER READING

Books

Michael Beschloss and Strobe Talbott, *At the Highest Levels,* Boston: Little, Brown, 1993.

I. M. Destler, *Presidents, Bureaucrats and Foreign Policy: The Politics of Organizational Reform.* Princeton, NJ: Princeton University Press, 1974.

Theodore Draper, *A Very Thin Line,* New York: Hill and Wang, 1991.

Alexander George, *Presidential Decisionmaking in Foreign Policy,* Boulder, CO: Westview Press, 1980.

Alexander George, *Bridging the Gap: Theory and Practice in Foreign Policy,* Washington, D.C.: United States Institute for Peace Press, 1993.

Michael Glennon, *Constitutional Diplomacy,* Princeton, NJ: Princeton University Press, 1990.

Louis Henkin, *Democracy and Foreign Affairs,* New York: Columbia University Press, 1990.

Loch K. Johnson, *America's Secret Power,* New York: Oxford University Press, 1989.

Barbara Kellerman and Ryan Barilleaux, *The President as World Leader,* New York: St. Martin's Press, 1991.

Harold Koh, *The National Security Constitution,* New Haven, CT: Yale University Press, 1990.

Thomas Mann, ed., *A Question of Balance: The President and Congress in Foreign Policy,* Washington, DC: Brookings Institution, 1990.

Documentary Sources

Commission on the Organization of the Government for the Conduct of Foreign Policy, *Final Report,* Washington: Government Printing Office, 1975.

President's Special Review Board (The Tower Commission), *Report of the President's Special Review Board,* Washington, DC: Government Printing Office, 1987.

Joel Brinkley and Stephen Engelberg, eds., *Report of the Congressional Committees Investigating the Iran–Contra Affair,* New York: Random House, 1988.

NOTES

1. William Quandt, *Carter and Camp David: Peacemaking and Politics,* Washington, DC: Brookings Institution, 1986.

2. Shimon Peres, *The New Middle East,* New York: Henry Holt, 1993; Amos Elon, "The Peacemakers," *The New Yorker,* December 20, 1993, pp. 77–85.

3. *Washington Post National Weekly Edition,* November 7, 1983, p. 37.

4. Arthur Bestor, "Separation of Powers in the Domain of Foreign Affairs: The Original Intent of the Constitution Historically Examined," *Seton Hall Law Review,* Vol. 5, no. 2, Summer, 1994, pp. 529–665.

5. *U.S. v. Curtiss-Wright,* 399 U.S. 304, 1936.

6. David Halberstam, *The Best and the Brightest,* New York: Fawcett Publishing, 1969, p. 181.

7. *Congressional Record,* January 4, 1977, pp. 246–247.

8. Jack N. Rakove, "Solving a Constitutional Puzzle: The Treatymaking Clause as a Case Study," *Perspectives in American History,* N.S., Vol. I, 1984, pp. 233–281.

9. Edward Corwin, *The President: Office and Powers,* New York: New York University Press, 1948, pp. 255–257.

10. See, generally, Joseph R. Biden, Jr., and John B. Ritch III, "The Treaty Power: Upholding a Constitutional Partnership," *University of Pennsylvania Law Review,* Vol. 137, no. 5, May, 1989, pp. 1529–1558.

11. Thomas Franck and Edward Weisband, *Foreign Policy by Congress,* New York: Oxford University Press, 1979, p. 137.

12. Louis Fisher, "Congressional Participation in the Treaty Process," *University of Pennsylvania Law Review,* Vol. 137, no. 5, May, 1989, pp. 1511–1522.

13. Abram Chayes and Antonia Handler Chayes, "Testing and Development of 'Exotic' Systems Under the ABM Treaty: The Great Reinterpretation Caper," *Harvard Law Review,* Vol. 99, no. 8, December, 1986, pp. 1956–1971; David A. Koplow, "Constitutional Bait and Switch: Executive Reinterpretation of Arms Control Treaties," *University of Pennsylvania Law Review,* Vol. 137, no. 5, May, 1989, pp. 1353–1437.

14. Quoted in Walter LaFeber, "Betrayal in Tokyo," *Constitution,* Vol. 6, no. 2, Fall, 1994, p. 11.

15. John R. Stevenson, "Constitutional Aspects of the Executive Agreement Procedure," *Department of State Bulletin,* Vol. 66, June 19, 1972, pp. 840–851.

16. *Holmes v. Laird,* 459 F. 2nd 1211, D.C. Cir., 1972; *Ozonoff v. Berzak,* 744 F. 2nd 224, 1st cir., 1984.

17. *Reid v. Covert,* 354 U.S. 1, 1957.

18. Ryan J. Barrilaux, "Parallel Unilateral Policy Declarations: A New Device for Presidential Autonomy in Foreign Affairs," *Presidential Studies Quarterly,* Vol. 17, no. 1, Winter, 1987, pp. 107–117.

19. Edward Corwin, *The President: Office and Powers,* 4th rev. ed., New York: New York University Press, 1957, p. 171.

20. *The Federalist Papers,* no. 64.

21. *New York Times,* June 2, 1987, p. B-6.

22. Thomas Mann, ed., *A Question of Balance: The President, the Congress and Foreign Policy,* Washington, DC: Brookings Institution, 1990, pp. 2–34.

23. Quoted in James Sundquist, *The Decline and Resurgence of Congress,* Washington, DC: Brookings Institution, 1982, p. 300.

24. Warren Christopher, "Ceasefire between the Branches: A Compact in Foreign Affairs," *Foreign Affairs,* Vol. 60, no. 5, Summer, 1982, pp. 989–1005.

25. Martha Liebler Gibson, *Weapons of Influence,* Boulder, CO: Westview Press, 1992, pp. 61–82.

26. Thomas Franck and Edward Weisband, *Foreign Policy by Congress,* New York: Oxford University Press, 1979, pp. 155–164; J. William Fulbright, "American Foreign Policy in the 20th Century under an 18th Century Constitution," *Cornell Law Quarterly,* Vol. 47, no. 1, Fall, 1961, pp. 1–13; Barry M. Goldwater, "The President's Constitutional Primacy in Foreign Relations and National Defense," *Virginia Journal of International Law,* Vol. 13, no. 4, Summer, 1973, pp. 463–484.

27. *Newsweek,* July 7, 1986, p. 27.

28. Ann Devroy and Daniel Williams, "Seeking to 'Carterize' Clinton," *Washington Post National Weekly Edition,* August 1–7, 1994, p. 16.

29. Quoted in Morton Halperin, *Bureaucratic Politics and Foreign Policy,* Washington, DC: Brookings Institution, 1974, p. 219.

30. Roger Hilsman, "Congressional-Executive Relations and Foreign Policy Consensus," *American Political Science Review,* Vol. 52, no. 3, September, 1958, pp. 725–744.

31. Elaine Scolino, "Top U.S. Officials Divided in Debate on Invading Haiti, *New York Times,* August 4, 1994, p. 1.

32. Theodore Sorensen, "The President and the Secretary of State," *Foreign Affairs,* Vol. 66, no. 2, Winter, 1987–88, pp. 231–248.

33. Alexander Haig, "Memorandum to the President," January 6, 1981.

34. *New York Times,* March 25, 1981, p. 1.

35. John M. Goshko, "Undiplomatic Doubts at Foggy Bottom," *Washington Post National Weekly Edition,* June 27–July 3, 1994, p. 31.

36. *New York Times,* December 26, 1993, p. A-1.

37. Walter Pincus, "From the CIA, the PDB, FYI, Each A.M.," *Washington Post National Weekly Edition,* September 5–11, 1994, p. 31.

38. R. Jeffrey Smith, "A Director Who Has Trouble Reading the Political Tea Leaves," *Washington Post National Weekly Edition,* May 30–June 5, 1994, p. 7.

39. Charles Babcock, "When Analysis Doesn't Mix," *Washington Post National Weekly Edition,* August 10, 1987, p. 12.

40. Tim Weiner, "Tension with White House Leaves C.I.A. Chief out in the Cold," *New York Times,* December 25, 1993, p. A-10.

41. Harold Koh, *The National Security Constitution,* New Haven, CT: Yale University Press, 1990, pp. 101–116.

42. Anna K. Nelson, "President Truman and the Evolution of the National Security Council," *Journal of American History,* Vol. 72, September, 1985, pp. 360–378.

43. Stanley L. Falk, "The National Security Council under Truman, Eisenhower and Kennedy," *Political Science Quarterly,* Vol. 79, no. 3, September, 1964, pp. 403–434.

44. *New York Times,* January 6, 1982, p. A-19.

45. I. M. Destler, "National Security Management: What Presidents Have Wrought," *Political Science Quarterly,* Vol. 95, no. 4, Winter, 1980–1981, pp. 573–588.

46. Zbigniew Brzezinski, "The NSC's Midlife Crisis," *Foreign Policy,* no. 69, Winter, 1987–1988, pp. 80–99.

47. Thomas G. Paterson and William J. Brophy, "October Missiles and November Elections: The Cuban Missile Crisis and American Politics, 1962," *Journal of American History,* Vol. 73, no. 1, June, 1986, pp. 87–119; Richard Lebow, "Domestic Politics and the Cuban Missile Crisis: The Traditional and Revisionist Interpretations Reevaluated," *Diplomatic History,* Vol. 14, no. 4, Fall, 1990, pp. 471–492.

48. Graham Allison, *Essence of Decision,* Boston: Little, Brown, 1967, pp. 197–200.

49. Abram Chayes, *The Cuban Missile Crisis: International Crises and the Role of Law,* New York: Oxford Unversity Press, 1974, pp. 25–40.

50. Raymond L. Garthoff, "Cuban Missile Crisis: The Soviet Story," *Foreign Policy,* no. 72, Fall, 1988, pp. 61–80.

51. Barton Bernstein, "The Cuban Missile Crisis: Trading the Jupiters in Turkey," *Political Science Quarterly,* Vol 87, no. 1, Spring, 1980, pp 97–125; Richard Ned Lebow, "The Cuban Missile Crisis: Reading the Lessons Correctly," *Political Science Quarterly,* Vol. 98, no. 3, Fall, 1983, pp. 431–459; James A. Nathan, "The Missile Crisis: His Finest Hour Now," *World Politics,* Vol. 27, no. 2, January, 1975, pp. 256–281.

52. The size of the Soviet commitments were not revealed to the American side until a series of five meetings held between 1987 and 1992 between the Soviet and American participants, at which time national security secrets of both sides were exchanged. Seymour Hersh, "Were Cuban Fingers on the Trigger in the Cuban Missile Crisis?' *Washington Post National Weekly Edition,* October 19, 1987, p. 23.

53. Quoted in Terry Eastland, *Energy in the Executive,* New York: Free Press, 1992, p. 221.

54. Secretary of State George Shultz's and Secretary of Defense Caspar Weinberger's testimonies before Congress, July 24 and August 1, 1987, in House Select Committee to Investigate Covert Arms Transactions with Iran and Senate Select Committee on Secret Military Assistance to Iran and the Nicaraguan Opposition, *Joint Hearings,* 100th Cong., 1st sess., 1987.

55. President's Special Review Board (Tower Commission), *Report of the Special Review Board,* Washington, DC: Government Printing Office, 1987, "The Reagan Model."

56. National Security Decision Directive 266.

57. William Boot, "Iranscam: When the Cheering Stopped," *Columbia Journalism Review,* Vol. 25, March/April, 1987, pp. 25–30; Elliott King and Michael Schudson, "The Myth of the Great Communicator," *Columbia Journalism Review,* November/December, 1987, pp. 37–39.

58. *New York Times,* July 16, 1987, p. A-16.

59. 18 U.S.C. sec. 641; 31 U.S.C. sec. 3302(b); 31 U.S.C. sec. 1341(a)(1)(A); Kate Stith, "Congress' Power of the Purse," *Yale Law Journal,* Vol. 97, no. 7, June, 1988, pp. 1343–1396.

60. Intelligence Oversight Act of 1980, 22 *U.S.C.* sec. 2422, 1982.

61. "Note: The Boland Amendments and Foreign Affairs Deference," *Columbia Law Review,* Vol. 88, no. 7, November, 1988, pp. 1534–1574.

62. Executive Order 12333, 46 *Federal Register* 59,942.

63. Lt. Col. Oliver North's testimony, July 8 and 9, 1987, in House Select Committee to Investigate Covert Arms Transactions with Iran and Senate Select Committee on Secret Military Assistance to Iran and the Nicaraguan Opposition, *Joint Hearings,* 100th Cong., 1st sess., 1987.

64. *U.S. v. North, et al.,* 708 F. Supp. 380, D.D.C. 1988.

65. Richard V. Secord's testimony, May 7, 1987, in House Select Committee to Investigate Covert Arms Transactions with Iran and Senate Select Committee on Secret Military Assistance to Iran and the Nicaraguan Opposition, *Joint Hearings,* 100th Cong., 1st sess., 1987.

66. U.S. House of Representatives, *Conference Report,* no. 102-166, 102nd Cong., 1st sess., 1991, pp. 27–28.

67. George Schultz, "Morality and Realism in American Foreign Policy," *Department of State Bulletin,* December, 1985, p. 26.

68. Ibid., p. 26.

CHAPTER 15

Presidential War Making

Allow the President to invade a neighboring nation, whenever he shall deem it necessary to repel an invasion, and you allow him to do so, whenever he may choose to say he deems it necessary for such purpose—and you allow him to make war at his pleasure. . . . This, our Convention understood to be the most oppressive of all Kingly oppressions; and they resolved to so frame the Constitution that no one man should hold the power of bringing the oppression upon us.

—*Abraham Lincoln*

INTRODUCTORY CASE: BUSH, CLINTON, AND SOMALIA

The students listened attentively to former president George Bush, speaking at their public school on a cold crisp autumn day in October, 1993. Bush talked of the American military presence in Somalia. He had sent 28,000 American troops there to protect humanitarian workers feeding hundreds of thousands of innocent victims of famine and civil war, planning to turn operations over the United Nations (UN) shortly thereafter. "For reasons I'm not sure of," he complained, "the mission has been redefined." Bush argued that President Clinton had bungled a straightforward mission by attempting to arrest a Somali warlord, General Mohammed Aidid. Bush suggested that a president must know the answers to three questions before using force: What is the goal? How will it be accomplished? How will the troops get out? He faulted Clinton for lacking an "exit strategy" for American forces. His implicit contrast was to the Persian Gulf War: After the United States evicted the Iraqis from Kuwait in 1991, Bush quickly brought the entire force home without yielding to the temptation to occupy Iraq.

His successor had gotten himself into a quagmire in Somalia. After Bush had withdrawn most of the troops there, President Clinton had placed most of the remainder under United Nations command.[1] Because the United Nations was stretched thin with many other peacekeeping commitments, the peacekeepers (especially those from other nations) were too few, ill equipped, and poorly trained for the Somali mission. Ugly incidents escalated: Somali sniper fire on UN encampments and convoys led to UN retaliation. Then, on June 5, a group of Pakistani soldiers fought with urban guerrillas loyal to General Aidid; dozens of women and children were injured in the firefight and twenty-four Pakistanis killed. The UN mission put a price on General Aidid's head and vowed to arrest him.

American gunships attacked General Aidid's forces, and on June 17th President Clinton said "the military back of Aidid has been broken."[2] Clinton was mistaken: most of the capital of Mogadishu, loyal to the General, harassed UN and U.S. forces. A contingent of U.S. Army Rangers was sent by Clinton to capture the general in August. Its raids produced many Somali casualties and prisoners, but not the general, who gained more support each day. As U.S. and UN forces found his arms caches, he resupplied with weapons from Iran and Sudan. After some U.S. soldiers were ambushed on September 9, Secretary of Defense Les Aspin denied a request by U.S. commanders in Somalia for additional tanks and armored personnel carriers.

On October 3 the Somalis downed two U.S. helicopters during a raid on Somali arms caches. A U.S. Ranger unit under American command, sent to rescue the crews, was attacked by hundreds of Aidid's troops in a well-planned ambush (despite intelligence assessments that he could not mount large attacks). The U.S. forces had not coordinated their efforts with the UN contingents, and it was hours before they were relieved by UN forces. More than 300 Somalis were killed and more than 700 wounded in the rescue attempts, with 18 U.S. Rangers killed and 75 wounded.

With images of the failed raid (and a captured U.S. soldier) on American television, public opinion turned strongly against continued involvement in Somalia. Although President Clinton had received a congressional endorsement for the American presence in February and May 1993, when the Senate and the House had passed resolutions authorizing U.S. forces to remain for up to a year under UN command, the mood in Congress and in the country was to end the commitment as soon as possible.[3] Representative Ben Gilman, Republican from New York, introduced H. Concurrent Resolution 170, which would have set a January 31 deadline for withdrawal of troops from the Somalia humanitarian mission. The amendment was designed to unite the Republicans, split the Democrats, and win political points. The Democrats countered with an amendment keeping the troops in Somalia until March 31, 1994. In a zigzagging set of votes in the House, first the Republicans and twenty-two Democratic defectors voted for the early deadline; then the Democrats (including the twenty-two defectors) voted for the later deadline.

President Clinton promised that U.S. forces would be withdrawn within six months, and he soon took out the Ranger units assigned to capture General Aidid. By the summer of 1994, peace talks had collapsed and feuding clans once again left the nation in anarchy. The situation was left to diplomats from neighboring nations and the Organization of African Unity to sort out. The United States no longer treated General Aidid as a fugitive from justice. He was recognized as an indispensable figure in efforts to restore a government to Somalia, and the U.S. military even transported him to the peace talks in Addis Abbaba, Ethiopia. On September 15, 1994, the United States ended its last military and diplomatic presence in Somalia—the same day President Clinton put U.S. forces in Haiti, in yet another risky effort at bringing democratic government to a Third World "failed nation." On March 3, 1995, Clinton sent marines to escort the last of the UN humanitarian workers and peacekeeping troops out of the country.

The Somalia case study raises questions of presidential decision making involving the use of the armed forces in the post–Cold War era. No longer is the

United States threatened by nuclear annihilation from Soviet missiles. No longer is Western Europe threatened by a conventional assault from Warsaw Pact nations across the Iron Curtain. Presidential use of the military has reverted to the nineteenth-century patterns: to maintain U.S. influence, protect U.S. lives and property, or provide humanitarian assistance. The casualties U.S. forces took in Somalia were minuscule compared with the carnage of the World Wars I and II, Korea, and Vietnam. Yet the American people wanted the mission ended as soon as a single soldier was captured, and President Clinton was whipsawed between domestic opponents (stirred up by former President Bush) and his international commitments to the United Nations. He almost got himself into a nasty constitutional dispute with Congress over the scope of his powers as commander in chief, and only his willingness to withdraw kept him from suffering major political losses.

Throughout American history, presidents have engaged in major wars, limited wars, and approximately 250 other uses of the armed forces in minor hostile engagements. Some have succeeded brilliantly, while others have been ghastly failures, weakening the authority and legitimacy of the presidency itself.

THE POWERS OF THE PRESIDENT AS COMMANDER IN CHIEF

What are the powers of the president as commander in chief? The Constitution does not provide us with authoritative answers. Presidential decisions to use force, not constitutional understandings, have defined the contours of presidential war powers.

Constitutional Provisions

It is difficult to determine the full intent of the framers from the debates of the Constitutional Convention.[4] In discussing war powers, it focused on the power of the Congress to declare war, especially in its debate on August 17, 1787.[5] Charles Pinckney opposed vesting the war power in Congress, because it would be in session too infrequently and would have too many members for quick deliberation. He preferred to vest the power for war or peace in the Senate. Pierce Butler objected against vesting any war powers in Congress, arguing that the president should make these decisions, because he "will not make war but when the nation will support it."[6] James Madison and Elbridge Gerry made a motion to insert "declare war" and strike "make" war from the congressional war power, leaving it to the president to repel sudden attacks, which seemed to be a concern of some delegates if war powers were vested in Congress. But Roger Sherman thought that the change would narrow the war powers of Congress too much. Colonel Mason said that he was against giving any war power to the president, because he was not to be safely trusted with it. He was for "clogging war, rather than facilitating war," but preferred "declare" to "make," agreeing with Madison about defensive actions. Madison's motion was agreed to, ayes 7 states, nays 2 states, with 1 state absent.[7]

The debate at the Convention tells us only that the delegates intended presidents to have the power to use the military on their own prerogative to repel attacks against the nation. Not to give the president such a power would have been irresponsible, because it would have been an open invitation to a foreign nation to invade, prevent Congress from meeting, and thereby render the government helpless.

We get no guidance from the *Federalist Papers* about the scope of presidential war powers. The issue was addressed by Hamilton in *Federalist* no. 69. He claimed that the president's powers as commander in chief would "resemble equally that of the King of Great Britain and of the governor of New York." Unlike those offices, the president would not control the entire militia, but only the part called into federal service. Therefore, Hamilton concluded, "the power of the president would be inferior to that of either the monarch or the governor." As for the power of the president as commander in chief, Hamilton argued that it would be quite limited:

> It would amount to nothing more than the supreme command and direction of the military and naval forces, as first general and admiral of the confederacy, while that of the British king extends to the declaring of war and to the raising and regulating of fleets and armies, all of which, by the constitution under consideration, would appertain to the legislature.[8]

We need not take this commentary seriously. Hamilton wrote it to win ratification of the Constitution, and to do so he had to minimize the scope of presidential war powers. Advised by Hamilton, President Washington's initial uses of force against Indian tribes, and his use of force to put down the Whiskey Rebellion, both relied on prior statutory authorization by Congress rather than claims of inherent presidential prerogative.[9]

What then, was the original intent of the framers? Thomas Jefferson, writing on Madison in 1789, observed that "we have already given one practical check to the dog of war by transferring the power of letting him loose from the executive to the legislative body." Madison, writing to Jefferson in 1798, summarized his understanding that the Constitution "supposes, what the History of all Governments demonstrates, that the Executive is the branch of power most interested in war, and most prone to it. It has accordingly with studied care, vested the question of war in the Legislature."[10] The Constitution gives to Congress the power to declare war in Article 1. It seems clear that the president could repel an attack: as Justice Paterson put it in 1806, "If, indeed, a foreign nation should invade the territories of the United States, it would, I apprehend, be not only lawful for the president to resist such invasion, but also to carry hostilities into the enemy's own country.[11] But could the president engage in "anticipatory self-defense" if he believed an attack were imminent? Could a president use the armed forces in hostilities without a declaration of war? Did the defense of the United States extend beyond its borders and possessions, to include defending American lives and property abroad? Did defending the United States mean that the president could execute treaty obligations involving the armed forces unilaterally? Could the president threaten to use the armed forces in an exercise of "coercive diplomacy" to get rulers of other nations to accede to his wishes? The constitutional debates provide no answers to any of these questions.

The Constitution gives Congress specific powers over the military in Article 1. Congress creates the military services, and organizes and funds them. It provides for a code of military justice and other regulations. It authorizes procurement and funding of weapons acquired by the military. The Constitution clearly intends to give Congress the preeminent role in establishing and maintaining the military establishment. Because of the ambiguities in Article 2, it is not as clear that Congress would always control how that establishment would be used.

Presidents and the Military Establishment

The commander in chief clause allows the president to supervise the Armed Forces. Presidents recommend defense budgets to Congress, as well as reorganization plans. When they call for massive buildups, like Truman and Carter and Reagan, they usually get Congress to go along. When they call for significant cutbacks, like Eisenhower and Nixon and Clinton, they are also successful, though the Pentagon may fight a rearguard action to stretch out cuts. They usually can enforce their overall ceilings on defense spending, although congressional committees often force modifications about particular weapons.

Presidents initiate most of the personnel policies. In 1948 President Truman issued an order desegregating the formerly racially segregated units in the armed forces. His proposal initially met with great resistance in the military, for many officers believed that it would increase racial tensions. Yet once Truman issued his order, the military quickly complied, and there were no instances of resistance to it. Similarly the expanded role of women in the armed forces was pressed by the White House over the opposition of military chiefs in the 1970s and 1980s.

Congress decides whether to institute a military draft, but the president can influence its actions. During the Vietnam War, for example, President Nixon asked Congress to establish a "lottery" system: those with low numbers would be drafted, but everyone else would be exempt. In effect the system was a "divide and conquer" strategy, because two-thirds of those picking numbers knew that they were "safe" from the draft, it gave young people less of a personal incentive to protest against the war. Later the Nixon administration proposed the all-volunteer army, designed not only to raise the standards of military personnel, but also to give the president greater flexibility in using the armed forces, the theory being that the American public would have fewer objections to casualties if they were sustained by volunteers (an erroneous assumption).

Presidents nominate, and by and with the consent of the Senate, they appoint all commissioned officers of the military. At the lower ranks, this duty is routine, but in making appointments to the Joint Chiefs of Staff and to positions of commander in chief of military forces in various regions, or to positions in international organizations traditionally held by an American (Supreme Allied Commander in Europe, heading NATO military forces), the president has wide discretion, and will appoint officers who support his policies. The president also reprimands and if necessary removes officers who are insubordinate. President Truman fired General Douglas MacArthur in the middle of the Korean War because MacArthur refused to submit his speeches for prior clearance by the Pentagon, and in them called for widening the Korean War to include bases in China and invading North Korea for a second time to win the war. In 1978 President Carter reassigned the deputy commander of U.S. forces in Korea after he publicly challenged the wisdom of Carter's decisions to remove some of the forces from the peninsula.

Presidential Military Experience

The president's own military experience may affect his authority as commander in chief. A few presidents have been victorious commanders: these include Washington, Jackson, William Harrison, Taylor, Grant, and Eisenhower. Several other presidents have been treated as war heroes, including Theodore Roosevelt, John Kennedy, and George Bush, and many others (such as Jimmy Carter) served in the military. Yet a president need not have served to be a successful commander in chief. James Polk led the United States to its victory over Mexico and acquisition of the southwest and California. Abraham Lincoln had only the briefest of military service with a state militia yet saved the Union. Woodrow Wilson had been a political science professor and university president, but his decision to intervene in World War I was crowned with success. Franklin Roosevelt's closest military experience was a brief stint as Woodrow Wilson's assistant secretary of the navy, and he presided over the allied victory in World War II.

Lack of a military record can hurt in some circumstances. President Clinton's participation in protests against the Vietnam War while he was at Oxford University in the 1970s soured many military officers on him, and he never won their confidence. His first defense secretary, former Wisconsin Representative Les Aspin, took the brunt of the military criticism for Clinton's budget cuts and controversial personnel policies, and was eased out of office. To gain some credibility with the military, Clinton then nominated former CIA director and retired admiral Bobby Inman. One of the most bizarre public events in the history of nominating announcements ensued: The White House held a big news conference for Inman, at which he stated that he had not sought the job but had acceded to Clinton's requests, and hinted that Clinton had promised him that no further cuts in defense spending would occur. "Mr. President, as you know, I had to reach a level of comfort that we could work together, that I would be very comfortable in your role as the commander in chief while I was secretary of defense," he observed, adding a reassurance to the military, "and I have found that level of comfort."[12] Rather than add to Clinton's credibility, these condescending remarks undercut him further. The president seemed relieved when Inman decided shortly after to bow out before Senate confirmation. Clinton then turned to a seasoned defense executive, Deputy Secretary William Perry, to take control of the department. Later, Clinton's fitness as commander in chief was challenged by Republican Senator Jesse Helms, prompting a spirited defense by the chair of the Joint Chiefs of Staff and Secretary Perry.

The Military Chain of Command

The Constitution makes the president the commander in chief of the armed forces of the United States, and of the militia when called into federal service. The president issues orders and takes salutes. (As a civilian he is not supposed to give salutes, but some presidents, including Clinton, have done so.) Congress, through the "necessary and proper" clause, legislates to establish and regulate the chain of command that flows from the president to military officers. The Supreme Court has ruled that the president, as commander in chief, "is authorized to direct the movements of the naval and military forces placed by law at his command, and to employ them in the manner he may deem most effectual to harass and conquer and subdue the enemy."[13] This is not a plenary grant of power: they apply when the forces have been "placed by law" at his command.

The statutes Congress passes are designed to maintain civilian control of the military, prevent the accumulation of command authority by the Joint Chiefs of Staff (JCS) or any individual service chiefs, and provide a "fail-safe" system to ensure that lawful presidential orders are carried out. The Goldwater-Nichols Act of 1986 provides that the chain of command runs "(1) from the president to the secretary of defense; and (2) from the secretary of defense to the commander of the combatant command."[14] In the Defense Department itself, the secretary is often considered to be "deputy commander in chief," though there is no constitutional or statutory basis for that title. The law allows the president to "direct" that the chairman of the Joint Chiefs of Staff be a link in the communications between the secretary of defense and the commanders of military units (CINCS), but the chair of the JCS has no military authority to command units, nor do any of the chiefs of the JCS. All directives from the Chiefs that require units to move their location, go to an area of imminent hostilities, or engage hostile forces, must be approved by the secretary of defense, ensuring civilian control of the military.

To ensure that a president cannot "go haywire" and start issuing insane or unconstitutional orders to the military, Congress has specified that the president has no statutory authority to issue direct commands to anyone below the commander of the CINC. (Covert national security operations fall under different law.) In the midst of the Watergate crisis, for example, Secretary of Defense James Schlesinger issued orders to all military commands reminding them that operational orders ran through his office.

In practice, these strict legal separations are not always enforced. Presidents do issue orders directly to unit commanders and even combat forces, as President Bush did during the Persian Gulf War, using a special headset provided for him by military communications specialists at the White House. The JCS usually become intimately involved in the chain of command. As Brigadier General Amos Jordan and Colonel William Taylor describe actual command and control arrangements: "In strict legal terms, the JCS is not in the chain of command; in practice, defense secretaries involve the chiefs, drawing on their professional advice on policy and operational means to implement directives from the President."[15]

The president establishes new military commands only through the secretary of defense. He issues written directives to the secretary of defense specifying the command and the units to be moved, and specifying the force structure. A "report-and-wait" provision provides that the president must give Congress 60 days notice in peacetime in case it wishes to block the decision. Similarly, the president may not issue orders to a unit to leave a command without transmitting it through the secretary of defense and giving Congress 60 days notice. Commanders of combatant commands perform their duties "under the authority, direction and control of the secretary of Defense, and are responsible to the Secretary for preparedness and carrying out of missions assigned to the command by the secretary."[16]

The best chain of command does not always prevent unauthorized actions by military commanders, though such incidents are rare. One of the most important breeches involved General Curtis LeMay, the air force chief of staff during much of the Cold War. The air force conducted unauthorized spy flights over the Soviet Union in violation of a May 1950 directive from JCS ordering reconnaissance flights to keep to international waters. President Eisenhower had reiterated the policy in 1953; nevertheless, on May 8, 1954, an R47 stratojet of the 91st Reconnaissance Wing based in Britain penetrated hundreds of miles into the Soviet Union. In April of 1956, nine RB-47s from the 26th Strategic Reconnaissance Wing flew into the Soviet Union from Greenland, and in 1957 a third flight went over Vladivostok and Western Siberia.[17] At least one plane was hit, and Soviet protests kept Cold War tensions high, undercutting President Eisenhower's own "Open Skies" disarmament proposals.

THE ULTIMATE DECISION

The most important decision the president can make is the decision for peace or war. It often determines the success or failure of his entire presidency.

Presidential Use of the Armed Forces

Presidents have used the armed forces with congressional declarations of war only eight times in American history, in each case to fight a large-scale war: the War of 1812 against Great Britain; the Mexican-American War of 1848; the Spanish-American War of 1898; World War I against the Central Powers; and World War II against the Axis Powers (which involved four separate declarations). In more than 230 other minor instances, they have relied on their constitutional prerogatives as commander in chief to use the armed forces in hostilities, with fewer than half involving any prior legislative authorization.[18] These include (but are not limited to) the following:

- Actions against politically unorganized pirates and bandits, drug smugglers, and terrorists, which may involve limited incursion into another state or its airspace or territorial waters.
- Evacuation of U.S. citizens and interventions to protect American lives and property during disorders in foreign nations. In some situations the United States may be involved unilaterally or multilaterally in efforts to restore law and order in other nations. In 1989 President Bush ordered "Operation Just Cause," an invasion of Panama, in part because U.S. civilians and members of the military had been harassed by Panamanian soldiers and police.
- Intervention on behalf of American colonists. In the nineteenth century this led to the acquisition of Florida, Texas, California, and Hawaii. In the last half of the nineteenth century the U.S. Army fought frontier wars against Indian tribes.
- Interventions in foreign nations to administer their assets on behalf of their creditors. In the first half of the twentieth century these included Haiti, Nicaragua, the Dominican Republic, and Cuba.
- Intervention to topple regimes unfriendly to the United States, such as the Dominican Republic in 1965, Grenada in 1982, and Panama in 1989.

- Enforcement of blockades and quarantines, such as the quarantine of Cuba in 1962 to force removal of Soviet nuclear missiles from the island, the blockade of Iraq in 1990 to pressure that nation to withdraw from Kuwait; and the blockade of Haiti in 1993 to force the military to allow an exiled democratically elected president to assume power.
- Wars and police actions such as with North Korea (1950–1953), North Vietnam (1964–1973), and Iraq (1991).
- United Nations or other multilateral peacekeeping, humanitarian, or monitoring operations, such as the protection of foreign-aid workers in Somalia in 1992–1993 and the relief of famine in Rwanda in 1994.

Almost all uses of force by presidents in the nineteenth century without a declaration of war involved minor incidents, mostly against pirates and brigands and bandits, while some of the uses of forces in hostilities without congressional sanction in the twentieth century involved much larger operations against organized governments and large numbers of American soldiers killed or wounded in pursuit of U.S. foreign policy goals.

The Political Stakes in Using Force

Presidential use of the armed forces is sustainable only when Congress and the American people support it. To win that support, the president can emphasize the danger to our national interests. The president can talk about casualties or hostages or deaths resulting from actions by foreign forces. The administration can stress our obligations to provide humanitarian assistance, as George Bush did in sending forces to Somalia. The president can talk about repelling aggression, bolstering collective security, and the "domino effect" of allowing an aggressor nation to succeed.

In the early stages of a military operation, the public rallies around the armed forces and the president who sent them into danger. When Eisenhower sent forces into Lebanon in 1958, he went up in the polls six points; when Kennedy set up a blockade around Cuba in 1962, he went up thirteen points; when Lyndon Johnson invaded the Dominican Republic in 1965, he went up six points; when George Bush used forces in the Persian Gulf in 1991, his support skyrocketed to the highest levels ever recorded for a president.

Yet the "rally-round-the-flag" effect has its limits. Protracted hostilities, large-scale casualties, and discord between president and Congress are all associated with falling presidential popularity. The Korean War dragged on, as did the Vietnam War, and in each case public support dropped as casualties increased, and the public could not discern an end to hostilities. Presidential approval ratings declined, the president's party suffered heavy losses in midterm elections, and its congressional leaders began to criticize his conduct of the war. Interventions in Lebanon in 1983 and Somalia in 1994 were concluded because of precipitous drops in support after U.S. casualties were taken.

When presidents use force they are likely to be successful if the intervention is limited in duration, when the mission has a precisely defined outcome achievable through military force; when overwhelming force routs a feeble enemy; and when forces are withdrawn quickly. A president who gets drawn into a quagmire, in which the goals are unclear and military force is not likely to attain them (i.e., if a political compromise is necessary), or where the forces within the combat theater are evenly matched and the enemy is fighting on home turf, is likely to lose political support, and eventually the military mission is likely to be scaled down or withdrawn.

Even when presidents win wars that have been declared or authorized by Congress, with great gains or minimal losses, their party often suffers. After the Mexican-American War, known as "Mr. Polk's war," the Democrats lost Congress and then the White House, even though Polk had gained a great amount of territory in the southwest with minimal losses of American life. After World War I, the Democrats again lost Congress in midterm elections and then the White House, though Wilson had intervened at a decisive moment, and again the United States won victories without sustaining the same level of casualties as our allies. After World War II, the pattern repeated itself partially, as the Democrats lost control of Congress in the first postwar midterm elections, though they did not lose the White House until 1952. Even after the U.S. victory in the Persian Gulf War of 1991, the Republicans lost the White House the following year. Clinton's successful military occupation of Haiti did nothing to help him in the midterm elections of 1994 when Republicans gained control of Congress.

Conversely, most presidents who withdraw from losing situations suffer no political fallout for their party (the major exception being John Adams and the undeclared naval war against France of 1798). The U.S. setbacks in the War of 1812 did not weaken the Democratic-Republicans, who maintained control of the government, though had they continued the war it might have led to the dismemberment of the Union. Eisenhower's acceptance of a negotiated truce in Korea gained him great popularity and a second term in 1956. Nixon's "Vietnamization" policy, involving withdrawal of most American troops and consequent reduction in U.S. casualties, ensured him a second term in 1972 against anti-war candidate George McGovern. Reagan's withdrawal of marines from Lebanon after suffering 250 casualties in a bombing of the marine barracks in 1982 kept his ill-fated intervention from affecting his reelection prospects. Clinton's withdrawal from Somalia in 1994 fits right into the "no loss" pattern: it was followed by a period of rising presidential approval ratings.

Escalation and Deception

The worst thing a president can do is deceive the American people, as Lyndon Johnson did with the "Gulf of Tonkin incidents" to gain congressional support for his escalation of the Vietnam War. On August 2, 1964, according to President Johnson, several North Vietnamese torpedo boats closed in on the destroyer *USS Maddox* and released torpedoes, which the *Maddox* was able to evade. Fighter planes sent from the aircraft carrier *USS Ticonderoga* damaged two of the torpedo boats. On August 4, according to the administration, the destroyers *Maddox* and *Turner Joy*, on patrol in international waters 65 miles from the Vietnamese coast, made radar contact with five torpedo boats, reported themselves under torpedo attack, fired their own weapons, and sank two boats. In response to these alleged provocations by North Vietnam, President Johnson ordered a retaliatory raid on August 5, destroying or damaging 25 enemy patrol boats. Congressional leaders agreed to introduce the Gulf of Tonkin Resolution, prepared by Johnson, by which Congress supported "the determination of the president, as Commander-in-Chief, to take all necessary measures to repel any armed attack against the forces of the United States and to prevent further aggression."[19] Moreover, the resolution also stated that "the United States is, therefore, prepared, as the President determines, to take all necessary steps, including the use of armed force, to assist any member or protocol state of the Southeast Asia Collective Defense Treaty requesting assistance in defense of its freedom," a provision covering South Vietnam.

Years later, an investigation by the Senate Foreign Relations Committee and revelations by pilots who flew over the Gulf gave a different version of events. The *Maddox* was *not* on a routine patrol and it was *not* 65 miles away in international waters; it was 8 or 9 miles off the coast, within the 12-mile limit claimed by North Vietnam. It was conducting electronic surveillance, sailing at the same time and in the same place as a South Vietnamese naval mission directed against the North, Operation 34-A. At the time of the first incident, the *Maddox* was near a North Vietnamese naval base that had been recently attacked by the South Vietnamese and was on a high state of alert—a fact known by the navy, which had intercepted its communications. The *Maddox* fired first, before the North Vietnamese fired their torpedoes. The North Vietnamese had not provoked an incident but were engaged in what they thought were defensive maneuvers to protect against further attacks. The second incident reported by the president may not even have happened. Visibility was poor, and enemy boats were never seen visually but only picked up on ships' sonar. The destroyers may have had a faulty sonar system, and one of the sonar operators on duty was an apprentice, inexperienced in distinguishing enemy torpedoes from other sounds (such as his ship's propellers).[20]

Johnson also deceived Congress and the American people in the 1964 presidential campaign, by portraying himself as a man of peace who would not escalate the war in Vietnam. The administration did warn that if we started winning the war, the other side might escalate hostilities, which we would have to match. In fact, we were doing more escalating than the other side, to prop up the South Vietnamese government, which was losing the war. As Johnson was making the decision to send several hundred thousand troops into Vietnam, he kept that information not only from the American people but also from much of his own government. His economic advisors and budget officials thought that the intervention was limited and the costs were low, and planned their fiscal policy and spending programs accordingly. The result of LBJ's deceptions: an economy that went into an inflationary spiral, military expenditures that skyrocketed, and a Congress that by 1966 began cutting domestic programs to pay for the war.[21] The administration suffered from a "credibility gap" with the media and the public that severely hampered its efforts to prosecute the war.

LEGITIMIZING PRESIDENTIAL WAR MAKING

Presidents claim a broad range of constitutional and legal justifications for their prerogative war making powers. Their critics, in turn, argue that none of these arguments justify war making without congressional participation in the decision.

Using International Police Powers

Grover Cleveland and Theodore Roosevelt were the first presidents to claim international police powers. They argued that the power of the president to take care that laws be faithfully executed extended to international law and treaty obligations of the United States, and could be applied against foreign nations. As Roosevelt put it:

> If a nation shows that it knows how to act with reasonable efficiency and decency in social and political matters, if it keeps order and pays its obligations, it need fear no interference from the United States. Chronic wrongdoing, or an impotence which results in a general loosening of the ties of civilized society, may in America, as elsewhere, ultimately require intervention by some civilized nation, and in the Western Hemisphere, the adherence of the United States to the Monroe Doctrine may force the United States, however reluctantly, in flagrant cases of such wrongdoing or impotence, to the exercise of an international police power.[22]

Both presidents used the Monroe Doctrine to keep European powers from using their navies to collect debts owed them by Latin American nations. Instead, the United States occupied Haiti and the Dominican Republic, and forced Venezuela into a compromise, to satisfy their debtors.

Collective Security Obligations

Presidents claim that the collective security obligations of the United States give them the authority to use military force without waiting for congressional approval. To justify presidential use of force in the Vietnam War, for example, the Johnson administration argued that South Vietnam was a state that has been attacked by North Vietnam. It was covered by the South East Asia Treaty Organization (SEATO), a treaty commitment of the United States, as well as UN obligations to resist aggression. Critics of presidential war making responded that South Vietnam was not a state under international law: it was a "military regroupment zone" under the Geneva Accords of 1954 that ended the French war in Indochina. It was supposed to permit all-Vietnam elections, but refused to do so (with U.S. backing) for fear that the communist nationalist hero Ho Chi Minh would win and take over power. Critics argued that we were intervening in a civil war between various Vietnamese factions, rather than attempting to stop aggression by one state against another.

Critics also claimed that we were under no obligation to assist South Vietnam, because the SEATO treaty required instead that a member state "consult immediately (with other members) to agree on measures that would be taken for the common defense." The United States did not consult other members before intervening: This lost us the support of the French, the British, and the Pakistani governments, all SEATO members. We were under no obligation as a member of the UN to intervene in Vietnam. Article 33 of the UN charter calls on nations to attempt peaceful resolution of disputes before resorting to arms. The United States made no attempt to use the UN, which led to Secretary General U Thant strongly criticizing U.S. involvement in the war. Nothing in the SEATO treaty or UN charter is self-executing; the decisions about U.S. involvement could have been made by Congress through its power to declare war or otherwise authorize limited hostilities.

Mutual defense treaties do not make a congressional declaration of war obsolete. For one thing, the president and Senate cannot consent to a treaty that would remove from the House of Representatives its share of Congress's constitutional prerogative to declare war (or refuse to declare war).[23] Neither can the president and Senate agree with another nation on a "self-executing" commitment to use force in the event of hostilities, because that too would take away from Congress its prerogative to decide whether and how to meet treaty commitments by authorizing and financing hostilities.

United Nations Resolutions

Presidents claim that their commander-in-chief powers must be used to enforce our obligations under the UN, because these obligations are "self-executing" and not subject to congressional approval. Since the Vietnam War, the issue of whether a UN resolution is "self-executing" or must be further authorized by Congress has become controversial, with a large majority in Congress favoring the latter position.[24] In August of 1994, the U.S. Senate passed a resolution explicitly stating the sense of Congress that a UN resolution could not authorize hostilities or commit Congress to authorize them—a position supported by President Clinton.[25]

Article 51 of the UN Charter recognizes the right of self-defense against aggression and the right to collective security, and Article 53 permits regional security pacts that can repel aggression. Under these provisions the United States took the lead after World War II in organizing NATO (Western Europe, the United States, and Canada), the Rio Pact (the United States and Latin America), the SEATO Treaty (United States, Britain, France, and several Southeast Asian nations), and METO (United States, Britain, and several Middle Eastern states) as pacts designed to deter aggression by the Soviet Union or communist China. These pacts contain provisions that members may use their armed forces "in accordance with their constitutional processes," ambiguous language that begs the question of whether the U.S. "constitutional process" permits the president to act on his own in using troops to meet these treaty obligations, or whether Congress must participate by voting a declaration of war or other authorization.

When the United States joined the UN, Congress passed the United Nations Participation Act, a law that regulates U.S. involvement in the international organization.[26] Section 6 requires congressional approval of collective security actions when the Security Council of the UN approves such actions. Under Article 43, each member state is supposed to negotiate an agreement with the Military Staff Committee of the Security Council that specifies the forces available for enforcement operations. Congress specified that it would have to give approval by joint resolution before any such agreement could take effect. Moreover, in a large operation Congress would have to approve if the level of U.S. forces went beyond the small number committed under the Article 43 agreement.[27] Testifying before a Congressional committee before passage of the law, Secretary of State Dean Acheson agreed that the president could not furnish troops until Congress had agreed, could not furnish more troops than Congress had agreed on, and could not make any other agreement with the UN that would circumvent congressional approval under these procedures.[28] The only forces exempt from these provisions were to be a small U.S.

contingent that might be used for humanitarian missions. Given these understandings from the Truman administration, Congress passed the law.

Presidents have ignored the United Nations Participation Act and its Section 6 procedures. They have combined their constitutional powers as commander in chief with the obligations imposed on the United States by the United Nations Charter to use U.S. forces in "police actions" and other missions aimed at deterring or ending aggression. The State Department used this justification to defend President Truman's use of force in Korea without obtaining a declaration of war.[29] Counseled by Acheson, President Truman did not negotiate an Article 43 agreement, nor did he seek congressional authorization as required by the Act. He sent troops to Korea to try to repel the invading North Korean army, then a day later won a 9–0 vote in the Security Council (with the Soviet Union absent) authorizing a "police action" on behalf of South Korea. Truman and Acheson established the historical precedent that U.S. forces *could* be used in UN peacekeeping operations or police operations without congressional authorization.[30] There was little congressional opposition. As Senator Paul Douglas put it, "International situations frequently call for the retail use of force in localized situations which are not sufficiently serious to justify wholesale and widespread use of force which a formal declaration of war would require."[31] Douglas, referring to North Korea as a pygmy state, thought it would take a short time to repel its army—a miscalculation almost made by Truman. Had Congress known in advance the extent of the war making inaugurated by the president, it might have insisted on a role in authorizing hostilities.

Similarly, there was no Article 43 agreement when the United States helped Kuwait repel aggression from Iraq in 1991, even when the Security Council passed S/678 permitting "other means" to be used to enforce its resolutions against Iraq. President Bush and Secretary of State James Baker went to great lengths to win the support of the Soviet Union for the U.S. action, and got the Soviets to drop their insistence that the UN military staff committee be involved, a procedure that would have triggered calls for congressional approval of the staff committees plan. Some critics of Bush's use of prerogative power argued that Bush should have negotiated an Article 43 agreement with the UN, because the action was not a small enforcement action but was a war, requiring congressional declaration or the equivalent. Although the Korean War precedent has been reinforced by the Persian Gulf precedent, both ignored the clear language of the UN Participation Act and the pledges of Franklin Roosevelt and Harry Truman in 1945 that Congress would codetermine and approve U.S. participation in international peacekeeping actions.

In October 1994, when Saddam Hussein again sent forces toward Kuwait, Clinton responded with a strong show of force that sent to Iraqi Republican Guard packing back north and ended the crisis. Although Clinton made the customary pro forma notification to Congress, he and his defense secretary made it clear that military force would be used against Iraq if the forces were not removed. Clinton did not intend to seek authorization from Congress for this action, nor from the United Nations. The administration argued that existing cease-fire resolutions passed by the UN Security Council in the aftermath of the 1991 Persian Gulf War were still applicable, and under them the president could, on his own authority, take actions he deemed necessary—a position contested by Russia and France. As part of these actions, for example, U.S. warplanes on presidential orders flew over positions in southern Iraq on simulated "bombing runs" doing everything but actually releasing the ordnance on the Iraqi forces below.[32]

Maintaining Nuclear Deterrence

Presidents claim power to use nuclear weapons without consulting Congress. President John Kennedy during the Cuban Missile Crisis of 1962 announced that he would launch nuclear weapons against the Soviet Union and Cuba in the event a missile were launched from Cuba. "I have full authority," Kennedy claimed about his efforts to quarantine Cuba during the crisis, and he saw no need to obtain authorization from Congress for his blockade or his threats of nuclear strikes.[33] These might involve "launch on warning" if our radar picked up evidence that an enemy had launched a strike against us; alternatively we might launch our own preemptive strike (first strike) if we knew that by doing so we could eliminate the first strike an enemy was about to launch. A president also must be able to launch a second strike after the United States has been attacked, because, unless an adversary believed that that might be done, no stable "balance of terror" could be achieved; an enemy might be tempted to strike first and eliminate our retaliatory response. Throughout most of the Cold War, Congress acquiesced in presidential nuclear powers. Senator William Fulbright, writing in 1961, argued that "the President has full responsibility, which cannot be shared, for military decisions in a world in which the difference between safety and cataclysm can be a matter of hours or even minutes."[34]

These nuclear war powers have been employed several times by presidents to maintain a stable nuclear balance or deter actions by other nations. In the 1950s the Eisenhower administration relied on a policy of "brinkmanship" in dealing with some communist states rather than matching them with conventional forces. There is some evidence that the North Koreans were induced to end the Korean War because they thought that Eisenhower might otherwise consider using nuclear weapons against them.[35] Communist China called off its bombardment of islands controlled by the nationalist Chinese when similar hints of a U.S. nuclear response were given.[36]

Some observers are uneasy about the vast nuclear war powers of the president. They have called for a "nuclear war cabinet" or joint congressional–executive committee that would meet (if possible) to consider presidential proposals to use nuclear weapons. Unless the committee were prevented from meeting (by a full-scale attack on the United States, for example), its approval would be required before the president could give the order to use nuclear weapons.[37] They also argue that a presidential "first use" of nuclear weapons to prevent a military defeat by other nation's conventional forces would also be unlawful and unconstitutional.[38] Critics of these proposals argue that they would erode the nuclear deterrent and that they go against the intent of the framers, which was to permit the president to protect against attack.

CONGRESS AND PRESIDENTIAL WAR POWERS

Congress has many war powers of its own, explicitly assigned in Article I. It not only declares war, but also can authorize hostilities in "imperfect wars" by passing laws or appropriations for conflict.[39] In 1839, for example, Congress passed "an Act Giving to the President of the United States Additional Powers for the Defense of the United States" as a signal to Great Britain to come to an agreement in a border dispute involving its Canadian province and the state of Maine.[40] In 1955 Congress authorized President Eisenhower to use military force to defend the nationalist Chinese regime on Formosa and its islands in the Pescadores from armed attack by the communist Chinese, and in 1958 Congress authorized the use of armed forces in the Middle East to protect pro-Western regimes "from any country controlled by international communism."[41]

Regulating War Powers

Congress can use its legislative powers to regulate presidential war making. It can determine war aims and prohibit military activities in conflict of which it disapproves. In a naval war with France, for example, Congress authorized the navy to seize vessels sailing *to* a French port; when a U.S. captain exceeded the law and followed President John Adams's orders to seize a ship sailing *from* a French port, the Supreme Court in *Little v. Barreme* held that Captain Little's actions were illegal and that he could be sued by the ship's owners.[42] In 1806 congressional power to regulate military actions was upheld by a circuit court in *U.S. v. Smith.*[43] Congress had already passed the Neutrality Act forbidding private U.S. citizens from engaging in hostilities against foreign nations. An individual indicted under the act claimed that his military activities against Spanish territory in the Americas had been authorized "with the knowledge and approbation of the executive department." The court held that the president could not "control the statute, nor dispense with its execution, and still less can he authorize a person to do what the law forbids." Thus, the president could not direct individuals to conduct hostilities against nations with which the United States was at peace.[44] Congress may prohibit the use of military forces in particular theaters: in 1940, before U.S. entry into World War II, Congress provided that persons inducted into the Army "shall not be employed beyond the limits of the Western Hemisphere" except in U.S. possessions such as the Philippines.[45]

Congress has the power of the purse and can cut off funds for military activities. In 1969, to reduce the U.S. commitment in the hostilities in Indochina, it prohibited funds for the Pentagon from being used to "finance the introduction of American ground combat troops into Laos or Thailand."[46] In 1971 it applied a similar funding cutoff to the use of ground troops into Cambodia.[47] After August 15, 1973, President Nixon stopped the bombing of Cambodia to comply with another congressional statute.[48] In 1986, Congress provided that no U.S. forces could provide training or any other service to the contras within twenty miles of the Nicaraguan border and prohibited these forces from entering Nicaragua.[49]

Sometimes an attempt by Congress to regulate presidential war making with its power of the purse can backfire. In 1993 Congress passed a Defense Department

Appropriations Act that contained a "sense of Congress" resolution that funds should not be "obligated or expended for United States military operations in Haiti" unless certain conditions were met. But the president could use the military if he certified to Congress in advance that national security interests were at stake, that rules of engagement would ensure that U.S. personnel "will not become targets due to the nature of the rules of engagement," that the mission and objectives were more appropriate to the armed forces than civilian personnel or armed forces from other nations, that the forces were "necessary and sufficient to accomplish the objectives of the proposed mission," that the president had clear objectives for the mission and an exit strategy, and that the mission would be undertaken only after costs were estimated.[50] Although the language of the law clearly contemplated a peacekeeping mission to uphold United Nations resolutions rather than use of military force in an invasion, President Clinton's constitutional lawyers later relied on this statutory language to justify his authority to order an invasion of Haiti without further congressional approval.

Congress may also take away statutory authority or repeal a prior resolution of support. In 1970 Congress repealed the Gulf of Tonkin Resolution, a sign to the Nixon administration that it would soon have to withdraw from Vietnam. In 1971 it passed the Mansfield Amendment to a military procurement authorization act, declaring that it was U.S. policy to

> terminate at the earliest practicable date all military operations of the United States in Indochina, and to provide for the prompt and orderly withdrawal of all United States military forces at a date certain, subject to the release of all American prisoners of war held by the Government of North Vietnam and forces allied with such Government and an accounting for Americans missing in action who have been held or known to such Government or such forces.[51]

Nixon ignored this amendment, declaring it an unconstitutional infringement on presidential war powers and the commander in chief clause, and considered it without force or effect.[52]

Congress does not regulate presidential war powers in the abstract. For Congress to take action, a presidential policy must be perceived as a failure. Mounting casualties; changes in goals, strategies, or tactics; enemy actions that prolong hostilities; a split in the president's party as public approval ratings for the administration and its policies drop; and a consensus among congressional leaders that action is necessary—these are the preconditions for effective congressional action.

Even when Congress is considering acting, it may give the president any number of loopholes to continue hostilities. On October 16, 1993, Senator Robert Dole proposed an amendment to a military appropriations bill that would have barred the United States from using forces in Haiti to restore exiled president Bertrand Aristide. Yet the Dole amendment would have permitted the president to use troops to evacuate U.S. citizens, or for any other national interest certified by the president, provided the president specified U.S. objectives, the international threat that the military regime in Haiti posed, the timetable for a U.S. pullout, and the costs of intervention. With enough loopholes, even Clinton supported it (as the Dole-Mitchell amendment applied to potential intervention in Haiti and Bosnia) and the language made it clear that it was not "binding."

Congress at the time rejected a proposal that would have prohibited the president from assigning U.S. troops to a UN command, except with thirty days' notice and approval by congressional joint resolution. Instead, Congress substituted the Nunn-Warner resolution, a nonbinding "sense of Congress" resolution that asked the president to consult with Congress and report within forty-eight hours of making such an assignment of U.S. forces to the UN. It also rejected an amendment offered by Senator Jesse Helms prohibiting the president from using U.S. forces in Haiti except to evacuate U.S. citizens. "I would strenuously oppose such attempts to encroach on the President's foreign policy powers," Clinton argued.[53] The failure of Congress to pass these amendments, even when U.S. public opinion overwhelmingly favored immediate withdrawal from Somalia and a policy of nonintervention in Bosnia and Haiti, shows that a president determined to protect his or her prerogatives as commander in chief can do so by cutting losses in a "no-win" military situation and by following a policy of restraint in other situations. By doing so, the president can gain a measure of bipartisan support against attempts to limit the constitutional powers of the commander in chief. Even so, after Republicans gained control of Congress in 1995, one of their proposals in their "Contract with America" was the "National Security Revitalization Act" to limit command of armed forces to U.S. military officers and to prevent the president from concluding military agreements with the United Nations to put American troops under the command of foreign officers.

The War Powers Resolution

After U.S. involvement in the Vietnam War and the U.S. bombing of Cambodia had ended, Congress passed the War Powers Resolution (WPR) on November 7, 1973, over President Nixon's veto.[54] The purpose of the resolution was to

> insure that the collective judgment of both the Congress and the President will apply to the introduction of United States Armed Forces into hostilities, or into situations where imminent involvement in hostilities is clearly indicated by the circumstances, and to the continued use of such forces in hostilities or in such situations.[55]

Congress wanted to create a consultative and collaborative process in which it would play an important role in the decision to commence hostilities. It also intended to define more clearly the presidential war powers. The act defined these powers in terms of three conditions:

> The Constitutional powers of the President as Commander-in-Chief to introduce United States Armed Forces into hostilities, or situations where imminent involvement in hostilities is clearly indicated by the circumstances, are exercised only pursuant to (1) a declaration of war; (2) specific statutory authorization, or (3) a national emergency created by attack upon the United States, its territories or possessions, or its armed forces.[56]

The first circumstance is a reiteration of the constitutional understandings regarding presidential war powers. The second requires that the authority that Congress grants must be specific and directed toward hostilities—the president no longer can claim "joint concert" if Congress simply passes Defense Department appropriations, or a Selective Service Act allowing the president to draft soldiers. The third condition is quite broad: The attacks on U.S. forces can take place anywhere in the world. This means that if the president deploys forces provocatively and gets an adversary to engage them, the administration can claim use of force in self-defense.

These two provisions are the "purpose and policy" section of the WPR. Although they seem to limit the president and require collaborative government, in fact they do no such thing. The purpose and policy section of any law is simply window-dressing: It has no force or effect and is generally not implemented by the executive nor enforced by the courts. Presidents treat these provisions as inoperative, because they do not specify all the circumstances in which the president might have to use force to protect U.S. interests.

The WPR does contain operative provisions. Section 3 requires that "the President, in every possible instance, shall consult with the Congress before introducing United States Armed Forces into hostilities." Yet this provision is poorly drafted: What does "every possible instance" mean? Does "Congress" here mean that the president must consult with all 435 members of the House and 100 members of the Senate? And what does "consult" mean: merely a briefing by the president, or an exchange of opinions? The House Committee on Foreign Affairs, when it reported the legislation to the full House for a vote, defined consultation as follows:

> Consultation in this provision means that decision is pending on a problem and that the members of the Congress are being asked by the President for their advice and opinions and, in appropriate circumstances, their approval of action contemplated. . . . The president himself must participate and all information related to the situation must be made available.[57]

In practice, presidents have ignored the consultation clause. At best, they have provided congressional leaders with briefings, just before or after commencing military operations.[58] George Bush gave several congressional leaders one-day advance notice of his planned deployments in the Persian Gulf. When Bush met with congressional leaders, it was to brief them on developments and debate with them the constitutional issues as to whether congressional authorization was necessary—but the meetings were not consultations to get congressional advice about the use of force. President Clinton did not give Congress prior notice when he sent troops from the Special Operations Command into Haiti in early September, 1994, on a mission to prepare for the kidnapping of Haitian general Raul Cedras, nor when he sent Navy Seals into Haiti ten days before a planned invasion to reconnoiter the beaches.[59]

The WPR in Section 3 goes on to state that "after every such introduction" [of the military into hostilities] the president "shall consult regularly with the Congress until United States Armed Forces are no longer engaged in hostilities." Again, the provision was poorly drafted. What does "regularly" mean? Every week? Once a year? If the president does not wish to consult, there is no mechanism whereby Congress can force it to be done.

Congress also provided in the WPR that the president must make certain reports when the following circumstances occur: using the armed forces in hostilities or introducing them into situations in which hostilities are imminent; introducing forces equipped for combat when hostilities are *not* considered imminent; or building up forces already introduced in either of the other circumstances. Only in the event that forces are involved in hostilities or if hostilities are "imminent" must the president submit a written report to Congress within 48 hours of their introduction: In this report, the circumstances must be indicated, along with the constitutional and legal authority in using force and the estimated scope or duration of the hostilities or involvement. Every six months, a similar report must be issued.

The reporting provision does not cover naval forces sent near another nation, provided they stay outside its territorial waters. It does not cover "training exercises" with another nation's forces, even if our forces are kept in the field for months as a deterrent against hostilities by another nation. It does not cover forces that the Pentagon designates "not equipped for combat," such as peacekeeping forces on multinational or UN missions. Presidents use these loopholes and often do not issue reports. In Central America, even when a U.S. training mission took casualties in El Salvador, the Reagan administration argued that the military personnel were not equipped for, and not intended to be used in, combat: Even though they were fired on, it was U.S. intent, not conditions on the ground, that determined whether a report had to be made.

Congress gave itself the power to end presidential war making or use of force through the subsequent restraint section of the WPR, which provides that:

> Within sixty calendar days after a report is submitted or is required to be submitted.... The president shall terminate any use of United States Armed Forces.... Unless Congress (1) has declared war or has enacted a specific authorization for such use; (2) has extended by law such sixty-day period, or (3) is physically unable to meet as a result of an armed attack.[60]

This provision does not allow a war to continue by default. If Congress does not actively support the president's policies, the war or mission must come to an end. The onus is on those who wish to continue to fight to organize in Congress to support the president; if they fail to do so, the hostilities must end. The 60-day "clock" begins ticking regardless of whether the president actually submits a report: Provided circumstances exist that require a report, Congress (and the courts if they wish) can consider the clock to have been started by the president's actions in ordering troops into hostilities or imminent hostilities.[61] In fact, although presidents submitted more than 25 reports under the WPR through 1991, only one time was the 60-day clock triggered (during a rescue attempt of the merchant ship *Mayaguez* in 1975 in Cambodia).[62]

Congress went even further: It gave itself a legislative veto over presidential war making that could be applied at any time, not just at the end of a 60-day period. It provided that:

> Notwithstanding [the 60-day provision], at any time that United States Armed Forces are engaged in hostilities outside the territory of the United States, its possessions and territories, without a declaration of war or specific statutory author-

ization, such forces shall be removed if the Congress so directs by concurrent resolution.[63]

Because the concurrent resolutions form of legislative veto was declared unconstitutional by the Supreme Court in *Chadha v. INS,* in 1983 Congress passed an amendment substituting a joint resolution.[64] The significance is that a joint resolution must be submitted to the president, who can then veto it. A presidential veto is sustained by one-third of one congressional chamber; thus the ability of Congress to force a president to withdraw troops would be dependent on support of at least two-thirds of each chamber, raising the hurdles for decisive congressional opposition to presidential war making.

The legislative veto can be exercised at any time. Congress does not have to wait 60 days. Once it passes, the president has 30 days to complete military withdrawal if it is determined that such time is needed because of "unavoidable military necessity respecting the safety of the United States Armed Forces." Critics of the WPR argue that this gives the president a 30-day blank check to use massive force, even after Congress has ordered an end to the venture. The legislative veto refers only to actual uses of the armed forces. The veto cannot be used to inhibit the president from building up forces or starting hostilities: Until the shooting starts, the president has absolute power over the deployment of forces.

The legislative veto may not be operative in all circumstances in which force is used. Consider the following scenario: The president introduces force, and Congress passes an authorizing resolution. Later Congress has second thoughts and repeals its resolution. Can it now use a legislative veto and order the president to remove the armed forces? It would seem that it can, provided we think of the resolution as a legislative act, for Congress can always repeal that which it has enacted. Not all "acts" of Congress are repealable, though: Senate consent to a treaty cannot be withdrawn, nor can Senate consent to a nomination; an impeachment cannot be reversed, nor a conviction. The president might argue that a declaration of war or authorization for war fits into the category of "nonreversible acts." In that case, once Congress commits itself to support the president, it cannot later reverse itself and then use the WPR to force the president to end hostilities. The president will argue that Congress gets an initial choice: Back the president or use the WPR to force an end to hostilities. Congress does not get a chance to change its mind.

PRESIDENTIAL OPPOSITION TO CONGRESSIONAL RESTRICTIONS

President Nixon vetoed the WPR on October 24, 1973, calling it "unconstitutional and dangerous to the best interests of the nation, because it would "attempt to take away, by a mere legislative act, authorities which the President has properly exercised under the Constitution for almost 200 years."[65] He particularly objected to the 60-day cutoff provisions and the ability of Congress to force a withdrawal by concurrent resolution. "In effect, the Congress is here attempting to increase its policy-making role through a provision which requires it to take absolutely no action at all."[66] Nixon concluded that "both these provisions are unconstitutional. The only way in which the constitutional powers of a branch of the Government can be altered is by amending the Constitution—and any attempt to make such alterations by legislation alone is clearly without force."[67] Congress repassed the act over his veto, but Nixon signaled that he would not be bound by its provisions. He and all other presidents have argued that it undercuts the credibility of the president with our allies, it gives our adversaries reason to doubt our determination to use force or "stay the course," and it infringes on presidential prerogatives.[68] In 1975 the legal advisor to the State Department testified on legislative veto of WPR, arguing "that power [the presidential power to put troops into combat] could not be taken away by concurrent resolution because the power is constitutional in nature."[69]

Presidential Evasion of the WPR

Presidents have routinely ignored, evaded, or otherwise minimized the reach of the WPR. President Gerald Ford used the navy and marines in 1975 to evacuate Americans, Europeans, and Vietnamese from South Vietnam when it fell to the communist armies of North Vietnam in 1975. Ford sent Congress a report that did not refer to imminent involvement in hostilities (even though U.S. forces were being shot at) and did not put forces under the 60-day limit. His report did not even recognize the WPR: Ford wrote that he was reporting "in accordance with my desire to keep the Congress fully informed," and his report was less than two pages. Subsequent presidents have also used the formula of "taking note of" the WPR, or issuing reports "consistent with" the law, rather than "in compliance with" or "in pursuance of" its provisions.

Ford ignored not only the WPR, but also seven other laws that Congress had passed between 1973 and 1975 that prohibited combat activities or paramilitary activities in, over, or off the shores of Indochina. Ford asked a joint session of Congress for a law to clarify these restrictions and permit the evacuations; Congress refused, with some members suspicious that, if they passed such a law, Ford would use it to escalate the war in Vietnam again. Ford justified the evacuations with a 1961 law permitting the navy to transport refugees—a loophole that permitted him to claim legal authority to act, but one that could not be used to escalate the war.

Shortly thereafter, Ford again ignored the letter and spirit of the WPR. On May 12, 1975, the *USS Mayaguez* was captured by a Cambodian torpedo boat, boarded, and taken to the island of Kho Tang. Ford ordered ships to the area and sent a message to the Cambodian communist government (through the good offices of China) that the ship and crew must be released. On May 13 Ford briefed House and Senate leaders but did not discuss any military options. Despite recommendations by his Joint Chiefs of Staff, Ford ordered a punishing military response. On May 14, without any congressional consultation, American aircraft sank three Cambodian patrol boats. The military then gave briefings to the House International Relations and Senate Foreign Relations Committees. Ford then ordered the bombing of an airfield and oil refinery (neither of which were operable) and an operation to recapture the *Mayaguez* and rescue the crew. Just before the mission got underway, the Cambodians released the crew in a small boat and the ship was set adrift: U.S. forces were unaware that the Cambodians had acted to defuse the crisis. The U.S. Marines stormed Kho Tang, ran into an ambush, and suffered eighteen dead and

Helicopter crews help evacuate Americans, South Vietnamese, and foreign nationals from Saigon at the end of April, 1975. Days later, all of Vietnam was controlled by the communists, marking the end of two decades of American attempts to keep Indochina free from communist control.

fifty wounded in an operation that need not have taken place.[70] Had the president consulted with Congress, the very process of consultation would have slowed events down for another day, and the United States would have not suffered any casualties. Ford later claimed that the WPR consultation clause was unworkable, because it was too difficult to find members of Congress, especially on long weekends—a claim that flies in the face of the White House boast that its telephone operators can get in touch with anyone, anywhere, at a moment's notice.[71]

President Jimmy Carter also played fast and loose with the WPR. He sent an aircraft carrier near Iran, but did not report to Congress. He ordered surveillance flights over North Yemen when that nation was invaded by South Yemen, but issued no report because it claimed that the planes were unarmed—even though they could be shot down. When he ordered the air force to transport Moroccan troops with French officers into Zaire's mineral-rich Shaba province to put down a secession attempt, he claimed that no report was required because the planes were landing behind the front lines: yet buildups and reinforcement actions are covered by the plain language of the law. The Carter administration never conceded the constitutionality of the veto or cutoff provisions of the law, though it did say as a matter of political expediency that it would abide by a congressional cutoff, since if it continued hostilities against congressional opposition it would irreparably split the Democratic Party.[72]

Reagan Outmaneuvers Congress

President Reagan extended the practices of Nixon, Ford, and Carter: He denied the act was constitutional, refused to comply with its provisions, and narrowed its reach. Reagan's invasion of Grenada demonstrated the political constraints on Congress in invoking the WPR. The president sent six thousand Marines and airborne troops to rescue American medical students, restore democracy on the island, and end the threat the regional peace posed by an anti-American leftist government. The president acted pursuant to a request from the Organization of Eastern Caribbean States, pursuant to the goals of the Organization of American States (preserving regional stability). But the OAS condemned the invasion as a violation of Grenadian sovereignty, as did the British Commonwealth, of which Grenada was a member. Reagan did not consult with Congress, but informed it after the operation had begun. He did not invoke the WPR, but sent a letter to Congress in lieu of a report within 48 hours. Yet U.S. forces had been involved in combat, taken light casualties, received combat pay and campaign medals. Prisoners were treated according to the rules of war.

The initial congressional response was concern that the WPR had not been invoked. The House voted 403–23 to invoke the WPR itself, with 147 Republicans deserting the administration. The Senate did likewise, with 25 Republican Senators including key Republican Party leaders Baker, Dole, Laxalt, and Percy joining 39 Democratic senators. Reagan received the support of only 20 relatively junior Republicans. Senators Percy and Baker joined with Democrats in calling for a congressional investigation of the wisdom of the invasion.

Within two days, public opinion strongly shifted toward the president, after the American people saw evening news reports of medical students who had been evacuated from Grenada kissing the tarmac at a U.S. airfield and thanking the airborne troops who had rescued them. Members of Congress quickly dropped plans for an investigation and joined in the general chorus of approval. Within a week, U.S. forces were withdrawn, and a contingent of police from several Caribbean islands had taken over peacekeeping. The lesson of Grenada seemed to be to use overwhelming force, influence U.S. public opinion (the Pentagon imposed tight censorship and let the media get news reports from an aircraft carrier, denying reporters access to the island), and get out quickly.[73]

Reagan adopted a conciliatory policy in dealing with Congress in a more controversial operation involving American marines in Lebanon: He cooperated with Congress rather than confront it over the WPR, yet never gave up his claims to any of his constitutional war-making powers. American involvement began on August 25, 1982, when 800 marines entered Beirut to assist in the evacuation of Palestine Liberation Organization fighters after the Israeli army had occupied much of the city. On September 24, 1,200 Marines returned as part of a multinational peacekeeping force to take control of Beirut from the withdrawing Israelis. The marines soon turned from impartial peacekeepers to guarantors of the Lebanese government, then locked in a civil war with a coalition of forces backed by Syria. Because Reagan wished to skirt the WPR, they were not armed with heavy weapons: Reagan notified Congress on September 24 in a letter that did not mention the WPR and did not trigger a 60-day clock. After a year of sniping, land mines, car bombings, artillery barrages, and several marine deaths, Reagan finally issued a WPR report on August 30, 1983. But his report indicated that U.S. marines were not involved in hostilities or in situations in which hostilities were imminent, and he still did not trigger the 60-day clock.

Congress and Reagan then agreed to authorize the use of troops for eighteen months, and Congress passed the "Beirut Resolution," giving such authorization under the WPR. Members of Congress believed that this was a great victory: For the first time a sitting president recognized the validity of the WPR. Under its Beirut Resolution, Congress started a clock by itself and set the timetable for the president. It stated that "nothing in this resolution shall preclude the Congress by joint resolution from directing a withdrawal," establishing the principle that Congress could decide to get out even after it agreed to allow hostilities.[74] Reagan signed the resolution at an elaborate ceremony at the White House, designed to showcase congressional support for his policy. Yet Reagan actually had conceded none of his war powers. A signing statement issued at the same time stated his position: Congress cannot set a clock that limits presidential deployment of forces; it cannot set a 60-day limit or any deadline on deployment; the initiation of isolated or infrequent acts of violence against marines does not constitute imminent involvement in hostilities; nothing in the Beirut Resolution "may be interpreted to revise the President's constitutional authority to deploy United States Armed Forces."[75]

By the end of the Reagan administration Congress had given up on using the War Powers Resolution. In 1987 President Reagan permitted Kuwait to fly its oil tankers under the U.S. flag, so that the U.S. Navy would protect them from attempts by Iran to blockade its enemy Iraq. That brought the United States into conflict with Iranian patrol boats and other naval forces on several occasions. After these incidents Reagan did not invoke the WPR or issue a report. The response in Congress was to bypass the WPR altogether in an attempt to limit the administration's war-making prerogatives. Senators Robert Byrd and John Warner fashioned a bipartisan resolution to allow congressional participation. It would have required an affirmative vote by Congress to get the U.S. Navy out of the Gulf. Yet the whole point of the WPR had been to force a President to withdraw forces if he could not get an affirmative vote to keep them involved.[76] Congress had conceded the unworkability of the WPR.

Clinton and Presidential Use of the War Powers Resolution

In September of 1994, as it was intensifying pressure on the ruling junta in Haiti, the administration argued that the War Powers Resolution gave the president authority to initiate military actions for a 60-day period without obtaining prior authorization from Congress. Clinton actually sent a military force on airplanes toward the island on the evening of September 18, though he recalled the planes when the junta agreed to a peaceful U.S. occupation for the following morning. Clinton acted on his own prerogative, despite overwhelming opposition in Congress (which was set to vote a prohibition on such action on Monday) and despite public opinion: 78 percent of the public opposed an invasion, and 73 percent thought Clinton had to obtain prior authorization from Congress.[77] Yet once Clinton had sent troops, public opinion switched, with a majority backing the action. Congress, in response, passed resolutions backing the president. The Senate voted 94–5 to commend the president for avoiding bloodshed, expressed support for U.S. forces, and urged a withdrawal "as soon as possible"—covering all bases for supporters and opponents alike.

Clinton's lawyers in the Justice Department made several arguments about the War Powers Resolution. In a letter to several Republican members of Congress, they argued that "the structure of the War Powers Resolution recognized and presupposes the unilateral Presidential authority to deploy armed forces 'into hostilities' or imminent hostilities."[78] They also claimed that because U.S. troops had been invited by the legitimate government in exile, hostilities would not have been a war—conveniently ignoring the fact that the legitimate government was nowhere to be found on the island, and that Haitian troops were under the orders of an illegitimate regime with de facto power to resist.

The Courts and the War Powers Resolution

The federal courts have indicated their doubts about the constitutionality of many provisions of the War Powers Resolution. In *Crockett v. Reagan,* several members of Congress took Reagan to court, claiming that he had violated the WPR by not issuing a report to Congress after sending military advisors to El Salvador. Judge Joyce Green refused to decide the case, claiming it was a "political question" to be decided by the president and Congress, because the court lacked the expertise or information to determine if in fact the training mission was in "imminent involvement" in hostilities.[79] Green also held that even if it were not a political question, a court could not start the clock retroactively from the time a report had been required, but could only start a new 60-day clock. For a federal judge to set the clock retroactively more than sixty days in the past, would deny members of Congress the chance to vote on the president's use of force, because the 60-day deadline for congressional approval would have passed. If the clock were set to provide a new 60-day period, however, Congress would then be able to approve the president's policies. Green's decision ran against the original intent of Congress in passing the WPR. The law originally contemplated that if the president used force, Congress would have to approve within 60 days or the president must withdraw. Yet if a president does not issue a report, according to Green's approach Congress would have to vote affirmatively to require a report or take other action to stop presidential war making. Congressional inaction would permit the president to continue hostilities—the situation that had existed before passage of the WPR.

When President Reagan reflagged Kuwaiti ships and used the navy to protect them against Iran in 1987, a number of members of Congress sought to invoke the WPR by bringing a court case. In *Lowry v. Reagan,* a federal judge held that the conflict seemed to be between members of Congress who wanted to use the WPR and members who did not; until Congress passed a joint resolution invoking the resolution, the Court would not decide any case involving the resolution.[80] During the Persian Gulf War, a sergeant with health problems challenged his deployment to

Saudi Arabia, arguing that he could not be sent without Congressional authorization. In *Ange v. Bush* a federal judge dismissed the complaint, holding that the president's actions as commander in sending soldiers to the Persian Gulf involved a political question, not subject to judicial review.[81] In *Dellums v. Bush,* 53 members of the House and one senator sought a court order in 1990 prohibiting President Bush from using the forces in Desert Shield to defend Saudi Arabia against Iraq without congressional authorization. Although Judge Harold Greene seemed sympathetic with the argument that congressional war powers might be usurped, he argued that the case was not "ripe" for decision. He insisted that the full Congress must vote a resolution prohibiting the use of the armed forces without authorization before he could decide the issues in the case.[82]

In each of these cases, the holding of the court would require Congress to go on record before the case could be decided. Yet the principle behind the War Powers Act was that Congress need not go on record to end presidential war making; the courts clearly were not impressed with a law that forced the president to limit his activities without even so much as a vote on the policy by Congress. To compel court action, members of Congress proposed various remedies: One would authorize any member of Congress to bring an action for a declaratory judgment. The proposed law would prohibit courts from refusing to make a determination on the merits on the grounds of political question, remedial discretion, equitable discretion, or any other finding of nonjusticiability (unless required by Article 3).[83] Another proposal would give members standing whenever the president failed to start the clock. Federal judges could not invoke standing, political question, ripeness, or any other threshold to avoid decision.[84] These proposals have been criticized by those who point out that Article 3 gives the federal courts power to decide what a case or controversy is; Congress cannot regulate this power by statute. Members of Congress might not like the result even if they could get a judicial decision; it might very well be the case that the federal courts would strike down key provisions of the WPR.

"SOFT" PREROGATIVE: PRESIDENT BUSH AND THE PERSIAN GULF WAR

On August 2, 1990, Iraqi dictator Saddam Hussein ordered his army to invade Kuwait and occupy it. After some initial vacillation, President Bush responded on August 4 that "this invasion will not stand."[85] Relying on his prerogatives as commander in chief, and bolstered by British Prime Minister Margaret Thatcher, President Bush on August 8 sent American warplanes and a brigade into Saudi Arabia, announcing the start of Operation Desert Shield to protect Saudi Arabia from potential Iraqi aggression. The president notified Congress on August 9, "consistent with" but not pursuant to the WPR, claiming that the mission was defensive. His letter did not start the 60-day clock because he claimed hostilities were not imminent.[86] By early September, 100,000 troops were in place. Secretary of Defense Richard Cheney observed, "It was an advantage to us that Congress was out of town" when the forces were sent to Saudi Arabia, because "we could spend August doing what needed to be done rather than explaining it to Congress."[87] On October 30 Bush decided to send an additional 400,000 troops. He did not consult with Congress or seek its permission to act, and he kept the decision secret until after the November elections.

Dealing with Allies: The Postmodern Presidency

President Bush operated according to a "postmodern presidency" model in putting together an international coalition. Saudi Arabia and Egypt asked for U.S. military assistance based on Article 51 of the UN Charter. Bush won Arab League condemnation of the invasion and a decision to defend Saudi Arabia with a multilateral force. He also won United Nations resolutions demanding Iraqi withdrawal under Article 41 of the Charter and implementing a trade embargo under Article 42. Under that same article, the Security Council authorized the use of "other means" (i.e., military force) if Iraq did not withdraw by January 15, 1991. The Security Council could "undertake such aerial, naval, or other operations as may be necessary to maintain or restore international peace and security." The Bush administration even got the allied coalition to provide $50 billion to fund military operations (much of the money provided by Japan and West Germany, neither of whom could provide military forces because of provisions in their constitutions).

Dealing with Congress: The Prerogative Presidency

Throughout the fall, Bush tried to bypass congressional war powers. He announced a $20 billion arms deal to Saudi Arabia, bypassing traditional consultation with congressional committees, then backtracked and cut the proposal to $7 billion when Congress objected to supplying the Saudis with tanks more modern than those given to U.S. forces. He announced that the United States would forgive Egypt's $6.7 billion debt, but did not clear it with congressional committees; the administration had to back off until it got congressional approval. He even asked Congress for authority to receive the financial contributions from other nations and divert them directly to the Pentagon, rather than place them in the Treasury and wait for congressional appropriations of funds to the military. Congress rejected this plan outright, and instead set up a "Defense Cooperation Fund" in the Treasury, under the control of the appropriations committees, to accept foreign contributions.

Congress was initially reluctant to move beyond the defense of Saudi Arabia with military forces, preferring to see if the embargo ordered by the UN could convince the Iraqis to withdraw from Kuwait. A resolution passed by the House of Representatives (by a 380–29 bipartisan vote) said:

> The United States shall continue to use diplomatic and other nonmilitary means, to the extent possible, in order to achieve those objectives and policies, while maintaining credible United States and multinational deterrent military force.[88]

Eventually Bush decided to seek congressional authorization for a change in the mission from a purely defensive operation (protection of Saudi Arabia) to an offensive mission (expelling the Iraqis from Kuwait). He did not offer a convincing rationale for possible military action. Many leading media commentators took a highly critical approach to Bush's policy, and his approval ratings on "handling the Persian Gulf conflict" steadily declined from August through late November.[89] Two former chairmen of the Joint Chiefs of Staff testified before a congressional committee that economic sanctions, not an invasion, would be the best course. Polls showed the American public would not want to use force if casualties were high: Support for fighting dropped to 44 percent if "more than 1,000 American troops were lost."[90] Most Americans wanted to give diplomatic negotiations a chance. By mid-December, a 48–45 margin of the public wanted to continue with the embargo rather than start military action if the January 15 deadline went by without an Iraqi withdrawal.[91] Most important, by a 3–1 margin, Americans believed that George Bush should go to Congress to get permission to use forces against Iraq.[92]

Congressional Republicans, reflecting public opinion, insisted on a congressional vote. They wanted to see Democrats go on record opposing the president. Although in October, Bush and his secretaries of state and defense were arguing that the administration did not need congressional authorization, by mid-November, House Republican William Broomfield told the president that failure to consult with Congress "is the main reason support for the policy is eroding."[93] The House Democratic caucus resolved on December 4, 177–37, that the president should seek congressional authorization to begin hostilities unless American lives were in danger.

President Bush surrounded by American soldiers in Saudi Arabia on Thanksgiving Day, 1990. Operation Desert Shield, to protect the Saudis after Iraq invaded Kuwait, was superseded in January, 1991, by Operation Desert Storm, which liberated Kuwait and destroyed much of Iraq's military capability.

Bush eventually bowed to the political pressure. On January 3, 1991, as a new Congress convened, he agreed to seek congressional "support" (doing so formally by letter on January 8), and Secretary of State Baker described a vote as "helpful." Even so, when Bush was asked by reporters the following week if he needed the vote, he responded, "I don't think I need it . . . I feel that I have the authority to fully implement the United Nations resolutions."[94]

Congress passed a joint resolution titled "Authorization for Use of Military Force against Iraq," on January 13, 1991. It authorized force pursuant to United Nations Resolution 678. The president could make a determination that force was necessary and communicate that determination to the speaker of the House and the president pro tempore of the Senate. Once he began using the armed forces, he would report to Congress every sixty days.

To win passage of the resolution the White House put together a bipartisan coalition, led by Republican House leader Robert Michel and Democrat Stephen Solarz, a prominent member of the House Foreign Affairs Committee with vast expertise in dealing with issues involving the Middle East. Bush held almost all Republicans, and with the help of Solarz, got more than half the southern Democrats, some Democratic committee leaders, and half the Jewish Democrats (concerned with ending the Iraqi threat to use nuclear weapons against Israel). The vote was 250 to 183 in the House. In the Senate Bush also won, 52–47, after targeting six southern Democrats.

Passage of the Michel-Solarz Resolution was not the end of the story, however. The House also passed the Durbin-Bennett Resolution, which stated that:

> The Congress finds that the Constitution of the United States vests all power to declare war in the Congress of the United States. Any offensive action taken against Iraq must be explicitly approved by the Congress of the United States before such action may be initiated.[95]

The vote on this resolution was 260 Democrats in favor, along with 41 Republicans and 1 independent, against 126 Republicans and 5 Democrats opposed.

Although Bush welcomed passage of the authorization to use force, he reaffirmed his own constitutional prerogatives. In a statement released on signing the bill, he said:

> My signing this resolution does not constitute any change in the long-standing positions of the executive branch on either the president's constitutional authority to use the armed forces to defend vital U.S. interests, or the constitutionality of the War Powers Resolution.[96]

Bush's actions in the Persian Gulf crisis were a mixture of the modern presidency (taking responsibility for solving an international crisis), the postmodern presidency (forging an international coalition to do so and relying on its financial resources), and the "soft" prerogative presidency (bypassing Congress in making the key decisions but utilizing congressional authorization for strategic political and diplomatic purposes). Bush made decisions unilaterally without congressional input throughout the crisis: the decision to send forces to the Saudis, the decision to build up forces (not announced until after the elections), the decision to attack Iraqi forces in Kuwait.[97]

The resolution of the conflicts between Congress and the president have demonstrated the utility of softening claims to prerogative powers without actually giving them up. When the president considered invading Haiti in August, 1994, the Senate passed a nonbinding resolution expressing its sense that the Constitution required congressional approval before the president used military force. When asked his position at a news conference on August 3, President Clinton responded as Reagan and Bush had: "I would welcome the support of the Congress and I hope that I will have that." But he added, "like my predecessors in both parties, I have not agreed that I was constitutionally mandated to get it."[98] Ultimately Clinton ordered the use of force in Haiti without asking Congress, and in fact did so just one day before Congress was to vote on a new set of resolutions expressing its disapproval.

POSTMODERN PRESIDENTIAL USE OF THE ARMED FORCES

Some political scientists have argued that the "postmodern" presidency can no longer project American force to solve international problems in the manner of the modern presidents during the Cold War.[99] Their reasoning is that the United States has neither the wallet (in an era of huge budget deficits and cutbacks in domestic programs) nor the will (in a post–Cold War era) for global interventionism. Interventions are more costly than ever, because the U.S. military machine is costly to maintain, transport, and install in other nations. Yet the U.S. public is uninterested in tax increases (or inflationary impacts) that would result if the nation paid for its interventionist policies. Interventions are also costly in human lives: Firepower on all sides is now so great that any use of military force may involve enormous casualties, not only to the combatants, but also to civilians. The U.S. public has no toleration for casualties, prisoners of war, or for loss of civilian life.

Other evidence for a swing away from interventionism is the attitude of the Pentagon. Secretary of Defense Caspar Weinberger formulated the "Weinberger doctrine" in the 1980s, to which most of the military subscribes: The United States should not use military force to "signal" other nations diplomatically, but should reserve force for crises in which the military is the only means that can resolve it; the use of force should be preceded by consultation and political support in Congress; it should be overwhelming force so that we do not get involved in drawn out hostilities; force should only be used to support national interests of the United States, interests that are understandable to, and supported by, the American people. In practice, the Weinberger doctrine would act as a constraint on presidents, who would find fewer occasions to use the military, and would find the JCS and Pentagon reluctant to back a presidential policy that diverged from these principles.

To some extent the Weinberger doctrine has become a part of U.S. strategy. The military has been reduced in size, with more emphasis put on the Ready Reserve rather than active duty units, even for foreign peacekeeping missions. Forces have been withdrawn from Europe and many other areas of the world, and the United States maintains fewer bases in foreign nations. Military doctrines call for rapid interventions and rapid execution, rather than drawn-out involvements. Yet postmodern presidency theorists could not have predicted U.S. intervention in the

Persian Gulf, nor U.S. involvement in Somalia. It is not clear whether President Bush acted more as a modern or as a postmodern president in the Gulf War. He asserted the traditional U.S. leadership of an allied coalition (modern presidency) but got coalition members to fund the military effort (postmodern presidency). He needed, and won, the cooperation of the Soviet Union (postmodern). He eventually agreed to a congressional authorization for hostilities (postmodern) but reserved the right to act unilaterally (modern).

Was Clinton acting as a postmodern president in Somalia and Haiti? It depends on our definition. If the modern president emphasizes U.S. power against another superpower (i.e., the Cold War), and the postmodern president emphasizes international cooperation, then to some extent the Somalia and Haitian operations were postmodern events. There was no compelling U.S. national interest in Somalia, but the sight of starving and tortured people influenced U.S. public opinion and the decision that Presidents Bush and Clinton made to intervene. Clinton's cooperation with UN peacekeeping efforts in Somalia was intended to be the start of a more ambitious U.S. role in international humanitarian and peacekeeping operations. If Somalia was a postmodern presidential operation, its failure—and the passage of congressional legislation mandating a withdrawal of U.S. forces—indicates that the postmodern presidency, with its emphasis on international cooperation, may be a presidency whose time has come—and gone.

Throughout the twentieth century, presidents have been burdened with the twin responsibilities of deterring and prosecuting major wars and minor military operations. They have carried the nuclear codes ("the football") with them, and had the power to destroy the world with their commands. With the end of the Cold War, the rationale for such awesome power is gone, yet the unilateral power to make decisions about peace or war remain. Presidents Bush and Clinton did not demobilize the military nor cease using it after the Cold War ended. Both presidents were engaged in several military operations and constantly had to consider using force in many others. Neither the United Nations nor multilateral peacekeeping efforts proved to be an effective substitute for unilateral use of American force, yet presidents at the end of the twentieth century had yet to find a completely viable constitutional balance within the U.S. political system when they used force, nor had they found fully viable policies that would promote their authority when they made the ultimate decision.

FURTHER READING

Books

Barry Blechman and Stephen Kaplan, eds., *Force without War: U.S. Armed Forces as a Political Instrument,* Washington, DC: Brookings Institution, 1978.

John P. Burke and Fred Greenstein, *How Presidents Test Reality: Decisions on Vietnam, 1954 & 1965,* New York: Russell Sage Foundation, 1989.

Joseph Dawson, ed., *Commanders in Chief,* Lawrence, KS: University Press of Kansas, 1993.

John Hart Ely, *War and Responsibility: Constitutional Lessons of Vietnam and Its Aftermath,* Princeton, NJ: Princeton University Press, 1993.

Louis Fisher, *Presidential War Power,* Lawrence, KS: University Press of Kansas, 1995.

John Norton Moore, *Crisis in the Gulf: Enforcing the Rule of Law,* Dobbs Ferry, NY: Oceana, 1992.

James Pfiffner, *The Presidency and the Crisis in the Gulf,* Westport, CT: Praeger, 1993

Clinton Rossiter and Richard Longaker, *The Supreme Court and the Commander in Chief,* Ithaca, NY: Cornell University Press, 1976.

Arthur Schlesinger, *The Imperial Presidency,* Boston: Houghton Mifflin, 1973.

Gary M. Stern and Morton H. Halperin, eds., *The U.S. Constitution and the Power to Go to War,* Westport, CT: Greenwood Press, 1993.

Francis Wormuth and Arthur Firmage, *To Chain the Dog of War,* 2nd ed., Urbana, IL: University of Illinois Press, 1989.

Documentary Sources

The War Power after 200 Years: Congress and the President at a Constitutional Impasse, Hearings before the Special Subcommittee on War Powers, Committee on Foreign Relations, U.S. Senate, 100th Cong., 2nd sess., 1988.

The Crisis in the Persian Gulf Region: U.S. Policy Options and Implications, Hearings before the Senate Committee on the Armed Services, 101st Cong., 2nd sess., 1990.

The Constitutional Roles of Congress and the President in Declaring and Waging War, Hearings before the Committee on the Judiciary, U.S. Senate, 102nd Cong., 1st sess., 1991.

NOTES

1. United Nations Security Council Resolution 794.

2. *New York Times,* October 18, 1993, p. A-18.

3. United States Senate, Joint Resolution 45, 1993.

4. Charles Lofgren, "War-Making under the Constitution: The Original Understanding," *Yale Law Journal,* Vol. 81, no. 2, December, 1971, pp. 672–702; W. Taylor Reveley III, "Constitutional Allocation of the War Powers between the President and Congress, 1787–1788," *Virginia Journal of International Affairs,* Vol. 15, no.1, Fall, 1974, pp. 73–147; David Gray Adler, "The Constitution and Presidential Warmaking: The Enduring Debate," Political Science Quarterly, Vol. 103, no. 1, Spring, 1988, pp. 1–36.

5. Max Farrand, *The Records of the Federal Convention of 1787,* New Haven, CT: Yale University Press, 1937, Vol. 2, p. 318.

6. Ibid., pp. 318–319.

7. Ibid., p. 319.

8. Alexander Hamilton, *The Federalist Papers,* no. 69.

9. 1 Stat. 96, sec. 5 (1789) and 1 Stat. 121, sec. 16 (1790), authorizing defensive actions to protect the frontiers; 1 Stat. 264, sec. 1 (1792), permitting the president to call out state militia to enforce laws if notified by an associate justice of the Supreme Court or federal district judges that federal laws had been opposed "by combinations too powerful to be suppressed by the ordinary course of judicial proceedings, or by the powers vested in the marshals by this act."

10. Gaillard Hunt, ed., *The Writings of James Madison,* Vol. 6, New York: Putnam, 1906, p. 312.

11. *U.S. v. Smith,* 27 F. Cas. 1192, C. C. D. N. Y. 1806.

12. *New York Times,* December 18, 1993, p. A-8.

13. *Fleming v. Page,* 50 U.S. 602, 1850, p. 614.

14. P.L. 99–433, October 1, 1986.

15. Amos Jordan and William Taylor, *National Security Policy,* Baltimore, MD: Johns Hopkins University Press, 1981, pp. 97–98.

16. Sec. 164(b)(2).

17. Paul Lashmer, "Stranger Than 'Strangelove,'" *Washington Post National Weekly Edition,* July 11–17, 1994, p. 24.

18. A listing of approximately 200 incidents through 1977 is contained in Barry M. Blechman and Steven S. Kaplan, *Force without War,* Washington, DC: Brookings Institution, 1978; see also Louis Fisher, "Historical Survey of the War Powers and the Use of Force," in Gary M. Stern and Morton H. Halperin, eds., *The U.S. Constitution and the Power to Go to War,* Westport, CT: Greenwood Press, 1993, pp. 11–27.

19. 78 Stat. 384, August 10, 1964.

20. "The Gulf of Tonkin: The 1964 Incidents," *Hearings before the Senate Committee on Foreign Relations,* 90th Cong., 2nd sess., February 20, 1968.

21. Jeffrey Helsing, *Guns and Butter: Minimizing the Military Escalation in Vietnam,* Ph.D. dissertation, Columbia University Department of Political Science, New York, 1991.

22. James Richardson, *Messages and Papers of the Presidents,* Washington, DC: Bureau of Arts and Literature, 1900, Vol. 14, p. 6923.

23. Michael J. Glennon, "United States Mutual Security Treaties: The Commitment Myth," *Columbia University Journal of Transnational Law,* Vol. 24, no. 2, April, 1986, p. 509.

24. Michael J. Glennon, "The Constitution and Chapter VII of the United Nations Charter," *American Journal of International Law,* Vol. 85, no. 1, January, 1991. pp. 74–88.

25. Presidential News Conference, August 3, 1994.

26. *United Nations Participation Act,* 22 U.S. C., 1945, secs. 287a,d.

27. Jane Stromseth, "Rethinking War Powers: Congress, the President and the United Nations," *Georgetown Law Journal,* Vol. 81, no. 3, March, 1993, p 604.

28. Testimony by Secretary of State Dean Acheson, "Participation by the United States in the United Nations Organization," *Hearings before the House Committee on Foreign Affairs,* 79th Cong., 1st sess., Washington, DC: Government Printing Office, 1945), pp. 22–26.

29. *Department of State Bulletin,* Vol. 23, no. 578, July 31, 1950, pp. 173–179.

30. Truman had gone back on his own word to Congress, cabled from the Potsdam Conference, that U.S. troop commitments to the UN would have to be approved by the legislature. See Edwin Borchard, "The Charter and the Constitution," *American Journal of International Law,* Vol. 39, 1945, pp. 767–768.

31. *Congressional Record,* Vol. 96, July 5, 1950, p. 9648.

32. Joseph Treaster, "U.S. Jets Fly Dry Runs on Iraq Targets to Show 'We're Here,'" *New York Times,* October 18, 1994, p. A-17.

33. *Public Papers of the Presidents,* Washington, DC: Government Printing Office, 1962), p. 674.

34. J. William Fulbright, "American Foreign Policy in the 20th Century under an 18th Century Constitution," *Cornell Law Quarterly,* Vol. 47, no. 1, Fall, 1961, pp. 1–13; see also Barry M. Goldwater, "The President's Constitutional Primacy in Foreign Relations and National Defense," *Virginia Journal of International Law,* Vol. 13, no. 4, Summer, 1973, pp. 463–484.

35. Daniel Calingaert, "Nuclear Weapons and the Korean War," *The Journal of Strategic Studies,* Vol. 11, no. 2, June 1988, pp. 171–202.

36. H. W. Branda, "Testing Massive Retaliation: Credibility and Crisis Management in the Taiwan Strait," *International Security,* Vol. 12, no. 1, Spring, 1988, pp. 124–151; Gordon W. Chang, "To the Nuclear Brink: Eisenhower, Dulles, and the Quemoy-Matsu Crisis," *International Security,* Vol. 12, no. 1, Spring, 1988, pp. 96–123.

37. Arthur S. Miller and H. Bart Cox, "Congress, the Constitution and First Use of Nuclear Weapons," *Review of Politics,* Vol. 48, no. 3, Summer 1986, pp. 424–455; William L. Banks, "First Use of Nuclear Weapons: the Constitutional Role of a Congressional Leader-

ship Committee," *Journal of Legislation,* Vol. 13, no. 1, January, 1986, pp. 1–21; Stephen L. Carter, "The Constitution and the Prevention of Nuclear Holocaust: A Reaction to Professor Banks," *Journal of Legislation,* Vol. 13, no. 2, April, 1986, pp. 206–215.

38. Jeremy Stone, "Presidential First Use Is Unlawful," *Foreign Policy,* No. 56, Fall, 1984, pp. 94–112; Marc Trachtenberg, "The Question of No First Use," *Orbis,* Vol. 29, no. 4, Winter, 1986, pp. 753–769.

39. In *Bas v. Tingy,* 4 U.S. 37, 1800, the Supreme Court upheld the legality of an undeclared naval war with France based on prior and concurrent congressional authorizations and appropriations.

40. 5 U.S. Stat. 355, March 3, 1839.

41. 69 U.S. Stat. 7, 1955; P.L. 85–7, 1958.

42. *Little v. Bareme,* 6 U.S. 169, 1804.

43. *U.S. v. Smith,* 27 Fed. Cas. 1192, C. C. N. Y. 1806.

44. Ibid., p. 1230.

45. 59 U.S. Stat. 885, September 16, 1940.

46. P. L. 91–171, December 29, 1969.

47. P. L. 91–652, January 5, 1971.

48. 87 Stat. 130, 1973.

49. 100 U.S. Stat. 3341–307, sec. 216(a), 1986; 100 U.S. Stat. 1783–298, sec. 203(e), 1986.

50. *Defense Department Appropriations Act of 1994,* sec. 8147, 1994.

51. 85 U.S. Stat. 423, 1971.

52. 85 U.S. Stat. 430; Nixon's response in *Weekly Compilation of Presidential Documents,* Vol. 7, November 22, 1971, p. 1531.

53. *Weekly Compilation of Presidential Documents,* Vol. 29, 1993, p. 2097.

54. P. L. 93–148; 87 U.S. Stat. 555; 50 U.S.C., sec. 1541–48.

55. P. L. 93–148, sec. 2(a).

56. Sec. 2(c).

57. *Conference Report,* no. 93–547, October 4, 1973, pp. 13–14.

58. John Hart Ely, "Suppose Congress Wanted a War Powers Act That Worked?" *Columbia Law Review,* Vol. 88, no. 5, November, 1988, pp. 1379–1431.

59. "U.S. Plan to Seize Haitian Ruler Is Denied," Associated Press, September 20, 1994.

60. P. L. 93–148, sec. 5(B).

61. Michael Glennon, *Constitutional Diplomacy,* Princeton, NJ: Princeton University Press, 1990, pp. 91–92.

62. Ellen C. Collier, "War Powers Resolution: Presidential Compliance," Congressional Research Service Issues Brief IB81050, Washington, DC: Congressional Research Service, 1991.

63. P. L. 93–148, sec. 5(C).

64. State Department Authorization of 1983, S. 1324.

65. "Veto Message to Congress," *Public Papers of the President,* Richard M. Nixon, Washington, DC: Government Printing Office, 1994, vol. 5, pp. 893–895.

66. Ibid., p. 894.

67. Ibid., pp. 893–895

68. For a presidential critique, see Gerald Ford, "The War Powers Resolution: Striking a Balance between the Executive and Legislative Branches," reprinted in "War Powers Resolution," *Hearings before the Committee on Foreign Relations,* U.S. Senate, 95th Cong., 1977, pp. 325–331 (hereafter "War Powers Resolution").

69. *"War Powers: A Test of Compliance," Hearings before the House Committee on International Relations,* 94th Cong., 1st sess., 1975, p. 91.

70. Jordan J. Paust, "The Seizure and Recovery of the Mayaguez," *Yale Law Journal,* Vol. 85, no. 4, April, 1976, pp. 774–806; "Recapture of the S. S. Mayaguez: Failure of the Consultation Clause of the War Powers Resolution," *New York University Journal of International Law and Politics,* Vol. 8, no. 1, Winter, 1976, pp. 457–478.

71. *"War Powers Resolution,"* p. 200.

72. *"War Powers Resolution,"* p. 207.

73. Michael Rubner, "The Reagan Administration, the 1973 War Powers Resolution and the Invasion of Grenada," *Political Science Quarterly,* Vol. 100, no. 4, Winter, 1985/6, pp. 627–647.

74. House Joint Resolution 159, October 11, 1983.

75. Signing statement, Beirut Resolution, *New York Times,* October 13, 1983, p. A-12.

76. Richard M. Pious, "Presidential War Powers, the War Powers Resolution, and the Persian Gulf," in *The Constitution and the American Presidency,* Martin L. Fausold and Alan Shank, eds., Albany, NY: State University of New York Press, 1991, pp. 195–210.

77. ABC News poll, reprinted in *New York Times,* September 13, 1994, p. A-12.

78. Letter from Walter Dellinger, assistant attorney general, Office of Legal Counsel, to Senator Robert Dole, reprinted in part in *New York Times,* September 29, 1994, p. 30.

79. *Crockett v. Reagan,* 558 F. Supp. 893, 1982; affirmed per curium, 720 F. 2nd 1355e D.C. Cir., 1983; cert. denied, 467 U.S. 1251, 1984.

80. *Lowry v. Reagan,* 676 F. Supp. 333, D. D.C. 1987.

81. *Ange v. Bush,* 752 F. Supp. 509, D. D.C. 1990.

82. *Dellums v. Bush,* 752 F. Supp. 1141, D. D.C. 1990.

83. Joseph R. Biden and John B. Ritch. III, "The War Power at a Constitutional Impasse: A 'Joint Decision' Solution," *Georgetown Law Review,* Vol. 77, 1988, pp. 409–410

84. John Hart Ely, *War and Responsibility,* Princeton, NJ: Princeton University Press, 1993, pp. 60–63.

85. *New York Times,* August 5, 1990, p. A-1

86. Charles Tiefer, *The Semi-Sovereign President,* Boulder, CO: Westview Press, 1994, p. 125.

87. *Congressional Quarterly Weekly Reports,* October 13, 1990, p. 3441.

88. *House Joint Res.* 658, 1990.

89. Brigitte Lebens Nacos, "Presidential Leadership during the Persian Gulf Conflict," *Presidential Studies Quarterly,* Vol. 24, no. 3, Summer, 1994, pp. 543–562.

90. *Washington Post National Weekly Edition,* January 14–20, 1991.

91. *New York Times* Poll, December 9–11, 1990. A *Washington Post* survey, January 6, 1991, showed only 29 percent favored starting hostilities after the deadline; 43 percent wanted to wait another month, and 14 percent wanted to wait longer.

92. *Washington Post/ABC News* Poll, *Washington Post National Weekly Edition,* December 10–16, 1990, p. 37.

93. *Congressional Quarterly Weekly Reports,* November 17, 1990, p. 3880.

94. *Weekly Compilation of Presidential Documents,* Vol. 27, 1981, p. 25; Matthew Berger, "Implementing a United Nations Security Council Resolution: The President's Power to Use Force without the Authorization of Congress," *Hasting International and Comparative Law Journal,* Vol. 15, no. 1, 1991, pp. 83–109; Thomas Franck and Faiza Patel, "UN Police Action in Lieu of War: 'The Old Order Changeth,' " *American Journal of International Law,* Vol. 85, no. 1, January, 1991, pp. 63–73.

95. H. Con. Res. 32, 102nd Cong., 1st sess., January 12, 1991.

96. *The Public Papers of the Presidents,* Vol. 14, January 14, 1991.

97. Michael J. Glennon, "The Gulf War and the Constitution" *Foreign Affairs,* Vol. 70, no. 2, Spring, 1991, pp. 84–101.

98. *Presidential News Conference,* August 3, 1994.

99. See especially Richard Rose, *The Postmodern President,* 2nd ed., Chatham, NJ: Chatham House, 1991.

CHAPTER 16

Reinventing the Presidency

Some men look at constitutions with sanctimonious reverence and deem them like the ark of the covenant, too sacred to be touched. They ascribe to the men of the preceding age a wisdom more than human, and suppose what they did to be beyond amendment. . . . Institutions must advance also, and keep pace with the times.

—Thomas Jefferson

INTRODUCTORY CASE: WOODROW WILSON AND REFORM OF THE PRESIDENCY

When Woodrow Wilson was a student at Princeton University he wrote his senior thesis on the reasons why our national government should change from a system of separated of powers to cabinet government. Wilson had been influenced by the British constitutional historian Walter Bagehot, whose writings had contrasted the highly disciplined and principled behavior of British politicians in Parliament with the corrupt spoilsmen in the American Congress and executive branch. So many high-level officials had resigned because of scandals during Ulysses S. Grant's recent administration that the term *Grantism* had been coined to describe systematic looting of the treasury. While Wilson was writing his thesis, President Rutherford B. Hayes was fighting against the endemic corruption in government departments fostered by party machine politicians.

Wilson was repelled by the corruption in Washington, and agreed with Bagehot's observation that "cabinet government educates the nation; the presidential . . . may corrupt it."[1] In his thesis he argued that cabinet government was more responsive, efficient, honest, and accountable to the people. It was also more flexible, because the parliament could replace one prime minister with another at a moment's notice. Could such a system be adopted in the United States? In an article titled "Cabinet Government in the United States," published two years after graduating from college, Wilson proposed that the president select members of his cabinet from Congress.[2] By constitutional amendment these secretaries would be permitted to retain their seats in Congress. The cabinet would resign, to be replaced by different members of Congress, if a majority of the legislators voted against its program. Wilson believed that by instituting a form of cabinet government, principled parties would emerge to replace those fueled by graft and patronage. Four years later, as a graduate student completing his doctoral thesis in 1884 at the Johns Hopkins University, Wilson returned to his theme, proposing to amend the separation clause of the Constitution (Article 1, section 6), by adding these four underlined words to the existing language: "No person holding any <u>other than a cabinet</u> office under the United States shall be a Member of either House during his continuance in office," a change that would permit members of Congress to serve as department secretaries.

Wilson became a distinguished political scientist at Princeton, then governor of New Jersey, and finally president of the United States. By 1908, in his book *Constitutional Government in the United States,* Wilson recognized that a strong president facing off against an equally powerful Congress was a fixture of American politics, and cabinet government could not be instituted.[3] By 1912, newly elected President Wilson paid no heed to outgoing President William Howard Taft's recommendation, in a parting message to Congress, that cabinet secretaries sit in Congress: *Professor* Wilson had been an avid theorist of reforms, but *President* Wilson worked within the existing constitutional system.

Yet Wilson did pioneer many innovations. He addressed Congress in person, held news conferences, introduced a comprehensive legislative program, and reformed the budget process to advance presidential control. His career illustrates how the presidency actually adapts to new circumstances: through our "unwritten" constitution of custom and precedent, along with statutes passed by Congress that establish new frameworks of presidential–congressional relations.

Political scientists, historians, and constitutional lawyers have many ideas about reinventing the presidency: instituting cabinet government; eliminating the possibility of divided party control of the White House and Congress; instituting new forms of collaborative government in decision making to give Congress a greater role; and, if all else fails, getting rid of a "failed presidency" through a vote of no-confidence. Our study of the presidency would be incomplete without assessing these proposals.

CABINET GOVERNMENT

As early as 1809, the first major study of the presidency by Augustus Woodward argued for its transformation into cabinet government.[4] In 1840 Abel Upshur (soon to be named secretary of war), wrote a constitutional law treatise that argued that "the most defective part of the Federal Constitution, beyond all question, is that which relates to the executive department."[5] He too was impressed with cabinet government. Shortly after the end of the Civil War, New York attorney Henry C. Lockwood called for the abolition of the presidency.[6] He proposed that Congress appoint officers to an Executive Council, to be chaired by the secretary of state. Its members would sit in Congress, initiate legislation, and participate in debates. Members could be removed by Congress if they lost the confidence of the majority. The Senate, which did not fit into this scheme, would be abolished. "In its essential properties," Lockwood admitted, "it would be the same as the English cabinet system."[7]

The Pros and Cons

Why have reformers tried to institute parliamentary government when it is so alien to American institutions such as separation of powers and checks and balances? They believe that the framers' concern about abuses of power and excesses of the executive are misplaced, and that conflicts between president and Congress create a government that lacks energy, accountability, or principles. Like Alexander Hamilton, they want more efficient and energetic government, and they think they can get it with a Congress controlled by the president and cabinet. The president could institute prerogative government confident that Congress would back him up. The government would be unified, with the executive and Congress supporting the same principles and implementing the same program. Congressional debates would be well attended, and speeches would be reported by the media, forming the basis for fundamental national debates on the issues. Voters, educated by these debates, could hold such a government fully accountable for its failures, or reward it for its successes.

Cabinet government has many disadvantages, however. Because the cabinet controls both the executive and legislature, it can implement programs according to party principles—but if it loses the election, the opposition coalition takes its turn at the helm. The resulting fluctuations in public policy are often greater than in a presidential system.[8] It is an open question whether cycles of nationalization and denationalization of industry, which occur in the United Kingdom, France, Italy, and Greece, are a more efficient approach to governance for the long term than the more incremental regulatory changes that occur in the United States.[9] Since American civil service reforms and ethics legislation, there is little evidence that American corruption is greater than the parliamentary variety in nations such as Britain, Italy, and Japan, for example, or that the White House is a major source of corruption. Nor is there any evidence that cabinet government provides better decisions than presidential government: If it were so, Great Britain, the model for cabinet government usually cited, would have a much better record in its economic performance and diplomacy over the past half-century.

Cabinet government has no checks and balances to hold executives accountable for abuses of power or corruption and conflicts of interest. The legislature engages in little administrative oversight or policy innovations. Courts do not have the power of judicial review of the constitutionality of executive action. In cabinet government scandals such as Watergate and Iran–contra are often swept under the rug. When a scandal is uncovered, the entire mechanism of government remains paralyzed until the governing party changes the prime minister or is defeated in the next elections. When an American president is involved in charges of abuse of power, Congress can act autonomously and in crises can work with the secretaries of defense and state, or with the president's chief of staff, to make important decisions and keep the national government functioning, even when the White House is paralyzed.

Cabinet government works well when one party has a majority in the legislature, but in many nations with multiparty systems, cabinet government means coalition government: several parties have seats in the cabinet. At that point, any assumed advantages of cabinet government over our presidential system disappear: Multiparty cabinets are usually fractious, inconsistent, and politically weak. The parties within them are not accountable for governmental policies, because policy usually involves unprincipled compromises designed to keep the coalition afloat. The government is in constant turmoil, and its energy is enervated by the constant effort to placate shaky coalition partners, and maintain a parliamentary majority. The government may hesitate to move against corruption in parties that form part of the majority coalition, lest it bring down the governing coalition.

British commentators have been dissatisfied with the performance of parliamentary government. They have turned to American innovations, and have attempted to give their Parliament more autonomy from the cabinet. It has now been equipped with staff members, and has committees that can investigate and conduct legislative oversight of the ministries of government. The tendencies toward establishing at least a limited separation of powers and checks-and-balances system in British government and in many other parliamentary systems have increased.

SEMIPRESIDENTIAL GOVERNMENT

If full-fledged cabinet government is unsuitable for the United States, are there ways in which the best attributes of cabinet government might be imported into our system? Many reformers, like Woodrow Wilson, wanted to institute *semipresidential* government, combining elements of a presidential and parliamentary system. Executive power would be exercised by department secretaries, collectively known as the cabinet, who would serve in the legislature and command its confidence. The members of the cabinet would lead their party in legislative debates and defend their programs against the opposition party. The cabinet would "fall" and would resign from office if it lost a formal "vote of confidence" or if it could not get its program passed, or if it were defeated by the opposition party in elections and lost its majority position in the legislature to another party or coalition of parties.[10] The president would retain constitutional and statutory powers, would be the strongest influence in foreign affairs, and would continue to serve as commander in chief.

Many nations have instituted semipresidential systems, in which a president is head of state and handles national security matters, while a cabinet and prime minister responsible to parliament are responsible for domestic programs. In Western Europe, France has been governed under such a system since 1960 when the Fifth Republic was instituted, and it is found in the former French colonies in Africa. In Eastern Europe and the Commonwealth of Independent States (the former Soviet Union), semipresidential government modeled after the French system has taken root as well.[11]

A Legislative Role for Cabinet Secretaries

To establish such a system in the United States, it would be necessary to provide a close link between cabinet and Congress. One idea is to allow department secretaries the right to appear on the floor of Congress, lead the debates on measures they have proposed for congressional consideration, and manage the bills as they move through the legislative process. It is doubtful that congressional leaders, or even the White House legislative liaison office, would be in favor of such a reform, though many department secretaries would favor it. A related idea is to borrow the British custom of a question period: At set times, cabinet secretaries could appear before Congress and answer questions posed by the opposition party, providing for a general debate on government policy. The question period would give presidents an incentive to appoint telegenic and fluent secretaries, because the debates would not only be televised but would also become a staple of evening news broadcasts and newspaper stories.

The question period was first proposed in the 1870s, as a way to end patronage abuses and corruption in the departments, by Gamaliel Bradford, a retired investment banker.[12] Nothing has come of it because neither the White House nor Congress has ever seen much point to it. Presidents prefer to control national agenda politics directly, through the White House, and have no incentive to bolster the public standing of their cabinet secretaries. Members of Congress, most of whom specialize in particular areas, prefer to question cabinet secretaries in committee rooms during hearings, and would not be happy to "share" their secretaries with noncommittee members during the question period. In periods of split government, the party controlling Congress might wish for a question period, but the president would have even less incentive to agree.

By 1878 Bradford himself abandoned the idea in his address to the annual meeting of the American Social Science Association that year. Instead, he suggested that cabinet secretaries be seated in Congress and become the spokespersons for the administration. Sitting in the audience and taking notes was George H. Pendleton, an Ohio railroad president and former House member who had already been active in efforts for parliamentary reform. The following year, newly seated Republican Senator Pendleton introduced a measure resolving that "the principal officers of each of the Executive Departments may occupy seats on the floor of the Senate and House of Representatives."[13] Pendleton chaired a Select Committee of Ten to study the measure and report to the Senate. In 1881 his committee reported such a proposal to the Senate, stating that cabinet secretaries "are the creatures of the laws of Congress, exercising only such duties as the laws prescribe." Pendleton was attempting to create a two-tiered government: the president would serve as chief of state with diplomatic and war powers; a unitary parliamentary system would evolve for routine domestic policy making. Pendleton's reforms went nowhere in the Senate.

Dolefully summing up his experience as a constitutional reformer, Bradford concluded that his proposals "had never received the slightest attention from either House of Congress, or from the executive."[14] Because cabinet secretaries already testified at committee hearings, legislative leaders saw no reason to seat them in Congress, particularly if it meant ceding leadership to the secretaries during debates and parliamentary maneuvers. Neither did secretaries want to spend much of their time on Capitol Hill at floor debates; they already complained that they spent too much time there testifying before committees and subcommittees. The weight of opinion at the time lay with Professor A. Lawrence Lowell of Harvard University, who argued that "a responsible ministry cannot be grafted onto our institutions without entirely changing their nature, and destroying those features of our government which we have been in the habit of contemplating with the greatest pride."[15]

The White House also saw no advantage in Pendleton's proposals. They were endorsed by President Taft in his last message to Congress simply to put Wilson on the spot. Later President Harding claimed he favored it but took no action to advance it. When Senator Estes Kefauver advanced the idea in 1943, Franklin Roosevelt opposed it as a favor to his speaker of the House.[16] It might provide popular members of the cabinet an independent power base in Congress. It could eventually lead to a return to the "conciliar" government of the early 1800s if secretaries gained a "veto" over White House initiatives by virtue of their strength in Congress and their popularity with the people. Why would presidents want to establish a system of governance that allowed subordinates to steal their thunder and upstage them?

A Joint Legislative–Executive Cabinet

A more comprehensive approach to semipresidential government would be to permit members of Congress to sit with the cabinet or even become part of it. Political scientist Edward Corwin called for an advisory joint cabinet in 1940 consisting of department secretaries and chairs of standing legislative committees. In 1945 Secretary of the Air Force Thomas Finletter and Senator Alexander Wiley proposed a joint "legislative–executive cabinet" or a set of functional policy councils consisting of nine department secretaries working along with nine committee leaders, as a way to increase the efficiency of the American government.[17] William Yandell Elliott of Harvard later proposed creating six "joint councils," each one with a different functional area of responsibility. In 1946 Senator Robert M. LaFollette introduced a comprehensive act to reorganize Congress. Among other provisions, LaFollette proposed that the majority party committees of the two chambers meet formally with the cabinet, creating a joint legislative–executive council. To win passage of his proposals for congressional reorganization, however, he and the other members of the Joint Committee on the Organization of Congress had to jettison the idea.

Opponents have argued that such a system would require a constitutional amendment, but that is incorrect. There is no constitutional prohibition against legislators participating in cabinet meetings, provided that they do not hold formal offices as secretaries of departments, or exercise the duties of "officers of the United States." Membership in the cabinet is not itself an office of trust or profit, and an invitation to join the cabinet does not make anyone an "officer of the United States," subject to restrictions on holding legislative office. If presidents wish, they can assign the cabinet's function of providing advice and political strategy to congressional party leaders, meet with such leaders whenever convenient, and refer to *them* as the cabinet.

Presidents need some incentive to include legislators in their cabinet sessions, and as yet they have found none. When the White House and both chambers of Congress are controlled by one party, there is no need for a formal arrangement, be-

President Clinton meets with incoming Senate Majority Leader Bob Dole and incoming Speaker of the House Newt Gingrich in December, 1994. They pledged to work together constructively whenever possible. For only the third time in the twentieth century (the others involved Wilson and Truman), a Democratic president would face a Republican Congress.

cause congressional party leaders routinely meet with the president and top White House aides, working with them and with members of the cabinet to consider legislative strategy and party politics. They do not call it cabinet government—they call it lunch. In times of split-party government, when one or both chambers of Congress are controlled by the opposition party, it is doubtful that a president would want to bring opposition party leaders into the inner councils of his government. Reformers claim that cabinet government sharpens the partisan debate and educates the electorate: They cannot simultaneously propose a "legislative–executive cabinet" that includes members of the opposition party and maintain that claim.

If the president includes leaders of the opposition party in cabinet meetings, he or she can no longer turn to the cabinet for political advice, which after all is its main function. And why would the opposition leaders wish to accept a presidential invitation to join the cabinet? They might be coopted by the president, and after participating in cabinet deliberations they would lose the opportunity to criticize the White House. If they maintained their critical stance, the president might "invite them out" and accuse them of obstructionism. Either way, it is hard to see what is in it for the opposition party.

The Reuss Amendment

In the aftermath of the Watergate crisis, Representative Henry Reuss (Democrat from Wisconsin) proposed a constitutional amendment providing that "Congress shall have the power by law to designate offices in the Executive Branch, not to exceed fifty in number, to which members of the Senate and the House of Representatives would be eligible for nomination and appointment . . . without being required to vacate their offices in the Senate or House of Representatives."[18] This proposal to end the separation of powers raises many questions. To which branch of government would these officials be accountable, the executive or the legislative? Would they have divided loyalties? Would the infusion of so many members of Congress into the top levels of the administration diffuse power away from the White House and blur lines of institutional responsibility? Such an appointment system might clog the administration by preventing a president from bringing in "new blood" to shake up a complacent Washington establishment. In periods of split government, would it be reasonable to assume that the president would pick cabinet secretaries and other officials from the party that controlled Congress? What incentive would the president have to turn over the administration to the other party? Yet if executive positions were filled with members of the president's own party, what advantage would there be if that party did not control Congress? Between 1969 and 1993, a system in which a Republican president put the minority congressional party (i.e., Republicans) into executive offices might have given the majority congressional party (Democrats) every incentive to subvert and sabotage Republican efforts to run an effective administration. And can anyone imagine President Clinton replacing his appointees with fifty congressional Republicans loyal to Newt Gingrich and Bob Dole in the aftermath of the 1994 midterm elections?

The Speaker as "Premier"

To establish a semipresidential system the United States would need some official to function as "prime minister." The only cabinet officer who ever played that role was Alexander Hamilton in the early 1790s, and that failed to become institutionalized. No leader in Congress has ever played such a role, although between 1890 and 1912 the two speakers of the House of Representatives seemed to be transforming themselves into versions of the British prime minister, at least for domestic affairs.

A series of rules changes in the early 1890s transformed the House of Representatives from a "mere debating society" (as Teddy Roosevelt characterized it at the time), dominated by committee chairmen representing special interests, and lacking party discipline in voting on party measures, into an institution that enabled the speaker to dominate committee rosters, "pack" the rules Committee (that developed legislative strategy and controlled congressional debate), and round up votes from his party caucus to pass the party's program.[19] Harvard historian Albert Hart in 1891 observed that "since the legislative department in every republic constantly tends to gain ground at the expense of the executive, the Speaker is likely to become, and perhaps is already, more powerful, both for good and for evil, than the President of the United States. He is Premier in legislation; it is the business of his party that he be also Premier in character, in ability, in leadership, and in statesmanship."[20]

Five years later one of the first women political scientists, Mary P. Follett, published *The Speaker of the House of Representatives,* which became the standard work on the speakership for two decades. She extended Hart's analysis, referred to the speaker as "premier," and convinced many reformers that the evolution of our system in a parliamentary direction was occurring.[21] Analyzing American politics at the end of the nineteenth century, journalist Henry Jones Ford predicted that Congress would soon dominate the departments, that the management of the nation's affairs would rest with trained statesmen under the scrutiny of the legislature, and that "the presidency will tend to assume an honorary and ceremonial character."[22] In 1908 Woodrow Wilson observed that "when matters of legislation are under discussion the country is apt to think of the Speaker as the chief figure in Washington rather than the President."[23] The following year the lawyer Hubert Fuller claimed in his book *The Speakers of the House* that "there is some room for saying that he is even more powerful than the President of the United States."[24]

But the commentators had it all wrong. Parliamentary government would not come to the United States. Speaker Thomas Reed himself opposed the idea of allowing cabinet secretaries to sit in Congress, because he believed that they would not be accountable to the House and would try to control it on behalf of the White House. Powerful senators had no intention of giving up their constitutional prerogatives (appointment and treaty consent) to become a symbolic chamber like the British House of Lords. Senate leaders such as Henry Lodge of Massachusetts, Nelson Aldrich of Rhode Island, Mark Hanna of Ohio, and Thomas Platt of New York were the most powerful leaders of the Republican party, and they controlled the Republican presidential nominating conventions. They had no intention of ceding any of their senatorial or party power to a speaker acting as "prime minister" of government.

The speaker might have been the most powerful figure in domestic politics in the 1890s, but the presidency was becoming the most important figure in international affairs. When Thomas Reed condemned the Spanish-American War and afterward became a leading figure in the anti-imperialist movement, he was forced to resign his speakership because a majority of his party sided with President William McKinley and favored a treaty with Spain granting the United States the Philippines and Puerto Rico. Thereafter McKinley won a series of victories in Congress that expanded presidential power in foreign affairs: tariff reciprocity treaties (even though they went against Republican principles of a high protective tariff); the Spooner Amendment, which enabled him to establish a military regime in the Philippines; and the Platt Amendment, authorizing American intervention in Cuban affairs. No speaker ever wielded such influence on foreign affairs.

The final reason cabinet government never came to America had to do with House politics. In 1903 Reed's former lieutenant Joseph G. ("Uncle Joe") Cannon became speaker. He enforced strict discipline on Republicans and was vindictive against those who dared vote against his program. When some progressive Republicans did so, he dropped them from choice committee assignments. He ignored the Democratic Party leaders and treated them with open contempt: In the elections of 1908, the Democrats went on record against "Czar" Cannon, equating their lot with that of Russian serfs. In 1909 he even exercised his prerogative to appoint Democratic members of House committees, instead of accepting the Democratic list, as all his predecessors had done. That year, an alliance of Democrats and Republican insurgents won changes in the House rules to make consideration of bills opposed by the speaker possible. In 1910 the same coalition (150 Democrats and 43 Republicans) took control of the Rules Committee from the speaker—the committee that controlled House procedures. In 1911 when the Democrats became the majority party in the House after the midterm elections, they appointed their own speaker, but stripped him of the power to appoint and remove committee members, instead providing for elections to the Rules Committee and standing committees by the whole House. They gave the power to make up Democratic committee rosters to the Democrats on the House Ways and Means Committee. By 1913, when the Democrats elected Woodrow Wilson president, the idea of the speaker as "premier" was dead.[25]

In 1995 Newt Gingrich became the most powerful speaker since "Czar" Cannon. He too could dispense with seniority to put loyalists into key positions, unify his Republican majority around measures to streamline House procedures and centralize power, and command the votes to pass an enormous amount of legislation. Even though he could compete with President Clinton to define the domestic agenda, he was no "premier" of government, and for much the same reasons that a century before had limited the growth of the speakership: the coordinate role of the Senate, sometimes operating at cross-purposes with the House; the prerogative power of the president, especially in foreign affairs; and, above all, the limits to the speaker's ability to command his fellow partisans in the House.

THE "NO-CONFIDENCE" VOTE

In the aftermath of the Watergate scandal some political scientists and members of Congress looked for ways to get rid of a "failed presidency" without waiting for impeachment or resignation. Representative Henry Reuss proposed a constitutional amendment providing that extraordinary three-fifths majorities of the House and Senate should be able to vote "no-confidence" in a president and call for new presidential and congressional elections to be held within three months. The incumbent president would serve until his elected successor assumed the office for the remainder of his original term.[26] A president who had been removed from office would remain eligible to compete in the interim presidential election. This proposal went counter to the original constitutional experience: a vote of no-confidence, to be exercised by governors of the states or congressional majorities, was rejected by the framers at the Convention in 1787 to preserve presidential independence from Congress.

In the 1980s a group of political scientists affiliated with a constitutional reform study group known as the Committee for the Constitutional System proposed constitutional amendments to permit a president to dissolve Congress and call for new legislative elections or to allow two-thirds of either chamber of Congress to call for new presidential elections—mechanisms that would enable either institution to take the initiative in ending the deadlock associated with split government.[27]

Proponents of such a vote want it to apply in cases of "general incompetence, misfeasance, abuse of power, and even mental or emotional breakdown," rather than partisan disagreement.[28] Opponents have argued that it would be a recipe for the destruction of the presidency, as it would "transform the present system of presidential–congressional government into a system of congressional government."[29] Presidents must sometimes take unpopular actions, but the vote of no-confidence might discourage them from doing so. Members of both parties might intrigue to bring a president down in a negative "coalition of resentment." Moreover, the long transition period (ninety days) would give an outgoing president temptations to institute prerogative government, to retaliate against his opponents, and to reward his supporters. The special election, if it had come about because of cynical congressional dealings, might inspire a low voter turnout, and the new president would have little legitimacy, a replay of the situation confronting John Quincy Adams in 1824.

In periods of party government it might not work as planned, because the party might be tempted to cover up wrongdoing by a president. It might provide a mechanism for party leaders to force out an unpopular president and replace him with a more popular vice president in a "party putsch." Or it might lead to replacement of a president after a disastrous midterm election. In periods of split government, the opposition party might be accused of political opportunism if it brought down a popularly elected president.

The proposed no-confidence vote weakens the president, because he cannot make unpopular decisions that have major consequences without worrying about removal from office. In crises a president may have to spend time and energy fending off the possibility of a no-confidence vote, rather than dealing with the issues at hand. An interim president elected under these circumstances is likely to be a caretaker, with no real mandate, and power will be diffused into Congress and the departments, with a corresponding *loss* of executive accountability rather than a gain.

Under the Constitution the president is supposed to play an independent and coordinate role in making and implementing policy, and popular election provides political as well as constitutional legitimacy. To pull the rug out from under the president when Congress has policy differences would cost both institutions legitimacy because the American people would probably view such an action as an unfair political maneuver that nullified the popular vote in the presidential election. Proponents argue that a no-confidence vote would be used sparingly and not for mere partisan political purposes, but how can we be sure of developing the customs and usages of a parliamentary system to ensure such restraint? And if the mechanism would be used so rarely, one might ask, what is the point of the reform?

The vote of confidence is not a weaker form of the impeachment mechanism, nor a sanction to be used against presidential abuse of power, and it should not be evaluated as if it were. If it is promoted as a prescription for dealing quickly with abuses of power, it does not fit in with the principles of our impeachment process, which relies on due process—a more legitimate approach to removing a president, and one that has commanded the confidence of the people. Had the vote of confidence existed during the Watergate crisis, the Democrats might have been tempted to vote against Nixon. Had Republicans then rallied around him to stave off what they would have viewed as a political challenge, the vote might have prematurely "closed" the issue (with Nixon "winning" the vote) before the accumulated weight of evidence turned public and congressional opinion against him. During the Iran–contra affair, some Democrats might have been tempted to try for a removal. Had they failed, they would have suffered a disastrous political defeat, and the entire affair would have been viewed as a partisan issue. Had they succeeded; they would simply have put George Bush in the White House. Had they declined to act at all (the most likely scenario, considering the two unsatisfactory outcomes of action), Reagan could have argued that the Democrats were afraid of calling for a vote because they lacked either support or a convincing argument to remove the president from office.

By providing only for a quasi-judicial process and by limiting removals to abuses of power, the framers protected those attempting to impeach a president from charges of political opportunism. Because cases are first taken to quasi-judicial congressional hearings, and then (if impeachment is voted) must be proven in a Senate trial, presided over by the chief justice of the United States, the process is "legalized"—and therefore legitimized—in a way that no congressional majority acting on political grounds might claim. Unless one is prepared to embrace all the mechanisms of parliamentary government, grafting a vote of confidence onto a presidential system only reduces the legitimacy of a congressional majority tempted to use it.

PARTY GOVERNMENT

One of the obstacles standing in the way of the strong presidency is split government: when the president is chosen from one party and one or both houses of Congress are controlled by another. Between 1969 and 1993, for example, Republicans controlled the presidency for all but four of those years, yet at no time did they have control of both houses of Congress.

In a parliamentary system divided party government cannot occur. The voters choose a member of the legislature, who in turn votes for a prime minister, and the prime minister always comes from a majority party or majority coalition. In the United States, of course, a voter chooses a member of Congress, a senator, and a president, and may split his or her ballot between parties. Up to 40 percent of the voters take advantage of that option in presidential election years.

Responsible Party Government

Some reformers would eliminate the separate ballots or use other mechanisms that would guarantee a president a majority in Congress. They want to institute *responsible party government:* both the Congress and the Executive are controlled by the same party, which has put before the voters a platform based on political principle and which carries out its program when elected to office. In a responsible party system, the voters choose policy alternatives as well as elect politicians to office.

The conditions for responsible party government are best met in a parliamentary system with two competing parties, each capable of forming a majority. The voters give one party a majority in parliament, which then forms a party government that is capable of carrying out its program in its entirety. In a presidential system it is very difficult to have responsible party government, not only because Congress will not carry out the entire program of the executive even if a majority is from the same party, but also because one or both chambers of Congress are often controlled by the opposition party. Putting an end to the possibility of split government is, therefore, a prerequisite for party government.

Preventing Split Government

How can split government be prevented? One approach is to augment presidential coattails. If members of the House served for four years and members of the Senate for eight, everyone in Congress could be elected in a presidential election year, when presumably the influence of a popular presidential candidate is greatest. At the very least, such a system would prevent midterm losses by the president's party, which tend to weaken the president's success as a legislative leader in the last two years of each term. Yet such a proposal has no chance of being adopted, because the mood among much of the public is to hold the representatives' feet to the fire in elections. The notion of *increasing* their terms of office and holding elections less frequently flies in the face of anti-incumbent public sentiment, which is more likely to call for term limitations and other ways to get officeholders out sooner rather than keep them in longer.

Another proposal assumes that voters would prefer party government to split government, and, to make sure voters can exercise this preference, presidential and congressional elections would be held on separate dates. Elect the president first, goes the argument, and then some voters will shift their support to congressional candidates of the newly elected president's party in the congressional elections. Alternatively, Congress could be elected first, and then the presidential candidate of the victorious party could make a case to voters that they should elect him or her to keep the government unified. Of course, those voters who prefer split government might vote in a way that confounds the intentions of this reform: in elections of 1984, 1988, and in the midterm election of 1994, a majority of voters preferred split to party government, leaving the viability of staggered elections somewhat suspect.

Because presidential coattails are often weak or nonexistent, or may even work in negative fashion, some reformers have proposed mechanisms to artificially create presidential coattails, so that the election of a president automatically provides a majority in the House of Representatives for the winner. These include the following ideas:

- *Party slate voting.* A single ballot is cast for president, U.S. senator, and U.S. representative. The winning presidential candidate will then have a majority of senators and representatives in Congress at the start of the term. Of course, mandatory slate voting restricts the freedom of choice of voters. It also increases the vulnerability of members of Congress who at present can distance themselves from an unpopular presidential candidate of their own party—it would probably be especially unpopular in southern congressional districts held by Democrats and the few northern urbanized and suburban districts that go "presidentially" Democrat but have Republican representatives.
- *Optional party ballot.* Voters could choose to cast a single ballot (or pull a single lever) and vote for all party candidates running in the election. Because it would be optional,

this system would not take away anyone's freedom of choice; yet it might encourage enough party voting to provide some presidential coattails. Because voters may vote a straight ticket already, and many seem disinclined to do so, it is hard to see how this reform can eliminate or significantly reduce the likelihood of split government.

- *Bonus seats.* A constitutional amendment would automatically give the party that won the presidency a bonus of additional Senate and House seats. If enough seats were awarded, even a party that had "lost" the geographic seats would gain enough additional seats to control Congress.[30] In one fell swoop a quasi-parliamentary system would be created, because the president would always have enough followers from his or her own party to control Congress.

The bonus proposal raises all sorts of issues. How would the seats be allocated geographically? If states received additional senators, it would change the most fundamental understanding in the Constitution: the Connecticut Compromise of two senators to each state, no more, no less. If House delegations added more members, it would violate provisions that apportion House delegations among the states based on population. To say that "at-large" members would represent no geographic areas would be disingenuous: They would either come from all over America (in which case the geographic issues of representation exist in fact, if not in theory) or would be taken from Washington, DC, and other centers of intellectual and political life, in which case they would represent merely a "presidentialist claque" with no grassroots legitimacy.

Would these "representatives" be accorded the same respect as members who won their seats by majority vote? Because most members of Congress conduct their activities and base their votes on geographic and constituency cues, how would these additional members function? Because their only job would be to support the presidential program, strong and independent-minded people would not likely accept it, and the position would be filled by presidential camp-followers and party hacks. Increasing the size of the Senate would convert it from a small deliberative body into a large assembly. It is doubtful that senators would accord any respect to the "mouthpieces" put in to solidify presidential control of their chamber. If these bonus members were elected for the length of a president's term, the electorate could not in midterm elections punish a failed president and his party, give the opposition control of Congress to embark on a new direction, and "send a message" to Washington. Any system designed to give a president automatic congressional majorities would weaken congressional independence, and the checks-and-balances system, particularly in the Senate where the appointment and treaty powers would be affected. The bonus members would support presidential vetoes and prevent Congress from overturning them, giving the president a dominant position in fashioning legislation.

Those who support the bonus system are put in the awkward position of seeking mechanisms to nullify the inclinations of the voters, especially in periods when voters seem intent on "Madisonianism" by voting for a Congress of one party to counterbalance the executive controlled by the other. Like other proposals to strengthen the prospects for party government, it has no chance of passing Congress, because it cheapens and demeans the role of the legislature. In the guise of promoting more efficient government, it would reduce the quality of representation and debate in Congress, erode the system of checks and balances, and make it less likely that executive incompetence and abuses of power would be uncovered or dealt with.

COLLABORATIVE GOVERNMENT

Secretary of State Henry Kissinger observed in the aftermath of the Watergate scandal that "comity between the executive and legislative branches is the only possible basis for national action," adding, "the recognition that the Congress is a coequal branch of government is the dominant fact of national politics today."[31] Since then a number of practical measures, known as "framework" statutes, have been passed by Congress to establish a measure of collaborative government. These laws have the potential to change the way the presidency functions—but only if the White House makes a good-faith effort to comply with their intent, and is willing to back additional framework laws.

A National Security Charter?

Congress often passes laws requiring the president or other executive officials to collaborate with Congress in developing and implementing national policy, such as fiscal policy, impoundments for deficit reduction, arms sales, intelligence operations, nuclear technology transfers, and use of the armed forces in military operations. To keep officials in a consultative frame of mind, proposals have been made that top national security advisers should be subject to Senate confirmation and should convene joint meetings of the National Security Council and other policy-making groups with various congressional committees. A fundamental reform of the national security powers of the presidency would occur if proposals for a National Security Charter were implemented. It would be a framework law that embodied the National Security Act of 1947, the War Powers Resolution of 1973, the International Emergency Economic Powers Act of 1977, the National Emergencies Act of 1976, the Intelligence Oversight Act of 1980, and similar measures, such as those regulating arms sales and technology transfers.[32] The charter would eliminate loopholes that give the president an incentive not to consult or inform or collaborate with Congress when making important decisions. It would require that proposed national security activities be reviewed by either National Security Council lawyers or the Office of Legal Counsel of the Department of Justice to ensure that all proposed initiatives were constitutional and legal.

Presidential Attitudes toward Collaborative Government

Presidents have exhibited suspicion or outright disdain for framework laws, especially when these laws regulate what they believe to be their constitutional prerogatives. Whether they involve presidential war powers, budget mechanisms such as the deferral or rescission of funds, "report and wait" and legislative vetoes, or oversight mechanisms involving foreign covert intelligence operations, presidents and their subordinates sometimes refuse to comply with procedures established in these laws, or exploit their loopholes.[33] Without presidential cooperation, there can be no "collaborative" government.

Congressional Capacity for Collaborative Government

Those who want Congress to play a more important role in important presidential decisions argue that Congress is neither institutionally nor intellectually equipped to do so without fundamental reforms. Congressional committees must be given jurisdictions that correspond to the problems with which the administration will be dealing. Congress could create a "core consultative group" of committee leaders with whom the president would meet and brief on national security matters. It would be given sensitive intelligence information so that it could give an informed judgment to the president.[34]

Reformers tend to be skeptical about the willingness of Congress to reorganize itself and to take political responsibility for collaborative government. Committee fragmentation gives lots of legislators a taste of power and status, and so committees and subcommittees continue to proliferate, making a rational "fit" with executive policy councils impossible. Congress's agenda is crowded with measures designed for constituents, and when the executive proposes new initiatives, policies with principles are turned into programs with specific projects for influential constituents. It may be difficult for the president to engage in consultation with congressional leaders, given their tendency to schedule congressional sessions on a Tuesday–Thursday schedule that gets most members out of Washington for much of the week.

A national security charter might be a good idea, but there is little reason to assume that it too would not be riddled with bad drafting, loopholes, presidential certifications and exemptions, and alternative procedures—in short, all the provisions that were required to take into account the interests of the White House when these provisions were first passed. There is little evidence that Congress wishes to pass well-crafted legislation that requires the president to act in concert with it. And there is even less evidence that it is willing to use the laws that are already on the books that supposedly require collaboration. Congress still suffers from an institutionalized "inferiority complex" when it comes to national security matters. It is more comfortable with traditional "after the fact" oversight because it can continue to pass the buck, avoid responsibility, and distance itself from potential fiascoes.

A national security charter that constrained presidential war making and intelligence operations would eventually lead to court challenges if a president disregarded them. The Supreme Court might dismiss challenges to the presidential action (or inaction) on political grounds, or else render a decision striking down the constraints. Certainly the composition of the Court in the early 1990s gives us little reason to believe that many restrictions on presidential powers under a national security charter would be upheld by the courts. Reformers who call for a national security charter and other collaborative legislation have provided an ambitious agenda for Congress, but as yet there is no hint of any legislative willingness to act on any part of it. Indeed, one might argue that a Congress that has shown itself unprepared to use the framework laws already in existence is hardly likely to pass an omnibus version with real teeth in it.

The Rule of Law and Presidential Power

Reformers concerned with keeping presidential power accountable and legitimate have made a number of suggestions which strengthen the role of the courts in the checks and balances system. They have proposed that Congress pass laws making it easier for legislators or "private attorneys general" (i.e., lawyers for advocacy groups interested in public policy) to obtain standing to sue the president or other executive officials. They would have Congress limit by statute the immunity that a president may claim, stating specific exceptions to the general rules that protect a president from suit or damages if he takes actions within the scope of his official duties. They would have Congress go on record with a resolution that presidential violations of statutes requiring collaboration should not be treated by the courts as "political questions" between the two branches (and therefore dismissed), but should be treated as violations of law, subject to judicial remedies and penalties. They would have Congress pass laws that allow the courts to issue injunctions against national security officials, injunctions that might prevent national security decisions from being implemented.[35]

CONSTITUTIONAL REFORMS OR INSTITUTIONAL ADAPTATION

Constitutional reforms of the presidential office have not involved the essential questions of presidential power but have focused instead on the road to the White House: The Twelfth Amendment cleared up a problem that surfaced in the elections of 1800 involving votes for president and vice president by providing for separate ballots for each office; the Twentieth Amendment solved some problems of presidential succession and House and Senate contingency elections for president and vice president, and made minor changes in the inauguration date (moving it from March to January); the Twenty-Second Amendment limited the president to two elected terms in office; and the Twenty-Fifth Amendment dealt with presidential disability and vacancies in the vice presidency (providing for presidential nomination and congressional ratification of a vice president to fill a vacancy). These and most other constitutional amendments (such as providing for popular election of senators, outlawing the poll tax, providing for eighteen-year-olds voting, preventing states from denying the suffrage to women and former black slaves, providing representation in the electoral college for the District of Columbia) concentrate on democratizing the electoral process. In point of fact, not a single constitutional amendment has affected the powers of the president once in office.

The presidency is not reformed by constitutional amendments, but is transformed and reinvented by institutionalized practices. Change occurs when the president asserts constitutional prerogatives, Congress acquiesces and supports them, and the courts legitimize the claim or avoid the issue—or alternatively, when Congress and the courts check and balance the president. It also occurs when Congress passes statutes that delegate vast powers to the presidency (such as the item veto), or passes framework statutes that require presidents to move from unilateral to collaborative decision making.

The real changes that take place in presidential–congressional relations occur at the statutory, or "subconstitutional" level, but not through comprehensive new charters. Instead, smaller-scale statutes passed by Congress under its "necessary and proper" clause endow the president with new institutional resources, enlarge the presidency with broad delegations of power, constrain the president with new ethical standards, or create new patterns of congressional–presidential interactions by instituting forms of collaborative government. "While the Constitution diffuses power the better to secure liberty," Justice Jackson wrote in the *Youngstown* case, "it also contemplates that practice will integrate the dispersed powers into a workable government. It enjoins upon its branches separateness but interdependence, autonomy but reciprocity."[36]

The politics of presidential reform works best when it follows original constitutional precepts rather than attempts to redefine the constitutional system. It succeeds when a strengthened presidency is needed to meet authentic emergencies facing the nation, or alternatively, when an exercise of presidential prerogative is politically unsustainable and the office must be cut down to constitutional size. The failure of framework legislation and collaborative government to work effectively is in part due to presidential subversion and in part due to congressional buck-passing and political cowardice, and the prospects that Congress can successfully "reinvent the presidency" and fully institutionalize its powers either by legislation or constitutional amendment remain limited.

THE FUTURE OF THE PRESIDENCY

And what of the future? If the past is any guide, the office of president will draw its authority and legitimacy from two enduring and antithetical strands of the American political culture: the strong desire for national security in a turbulent and unpredictably dangerous world; and the strong antipathy for centralized government and technocratic programmatic politics. The national security presidency remains alive and well in Washington. Although the Cold War may be over, peacekeeping and humanitarian missions, quarantines and blockades, covert actions and anti-terrorism activities, and stepped-up efforts to regain control of American borders will all provide presidents with a full national security agenda. There is nothing in our recent history to suggest that presidents will not be able to continue to marshal public opinion to deal with genuine national security threats, or will not be able to use their prerogatives for small-scale uses of force and covert actions.

Although it is true that the modern presidency of Franklin Roosevelt and his successors was based in part on domestic welfare state activism, the vast sweep of American history draws a somewhat different lesson about presidential strength: Jefferson, Jackson, and the line of Republican presidents since Lincoln have all drawn political strength from the American suspicion of concentrated power and governmental activism. Over the long run, presidential skepticism about such power has proven more politically viable than a presidential embrace of the potentialities of government. Some call this tendency postmodern government, but in fact it resonates with the politics of two centuries of American political history. Although this history will continue to be punctuated with periodic bursts of presidential activism and accomplishment, it is likely in the future, as in the past, that many presidents—and those who would be presidents—will gain greater ground by rethinking the role of government in the economy and society, and by "reinventing government" to make it a more effective instrument of governance. "Those who question power make an indispensable contribution to American democracy," John Kennedy once said, and it is almost certainly the case that a president who questions power and tries to reinvigorate and reinvent national government institutions makes an even greater contribution.

FURTHER READING

Books

Larry Berman, *The New American Presidency,* Boston: Little, Brown, 1987.

Charles Hardin, *Constitutional Reform in America,* Ames, IA: Iowa State University Press, 1989.

Stephen Horn, *The Cabinet and Congress,* New York: Columbia University Press, 1960.

Thomas Langston, *With Reverence and Contempt: How Americans Think about Their Presidents,* Baltimore, MD: Johns Hopkins University Press, 1995.

Donald Robinson, *To the Best of My Ability: The Presidency and the Constitution,* New York: W. W. Norton, 1987.

Theodore Sorensen, *A Different Kind of Presidency: A Proposal for Breaking the Political Deadlock,* New York: Harper and Row, 1984.

James Sundquist, *Constitutional Reform and Effective Government,* Washington, DC: Brookings Institution, 1986.

Woodrow Wilson, *Constitutional Government in the United States,* New York: Columbia University Press, 1908.

Documentary Sources

Donald Robinson, ed., *Reforming American Government: The Bicentennial Papers of the Committee on the Constitution System.* Boulder, CO: Westview Press, 1985.

Report and Recommendations of the Committee on the Constitutional System, "A Bicentennial Analysis of the American Political Structure," *Committee on the Constitutional System,* January, 1987, pp. 1–20.

NOTES

1. Walter Bagehot, *The English Constitution,* Ithaca, NY: Cornell University Press, 1966, p. 72.

2. Woodrow Wilson, "Cabinet Government in the United States," *International Review,* Vol. 7, August, 1879, pp. 146–163.

3. Woodrow Wilson, *Constitutional Government in the United States,* New York: Columbia University Press, 1908.

4. Augustus Woodward, *Considerations on Executive Government in the United States,* Flatbush, NY: I. Riley, 1809; Augustus Woodward, *The Presidency of the United States,* New York: D. Van Veighton, 1825.

5. Abel Upshur, *A Brief Inquiry into the Nature and Character of Our Federal Government,* New York: Da Capo Press, reprint, 1971, p. 116.

6. Henry C. Lockwood, *The Abolition of the Presidency,* New York: R. Worthington, 1884.

7. Ibid., p. 305.

8. On the advantages and disadvantages of instituting the British system of parliamentary government, especially for practical problems of governance, see Richard E. Neustadt, "Shadow and Substance in Politics: The Presidency and Whitehall," *The Public Interest,* Vol. 2, Winter, 1966, pp. 55–69.

9. Demetrios Caraley, ed., *Parliamentary and Presidential Systems: Which Works Best,* New York: Academy of Political Science, 1994.

10. On cabinet government, see Ivor Jennings, *Cabinet Government,* rev. ed., Cambridge, UK: Cambridge University Press, 1959; P. Weller, *First among Equals: Prime Ministers in the Westminster Systems,* Boston: Allen and Unwin, 1985.

11. Maurice Duverger, "A New Political System Model: Semi-Presidential Government," *European Journal of Political Research,* Vol. 8, no. 2, June, 1980, pp. 165–188.

12. Gamaliel Bradford, "Congressional Reform," *North American Review,* Vol. 111, 1870, pp. 331–351.

13. On Pendleton's proposal, see Stephen Horn, *The Cabinet and Congress,* New York: Columbia University Press, 1960, pp. 95–97; Estes Kefauver, "The Need for Better Executive-Legislative Teamwork in the National Government," *American Political Science Review,* Vol. 38, no. 4, December, 1944, pp. 317–325.

14. Gamaliel Bradford, "Congress and the Cabinet," *Annals of the American Academy of Political and Social Science,* Vol. 363, November, 1891, p. 294.

15. A. Lawrence Lowell, *Essays on Government,* Boston: Houghton Mifflin, 1889, pp. 23–24.

16. Estes Kefauver, "The Need for Better Executive-Legislative Teamwork in the National Government," *American Political Science Review,* Vol. 38, no. 4, December, 1944, pp. 317–325.

17. Thomas Finletter, *Can Representative Government Do the Job?,* New York: Reynal and Hitchcock, 1945; Edward Corwin, *The President: Office and Powers,* New York: New York University Press, 1940. Corwin called for an advisory joint council consisting of all the department secretaries as well as chairs of the appropriate standing legislative committees.

18. U.S. Congress, House Committee on Banking, Finance and Urban Affairs, *Looking Toward the Constitutional Bicentennial—A Proposed Amendment to Permit Members of Congress to Serve in Key Executive Branch Offices,* 96th Cong., 1st sess., January, 1980.

19. On rule changes, see Thomas Reed, "Reforms Needed in the House," *North American Review,* Vol. 149, May, 1890, p. 544; Henry Cabot Lodge, "Parliamentary Obstruction in the United States," *North American Review,* Vol. 151, March, 1891, p. 427.

20. Albert Hart, "The Speaker as Premier," *Atlantic Monthly,* March, 1891, p. 19.

21. Mary P. Follett, *The Speaker of the House of Representatives,* New York: Longmans Green, 1896, p. 272.

22. Henry Jones Ford, *The Rise and Growth of American Politics,* New York: Macmillan, 1898, ch. 28: "The Ultimate Type."

23. Woodrow Wilson, *Constitutional Government in the United States,* op. cit., p. 107.

24. Hubert Fuller, *The Speakers of the House,* Boston: Little, Brown, 1909, pp. 19–20.

25. Richard M. Pious, "A Prime Minister for America," *Constitution,* Vol. 4, no. 3, Fall, 1992, pp. 4–12.

26. James Sundquist, "The Case for an Easier Method to Remove Presidents," *George Washington Law Review,* Vol. 43, no. 2, January, 1975, pp. 472–484; Allen P. Sindler, "Good Intentions, Bad Policy: A Vote of No Confidence on the Proposal to Empower Congress to Vote No Confidence in the President," *George Washington Law Review,* Vol. 43, no. 2, January, 1975, pp. 437–458.

27. Lloyd Cutler, "To Form a Government—On the Defects of Separation of Powers," in Donald Robinson, ed., *Reforming American Government,* Boulder, CO: Westview Press, 1985, pp. 11–23; also see the discussion in James Sundquist, *Constitutional Reform and Effective Government,* Washington, DC: Brookings Institution, 1986, pp. 7–10.

28. Henry Reuss, "An Introduction to the Vote of No Confidence," *George Washington Law Review,* Vol. 43, no. 2, January, 1975, pp. 333–335.

29. Louis Koenig, "Symposium on the No-Confidence Amendment," *George Washington Law Review,* Vol. 43, no. 2, January, 1975, p. 376; Sindler, op. cit.

30. Charles Hardin, *Presidential Power and Accountability,* Chicago: University of Chicago Press, 1974, pp. 182–189.

31. Henry Kissinger, *Department of State Bulletin,* Vol. 73, 1975, p. 562.

32. Harold Koh, *The National Security Constitution,* New Haven, CT: Yale University Press, 1991, pp. 153–207.

33. Nancy Kassop, "From the Imperial Presidency to the Arrogant Presidency in Separation of Powers Conflicts," paper delivered at the 1994 Annual Meeting of the American Political Science Association, New York City, September 4, 1994, p. 4.

34. Koh, op. cit., p. 192.

35. Koh, op. cit., pp. 182–183.

36. *Youngstown Sheet and Tube v. Sawyer,* 343 U.S. 579, 1952, p. 635.

Appendix A

Constitutional Provisions Relating to the Presidency

THE CONSTITUTION AS WRITTEN IN 1787

Article 1

Sec. 2, paragraph 5. The House of Representatives . . . shall have the sole power of impeachment.

Sec. 3, paragraph 4. The vice-president of the United States shall be president of the Senate, but shall have no vote, unless they be equally divided.

Sec. 3, paragraph 5. The Senate shall choose their other officers, and also a president pro tempore, in the absence of the vice-president, or when he shall exercise the office of President of the United States.

Sec. 3, paragraph 6. The Senate shall have the sole power to try all impeachments. When sitting for that purpose, they shall be on oath or affirmation. When the president of the United States is tried, the chief justice shall preside: And no person shall be convicted without the concurrence of two-thirds of the members present.

Sec. 3, paragraph 7. Judgment in cases of impeachment shall not extend further than to removal from office, and disqualification to hold and enjoy any office of honour, trust or profit under the United States; but the party convicted shall nevertheless be liable and subject to indictment, trial, judgment and punishment, according to law.

Sec. 6, paragraph 2. No senator or representative shall, during the time for which he was elected, be appointed to any civil office under the authority of the United States, which shall have been created, or the emoluments whereof shall have been increased during such time; and no person holding any office under the United States, shall be a member of either house during his continuance in office.

Sec. 7, paragraph 2. Every bill which shall have passed the House of Representatives and the Senate shall, before it becomes a law, be presented to the president of the United States; if he approve, he shall sign it, but if not, he shall return it, with his objections, to that house in which it shall have originated, who shall enter the objections at large on their journal, and proceed to reconsider it. If after such reconsideration, two thirds of that house shall agree to pass the bill, it shall be sent, together with the objections, to the other house, by which it shall likewise be reconsidered, and if approved by two-thirds of that house, it shall become a law. . . . If any bill not be returned by the president within ten days (Sundays excepted) after it shall have been presented to him, the same shall be a law, in like manner as if he had signed it, unless the Congress by their adjournment prevent its return, in which case it shall not be a law.

Sec. 7, paragraph 3. Every order, resolution, or vote to which the concurrence of the Senate and House of Representatives may be necessary (except on a question of adjournment) shall be presented to the president of the United States; and before the same shall take effect, shall be approved by him, or, being disapproved by him, shall be re-passed by two-thirds of the Senate and House of Representatives, according to the rules and limitations prescribed in the case of a bill.

Sec. 8. Congress shall have the power . . . [*paragraph 18*] To make all laws which shall be necessary and proper for carrying into execution the foregoing powers, and all other powers, vested by this constitution in the government of the United States, or in any department or officer thereof.

Sec. 9, paragraph 2. The privilege of the writ of *habeas corpus* shall not be suspended, unless when in cases of rebellion or invasion the public safety may require it.

Sec. 9, paragraph 7. No money shall be drawn from the treasury, but in consequence of appropriations made by law, and a regular statement and account of the receipts and expenditures of all public money shall be published from time to time.

Article 2

Sec. 1, paragraph 1. The Executive Power shall be vested in a president of the United States of America. He shall hold his office during the term of four years, and, together with the vice-president, chosen for the same term, be elected, as follows:

Sec. 1, paragraph 2. Each state shall appoint, in such manner as the legislature thereof may direct, a number of electors, equal to the whole number of senators and representatives to which the state may be entitled in the Congress; but no senator or representative, or person holding an office of trust or profit under the United States, shall be appointed an elector.

Sec. 1, paragraph 3. The electors shall meet in their respective states, and vote by ballot for two persons, of whom one at least shall not be an inhabitant of the same state with themselves. And they shall make a list of all the persons voted for, and of the number of votes for each; which list they shall sign and certify, and transmit sealed to the seat of the government of the United States, directed to the president of the Senate. The president of the Senate shall, in the presence of the Senate and House of Representatives, open all the certificates and the votes shall then be counted. The person having the greatest number of votes shall be president, if such numbers be a majority of the whole number of electors appointed; and if there be more than one who have such majority, and have an equal number of votes, then the House of Representatives shall immediately choose by ballot one of them for president; and if no person have a majority, then from the five highest on the list, the said House shall, in like manner, choose the president. But in choosing the president, the votes shall be taken by states, the representation from each state having one vote; a quorum for this purpose shall consist of a member or members from two-thirds of the states, and a majority of all the states shall be necessary to a choice. In every case, after the choice of the president, the person having the greatest number of votes of the electors shall be the vice-president. But if there should remain two or more who have equal votes, the Senate shall choose from them by ballot the vice-president.

Sec. 1, paragraph 4. The Congress may determine the time of choosing the electors, and the day on which they shall give their votes; which day shall be the same throughout the United States.

Sec. 1, paragraph 5. No person except a natural born citizen, or a citizen of the United States, at the time of the adoption of this constitution, shall be eligible to the office of president; neither shall any person be eligible to that office, who shall not have attained to the age of 35 years, and been fourteen years a resident within the United States.

Sec. 1, paragraph 6. In case of the removal of the president from office, or of his death, resignation, or inability to discharge the powers and duties of the said office, the same shall devolve on the vice-president, and the Congress may by law provide for the case of removal, death, resignation, or inability, both of the president and vice-president, declaring what officer shall then act as president, and such officer shall act accordingly, until the disability be removed, or a president shall be elected.

Sec. 1, paragraph 7. The president shall, at stated times, receive for his services a compensation, which shall neither be increased nor diminished during the period for which he shall have been elected, and he shall not receive within that period any other emolument from the United States, or any of them.

Sec. 1, paragraph 8. Before he enter on the execution of his office, he shall take the following oath or affirmation: "I do solemnly swear (or affirm) that I will faithfully execute the office of president of the United States, and will to the best of my ability, preserve, protect and defend the constitution of the United States."

Sec. 2, paragraph 1. The president shall be commander in chief of the army and navy of the United States, and of the militia of the several states, when called into actual service of the United States; he may require the opinion, in writing, of the principal officer in each of the executive departments, upon any subject relating to the duties of their respective offices, and he shall have power to grant reprieves and pardons for offences against the United States, except in cases of impeachment.

Sec. 2, paragraph 2. He shall have power, by and with the advice and consent of the Senate, to make treaties, provided two-thirds of the senators present concur; and he shall nominate, and by and with the advice and consent of the Senate, shall appoint ambassadors, other public ministers and consuls, judges of the supreme court, and all other officers of the United States, whose appointments are not herein otherwise provided for, and which shall be established by law. But the Congress may by law vest the appointment of such inferior officers, as they think proper, in the president alone, in the courts of law, or in the heads of departments.

Sec. 2, paragraph 3. The president shall have power to fill up all vacancies that may happen during the recess of the Senate, by granting commissions, which shall expire at the end of their next session.

Sec. 3, paragraph 1. He shall, from time to time, give to the Congress information of the state of the union, and recommend to their consideration, such measures as he shall judge necessary and expedient; he may, on extraordinary occasions, convene both houses, or either of them, and in case of disagreement between them, with respect to the time of adjournment, he may adjourn them to such time as he shall think proper; he shall receive ambassadors and other public ministers; he shall take care that the laws be faithfully executed, and shall commission all the officers of the United States.

Sec. 4, paragraph 1. The president, vice-president, and all civil officers of the United States, shall be removed from office on impeachment for, and conviction of, treason, bribery, or other high crimes and misdemeanors.

Article 4

Sec. 4, paragraph 1. The United States shall guarantee to every state in this union, a republican form of government, and shall protect each of them against invasion; and on the application of the legislature, or of the executive (when the legislature cannot be convened), against domestic violence.

Article 6

Paragraph 2. This constitution, and the laws of the United States which shall be made in pursuance thereof; and all treaties made, or which shall be made, under the authority of the United States, shall be the supreme law of the land; and the judges in every state shall be bound thereby, any thing in the constitution or laws of any state to the contrary notwithstanding.

Paragraph 3. . . . no religious test shall ever be required as a qualification to any office or public trust under the United States.

AMENDMENTS TO THE CONSTITUTION AFFECTING THE PRESIDENCY

Amendment 12

The electors shall meet in their respective states, and vote by ballot for President and Vice-President, one of whom at least shall not be an inhabitant of the same state with themselves; they shall name in their ballots the person voted for as President, and in distinct ballots the person voted for as Vice-President; and they shall make distinct lists of all persons voted for as President, and of all persons voted for as Vice-

President, and of number of votes for each, which lists they shall sign and certify, and transmit, sealed, to the seat of the government of the United States directed to the president of the Senate; the president of the Senate shall, in the presence of the Senate and House of Representatives, open all the certificates, and the votes shall then be counted; the person having the greatest number of votes for President shall be the President, if such number be a majority of the whole number of electors appointed; and if no person have such majority, then from the persons having the highest numbers not exceeding three, on the list of those voted for as President, the House of Representatives shall choose immediately, by ballot, the President. But in choosing the President, the votes shall be taken by states, the representation from each state having one vote; a quorum for this purpose shall consist of a member or members from two-thirds of the states, and a majority of all the states shall be necessary to a choice. And if the House of Representatives shall not choose a President, whenever the right of choice shall devolve upon them, before the fourth day of March next following, then the Vice-President shall act as President, as in the case of the death or other constitutional disability of the President. The person having the greatest number of votes as Vice-President, shall be the Vice-President, if such number be a majority of the whole number of electors appointed, and if no person have a majority, then from the two highest numbers on the list the Senate shall choose the Vice-President; a quorum for the purpose shall consist of two-thirds of the whole number of senators, and a majority of the whole number shall be necessary to a choice. But no person constitutionally ineligible to the office of President shall be eligible to that of Vice-President of the United States.

Amendment 14

Sec. 3, paragraph 1. No person shall be . . . elector of President and Vice-President, or hold any office, civil or military, under the United States, or under any state, who, having previously taken an oath, as a member of Congress, or as an officer of the United States, or as a member of any state legislature, or as an executive or judicial officer of any state, to support the Constitution of the United States, shall have engaged in insurrection or rebellion against the same, or given aid and comfort to the enemies thereof. But Congress may, by a vote of two-thirds of each House, remove such disability.

Amendment 20

Sec. 1, paragraph 1. The terms of the President and Vice-President shall end at noon on the 20th day of January . . . and the terms of their successors shall then begin.

Sec. 3, paragraph 1. If, at the time fixed for the beginning of the term of President, the President elect shall have died, the Vice-President elect shall become president. If a President shall not have been chosen before the time fixed for the beginning of his term, or if the President elect shall have failed to qualify, then the Vice-President elect shall act as President until a President shall have qualified; and the Congress may by law provide for the case wherein neither a President elect nor a Vice President elect shall have qualified, declaring who shall then act as President, or the manner in which one who is to act shall be selected, and such person shall act accordingly until a President or Vice-President shall have qualified.

Sec. 4, paragraph 1. The Congress may by law provide for the case of the death of any of the persons from whom the House of Representatives may choose a President, whenever the right of choice shall have devolved upon them, and for the case of the death of any of the persons from whom the Senate may choose a Vice-President, whenever the right of choice shall have devolved upon them.

Amendment 22

Sec. 1, paragraph 1. No person shall be elected to the office of the President more than twice, and no person who has held the office of President, or acted as President, for more than two years of a term to which some other person was elected President shall be elected to the office of the President more than once. But this Article shall not apply to any person holding the office of President when this Article was proposed by the Congress, and shall not prevent any person who may be holding the office of President, or acting as president, during the term within which this Article becomes operative from holding the office of President or acting as President during the remainder of such term.

Amendment 23

Sec. 1, paragraph 1. The District constituting the seat of Government of the United States shall appoint in such manner as the Congress may direct: A number of electors of President and Vice-President equal to the whole number of Senators and Representatives in Congress to which the District would be entitled if it were a State; but in no event more than the least populous State; they shall be in addition to those appointed by the States, but they shall be considered, for the purpose of the election of President and Vice-President, to be electors appointed by a State; and they shall meet in the District and perform such duties as provided by the twelfth article of amendment.

Amendment 24

Sec. 1, paragraph 1. The right of citizens of the United States to vote in any primary or other election for President or Vice-President, for electors for President or Vice-President, or for Senator or Representative in Congress, shall not be denied or abridged by the United States or any State by reason of failure to pay any poll tax or other tax.

Amendment 25

Sec. 1, paragraph 1. In case of the removal of the President from office or of his death or resignation, the Vice-President shall become President.

Sec. 2, paragraph 1. Whenever there is a vacancy in office of the Vice-President, the President shall nominate a Vice-President who shall take office upon confirmation by a majority vote of both Houses of Congress.

Sec. 3, paragraph 1. Whenever the President transmits to the President pro tempore of the Senate and the Speaker of the House of Representatives his written declaration that he is unable to discharge the powers and duties of his office, and until he transmits to them a written declaration to the contrary, such powers and duties shall be discharged by the Vice-President as Acting President.

Sec. 4, paragraph 1. Whenever the Vice-President and a majority of either the principal officers of the executive departments, or of such other body as Congress may by law provide, transmit to the President pro tempore of the Senate and the Speaker of the House of Representatives their written declaration that the President is unable to discharge the powers and duties of his office, the Vice-President shall immediately assume the powers and duties of the office as Acting President.

Sec. 4, paragraph 2. Thereafter, when the President transmits to the President pro tempore of the Senate and the Speaker of the House of Representatives his written declaration that no inability exists, he shall resume the powers and duties of his office unless the Vice-President and a majority of either the principal officers of the executive departments or of such other body as Congress may by law provide, transmit within four days to the Speaker of the House of Representatives their written declaration that the President is unable to discharge the powers and duties of his office. Thereupon Congress shall decide the issue, assembling within forty-eight hours for that purpose, if not in session. If the Congress, within twenty-one days after receipt of the latter written declaration, or, if Congress is not in session, within twenty-one days after Congress is required to assemble, determines by two-thirds vote of both Houses that the President is unable to discharge the powers and duties of his office, the Vice-President shall continue to discharge the same as Acting President; otherwise, the President shall resume the powers and duties of his office.

Appendix B

Presidential Terms of Office, 1789–1997

Name	Term of Office	Political Party	State of Residence	Inaugu-ration Age	Vice President
George Washington	1789–1793	Federalist	Virginia	57	John Adams
	1793–1797				John Adams
John Adams	1797–1801	Federalist	Massachusetts	61	Thomas Jefferson
Thomas Jefferson	1801–1805	Democratic–Republican	Virginia	57	Aaron Burr
	1805–1809				George Clinton
James Madison	1809–1813	Democratic–Republican	Virginia	57	George Clinton
	1813–1817				Elbridge Gerry
James Monroe	1817–1821	Democratic–Republican	Virginia	58	Daniel Tompkins
	1821–1825				Daniel Tompkins
John Q. Adams	1825–1829	National Republican	Massachusetts	57	John Calhoun
Andrew Jackson	1829–1833	Democrat	Tennessee	61	John Calhoun
	1833–1837				Martin Van Buren
Martin Van Buren	1837–1841	Democrat	New York	54	Richard Johnson
William Harrison	1841	Whig	Indiana	68	John Tyler
John Tyler	1841–1845	Democrat*	Virginia	51	
James Polk	1845–1849	Democrat	Tennessee	49	George Dallas
Zachary Taylor	1849–1850	Whig	Louisiana	64	Millard Fillmore
Millard Fillmore	1850–1853	Whig	New York	48	
Franklin Pierce	1853–1857	Democrat	New Hampshire	50	William King
James Buchanan	1857–1861	Democrat	Pennsylvania	65	John Breckenridge
Abraham Lincoln	1861–1865	Republican	Illinois	52	Hannibal Hamlin
	1865				Andrew Johnson
Andrew Johnson	1865–1869	Unionist†	Tennessee	56	
Ulysses Grant	1869–1873	Republican	Ohio	46	Schuyler Colfax
	1873–1877				Henry Wilson
Rutherford Hayes	1877–1881	Republican	Ohio	54	William Wheeler
James Garfield	1881	Republican	Ohio	49	Chester Arthur
Chester Arthur	1881–1885	Republican	New York	50	
Grover Cleveland	1885–1889	Democrat	New York	47	Thomas Hendricks
Benjamin Harrison	1889–1893	Republican	Indiana	55	Levi Morton
Grover Cleveland	1893–1897	Democrat	New York	55	Adlai Stevenson
William McKinley	1897–1901	Republican	Ohio	54	Garrett Hobart
	1901				Theodore Roosevelt
Theodore Roosevelt	1901–1905	Republican	New York	42	
	1905–1909				Charles Fairbanks
William Taft	1909–1913	Republican	Ohio	51	James Sherman

Name	Term of Office	Political Party	State of Residence	Inauguration Age	Vice President
Woodrow Wilson	1913–1917	Democrat	New Jersey	56	Thomas Marshall
	1917–1921				Thomas Marshall
Warren Harding	1921–1923	Republican	Ohio	55	Calvin Coolidge
Calvin Coolidge	1923–1925	Republican	Massachusetts	51	
	1925–1929				Charles Dawes
Herbert Hoover	1929–1933	Republican	California	54	Charles Curtis
Franklin Roosevelt	1933–1937	Democrat	New York	51	John Garner
	1937–1941				John Garner
	1941–1945				Henry Wallace
	1945				Harry Truman
Harry Truman	1945–1949	Democrat	Missouri	60	
	1949–1953				Alben Barkley
Dwight Eisenhower	1953–1957	Republican	New York	62	Richard Nixon
	1957–1961				Richard Nixon
John Kennedy	1961–1963	Democrat	Massachusetts	43	Lyndon Johnson
Lyndon Johnson	1963–1965	Democrat	Texas	55	
	1965–1969				Hubert Humphrey
Richard Nixon	1969–1973	Republican	California	56	Spiro Agnew
	1973–1974				Spiro Agnew
					Gerald Ford
Gerald Ford	1974–1977	Republican	Michigan	61	Nelson Rockefeller
Jimmy Carter	1977–1981	Democrat	Georgia	52	Walter Mondale
Ronald Reagan	1981–1985	Republican	California	69	George Bush
	1985–1989				George Bush
George Bush	1989–1993	Republican	Texas	65	J. Danforth Quayle
Bill Clinton	1993–	Democrat	Arkansas	46	Albert Gore

*Tyler was a Democrat elected on the Whig ticket with William Henry Harrison.

†A. Johnson was a Democrat elected on the Unionist and Republican slates with Abraham Lincoln.

Appendix C

Vice Presidential Terms of Office, 1789–1997

Name	Term of Office	Political Party	State of Residence	Inauguration Age
John Adams	1789–1797	Federalist	Massachusetts	54
Thomas Jefferson	1797–1801	Democratic–Republican	Virginia	54
Aaron Burr	1801–1805	Democratic–Republican	New Jersey	45
George Clinton	1805–1812	Democratic–Republican	New York	66
Elbridge Gerry	1813–1814	Democratic–Republican	Massachusetts	67
Daniel Tompkins	1817–1825	Democratic–Republican	New York	43
John Calhoun	1825–1832	No party nomination	South Carolina	43
Martin Van Buren	1833–1837	Democrat	New York	51
Richard Johnson	1837–1841	Democrat	Kentucky	57
John Tyler	1841	Whig	Virginia	51
George Dallas	1845–1849	Democrat	Pennsylvania	53
Millard Fillmore	1849–1850	Whig	New York	49
William King	1853	Democrat	North Carolina	67
John Breckenridge	1857–1861	Democrat	Kentucky	36
Hannibal Hamlin	1861–1865	Republican	Maine	52
Andrew Johnson	1865	Union	North Carolina	57
Schuyler Colfax	1869–1873	Republican	New York	46
Henry Wilson	1873–1875	Republican	New Hampshire	61
William Wheeler	1877–1881	Republican	New York	58
Chester Arthur	1881	Republican	Vermont	51
Thomas Hendricks	1885	Democrat	Ohio	66
Levi Morton	1889–1893	Republican	Vermont	65
Adlai Stevenson	1893–1897	Democrat	Kentucky	58
Garrett Hobart	1897–1899	Republican	New Jersey	53
Theodore Roosevelt	1901	Republican	New York	43
Charles Fairbanks	1905–1909	Republican	Ohio	47
James Sherman	1909–1912	Republican	New York	54
Thomas Marshall	1913–1921	Democrat	Indiana	59
Calvin Coolidge	1921–1923	Republican	Vermont	49
Charles Dawes	1925–1929	Republican	Ohio	60
Charles Curtis	1929–1933	Republican	Kansas	69
John Garner	1933–1941	Democrat	Texas	65
Henry Wallace	1941–1945	Democrat	Iowa	53
Harry Truman	1945	Democrat	Missouri	61
Alben Barkley	1949–1953	Democrat	Kentucky	72

Name	Term of Office	Political Party	State of Residence	Inaugu-ration Age
Richard Nixon	1953–1961	Republican	California	40
Lyndon Johnson	1961–1963	Democrat	Texas	53
Hubert Humphrey	1965–1969	Democrat	Minnesota	54
Spiro Agnew	1969–1973	Republican	Maryland	51
Gerald Ford	1973–1974	Republican	Michigan	60
Nelson Rockefeller	1974–1977	Republican	Maine	66
Walter Mondale	1977–1981	Democrat	Minnesota	49
George Bush	1981–1989	Republican	Texas	57
J. Danforth Quayle	1989–1993	Republican	Indiana	42
Albert Gore	1993–	Democrat	Tennessee	46

Appendix D

Presidential Election Statistics, 1789–1992

Year	Candidates	Party	Popular Vote	Electoral College Vote
1789	George Washington	Federalist	—	69
1792	George Washington	Federalist	—	132
1796	John Adams	Federalist	—	71
	Thomas Jefferson	Democratic–Republican	—	68
1800	Thomas Jefferson	Democratic–Republican	—	73
	John Adams	Federalist	—	65
1804	Thomas Jefferson	Democratic–Republican	—	162
	Charles Pinckney	Federalist	—	14
1808	James Madison	Democratic–Republican	—	122
	Charles Pinckney	Federalist	—	47
1812	James Madison	Democratic–Republican	—	128
	George Clinton	Federalist	—	89
1816	James Monroe	Democratic–Republican	—	183
	Rufus King	Federalist	—	34
1820	James Monroe	Democratic–Republican	—	231
	John Q. Adams	Democratic–Republican	—	1
1824	John Q. Adams	Democratic–Republican	108,740	84
	Andrew Jackson	Democratic–Republican	153,544	99
	William Crawford	Democratic–Republican	46,618	41
	Henry Clay	Democratic–Republican	47,136	37
1828	Andrew Jackson	Democrat	647,286	178
	John Q. Adams	National Republican	508,064	83
1832	Andrew Jackson	Democrat	687,502	219
	Henry Clay	National Republican	530,189	49
	Electoral votes not cast			2
1836	Martin Van Buren	Democrat	764,176	170
	William Harrison	Whig	550,816	73
	Hugh White	Whig	146,107	26
	Daniel Webster	Whig	41,201	14
1840	William Harrison	Whig	1,274,624	234
	Martin Van Buren	Democrat	1,127,781	60
1844	James Polk	Democrat	1,338,464	170
	Henry Clay	Whig	1,300,097	105
1848	Zachary Taylor	Whig	1,360,967	163
	Lewis Cass	Democrat	1,222,342	127
	Martin Van Buren	Free Soil	291,263	—
1852	Franklin Pierce	Democrat	1,601,117	254
	Winfield Scott	Whig	1,385,453	42
	John Hale	Free Soil	155,825	—

Year	Candidates	Party	Popular Vote	Electoral College Vote
1856	James Buchanan	Democrat	1,832,955	174
	John Frémont	Republican	1,339,932	114
	Millard Fillmore	Whig–American	871,731	8
1860	Abraham Lincoln	Republican	1,865,593	180
	John Breckenridge	Democratic	848,356	72
	Stephen Douglas	Democrat	1,382,713	12
	John Bell	Constitutional Union	592,906	39
1864	Abraham Lincoln	Unionist (Republican)	2,206,938	212
	George McClellan	Democrat	1,803,787	21
	Electoral votes not cast			81
1868	Ulysses Grant	Republican	3,013,421	214
	Horatio Seymour	Democrat	2,706,829	80
	Electoral votes not cast			23
1872	Ulysses Grant	Republican	3,596,745	286
	Horace Greeley	Democrat	2,843,446	(died)
	Thomas Hendricks	Democrat		42
	Benjamin Brown	Democrat		18
	Charles Jenkins	Democrat		2
	David Davis	Democrat		1
1876	Rutherford Hayes	Republican	4,036,572	185
	Samuel Tilden	Democrat	4,284,020	184
	Peter Cooper	Greenback	81,737	—
1880	James Garfield	Republican	4,453,295	214
	Winfield Hancock	Democrat	4,414,082	155
	James Weaver	Greenback–Labor	308,578	—
1884	Grover Cleveland	Democrat	4,879,507	219
	James Blaine	Republican	4,850,293	182
	Benjamin Butler	Greenback–Labor	175,370	—
	John St. John	Prohibition	150,369	—
1888	Benjamin Harrison	Republican	5,447,129	233
	Grover Cleveland	Democrat	5,537,857	168
	Clinton Fisk	Prohibition	249,506	—
	Anson Streeter	Union Labor	146,935	—
1892	Grover Cleveland	Democrat	5,555,426	277
	Benjamin Harrison	Republican	5,182,690	145
	James Weaver	People's	1,029,846	22
	John Bidwell	Prohibition	264,133	—
1896	William McKinley	Republican	7,102,246	271
	William Jennings Bryan	Democrat	6,492,559	176
	John Palmer	National Democratic	133,148	—
	Joshua Levering	Prohibition	132,007	—
1900	William McKinley	Republican	7,218,492	292
	William Jennings Bryan	Democrat	6,356,734	155
	John Wooley	Prohibition	208,914	—
	Eugene Debs	Socialist	87,814	—
1904	Theodore Roosevelt	Republican	7,628,461	336
	Alton Parker	Democrat	5,084,223	140
	Eugene Debs	Socialist	402,283	—

Year	Candidates	Party	Popular Vote	Electoral College Vote
	Silas Swallow	Prohibition	258,536	—
	Thomas Watson	People's	117,183	—
1908	William Taft	Republican	7,675,320	321
	William Jennings Bryan	Democrat	6,412,294	162
	Eugene Debs	Socialist	420,793	—
	Eugene Chafin	Prohibition	253,840	—
1912	Woodrow Wilson	Democrat	6,296,545	435
	William Taft	Republican	3,486,720	8
	Theodore Roosevelt	Progressive	4,118,571	88
	Eugene Debs	Socialist	900,672	—
	Eugene Chafin	Prohibition	206,275	—
1916	Woodrow Wilson	Democrat	9,127,695	277
	Charles Hughes	Republican	8,533,507	254
	A. L. Benson	Socialist	585,113	—
	J. Frank Hanly	Prohibition	220,506	—
1920	Warren Harding	Republican	16,143,407	404
	James Cox	Democrat	9,130,328	127
	Eugene Debs	Socialist	919,799	—
	P. P. Christensen	Farmer–Labor	265,411	—
	Aaron Watkins	Prohibition	189,408	—
1924	Calvin Coolidge	Republican	15,718,211	382
	John Davis	Democrat	8,385,283	136
	Robert LaFollette	Progressive	4,831,289	13
1928	Herbert Hoover	Republican	21,391,993	444
	Alfred Smith	Democrat	15,016,169	87
	Norman Thomas	Socialist	267,835	—
1932	Franklin Roosevelt	Democrat	22,809,638	472
	Herbert Hoover	Republican	15,758,901	59
	Norman Thomas	Socialist	881,951	—
	William Foster	Communist	102,785	—
1936	Franklin Roosevelt	Democrat	27,752,869	523
	Alfred Landon	Republican	16,674,665	8
	William Lemke	Union	882,479	—
	Norman Thomas	Socialist	187,720	—
1940	Franklin Roosevelt	Democrat	27,307,819	449
	Wendell Willkie	Republican	22,321,018	82
1944	Franklin Roosevelt	Democrat	25,606,585	432
	Thomas Dewey	Republican	22,014,745	99
1948	Harry Truman	Democrat	24,179,345	303
	Thomas Dewey	Republican	21,991,291	189
	Strom Thurmond	Dixiecrat	1,176,125	39
	Henry Wallace	Progressive	1,157,326	—
	Norman Thomas	Socialist	139,572	—
	Claude Watson	Prohibition	103,900	—
1952	Dwight Eisenhower	Republican	33,936,234	442
	Adlai Stevenson	Democrat	27,314,992	89
	Vincent Hallinan	Progressive	140,023	—

Year	Candidates	Party	Popular Vote	Electoral College Vote
1956	Dwight Eisenhower	Republican	35,590,472	457
	Adlai Stevenson	Democrat	26,022,752	73
	T. Coleman Andrews	States' Rights	111,178	—
	Walter Jones	Democrat	—	1
1960	John Kennedy	Democrat	34,226,731	303
	Richard Nixon	Republican	34,108,157	219
	Harry Byrd	Democrat	—	15
1964	Lyndon Johnson	Democrat	43,129,566	486
	Barry Goldwater	Republican	27,178,188	52
1968	Richard Nixon	Republican	31,785,480	301
	Hubert Humphrey	Democrat	31,275,166	191
	George Wallace	Independent	9,906,473	46
1972	Richard Nixon	Republican	47,170,179	520
	George McGovern	Democrat	29,171,791	17
	John Hospers	Libertarian		1
1976	Jimmy Carter	Democrat	40,830,763	297
	Gerald Ford	Republican	39,147,793	240
	Ronald Reagan	Republican	—	1
1980	Ronald Reagan	Republican	43,904,153	489
	Jimmy Carter	Democrat	35,483,883	49
	John Anderson	Independent	5,719,437	—
1984	Ronald Reagan	Republican	54,455,074	525
	Walter Mondale	Democrat	37,577,137	13
1988	George Bush	Republican	48,881,278	426
	Michael Dukakis	Democrat	41,805,374	111
	Lloyd Bentsen	Democrat	—	1*
1992	Bill Clinton	Democrat	43,727,625	370
	George Bush	Republican	38,165,180	168
	Ross Perot	Independent	19,236,411	0

*Lloyd Bentsen, Democratic vice-presidential nominee in 1988, received one electoral vote for president.

Note: This table includes all persons who received electoral college votes, whether or not they were candidates. It omits candidates who received less than 100,000 popular votes and no electoral college votes. In 1872 the Democratic presidential nominee, Horace Greeley, died after the popular votes were cast but before the electors had met. Because the Democrats had lost the election to the Republican candidate, President Ulysses Grant, the Democratic electors that Greeley had won felt no need to unite behind a single candidate. Instead, they split their votes among four Democratic politicians who had neither run for the presidency nor received any popular votes in the election. In 1956 a Stevenson elector in Alabama cast his ballot for Walter Jones. In 1960 Senator Harry Byrd of Virginia won the electoral votes of his state, because an uncommitted slate in Virginia won the support of the voters. Byrd also picked up an electoral vote in Oklahoma from a Nixon elector. In 1968 a Nixon elector in North Carolina voted for George Wallace. In 1972 a Nixon elector in Virginia voted for John Hospers. In 1976 a Ford elector in Washington voted for Ronald Reagan.

Sources: Bureau of the Census, "Electoral and Popular Vote Cast for President, by Political Party: 1789 to 1968," *Historical Statistics of the United States, Colonial Times to 1970,* Part 2, Series Y 79–83, Washington, DC: Government Printing Office, 1975; 1972–1988 data from *Presidential Elections since 1789,* 5th ed., Washington, DC: Congressional Quarterly, 1991.

Index

Page references followed by *f* or *t* indicate figures or tables, respectively. Names given in source citations have not been indexed; for these, refer to the Further Reading and Notes sections at the end of each chapter.

About the Author

Richard M. Pious is a professor of political science at Barnard College, the School of International and Public Affairs, and the Graduate Faculties, all affiliated with Columbia University, where he has taught since 1968. His books include *The American Presidency* (1979); *The President, Congress and the Constitution* (1984); and *American Politics and Government* (1986). He edited the centennial volume of the Academy of Political Science, *The Power to Govern* (1982), and its subsequent volume, *Presidents, Elections and Democracy* (1992). He has published articles in numerous journals, including *Political Science Quarterly, The Wisconsin Law Review,* the *Journal of International Affairs,* and the *Journal of Armed Forces and Society.* He has written articles in Russian for *Za Rubeshom* and *USA,* the journal of the Institute for the USA and Canada of the Russian Academy of Sciences. He wrote the biographical article on Richard Nixon for the *Encyclopedia of American Presidents* (1984) and nine articles for the *Encyclopedia of the American Presidency* (1993). Dr. Pious is the author of the *Young Oxford Companion to the Presidency of the United States* (1993), a reference work presented to President Bill Clinton at a White House ceremony in 1994, as well as several other reference works and textbooks for young adult readers.

Dr. Pious has been a consultant in several presidential election campaigns, an advisor to congressional committees dealing with presidential war powers, a consultant to numerous foreign governments, and a source for journalists writing about the presidency for leading news magazines. He has served on the international advisory board of *Journal des Elections* in Paris and is a member of the editorial advisory boards of *Political Science Quarterly* and *Presidential Studies Quarterly* in New York City. Dr. Pious grew up in Brooklyn, New York, where he graduated from Erasmus Hall High School. He graduated from Colby College in Waterville, Maine, in 1964. He received his doctorate from Columbia University in 1971. He and his family reside in South Salem, New York, where they live in a colonial house that dates back to 1791.